THE DAUGHTERS OF KOBANI

Gayle Tzemach Lemmon is the author of the *New York Times* bestsellers *Ashley's War* and *The Dressmaker of Khair Khana* and an adjunct senior fellow with the Women and Foreign Policy Program at the Council on Foreign Relations. She has written about women's entrepreneurship, girls' education, and child marriage and spoken at venues including the World Bank and TEDWomen. A graduate of Harvard Business School and the University of Missouri School of Journalism, Gayle previously worked in the emerging technology and financial services sectors. She serves on the board of Mercy Corps and is a member of the Bretton Woods Committee.

Praise for *The Daughters of Kobani*

"An inspiring look at the all-female militia that helped fight ISIS—and shined a light on women's capabilities and rights—in Syria." —*People*

"Fascinating . . . The inspiring story about the Kurdish women warriors who took on the terrorists of the Islamic State in Syria and won." —*Good Morning America*

"For many people outside Iraq and northeastern Syria, the Islamic State remains an abstraction. For the commanders of the Kurdish Women's Protection Units (YPJ), one of the most intrepid fighting forces on the ground, the terrorist group was anything but. . . . Few, if any, writers have told their story better than Gayle Tzemach Lemmon . . . [who] vividly chronicles the YPJ's grueling fight with the Islamic State on the battlefield. . . . The reader can feel the tension in a sniper's knees as she crouches for a shot and hear the hiss of Islamic State fighters taunting the female commanders over the radio." —*Foreign Policy*

"A riveting story of women in combat . . . Compelling . . . A tale that's sure to shock anyone who believes that combat is exclusively a man's job." —*Military.com*

"A must read for anyone who wants to feel inspired by women defying the odds to create change." —*Marie Claire*

"A story not only about the warriors who battled ISIS against all odds, but also a reminder of the ways in which the world is still divided by gender—and how that's changing in Syria, the Middle East, and the world at large." —*Town & Country*

"Handling difficult topics with adroit respect and care, Lemmon offers a story that's eminently relatable and speaks to the ongoing fight for women's rights the world over. This is a story that needed to be told and needs to be heard. Highly recommended to anyone with an interest in current events and women's history." —*Library Journal* (starred review)

"Lemmon's books . . . have extolled heroic women fighting sexism in the Islamic world. Now she's back with *The Daughters of Kobani*, a remarkable true story about an all-female Kurdish militia who helped drive ISIS from northern Syria." —CNN.com

"A fascinating portrait of Kurdish female fighters and their role in the Syrian civil war and the fight against the Islamic State. . . . Riveting . . . [Lemmon] unravels the complex history of the region with skill. This deeply reported account enthralls and informs." —*Publishers Weekly* (starred review)

"*The Daughters of Kobani* is proof of the power of women to shape their future and the power of girls to create the world in which they want to live. The brave example these women have set against the longest odds should inspire us all."
—Reshma Saujani, founder and CEO of Girls Who Code and author of *Brave, Not Perfect*

"A well-told story of contemporary female warriors and the complex geopolitical realities behind their battles." — *Kirkus Reviews*

"*The Daughters of Kobani* is an unforgettable and nearly mythic tale of women's power and courage. The young women profiled in this book fought a fearsome war against brutal men in impossible circumstances—and proved in the process what girls and women can accomplish when given the chance to lead. Brilliantly researched and respectfully reported, this book is a lesson in heroism, sacrifice, and the real meaning of sisterhood. I am so grateful that this story has been told."
—Elizabeth Gilbert, author of *Big Magic* and *Eat, Pray, Love*

"One of America's premier storytellers has risked her life to research perhaps the most important subject of our times: the empowerment of women and the establishment of a truly egalitarian society. Documenting the extraordinary struggles of a small group of women battling ISIS, Lemmon has showed us unequivocally what female leadership can do for a society. It is breathtaking to behold." —Sebastian Junger, author of *Tribe*

"Absolutely fascinating and brilliantly written, *The Daughters of Kobani* is a must read for anyone who wants to understand both the nobility and the brutality of war. This is one of the most compelling stories in modern warfare." —Admiral William H. McRaven, author of *Make Your Bed*

"This book is the extraordinary and humbling story of the women leading the fight against ISIS." —Angelina Jolie, actor, director, and activist

"*The Daughters of Kobani* is real-time history told with rigor and heart. Marrying two important narratives—the United States's entry into the Syrian conflict from the air and the lived experience of Syrians fighting ISIS on the ground—it is a remarkable contribution." —Hassan Hassan, coauthor of *ISIS: Inside the Army of Terror*

"This passionate and incisive book takes us into the radically brave hearts of the women who fought ISIS. *The Daughters of Kobani* is a gift to the women of the Middle East and to us, inscribing their sacrifice onto the history of a war no one will soon forget." —Azadeh Moaveni, author of *Guest House for Young Widows*

"Moving and inspiring, Gayle Tzemach Lemmon's *The Daughters of Kobani* vividly recounts the astonishing story of the all-women's army that fought and died to stop ISIS. These are fiercely brave women whose courage is unforgettable." —David Ignatius, columnist for *The Washington Post* and author of *The Paladin*

"*The Daughters of Kobani* offers a courageously reported, must-read account of a group of women fighters who risked everything to defeat ISIS and take their future into their own hands. Gayle Tzemach Lemmon has written an invaluable book for those seeking to understand the direction of twenty-first century conflict." —August Cole, coauthor of *Burn-In*

Look for the Penguin Readers Guide in the back of this book.
To access Penguin Readers Guides online, visit penguinrandomhouse.com.

THE
DAUGHTERS
OF
KOBANI

A STORY OF REBELLION,
COURAGE, AND JUSTICE

Gayle Tzemach Lemmon

PENGUIN BOOKS

PENGUIN BOOKS
An imprint of Penguin Random House LLC
penguinrandomhouse.com

First published in the United States of America by Penguin Press,
an imprint of Penguin Random House LLC, 2021
Published in Penguin Books 2022

Map by Jeffrey L. Ward

Interior insert images: page 7, top and bottom: Getty/AFP Contributor; page 8,
top: Getty/Delil Souleiman. All other images courtesy of the author.

ISBN 9780525560708 (paperback)

THE LIBRARY OF CONGRESS HAS CATALOGED THE HARDCOVER EDITION AS FOLLOWS:
Names: Lemmon, Gayle Tzemach, author.
Title: The daughters of Kobani: a story of rebellion, courage,
and justice / Gayle Tzemach Lemmon.
Description: New York: Penguin Press, [2021] | Includes bibliographical
references and index.
Identifiers: LCCN 2020027506 (print) | LCCN 2020027507 (ebook) |
ISBN 9780525560685 (hardcover) | ISBN 9780525560692 (ebook)
Subjects: LCSH: Kurds—Syria—'Ayn al 'Arab—History. | Kurdish Women's
Protection Units (Organization) | Women soldiers—Syria—'Ayn al 'Arab. |
'Ayn al 'Arab (Syria)—History, Military—21st century. |
Syria—History—Civil War, 2011—Women. | IS (Organization) |
Special operations (Military science)—Syria. | Insurgency—Syria.
Classification: LCC DS99.A926 L46 2021 (print) |
LCC DS99.A926 (ebook) | DDC 956.9104/234082—dc23
LC record available at https://lccn.loc.gov/2020027506
LC ebook record available at https://lccn.loc.gov/2020027507

Printed in the United States of America
1st Printing

DESIGNED BY MEIGHAN CAVANAUGH

To Frances Spielman and Rhoda Spielman Tzemach,
who taught me everything.

To Eli Tzemach, who taught me about pistachios,
backgammon, the proper taste of watermelon,
Marlboro Reds, and so much more.

And to all those women whose stories
will never be told.

"The best revenge is not to be like your enemy."

MARCUS AURELIUS,
Meditations

CONTENTS

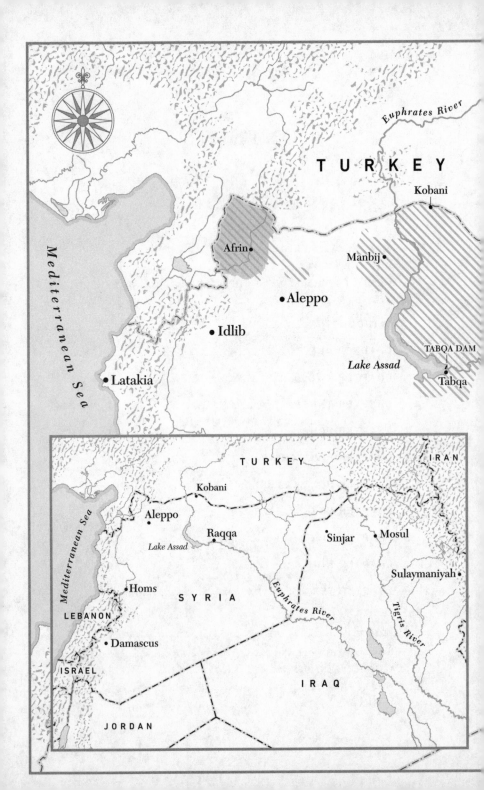

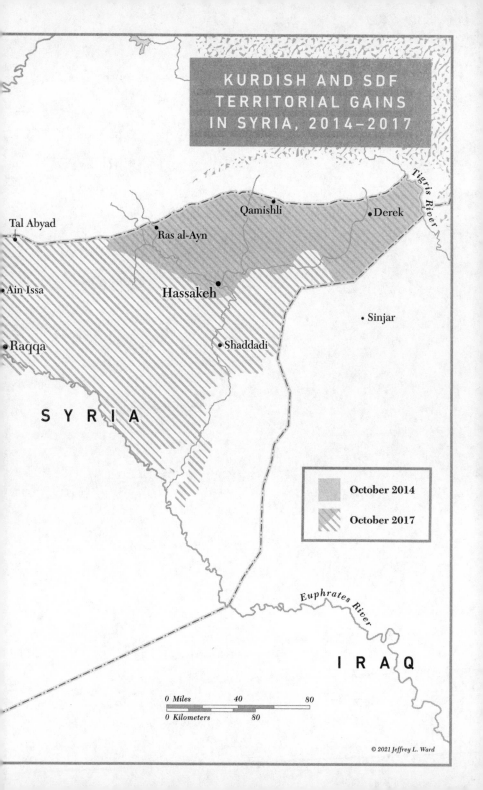

AUTHOR'S NOTE

The stories in this book reflect three years of research and on-the-ground interviews across three countries. This includes seven reporting trips to northeastern Syria between 2017 and 2020, along with more than one hundred hours of interviews across the United States and in northern Iraq.

My focus has been to provide the most precise accounting possible of the history that follows. I have worked hard to ensure the accuracy of the dates, times, and narratives reconstructed in this story, including conversations between characters built from interviews with multiple people holding different perspectives.

Security in northeastern Syria evolved throughout this time, as did America's presence in the area. Out of respect for the security and privacy of some who spoke with me, I have changed the names of several U.S.-based characters and omitted identifying details. For some people, including YPJ fighters, I have used only first names.

GUIDE TO THE STORY'S CHARACTERS

SYRIAN CHARACTERS

Nowruz: Women's Protection Units commander

Rojda: Women's Protection Units member

Azeema: Women's Protection Units member

Znarin: Women's Protection Units member

Mazlum Abdi: Head of the People's Protection Units, later head of the Syrian Democratic Forces

Ilham Ahmed: Copresident of the Syrian Democratic Council

Fauzia Yusuf: Political leader

AMERICAN CHARACTERS

Mitch Harper: U.S. Special Operations

Leo James: U.S. Special Operations

Brady Fox: U.S. Special Operations

Jason Akin: U.S. Special Operations

Brett McGurk: Special presidential envoy to the Global Coalition to Defeat ISIS

Amb. William Roebuck: Senior adviser to Special Presidential Envoy Brett McGurk; deputy special envoy to the Global Coalition to Defeat ISIS

INTRODUCTION

I made the trip to the Iraqi-Syrian border with some reluctance. I told myself that I had given up war—at least for a bit. I felt deeply guilty that I enjoyed the luxury of making that choice while so many I had met in the past decade and a half did not, but I was homebound and determined to stay that way.

I had spent years telling stories from and about war. My first book, *The Dressmaker of Khair Khana*, introduced readers to a teen-age girl whose living-room business supported her family and families around her neighborhood under the Taliban. During years of desperation, it created hope. I came to love Afghanistan—the strength and resilience and courage that I saw all around me and that rarely reached Americans back home. I wanted readers to know the young women I met who risked their lives each day fighting for their future.

The Dressmaker of Khair Khana led to my next story, *Ashley's War*, about a team of young soldiers recruited for an all-female special operations team at a time when women were officially banned from ground combat. That book changed me, just as the first book had.

Once more, the upheaval of war created openings for women. I felt personally responsible for bringing this history to as many readers as I could, given the grit and the heart of the women I met in the reporting process and their valor on the battlefield in Afghanistan.

The post-9/11 conflicts had come to shape my life: I got married only a few days before heading to Afghanistan for the first round of research for *Dressmaker*. I found out I was pregnant with my first child while in Afghanistan two years later, when I was finishing the book. For *Ashley's War*, I spent years not long after my second pregnancy immersed in the workings of the special operations community, and I was in constant touch with a Gold Star family forever changed by their daughter's deployment. They taught me what Memorial Day actually means.

I felt deeply proud of the work. And I also felt emotionally spent, trying to make Americans care about faraway places and people that meant so much to me personally. I was tired of living two lives, the one at home and the one immersed in war, and I thought often of that moment in the film *The Hurt Locker* when you return full of fervor to persuade Americans to care about their conflicts and then wind up in the grocery store, looking at stacks of cereal boxes on the shelf, and realize no one back home even remembers these wars remain under way.

I would recharge for a bit, I decided. Tell a story about the community of single moms who raised me.

And then I received a phone call that changed everything.

"Gayle, you have to see what's happening here. I'm not joking—it's unbelievable," Cassie said when I picked up her call from a number I did not recognize one afternoon in early 2016. She was a member of an Army special operations team deployed to northeastern Syria, where U.S.-backed forces were fighting the extremists of the Islamic State of Iraq and Syria, or ISIS. This was her third deployment. She had served in Iraq in 2010 as a military police officer. Then she signed up to go to Afghanistan in 2011 as part of the Cultural Support Teams, serving alongside the Seventy-Fifth Ranger Regiment; she belonged to the all-women's team I chronicled in *Ashley's War*. A few years after her Afghanistan tour, she joined Army Special Operations Forces, and that work led her to Syria and the ISIS fight.

Cassie told me that in Syria she had worked with women fighting ISIS on the front lines and that they had started a revolution for women's rights. These women now were part of the U.S.'s partner force—the fighters the U.S. had aligned with to counter the Islamic State. These women followed the teachings of the jailed Turkish Kurdish leader Abdullah Ocalan, whose left-leaning ideology of grassroots democracy insisted that women must be equal for society to truly be free. They belonged to a group called the YPJ, the Kurdish Women's Protection Units. Cassie explained that they had been fighting for the Kurds since the beginning of the ISIS battle and well before. How they led men and women alike in the fight. How their members had blown themselves up when it looked as if ISIS fighters would capture them. How they faced none of the restrictions American women confronted when they went to war—no rules about which jobs were open to them and which remained off-limits—and instead served as snipers and battlefield commanders and in a whole host of other frontline leadership roles. How they all shared the same messages and talking points about women's equality and women's rights, leading the Americans to consider them both incredibly effective leaders and ideological zealots. How they said women's rights had to be achieved now, today; they would not wait until after the war ended to have their rights recognized. Most remarkable, Cassie said, was that they had the full respect of the men they served with in the YPG: the People's Protection Units, which were the all-male YPJ counterpart.

"Honestly, I'm kind of jealous of them," Cassie said. "The men have no issue with them at all. It's almost bizarre.

"Seriously, Gayle, these women have some incredible stories. You've gotta come."

I thought about our conversation for days. It just didn't make sense that the Middle East would be home to AK-47-wielding women driven to make women's equality a reality—and that the Americans would be the ones backing them.

Syria's civil war had begun as a peaceful protest by children at a school in 2011 and morphed into a humanitarian catastrophe that world leaders proved utterly impotent to resolve and to which regional and global powers sent proxies to fight. The Russians, the Qataris, the Iranians, the Turks, the Saudis, and the Americans— all played their roles in the history of this war. I had written about America's tortured efforts to settle on a Syria policy back in 2013 and 2014 and about its ultimate decision to enter the ISIS fight without taking on the Syrian regime. I had traveled to Turkey on my own to interview Syrian refugees in 2015 and share their stories. The Syrian civil war by 2016 had turned from a democratic uprising to a locally led rebellion to a full-throttle proxy war dividing those who supported the Syrian regime of Bashar al-Assad (Russia and Iran, most notably) and those who did not (Turkey, Qatar, Saudi Arabia, to name a few). The Islamic State had taken advantage of the power vacuum and the broader civil war to make its name and take control of territory. But it was only one group in one part of the country: rebels of different stripes with differing ideologies controlled different sections of Syria. The Assad regime held the majority of the country, including the capital, Damascus, and by 2016 the second city, Aleppo, which by then the Russians had bombed into submission.

I knew far less about this all-women's force Cassie said I had to see. I had spotted some short pieces online and caught a CNN segment on TV, plus I saw a few photos on Twitter, which others immediately labeled "fakes" and "propaganda." It was hard to separate the real from the fake without seeing it firsthand.

The story raised for me a whole series of questions: How had ISIS inadvertently forced the world to pay attention to an obscure militia launching a long shot of a Kurdish and women's rights revolution in the Middle East? Does it take violence to stop violence against women? Is it possible that a far-reaching experiment in women's emancipation could take root on the ashes of ISIS, a group that placed women's subjugation and enslavement right at the center of its worldview? Would real equality be possible only when women took up arms?

Geography made this particular war story even more personal. Part of my father's family came from the Kurdish region of Iraq. He was born in Baghdad and spent his early childhood in Iraq. He became a refugee while still a child because of his religion. In fact, while traveling in northern Iraq and Syria, I carried with me a passport photo of my seven- or eight-year-old father sitting with his brothers and sisters. Alongside the picture is a stamp from the Iraqi government saying that the family had ten days to exit their own country and would never be permitted to return.

The region didn't leave my father, even when he left it for the United States. As a girl growing up in Greenbelt, Maryland, I spent weekend afternoons with my father playing soccer and back-gammon, our fingernails turning red from snacking on pistachios whenever he paused his chain-smoking of Marlboro Reds. He always found the notion of women's equality confounding. When I was ten, my father turned to me during a heated discussion I'd started about why women in his family cooked for men and waited to eat dinner until after they served their husbands and sons. He asked me one question that expressed everything:

"Do you *really* think men and women are equal?"

His bafflement was entirely genuine. To him, and the society in which he and his siblings had been raised, the idea could not have sounded more absurd. So I could imagine what these young women Cassie told me about faced when it came to persuading their parents to let them pick up a weapon and head into war. What I still couldn't imagine was how they had traveled from that mindset to this moment.

A few days later I picked up my phone and wrote to Cassie on WhatsApp. One year later, in the summer of 2017, I landed in northeastern Syria.

A YOUNG WOMAN wearing olive-green fatigues and a hat pulled down low to shield her from the August Raqqa sun stepped into the concrete courtyard where we had spent the past several hours waiting. To combat boredom while the afternoon stretched on, my colleagues and I there with the *PBS NewsHour* had climbed onto the rooftop of the abandoned house serving as a collection point for journalists hoping to witness firsthand the fight against ISIS. We had listened to the sound of gunfire and mortars targeting the Islamic State's positions and taken turns guessing how close the front line came to where we stood. Sometimes our minders asked us to come down; they worried that our presence on the roof distracted those charged with protecting us and didn't want to make more work for them. Otherwise, we sat around on plastic chairs in this makeshift press center in the 118-degree heat, pleading with the Syrian forces to take us where no one with even a hint of good sense would go: the front line of the U.S.-backed Syrian Democratic Forces', or SDF's, battle to retake the capital of the Islamic State.

The hat-wearing young soldier walked toward the stoop where we sat and began speaking with one of the young men in uniform, who pointed in our direction. Sensing that our fate was the topic of discussion, our Syrian colleague, Kamiran, stepped over to join the conversation and began explaining in Kurmanci, a Kurdish dialect, that we had only today, that we really needed to get to the front line, and that we wanted the local commander running the battle to take us.

A few minutes later, the commander for whom we had waited all day at last arrived. The moment she strode through the metal gate of the house turned press pen, we all knew who she was. The rush of our male hosts to straighten the wrinkles out of their camouflage uniforms, to stand up and outstretch their right arms to shake her hand, cemented my impression.

Klara wore a dark green, brown, and black camouflage uniform and light grey hiking boots with even lighter grey laces. Her untucked shirt draped past her waist and reached just about to the pockets of her pants, but there was nothing informal or sloppy about her. A forest-green scarf with pink, red, and yellow flowers painted on its center and fringed tassels hanging from the edges covered her hair under the throbbing sun. She looked tan from all the days out fighting in the city's streets. I kept noticing the dimple-like cheek lines that appeared as she spoke. They seemed out of place somehow on a face that had weathered so much war.

She arrived late, she explained, because she had just visited the survivors of an ISIS car-bomb attack against a family trying to flee the city that morning. Our team had heard the "boom" earlier, but we hadn't known its source. Most who could flee Raqqa already had by this point, but some had stayed out of the fear of the snipers and land mines they would face while attempting to escape, not to mention the U.S.-backed coalition airstrikes bombarding the city to force ISIS out of it. Some civilians didn't want to leave their homes or couldn't afford to give every last cent they had to smugglers, who earned their fortunes ferrying families from ISIS-held areas to liberated territory. Thousands already sat in the August heat waiting for the battle to end in a camp for the displaced in the town of Ain Issa.

Klara had gone to see the children who had survived the ISIS car bomb at a makeshift field hospital. Some of the kids had come out of the bombing unscathed. At least one of the parents had not been as lucky. After checking on the wounded, Klara had come to see us. Kamiran pleaded our case to her with a mix of charm and confidence, just as he had to her press office colleagues. I thought back on my earlier conversation with the SDF equivalent of a press representative, an Englishman.

"We aren't taking anyone to the front line today," he had said.

"But what if Klara is willing to take us?" I asked.

"Well, then you can go; Klara is a commander," he answered in a tone that made it sound as though I should know this already. Klara led, he served under her, and if she said we could go, we could go.

Now Klara listened to Kamiran argue our case and agreed to

take us to the front line. We would see what it looked like to fight ISIS, block by block.

Half of our team climbed into Klara's black HiLux pickup truck, the word TOYOTA spelled out on its back in big white block letters. (The Taliban also loved this make of truck, as I learned in Afghanistan while writing *Dressmaker*.) As it turned out, the first soldier we had seen, wearing the same uniform as Klara and the same black digital watch on her right wrist, plus the hat shoved down over her eyebrows, was Klara's driver. With her at the wheel, and Klara in the passenger seat, they set off. The only "armor" I could see protecting the pickup truck was a black scarf stretched out to cover the HiLux's back window.

If this is what it means to be backed by the Americans, I thought as I climbed into our team minivan right behind them, *I'd ask for better equipment.*

Driven by our British security leader, Gary, we traversed a gutted moonscape free of people and blanketed by silence. I kept looking through the window at the carcasses of the houses we passed. *Who lived in these homes, and when would they return? What did they see and survive under ISIS? And what would come next for them once Klara and her fellow fighters finished the battle?*

We came to a small bridge and our car slowed to a near stop.

If you're a sniper, it must look like a bull's-eye is painted on the roof of our minivan, I thought. *If ISIS guys want to hit us, now would be the time.*

I thought of Klara and the young women who served under her. They made this drive to the front line every single day; this was their commute to work. I wondered if over time the bridge lost its power to terrify. At a certain point in war, everything can become normal.

Ten minutes later—which felt like sixty—we arrived at our destination. This was as close to the front as the SDF would take us. Before us I spotted a burnt-out truck. Just that day it had been used as a bomb. Grey-black streaks of smoke still poured from its charred innards. This truck-borne explosive clearly hadn't gone off very long ago.

Klara strode around the truck, waving her right arm here and her left arm there, pointing out the location of the attack with an unfazed air, as if she were a tour guide at a museum. She spoke of the ISIS men targeting her teammates as if she knew them. I understood why: their interaction, their proximity and mutual understanding of one another's tactics, fighting force versus fighting force, had begun three years earlier. Our team wore body armor on our heads and torsos while Klara walked around with no armor at all, her head covered only by her green scarf.

Klara agreed to let us visit some of her troops on the way back to the press pen. At the entrance to the soldiers' base, a house gated by black wrought iron, we stopped our convoy. Sweat dripped from my helmet onto the once white oxford I wore beneath the body armor.

As I got out of the truck and prepared to meet Klara's forces, I realized my mistake. None of the troops we had come to see were women. And they were not Kurdish. They were young Arab men who served under Klara and the other SDF commanders.

Klara stepped out of the car and shook the men's hands, one by one, chatting with them as she went down the row and admonishing them not to smoke cigarettes in front of the camera. She asked them about the day's fight, talked to them about what they had seen. Some of the young men sported bandanas around their foreheads and ears to block their sweat and protect them from the heat. All of them looked exhausted. "Keep up the fight," Klara said, offering encouragement and a flash of a dimpled smile as she left.

Fifteen minutes later, we landed at the temporary base where the young women who served under Klara stayed. The women, who ranged in age from eighteen or nineteen to forty, milled around, still in their camouflage after the day's fight, but now lounging in stocking feet rather than standing at attention in hiking boots. They sat together in their shared living room, quietly puffing on cigarettes (the camera had been put away for the moment) and drinking cups of tea: an army of women with dark hair, black digital watches, side braids, and red-and-pink smiley-face socks. In a corner of the darkened room near the doorway, their weapons stood at the ready.

When we spoke, they made clear that their ambition went well beyond this sliver of Syria: they wanted to serve as a model for the region's future, with women's liberation a crucial element of their quest for a locally led, communal, and democratic society where people from different backgrounds lived together. This story was not only a military campaign, I realized, but also a political one: without the military victories, the political experiment could not take hold. For the young women fighting, what mattered most was long-term political and social change. That was why they'd signed up for this war and why they were willing to die for it. They believed beating ISIS counted as simply the first step toward defeating a mentality that said women existed only as property and as objects with which men could do whatever they wanted. Raqqa was not their destination, but only one stop in their campaign to change women's lives and society along with it.

I could not help thinking about the parallels between these

women and their enemies—not, of course, in substance, but in their commitment and their ambition. ISIS shared the grandeur and the border-crossing scope of the YPJ's vision—in the exact opposite way. The Islamic State's forces believed that their work would return society to the glories of the Islamic world of the seventh century. They invoked the idea of a "caliphate" ruled by a caliph, or representative of God, with centralized power and influence. The men belonging to this radical Islamist group, which trafficked in public displays of its interpretation of Sharia law, including whippings and maimings, believed that their efforts would write a new chapter not only for Syria and Iraq, but also for the entire Middle East and well beyond. ISIS placed the subjugation, enslavement, and sale of women right at the center of its ideology.

Every day, these two dueling visions of the future—and women's roles in it—clashed in Raqqa, as they had across northeastern Syria for more than three years. The men who enslaved women faced off against the women who promised women's emancipation and equality. Whose revolution would carry the day?

ON THE DRIVE out of Raqqa that August night in 2017, our team silent in our minivan from a mixture of heat and fatigue and released relief, I worked to stretch my imagination around what we had seen. Never had I encountered women more confident leading people, more comfortable with power and less apologetic about running things.

Whatever ambivalence I felt at the outset, this story mattered. Its impact would be felt well beyond one conflict, even a war with as much consequence as the Syrian civil war. The story had found me. I knew by then that when that happens, when a story grabs you, digs into your imagination, and presents you with questions you simply cannot answer, you either embrace the inevitable and get to work reporting or store it away in your mind and know it will find you and haunt you and gnaw at you regardless. I chose to get to work.

CHAPTER ONE

Azeema paced her breath—making it move through her quietly, nearly silently—and coached herself to do something that did not come naturally to her.

Be patient.

"Stay in your position. Hunt the enemy. You must be calm to succeed," she said to herself. "Especially when your goal is right before you."

If you asked any of her eleven sisters and brothers to describe her when she was young, none of them would have included the word *patient* in their answer. "Intense," they would have said. "Take charge, a leader," they would have said. Someone who acts immediately. "Determined."

And yet here she sat, now hovering around the age of thirty, hunched over on all fours in the sniper's perch in full stillness, her knees tucked beneath her, her body forming a near-perfect letter *S* as she rounded her neck to peer into the narrow square of daylight through which she would shoot her weapon. Her life and—more important, in her view—the lives of her teammates hinged on her ability to bide her time, to know just the right moment to shoot—not a fraction of a second sooner. Snipers like her played a central role in the situation in which they now found themselves: under siege in Kobani, a Kurdish town of around four hundred thousand pressed right up against the Syrian-Turkish border. Azeema and her comrades in arms had one job: defend Kobani.

"The secret is to keep calm," she had been telling the newer snipers working alongside her and looking up to her. "No movement, no excitement. Any excitement at all, and you won't hit your target."

Azeema slowly leaned onto her right elbow, tilting her head ever so slightly as she looked down the barrel of her rifle. Her thick brown-black hair tried to escape the flowered blue, white, and purple scarf that covered it, but Azeema pulled the scarf down farther to fix it firmly in place. She moved her other elbow, propped up on a tan-colored sandbag, just a fraction of an inch to the left, and stayed as close to the ground as she could while she shifted her weight. Every movement mattered.

FOR AZEEMA, as for many other members of the Syrian Kurdish People's Protection Units, the path to the Kobani battlefield in 2014 had started during street protests in her hometown of Qamishli ten years earlier.

The Kurds made up Syria's largest ethnic minority at roughly 10 percent of a country of around twenty-one million. The Kurds were a people split across four countries, the largest ethnic group with no state of its own. This hadn't been the plan: The 1920 Treaty of Sèvres had promised the creation of a Kurdish state, but Turkey's first president, Mustafa Kemal Atatürk, rejected the treaty immediately upon taking office in 1923. The Treaty of Sèvres soon gave way to the Treaty of Lausanne, negotiated with Atatürk's new government, which did not reference a Kurdish homeland at all. Lacking their own state, thirty million Kurds found themselves spread across what became, in the post-Ottoman era, modern-day Turkey, Iraq, Syria, and Iran. Turkey was home to the largest Kurdish population.

None of these four countries embraced Kurdish identity or the Kurds' push for their own land. With the rise of Arab nationalist governments in Syria, the rights Kurds did enjoy began to narrow: Kurdish-language media outlets shuttered and teaching in Kurdish became illegal. By the end of the 1950s, Kurds could not apply for positions in either the police or the military.

The Syrian Kurds in many ways lived as outsiders within their nation, a regime officially known as the Syrian Arab Republic. The national government denied citizenship to tens of thousands of Syrian Kurds who missed the surprise one-day census in 1962 in the Kurdish-dominated province of Hassakeh. As a result, Kurds were unable to attain marriage and birth certificates, university slots, and passports; officially, they were stateless. The repression grew in 1963 when a coup brought the Baath Party to rule in Damascus. A decade later, the Syrian regime's "Arab cordon" policy took Kurdish lands along the borders with Iraq and Turkey. As part of the policy, the government brought Arab families to live on these lands owned by Kurds and now confiscated by Damascus. Syrian regime teachers taught in Arabic in Kurdish-area schools— no Kurdish permitted. Kurds had no legal right to speak Kurdish and publishers no legal right to print Kurdish text. Kurds had only a minimal right to own property, no right to celebrate traditional Kurdish holidays, which remained illegal by law, and no ability to name their children in their own language or to play their own music. Anyone—Kurd or Arab—who opposed the regime faced jail or worse, and the Syrian government's security apparatus monitored the area closely. Stepping out of line or moving against these rules meant defying a watchful regime that regularly jailed, tortured, and disappeared its enemies.

For decades, young Kurds had gone along with their elders as they sought to live their lives within the regime's boundaries. The regime officially outlawed political parties other than its own, but Kurds still organized loosely in an alphabet soup of political organs. Yet by 2004, the winds were shifting, in no small part because Kurds across the border in Iraq had won more rights as a result of the U.S. ousting Saddam Hussein. A no-fly zone in place for decades had offered a de facto safe neighborhood for Iraqi Kurds. The 2003 ousting of the Iraqi leader who had murdered and gassed his Kurdish population had opened the way for greater recognition of Kurds' rights in the Iraqi constitution—and had been greeted enthusiastically by young Syrian Kurds. News that U.S. president George W. Bush might soon turn to sanctioning the Syrian regime was not lost on this group.

Against this backdrop came the fateful March 2004 championship soccer match, which took place on a Friday in the largely Kurdish town of Qamishli but would have consequences across Kurdish areas. Facing off were rival soccer clubs from Qamishli and the majority-Arab town of Deir Ezzor. The usual trash-talking between fan groups soon turned ugly and political. Some reports said Kurdish fans kicked off the confrontation when they waved Kurdish flags and held signs praising George W. Bush. Others said fans from Deir Ezzor started it by holding signs with images of Saddam Hussein and by chanting insults about Iraqi Kurdish leaders. Before long, a brawl broke out. In response, the local authorities of the Syrian regime opened fire on the Kurdish side, killing more than two dozen unarmed fans and injuring around a hundred. Riots and attacks on government buildings and offices by young Kurds—including the defacing of murals honoring the now deceased Hafez al-Assad—followed. By Saturday night, Syrian state television had announced that the government would investigate the riots, which the regime blamed on some rogue elements reliant on "exported ideas." The unrest spread to other towns in the area and became the biggest civil uprising Syria had seen in decades. Government offices were destroyed, thousands of Kurds were thrown in jail by the Assad regime, and hundreds were left wounded.

By the end of March, after nearly two weeks of upheaval, the regime had imposed order once more. Bashar al-Assad, who had taken over ruling Syria four years earlier, following his father's death, sent tanks and armed police units into Kurdish areas, and quiet returned.

The 2004 protests marked a significant shift: Assad was growing more isolated as change came to Iraq. Young Syrian Kurds had shown that they would defy their elders and go out into the streets, despite the dangers and the risk of jail. The uprising laid bare a generational divide and exposed the will of young Syrian Kurds like Azeema, who felt impatient both with the rulers in Damascus and with their own Kurdish political leaders, who favored continued dialogue and quiet back channels over direct confrontation with Assad. Indeed, Kurdish leaders vied for the role of key interlocutor in any future talks about Kurdish rights with the Syrian regime. Some had condemned the defacement of government installations during the protests and urged an end to the unrest.

To Azeema and other young Kurds determined to shape a political future different from that of their parents, the events of March 12, 2004, showed the need for organization. The Kurds who came out to protest had no weapons and no strategy to protect themselves against the armed security forces of the Syrian regime, men willing to deploy any violence required on civilians. As Amnesty International noted, the aftermath of the incident in Qamishli brought "widespread reports of torture and ill-treatment of detainees, including children. At least five Kurds have reportedly died as a result of torture and ill-treatment in custody." As Azeema and her friends saw it, the disarray of the Syrian Kurds during those weeks cost dearly in lives. They vowed they would be armed and far better organized the next time an opening arose.

In the wake of the 2004 protests, a Syrian Kurdish political opposition group, the recently created Democratic Union Party, went to work recruiting and organizing members. This political party traced its origins directly to a Turkish Kurdish party, the PKK, or Kurdistan Workers' Party. Illegal like all opposition parties in Syria, the Democratic Union Party worked in secret to spread its ideas and gather followers, drawing on nearly two decades of PKK presence inside Syria.

The PKK had taken root in Syria in the late 1970s when its founder, a charismatic college dropout from southeastern Turkey named Abdullah Ocalan, brought his Marxist-Leninist movement for an independent Kurdish homeland from Turkey to Syria. Turkey had long denied Kurds nearly all their rights and even took issue with the idea that an ethnic Kurdish identity existed, instead calling the Kurds "mountain Turks." The rebellion for Kurdish rights was bolstered following the imposition of martial law after the 1980 military coup and the enactment of the 1982 constitution, which named citizens members of the "Turkish nation" without regard for minority rights.

Ocalan came from a poor family of farmers with seven children, including a beloved sister who was married off for some money and several sacks of wheat. He studied political science at Ankara University and began to embrace Marxism while advocating for the Kurdish cause. He ended up dropping out of university after being jailed for distributing brochures and founded the PKK. Inspired by Marxist-Leninist thought, the group called for the establishment of an independent Kurdistan, with its most urgent priority the liberation of what it called northern Kurdistan, a part of Turkey. The PKK carried out its first paramilitary attack against Turkish government forces on August 15, 1984, killing two government soldiers in a coordinated assault in two southeastern provinces. One year later, a CIA memo noted that the insurgents had clashed with Turkish security forces more than thirty times and in the process taken the lives of fifty-six Turkish soldiers. These attacks grew in scale and reach over the next decade, and so did the range of targets, with the PKK using bases in the mountains of northern Iraq and in Syria as refuge.

At this time, the Syrian leader was Hafez al-Assad, Bashar's father, who ruled until his death in 2000. At Assad's invitation, Ocalan fled from Turkey to Damascus, Syria, in 1979, one year after the PKK's formation in a Turkish teahouse. The Assad regime, which denied Syrian Kurds their rights and shared none of Ocalan's goals, hosted the Turkish Kurdish leader as a means of spiting the enemy Syrians and Kurds shared: Turkey. Syria clashed with Turkey on a number of issues, including access to water from the Euphrates River. The two also landed on opposite sides of the Cold War, with Turkey joining NATO in 1952 and the Soviet

Union backing Assad's regime. For Assad, hosting Ocalan and the PKK would keep his rivals in the Turkish capital of Ankara insecure and off-kilter. In exchange, Ocalan kept his focus on Turkey, not Syria. For two decades, Ocalan built and operated a PKK organization out of Syria and ran training camps in Lebanon from there. Quietly, his adherents taught families like Azeema's about Kurdish rights, economic justice, and—right at the center of the work—women's equality, even while the PKK escalated attacks in Turkey, which saw Ocalan and his organization as its chief security threat. The Syrian regime sometimes allowed Kurds to serve in the PKK's armed wing instead of completing their state-mandated military service in the Syrian Army.

By the late 1990s, Turkey, by then growing in military and economic strength and forging diplomatic and military ties with Israel, grew impatient of demanding Ocalan's expulsion. Ankara at last ended Syria's support of Ocalan by repeatedly threatening military action and suspension of Syria's water supply. Assad, no longer enjoying Soviet backing, agreed to Turkey's decades-long demand to evict the PKK's founder. The Syrian regime threw Ocalan out of the country in October 1998, forcing him to hunt for asylum and his PKK forces to find refuge in northern Iraq's Qandil Mountains, thus ending two decades of Ocalan's presence and influence in Syria. By then, Turkey also had persuaded the Americans to get involved in cracking down on Ocalan and the PKK: In 1997, the U.S. agreed to Turkey's request to designate the PKK, which Turkey counted as responsible for close to forty thousand deaths, as a terrorist organization. Not long after Ocalan fled Syria, U.S. surveillance information helped Turkey arrest him as he sought safety in Nairobi, Kenya. Turkey sentenced its highest-profile prisoner to death in 1999, but revised the sentence to life in prison after abolishing the death penalty in 2002. Since 1999, Turkey has imprisoned Ocalan in a one-man jail on Imrali Island in the Marmara Sea.

Turkey may have considered Ocalan its most-wanted man, but for the Syrian Kurds who followed him, Ocalan lived in the public imagination somewhere between Nelson Mandela and George Washington. Central to his teachings was the position that Kurdish rights could not be divorced from women's liberation because the enslavement of women had enabled the enslavement of men. Ocalan stated that the Neolithic order of a matriarchal society in which everyone was protected and people enjoyed communal property, sharing of resources, and a lack of social and institutional hierarchy had given way to a social order in which women's work became relegated to the home, women's rights had been denied, and women faced what he termed the "housewifization" of their contributions. Modern capitalism had taken people's freedoms and exploited its workers, spreading sexism and nationalism:

> The 5,000-year-old history of civilization is essentially the history of the enslavement of woman. Consequently, woman's freedom will only be achieved by waging a struggle against the foundations of this ruling system.

IN 2011, the start of the Syrian civil war stirred fear among Kurds determined to protect their lands. What the next months would bring as the Syrian regime moved to put down the first armed threat to its rule was anyone's guess. A mix of young people from around the majority-Kurdish regions in northeastern Syria signed up to defend their neighborhoods under the umbrella of the newly formed People's Protection Units. Azeema was among the recruits who joined at this time. She felt as if she had to get involved to protect the Kurds from outsiders, whether they were anti-Assad rebels who wanted to take Kurdish land or regime forces rolling in to crack down even further on their area. She also strongly shared Ocalan's view that the Kurds couldn't be free if women weren't. Her father followed Ocalan, and Azeema and her siblings had been raised on his teachings. The children had heard the tale from their father about his grandmother, who had been an elder in charge of her Turkish Kurdish village at a time when all the other leaders were men. Politics in Syria remained largely dominated by men, regardless of community, but women across the country were coming out into the streets to organize protests. Among the Syrian Kurds, women played a growing role. Azeema intended to be part of the movement.

When she was thirteen, Azeema sat outside in the courtyard of her house in Qamishli with one of her older sisters, trying to survive the summer's oppressive nighttime heat by watching her favorite Syrian soap opera, which aired each night at 7:00 p.m. One of the main characters faced beatings and abuse from her husband, and no one stood up to help her. Azeema's sister had gotten engaged not long before, and Azeema began to connect the woman on the television with her sister sitting next to her.

"You shouldn't get married," Azeema told her. "How can you possibly think of it?"

Her sister sat on the rug, propped up on one of their plush pillows, hunting for a breeze and trying to relax. "You're crazy," she said. "Marriage isn't like that. Mine isn't going to be, at least. Just watch the show."

"Maybe I'm crazy," Azeema said, sitting up, her pursed lips

showing she thought no such thing. "But I am not going to get married. Haven't you been watching? Why would you get married? Look what this thing is like."

She gestured toward the TV and kept speaking, despite being aware that her sister was no longer listening.

"I don't see how you can watch this show, know that *this* is what goes on, and still want to marry anyone," Azeema said. "I'm never getting married. Ever. And you should break off your engagement."

Her position on marriage had not softened over the decade and a half since.

When Azeema first took up arms in 2011, she didn't join the People's Protection Units expecting she would actually end up killing anyone. Indeed, the YPG didn't yet exist; she joined the training academy of the YXK, Yekîtiya Xwendekarên Kurdistanê, or Student Union of Kurdistan. The idea was to protect Kurds against the Syrian regime—as they had failed to do in 2004—if it came barreling through with its tanks to crack down harshly on the area, and to keep out others who wanted to try to take over their land, including any Islamist extremists hostile to Kurdish rights.

At her first meeting to learn more about the self-defense units, Azeema gathered with a handful of others in secret in a local hall in Qamishli. Everyone feared the government would find out about their assembly, even though Assad's men had their hands full dealing with opposition forces seeking to topple the regime. At the meeting, Syrian men who had been trained by the PKK in northern Iraq's Qandil Mountains, and who had returned home once the civil war started, talked to the gathered twentysomethings about the need to organize and learn the basics of weaponry and military tactics.

As she looked at the two or three dozen people who had come together in that unremarkable room with its bare walls in her hometown of Qamishli, Azeema felt excitement and pride. This was what she had hoped to join since 2004: a movement of Kurds standing up to protect themselves. She knew that being part of a militia carried risks and that she would face imprisonment and perhaps torture if the regime caught her, but despite the danger, she felt as though her life finally was beginning to take the shape she wanted. She had stood out for years as a leader: in high school, she made her name as a volleyball star skilled enough to help lead her team to victory at a regional competition in the coastal resort town of Latakia. She loved the sport's intensity, relentlessness, and teamwork. Her skill landed her a photo spread in a local magazine, which her younger sister proudly shared with the entire family.

Looking across the room to see who else had dared to join this clandestine gathering, Azeema raised her eyebrows and felt her serious expression give way to an unguarded smile: her childhood friend and distant relative Rojda was there, too. Azeema could be brash and loud, shouting plays to her volleyball teammates across the court in an unmissable bellowing baritone. Rojda, who loved soccer enough to defy every family admonition that it was a sport that belonged to boys, had never bellowed at anyone in her life, even while calling for the ball. Indeed, no one had ever seen her temper escalate or heard her voice rise above a firm, quiet tone. The extroverted Azeema would take on anyone she encountered and shout down anyone who got in her way. The introverted Rojda, on the other hand, preferred picking up a new book to meeting a new person, and if someone gave her a hard time, she would tell Azeema, knowing that her outspoken friend would either beat them up or scare them away with the threat of doing so.

One of Rojda's uncles lived near Azeema, and Rojda regularly ended up at Azeema's house after school. Together with their friend Fatima, they would make their way through Azeema's neighborhood each day when classes ended and pick up their favorite ice cream on the way to Azeema's house. Boys would catcall them and try to follow them home, but Azeema would turn around and shoo them away. "Get lost," she would shout. "*No one* wants to talk to you." Fatima and Rojda would hide behind Azeema while she went on the offensive. "Azeema," Rojda joked, "no one is going to marry you. You are just like the boys!"

Azeema laughed. "Rojda, you know I am never getting married."

"But you have to," Fatima said. "What are you going to do, live at home forever?"

"Never," Azeema insisted, staying true to the pledge she'd made while watching the soap opera with her sister. Rojda never said so, but she mostly shared her friend's view of marriage. She had no desire to become a wife; right now, with the Syrian uprising under way, she felt she had more urgent work in front of her.

People sometimes mistook Rojda's quiet calmness for passivity. They usually made that error only once. It obscured a will that did not bend, a fact that her mother would often bemoan through tears.

Rojda loved soccer deeply as a girl and played it everywhere she could, including against boys at the school she and Azeema attended in Qamishli. The second-oldest of eight children, she always had siblings to play with and took her ball everywhere. On TV she followed Brazilian soccer and idolized its players. She also revered the Argentine legend Diego Maradona. One summer, during her family's annual visit to her grandmother's village, Qirat, she enlisted her cousin to play soccer with her. Her uncle, devoutly religious and conservative, could not believe it when he spotted the girls kicking the ball around the tree near the village's mosque. Already he had shooed them off the tractor, telling them that only boys did such work.

"*Stop*," he shouted. "What are you doing? This is haram, forbidden. It is not for girls to play this sport. That is shameful."

"You're wrong; football is for everyone," Rojda answered him in a bold display of disobedience, which her uncle later shared with her parents. "We want to play." The girls ran to the other side of their grandmother's house and kept playing.

A few days later they had the ball out, and as Rojda went to score a goal, her cousin screamed. A figure dressed in a white sheet came running at the girls. Rojda realized it was no ghost, only her uncle dressed up to look like one to scare the girls out of shaming their family by daring to play soccer. Unimpressed, Rojda told her cousin they had to keep going. No one was doing anything wrong, she told her. To keep peace, they stopped playing for a week—and then went back to the game they loved.

Growing up, Rojda was fascinated by the military and watched every military TV show she could. She saw a story once about Syrian women who attended a military college, and wanted to join them immediately. She loved organization and planning and received only good grades in school. Rojda dreamed of becoming a pharmacist so that she and her brothers, who wanted to be doctors, could work together. Then the 2004 protests following the soccer match in Qamishli shattered her conception of the future. Those protests changed Rojda, just as they had Azeema.

When Rojda spotted Azeema at that first YXK self-defense meeting in 2011, the young women locked eyes and shared a silent laugh across the room. "Shhhh," Azeema gestured to Rojda, putting her index finger over her mouth. Both young women knew they couldn't tell their families about this.

Weeks later, though, Rojda did tell her mother about joining these self-defense units. A dutiful daughter always close to her mother, she struggled to keep secrets from her family and felt that her relatives would find out regardless. Her mother's immediate reaction was a tsunami of tears. She blamed Azeema for her daughter's decision. No way her orderly, well-behaved child would make such a brash choice to put her life at risk. Her mother didn't care that they intended only to protect the area; she believed Rojda was endangering herself, and she wanted none of it.

"Azeema brought you to this," Rojda's mother cried. She called Azeema's relatives and scolded them through her tears.

"Your Azeema is the reason my daughter is making this mistake; she is always leading Rojda down the wrong path," she said. "This is her fault. She is going to break my house."

When Rojda heard about all the grief-stricken calls her mother had made to Azeema's family, she pleaded with her to put down the phone and never raise the subject again. "Mother, you have to stop this," Rojda told her. She spoke gently; she meant no disrespect. "This is *my* decision to join."

At Rojda's first weapons training, she felt immediately that she was in the right place, even if they had only one rifle for every two people. She felt full of fear when she first picked up a gun, but she quickly came to love it because it signified the power of self-defense.

"In 2004, we had nothing," she told her mother, trying to make her understand her decision. "You cannot be empty-handed when someone attacks you."

. . .

NOWRUZ WAS NEARLY a decade older than Rojda and Azeema and carried herself with the calm reassurance of a seasoned leader. While she shared Azeema's penchant for action, she also understood the need for patience and discipline. She wasted neither movements nor words and observed people as intently as athletes study their opponents. From girlhood, Nowruz knew that she saw the world differently from most of those around her. She would argue about the role of girls and women with the men in her family, asking them why girls had so little voice in their own lives. Her constant questions led her brothers and sisters to predict that she would become a lawyer. She herself wanted to serve as a doctor, to devote her life to healing.

Some of the explanation for Nowruz's worldview traced back to her mother. Uneducated and illiterate but observant and strong-willed, Nowruz's mother had had little say in her own marriage and gave birth to and raised eight children. Despite the chasm of experiences that separated their generations, Nowruz's mother served as one of her biggest influences.

"Don't be like me. Make sure your life looks different," she would tell Nowruz at night as the children went to sleep. "Never rely on others for your future."

Her mother's warning stayed with Nowruz. As she grew older, she watched girls she knew from her neighborhood, who studied hard and earned good grades, face marriage whether they wanted it or not, usually to someone their relatives had chosen. Nowruz felt lucky that her own father opposed arranged marriage, but he still wanted her to wed.

"You'll study, you'll reach a point, and then what? Sooner or later you have to get married," he told her, even while she told him that she had no interest in finding a husband.

As a teenager, Nowruz felt certain that marriage would not be part of her future, though she loved children. But even as she resisted the conventional domestic path of marriage, she had no idea that war would define her future instead.

The first time she picked up a weapon, she was a teenager at a summer camp run by her school. Hafez al-Assad was in power and Syria had intervened in the Lebanese civil war, sided with Iran in the Iran-Iraq war, and joined the American coalition opposing Iraq's invasion of Kuwait. Some of the girls in her class felt nervous about shooting a gun. Nowruz watched the boys, full of excitement, and told herself that if they could do it, so could she. When her turn finally arrived she looked at the target, squinted, and shot.

That first thrill of hitting her mark stayed with her.

She came from Hassakeh, a Kurdish town Bashar al-Assad visited in 2002—marking the first presidential touchdown in a Kurdish area in more than fifty years and potentially signifying an opening in regime relations with the minority group—and grew up wanting to change both women's lives and the Kurds' situation. She watched her parents unable to celebrate their holidays, saw kids she grew up with get in trouble for speaking Kurdish, and then, in 2004, witnessed her friends and family face arrest after taking part in the Qamishli protests. She possessed more of a professor's unruffled calm than a renegade's impatience; indeed, imagining her performing patient rounds as the doctor she would have been if politics hadn't overtaken her life was easy. But what she wanted more than anything was for her nieces and nephews to grow up in a neighborhood where they could celebrate their holidays, speak their language, and write and publish in it, too. She was looking for somewhere to direct that conviction.

At the outset of the civil war, in 2011, men outpaced women in joining what had officially become known in that year as the People's Protection Units, or the YPG. Some looked askance at Nowruz, a woman among them at the time of the group's founding. They asked her why she thought the new forces needed women when they already had so many men willing to enter battle. But a trickle of young women, including Azeema and Rojda, signed up nonetheless. They faced objections from their families, who believed, like Nowruz's, that girls should become brides, not fighters, but they came anyway. And as more women joined, their desire for more professional training grew.

The YPG formalized its coed training and divided it into two parts: ideology and tactics. Pages and pages of Ocalan's writings had been released since his imprisonment on Imrali Island, including texts on the history of civilizations on the banks of the Tigris and Euphrates Rivers, the histories of Christianity and Islam, and the roles of patriarchy and class in stunting society's development. The tactics the self-defense units taught were more straightforward: how to shoot a weapon, how to apply basic first aid, how to maneuver against a force much larger than your own—strategies shared by those who had trained with the PKK—and physical training that started at dawn.

The ideological side—and, most urgent, the notion of women's emancipation—was what initially drew in Znarin, another young recruit. She signed up for the People's Protection Units in 2012. Closing in on thirty with long brown hair, a round face, and kind brown eyes, Znarin possessed an ability to listen with stillness and project empathy with a smile that shot out of nowhere. She had come to the YPG as a decidedly naive entrant into militia life. She didn't really know what she wanted to get out of joining or what to expect. What she did know was that, in her gut, she felt drawn to join the ranks of the women she knew who had signed up already.

Znarin had grown up in the town of Manbij, home to an Arab majority and a sizable Kurdish minority, though her conservative family originally hailed from Kobani. When she was seventeen, Znarin's father told her she could no longer go to school. She was devastated: The only thing she loved was going to class each day and learning, and she was a good student. She dreamed of becoming a doctor—just like Nowruz, the woman who one day would change the shape of Znarin's life. Just then Znarin had been studying for her high school examinations.

Her father told her he did not oppose her getting an education. But his older brother did. Znarin's uncle was the patriarchal head of the family and what he said, went. Girls attending school fell squarely on his list of prohibited activities.

"I can't oppose my brother," her father told her. "It is his decision."

The fight went on for weeks. Znarin shuffled around the house like a ghost without a sheet to hide under. She cried in the morning while she swept the kitchen and helped her mother prepare breakfast. She cried to herself at night in bed. In between, she would not emerge from the room she shared with one of her sisters unless it was to clean or cook or help take care of her siblings. She did not speak to anyone, including her mother, who herself had never gotten the chance to go to school.

Znarin's resistance became the subject of dinnertime family

gossip. A rift grew between her father and her uncle. All her aunts talked about Znarin's defiance—none of them approvingly. At last, Znarin realized that she could not win and that prolonging the clash would only cause even greater problems for her mother and father.

Znarin gave up her battle for university, abandoning her dream of becoming a doctor and resigning herself to letting her uncle win. But she did so grieving for the person she would never become, filled with bitterness laced with determination.

By the time she reached her twenties, her relatives moved on from gossiping about her fight for education to gossiping about her need for a husband. Her family lived in Kobani now, and Znarin worked to settle into life in a new town. She felt even more constricted, given how conservative her extended family in Kobani was.

But then, as she neared the end of her twenties, her luck seemed to be changing: she found love.

The young man came from the outskirts of Kobani. He had a high school degree and pledged to marry her and take care of her. They would meet in town and talk without their families' knowing, which was no small feat considering the scrutiny the women in Znarin's family came under from older relatives bent on preserving their "honor" and good name.

Znarin told her parents that a young man would come to their house to ask for her hand. He was sweet and kind, she assured them, and they would get married and have children. But then, at almost exactly the same time, one of Znarin's cousins—a son of the uncle who had halted her studies—declared that he wanted to marry her. Her uncle came to her father's home to formalize the match. He said that he had decided: Znarin had to marry his son. It would be a good match for everyone.

Znarin had finally recovered from the loss of her education, and now her family wanted to keep her from marrying the man she loved—her only source of joy and light since her family had suffocated her university dreams.

She refused to give up on her love and took the outrageous step of telling her family "no" to the proposal. This provoked a fire of outrage among her relatives.

She listened to all the discussions from different rooms of her family's house. The debates went on for months. She prayed at night that the fight in her family would finish so that she could fulfill the only dream that now mattered to her.

Finally her uncle came to speak to her directly. Clan tradition dictated that she treat him with the greatest respect even while he worked to deprive her of her greatest hope.

"You have to marry my son," her uncle said to her in the family's living area. "This is the way it has to be."

Znarin said nothing. She sipped her tea and planned an escape. She assessed the look of determination on her uncle's face and mustered her own in response, promising herself one thing: that if she couldn't marry the person she loved, then she wouldn't marry anyone—not her cousin, and not anyone else her uncle chose.

As the months passed, the parents of the young man she loved tired of Znarin's family drama. Eventually they persuaded him to move on. The following year he married someone else. Znarin received word through a friend that he and his new wife planned to move: it was too hard for him to be in Kobani knowing that Znarin lived there.

Znarin considered running away from Kobani. But she had no-where to go. Men made all the decisions about women's lives. And until that changed, she could do almost nothing. She wondered: Was she the only person who felt this way? The only person who believed that things shouldn't be the way they were?

Two years after she at last gave up the idea of marrying and a decade after her uncle had put a stop to her education, a political earthquake arrived to shake up her life in the benign form of a knock at her door. A woman came to her family's house in Kobani and asked if she wanted to help women in the community.

The woman represented the organization Union Star, which later became Congress Star, a women's organization affiliated with the Democratic Union Party, which itself remained affiliated with the PKK. Congress Star had mobilized as a kind of group of travel-ing saleswomen going door to door in Kurdish neighborhoods, sell-ing Abdullah Ocalan's ideas. This woman began telling Znarin about the teachings of Ocalan and how no society could be free, could shake off its enslavement, without women playing an equal role in their communities.

For many Syrian Kurdish families like Znarin's, these ideas reached much too far, too fast. Few men wanted to hear about the rights of women as connected to the rights of Kurds or about why the family supremacy they took for granted should be questioned. Few women dared oppose the men in their families—the ideas that the Congress Star women brought to their front doors defied all they knew and accepted as truth. But for Znarin herself, joining Congress Star brought the thunderbolt of a realization: that other people thought just as she did that women should have a say in their lives. Soon she began accompanying the women of Congress

Star on their family visits to gather more recruits, even though many doors got slammed in their faces. She began learning more about Ocalan and reading his writings about the rights of women; she had never before heard anyone use the phrase "women's rights." For the first time, she didn't feel alone.

Znarin's relatives urged her father to put a stop to his daughter's political awakening. Her aunts began gossiping that she would disgrace her family. Znarin's father didn't want trouble from his family, but he also realized he already had denied his daughter her two great passions: education and love. He didn't have the heart to deny her a third time, especially because, so far as he could see, she worked and talked only with women. He kept his family at bay and pleaded with her to keep her activities quiet. "Do not give people an excuse to speak against you," he urged her. "You know they will only cause problems for the whole family."

But by now Znarin had been radicalized to the cause of women's rights and, as a consequence, Kurdish rights. The natural next step for her, she felt, was to take up arms to defend both. She had absolutely nothing to lose.

AT AROUND THE TIME ZNARIN joined the YPG, in 2013, the organization's women members formed their own group, the YPJ, or Women's Protection Units. In the roughly two years since the establishment of the People's Protection Units, women had worked alongside men. They wanted credit for it.

The YPG already had begun to see more fighting than many of its members had expected at the outset. Starting in 2012, the YPG clashed with members of the Free Syrian Army (FSA), a loose collection of rebel groups opposing Assad. Founded in 2011 by former Syrian military leaders who had defected from Assad's forces, the FSA led the beginning of armed insurrection against the Syrian leader. In 2012, both sides took losses in battles around the city of Aleppo. Confrontations continued even as leaders said they wanted no further bloodshed. While the FSA sought to oust the Assad regime, the YPG's stated sole objective was to be the dominant force in Kurdish areas and to remain neutral in the broader conflict over national rule, thereby opening itself to charges that it would be willing to work with the barbaric Syrian regime if it meant blocking anti-Assad rebels from its areas. Indeed, the ever-pragmatic Kurds, seeking to survive, coordinated with the Syrian regime against other rebels on the occasions when it protected their purposes and their people. But for the YPG that narrative of active alignment with Assad was too simple, and it left out the lessons of 2004 and all the years the Kurds had suffered at the hands of the regime. What Kurdish leaders sought was self-rule: not separatism, but the right to govern themselves. They had been arrested, tortured, and forced into exile by the regime, and if there were alliances to make with Assad's forces, they were based not on coexistence but on an understanding of the realities of power. What the Kurds feared most in this moment was rising Islamic extremism among those seeking to oust Assad, including the 2012 creation of Jabhat al-Nusra, an extremist group linked to Al Qaeda that showed no interest in minority rights. Fighting with Nusra and other groups continued into 2013 as the YPG became known for effectively defending Kurdish areas from rebels.

Against this backdrop—a chaotic Syrian civil war whose opposition forces were splintering and multiplying, sometimes under the more moderate FSA banner and sometimes outside it, and a

Syrian regime that displayed brutality and a willingness to kill all opponents—the YPJ was formed.

The YPJ would become a separate and equal part of the YPG. By creating all-female units, Nowruz, Azeema, and a few hundred others made clear that women would be responsible for their own decisions and their own defense: women could and would lead men in battle, but women would not be led by men, falling exclusively under an all-female command structure. The YPJ released a statement noting that the goal of the group was to build a democratic and egalitarian society and to defend women from around the region wherever they faced discrimination or persecution, not just in Kurdish areas.

The move reflected Ocalan's idea that "the struggle for women's freedom must be waged through the establishment of their own political parties, attaining a popular women's movement, building their own non-governmental organisations and structures of democratic politics." Women in the PKK in Turkey had established their own armed units twenty years earlier. Now Syrian women would do the same for themselves.

Men didn't love the idea. Nowruz, who, two years in, was among the key female leaders in the YPG, kept hearing that men and women should work together, that it was too early for a women's force. But women already had died defending Kurdish areas against both FSA and Nusra forces and in clashes with the Syrian regime. If they had "martyrs," how could they not have their own units? Nowruz and others said the moment was now, given how uncertain the future looked. Why wait?

Rojda, ever a quiet but unmovable force, had argued strongly in favor of the YPJ's creation.

"Why should men take credit for our work?" she demanded in

discussions before the group's formal declaration. "Women already have proven themselves in battle. They should know they have strength and bravery within them. And it will build the confidence of women."

The YPJ came into existence officially on April 4, 2013, Ocalan's sixty-fifth birthday. Nowruz, Rojda, and Azeema attended a gathering of several hundred women in the northeastern town of Derek (known as Al-Malikiyah in Arabic), a dozen miles west of the Tigris River, close to the Iraqi and Turkish borders. After the announcement, noticed by few outside northeastern Syria and southeastern Turkey, the women sang and held hands and danced in a circle to celebrate the new force's beginning. They announced that they would open training camps exclusively for women—one there in Derek and another in the town of Afrin.

In December 2013, the YPG released what it termed its "balance sheet" of that year's war. The statement said that 376 Syrian regime soldiers and 2,923 members of ISIS and Nusra were killed in battles with YPG forces. And it noted that "clashes throughout the year also left 379 members of the YPG and YPJ (Women's Defense Units) dead." The YPJ was now real, and so were its losses.

NOW, IN KOBANI, Azeema at last heard the sounds she craved: men of the Islamic State on the radio, talking to one another. Her own radio sat tucked in one of the pockets of the cargo vest she wore every day. She knew the men she hunted were about to make their move, which meant she had better be prepared to make hers.

Kobani was not the first battle in which Azeema had faced off against the men of the Islamic State. In 2013, the Kurds began fighting ISIS and other Islamist groups, including Nusra, primarily to push them out of the northeastern Syrian areas they controlled. In July, the YPG and newly created YPJ fought in the campaign to defend the town of Ras al-Ayn near the Turkish border. A few months later, the Kurds launched a successful October operation to retake the border town of Yaroubiya, close to northern Iraq, giving the YPG control of the Syria-Iraq crossing there. Shortly thereafter, the People's Protection Units moved to take villages near the town of Tal Tamr.

At the start of 2014, in Tal Abyad, ISIS launched an offensive to retake towns in the Hassakeh province, to which the YPG responded with its own counteroffensive. At one point ISIS had shocked the Syrian Kurds by launching several car-borne explosives and suicide bombers in the streets and had shown its advanced equipment, such as GPS. The Syrian Kurds had lost around a hundred friends and teammates that day, and they had sought afterward to figure out how to fight this new enemy. In May, ISIS forces released photos on Twitter of YPG and YPJ members they had killed south of Kobani.

Azeema peered into her rifle-mounted scope, looked at the mound of grey, black, and brown collapsed concrete on the street below, and saw fighters moving. She held her breath and counted. Then, gently, she squeezed her left eyelid while she used her right index finger to release her weapon several times in quick succession.

She looked out to see her work's results.

Her bullets had found their target on the narrow street; she saw a body crumple. She felt a jolt of satisfaction and then immediately turned back to scan for more ISIS fighters.

She released her rifle once more, knowing that in seconds the men she aimed at would scatter—and that others would turn their weapons in her direction, if they hadn't already. She heard her heart beating in her ears. She needed to move. These men knew war more intimately than she did; some of them had fought for well over a decade in Iraq and beyond. They had built tunnels within walls to crawl through buildings rather than walk on the street. The tunnels protected them from snipers like Azeema: if they never went outside, they could never land in her rifle's crosshairs.

Azeema unfolded her body, listening to hear whether ISIS commanders would begin talking about her kill on the radio. Gathering up her weapon and preparing to exit the sniper position, she crawled away from the window toward the back of the room and stood upright once more against a side wall. She patted her palms against the pant legs of her hand-sewn green, black, and brown uniform, sending waves of dust into the air, tightened the blue laces of her black tennis shoes, and began checking her rifle as she prepared to throw it over her shoulder.

"Maybe that will keep them quiet on the radio, at least for a minute," Azeema said to Miriam, one of her teammates, tilting her head toward the window and the dead ISIS fighter below. "Now they can talk to each other about getting killed by women instead of just beheading and enslaving them."

Miriam laughed. The women found motivation in hearing these ISIS men chat on their radios. Azeema had made a point to try to learn the identities of her enemies—because they were making a point to know hers.

"I am going to behead you, Azeema," she had heard one ISIS leader say over the radio. He was known by his nom de guerre: the Sheikh.

Azeema had wanted to answer him directly. But she would never be so foolish. These men would never be permitted to get to her and crawl into her head, she thought. She didn't need to talk trash. She wanted to fight.

Her troops, however, had a different idea.

"Comrade, if you want to behead Azeema, come out and let's see you," one of her male fighters had answered. "Come out here and show yourself, let us know who you are, and then you can come behead her."

Azeema smiled. Her brown-black eyes brightened her face while she shook her head in feigned disapproval at soldiers who sought to defend her and to draw out their enemy. The Sheikh paid her the compliment of saying that she was important enough—skilled enough—for them to know her name and want to behead her.

She had picked up a cigarette at the mention of her name and offered her soldiers another sideways smile, marked by a raised right eyebrow and the upturn of the left side of her mouth.

"Let's go, *Haval*," Azeema said to Miriam now, using the Kurdish word for "comrade." Darkness was coming, and Azeema wanted to seize the house ISIS had just fled while they could still see.

The two women descended the staircase and ran together into the night.

CHAPTER TWO

On the rainy morning of January 15, 2014, the streets of the town of Qamishli filled with the footsteps of funeral goers. Shops closed to mark the occasion, and red, green, and yellow YPG banners flapped in the wind alongside photos of Abdullah Ocalan as the procession proceeded. The mourners came to pay respects to thirty-nine YPG fighters who had been killed in battles with the extremist groups Jabhat al-Nusra and ISIS and would be buried that day. ISIS had set off a car bomb in the town a month earlier.

QAMISHLI IS THE CASTLE OF RESISTANCE IN ROJAVA, one sign read. Rojava, Kurdish for "land where the sun sets," was the name Kurds used for the areas of northern Syria they now held.

Kurds from towns around Qamishli gathered that morning in the city where unarmed soccer fans had faced bullets from regime security forces a decade earlier. Only now they did not feel fear of Syrian regime reprisal or hurry home to avoid arrest. Indeed, in a turn of events Azeema's family would have found unbelievable back in 2004, the regime maintained only a limited presence in the town now. The Kurds of the YPG and the political party with which they were affiliated, the Democratic Union Party, now controlled the area. The YPG stood watch at its checkpoints. The Kurdish dialect of Kurmanci could be heard on the streets and in the office buildings of those in charge of city services. War had brought about many changes, and the morning's ceremonies showcased nearly all of them. Lives had been lost a decade earlier and war continued now. But for the first time, Kurds had control of their towns, Kurdish language could be spoken freely, and Kurdish dead could be remembered without reprisal from the government that had taken their lives.

THE SYRIAN CIVIL WAR began in February 2011 as a peaceful protest against forty years of Assad family rule. People marched against the Syrian regime for its torture of teenagers from the town of Deraa. A group of schoolboys had spray-painted slogans and support for the Arab Spring, a series of pro-democracy public uprisings across the Middle East that led to the end of decades-long rule by the presidents of Tunisia and Egypt. The graffiti the boys from Deraa scrawled on their school wall read, "Your turn next, Doctor"—a word of warning to Bashar al-Assad, who had inherited his father's presidency back in 2000. The French-speaking, London-trained doctor from the minority Alawite community had assumed power at the age of thirty-four, following his father's death after thirty years of rule and repression. Talk of the young doctor becoming a reformer ended quickly as the new president continued the legacy of his father's brutality—and then some. The Assad regime, unwilling to allow a contagion of hope for political transition, democracy, and freedom of expression to spread, reacted with ferocity, rounding up and arresting the boys. Then the regime's security men tortured the children—beating them, electrocuting them, and hanging them upside down—and refused to let their parents see them. Led by the boys' fathers, protesters soon took to the streets of Deraa. The regime opened fire on them as they shouted and marched in entirely peaceful protest. By the sixth day of protest, more than a dozen had been shot and killed by the regime. By October 2011, a group of men—young and old—from around Deraa became the first to take up weapons against Assad and his security forces.

The uprising against Assad spread. Protests ballooned in size in the town of Homs and in the suburbs of Damascus. Yet even while the country caught fire all around them, the Kurds, who wanted their rights and came out in favor of the protests, did not join in armed resistance against Syria's regime. There were several reasons for this: Older generations knew the regime's brutality and wanted no problems for themselves or their children. Some were still smarting from a lack of Arab support when the Kurds protested Assad in 2004 after the Qamishli soccer match. The Kurds also feared that the armed Arab rebel groups of the FSA and Nusra fighting the regime would be no better in defending their rights—indeed might be far worse, given statements about the Kurds from some opposition leaders. When no guarantees of recognition or protection for their communities came from the largest armed opposition groups, the Kurds focused primarily on defending their region without going on the offensive against Assad.

For its part, the Assad regime faced more urgent problems than the Kurds as it sought to characterize the upheaval as an isolated sectarian revolt rather than a full-throttle democratic uprising against its savagery. Indeed, early in the crisis, the regime tried to win the

Kurds over to its side. In April 2011, it issued Decree 49, which offered a path to citizenship to one portion of the three hundred thousand or so stateless Kurds who had been forced to live without the rights to travel abroad, own property, or take university slots because the regime had long denied them national identification cards. The Kurds saw the move as an attempt to buy their support. Eyeing developments with a wariness encouraged by their elders, many Kurds showed support for the anti-Assad marches spreading elsewhere in the country. Young Kurds—if not their political leaders—began protesting publicly, in solidarity and agreement with young Arabs taking to the streets against Assad, chanting, "The Syrian people are one."

In July 2011, more than one hundred thousand Syrians dared to protest the Assad regime. Soon afterward, a handful of Syrian Army officers defected and created the opposition Free Syrian Army. U.S. president Barack Obama released a statement saying that "for the sake of the Syrian people, the time has come for President Assad to step aside." The following February, the Syrian regime launched an offensive against the city of Homs, which it now saw as the rebellion's ground zero; Homs had become known as the "capital of the revolution" for its thousands of pro-democracy marchers. The Syrian military shelled the town, killing more than two hundred in one day. By July 2012, Assad's forces had killed hundreds in the nearby region of Hama, the site of a massacre at the hands of Hafez al-Assad's forces three decades earlier. Soon after that, the head of Al Qaeda spoke out publicly in favor of the anti-Assad movement. Scenes of joyful pro-democracy protesters who had peacefully filled the streets of Homs pushing for their freedoms became a painful, evanescent memory. The marchers' dreams had been suffocated by the Syrian regime and its supporters. The conflict had now shifted shape from local to global, seizing the attention of jihadists who saw Syria as inviting real estate for the realization of their dreams of extremist expansion. The next phase of what now was the Syrian civil war was under way.

UNTHREATENED BY THE KURDS, Assad would direct his brutality toward the communities most effectively opposing his rule. By the summer of 2012, the authorities in Damascus had pulled the bulk of their forces out of northeastern Syria, leaving the Kurds in charge of their own streets. Syrian regime forces remained stationed in Qamishli, but the two sides mostly left one another alone.

The regime's withdrawal offered the Syrian Kurds the opening they had sought. A number of Democratic Union Party leaders who had fled Syria, either to evade imprisonment or following their jailing and torture by the Assad regime, had begun returning home from the PKK's enclave in northern Iraq as soon as the civil war started. They wanted to get back to Syria to be part of shaping the region's future. These Syrian Kurds understood the urgency of organization and the need to fill political vacuums swiftly. They acted quickly to consolidate power.

The Democratic Union Party was hardly the only Kurdish political party to operate in the area. Indeed, many politically independent Kurds joined the protest movement against Assad. But it was the most effectively organized, even if few outsiders had noticed it before the civil war left an opening. Opponents included the Kurdish National Council (KNC), a collection of parties with ties to Iraqi Kurdish leaders allied with Turkey who stood against the ideas of Abdullah Ocalan. Even after the two sides came to a political agreement in June 2012, the Kurdish National Council accused the Democratic Union Party of steamrolling its political competitors and imprisoning all who stood against them. In the KNC's view, the Democratic Union Party was on a path to one-party rule at best and full-blown authoritarianism at worst. A local watchdog group accused the YPG of attacking demonstrators in the street and targeting KNC offices, while international rights groups accused the Democratic Union Party of harassing and arbitrarily jailing political competitors. The KNC offered an unequal match to the organizational and ideological strength of the Democratic Union Party, whose leaders were loath to share power amid the turmoil and willing to arrest opponents who they believed wanted to create parallel political structures.

Some political observers inside and outside the country also accused the Democratic Union Party, sister as it was to the PKK, of capitalizing on the uneasy but real ties between Ocalan and Damascus, built during the years of his stay in Syria, and argued that these Kurds colluded with Assad to keep the regime in place. That view, however, overlooked the reality that many Democratic Union leaders had been arrested, imprisoned, and forced into exile by Assad, and interpreted the Kurds' ambivalence toward the Syrian revolution and what would follow it as an embrace of Assad's regime.

What was clear was that the YPG, the Democratic Union Party's armed militia, had proved itself the most effective Kurdish force capable of controlling territory and defending Kurdish areas from the growing threat of armed extremists. The Democratic Union Party had the strongest political architecture to institute its revolution, and its armed side had attracted young people ready to commit their lives to Ocalan's ideas and Kurdish security. The stronger the Islamic extremists grew, and the greater the fight the

YPG put up against them, the more that apolitical Kurds came to see the People's Protection Units as the only group offering basic security.

Despite the optimism beyond Syria's borders that Assad would step down, few in the Democratic Union Party believed the regime's rule would end quickly; indeed, they felt Assad would dig in and do whatever necessary to stay in power. The experience of 2004 had taught them that much. In the meantime, they focused on establishing themselves as the single dominant political player in the Kurdish areas.

In the middle of a July night in 2012, Afrin became the first heavily Kurdish Syrian town whose checkpoints the YPG would control. Controlling checkpoints signaled responsibility for an area—and that the YPG, not the regime, was now in charge of the town. Kobani would soon follow Afrin. One older man crossed the first checkpoint the Syrian Kurds established in Kobani, only to cross it another time and then another. When one of the young women working at the checkpoint asked him whether everything was okay, the man answered that he was fine—he had just never heard his language, the Kurdish dialect Kurmanci, spoken at a checkpoint and wanted to enjoy it in case the regime returned.

IN 1999, after the Turkish authorities captured him, Ocalan proclaimed a "peace initiative" and things remained relatively quiet through 2004. Peace talks between the PKK and the Turkish government began then, only to end after the PKK killed a dozen Turkish soldiers. Talks eventually restarted, then stopped once more, then resumed for the third time in March 2013.

Prison offered Ocalan a lot of time to think, write, and further formalize his ideas, which those closest to him then shared with his followers. His goal evolved from a military campaign to create an independent and unified Kurdistan to a grassroots system in which Kurds exercised peaceful self-rule in the countries where they lived.

Among those who had shaped and influenced the evolution of Ocalan's political thinking was a Vermont-based writer few Americans have ever heard of: Murray Bookchin. Bookchin had undergone his own decades-long intellectual journey from communist to anarchist to architect of what he came to call "social ecology." His thought would push Ocalan from a focus on a nation-state to a belief that grassroots democracy and social justice offered the political answers he and the Kurds sought.

Born in New York City to Russian Jewish immigrants in 1921, Bookchin joined the Communist Party Young Pioneers at the age of nine after a pair of children from the group knocked on his apartment door and recruited him. As part of their work, the children would stand on soapboxes in New York City parks, speaking about the rights of the working class and the need for justice for workers. By the age of thirteen, Bookchin had read Marx's *The Communist Manifesto*; he then moved on to the works of Friedrich Engels and to Vladimir Lenin's *The State and Revolution*.

Raised by his grandmother until the age of nine, Bookchin cared and provided for an unstable mother. He turned to the Communist Party for both structure and intellectual training, spending his high school years into early adulthood reading all of Marx's fifty volumes and working all sorts of jobs—including selling ice cream from a freezer he carried around on his back across the city and selling the *Daily Worker* newspaper on street corners.

By 1939, Bookchin's concerns about the Communist Party and its leadership had sunk from mistrust into disgust. The pact between Adolf Hitler and Joseph Stalin proved too much for him; he could not be part of a party that aligned itself with fascists. He got a job in a steel factory in Bayonne, New Jersey, where he organized workers in the United Electrical Workers Union.

A decade later, Bookchin became part of a left-leaning think tank devoted to researching topics including the environment's health and the harm pesticides created for food supplies. The group arrived at the idea that the working class could no longer be counted on to change history; indeed, Bookchin's own experiences had taught him that most factory workers cared more about bringing home a bigger paycheck than bringing about political change.

Bookchin's ideas aligned with the anti-war, countercultural spirit of the 1960s. In 1964 Bookchin published an essay titled "Ecology and Revolutionary Thought," in which he wrote that no environmental issues could be resolved until all forms of hierarchy—including gender, sexual orientation, and age—ended. Bookchin had learned to love nature by living in his city. He would walk New York as a child, in that era before development overtook so much of its natural splendor, and hike his way out of the city.

He moved to Vermont in 1971, seeking to bring his ideas on local politics to a place that still held statewide town meetings. He aspired to make Burlington his own political laboratory—indeed, his former wife fought to stop the development of Burlington's waterfront, a plan advanced by Bernie Sanders, who was mayor at the time.

From Burlington, in 1982, Bookchin published what came to be his best-known work, the book that eventually would nest his ideas in the heart of the governance of northeastern Syria: *The Ecology of Freedom: The Emergence and Dissolution of Hierarchy.* The book chronicled the evolution of societies into "civilizations" underpinned by "two mutually reinforcing 'big lies': that in order for man to flourish, he must dominate nature; and that in order to dominate nature effectively, he must also dominate both women and his fellow men."

In the early 1990s, Bookchin began arguing that the path to achieving a just society could be found in what he termed "libertarian municipalism": neighborhood-level assemblies based on models such as the town halls of Revolution-era New England.

At around the same time, *The Ecology of Freedom* was published in Turkish. As Ocalan sought books from leftist thinkers, Bookchin's ideas landed in Ocalan's prison cell and became part of his ideology. Leaving behind Marxism and communism and influenced by Bookchin, Ocalan came to the idea that the Kurds did not need statehood. They needed self-governance with social justice and a structure reliant only on their ideas and organization, not the state.

Thus did a jailed, hard-line Turkish fighter for Kurdish rights find his ideas shaped by a self-educated former communist from New York City living in Vermont with politics to the left of Bernie Sanders. By 2014, this merged concept of New England–style townhall democracy with Kurdish rights and women's equality at its core would govern the political no-man's-land of Assad-abandoned northeastern Syria. Its founding document would reflect the intellectual voyages of both of its fathers.

At the start of the civil war in 2011, Kurds who had worked for years to organize against the Syrian regime now spotted an opening. The work they had done mobilizing women in secret would help them assemble them in public. They set out to put laws in place that guaranteed women a seat at the main table, starting now. Ocalan's philosophy directly informed their approach and their desire to be the Kurdish political party in charge of their areas. It also informed their goal: not an independent Kurdish state, but the establishment of a new set of grassroots political structures designed to support self-rule in a local, autonomous region.

The Democratic Union Party put the Charter of the Social Contract into effect in January 2014. This constitutional law for northeastern Syria formalized the area's "democratic autonomy" and established local councils. It outlawed torture and the death penalty, declared the YPG the "sole military force" of the region, and named Kurdish, Arabic, and Syriac the area's official languages. Ethnic minorities would enjoy full rights and could teach their children, name their children, and speak to one another in public in their own languages. The charter did not, however, promise a ban on arbitrary detention or guarantee access to a lawyer in criminal proceedings. This fueled further criticism that the Democratic Union Party did not tolerate political rivals and instead sought one-party rule. For the Democratic Union Party, the goal was indeed the party's ascent to power. The on-the-ground reality was that the party embraced ideas that few other Kurdish groups would in the creation of its radically new structures. The other truth was that no other party came close to matching its organizational discipline, nor its ability to provide security. This meant that it could proceed on its own political path while the chaos of the civil war swirled around it.

Ocalan's and Bookchin's fingerprints could be detected throughout the charter. The environment would be protected and conservation would be a priority. The importance of social justice and the elimination of hierarchies earned mentions.

Articles 27 and 28 focused on equal rights for women: "Women have the inviolable right to participate in political, social, economic and cultural life. Men and women are equal in the eyes of the law. The Charter guarantees the effective realization of equality of women and mandates public institutions to work towards the elimination of gender discrimination."

The charter also guaranteed 40 percent women's representation in the new local legislative assembly and "all governing bodies, institutions and committees." Upon its enactment, it became the most progressive governing "constitutional" document on women's rights in the region and went further than anything the United States or any other Western ally had ever attempted. Of course, it covered only the sliver of land the Kurds controlled and held no real political legitimacy outside the Democratic Union Party's ability to enforce it, given that Assad still legally ruled the entirety of Syria.

The focus on women's rights, of course, was no accident. Activists who had long awaited the opportunity to lead Kurdish areas and reshape their politics made sure that security gains achieved by the Women's Protection Units were matched by political gains for women.

One of these activists was Ilham Ahmed. When she was only twelve years old, Ilham had led an insurgency in her family when she refused to give in to her father's demand that she wear a headscarf in her grandmother's village. That rebellious streak never stopped. When she was a teen, the Syrian regime told Ilham's father that land he loved and tended to and owned no longer belonged to him. Protesting the decision meant prison. Those twin battles—arguing for women's equality and fighting for Kurdish rights—determined the course of her life.

The charter was just the beginning of codifying women's participation. Each town the Kurds led had a civil council with a man and a woman running it jointly. And each town had a women's council, where women organized to advocate for their own economic, social, and political opportunities, and where they could go for safety and arbitration if they faced beatings at the hands of their husbands or knew of a girl facing a forced marriage. The idea was to build women's communes, too, where women could live together with their own schools, bakery, farm, security, and medical clinic.

BY THE TIME the charter was finalized, in January 2014, Azeema, Nowruz, and Rojda had already seen combat. They had faced off against the Syrian regime and done battle against Al Qaeda–linked groups and the new jihadist organization known as ISIS, born the year before. The London-based Syrian Observatory for Human Rights estimated the death toll of the entire civil war at upward of one hundred thousand, but no one knew for certain. And there was no end to the fighting within sight.

Meanwhile, this isolated patch of northeastern Syria proceeded to put its ideas into practice. Turkey watched with increasing alarm as this group of Kurds gained control of the border and created a new hamlet of Kurdish rights and self-rule. For Turkey, toppling Assad was the goal at that time, but Turkey's leader made clear he could not support and would not tolerate the rise of a PKK-linked group along the country's border. Saleh Muslim, copresident of the Democratic Union Party, spoke often and publicly about how theirs was a Syrian, homegrown political party separate from and independent of the PKK even if related to it, but Turkey's concerns would not be assuaged. This meant that Ilham Ahmed and her fellow Democratic Union Party members had no supporters out-side their region and no international allies to turn to for backing or protection. It seemed that the Syrian Kurds would survive or die on their own as the war ground on and extremists threatened.

But in the summer of 2014, ISIS's moves to launch an attack on the town of Kobani would set into motion a chain of events even a region accustomed to the unexpected could not have predicted. The Syrian Kurds whom few had ever heard of, who lived in a town no one could even find on a map, would be catapulted onto the global stage.

CHAPTER THREE

2014 was the year ISIS shook the world.

Born in Iraq under the umbrella of Al Qaeda and in the wake of the U.S. military presence in the country following the 2003 invasion, ISIS possessed—and planned to make real—dreams of returning to the glory of Islam's seventh-century founding. ISIS had morphed from what had been known as Al Qaeda in Iraq into its own unique brand of terror. As early as 2004, the men who sowed the seeds for ISIS showed their enemies and followers alike their willingness to go even further than Al Qaeda's founder, Osama bin Laden, to kill, torture, and maim adversaries—so much so that even Al Qaeda eventually disavowed their tactics. Beheading those it conquered, caging and murdering innocent people who opposed the group's extremism, and enslaving, raping, and torturing women became a part of how ISIS did business as it sought to win the hearts and minds of new recruits. ISIS dealt savagely with people who stood against it and those it conquered from other religious ethnic groups, including Christians. In 2014, the group's name grew and spread as a result of a military winning streak that managed to surprise the world with its scale, speed, and staying power.

In Washington, the Obama administration was slow to respond to the seriousness of the ISIS threat. Pockets of experts and policy makers started arguing in favor of striking against the group in 2013, but they failed to convince those with decision-making power of the peril that ISIS posed and the need for action. Responding to the Syrian civil war had divided Obama's first-term administration from the conflict's outset. Some, including Secretary of State Hillary Clinton and CIA director David Petraeus, favored greater intervention early in the civil war to support the moderate opposition rather than allow extremists to fill the vacuum. The other side, including voices at the National Security Council, noted that any U.S. move would not take place in isolation. Obama feared that America's escalation would be greeted by escalation from Russia, Iran, and the Syrian regime. The president wanted to know whether those favoring intervention could be certain that U.S. action would not make things worse. For Obama, who had been elected on a platform of ending wars in the region, intervention seemed to offer only a path to quagmire, the start of yet another war that the U.S. would be unable to exit. Early on, in 2011, the White House had said that the time had come for Assad to step aside, but it didn't support the young generation of Syrian democratic activists who took to the streets to make that a reality. The president called the use of chemical weapons a red line, but without stating what the consequences of crossing it would be.

By August 2013, ISIS had fought and killed enough other rebels in enough cities to now count among the leading forces opposed to Assad. That same month, Assad crossed Obama's red line and used chemical weapons against Syrians in the Damascus suburbs.

Obama publicly vacillated between using or refraining from military action.

Meanwhile, ISIS gained strength and encountered little real opposition as its military campaigns pressed on.

In January 2014, Obama characterized ISIS as "junior varsity." The thinking inside the White House was that elevating the terror group with a presidential mention would only strengthen it further—and that "when the president of the United States gives a Churchillian speech, people expect Churchillian action." That same month, ISIS captured all of the Syrian city of Raqqa. Syria's once-diverse, sixth-largest population center became the first city of consequence to fall under ISIS control as the group declared it the capital of the Islamic State. Raqqa was a city rich with symbolic importance: ISIS aspired to invoke the memory of a "golden age" of Islam at the end of the eighth century, during which the Abbasid caliphate's ruler Harun al-Rashid named Raqqa his capital. Next, in February, the group took the northern town of Manbij, a mix of majority Arabs and a significant Kurdish minority, in Syria's Aleppo province along the border with Turkey. Manbij became the welcome center for foreign fighters, the crossroads through which the growing number of internationals joining ISIS passed to drop off their families and their passports before heading to the front. By the time summer rolled around, ISIS had come closer to reaching varsity status far more quickly than even those watching closely had ever expected.

On June 10, 2014, ISIS shocked the world by capturing, with only minimal effort, Iraq's second-largest city, Mosul, sending hundreds of thousands of its nearly two million residents fleeing. The Islamic State's militants reached within one hundred miles of the Iraqi capital, Baghdad, as Iraqi authorities abandoned Mosul.

Baghdad turned down offers of help from the Peshmerga, the Iraqi Kurdish military force, on the grounds that such help was unnecessary—only for truckloads of ISIS fighters to soon pour in from Syria and find the way relatively unimpeded.

Mosul was a wake-up call for Washington, which now could no longer ignore the problem of the Islamic State. "ISIS became the overwhelming priority," remembers one former senior official, though debate about how and whether to support opposition to Assad continued.

On June 29, a surging ISIS heady from its own wins announced the establishment of a caliphate in the territories it had conquered in Iraq and Syria. The elusive ISIS leader Abu Bakr al-Baghdadi declared that, from that day onward, he would be regarded as caliph and "leader for Muslims everywhere." From Mosul's Grand Mosque, al-Baghdadi laid out his vision for a caliphate tolerating only the most extreme interpretation of Sunni fundamentalist Islam and bringing to life once more an Islamic empire reaching across the Middle East and well beyond, into Europe and all the other lands of the nonbelievers. Sharia law as interpreted by ISIS would be the only law governing the land. It would be enforced without mercy.

Two months after ISIS captured Mosul, the group launched a campaign against the Yazidi minority in the town of Sinjar so brutal and medieval in its hellishness that it stunned even an indifferent world into shocked disbelief. ISIS considered Yazidis "devil worshippers" in a critical misreading of their religious teachings. The persecution of the small, close-knit group did not begin with ISIS; it had gone on for centuries through the modern era. After a period of relative stability following the overthrow of Saddam Hussein, in 2007 Al Qaeda began targeting Yazidis for their beliefs.

Things grew calmer for a time as Iraqi Sunni Muslims, allied with U.S. forces, fought Al Qaeda.

When the Islamic State reached the Iraqi town of Sinjar in August, however, fresh from victory in Mosul and feeling triumphant, it turned the full weight of its brutality and emerging strength on the Yazidis. ISIS fighters did not offer the Yazidis the chance it gave to Christians to provide a "tax payment" in return for the benefit of protection by ISIS; instead, they declared that they must convert to Islam or face mass killings. They set out to erase their community, estimated to number around six hundred thousand in Iraq. Men and boys were rounded up and shot. Young and old women were separated at collection points, then shuttled around the region and into Syria and distributed as spoils to ISIS fighters. Commanders received the youngest, most attractive girls and women. Then the trading and sale of the girls and women began, creating a market. Indeed, the men of the Islamic State built a system that not only justified but also enshrined enslavement of women into the center of its very code. Images streamed from televisions, phones, and websites of young girls torn from their screaming mothers' arms and shoved, wailing, into the hands of Islamic State fighters who would mete out rape, forced marriage, servitude, and torture. No one came to protect the girls as they shouted, pleading, for their families. Tens of thousands of Yazidis fled to Mount Sinjar, seeking to stave off their extermination, but without enough food or supplies to survive the hard conditions there.

The Yazidis' plight grabbed headlines as ISIS advanced toward the Iraqi Kurdish city of Erbil, home to U.S. forces and a U.S. consulate. The fate of the Yazidis had motivated the Obama administration to begin exploring options for a full rescue mission while

European powers intensified their efforts to get aid to the families stranded on Mount Sinjar in the August heat. After Mosul's fall, the growing strength of the Islamic State had seized Washington's attention. If ISIS reached Erbil, significant U.S. interests would be at risk, given that U.S. forces and diplomats enjoyed a meaningful presence in the largely open and welcoming town, U.S. officials in the area warned. The U.S. had invested a lot in the Kurdistan Regional Government of Iraq, which governed the region, and did not want to see its allies and its own regional hubs overrun by the Islamic State. On August 7, 2014, Obama, who had for so long sought to keep America out of further conflicts in the region, announced what he assured the nation would be a limited intervention.

"To stop the advance on Erbil, I've directed our military to take targeted strikes against ISIL terrorist convoys should they move toward the city," Obama said to America in an eight-minute primetime televised address from the State Dining Room. He then turned to the fate of the Yazidis and announced that the U.S. would undertake operations to help save Iraqi civilians and end the ISIS siege of Mount Sinjar, which had trapped Yazidis as well as Christians.

Obama's statement that night signaled America's first public steps into the fight against ISIS. At the same time, Obama made it clear that the intervention would not be open-ended, nor would it involve U.S. infantry troops on the ground. Obama would be forced to weigh in again soon. Barely a week later, ISIS beheaded American journalist James Foley, a Massachusetts native and veteran war reporter beloved by his colleagues, and shared the video immediately as a propaganda tool, stirring the American public's outrage and desire for action, which the White House felt. The following month the Islamic State converged on its next target: the obscure Syrian town of Kobani, just south of the Turkish border.

FROM HIS PERCH in the Middle East, Mitch Harper watched the president's early August statement and felt some relief. He had tracked the birth, growth, and expansion of ISIS and monitored its unfettered advance across Syria and Iraq for months. He wondered what it would take for the world to gather its will and act to stop ISIS. Mitch led a small team of special operations forces deployed to the region. His team consisted of elite soldiers trained in unconventional warfare who had earned their spots following years of training and assessments, and who specialized in reconnaissance and counter-terrorism operations.

As special operations forces became increasingly utilized in the post-9/11 conflicts, their lives had become a calendar of deployments. Mitch had come of age at war. He was among the special operations forces that had deployed to Iraq and Afghanistan again and again since 2003, and he knew the region well. By the time he found himself back in the Middle East in the summer of 2014, he had lost count of his overseas tours. He had come, over the past decade, to see the fight against extremism as generational, as something he would be forced to bequeath to his children. He wondered how the U.S. would ever manage to end the cycle of fighting the same people in different neighborhoods in an extension of the same war in a different year. It wasn't lost on him that each year that went by, fewer and fewer people in the rest of America even remembered that troops were still deployed to Afghanistan and Iraq, while his kids grew older thinking that that was all their dad did.

Mitch's family, of course, counted among America's exceptions. He belonged to the less than 1 percent who had fought continually in America's wars since 2001. The circadian rhythms of his sprawling home off a quiet gravel road that barely received cell service or found GPS centered on Mitch's deployment cycle. Everyone had grown used to it by now, children and parents—even the family's dogs—alike.

Mitch had left home for his deployment in 2014 focused on the Islamic State and the threat its rise presented to the United States. He worried that no one had yet moved to counter the military threat ISIS presented to the region or tried to puncture the self-styled air of invincibility created by ISIS videos that showed storming soldiers clad in black, mowing over everyone who stood against them.

And then ISIS got close—very close—to Erbil, the capital of Iraq's Kurdistan Regional Government, the closest thing the Kurds of the Middle East had to their own capital, and a town with a sizable presence of American diplomats and service members.

For more than two decades the U.S. military had worked closely with the Iraqi Kurds. Some, like Mitch, even stayed in regular touch with their Iraqi Kurdish counterparts while back home in the U.S.

In the diplomatic realm, the U.S. had built a tradition of supporting the Iraqi Kurds financially and militarily, only to abandon them. In the 1970s, the U.S. had supported the Kurds against the Iraqi Baath Party, only to back away once tensions cooled between Iraq and (pre-revolutionary) Iran. With Tehran and Baghdad friends, the Americans had no need to use the Kurds as leverage against Baghdad. In 1988, the Iraqi president Saddam Hussein unleashed his military's power and chemical weapons against the Kurds, who dared to argue for their rights. Up to five thousand civilians are estimated to have been killed in *just one* chemical weapons attack employing mustard gas and sarin.

During Iraq's 1990 invasion of Kuwait, America moved swiftly to build a coalition to counter Saddam's offensive and initiated a successful campaign to force Iraq out of the tiny Persian Gulf nation. In the wake of Saddam's February 1991 withdrawal from Kuwait and ensuing cease-fire, the Kurds—along with Shia in the south of Iraq—rose up to overthrow the dictator. The U.S. did not come to their aid, and the Kurds found themselves once more alone internationally and crushed by Saddam's Baath regime. The U.S. and several Gulf War allies, including the United Kingdom and France, established a no-fly zone over northern Iraq, thus offering the Kurds a reprieve from Saddam's deadly bombardments. One year later, Iraqi Kurds went to the polls and brought into office the first-ever Kurdistan Regional Government, including its own parliament.

During the 2003 U.S. invasion of Iraq, led by President George W. Bush, American forces toppled Saddam Hussein in a war that a decade later would be seen by most Americans and Iraqi Sunnis alike as a source of loss, grief, and destruction. But for Iraqi Kurds, the war had offered a lifeline. They went from a nearly starved minority fearful of being gassed by their government to a group on its way to enjoying the self-rule it had always sought but been denied in the wake of World War I.

The northern Iraqi Kurdistan Regional Government, or KRG, now became home to U.S. bases and an American presence in Erbil and beyond. Americans like Mitch fought alongside Iraqi Kurdish Peshmerga units. Then the U.S. withdrew from Iraq at the end of 2011. The move, supported by an overwhelming majority of the American public, left some U.S. foreign policy observers full of concern that the Americans would be back soon because the threats from extremists to the country and the region had not ended.

ISIS would force the Americans' return. With Mosul's collapse and the Sinjar massacres, along with the urgency of stopping ISIS before it reached the Mosul Dam and the city of Erbil, the Iraqi government in Baghdad and the KRG leadership alike were now ready to enlist American assistance. By August 2014, U.S. troops were headed back to Iraq.

What struck U.S. special operations leaders the most as they observed ISIS tear across Syria and Iraq, was how different the Islamic State looked and acted from the terrorist groups that had preceded it and from which it had emerged. This wasn't simply the Taliban in Afghanistan or Al Qaeda starting insurgencies to unseat governments it opposed. ISIS instead looked more like a regular conventional army belonging to a nation-state: the group boasted a quick reaction force prepared to act when battlefield plans went sideways, integrated radio networks to allow different groups to talk with one another, and a mobile force ready to respond with significant firepower.

Back in Washington, a question arose after Mosul inside the National Security Council and the interagency process spanning America's national security organs: If the U.S. wanted to do more to stop ISIS, who would be the ground force? Administration officials charged with presenting options about what to do in Syria noted that most discussions began by explicitly stating what America would not do: commit U.S. ground forces to the fight.

Few good options existed. Europe's powers had no more appetite for going back to war in the Middle East than the Americans.

The ghost of the Iraq War showed no favorites: it haunted Washington and capitals from London to Brussels alike. Turkey arose as an option for countering ISIS in Syria, and the U.S. and its NATO ally held a series of discussions about it. Already the U.S. had instituted a plan to arm Syrians opposed to Bashar al-Assad who fell under the heading of "politically moderate." But in the end, these conversations about an anti-ISIS force went nowhere. The Turks had backed groups seeking to overthrow the Assad regime and remained focused on that fight as priority one. The Turkish government faced questions about the porousness of its border, as many ISIS fighters were crossing into Syria from Turkey unimpeded. Ultimately, the Americans concluded that Turkey did not possess the combination of military ability and will to accomplish the mission they required.

The U.S. needed a force capable and determined enough to fight ISIS but willing to stop short of taking on Assad. America had no desire to institute a regime change in Damascus or to be responsible for the future of another nation in the Middle East. The Obama administration felt it had to defeat ISIS, saw no standing armies ready to do so, and had no intention of putting Americans on the ground.

So who did that leave?

In Sulaymaniyah, watching U.S. officials scout for suitable partners, Lahur Talabany, head of the KRG's Zanyari intelligence service and a longtime interlocutor of the Americans, suggested that they meet the Syrian Kurds of the People's Protection Units. Talabany vouched for the YPG, explaining that this force had stood up against ISIS and the extremist groups that came before it in Syria in 2012 and 2013. He said the U.S. could trust this little-known militia: They would not back away from the fight, because the

Kurds would be massacred if the Islamic State carried the day. They also would not seek to topple Assad, because they couldn't be sure that whoever came afterward would not be worse for the Kurds. Senior leadership inside U.S. special operations began talking over Talabany's recommendation. In the absence of any other good alternative, the conversation looked worth having.

Already Brady Fox, another special operations veteran, had gotten word through other channels and people he knew on the ground about the YPG's role in the ISIS fight so far. Like Mitch, Brady had spent the last decade-plus deploying to Iraq and Afghanistan. He had been tracking the YPG for months and told his teammates to take a look at their Twitter and Facebook feeds. They showed photos of men—and, to his surprise, women—fighting Nusra and ISIS.

The YPG's actions in Sinjar that August bolstered the Americans' confidence in what might be possible. The YPG battled ISIS to enter northern Iraq from Syria and to rescue from the mountain tens of thousands of stranded Yazidis. They loaded old men, babies, and parents, some with only the nightgowns in which they fled, into tractors and pickup trucks and Jeeps and brought them to the northern Syrian town of Derek, where they housed families in a temporary city of blue tents. For the People's Protection Units, rescuing the Yazidis felt like taking care of their own, given the Yazidis' status as ethnic Kurds and the savagery Yazidi women faced at the hands of ISIS. The rescue also allowed the Syrian Kurds to show that they would take the risks needed to protect this minority group from genocide while proving their mettle to Iraqi Kurds who opposed them politically. They would gain international press and a dose of diplomatic goodwill in the process.

The first discussions between the Americans and the YPG

occurred that summer in Sulaymaniyah. Polat Can—a university-trained historian who was conversant in six languages, had written books about the Kurds' history, and had worked as a freelance journalist before helping to found the YPG in 2011—was sent by the People's Protection Units leadership to sit down with the Americans. Close to a dozen U.S. officials, including military leaders and diplomats based in the region, piled into the office where they met. They pulled out a map of northeastern Syria and placed it on the meeting room's table, and the strategic discussions began.

Polat Can had not known exactly what to expect from the Americans. He had begun his diplomatic outreach campaign on behalf of the YPG in February 2014. The Syrian Kurds had recently lost one hundred of their fighters in a single day to the Islamic State, which used tactics the YPG and YPJ had never experienced, including suicide bombers and vehicle-borne explosives. The grim degree to which the Kurds were militarily outmatched affirmed their desire to seek international backing. Already Polat Can had met with representatives of more than a dozen countries to answer their questions about the YPG and request critical support. Polat Can himself had been injured twice, most recently fighting the Al Qaeda–linked Nusra Front. The only reason he'd survived was the quick work of his teammate Rangin, from the Women's Protection Units, who risked her life to rescue him after he was shot. He knew firsthand how much tactical training his forces needed and how much they would benefit from the help of even basic technologies, such as GPS. But none of these countries was prepared to lead militarily, and all seemed affected by Turkey's view of the YPG and the diplomatic blowback working with the group would inspire.

By late summer, discussions between the U.S. and the YPG had gathered momentum. Leo James arrived in northern Iraq to broker the relationship and to see how far it could take the Americans in countering ISIS. A veteran special operations soldier who had been fighting overseas for more than a dozen years, Leo arrived in Sulaymaniyah as part of the U.S. force sent to protect Erbil. Upon landing, he went straight to the same military base the Americans had abandoned in 2012. His first thought as he set foot in the camp: nothing had moved. Even the silverware and the dishes were in the same place the U.S. forces had left them when they'd shipped out of Iraq two years earlier.

Leo began meeting regularly with Polat Can. The two men formed an odd pair: Polat Can, the university-trained scholar turned fighter, prone to speaking in sentences that became paragraphs, and Leo, a direct, rarely effusive enlisted soldier from America's East Coast who had been in and out of minor scrapes during high school before joining the military, to his mother's relief. Leo had gone to war in 2001 at the age of eighteen and never left it. By now, he had become a skilled fighter and a teammate known for his calm in battle. He also had become a student of extremist movements. He had been tracking ISIS fighters on YouTube and the messaging app Telegram for more than a year.

Conversations progressed and a foundation for cooperation emerged. Colleagues at the State Department and the White House wanted to use this moment to learn from past mistakes and talk about governance right up front. America had learned that failing to get these things right at the beginning made it impossible to end wars.

Yet even as the dialogue between the Americans and the Syrian Kurds pushed forward, one formidable challenge stubbornly remained. America's NATO ally Turkey considered the YPG to be terrorists because of their association with the PKK and made no distinction between the two groups. For Turkey, Ocalan remained public enemy number one. The Turkish government was still engaging in talks with the PKK aimed at negotiating a settlement to the three decades of conflict; a fragile cease-fire held at the moment, but developments in northeastern Syria had exacerbated tensions. Turkey feared the Syrian Kurds' control of the border and campaign for self-rule now under way. The idea of the Americans getting behind the YPG pushed Turkish leadership to speak out angrily.

Still, for the United States, the YPG remained the only ground force that stood a chance of countering ISIS militarily, and the Kurds sought self-rule, not regime change. Turkish leaders faced questions about their willingness to tolerate ISIS, given their prioritization of removing Assad. Special operations forces drew up possible plans to support this small band of fighters that seemed to be managing to do what no one else had; the YPG and the YPJ had shown they could be tactically resilient and disciplined enough to take on ISIS. Most important to Mitch and his teammates, they entered the fight with a will to win.

Only weeks after the discussion between the Syrian Kurds and the Americans began, ISIS attacked Kobani. The U.S.'s willingness to trust a partner it had just met would face an immediate test.

CHAPTER FOUR

H aval Azeema, how is it? What's the situation?"
Azeema recognized the Kurdish word for "comrade" and
the voice of her commander, Nowruz, coming through the black
radio stuffed in her right vest pocket. The radio's rubber antenna
stretched toward the sky, but the device often struggled to connect on the ground, even on the quietest days. When the fighting
grew intense, Azeema had to yell to be heard over the roar of bullets flying and fighters shouting.

Right in that moment, Azeema and her soldiers were holed up
in a city block on the south side of Kobani. Her commanders had
divided what terrain they still held into four front lines to try to
keep the city from falling to ISIS. This one was Azeema's. The
former high school volleyball star relished the fight at the front.
Her gifts as a sniper and her loyalty to her comrades had earned
her not only respect from the soldiers but also a promotion: she
now led several hundred YPG and YPJ members in the mission to
keep ISIS from capturing the southern front line and had several

troop commanders who reported to her, while she, in turn, reported to Nowruz. Her fellow soldiers saw her as one of them, a leader who stayed at the front and who never asked anyone to do anything she wouldn't—or hadn't already.

In normal circumstances, war allowed a brief moment to exhale, a nighttime pause in which senior commanders could debrief the day's events and discuss tactics for the following day. But this was not a normal war. The entire town of Kobani felt like a front line. There wasn't a safe place to return to after the day's fighting had ended or a place to rotate forces out to rest. Instead, Nowruz talked to Mazlum Abdi, who helmed the entire YPG, over the radio and on her cell phone, and used her walkie-talkie or phone to order her leaders to pull back or push forward—usually pull back—as she saw ISIS destroy their positions. Sometimes Znarin, Nowruz's aide, whose relatives came from Kobani and who knew the town well, would carry orders and bring ammunition and other supplies to the frontline commanders, who included Azeema and Rojda, Azeema's friend and distant relative. But Nowruz rarely took that risk; most of the time she spoke to Azeema and the others on one of her radios.

The radio crackled as Azeema tried to make out what else Nowruz was asking. But she had already deciphered the gist: Nowruz had heard that Azeema's sector was under fire. She wanted to know what she could do to help Azeema—but first, she wanted to make sure she was still alive.

ISIS HAD BEGUN THE SIEGE of Kobani on September 15, 2014. The offensive opened with an assault in which ISIS used recoilless rifles, a series of rocket-launch systems, and artillery to bombard the city's outskirts—a combined arms attack planned expertly and designed to besiege the city on multiple fronts at once.

For ISIS, capturing Kobani presented several advantages. One was unimpeded domain over the road that connected its self-declared capital, Raqqa, to the Syrian city of Aleppo. It also offered a chance to conquer the Kurds, whom ISIS viewed as infidels. And there was this reality: if Kobani fell, the other Kurdish areas would surely fall, too; the land around the town was flat, giving the YPG no ability to use geography as a means of surprise. After taking Kobani, ISIS would soon control the entire Syrian-Turkish border. ISIS declared that Kobani would be one more win on the way to achieving its vision of regional domination and beyond. As more and more foreigners from Europe—including France, Germany, the United Kingdom, the Netherlands—and across the Middle East and North Africa—Egypt, Tunisia, and Morocco, to start— poured into Syria to join ISIS forces and fight for the dream of the caliphate, the group sent its most capable men to Kobani to take part in what it promised would be a historic battlefield victory.

For the Syrian Kurds, as the days passed and no one came to their aid—neither Turkey, which refused to close the border to ISIS members or send troops to stop ISIS fighters in Kobani, nor the U.S. and its allies, which refused to help with airstrikes on the Syrian side even while striking ISIS targets only a few dozen miles away in Iraq—Kobani became a rallying cry. The first of November became #GlobalDay4Kobane as a Twitterstorm promoted by Kurds in the Middle East, Europe, and around the world—and by their growing number of sympathizers—pushed the topic on social media. In the wake of the savagery in Sinjar, including gutting images of women being carried away screaming from their families to face rape and enslavement, an outcry grew among regular citizens, who questioned how the West could sit back and allow one more humanitarian disaster to unfold unchecked.

Kobani's proximity to Turkey proved both critical and decisive. Cameras in Turkey trained on the Syrian border captured the beating the town was enduring—on its own and without allies—at the hands of ISIS; Western reporters, who faced kidnapping and beheading if they dared to enter ISIS territory, could stay secure in Turkey as they filmed and photographed the unfolding scene and shared it around the world instantly. These images influenced Washington and European capitals, too. Social media amplified images of fighters from the People's Protection Units, standing alone to stop ISIS after its glittering string of wins: young men in fatigues and young women in braids with flowered scarves, staring down the barrels of their AK-47s. The more world leaders sought to ignore the situation, the longer the cameras rolled, the stronger—and more compelling—the narrative of the plucky ragtag militia taking on the savage global terrorists became. By refusing to aid the Syrian Kurds, leaders, including in Turkey, who awaited Kobani's fall inadvertently helped burnish their image and grow their myth.

By November, the YPJ's ranks had expanded from a few hundred there in Kobani at the start of the fight to around double that, despite a number of soldiers being killed. Women came from Iran and Turkey to join this historic battle against ISIS now grabbing the world's attention, and when local families saw TV stories about young women taking up arms against ISIS, they became somewhat more willing to let their own daughters join. Some of the YPJ's forces remained in other areas, such as Qamishli, but most members who could go were sent to Kobani, given the urgency of the fight.

Still, the battle from September until November had been disastrous for the Syrian Kurds, cameras or no cameras. Azeema had lost close to a dozen friends in the first week. Underestimating ISIS's firepower proved costly in terms of both lives and resources. Like the Americans, the Syrian Kurds, including Nowruz, had watched ISIS take Mosul and Sinjar and the Syrian town of Ain Issa, not far from Raqqa. But they had still been taken by surprise when ISIS came to Kobani in September—after launching smaller-scale attacks against the town over the summer—with thousands of fighters and a slew of heavy weaponry, some of it American and taken from the Iraqi military in Mosul that June. ISIS launched its Kobani offensive by pounding at the town's countryside from both the east and west, and quickly killed a number of YPG and YPJ members. Morale plummeted as the death toll climbed and ground was lost, and the Syrian Kurds began to feel certain that they could not hold the city.

Azeema had not only had to wait to earn a position of leadership but had also had to fight for her place on the battlefield to begin with. When she first told her commanders she wanted to go to Kobani, in the middle of September, they told her no. "You aren't ready," they said. "You need more time." Nowruz wanted her to stay in Qamishli to help lead and learn from those at headquarters.

"If you don't send me to Kobani, I won't stay in the YPJ," she insisted. She knew her job required her to follow orders. But she also knew that she could do the most good for *everyone* by leading from the battlefield, not from an office. Each day counted. And the YPG didn't have the luxury of resting its fighters or waiting for them to have as much training as their enemies.

"The fighting is heavy," she said. "You need me there. And I need to be there."

For three days she sulked wordlessly before trying again. Finally, her leaders gave in.

Her experience so far had been shaped by the 2013 and early 2014 battles she'd participated in against the Nusra Front and ISIS.

Earlier that year, the People's Protection forces took the fight to ISIS in areas close to Azeema and Rojda's hometown, Qamishli, mostly in villages with farmlands and open roads. Kobani could not have looked more different: the town was a web of narrow lanes and houses crammed up against each other. Right now Kobani was on the verge of becoming a death trap for the Kurds, who were battling some of the most experienced soldiers ISIS had. The foreigners who poured in to join ISIS had seen a veritable greatest-hits list of extremist battles: Afghanistan, Chechnya, Somalia, Libya, Iraq; some had gone up against the United States and its allied forces in more than one of those places.

By the end of September, ISIS had Kobani encircled and controlled three-quarters of the city. Each day, more villages surrounding the town fell to ISIS as the Islamic State sent what seemed to Azeema like an inexhaustible supply of men to defeat them. At the start of October, ISIS tanks rolled into the final village standing between the Islamic State and Kobani and captured Mishtanour, a strategic hilltop the Kurds had used to defend the city.

After days of one-sided fighting, the order came from YPG leaders to withdraw from Mishtanour and allow ISIS to take the hill; the Kurds would retreat farther into the town center and hold what precious little real estate they had left. But even as the withdrawal order came, some YPJ members stayed to fight. And one, a young woman who went by the nom de guerre Arin Mirkan, went further.

Already Mirkan had become known in the YPG for her bravery. In early October a Syrian Kurdish journalist from Kobani recorded Mirkan telling the story of how she retook a house from ISIS. At first, she said, it wasn't clear whether the men she saw on the other side of the wall in the courtyard where she stood wore YPG or ISIS uniforms. "Haval," she called out, only to hear the men respond with "Allahu Akbar." She realized her mistake and began shooting. She told the reporter, matter-of-factly but with pride, that she killed at least two of them.

Days later Mirkan ended up on Mishtanour as part of the team whose position on that hillside fell to ISIS. She strapped a grenade to the waist of her uniform, ran toward oncoming ISIS tanks, and detonated the explosive right next to one of them, killing all the fighters inside the tank as well as herself. Immediately the story hit Kurdish news and spread from there of the young woman who sacrificed herself to help her people when she had no other weapons left. While Mishtanour's fall signified defeat, the event symbolized the YPJ's will to battle ISIS to their very last fighter.

The only option the Kurds had now that Mishtanour had fallen into ISIS hands was to bring the war into the winding streets of the town center. Nowruz told all her frontline leaders to prepare to battle house by house, street by street, and to begin putting sandbags in place to fortify their positions. Mazlum, who commanded the People's Protection Units after nearly a half dozen arrests by the Syrian regime, and who had been part of the PKK's ranks and known Ocalan well from his time in Syria, had ordered a shift in tactics while urging the civilians who still remained in the city to evacuate.

First, to counter the ISIS onslaught of tanks and mortars that their side faced with only AK-47s and a smattering of rocket-propelled grenades, Mazlum, Nowruz, and the small group of fighters who worked directly with them divided the emptied town into four front lines. The strongest commanders in the field, including Rojda and Azeema, would take charge of one each. From there, they would divide their soldiers into small groups, some as small as four, to keep from losing too many people at any one time. Snipers would be deployed to watch over their positions and kill ISIS members as they neared. The Kurds also would assemble a team of Kobani natives who understood how to best defend the town and could use their familiarity with the area—one of their few advantages—against their enemy. These forces would go out into the countryside, enter ISIS territory, and launch attacks from the back of the ISIS front line to confuse them and make them feel more vulnerable than they actually were. ISIS should never feel safe in Kobani, Nowruz instructed her forces. The final piece of the strategy offered perhaps the greatest challenge: leadership and morale. They had to make those whom they led feel that victory was possible even while they watched their enemy pour into the city in long columns of HiLux trucks, waving their black flags. If field commanders came to believe defeat was inevitable, it would be, Nowruz was sure.

Nowruz had called Mazlum as soon as she arrived in Kobani, at the start of the battle, and delivered only one message:

"We are going to win."

But the days were getting long and loss-ridden. Mishtanour Hill's fall had shaken everyone. By the second week of October, the war took root in the city center.

THE FIRST TIME SHE FOUGHT house to house, Azeema took only one lesson from the experience: *If they discover weakness in us, they will win.*

That had become the truth of the battle for her. She could only think about her role in the fight in one way: *The enemy in front of*

me, this man standing nine feet away, he has come to kill me. He mas-
sacred my people. It's my job to kill him first. And that's all there is.

"Haval Azeema," the invisible voice spoke from her pocket
again. "What is happening there? What is the situation?"

Azeema stopped her work boring a hole through the wall in the
house they had just taken and squatted low to answer her commander.

"They have been rocketing us all day and their snipers killed
one of our fighters when we crossed the street," Azeema told
Nowruz. "We hung the black curtain across the buildings to protect our position, but they know this tactic and they shot where
they guessed we were and got lucky."

What Azeema left out, Nowruz already knew. After the ISIS
sniper killed Azeema's fighter, a young woman who also was a
friend, two other ISIS men ran out, grabbed her body, and dragged
her toward their position. Then they took out their once-glimmering
knives, now turned brown by Kobani's dust and rubble, and beheaded her corpse right there on the street for all their men to see.
Azeema watched as her friend's head with its brown hair rolled
away from her body and her blood turned the ground beneath her
from dull grey to deep red. In case Azeema or her teammates had
any doubt about what fate awaited them if captured, ISIS erased it.
Sometimes the Islamic State shared images of beheaded YPJ fighters on social media.

Azeema wanted revenge. The more friends and battlefield
buddies ISIS shot dead or rocketed or beheaded, the more motivated she and her forces grew to shove these men out of their town
and to hand them their first military defeat.

Sometimes in the middle of their offensives, while they shot
their weapons at Azeema and her unit, ISIS fighters would shout

"Allahu Akbar," or "God is great." Their cries would echo across the city's streets and interrupt the rat-tat-rat-tat sound of small-arms fire. Azeema's soldiers would shout back in Arabic, "Kobani is the greatest!"

In quieter moments, during pauses in the fighting, her forces would break out the tambor, an instrument akin to a banjo. A young fighter named Baran, who had a deep singing voice they all loved, would pick up his instrument and play songs about Kobani and the friends they had lost:

> *Today, I will make Kobani's resistance into a poem and*
> *   distribute it among all the people of the world.*
> *Ah, woe to me, I am gazing at the streets of Kobani and seeing*
> *   the mothers' tears.*
> *Children and the elderly are crying out; tears of children*
> *   are streaming through the streets of Kobani like the*
> *   Euphrates River.*

EVEN IF IT WERE YOUR last moment, Azeema decided, you could still sing and dance. You couldn't shed your humanity just because your enemy had lost theirs.

Azeema grew accustomed to the physical intensity of war and the noise and the smells. But she would never get used to the death of her friends. She would replay every loss in her mind. But as much as she wanted to dwell on each death, and learn from it, she knew she couldn't: she would lose many more of her forces if she didn't bring 100 percent of her focus to the sound of bullets coming for them. At night, if she could rest, she would think about those ISIS had killed while she waited for sleep.

Nowruz's voice came back in.

"Azeema, stay where you are," she said. "We are facing a big fight both on the west side and the east side of the city, and we need to defend the lines that we have. Do not move forward. Hold your position."

Azeema had expected that Nowruz would say this, but she also knew that her team had to make progress soon or ISIS would be able to connect their positions and encircle them fully. Azeema had earned a reputation for taking risks others wouldn't and maybe even shouldn't. When Nowruz had come to visit her the week before, she told Azeema something she would never share on the radio for others to overhear: that they already had lost enough commanders to ISIS bullets and mortars. They needed her to stay alive; they needed her leadership.

"Haval Azeema, you are doing just what we need you to right there. Hold the position and keep them back," Nowruz said again on the radio. Her voice came in firmer than usual.

"I understand," Azeema said. "Haval Nowruz, one other thing: we really need bullets here. We are running low on ammunition. When should we expect supplies?"

There was a pause on the other end of the radio. Then: "We are doing our best, Haval. We will get something to you by tomorrow."

Azeema trusted Nowruz, but she had a feeling that they were seriously low on both troop reinforcements and bullets. In this case, Azeema told herself, maybe it was best to know less instead of more. If ammunition wouldn't arrive for days, no point in hearing that now. She shoved her radio back into her vest and returned her focus to the fight.

Just then her silver cell phone rang.

"Azeema." It was Dilawer, one of the men who fought with her, along with Harun, his teammate. Dilawer's tone was calm. "We have a big problem. *Daesh* has a whole group of us pinned down over here; they have us under siege," he said, using another name for ISIS. "We are trapped."

The plan had been for three or four small groups of fighters to clear ISIS from a few houses they thought they could take over; the YPG forces set out to meet in one location, with reinforcements to follow quickly. ISIS, however, found the gap between the teams and exploited it; instead of one larger YPG group battling a smattering of ISIS men, Dilawer and his teammates had become sitting ducks in the two-story house where they had managed to hole up.

"Can you give me your grid coordinates?" Azeema asked.

"We can't." Dilawer reminded her of what she already knew: ISIS would be listening. He urged her to come to the school near Mishtanour Hill so they could try to show her a sign that would make clear their location.

"Okay. Don't worry," Azeema said. "We will get you out of there. And stay off the radios—I don't want anyone else from our side trying to be a hero and coming to rescue you while we figure out how we are going to get you out of there. Don't look out the windows, because the enemy is going to try to shoot you. And spread out, a few of you, on the first floor to make sure no one can enter."

She took a breath while she collected her thoughts.

"Just stay calm and I will get you out; no matter what we will get you out of there," she said, listening to the sound of gunfire directed at her fellow forces while she spoke.

She hung up the phone and stood motionless for just a moment. For the first time in Kobani, Azeema felt doubt and fear tug at her.

She hadn't eaten more than bread in close to forty hours and had barely slept in days—just thirty minutes here and there. When her fighters urged her to rest, she would always answer them in the same way: "When you feel like at any moment a bullet might travel right to your front line, it's impossible to sleep. We'll sleep when the fight is over." Now she needed to think and to focus her imagination on how she would get them out.

She called Nowruz and explained what had happened, careful not to use the radio. ISIS monitored their channels, just as the YPJ monitored ISIS exchanges by taking the radios of the ISIS men they killed. Better to use the cell phone network from the Turkish company Turkcell, even if it meant Turkey could hear every move they made.

She let Nowruz know that she was going to try to get closer to their position. If her forces could get near enough, they could shoot mortars that would create enough smoke and confusion for Dilawer's group to escape.

Azeema knew Nowruz needed her to stay put—she had already told her that. But now twenty-one of her friends and teammates would die if she did nothing, and she would never abandon her responsibility to bring them back safely.

Azeema nudged two of her fighters to come with her, a young woman she had fought with for months and a young man who came from Kobani and knew its neighborhoods well. Weapons pressed against their shoulders, the three of them ducked out of their covered position and set out to rescue their friends.

Arriving at the hillside school, Azeema called Dilawer and Harun back.

"I'm here at the school and I can't figure out which house is yours," Azeema said.

"It's the one that looks like it is still being built; you can see the beams," Harun said.

"That's about half the street." Indeed, all the houses she could see looked gap-toothed and injured. And Harun had lost count of how many houses stood to the left and right of the place where they now were pinned down. There was no way to know where they were.

"Okay, let's try this. Can you wave something white from the window?" Azeema asked. Another of their fighters, Israel, crawled toward the window of the building separating him and his team from their deaths and waved a white scarf for a few seconds, letting only his arm dangle out.

"Got you!" Azeema shouted. "Great. Now can you show a red scarf from the same window, so I can know it is you?"

Israel did as she asked.

She called Judi—a young man responsible for the few heavy weapons, such as mortars and machine guns, the YPG had in its possession—and told him to come to her location as soon as he could. They needed to move fast. Then she got back on the phone with Harun and told him to wait for her call and not to take instructions from anyone else. She knew that other fighters, worried about Harun and Dilawer and their teammates, were trying to offer advice over the radio about what they should do. A lot of what they were being told would get them all killed, Azeema felt certain. They had to follow only her instructions if she was going to be able to extricate them from this disaster.

Judi at last arrived at the school. Azeema pointed to where their teammates sat awaiting rescue, and Judi examined the distance from there to where they stood.

"Make sure you don't hit that house," Azeema said, pointing again to where the scarves had just flown from the window. "But you can hit anything else in that area. It is all ISIS. They have it surrounded."

"I don't know, Haval," Judi said. "We'll do our best, but I think we're likely to be too far away for mortars to make any difference."

By now it was close to 3:00 p.m., more than an hour after Azeema first received Dilawer's call. Time mattered and they were losing it.

Judi shook his head and began preparing. Azeema could tell he did not feel certain that firing mortar rounds would make any difference, and the truth was that she shared his concern. She had to move up, closer to the building, and see for herself how far away the mortar rounds fell.

"Come on, let's go see Judi's work," Azeema said. She shared a smile with the two fighters accompanying her, but none of them underestimated the danger they were charging into.

The whistling ping of bullets sliced the air around Azeema and her teammates as they ran, low to the ground in a high-speed, crouched blur, across the first paved street dividing their territory from that of ISIS. They shoved their bodies behind a gutted building and gathered their breath, finding safety against the wall. They made no sound and gestured toward the next street. They crossed three more streets the same way, fully exposed to ISIS fire. Then Azeema felt certain that they could move no closer without getting themselves killed. The noise of men shooting at them hung in her ears, but judging by the sounds the bullets made, none had landed close enough to really bring trouble. She craved a cigarette.

Ducking into a hollowed-out building close enough for her to see the Islamic State's forces and to make out their black uniforms with ease, Azeema called the group back. They needed to be ready to run, she explained—the smoke from the mortars soon to be fired would create only a brief moment of chaos and cover in which they could escape.

Azeema looked down at her black digital watch. Only about twelve or thirteen minutes had passed since she left Judi, though adrenaline made it feel like hours. By her assessment, the mortar rounds should have been falling by now. She wondered what the holdup could be. Two or three minutes later, the crackling boom of incoming mortars broke up her thoughts. She craned her neck in the direction of her forces and watched as Judi went to work.

His fears were realized: not one of his mortars landed near enough to create an opening for Harun, Dilawer, Israel, and the eighteen others ISIS held trapped. Even the closest one landed well short. No smoke at all in which they could make their escape.

Azeema paused and put her head in her hands while she looked at the ground and spoke to herself silently for a moment. She had to keep her team's spirits up, even if she felt sure they were running out of time and options.

She called her teammates again. "Dilawer, don't worry—we have another plan," she said. She made sure to sound more confident than she felt in that moment. "Just don't listen to anyone else—and stay off the radio."

She had only one option left.

ON THE TWENTY-SEVENTH OF SEPTEMBER, the U.S. had launched its first strikes in the area of Kobani, with Air Force

F-15Es targeting an ISIS command and control center. Four days later, Adm. John Kirby of the Navy, the Pentagon press secretary, announced that America had conducted seventy-six airstrikes.

But if U.S. airpower sounded game-changing from a podium, it sure didn't look like it on the ground. By October, ISIS had managed to back Azeema and Nowruz and their teammates into just a handful of square kilometers of the city. As far as weaponry went, the YPG and the YPJ had only AK-47s, a random smattering of heavy weapons, and some PKMs, a machine gun designed decades earlier. ISIS had tanks, artillery systems, and even 155-millimeter Howitzers they had taken from Iraqi forces, who had received the equipment from America. They had armor. They showed up to the fight with weaponry created not to pick off a fighter here and there, but to kill their opponents in large numbers.

Just a few days after the U.S. airstrikes began, ISIS dominated the media narrative by raising two of its black flags on the east side of the city. On October 7, the Turkish president, Recep Tayyip Erdogan, who loudly opposed American assistance to the YPG, put it succinctly: U.S. airstrikes had yet to make a dent in the ISIS steamroll.

"Kobani is about to fall," Erdogan told reporters. "I am telling the West: dropping bombs from the air will not provide a solution."

On the limitations of helping the Kurds only from the air, American political leaders agreed with Erdogan. They worked to lower the public's expectations even while TV images of a besieged Kobani increased pressure on the White House to do more to help.

"As horrific as it is to watch in real time what is happening in Kobani, it is also important to remember you have to step back and understand the strategic objective," Secretary of State John Kerry said in a press conference. The Global Coalition to Defeat ISIS, formed in September 2014, had political and military objectives whose scope went beyond any one battle. The fight against ISIS was about more than defending Kobani; it was about attacking the group's infrastructure and its ability to command and control its forces in both Syria and Iraq.

White House advisers made clear they believed that the fall of Kobani might be inevitable. Few could imagine how airpower alone, without a U.S. ground presence, would stop ISIS from conquering Kobani. Indeed, in acknowledging this reality, deputy national security adviser Tony Blinken urged reporters to realize the scale of the challenge and just how many towns across two countries faced the same threat from ISIS.

"There are other Kobanis in Iraq; there are other Kobanis in Syria on a daily basis," Blinken noted.

Of course, for those Americans working with the Syrian Kurds to keep the town from falling to ISIS—from special operations leaders in the U.S. to their forces on the ground in Iraq—there was only one Kobani, and it was taking a beating. Back in the U.S., special operations leaders and team members now played a key role in events happening half a world away. They catalogued a mental list of the ISIS advantages: access to night-vision gear, thermal weapons sights, and heavy weapons. A real knowledge of war, born of experience and fluency in siege warfare, with the ability to enter one home and pass through an entire city block undetected by crawling house to house through holes blown out between the walls. ISIS was no insurgent operation. Informed by more than a decade of fighting the Americans in Iraq, these men had mustered up a near-conventional military, a force skilled in tactics and aligned on strategy to take and keep territory.

By the end of the first week of October, right around the time of Secretary Kerry's statement, the situation in Kobani was so dire that members of the special operations team began to sleep in a conference room at their headquarters on two-inch-thick, rollout Tempur-Pedic mattresses. If the U.S. had the resources available to launch airstrikes—which at that time was a big "if," given the focus on Iraq, the limited airpower in the region only months prior, and the reality that no one had planned even six months earlier to provide aerial support to a ground force in Syria—and the Syrian Kurds and the Americans both had a confirmed location where they could strike ISIS with no civilians present, they wanted to do their part to help. The only way to ensure the team could be reached quickly once a location was confirmed? Never leave the office. No one knew whether being ready to strike at a moment's notice would help the Kurds hold off ISIS. But the team felt certain that if they didn't stay ready, they would lose valuable time and even more fighters to the Islamic State.

At home, some of their wives asked about the female forces they saw on TV, and whom America now supported from the skies. Many had long tracked their husbands' work, but it almost always fell under the impenetrable canopy of "top secret," so no details could be shared. This was different. Just about the entire battle played out on phones and screens every day. Some went on social media to learn more about Rojda and Azeema and the others in the all-women's force, and started following them on Twitter and

Facebook. They would ask their husbands about how the day had gone based on what the YPG and the YPJ posted. For Mitch's teammates back home, Kobani was a new turn: never before had their families been able to watch their work in real time.

Still, by the second week of October, the U.S. was authorizing airstrikes to support the ground forces only in a trickle and rarely in time to make a difference. Leo James, who helped build the foundation for U.S.-YPG cooperation with Polat Can over the summer, called his leaders from Sulaymaniyah to argue his case in the clearest language possible.

"We are going to lose here—in a big, big way. And we are going to lose in the next twenty-four hours if we don't change things," Leo said. He himself was fighting ISIS on the ground in the Iraqi town of Kirkuk—a forty-minute drive from Sulaymaniyah—whenever he wasn't at the operations center monitoring events in Syria. This was what Kerry and Blinken had meant when they said the U.S.-led coalition's effort to stop ISIS covered two countries and was more than just one town in northern Syria. "This partner is going to be defeated and with it we will lose our best—probably our only—chance to stop these guys. They cannot fall back any further. They are going to fight until the last person dies, and then this whole thing is all over. People here *cannot* believe that we can't do more. You want to talk about the story ISIS is going to sell out of this? Are we prepared to watch the victory lap they are about to take?"

As October wore on, the U.S. stepped deeper into the fight. Kobani had become a symbol of resistance, fueled by the satellite feeds that traveled from cameras on a Turkish hilltop to televisions all around the world. Inside the Obama administration, there was a feeling that the White House had to do something. "We ended up acting there even though we didn't act in a number of similar situations; it was just in the world's eye," one official recounted years later. Television images made it that much more difficult to stand by and let the town fall.

The strikes began to make a difference as they came in greater number and with greater frequency; on October 14, U.S. Central Command announced that it had carried out more than twenty airstrikes near Kobani, seriously damaging crucial ISIS staging areas.

STILL, THE People's Protection Units couldn't always get U.S. airpower when they needed it; indeed, most of the time it took a minimum of an hour for the U.S. to confirm locations, make certain no civilians could be found there, and get the resources necessary for a strike. That lag had led to lost lives. Azeema knew this when she called Bavar, a Syrian Kurd from Kobani who worked as the go-between for the YPG and the U.S. Bavar had a tablet with the town's coordinates and Google Earth access. He worked with his fellow fighters to find the exact coordinates of the locations where ISIS gathered. He passed these coordinates to Polat Can or others back in Sulaymaniyah, who then shared them with the Americans, who began their verification process.

Azeema called Bavar with her walkie-talkie while keeping Dilawer on the line, her cell phone pinned to her right ear. She kept her voice calm, urging Dilawer to stay with her and not give up and not listen to anyone trying to put forward another plan; help would arrive. She just had to get everyone to hang in there a bit longer.

"Hold on, Dilawer," Azeema said, handing the phone to a

teammate as Bavar answered her call on the radio. Azeema began describing in short sentences exactly where her forces sat trapped. Static interfered every fifth or sixth word. She repeated their location to make sure he heard.

"Look, I know the Americans can't answer every request for strikes, but we have close to twenty-five people in there," she said. "We have no other option if ISIS isn't going to kill them."

Bavar acknowledged the grid coordinates and went on to transmit his message: Kobani to Sulaymaniyah, Sulaymaniyah to the U.S., and the U.S. back to the Middle East, where American airplanes awaited approvals.

Azeema paced in the shell of a structure where she now holed up, waiting to see what would happen, while her request for a strike traveled across the globe.

She got back on the phone with Dilawer's group and yelled at them to crouch in corners, away from windows, with their hands over their ears.

Minutes passed. She started to think about what would happen if she had to recover bodies instead of her teammates alive.

Suddenly the clatter of a B-1 bomber overhead shook the earth on which Azeema was pacing.

A whizzing roar overwhelmed her ears as the bomber unleashed its munitions. Seconds passed as she saw the explosives fall toward the earth.

She stopped breathing.

Finally, only moments later, Azeema watched buildings buckle toward the ground and, with them, all those inside. Smoke billowed and rolled down the street in waves as the charred structures leveled by the strike exhaled black.

Azeema called Harun, but he didn't answer. She ran forward, straight toward the building too dangerous to approach only a few minutes earlier. She wanted to be the first to greet her teammates if they actually made it out.

And then she saw it: the huge smile of Dilawer as he ran toward her, full of joy. Azeema caught him in her arms and the two hugged.

"The others?" she asked.

"Everyone is alive."

Azeema doubled over, her chest touching her knee for a moment as the news that no one was dead sank in. One of their teammates, a young woman, had been shot in the leg. Shrapnel had hit Harun in the forehead and left a gash. But they had all survived.

One of Azeema's fighters called on the radio for a car to whisk their injured teammates to the hospital. They needed care right away—they had lost a lot of blood. But both were conscious and looked remarkably happy for people who had been wounded.

By the time Azeema and her forces—including the uninjured nineteen who had made it through the day's events—returned to their positions on the southern front line, night and its crisp coolness had arrived.

"Rest tonight," Azeema told her troops. She gave the fighters who had been by her side all day a wink. "Get sleep. Tomorrow is guaranteed to bring more adventure."

She at last took her rifle off her shoulder and carefully placed it next to her.

"First World War I, then World War II, now Kobani," Azeema said, lighting the cigarette she had thought of for hours, a twinkle of mischief in her dark brown eyes. "The world is never going to forget this fight."

ISIS still had the momentum—the YPG and YPJ hadn't yet been able to pull it away from their enemy. That would change, Azeema told herself. But tonight they would enjoy a bit of tambor and do some dancing to keep the cold away and celebrate their survival.

CHAPTER FIVE

November 2014 began with ISIS controlling nearly 60 percent of Kobani. But as the month wore on, a few factors converged that began, slowly, to shift momentum in favor of the Syrian Kurds. First, roughly 150 Peshmerga fighters from Iraqi Kurdistan arrived to serve as reinforcements. The Americans helped broker a deal in which Turkey allowed Iraqi Kurds to join their Syrian counterparts in battle, assisted by strong relations between the Iraqi Kurds and Turkey. Arab forces from the Free Syrian Army who had fought ISIS elsewhere joined the fight as well.

The Americans, too, expanded their aid to the Syrian Kurds in a decision made by President Obama in late October that angered Turkey and further strained the relationship between Ankara and Washington. Using C-130 planes, the U.S. launched a nighttime airdrop of small arms, ammunition, and medical supplies into Kobani. One of the three doctors left in the town burst into tears and shouts in the middle of a blackened, empty street, raising his hands to the sky in elation, the first time he saw medical supplies slam

down where his makeshift hospital, starved for bandages and anes-
thesia, struggled each day to treat its wounded.

Obama himself informed the Turkish president of his decision
to launch the airdrops, following an extensive and sometimes con-
tentious White House deliberation in which advisers underscored
the fury with which Turkey would react. The move marked a significant step from the Americans toward entering the ISIS fight
in alliance with the People's Protection Units. The truth was, in
the view of those inside the Obama administration who argued
for the airdrop, no one else had a better plan for stopping the Islamic State.

America's F-15s, A-10s, and B-1s had begun making regular appearances above Kobani. B-1 crews from the Ninth Bomb Squadron stationed at Dyess Air Force Base in Texas rerouted from a
planned deployment focused on fighting the Taliban in Afghanistan to one aimed at stopping ISIS in Syria. Military leaders had
been preparing to eventually take the B-1 out of circulation; now
the war in this contested sliver of northern Syria had given the
aircraft an unlikely new lease on life.

Beyond the Kurds' northeastern corner of the country, the Syrian regime remained locked in a battle with rebels who wanted to
oust Assad. The Syrian Army had begun advancing toward the
north of Aleppo, the most populous city, blocking supply lines into
the area, and had retaken a town from opponents in Damascus's
Eastern Ghouta. The Syrian Army also regained a town north of
Hama as it sought to stabilize its hold on the west. For Syrians
fleeing the war, there were fewer and fewer places to go; in October, Lebanon shuttered its border crossings and said it would take
no more Syrians after more than a million had come seeking safety.

By November, ISIS had lost enough fighters in Kobani that the group began to call for thousands of reinforcements. For the Islamic State, which had been feeling invincible after a string of wins, defeat in Kobani—to an unknown, unsophisticated, and far less experienced opponent—felt inconceivable. And it was bad for recruiting and propaganda.

Still, their battle strategy was relentless: ISIS turned trucks and cars into explosives multiple times a day to break through the lines Nowruz and her fellow commanders had fought so hard to establish. For Nowruz, each day couldn't end soon enough. She stood for hours at tables in the group's makeshift headquarters, a cement-walled school located on the corner of what once was a quiet street, and spoke to Rojda and Azeema on the radios, listening to their channels as the fight played out. Znarin, Nowruz's aide, urged her boss to eat, bringing her plates of bread and canned meat she left untouched. Znarin would stand at the back of this impromptu command center, watching Nowruz's example of calm amid calamity.

At night, Nowruz could sometimes send reinforcements to help her frontline commanders get a bit of rest; only generous neighbors opening up their cabinets filled with tins of meat and cheese to YPG fighters saved the group from running out of food. Nowruz warned all her team against eating the chickens they saw roaming around the city: the animals feasted on the remains of fighters killed in the battle. Eat the chicken, Nowruz said, and you would be eating dead bodies.

Some late evenings, when stars sparkled overhead and silence finally arrived, Nowruz allowed herself this thought: *One day we will be finished with this war. And then people will know that women showed their power on the front lines.* At the end of November, however, as she walked around the command center, she did not know whether the front lines would even hold through the night.

. . .

THE DAY BEGAN with a BOOM. Nowruz heard it from the school and felt it, too. She grabbed one of the four radios in front of her and reached out to Azeema, who said she had heard it but hadn't been touched by it. Then she radioed Rojda.

"Haval Rojda, what is happening?" Nowruz asked.

"We've been taking fire for hours and it looks like we will have to find another position," Rojda answered. The radio crackled and gunfire muffled the sound of her voice. "We can't move anywhere—maybe we've gained a meter. Not more.

"We're conserving our bullets, but that means we have to let Daesh get close enough to kill them, which means close enough for their bullets to get us, too," Rojda said.

Rojda now led parts of the western front line. Like Azeema, she hadn't started the Kobani battle in charge of this sector, but had ended up being chosen for command by Nowruz and Mazlum. Rojda, soft-spoken and rarely brash, at first glance the opposite of Azeema, had impressed her superiors with her decisiveness in battle. She didn't need bravado to lead; her own quiet style inspired confidence in a different way. Rojda hadn't spoken with Azeema in weeks—there was no time for that in the middle of this war for survival—but she thought of her childhood friend often and listened for news of her on the radio channels. (Rojda's mother, who still blamed Azeema for Rojda's being there, asked about Azeema nearly every time she called Rojda, which was every day.)

ISIS had attacked Rojda's front line and they had no place to go.

"They are attacking from four directions and from the Turkish border," Nowruz told Rojda. "They have just sent a car bomb through the Turkish crossing, and they are penetrating the front line." ISIS's strategy was to surround the YPG forces and give them no space to maneuver.

It wasn't just ammunition that was running low. Nowruz worried that her field commanders were running low on hope. She needed them in the fight and all she had were words to convince them they could push ISIS back.

"Think about all those women in Sinjar," Nowruz said to Rojda, speaking of the Yazidis ISIS now raped, traded, and tortured. She held her radio only a few inches from her mouth and spoke loudly so Rojda could hear through the din of battle. She paced in the classroom while she spoke. She couldn't deliver more forces or more ammunition, but what she could do for her fighters was remind them of the importance of their mission and inspire them to ignore all the things they lacked, because they remembered why they fought. "They would do the same to us. You must take revenge for the Yazidis and for all the women they have brutalized. Daesh thinks you are useless, that you are nothing, that you have no value at all. Show them what you are capable of. Prove yourself in this battle. And remember that this fight is not just for you. It would be better to die with dignity here, today, than to become their slave."

"I understand," Rojda said into her walkie-talkie when Nowruz finished. "We are here. We won't give up."

Rojda put down her radio and worked to figure out how to keep her front line intact.

Then: BOOM. Another car bomb sent stacks of black smoke climbing upward, as if a night-colored blanket had been dropped over a narrow band of sky. The voice of an ISIS fighter traveled over the radio and stopped her thoughts.

"Women, surrender," came the man's voice. Rojda worked to identify his accent. She had heard that Indonesians had come to fight for ISIS, but she had no idea what they sounded like. This man didn't come from Syria—that much she knew. "We are coming for you and we are going to take you as our slaves. We are going to rape each one of you and then we are going to kill you. Your families will see it all."

"We are coming," the fighter said. "I myself will see you soon."

Rojda tuned out his words as she tried to figure out where they could retreat to if they had no more room left. She sat for a moment with her hands at her ears, considering what options she had.

But her forces saw an opportunity.

"Hey, if you are really a man, then come out and show yourself," a young YPJ fighter with curly brown hair shouted into the radio in Arabic. "You talk about killing us. We are going to come and kill you first. And then where will you be when it comes time to go to paradise?

"We know you are in the house across from the old bakery—"

The ISIS fighter interrupted her.

"No, we are in the house behind it," he said.

That was all the help Rojda's team needed. The ISIS fighters had just given away their position.

Rojda heard more explosions coming from the eastern side, close to the Turkish border, and turned back to her battle plans.

"HAVAL AZEEMA, can you hear me?" She recognized the voice of Ferzan, one of her fighters.

"Yes, Haval, what do you need?"

"We are seeing some people here near our position," he said. "They look like ISIS and there is a woman with them.

"What should we do?" he said. "It looks like she might be a sniper. We can't kill a woman, can we?"

Azeema knew ISIS had women among its fighters—or at least she had heard it. But she hadn't seen any for herself. She wondered what could persuade a woman to fight on the side of these men who enslaved women.

"You have to get closer," Azeema said. She now spoke to a different fighter, the leader of the group, which was composed of four women and two men. "See if she is actually a shooter. If she is, then you have to kill her."

Azeema picked up immediately when another in the group called to report back. This time it was Zuzana, a young woman from Kobani there to protect her town.

Zuzana told Azeema that the woman who stood with the ISIS fighters, now about twenty meters away, carried a sniper rifle. She was the only woman among six or seven men. She was tall, thin, and blond, Zuzana said, and wore the clothing of a foreigner—a T-shirt and what looked like jeans. The blond shooter stood out; she didn't look like any other women they had seen in Kobani.

Azeema lit a cigarette as she figured out her day's defenses. Her silver phone chimed again.

"Azeema, Ferzan says as a man he cannot target a woman," Zuzana said. "He said you have to okay it—he wants to hear it from you."

Zuzana passed the phone to Ferzan.

"Ferzan, this is on my conscience, not yours," Azeema said. She understood his sensitivity about killing women, but this was war.

"I am a woman telling you it is okay to kill another woman. It's on me. You can't let her stay there shooting at us."

Ferzan and Zuzana went up to the window position where they had an AK lodged in a hole in the wall. Ferzan called Azeema back a half hour later. The job was done.

THE ENDLESS DAY wound on for Nowruz. She stood in front of her row of radios, talking with Rojda and Azeema and Sozdar—a dear friend and fellow female fighter with whom she worked closely on planning and who was more senior to field commanders Rojda and Azeema—figuring out where to send which unit next as front lines gave way. They had lost count of the day's dead. The People's Protection Units took fire from four directions and couldn't fully defend any. The Americans landed airstrikes against two targets: a staging area from which ISIS launched attacks and one of the buildings it used to house its forces. Neither made much of a difference.

Rojda needed bullets. They had just begun to call around to all the front lines and get the casualty counts, but they knew already that ISIS had hit their western front, which she now led, hard. The clapping roar of car bombs and rocket-propelled grenades striking her forces interrupted the sounds of incoming mortar rounds and small-arms fire.

Nowruz asked Znarin to take some ammunition over to Rojda. As she sped through the streets, Znarin scanned the rooftops and blasted-out windows, searching for snipers and suicide bombers. She felt more alive than she ever had, even while living closer to death than ever before. Her family had denied her the right to make her own choices, first taking away her education and then the man she loved. But she had made her own decision to be here.

When she arrived at Rojda's position in an apartment building on the western side of the town center, the two women embraced. The street outside had been utterly destroyed: all along it stood sagging buildings buckled by war, looking like survivors of the apocalypse. Znarin left Nowruz's truck running while she made her delivery; moving quickly was better for everyone.

"Thank you for bringing this, Haval," Rojda said with a sideways smile, looking equal parts resolute and exhausted. "This day has been very, very long."

Znarin looked at Rojda and felt a surge of pride to see this young woman with a quiet laugh and a long braid leading her forces against this enemy.

Back at the base, Nowruz and the YPG had stopped issuing statements to local media. They simply didn't know what to tell them. Still, Nowruz refused to say they had surrendered. She paced their command center, looking at maps and talking to her field commanders and to Mazlum, figuring out what their next move could be.

When dawn arrived, they still held on to a handful of blocks in the city. A victory in itself.

FIVE WEEKS after that endless day, Azeema picked up her ringing flip phone and prepared to tell Nowruz her next steps.

"Haval," she said, "here's my plan—"

"Azeema?" Azeema recognized the voice of her youngest sister, Wahida. "How are you?"

Azeema felt a surge of irritation. She had told her sister a few weeks earlier not to call. She needed to focus on the fight. She didn't have time to offer hourly updates to her family, who were tracking every moment of the battle for Kobani on Facebook and WhatsApp, and she let Wahida know as much, her voice rising.

"Do I need to sit next to you on the couch and hold your hand?" she demanded. "We are trying to win a fight here." Then she softened toward her sister, but only a bit. "I promise you the first moment the city is free I will call you. Until then, don't worry—and don't call."

She clapped her phone closed—and realized her whole team had overheard her tirade. Their current position in an old apartment building made it hard to have even a moment of privacy.

"Okay, okay," she said, laughing about the scene her troops had enjoyed and picking up her waiting cigarette. "Back to work."

Lighter moments remained precious, but there was reason for optimism among the YPJ ranks. American airstrikes were making a difference, slowly, incrementally, and not at all inevitably, as Secretary of State Kerry had noted early on. Each day, the U.S. targeted ISIS fighters' convoys and weapons supplies. Add to this the small groups of forces that had joined the YPG from northern Iraq and the Free Syrian Army, who opposed both Assad and ISIS, and the band of fighters defending Kobani had clawed their way to retaking territory in December. They stood now, at the beginning of January, in a better position than they had since September.

To Western foreign policy watchers, American airpower was all that stood between ISIS and the conquering of Kobani. Inside the town, it was clear that the strikes made a difference. But the weapons drop from the U.S. had mattered, too. Without a ground force standing on its own and doing the fighting, airstrikes alone would not have been enough to keep the city out of ISIS hands.

Her family drama over for the moment, Azeema sat thinking about how she would counter that day's ISIS offensive. Nowruz had contacted her on the radio earlier and advised her to stay in her current position on the southern front line, given heavy clashes elsewhere in the city. ISIS wanted to turn its focus to the eastern border and to retake the school where Azeema's forces were stationed. The Islamic State was on the hunt for a symbolic victory.

"ISIS wants two things," Azeema told her fighters a few minutes later as they stood in a huddle, eating two-day-old bread for breakfast. "They want to hold Mishtanour Hill. And they want to take control of the border gate." This was the divide separating Kobani from Turkey. Sending up the black ISIS flag from these locations would show the Americans that the fight was over; ISIS would hold the highest ground and control the terrain onto which the Kurds would otherwise try to fall back.

"We can't let them achieve either," she said. "We have to be ready for them."

Her radio sounded.

"Azeema, take care. There are clashes on the front line now— very heavy ones," Nowruz told her. "Try and guide your forces out of there. Make sure everyone is safe. I am going to try and send reinforcements if I can find them."

Azeema knew she had to heed her commander. But she also knew she was needed up at the front.

One of the YPG commanders leading a unit in the east called Azeema on her cell phone after her discussion with Nowruz. He needed help. She knew this wasn't the normal battle order, which would have seen Azeema taking instruction from Nowruz, but he had to have reinforcements now.

Crawling through buildings so that they would not get shot on the street, Azeema and her soldiers started toward the eastern front line. They reached one of the last streets between ISIS fighters and the border gate.

She called Nowruz.

"I had to advance a little bit," Azeema said. "The situation on the front line is very tough and they needed help."

"Send someone else, Azeema," Nowruz said. "Don't go yourself."

Azeema looked down at the radio and was quiet for a second or two.

"I'll do my best," she said.

The whistling sound of bullets flying ended the discussion.

Azeema's unit crouched below a courtyard wall separating a house from the street. All around came the percussion of gunfire. A bullet landed three feet away.

Another bullet sank into the earth right in front of Azeema. She waited for a pause, then bobbed up above the wall and shot back.

"Haval, if I get wounded here, do not leave your place," Azeema shouted at Mustafa, one of the men she led. "Keep fighting no matter what."

On the other side of the wall, Azeema counted eight ISIS fighters targeting her team from a house across the street. And now, she realized, bullets came at them from the east side of the house, too.

Azeema peered over the wall and saw fighters aiming at their position. She shot one, then two. And she heard what she thought was the sound of bodies hitting the ground.

"Two down," Mustafa said. Azeema acknowledged his words with a nod and reloaded her AK-47. Only six more to go.

An ISIS tank lumbered down the street, its guns aimed at her team. Azeema's soldiers fired at it, but the M1 moved forward unimpeded. The tank's fire hit the house behind them and demolished its entrance, but failed to kill any of her soldiers. Azeema knew they wouldn't be so lucky again. When the tank circled around a few minutes later, her soldiers stood ready. Mustafa tossed a grenade that landed beneath it, and the tank exploded.

"We have to make our way toward the school—we can't let them take it," Azeema said to her fighters. She stooped low and began sprinting, her teammates following suit.

She heard the ISIS guns firing but kept her mind trained only on moving as fast as she could.

They reached the school's courtyard and crouched behind its exterior wall. While she'd run toward the school, she'd registered a bald man with brown eyes and a brown-and-grey beard standing on the opposite side of the wall there on the street. His weapon was aimed at her. She lifted her gun and peered over the wall, looking for him.

A bullet whizzed by her brow, missing her by maybe three inches. She placed her body against the wall and pushed herself upward. The moment she could see the bald fighter's position, she shot at him. He shot back again.

Azeema reached for her Kalashnikov. Suddenly, she realized her left hand could not bear the weapon's weight. Her arm hung limply instead of grabbing the rifle; the limb refused to do anything her brain commanded. She moved upward again to peer through her sniper scope and shoot at her adversary. But she couldn't see a thing through the lens she had come to know so well. *What's wrong with my scope?* she thought to herself. *Everything looks so blurry.* She lifted her right hand to examine her left eye. It felt enormous, like a balloon filled with water. Returning her hand to her lap, she saw through her other eye only red liquid, sticky to her touch. Blood. The bald man must have gotten her.

She pulled her camouflage shirt away from her body so she could see the fabric. A red stain in the top left corner made her think that the bullets might have hit her heart.

Azeema heard Mustafa and her other fighters making plans to keep advancing.

"Go, go," she said, looking up from her self-exam and shooing them forward with a wave of her arm. "I will catch up."

"Azeema, you have to get to the doctor," Mustafa said. He sounded to Azeema as though he wanted her to think he was calm—only she knew better. "You have to get treatment. We are going to get you to the hospital."

"No way," Azeema said. "Not yet. You keep advancing and I will cover you."

What she wanted more than anything now was to kill the man who shot her. With her one good eye and her right hand, she targeted him where he stood; she felt certain he must be only three or four meters from her. She fired a first round of bullets and then a second. Then she felt a surge of satisfaction as she saw the bald man with the brown eyes crouching in the street for a moment. He grabbed his leg where she must have hit him. He hopped off the battlefield seconds later, moving as fast as his uninjured limb could carry him. Azeema shot at him again and missed.

Blood continued to redden her shirt. Azeema didn't want to leave her soldiers, but she knew it would be worse to stay and slow them down. She stood up on her own and limped toward the back of the front line to the collection point for injured fighters where she had taken so many of her friends. A black HiLux careened in to ferry her to the makeshift hospital—once a school, now treating Kobani's wounded.

When she arrived, Azeema saw dozens of other injured YPG and YPJ fighters on stretchers and lying on plush blankets on the floor of the building's basement. Some no longer had both legs; others wouldn't make it more than a few hours, judging by the amount of blood they were losing.

Only a handful of doctors remained in Kobani, and all they did was tend to the wounded. They knew when they decided to stay in the town that they might not survive. One had refused to leave even after he had gotten his family across the border to safety in Turkey. He saw Azeema come in and noted her ability to stand on her own. He assumed that she had only a flesh wound and went on tending to his most urgent cases, including a young man who would soon become an amputee.

A half hour or so after Azeema arrived, he began to examine her.

"Looks like it is just shrapnel," he said. "You should be fine; don't worry."

He offered a smile.

Azeema wished she could be as hopeful as he was that this wasn't serious.

The doctor asked her to raise her arms.

"My left hand is weak, Doctor," Azeema said. "I can't move it properly."

He picked up her hand and then pressed on her arm and followed it upward. As Azeema took off her vest, the source of her arm's weakness became clear. Blood soaked the entire left side of her camouflage shirt. The bullet from the bald, bearded fighter had penetrated her chest.

The doctor called his colleague over and his smile vanished.

"The bullet is very close to your heart," the first doctor said after seeing the wound. "If we operate now, you could lose your life. We want to keep you here to rest. We will keep close watch and wait for the bullet to move. Then we can operate."

"I can go back and rest with my fighters," she said. "It'll be fine."

"Absolutely not," he said. He reminded her that the bullet had nearly killed her and insisted she stay at the hospital, where they could monitor her condition. She felt her head throbbing and her arm aching. Finally she lay down on the stretcher where she had been sitting.

The only thought that comforted her as she closed her eyes: she had shot the man who shot her and forced him off the battlefield, too.

NOWRUZ LEARNED that Azeema had been shot almost as soon as it happened. She heard Azeema's forces call on the radio for the car to take her to the hospital. Her first thought was for Azeema's safety. Her second was that she had told her to remain back and that Azeema had gone forward anyway. She knew Azeema and understood that no matter what anyone said, she would never let her people face danger without her. But now Nowruz had a team without a leader. Another problem to solve.

Nowruz counted that January day as a success despite the ISIS attacks. The YPG and YPJ won back several schools and streets in the government district. As Azeema wanted, the YPG advanced in the direction of Mishtanour in the south of the city. The next day, the YPG launched its most significant counteroffensive in weeks, aided by three airstrikes from the American side. A few days later that number climbed to eight, and the YPG took advantage of the strikes to move forward and retake ground from the militants, increasing its control of parts of the government district. The group also beat back an offensive ISIS attempted to launch around a library and seized ISIS weapons. And the border gate remained in YPG hands, meaning that ISIS could not enter Kobani from Turkey's border. Momentum had begun to shift.

Nowruz went to see Azeema in the hospital the day after she was shot.

"Thank God you're safe," Nowruz said, leaning over the make-shift bed to hug Azeema gently. "You got lucky for the second time!"

A few weeks earlier, a bullet had grazed Azeema's right arm. That time, she'd had to remain in the hospital for only a few hours, just long enough for the doctors to clean up her wound and make sure it wasn't more serious. This was different.

"You know I am lucky," Azeema said. "They cannot get me." She smiled weakly at her leader.

"Just rest for a bit here, please, Azeema," Nowruz said. "As soon as your health improves you can go back to the front line. The doctor agrees. But for now, stay here and rest. And you have to listen to me this time. That is a command."

Soon after Nowruz, Rojda came to see Azeema. The doctors joked that she had too many visitors and needed more rest.

"You shouldn't have come," Azeema scolded her. "They need you to be fighting."

Rojda smiled at her childhood friend. When she'd first spotted Azeema at the students' union meeting four years earlier, she never imagined she would see her friend in this condition, lying in a hospital bed with a bullet lodged near her heart and a bandage around her head to protect the eye she had nearly lost.

She and Azeema used to lock arms while walking back to Azeema's house from high school, stopping to get ice cream and joke and visit with friends. Now Rojda held Azeema's hand and searched for a way to make her laugh.

"And I know how you think, Azeema," she said. "Don't you even try to jump up and escape from this hospital."

Rojda's mother called her soon after she saw Azeema. Rojda picked up and, instead of saying hello, held out the receiver so that her mother could hear the sound of gunfire for herself. Rojda had learned that if she didn't answer the call when her mother rang, she would simply keep trying her and then she would start calling their friends and relatives to find out if they had heard from her. Easier to answer her, even in a firefight.

"How is Azeema?" her mother asked, when Rojda finally spoke to her in a whisper. Though she blamed Azeema for Rojda's decision to join the People's Protection Units, Rojda's mother always worried for both her own daughter and her dear friend.

When Rojda told her mother that Azeema had been shot, her mother's wails were so loud that Rojda's forces heard them through the phone, even in the middle of the gunfire.

"Be careful, be safe, my daughter," Rojda's mother said, nearly shouting into the phone. Her tears stopped only long enough to allow her to get out her words and then they began again.

"Mother, of course I'll try," Rojda said, trying to soothe her and hang up the phone at the same time. She couldn't believe she had answered her mother so honestly; as soon as she told her about Azeema, she knew it was a mistake. Her forces needed to move, and she couldn't get her mother off the phone. "Please don't worry; I promise you I will try. But in the end it is war. We are fighting for our lives here."

. . .

BUILDING ON THE ASSISTANCE of the counter-ISIS airstrikes and the 150 Iraqi Kurdish Peshmerga forces on the ground, the Syrian Kurds at last succeeded in gaining territory, not just laboring to keep from losing it. By the twentieth of January, the Syrian Kurds controlled much of the city. The YPG flag now flew from the top of the tower on Mishtanour Hill. Soon afterward the YPG retook the biggest hospital in the city's southwest. In the process, the People's Protection Units won control of ISIS weapons and ammunition depots. Now ISIS held just two neighborhoods in the city, though the group continued to hold terrain in the countryside surrounding Kobani.

Azeema's confidence had been rewarded. The Kurds had not let the town fall, even though they had been holding just a few blocks only a few months earlier. In October, when the U.S. launched its first weapons drop to the Kurds, Secretary of State Kerry had called the Kurds' solo stand against ISIS "valiant" and noted it would be "morally very difficult" to do nothing in support of them. Three months later, the U.S. and the coalition it gathered against ISIS could say that their air support had helped keep the town out of the grip of these extremists, though the destruction on the ground was near complete.

Twenty days after Azeema arrived at the hospital, the YPG declared victory over ISIS in Kobani. The Syrian Kurdish forces and their allies—the Iraqi Kurds, the Free Syrian Army, and the Americans—had handed ISIS its first loss.

On January 26, Azeema stood with five male commanders in front of the yellow YPG flag to declare the formal end to the battle for Kobani. They congratulated their battlefield comrades, thanked the U.S.-led coalition for its support from the skies, remembered friends killed in battle, and vowed to fight on through the Kobani countryside to defeat ISIS.

Azeema had snuck out of the hospital to be there that day before the cameras and in front of the flags. The bullet from the bald ISIS fighter remained lodged near her heart and had not yet moved enough to allow doctors to operate. But she would not miss the day she had dreamed of since she first started fighting ISIS: the day that ISIS lost at her and her teammates' hands. She and Rojda and all the young women they served with had been part of reaching this moment, she thought. So many friends she loved and missed had died to make it possible. In the right corner of the yellow YPG flag hanging behind Azeema was the green flag with a red star belonging to the YPJ, created nearly two years earlier.

Azeema's entire chest hurt; she felt weak and hoped she wouldn't collapse in the middle of the press conference. The pain meant that she could carry only the lightest gear possible, including a magazine that held just a fraction of its usual ammunition. She bounced her right leg gently up and down while she stood in front of the rolling cameras, willing the media event to end quickly so she could go back to rest.

When her turn came to speak, she would share a few words she had prepared while lying in the hospital.

"Now that Kobani is free, what we want to tell the world is that women have played a great role in liberating this town."

CHAPTER SIX

His eyes looked light brown when she studied them closely. Sometimes, they turned grey-brown. Always he stood tall and stared directly at her with an intensity that made her feel the seconds pass. The baldness of his head contrasted with the fuzzy brown beard blanketing the lower third of his face and reaching down toward his collarbone.

Then he took his shot.

Azeema thought a lot about the man who had wounded her. Was he Chechen? She guessed so, but she would never know. Possibly from Eastern Europe?

He had hunted her specifically, she believed. The two would never meet again, but they had changed each other's lives. She kept scanning and rewinding in her imagination the tape of previous clashes in Kobani; she wondered if she had ever seen him before he injured her. He had aimed only at her and with persistence—and success.

For so long, she had trusted her instincts on the battlefield, and they had served her well. Now she played on a loop in her head the moment in which this man she so wanted to kill had managed to get her. To her troops she remained the invincible leader, the fighter who had crawled out from her hospital bed to tell ISIS before cameras and the world that her forces intended to go on and defeat them, the one who never doubted herself or feared her foe. The one who figured out how to rescue twenty-one of her fighters pinned down by ISIS that day in Kobani in the fall of 2014.

All day Azeema showered her fighters with her usual bravado, but at night she went to sleep unable to shake the sense that something terrible was about to happen. Her outer swagger and her inner dread competed. The former won the morning. The latter carried the night.

Nowruz urged Azeema to take some time off to rest and recuperate. The doctors had finally performed surgery on Azeema, and she had come through as well as anyone could have. Instead of resting, however, Azeema went directly to the town of Hassakeh to continue the fight. The Kurds had been facing off against ISIS there for months, but most of the YPG's resources had gone to the effort in Kobani. Not long before the Kurds declared victory in Kobani, ISIS began moving more of its forces to villages in the north of Hassakeh.

"I didn't come to the YPJ to rest," Azeema told Nowruz when they spoke by phone. "I came here to fight." Just a few months had passed since the January press conference, and Nowruz thought Azeema needed several months' more rest before heading back to war. Azeema wanted no part of that advice.

In the hospital, one of her fighters had come to her to deliver the news. Israel, who had been part of the large force trapped by ISIS the day she organized the rescue, had entered a building as part of the campaign to retake the Kobani countryside. He and his teammates thought ISIS had left the house, but it turned out the enemy lay in wait. As Israel stepped onto the first set of stairs to clear the second floor, an ISIS fighter picked him off, shooting him from behind. He died almost instantly there on the staircase.

Her very survival counted as an act of resistance against ISIS, she felt. Azeema had no choice but to flaunt it and toss it back in the faces of the men who tried to end her. Her forces served as her great motivator. She wanted revenge for all the friends ISIS had taken from her. She wanted them to feel the loss she did—but worse.

BY NOW, the Syrian civil war had carved up the country. In January, just as the Kurdish People's Protection Units had retaken Kobani, the Al Qaeda–linked Nusra Front, along with Ahrar al-Sham and Jund al-Aqsa, Islamist groups backed by Turkey and Saudi Arabia, had captured the northwestern Syrian town of Idlib. With a population of roughly one hundred thousand before the war, Idlib sat near the highway connecting the Syrian capital, Damascus, to the commercial hub, Aleppo. Now the Syrian regime had lost two provincial capitals: Raqqa and Idlib. The war already had claimed at least two hundred thousand Syrian lives.

ISIS had not stopped advancing inside Syria. In May 2015, the group captured the historic town of Palmyra, home to the rich Syrian cultural legacy of antiquities tracing back to the first century. Among them was the two-thousand-year-old Temple of Bel. No one doubted that ISIS would soon destroy these cultural treasures: the Islamic State saw all such preservation as a form of idolatry, and blowing up the sites offered powerful footage for the group's slick propaganda videos, grabbing the eyes of new recruits on Telegram. ISIS also seized the gas fields surrounding Palmyra and began preparing to take another key location: the eastern Syrian town of Deir Ezzor.

By the start of the summer, the Syrian Kurds began to retake territory from ISIS on two fronts: one in the direction of the towns of Tal Abyad and Ain Issa, the other toward Hassakeh, where clashes continued. The YPG and YPJ fighters who advanced toward Tal Abyad, on Turkey's border, were accompanied by Arab rebel groups. In June, they recaptured the town, considered the Islamic State's key passageway for both trade and their inflow of foreign fighters. The fall of ISIS's black flags in Tal Abyad offered cause for celebration among YPG supporters on social media, and U.S. special operations forces greeted the news as one more step toward slowing the flow of international ISIS members.

After Kobani, Azeema went directly to the Hassakeh front instead of resting in the hospital or taking a desk job at a base in Qamishli. She told her sisters and brothers, who asked why she wanted to go to Hassakeh after having endured so much in Kobani, that she simply had to keep going. The fighting hadn't stopped. She wanted to be with her soldiers.

The first thing Azeema thought upon taking command of several thousand troops in Hassakeh that summer was how much simpler this battle was than Kobani. All the Kobani veterans agreed. Kobani had been a war. Azeema and her forces would liberate two streets in a day, and a half dozen of their friends would be slain or injured in the process. No day left them untouched or fully intact. Israel was dead. Miriam, one of her teammates from the sniper's nest back in the fall, was dead.

They had lost so many. In Hassakeh, by comparison, the fight so far took place in the countryside, not the city center, and it proved far less bloody: they could liberate six or eight streets at a time and lose no one. In Kobani, they had confronted the best and most experienced foreign fighters who had come to be part of the big battle. Hassakeh claimed no such distinction, and Azeema noted to her troops the relative lack of sophistication among ISIS forces there. They used no human shields, and they rarely used vehicle-borne explosives, because they weren't as effective outside the claustrophobic streets of Kobani. As in Kobani, few civilians remained in their homes in the parts of the city where the fighters faced off. Most already had fled.

As eager as Azeema was to stay in the fight, she wondered whether she would be equal to the challenge of leading this many people, about four times the number she had commanded in Kobani. Liberating a town from ISIS might prove a lot harder than defending one. In towns ISIS already held, they had had a chance to dig in, to learn the terrain, to establish positions they could defend. They had chosen the locations where they would store their weapons and house their forces. So far, Azeema hadn't lost a single fighter in Hassakeh, and she was intent on keeping this record intact. She wanted to live up to the example of calm and care and courage that Nowruz offered her field commanders in Kobani. She hoped she would provide the same inspiration and leadership for the half dozen field commanders who now reported to her. Being out in the fight had energized her—and, for stretches of time, helped divert her mind from the man who shot her.

Her team planned to attack the village of Karama the next day, and already ISIS had its eye on her. Her fighters followed ISIS troops talking to each other on their radio channels, just as they had in Kobani.

"A woman is leading a lot of fighters in the battle, and we want to kill her," her forces had heard an ISIS fighter say in Arabic. Azeema's troops knew better than to answer, though they wanted to. Instead, a young man named Nouri who served with Azeema told her what he had heard.

"You're getting famous on ISIS radio!" Nouri said.

He joked, but his point landed with Azeema. ISIS fighters wanted to target her in particular. She couldn't be entirely certain that they had been talking about her, but her presence on the front lines—her loud voice, her bravado, her humor, her troublemaking smile—made her among the most visible YPJ leaders in Hassakeh.

Azeema brushed off Nouri's warnings and tried to reassure him. ISIS fighters had made the same threats in Kobani and she had ignored them then, just as she would now.

She thought back to Nowruz's example: Azeema had never heard her sound nervous, even when things unraveled.

But for the first time in her three years of war, a bad feeling balled up in a mangled knot in the bottom of her stomach and would not budge. She had never felt this way, even in Kobani. If she had listened to her gut, she would have postponed the offensive by a few days. But she and her team had put a plan in place involving thousands of fighters. A vague—if persistent—feeling of dread did not count as a good reason to diverge from the campaign they had prepared.

Two mornings later, they set out to retake Karama in the heat of the summer sun. By noon, things looked positive for Azeema's forces: they had already been able to clear a few streets and had not yet encountered significant opposition. Azeema felt good. *We just might be able to control this village by nightfall,* she thought to herself.

Azeema stepped into the aging armored personnel carrier that her team used, a hulking tan truck with bench seating for about a half dozen people. Across from Azeema's perch on the vehicle's right side, three of her field commanders, one man and two women, sat in a row and leaned toward her to discuss the morning.

"Have you heard from the other teams yet today?" Azeema asked them. She had been focused on the movements she led through Karama that morning and had not yet asked for news of other units as they moved into surrounding villages. She always felt better while out in battle, and today reminded her why: you couldn't think about anything other than your mission. You couldn't win without being prepared. But Azeema much preferred the actual fight to getting ready for it.

"Yes, I have been checking in with them," answered Sara, one of the field commanders. "I just heard on the radio—"

Sara's voice suddenly became overwhelmed by a sound that stopped everything: an explosion shattered their eardrums and their vehicle. The personnel carrier stopped advancing but kept shaking.

Azeema guessed that a rocket-propelled grenade or perhaps an improvised explosive device had hit them. She swallowed to show herself that she could. Then a bolt of terror ripped through her as she realized she couldn't see. Her eyes *felt* open. But she could decipher only greyish figures standing and yelling in the truck, a hole blown out across its right side.

Azeema recognized the stinging cut of shrapnel all across her face. Maybe only a minute had passed since the explosion, but she knew she was hurt.

"Get out of the car, Haval, get out of the car!" Hamudi, a soldier who had fought alongside her in Kobani, yelled at her. Azeema heard his voice and understood his words, but she did not move.

She commanded her legs to stand and they simply stayed put. *Something must be very wrong*, Azeema thought, *or I would already be out of here.*

"I can't." She couldn't tell whether she was shouting back at him or whispering. All she knew was that her mouth moved and her teammates heard her. Two of them grabbed Azeema's motionless feet, picking them up off the truck's ruptured floor, while another pulled her shoulders away from the metal sidewall and shimmied underneath her so that he and another teammate could lift her, inserting their outstretched arms between her ribs and her shoulders. Together, the four held her level and hoisted her off the personnel carrier.

Azeema's mind sprinted ahead of her body. She now could feel pain piercing both of her legs. Her hand hurt, too, but she couldn't get a good enough look at it to see what had happened.

What a disaster. Our attack failed, she thought. She pushed herself to stay alive.

I will not die. I will not give ISIS that gift. They will not kill me.

A few minutes later, sprawled out in the back of a HiLux truck while it zoomed to the field hospital a few miles away, her black-brown hair spilling out of her short ponytail, her body dripping blood, Azeema gave her forces her last orders of that day.

"Take me to the hospital and then go," she said, looking up at Hamudi and Sara, who stared back at her without speaking, their faces etched with pain and worry. Azeema could see a little bit better now, though everything was still blurry. They tried not to cry at seeing their leader blown up. "Don't you dare stay with me. Your job today is to get back there and win. You have to free Karama; please don't think about coming to the hospital until it is finished."

The two fighters knew they had no choice but to take orders.

"Keep me updated," she called to the pair as they left her at the hospital. Watching them go back to liberate Karama without her was more painful than the physical injuries now demanding her attention. Less than six months had passed since she had been shot by the bald and bearded ISIS fighter in Kobani, and now she again found herself in a hospital. This time, however, she could tell she was in far worse condition.

Late that night, while Azeema lay resting on a hospital gurney, her legs invisible beneath bandages and plaster casts and an off-white hospital sheet, some of her field commanders came to bring her an update from the front lines.

One of them issued a quiet gasp when he caught a look at her casts. Azeema told him the explosion had broken both her legs. She said it in a flat tone, no emotion attached. Without saying it, they all knew that she had been incredibly lucky. She had come close enough to touch and smell death for a second time here in Hassakeh. Now all she wanted was to hear the latest from the field.

"Karama is liberated," Nouri said, smiling at Azeema with real joy now that he realized she was out of immediate danger. "The fight went well. We didn't lose anyone."

Azeema, pale from pain, offered him as wide a smile as she could muster.

"Okay, good," she said. "What's next? Take out the map so we can talk about tomorrow."

He shook his head at his commander's determination. They had figured out by now that they had driven over a mine ISIS had laid for them in Karama. The mine exploded just beneath Azeema's seat. The driver sustained an injury from shrapnel flying in his face, but only Azeema had been seriously hurt. She needed to have metal inserted into her hip, and doctors predicted that she would not walk on her own, even with the help of a cane, for some months. If ever. Azeema listened to their predictions, but vowed to herself that she would be up and moving *far* sooner than they expected. In the meantime, she would relocate their command center to her hospital bed if she had to. No way would she not be part of beating ISIS in Hassakeh. Twice her enemies had gotten close to killing her and twice they had failed. Instead, she would live on and kill many more of them.

"Okay," Sara said, leaning over the bed to show Azeema the rectangular map she held, "here's what we are looking at."

DURING THE SUMMER OF 2015, the Americans who had taken part in the Kobani battle worked to build on the success of that campaign. As Leo and Mitch had thought might be the case a year earlier, at the start of the ISIS siege of Kobani, the YPG was a partner with whom they could work and build trust. Leo and the rest of the Americans had been impressed by the fortitude and flexibility of the militia's fighters: when things didn't work, they would talk, figure out why, plan, and go forward. To the special operations leaders who worked with them each day, these women and men had proved that they would be the U.S.'s best shot against ISIS in Syria. Without the Americans helping from the air, the Kurds would have faced obliteration in Kobani. And without the YPG on the ground, the Americans had no ground force strong enough to hold terrain and advance. Neither side could achieve its goals without the other, though one was a superpower and one a militia. But in order for the U.S. to work with the Kurds in ISIS strongholds outside majority-Kurdish areas, the YPG would have to expand to include Arab leaders. America had learned the hard way how badly things could turn when the force it partnered with shut out the majority of the region's population.

While the Obama administration deliberated on how to "degrade and ultimately destroy" the Islamic State, as the president had pledged to do in September 2014, U.S. military leaders argued that to be most effective, they would need to place American special operators inside Syria and establish a sustained presence and an operating base. Once they could see what things looked like for themselves, the Americans would have a far more detailed understanding of on-the-ground realities and the best insight into what should come next in the counter-ISIS campaign. Several U.S. diplomats, most notably Brett McGurk, who had focused on Iraq across two administrations now, joined in advocating for this small U.S. presence. They argued that the Syrian Kurds and the YPG were not the same as the PKK, which YPG leaders had insisted since they met the Americans in 2014. Indeed, in October 2014, the U.S. State Department noted that the Democratic Union Party was "a different group than the PKK legally, under United States law." In the eyes of those who favored working with them, Azeema and Rojda and Nowruz were not terrorists—they were the best chance America had to *stop* terrorists.

Others inside the administration with Middle East experience stressed that the U.S. could absolutely *not* do this, given Turkey's concerns. And they agreed with observers who called it an "illusion" to say that a distinction could be drawn between the PKK and the Democratic Union Party or its armed wing, the YPG. Turkey considered Mazlum, the head of the YPG, whose calm command of the battlefield and astute assessment of the forces operating inside Syria the Americans had come to trust, one of its most wanted men. Turkey's foreign minister accused the YPG of forcing Arabs out of the areas it led—a claim the Kurds denied—and drew absolutely no distinction between ISIS and the Syrian Kurds. "It doesn't matter who comes—the regime, Daesh, the Democratic Union Party— they are all persecuting civilians," he said.

Digestible truth lay nestled in between these two worldviews. The Syrian Kurds had distanced themselves from the actions of the PKK in Turkey and cared about their own country first. They had launched no attacks against Turkey from Syrian soil. The more they worked with the U.S., the more they developed their own leverage and matured in their own decision making. Yet the PKK remained closely connected to the YPG in leadership and in ideology—both groups saw Ocalan as their guiding force. The Qandil Mountains that served as the PKK's headquarters may have sat across the border in Iraq, but that didn't mean the ideas that emerged from Qandil didn't directly impact the direction of the Syrian Kurds.

The White House, in the meantime, approved in-and-out raids to pursue ISIS leaders in Syria. On May 15, 2015, Army special operations forces began a mission from Iraq and flew close to the eastern Syrian town of Deir Ezzor to find a Tunisian senior ISIS commander known as Abu Sayyaf, who helped lead the group's oil and gas operations. The forces quickly returned to Iraq, but not before freeing an eighteen-year-old Yazidi woman who had been held as a slave by Abu Sayyaf and his wife.

By the first week of October, after a National Security Council meeting at the Pentagon led by the president, plans took shape: The White House would bring to a close a congressionally approved $500 million Pentagon program to train and outfit moderate Syrian opposition fighters after it had delivered meager results, given the constraint that said these fighters could battle only ISIS, not Assad. Supporters said that those parameters and America's refusal to provide these rebels any defense from regime attacks meant the program was doomed from its launch. The goal had been to train a few thousand fighters; the program ended with fewer than 150. By contrast, in the past year, the YPG and YPJ had won back more than 6,500 square miles of territory from the Islamic State without any formal training or equipping support from the U.S. If the Syrian Kurds could expand their force and formally include Arabs already fighting alongside them to advance toward the ISIS "capital," Raqqa, the U.S. would support the combined force. In short order, a collection of Syrian rebel groups willing to align themselves with the Kurds became known publicly as the Syrian Arab Coalition. America answered Turkish objections about its new Kurdish partners by pledging that it would bolster only the Arab contingent with arms and ammunition, not the Kurds. The effort required more than a little policy acrobatics, but it sufficed for now.

For his part, Leo James felt that his conversations with Polat Can more than a year earlier in Sulaymaniyah had advanced as he had hoped back then might be possible. Arming the Syrian Arab Coalition and broadening the YPG was a first step. Others on the American military side, including colleagues in Army special operations, felt far less convinced that this partnership could last, and viewed it as a temporary alliance against a shared enemy. But even they believed that Mazlum and his forces offered America the best option to beat ISIS on the ground.

The new Syrian Arab Coalition would fall under another new entity, one through which America would bring far more resources to the ground fight against ISIS. America played a central role in the creation of this combined Kurdish and Arab militia that would fight ISIS in Syria. One of Mitch's teammates called Mazlum and said they needed a name for the new force. He threw out a few ideas. The name had to show that the force was inclusive of Syrians of all backgrounds. It also had to make clear that the Syrian Kurds did not seek their own Kurdish nation and represented a fighting force, not a nation-state. Mazlum called back with a name that hadn't appeared on anyone's list: the Syrian Democratic Forces. A dozen Arab tribes that had already fought alongside the People's Protection Units would make up the founding Arab component of the SDF, not those forces put forward by either Turkey or Iraq.

For the Americans, the SDF's creation marked the start of the next phase of the ISIS fight as Assad's backers entered the war and made clear that they would do anything required to keep the Syrian regime in power. On September 30, Russia launched its first airstrikes in Syria, including around the town of Homs, where rebels had made gains. The Russians insisted that they had targeted ISIS positions, but U.S. defense secretary Ash Carter told reporters that it appeared the strikes hit areas "where there probably were not ISIL forces," while Secretary of State Kerry noted that "strikes of that kind would question Russia's real intentions— fighting ISIL or protecting the Assad regime." On the second day of airstrikes, rebel forces reported "fast jets" from Russia striking a series of locations, killing civilians. Putin assured his nation that there would be no Russian "boots on the ground" in Syria. But his actions left no doubt: Russia would keep Assad in power and would strike anywhere, with overwhelming force and without precision, to guarantee the regime's survival. As the days went on and the Russian air campaign accelerated and claimed more lives, the U.S. and its European and Gulf allies spoke out to accuse Russia of working to kill Assad's opposition and civilians rather than stopping ISIS.

The day after the October announcement of the SDF's creation, American C-17 cargo planes dropped supplies to Arab fighters who had joined the new group. The operation looked a lot like the air drop the Americans had carried out to help Azeema, Rojda, and their teammates in October 2014 in Kobani. More than one hundred pallets of supplies, including fifty tons of ammunition, fell from the sky to Arab fighters waiting on the ground in Hassakeh. News reports immediately surfaced questioning whether the airdrops went right to the YPG as soon as the Arab forces received them. (An unidentified senior Obama administration official called the Syrian Arab Coalition a "ploy" to direct weapons to the Kurds, and it was hard to dispute that.) The Americans paid little heed to what they saw as background noise: they had now made clear their intention to double down on the ISIS fight with the new, broadened force they had helped create.

October 30 brought the announcement that Leo, Mitch, and others in the U.S. military, particularly in special operations, had worked toward since the summer: U.S. teams would be permitted to enter Syria. President Obama would authorize the deployment of "fewer than 50" American special operations forces to join the newly created Syrian Democratic Forces on the ground. The start of Russian airstrikes in Syria the month before also proved a powerful accelerant to the Washington policy-making machine: while some might have been ambivalent about the YPJ and YPG as partners, the administration could unify around the desire to curb Russian influence.

The announcement of U.S. ground forces deploying to Syria— even if only fifty and only to train and advise local SDF fighters— immediately sparked headlines, given the president's efforts since 2011 to keep American troops out of Syria's war. In September 2014, when Obama spoke to America about U.S. efforts to stop ISIS, he emphasized that the ISIS fight "will not involve American combat troops fighting on foreign soil." This was not Iraq in 2003, Obama made clear, and no Americans would be sent into an unwinnable war in the Middle East.

Yet several factors had combined to render the idea of putting special operations forces in Syria both urgent and politically acceptable. These included ISIS advances, the risks that attacks against U.S. targets were being planned in Syria, and escalating concerns about the rise of foreigners joining the Islamic State who would then return to Europe or the United States to carry out ISIS plots. The White House eventually agreed to allow these troops to enter Syria so long as they remained under fifty in total. No fighting, no front lines, *only* advising and support.

On November 13, terrorist attacks in Paris killed 130 people, including Americans. The number of wounded reached nearly five hundred. Television cameras captured the brutality and the stories of young people murdered while enjoying their city. Immediately suspicion fell on ISIS foreign fighters who had passed through the northern Syrian town of Manbij. ISIS claimed responsibility for the attacks, designed for the spectacle of maximum carnage. France declared a state of emergency and prepared a military response. In Washington, the sense of urgency to defeat ISIS in Syria before the group could attack the West intensified further. Three weeks later, Tashfeen Malik and her husband, Syed Rizwan Farook, killed fourteen people in San Bernardino, California. Malik had declared her allegiance to Abu Bakr al-Baghdadi, the leader of ISIS. Aiding the SDF with a presence in Syria looked increasingly to U.S. officials like a bet America had to make.

ONCE THE DECISION had been made to allow U.S. forces to enter Syria, the question became exactly where they would base their operations. The key was to be close to the Syrian fighters with whom they would partner, without coming near the front lines. The president had made clear that the Americans must stay far from combat—or as far as they could, given that they were entering an active war.

That task of finding and establishing a headquarters for the Americans in the area fell to a team that included Mitch. In early December 2015, he prepared to enter northeastern Syria for the first time. With Mazlum as his guide, he would at last set foot in the place he had seen so often from neighboring countries and from above in intelligence surveillance video. The U.S. had no official presence in the country and had not been on the ground directly since the Syrian civil war began. The American embassy in Damascus closed in February 2012 and no longer offered even consular services such as visas or passport help. Americans still in the country who needed diplomatic assistance had to contact the Czech Republic's embassy. If things went awry during the seven days of their planned visit, Mitch and his small team would more or less be on their own.

They landed in northeastern Syria on a starry, chilled December night. What struck Mitch first was the crisp air and the quiet; war felt distant, even though it could be found only a short drive away. The Syrian regime by then was enjoying the benefits of Russia's military campaign: Russian airpower had pummeled Homs, and the regime was on the verge of retaking its third-largest city after four years under Syrian rebels.

By now the battle against ISIS for Hassakeh had largely been won, at least along the main highway. That fall, the Syrian Kurds had connected the territories they controlled and, alongside Arab allied units, had pushed ISIS out of several major towns. Next up: the retaking of the Tishreen Dam, a strategic location central to the Islamic State's supply routes between Turkey's border and ISIS's de facto capital, Raqqa.

Mitch and his teammates spent their first nights in Syria at a granary north of Hassakeh. Mazlum, who came from Kobani, then invited them to stay at a relative's house. His own home, it turned out, had been destroyed in U.S. airstrikes during the Kobani fight. Mazlum and his fellow leaders kept quiet about the Americans' coming to Kobani as part of their security protocol, but their secret spread fast as soon as Mitch and his team hit the ground. The Americans had arrived, and everyone in the town knew it.

On the third morning of their trip, Mazlum took the Americans to see for themselves the town their strikes had both destroyed and kept out of ISIS hands. The U.S. air campaign had leveled the city—no building above two stories remained standing. The innards of destroyed structures piled up in different corners of the town as debris removal proceeded slowly, with no heavy equipment or bundles of reconstruction dollars to help. Kobani's residents had returned to rebuild their homes. Construction of new apartments on the west side had begun, but the town bore the footprints of the war that had ended less than a year earlier. Mitch noted that women and men he met talked to him not about the devastation of their city, but about its survival. *Their* little town had handed ISIS its first setback.

Mazlum and a local representative took Mitch and his team on a tour of the city center. They stopped to visit the elementary school Mazlum had attended as a child—the same place where Azeema had landed after being shot by the brown-eyed, bald ISIS fighter. Mazlum showed Mitch his old classroom. Then they stepped down into the basement, and Mazlum and Mitch's translator pointed out a few lines of graffiti written in black, which stood out against the white-yellow wall with paint peeling from it. Written in the Kurdish dialect of Kurmanci, it read:

WE WILL FIGHT TO THE LAST PERSON.
YPJ/YPG

Mazlum and the town representative noted as they exited the school that several women fighters had been killed by ISIS there on the street where they stood. At some point, they said, when they had time, the town's leaders would memorialize the site so that people would remember the young women's sacrifice.

Mitch turned to his sergeant major, a teammate and friend named Dan Gray with whom he had seen more than a decade and a half of war, to gauge Gray's reaction to the scene. Usually outspoken and gregarious, Gray stood silent. His eyes did not move from the graffiti. The two men hadn't ever really spoken about the presence of women in their partner's force. Before arriving in Kobani, neither could have said whether the Syrian women's role in the fight constituted window dressing for naive foreigners or a truly significant part of the Syrian Kurdish force.

Now, though, these Americans had matched the figures they had seen on video and from the air with the people they could see face-to-face on the ground. Mitch and his teammates received their hosts' message: the fight would not have been won without women. Mitch realized that neither he nor Gray had ever worked with women in a local fighting force before, anywhere they had served. Somehow, though, it didn't seem unusual here.

Mitch wondered who had scrawled that message on the wall and at what point in the fight she had written it. He and Leo, too, had thought they might lose the Kobani fight in those grim fall and winter months the year before. But it hadn't been their backsides on the line. Today, though, the mood in the town felt festive, as if, eleven months after the Syrian Kurds claimed victory in Kobani, everyone had gathered to show the Americans how proud they were of their survival. He understood that the Syrian Kurds wanted the Americans to come and stay and to offer their forces more support. To be a friend and ally who would provide recognition and protection—a path out of the questions about their allegiance to the PKK and toward international legitimacy. But Mitch viewed the visit foremost as a chance to see firsthand whether these fighters presented America a real path to defeat ISIS.

Later that day, Mazlum hosted the Americans at his uncle's home. They took a break from the discussions about the future fight and spent a few moments out on the veranda, enjoying the brisk air and the sunshine of the December afternoon. Mitch stood with Roger Spaulding, a team leader who, like himself, had spent his twenties and most of his early thirties deployed to the Middle East on behalf of his country.

A young woman, a relative of Mazlum's, wearing the dark-colored fatigues of a YPJ member, stepped out to join them, interrupting their reverie. She wore her long brown hair in a loose ponytail. Mitch guessed she might have been around twenty years old.

She said hello to the Americans in the passable English she had learned in school and asked how their visit was going so far. Mitch said that they had enjoyed seeing Kobani and found it quite moving.

"We're happy to see your town for ourselves," he said, in the formal tone of a guest to his host.

"You know, we were never going to abandon this city," she answered. Mitch noted to himself just how young she looked, this woman who couldn't have weighed more than a hundred pounds at most, and how focused. "Never."

She looked down at the ground for a brief moment. She wore a woolen shawl that was identical to the one Mitch had been holding when he arrived at the house. Black and fringed, the shawl had bright pink roses lined up in a pattern along its edges, nested in green leaves surrounded by yellow, orange, and green paisley swirls. Scarves just like it could be found all around the Syrian Kurdish region: Azeema had used one to cover her hair throughout the Kobani fight. Mitch had received a shawl like this as a present that morning from Mazlum, along with a wooden plaque with the YPG symbol, a photo of Kobani during the siege with KOBANE spelled out in block letters along the bottom of the frame, and an aging bolt-action rifle that had been recovered from the battlefield after the fight ended. The shawl belonged to one of the young YPJ troops killed fighting ISIS, Mitch's hosts told him, and they wanted him to have it. Mitch had received a lot of gifts in the past decade from a host of different forces he had worked with in Africa and the Middle East. This counted among the most meaningful presents he had ever received, he thought, because no one could ever bring back the woman who once wore it.

On the veranda, the young YPJ member sized up the two Americans. She turned slightly to focus her attention on Spaulding.

"Hey, how many ISIS did you kill?" she said in accented English, looking him in the eyes. Mitch glanced at Spaulding, a broad-chested, pumped-up man whose muscular physique reflected how much weight he lifted each week. "I bet I killed more ISIS than you did."

She smiled with a glint of mischief in her eyes and gave a laugh as she threw down her challenge to this special operations veteran who had supported Kobani from the air while she had fought for it, block by block, house by house, from the ground.

Spaulding laughed for a second.

"You know what?" he said. "I bet you did."

The young woman went on to tell the Americans about the night that the graffiti they had seen in the school had been written.

"We decided as a group that evening that we would stay until the end, however it ended," she said. "We would have died before handing them Kobani."

The memory of this young woman giving his grizzled teammate a ton of grief about her being more of a warrior than he was stayed with Mitch, just like the scarf in his backpack. He now inhabited a world where these women fought from the front while he and his special operations colleagues operated from the back and from the headquarters, where face-to-face contact with their enemy was neither likely nor expected.

A whole lot of "firsts" had taken place on this trip already, and a twenty-year-old woman trash-talking his teammate about how much more deadly she had been against ISIS was only one of them.

IN FEBRUARY 2015, just after the fight for Kobani's town center ended, ISIS carried out an offensive against three dozen Christian towns all at once. The extremists raided northern Syria's Khabour Valley and kidnapped hundreds of Assyrian Christians, who traced their roots in the region to the time of Christianity's founding. A community that already had lost so many of its young people to migration in Europe now found itself decimated and defenseless.

In February 2016, part of this small community of Christians who fought under the banner of the Syriac Military Council prepared to take back the town of Shaddadi from ISIS control.

One morning at the meeting point for all the forces gathered for the offensive, including young women who fought under the Syriac Military Council flag, one of Mitch's teammates, an enlisted special operations soldier named Dean Walter, stood watching the frontline preparations. He and a group of Americans had come to introduce themselves to SDF commanders, who happened to be women on this offensive. (They learned this after a few U.S. troops from another unit extended their arms to shake a male fighter's hand, mistaking him for the campaign's leader, only for him to point to his superior, a woman standing nearby.)

Walter marveled at just how happy everyone seemed, how much camaraderie they shared. Young women, some of whom wore the Bethnahrin Women's Protection Forces' royal blue and gold patch on their shoulders, climbed into the waiting HiLux pickup trucks, greeting one another with hugs and smiles. He watched them throw their arms around each other's necks in greeting and whoop it up as they prepared for war.

Competing emotions crashed into him, Walter later noted:

> I felt guilt that these young women were going off into battle on their own when we could have helped them more with training and expertise. Jealousy because they stood there with their friends filled with purpose and excitement as they prepared to enter a fight they believed in while we were simply standing by and going nowhere near the front. Admiration for the fact that these young fighters had the guts to put themselves on the line for their people. And pride in them and who they were, real warriors.

DOCTORS HAD SAID at the outset that it would take Azeema close to a year to walk, if she was lucky. She ignored her doctors in Hassakeh, just as she had ignored her doctors in Kobani. Within several months of the truck explosion, she was pacing around the hospital with her cane every day and riding in her teammates' trucks to the front line as often as she felt up to it.

Rojda came to see Azeema whenever she could. The two women with so many ties—family, childhood, school, and now war—sat and talked and snacked on sunflower seeds. By now the all-women's force of the YPJ had grown from several hundred to more than a thousand. Images of female fighters in Kobani had proved a powerful tool for winning new recruits and, as important, for convincing their fathers. Training centers had opened across northeastern Syria. Wahida, Azeema's sister, persuaded Azeema to come home to Qamishli for a few days; their aunts and cousins and neighbors wanted to see her. Azeema, just out of her full cast, held court in her family's Qamishli living room.

In February 2016, using only a cane to walk, she arrived at the send-off point in nearby Shaddadi where SDF soldiers—members of the YPJ and other coalition groups—gathered before heading off to the front. She wanted to see for herself this next phase of the campaign, which the Americans had been eager for them to launch, and to make sure her teammates had all that they needed.

Nowruz, who, like Rojda, had visited Azeema at the hospital in her own hometown of Hassakeh, did not know how Azeema recovered so quickly. She told Rojda that only Azeema's will and maybe some guardian angels could have enabled this result. She joked that Azeema's legs were too scared of her to stay broken. But ISIS forces had grazed her, shot her, and blown her up, and Nowruz would not give them a fourth chance to kill her friend. She sent Azeema to work in intelligence and to be part of the battle planning from headquarters. No objections permitted. Period.

"You have done more than your part, Haval," Nowruz said, enveloping her in a hug when she saw her just after the Shaddadi campaign at an SDF base. "Come back to work—but not on the front lines."

Two fighters—one male, one female—strategize during
the battle for Kobani in December 2014.

Azeema poses with the YPJ flag on
the outskirts of Kobani in 2015, with
the Euphrates River serving as the
backdrop.

Rojda in 2016, during the lead-up to the
Manbij campaign.

Nowruz in a command center during the battle for Raqqa in August 2017. By this point, the SDF controlled more than half of the city that the Islamic State had claimed as its capital, but the fight wasn't yet over.

Kurdish sculptor Zirak Mira, from the town of Sulaymaniyah in Iraq, created a statue honoring the women who fought ISIS. The monument was erected in the center of Kobani in March 2016, a year after the battle for the city ended. The sculpture now serves as a focal point and tourist destination in Kobani.

Roadside signs outside Kobani (above) and in Qamishli (below) celebrate YPJ.

My colleague Mustafa and I interview YPJ recruits in 2018. They spoke to us about the battles they waged within their own families to join the all-women's force.

Young women training to join the YPJ in northeastern Syria, 2018.

Photographs of YPJ and YPG fighters lost in battle adorn the walls of the headquarters of the Syrian Democratic Forces in Ain Issa in 2018.

I interview Mazlum Abdi, head of the Syrian Democratic Forces, on a trip to Syria in 2019.

Mazlum with Ilham (left) and Nowruz (center).

Rojda waves the SDF flag in Raqqa's Naim Square after leading the
U.S.-backed coalition, which included the YPJ, in its campaign to take
the city from the Islamic State, October 2017.

Women of the YPJ mark the end of the Raqqa fight in Naim Square, October 2017.

U.S. forces on patrol in northeastern Syria in 2019, with a YPJ billboard visible in the background.

Women and men dance at the ceremony to commemorate the opening of the Raqqa Women's Council, August 2018.

CHAPTER SEVEN

Nowruz stood on a hill overlooking the banks of the Euphrates River under a black night sky and watched the stream of rubber Zodiac boats set out on their crossing toward the town of Manbij. She barely noticed the booming sounds of mortar fire coming from her side, like a fireworks show that did not end, which was aimed at keeping ISIS at bay and preventing them from shooting at the SDF forces now gliding across the water. She thought only of her hope that the winds would stay manageable so that her troops would arrive safely at their destination, just as they had planned and prepared, over and over again, for two months. The waves churned high, and the skies looked as if they might open up and pelt rain down on them in an instant.

It cannot rain, she thought. *We need a quiet, clear night, just as the forecast promised.*

The commander held her radio in her right hand and checked her black digital watch: it read 11:03 p.m. on May 30, 2016. Nowruz looked down at the scene just beginning to unfold below and saw staggered rows of small boats, women fighters on each one, including the first. They had come to take back ISIS's last territorial connection to the outside world: its border with Turkey in the town of Manbij.

For two and a half years, the residents of Manbij had lived under the black flag of ISIS. Beheadings and hangings had become regular occurrences from which parents shielded their children by covering their eyes when they stepped out onto the streets. Home to an Arab majority, Manbij, whose population numbered around three hundred thousand, also included a Kurdish minority that accounted for around a quarter of citizens. The city had attracted attention because it served as the transit point for the foreign fighters who fueled the expansion of the Islamic State. When international ISIS followers arrived in Syria from across the globe—from Europe to the Middle East to Africa and beyond—they traveled through the town and, from there, to the front. Now those same fighters had been called back to Manbij to defend it against the impending attack from the U.S.-backed SDF forces, of which Nowruz and the women's units formed a crucial part.

Manbij's strategic significance to ISIS meant that the town was a crucial next target for the SDF. The fact that the men who carried out the November 2015 Paris attacks had come through Manbij strengthened their case with U.S. diplomats, who strongly agreed. For months, the U.S. delayed the offensive while discussing with Turkey whether the SDF in general and the Kurds specifically could cross the Euphrates River and push ISIS out or whether a Turkish-backed force would do it. At last, the debate ended with the decision that the SDF was the only force capable of the mission, and the U.S. pledged to Turkey that Arabs, not Kurds, would lead the operation.

Now, as Nowruz and her team faced the challenge of actually executing the mission alongside Arab forces, a slew of complications lay before them. The YPG had the command and control experience and the relationships with the Americans. Arab commanders, including those of the newly formed Manbij Military Council, would lead their forces to take terrain alongside the YPG and YPJ. No one involved had managed an operation this complicated, and while the groups would work together in the campaign under the same flag, the units would not have to integrate at the ground level. There was no bridge across the river; crossing by boat was the only way Nowruz's forces could reach Manbij. Nowruz watched while they began their biggest operation yet: a water crossing in the dead of night, with ISIS waiting to defend its stronghold on the other side.

She had worried for weeks while they planned the offensive. Crossing the water complicated just about everything. The boats couldn't carry heavy weapons. Her forces would be visible to ISIS fighters, who would have the high ground on the other side and could easily pick them off. They also would be vulnerable to the weather: if a surprise storm arose, they would have to figure out how to rescue their forces from the watery darkness, and their supplies could topple into the river, never to be recovered. *So much could go wrong*, she thought to herself. *Have we planned for all of it? Could we?*

And all those worries surfaced before the SDF even reached the other side. Crossing the Euphrates River was just one piece of the mission: after that, they had to fight to retake the town, and the offensive would doubtless be brutal and bloody. ISIS had spent more than two years digging into their positions in the city, and some of the most glittering names on the ISIS roster called it home. She had a YPJ team ready to de-mine the area where they would build the first road toward the city center; by now they knew ISIS would leave improvised explosive devices, or IEDs, all along the terrain from the river to the town.

War had made Nowruz even more of a planner than she had been as a girl who dreamed of becoming a doctor. Starting at the end of March, she and her fellow leaders met regularly with the Americans to discuss exactly how the mission should proceed. Leo James by now had come back to Syria from Iraq and formed part of the U.S. team that would advise on the mission, though Americans could not cross the river at the outset, given their mandate to stay behind the front line. All the senior SDF commanders who were involved gathered early in May to talk through the logistics of the operation.

Nowruz told the assembled field commanders that part of the overall campaign to push ISIS out of Manbij would include the YPJ executing the water crossing first; this would be the greatest tactical challenge they had yet faced as a fighting force. They would pursue the campaign from two points, the Qara Qowzak Bridge and the Tishreen Dam. To succeed, several thousand fighters would have to cross the water at night, knowing that explosives, snipers, and rocket-propelled grenades might well lie in wait for them on the other side.

The YPJ women would go first, and their fellow SDF forces, including the Arab fighters the U.S. had promised the Turks were at the fore of the campaign, would be right there behind them. Once they survived the nighttime water crossing, their job was to secure the riverbank. Then the SDF would bring across cars and tanks and heavy weapons. This was just the first of multiple phases of the campaign that would see a number of groups united under the SDF coalition enter the city at different locations and different times to keep ISIS on the defensive.

"We have to force Daesh to choose where to put their resources and their forces by attacking them from different sides and exploiting their weaknesses," Nowruz continued. "The Americans will help us from the air while we bring everybody across." Once they got over the hill on the riverbank and into the city, she told them, the fight would get harder. They would need to take as much terrain as they could while they still had an element of surprise.

Five days before the crossing, she and her fellow Syrian commanders from the SDF had convened for a final planning meeting. They had spent hours with the Americans poring over a three-dimensional model of the terrain, what they called a "sand table," so that everyone could talk through how the crossing would unfold and craft contingencies for what they would do if plans fell apart. A half dozen men and a few women had lined up around the rectangular replica, which consisted of rust-colored terrain surrounded by blue water and spanned much of the length of the room. They discussed the minute-by-minute details of the attack's sequencing, hashing out who would cross from which point on the bank at what point in the night.

Nowruz felt that the YPJ had shown sufficient discipline and effectiveness to launch the crossing. Arab fighters would be part of leading this attack, and she wanted her forces to go alongside them, clearing the path by leading in small units to repel ISIS. The all-women's forces knew how to set passable routes for people to safely cross newly held terrain, how to establish checkpoints, and how to control the land they had seized. Now they would take the lead in doing so.

Of course, Nowruz knew that the YPJ leading the boats across the Euphrates meant that if anything went wrong along the way, the all-female units would own the failure. It was only one part of the campaign, but a crucial piece that would set the tone for what followed.

Nowruz had spent the previous day getting ready—going without sleep for more than twenty-four hours—and had been on the radio since early evening, just after a group dinner of chicken and rice. She had listened to all the teams check in while preparations for the late-night crossing got under way.

Since the battle for Kobani, she had realized the importance of putting forward the most unflappable front possible; her troops knew her for her cool, even amid the choppiest waters. But here on this hilltop, cupping her radio in her hand as she strained to hear news of the crossing, her hair knotted in a short ponytail just below her ears, looking down at her lined white notebook full of plans, she felt the nerves in her stomach jangling.

The water crossing, she knew, was a tremendous risk. Some of her forces were scared of the river; few of them knew how to swim. The Americans had offered everyone flotation devices, but almost none of her team accepted them; the vests and other gear were too heavy. A sense of fatalism among the Syrians overrode the Americans' push for them to put on the survival gear.

"If I am going to make it, I'll make it," one of the young women had told Leo James when he and his counterparts from the U.S. Navy tried to give her their heavy flotation equipment. "If not, it's not your life vest that is going to make the difference. I won't wear that."

Nowruz and her fighters had trained and rehearsed again and again for this night. But all those plans would soon encounter the next force that would get a say in how smoothly the offensive went:

the Islamic State. And there was still that list of things she couldn't control: the weather, the waves, her teammates' fears, their inability to swim, the certain counterattack by ISIS—which combined to give her the most anxious night she had experienced since Kobani.

Just then she heard a voice on the radio. It was one of her commanders, a young woman named Raheema.

"Haval Nowruz, we are on the boat," she said.

"Okay, good, Haval, let me know how things proceed," Nowruz responded.

Less than ten minutes later, Raheema came back on the radio.

"We have started driving; we are on the water and moving forward," she said.

The offensive was officially under way.

On the hill above the riverbank, Nowruz paced back and forth while the scene unfolded below. The sight of the boats crossing against the grey-black of the sky was beautiful. She pushed from her mind her worst-case scenario: one of her fighters falling into the water as they battled thirty-to-forty-knot winds with no one aware until it was too late.

Raheema confirmed that they had reached the middle of the river a few minutes later. This time, Nowruz strained to make out the words over the sound of the Zodiac's motor and the waves crashing. She tried to imagine what the scene looked like to Raheema and the other women in the lead boats. Snipers, mines, grenades—she expected that ISIS had had time to put all of these in place, but she couldn't know for sure. They were sailing quite literally into the unknown as they crossed on the reinforced inflatable boats.

The radio sputtered, and Raheema's voice broke into her thoughts.

"We made it. We are across," Raheema said. She whispered into the radio, trying to speak loudly enough for Nowruz to understand her but quietly enough to keep ISIS from hearing.

Nowruz caught Raheema's words and allowed herself a moment of relief. But in the next moment, her thoughts shifted to twin concerns: She now had to follow Raheema and her team as they made their way to high ground in Manbij and to coordinate their positions while avoiding ISIS attacks. And she still had a whole night's worth of boat crossings to track.

FOR THE AMERICANS, the Manbij campaign was another first: the first contested wet gap crossing—an advancing of forces across a linear obstacle, in this case the Euphrates River, with adversaries waiting on the other side—since the Korean War.

Leo James had come in from northern Iraq for the campaign. He hadn't returned to the U.S. for any length of time since he first began supporting the Syrian Kurds against ISIS in Kobani two years earlier. The unusually long tour had destroyed his personal life—he had no time or emotional energy for anything but the ISIS campaign—but he had felt he had no choice. The work was urgent and important, and he wanted to be there with his teammates to see it through.

Joining Leo in advising on the Manbij mission was Gene Williams, another noncommissioned officer on his fifteenth or sixteenth special operations deployment. Williams was known to be particularly gruff and matter-of-fact among a crowd of people who shared those traits. Solving complex logistical challenges on the battlefield was the kind of puzzle he enjoyed most. He and Leo and a few others had spent the past two months walking through the details of exactly how they could best help Mazlum, Nowruz, and the SDF forces get across, and then how they would get trucks, supplies, and medical support to all those forces once they entered ISIS territory. In many ways, safely ferrying the women and men who would serve as the ground force in the Manbij campaign was one of the easier challenges. It would not be enough to simply get Raheema and all the others *into* Manbij; their forces had to keep advancing, or ISIS would shove them back toward the riverbank and push them into the water and to their deaths. Planning for traffic control and casualty evacuation, ensuring that doctors reached the right positions so they could quickly treat injured SDF fighters, figuring out what to do if one of the trucks broke down and needed to be repaired urgently—all those challenges faced the Americans as they supported the Syrians.

Supplying the SDF fighters would require a bridge strong enough to allow the transport of equipment, one that could be assembled fast and put to work quickly. Trucks and cars and heavy weapons couldn't travel into Manbij on Zodiacs, no matter how durable those small boats might be. Fortunately, Nowruz's forces unearthed a gift from the Russians—a discovery that would make a critical difference.

The PMP was a floating pontoon bridge, first used in the 1960s. Known as a "ribbon bridge," it could be split into pieces and moved by powerboats, and was durable enough to carry tanks and trucks. The SDF had been seeking a solution to Manbij's engineering problem and had seen the aging PMP parts submerged in water in the town of Derek, not too far from the Iraqi border. They had brought Williams to see it and asked whether he thought it would work if they found more of the pieces. The American spent days scouring Google, talking to Army engineers, and watching You-Tube videos to learn more about the PMP and what it could do. He ended up finding a user manual online, in Russian, and using Google Translate to turn the instructions into English. Once the Americans and the SDF realized that the Soviet-era bridge could perform the transport work, they rehearsed the assembly procedure: lifting the PMP onto a truck, then assembling it on the banks of a lake and driving it across four hundred meters of water, with winds kicking up throughout.

The night of the crossing, while Raheema and the rest of Nowruz's forces were in the Zodiacs, another group assembled the PMP using night-vision tools. They needed to be ready for daybreak, when they would bring across the heavy weapons and construction equipment, including excavators that would help them build a road from the riverbank into town.

The operation started at 11:00 p.m. By 3:58 a.m., five hundred SDF fighters had crossed into Manbij.

Leo sat on the hill near Nowruz and watched the mission unfold. The feeling of witnessing something historic grabbed him, and he felt honored to have played a small role in helping the crossing come to pass. When dawn arrived, he and Williams saw the crane drop as they had planned and practiced. The floating bridge entered the water and began to move, the Zodiacs serving as its engine.

FOR ZNARIN, Nowruz's former aide and one of the half dozen or so field commanders leading the offensive in Manbij for the YPJ, the campaign was a homecoming. She could have never imagined when her family left the city for Kobani more than a decade earlier that this was how she would return to it: in dark green camouflage with an AK-47 strapped across her back, leading fifty of her forces for the first time in their quest to liberate the city from the extremists who followed the Islamic State. Back then, she had been a teenager crushed by her uncle's disapproval of her dreams of education. She had felt only sadness as she drove out of the city: even if Manbij would always be lodged in her mind as the place where her future ended and her hope died, she still loved the city itself, its energy, its mix of people. She had thought then that perhaps she would return one day to live in her hometown, once events sorted themselves out and things grew calmer in her family.

That all felt like lifetimes back. So much had passed in the intervening years. She had used her trail of personal disappointments to fuel her quest for women's rights—first her own, then those of Kurdish women through Congress Star, and now as part of the YPJ, for women across the region and, she hoped, well beyond.

Kobani had been Znarin's training ground as she learned about leading in battle from her mentor, Nowruz, and watched Azeema and Rojda and so many other women; she had first learned there how to plan an offensive and how to defend terrain while front lines collapsed, how to take people terrified by war and inspire them to bravery in battle, how to protect fighters during an attack, how to coordinate medical care for the injured. Manbij offered a chance for her to share all that she had been taught with others. In the year and a half since the Kobani battle ended, Znarin had taken part in Hassakeh, Shaddadi, and other, smaller campaigns against ISIS, but she had never before had dozens of troops serving under her.

When she heard that her commanders, including Nowruz, had chosen her to lead in the Manbij battle, Znarin had felt joy and then, immediately, anxiety. She had hoped to be selected, and she felt ready for the responsibility, but as soon as she heard the news of her selection, she worried it was too much, too soon. Nowruz had reassured her without hesitating.

"None of that," she told Znarin. "We trust you and we know you'll do a great job leading. We would not have given you this chance otherwise."

Now that the night to which they had devoted so much preparation, including spending the past three days running reconnaissance missions to learn the terrain, had arrived, Znarin stood on the edge of the riverbank on the other side of the Euphrates from Nowruz, a sliver of moonlight illuminating the movements of her forces. She had traveled across on a Zodiac after most of her fighters had made it over. The quiet of the night surprised her; it somehow did not fit with the momentousness of the offensive.

Not too long after they crossed she heard a "pop, pop, pop." She grabbed her radio and lifted it to her ear. She knew she would not be the only one wanting to know what had happened. Sure enough, she soon learned the source of the sound.

"It's the rainstorms—they're making the IEDs ISIS left for us explode," one of their leaders called out on the radio. "Keep moving forward."

By this time, battling ISIS had become deeply personal to Znarin. She had seen its commanders; she had seen its prisoners. She had seen the women who fought as part of the Islamic State's forces—as Azeema's teammates had that day in Kobani, when they spotted a female sniper—and the women the ISIS men married. She also had seen the dead bodies of ISIS fighters decaying in the street. While the world considered ISIS a movement, Znarin saw it as far less grand than that: for her, ISIS was a group of men who brutalized women and who wanted to destroy her and her friends.

Taking on ISIS fighters meant thinking like them, learning from them. While she and her forces clambered up from the river-bank after the crossing and headed to the higher ground offered by the hillsides ten miles outside the city, she began putting her plans into action. She had to place her snipers in a location where they could give cover to those entering the villages on the western out-skirts of the city. The SDF had received reports that ISIS might withdraw from some of the less populated towns so that they could focus on the city center and the grain silos inside it; the SDF fight-ers must be ready for that, and ready for ISIS to be lying in wait to ambush them upon their arrival.

One of Znarin's fellow field commanders spoke over the radio.

"We are taking fire, and we have comrades who have been shot," she said. "We are requesting evacuation; we need medical support."

Znarin heard the update and assessed her plans. SDF com-manders already faced a logistical nightmare getting aid to the injured on this first brutal night of a new fight against a familiar enemy. She would stop her forces here on the hillside until dawn came. They did not need to risk any further chance of injury there in the dark. When morning arrived, they'd set off and enter the first set of villages with daylight on their side.

BY THE SIXTH DAY after the river crossing, Znarin's forces had endured losses.

ISIS snipers hit several young women fighters. ISIS also had mined the roads that the Arab and Kurdish forces used to approach the heart of the city. Several SDF members died while driving over them. The grueling fight Nowruz had expected had begun.

Every once in a while, good news buoyed them. A group of Yazidi girls held as sexual slaves by ISIS in Manbij for two years had been rescued. They would be taken to Kobani and then, Znarin guessed, back to their families in Sinjar.

Still, losses were rising. A friend and teammate died instantly after an ISIS fighter shot her when she entered a building to clear it. Znarin knew from Kobani that morale was a living, breathing thing that must be guarded, cared for, and cultivated. She spoke with her fighters in the same way that Nowruz had talked to her team in Kobani.

"They want to break us and to make us weak, but we can't let them," Znarin told her forces before they set off that morning to push ISIS from the next set of villages between them and the city center. Znarin mixed Nowruz's Kobani speeches with Ocalan ideology and added the realities of the ISIS fight. "We have come here to fight for our values, for our principles. For the liberation of the Yazidis they have committed crimes against. We're not just fighting for ourselves, but for humanity."

Each day, ISIS fighters sought to undermine the SDF's ability to maneuver and Znarin's ability to keep her troops' spirits high. They deployed the same tools they had used in Kobani but now even more effectively. Everywhere Znarin's forces went, ISIS explosives awaited them: in the hallways of houses and on street corners, in teapots in kitchens and in shop entrances. Several times a day, the Islamic State turned cars into bombs to kill as many of Znarin's SDF teammates as possible.

ISIS had booby-trapped doorways so that when Znarin's forces entered a building, they would step on a mine and die instantly or lose limbs. No place proved safe from explosives. Schools, shops, homes, side streets: ISIS mined them all. The city's Islamic State rulers, many of whom didn't come from Syria, had refused to let civilians leave and instead kept them as hostages, knowing that the presence of civilians would keep the U.S. from attacking. Those families who tried to flee faced the risk of land mines or ISIS bullets in their backs. The SDF responded by slowing the campaign; it became a harrowing slog in which advancing a single block took hours. The Americans couldn't assist with airstrikes the way they had in Kobani, where few civilians had remained during the battle. So the SDF ground it out, street by street, and discovered civilians held as hostages all along the way.

All of this complicated the SDF's mission to liberate the city. On the third week after the river crossing, Znarin's team reached the north of Manbij. ISIS fighters, dressed in SDF uniforms, entered one of the villages and began killing as many civilians as they could find. By now the Islamic State's forces had pulled out of much of the west side of the city to defend the grain silos that they had decided would become the site of their last stand. This allowed the U.S. to strike them, but then made it harder to get bread to the civilians trapped inside the city. Once the SDF forces controlled enough terrain and could safely encircle a portion of the city, they at last created a passage to usher thousands of civilians out of Manbij, but not before losing a number of fighters, including YPJ members, to ISIS bombs.

As the end of June approached, Znarin's forces prepared to capture the city center. They knew ISIS wanted to counterattack in the streets of Manbij and expected that the extremists would use car bombs from one side while pinning them down with their ground forces from the other. Znarin, in turn, worked with Nowruz and other senior commanders to think like ISIS and figure out how to attack their enemies from the rear of their own front line.

One morning, Znarin readied her forces to set out from their base on the western outskirts of the city and move toward Ketab Square. She had just finished reviewing plans for the day when she heard Yasmin, one of the more junior members of the all-women's force, calling her name.

Znarin, wearing an olive-green T-shirt and camouflage pants, came to the doorway where her young fighter stood. Yasmin looked like Znarin once had, wide-eyed and bewildered by war but trying to be stoic.

"What is it?" Znarin hadn't wanted to be curt, but they had to head out.

"There is a girl here to see you," Yasmin said. She pointed to a girl of maybe thirteen or fourteen, perhaps fifteen, who stood in front of the metal gate of the house they used for a base. She looked thin, and her eyes betrayed nothing. Znarin wondered for a moment whether the girl's arrival was part of an ISIS tactic. The SDF had only recently, in the past three days or so, liberated this village. Arab women and little girls had emerged from their houses to give Znarin and her fighters hugs. One older woman with a sun-etched face and deep lines in her forehead and around her mouth, which no longer held teeth, had asked the YPJ forces what in the world had taken them so long. She had stretched her arms out to the sky and then toward Znarin's fighters.

"All praise is due to God," she had said. "We thank God that you are here." She cupped Znarin's face in her hands and offered a wondrous smile full of kindness that made Znarin wonder what she had looked like as a girl.

That same morning, another woman, who appeared to be in

her late twenties or early thirties, had approached Shelan, one of Znarin's fighters. A twentysomething with a round face, dark eyes, and hair held in a loose bun by a rubber band, Shelan had come to be among Znarin's best fighters; she kept her calm no matter what.

"We thought people had invented you," the woman said to Shelan, who walked alongside her to guide her to a safer area, cleared of mines. The woman spoke in a near shout to counter the sounds of all the people, young and old, who had come out to see whether it was true that ISIS had withdrawn from their area. On her other side, Shelan held tightly on to the arm of an aging woman dressed in black, to help steady her gait. "We heard about these Kurdish women who were fighting, but we didn't believe it at all. But now we see *so many* of you!"

An older woman had come out of her house as the SDF cleared her village. She said that an ISIS fighter had slapped her down while she tried to buy food at a small grocery store near her house. She was nearly blind, she said, and she'd had to lift her veil a little bit to read the letters on a can of meat; just as she moved her veil, the ISIS member assaulted her for the "crime" of showing her face.

This same conversation kept greeting the YPJ fighters as they made their way toward the center, clearing Manbij of ISIS. Mothers and daughters, especially, would come out into the streets. The women from Manbij would stare at them, talk with them, and sometimes hug them wordlessly, their embraces expressing more than words could about just how much they had witnessed and suffered. Znarin realized how strange it must have been for women in these villages to see female soldiers come through with braids and ponytails, carrying rifles and dressed in camouflage; it was strange enough for the Kurdish families to whom these women belonged.

Znarin snapped her mind back to the moment and looked at this reed of a girl standing before her, wearing a niqab, a black veil that covered all of her face except her eyes. The girl had been savvy enough to make it this far, past two of the young women pulling security at the entrance to their makeshift base camp.

"Salaam alaikum," Znarin said to the girl. "How can I help you?"

The girl spoke in barely a whisper. Znarin could see how much courage it had required for her to come here. "I wanted to find out how I could join you."

As Znarin looked at the girl, she understood her. Of course, this girl could not yet join them. She didn't look nearly old enough, and her family would have a say in her decision. But Znarin would not be one more person in her life who told her "no."

"Well, we would be very glad to have you and all the other girls in the village who would want to join us," Znarin said. "Maybe we could talk to your father and mother about coming to us when you are ready? We would be very happy to have a girl as brave as you with us."

The girl still did not meet Znarin's gaze, but her eyes communicated everything. They lit up and shone with a glimmer of what might be possible.

The girl nodded and said little more. She didn't even give her name. But while she walked away she turned to wave—and even raised her eyes to meet those of Znarin, who thought about her for a very long time afterward.

MANBIJ HAD COST dearly in lives—more YPJ fighters than Znarin could count had died already in this horrible battle, many killed right at the start by either ISIS bullets or bombs—but it was also a turning point for the SDF, for the YPG and YPJ, and for herself. The Islamic State had viewed Manbij as a vital hub. Now, little by little, the SDF and its local partners were gaining. Coalition air support helped, too, though airstrikes often proved impossible given the presence of civilians who stayed because they feared dying while fleeing ISIS. By the end of June, the U.S. and its allies had carried out more than 250 strikes, including on the grain silos in which ISIS now holed up. With each passing week, Znarin trusted herself more and doubted her ability less, fueled by her team's results: they retook streets and villages, survived ISIS defenses, and were increasingly successful in outmaneuvering the enemy's vehicle-borne IEDs.

Yet ISIS was not done. On the first of July, the Islamic State counterattacked from all four sides, seeking to retake villages and free its encircled fighters. The Manbij Military Council, part of the SDF, released statements saying that the ISIS attack had failed, but the fact was that the Islamic State's use of human shields slowed the fight. ISIS released videos of SDF fighters it held, and shot families trying to flee the city. Its men changed into civilian clothes and blended in with the population, appearing as if they were innocent people to protect, not fighters to target.

ISIS continued to launch counterattacks, but one cost the group more than a hundred lives in a single day. By the middle of July the SDF had much of the city surrounded. ISIS now had a choice. As one SDF spokesman put it to a local reporter, "Either they will surrender and give up, or fight against us until they die." They chose the latter, going down fighting and taking civilians with them. In one airstrike launched by the U.S., local human rights groups said that at least seventy civilians were killed. The U.S. promised an investigation, but said that it was exercising great care to avoid civilian casualties and noted that ISIS was making the killing of civilians central to its survival strategy, using innocents as "bait" to draw fire. As U.S. defense secretary Ash Carter noted at a Washington event focused on defeating ISIS, Manbij was "one of the last key junctions connecting Raqqa to the outside world" and ISIS would not give it up easily. The SDF began to call in reinforcements from nearby Kobani as the fight dragged on and ISIS forces withdrew to their remaining pockets in the center of the city, leaving booby traps, mines, and all manner of explosives behind them as they retreated.

By now the SDF held between 80 and 90 percent of Manbij. The group made an offer to the ISIS fighters: release all the civilians you hold hostage and we will give you safe passage out. ISIS's response came swiftly: "Inform all our besieged brothers that we will never accept withdrawal and that they must endure even if only one of them remains," ISIS officials wrote to the man leading the now doomed defense of Manbij.

Only a few weeks later, on the twelfth of August, however, a withdrawal of a sort finally took place as ISIS judged it wiser to fight another day than to lose all its men in one city. A convoy of several hundred vehicles streamed out of Manbij, carrying Islamic State fighters, followers, their families, and hostages, whom ISIS kept as human shields to stop the U.S. from blowing up the HiLux trucks escaping toward the northern town of Jarablus.

Manbij marked the first time the SDF had assaulted an ISIS-held city of strategic importance, and the first time ISIS negotiated a chance to keep battling by using civilians as life insurance. It would not be the last time either occurred.

For Znarin, August 12 constituted her own "first." Two and a half months of her life had been devoted to expelling ISIS from the place where the extremists once greeted foreign recruits and welcomed their wives. Far from the driver and aide she was in Kobani, she had led forces from the field to retake her hometown and had learned a lot from tactical successes and even more from failures. Her fighters trusted her to put them first, and now she trusted herself to lead them no matter what. Two years after Kobani, she had finally succeeded in accomplishing what she had pleaded with Nowruz for back then: a chance to lead from the front.

CHAPTER EIGHT

As the relationship between the Americans and the Syrian Kurds on the battlefield grew stronger, the political discussion about governance naturally followed. The Americans were walking a diplomatic high wire on which it proved nearly impossible to stay standing. The U.S. struggled to keep NATO ally Turkey on its side while also deepening a military, and consequently political, alliance with the only candidate U.S. officials judged capable of becoming the infantry force against ISIS: the YPG, and now the SDF.

Critics said that the PKK, or Kurdistan Workers' Party, controlled everything happening in Syria from its base in northern Iraq, and that no distinction could be made between the PKK, designated as a terrorist organization by the U.S. and E.U., and its Syrian offshoot, the Democratic Union Party. For their part, Ilham Ahmed and Fauzia Yusuf, her fellow activist, and their colleagues from the Democratic Union Party swatted down the idea that Qandil controlled their activities. They answered that, yes, of course, the ideas of Ocalan informed their work, but that Syrian Kurds decided their own political fate and shaped their autonomy project. Life-sized posters hung by the Democratic Union Party all around northeastern Syria showed a younger, amiable-looking Ocalan, wearing a big smile and blessed with a full head of hair.

The influence of the PKK was both obvious and acknowledged. Yet the narrative that the PKK equaled the Democratic Union Party and the People's Protection Units was too simple. This was a Syrian branch of that ideology, advanced by Syrians who had risked their lives fighting for Kurdish rights in their country. This didn't mean a separate nation for Kurds, but a future in which Kurds had the dignity of being able to openly speak and publish and move about without being monitored by the regime's henchmen. The Syrian Kurds had continually called for negotiations with Turkey brokered by international allies. Seeing what the Democratic Union Party and the YPG and YPJ were putting in place on the ground, imperfect as it was, was a reminder that they took their governance project seriously, placed women at its center, and understood that U.S. support required them to create an inclusive government built on a separate—if tightly connected—path from the PKK.

In December 2015, six weeks after the U.S. had facilitated the creation of the Syrian Democratic Forces, the SDF's political counterpart was officially formed. Known as the Syrian Democratic Council (SDC), the organization defined itself as the "political branch of the Syrian Democratic Forces" in a five-page statement in Arabic released after two days of discussion in the town of Derek. Like the SDF on the military side, the Syrian Democratic Council aimed to send the message that it represented not just the Kurds. On the roster of the SDC's forty-two representatives:

members of the country's Arab majority, along with Turkmen, Ya-zidis, and Assyrian and Syriac Christians. These groups were among the region's ethnic minorities, like the Kurds.

At a rectangular table draped in white cloth that spanned nearly the length of the ballroom, Ilham sat on her matching fabric-covered chair, upright and attentive. More than a dozen local media outlets reported on the gathering.

When it came time for her to speak, Ilham declared that this new Syrian Democratic Council needed not only support from the region, but also significant international assistance to bring the Syrian civil war, then in its sixth year, to an end. At that moment, estimates put the number of people killed in the conflict at a quarter of a million. More than eleven million Syrians—more or less the entire population of New York City and most of Los Angeles—had been displaced.

Among the dead: hundreds of civilians killed by Russian airstrikes in Syria. Moscow was by now nearly three months into its air campaign in support of the Assad regime and showed no signs of letting up. Russia said its targets were ISIS; U.S. officials said the strikes were "probably not" in ISIS-held locations, but instead designed to offer air cover for the Syrian regime's operations. Russia's willingness to strike anywhere—including markets, medical facilities, and schools—was clear. An October Russian strike killed thirty-two children who sought shelter from the airpower in a building's basement, according to local first responders and international NGOs. Talk of a peace deal in Geneva continued, but no side seemed to really believe negotiations would lead anywhere, despite going through the motions.

Ilham was elected the co-head of the SDC. The council's first task: creating a constitution for *all* of northeastern Syria, including towns and villages being liberated from ISIS by the SDF that were not overwhelmingly Kurdish. These were places with Arab majorities and little knowledge of the ideals of Abdullah Ocalan—places where the idea of a Kurdish minority leading the Arab majority would be seen as grounds for further conflict, and where the idea of women's rights as central to political representation would be questioned from the outset.

Ilham and her colleague Fauzia Yusuf had a great deal of convincing to do among their new partners from the Arab, Assyrian, Syriac, and Turkmen communities, not to mention among older Kurds and Kurds of all ages who found their ideas too radical. Advancing women's rights had proved nearly impossible in their own areas. Only the extreme act of women taking up arms against ISIS in Kobani, fighting as snipers and field commanders and sacrificing their lives there, had at last led to the possibility of recognition of women as equal players within Kurdish society. As Fauzia put it, "the images of YPJ removed the idea that there was a difference between men and women." But for a lot of other communities, the concept of a Kurdish minority promoting an equal rights agenda sounded *more* than alien.

THE INTERNATIONAL SUPPORT that Ilham called for in that ballroom in Derek came soon after the SDC's launch. Brett McGurk, America's deputy special presidential envoy for the Global Coalition to Defeat ISIS, arrived in January 2016, having been charged with implementing an "Iraq first" policy, which had itself shaped the Obama administration's approach to the Syrian conflict. The idea was to stabilize Iraq because America could do little to shift events on the ground in Syria. America had a partner in the government in Baghdad, as well as a number of bases across the country. The U.S. also had a strong diplomatic presence in Iraq and a working relationship with government officials from across the nation's ethnic groups. In Syria, America had none of those tools at its disposal. McGurk had spent more than a decade focused on U.S. policy in Iraq, working for the post–Iraq War Coalition Provisional Authority and then moving on to the National Security Council and the State Department with portfolios that grew in size and profile over time. Now, in his role with the Global Coalition to Defeat ISIS, he broadened his focus to include Iraq *and* northeastern Syria, whose fates ISIS had bound together.

Unlike Mitch Harper's visit, which went unknown and unseen by nearly all outside Kobani, the Washington envoy's January 2016 weekend diplomatic touchdown on Syrian soil played out on social media and in the U.S. and international press, as it was intended. The message was clear: the Americans were now working with the Kurds.

McGurk, like many inside special operations, first took note of the Syrian Kurds and the YPG when they broke the siege of Mount Sinjar in the summer of 2014 and rescued the Yazidis who had fled ISIS only to end up hungry and cold, stranded on a mountain. By October of that year, McGurk had become one of the loudest diplomatic voices in the Obama administration arguing for the airdrop of supplies into Kobani in support of the People's Protection Units.

During the ISIS invasion of Kobani, McGurk stayed in Sulaymaniyah, and watched each day as the Syrian Kurds called for airstrikes against ISIS, even when that meant destroying their own homes and placing their lives at risk. He argued to senior leaders in the U.S. that if Kobani fell, the entire border with Turkey would land in ISIS hands. And if ISIS controlled that border, then the U.S. would never be able to keep ISIS out of Iraq and support the government in Baghdad. Iraqi and U.S. interests in a stable Iraq would be harmed because ISIS would operate unimpeded just across the border.

The counter-ISIL envoy planned his first on-the-ground visit in January 2016 to be a fact-finding trip to see the situation in northeastern Syria for himself. He also had a political mission: to persuade the Syrian Kurds to press forward with the ISIS fight. For the Kurds, moving past the Kurdish areas and into majority-Arab towns hadn't been part of their initial plan before the rise of ISIS. What they wanted was self-protection and legitimacy, the ability to exercise their rights inside Syria—what young people sought in 2004 in Qamishli—and for the international community to stop dismissing them as a proxy for the PKK. These Kurds wanted to see their vision of local democracy and self-rule cemented once the civil war ended, whenever that might be, and they wanted a seat at the table at internationally sponsored peace talks aimed at deciding Syria's future. Moving beyond that and stretching themselves thin by entering Arab areas was not part of their plan.

During his trip, McGurk met in Kobani with Ilham and other political leaders to talk about the future of the ground fight against ISIS. Mazlum, who had commanded the YPG and now led the entire SDF, and who had hosted Mitch in December, expressed concern to McGurk about the number of young people his forces would lose if they pressed forward with the war against ISIS. The battle already had proved costly: by the YPG's own count, 680 of its members had died in battle in 2015 alone. If the Syrian Kurds agreed to sacrifice lives and limbs for areas well beyond their own region, they needed assurance that the Americans would not withdraw their support the minute the ISIS fight ended. They wanted to know that the Americans would endorse giving the Kurds a seat at the table in the Geneva peace process on Syria, sponsored by the United Nations. So far, at Turkey's insistence, they had no such representation.

McGurk said he wouldn't make promises he couldn't keep and urged Mazlum, Ilham, and other Syrian Kurdish political leaders not to see the U.N.-backed Geneva peace process as the goal. Instead, McGurk recommended, the SDF should proceed to the Euphrates River and recruit the Arab forces needed to retake Raqqa. Territory would matter most when Syria's fate was decided down the road, not Geneva's moribund peace process, which had thus far yielded little.

The U.S. also wanted the SDF to retake the town of Shaddadi, a transit hub between Raqqa and Mosul, both of which ISIS continued to control. If the U.S. could disrupt the link between Raqqa and Mosul, it could deliver one more blow to the Islamic State while it figured out how to retake both cities in the coming year.

McGurk's trip was the first official U.S. visit to northeastern Syria, and for Ilham Ahmed and Fauzia Yusuf, it signaled a new chapter for their political movement. The Syrian Kurds had entered 2014 largely friendless and besieged and now, in 2016, received a U.S. diplomat not in a secret visit, but on a tour shared on Twitter and Facebook, the very same social media platforms ISIS used to recruit foreign women and foreign fighters to come to Syria. Turkey would be sure to notice that the Kurds were making new, powerful friends right out in the open, as would others trying to understand how committed the U.S. was to stopping ISIS.

"Spent two days in northern #Syria this past weekend to review ongoing fight against #ISIL. #ISIS #Daesh," McGurk wrote in a Tweet after he had safely departed the region. "Paid respects to over 1,000 Kurdish martyrs from #Kobani battle. #ISIL's siege was broken 1-year ago last week." Social media showed that one of McGurk's stops was the Kobani cemetery, which sat along the road that led to Raqqa; Azeema, Rojda, and Znarin had buried many of their friends there.

Polat Can traveled with McGurk on his visit. He, too, shared images of the American diplomat's trip on social media, unbeknownst to McGurk. One photo showed him offering McGurk a plaque of thanks emblazoned with the YPG logo: a red star surrounded by a yellow shield with two crossed assault rifles behind it. Mitch had received a similar wooden plaque in December, only his featured the letters *YPJ*. Turkey would surely be angered by both the American's visit and the sharing of it by the YPG. U.S. SPECIAL ENVOY MEETS WITH FORMER P.K.K. MILITANTS, read a Turkish newspaper headline, accompanied by an older photo of Polat Can wearing the olive-green uniform of the PKK.

McGurk went to see the spot in Kobani where the U.S. airdrop of medical supplies, weapons, and ammunition had landed in October 2014, and sat down with Arab, Christian, and Turkmen military forces now part of the SDF. Over tables filled with bottles of Pepsi, pita bread, rice, and meat, with hummus and baba ghanoush on the side, the American talked with his hosts about the region's chances for future stability and the opportunity for future cooperation between the U.S. and the SDF against ISIS.

McGurk returned from his travel to Syria feeling that the

United States had made the right decision to work with this partner. Days later he spoke of his trip in testimony before Congress
on America's counter-ISIS strategy. For their part, the Syrian Kurds
had received what they sought most: a dose of international legitimacy bestowed by the United States of America.

*IN POLITICS, you should be prepared for anything; you never know
what will come*, Fauzia Yusuf told herself in 2014 as she considered
what U.S. backing might mean for the Syrian Kurds and her own
Democratic Union Party. Years before, Fauzia had left her studies
as a young woman at Aleppo University to focus all her energy on
the movement for Kurdish and women's rights. By then, her activ-
ism on behalf of the Kurds had earned her the attention of the
Syrian regime's internal security services, who followed her. All
around her she saw friends being rounded up and arrested. She
escaped the same fate but felt she had to do something for the
Kurds. Fauzia became part of the Democratic Union Party's wom-
en's group, Congress Star, the same group that Znarin had joined
years earlier back in Kobani.

Her experience organizing for Congress Star and the Democratic Union Party made her a veteran of political action at a relatively young age. She had seen these groups grow from underground
movements in the early 2000s to organizations getting their first
taste of real power in the early 2010s to participants in discussions
with major Western powers.

They'd received no support from outside countries to this point,
but now their organization was drawing the attention of the world.
The Russians had come calling, and dialogue with Moscow about
possible assistance had been ongoing. After all, the Soviet Union

had backed the Kurds in Iraq for decades as a way of getting what they wanted from both Baghdad and Washington. In the 1980s, Abdullah Ocalan fled Turkey for Syria, which was allied with the Soviet Union, and received support for his Marxist-Leninist PKK from the Soviet Union while there. Russia continued to see the PKK as a tool to exercise leverage in its often fraught and only occasionally friendly relations with Turkey.

But now the Americans had become a new friend and partner for the Syrian Kurds, one that offered airpower and maybe even a path to international legitimacy if their alliance lasted longer than the ISIS fight, which was a big "if," Fauzia thought. Receiving support from the Americans, of all people, came as a surprise, and Fauzia felt they must be clear-eyed about it.

Alongside protecting the Kurds' self-rule, Fauzia kept her focus on her other objective: making sure women were included in the Kurds' political future and winning votes for language on women's rights in the new constitution for northern Syria. She faced pressure from men, both outside and within the Kurdish community, to slow down on the women's rights piece of the puzzle. The Kurds needed to build an inclusive political coalition so that people didn't think they just wanted to force their own very specific ideology on others. How could these political leaders, Fauzia and Ilham and the women from the Congress Star movement, think that such a vigorous push for equality would be accepted? Some working on the draft urged Fauzia to wait. Women would get their rights later; it didn't have to be now. Northern Syria had enough problems without creating a social hurricane. And it wasn't just men who urged a slowing of the charge on women's rights.

"Husbands should be able to marry another wife if the first wife can't have children," one woman told Fauzia, objecting to language outlawing polygamy. "Why would you stop this? This will create too much pressure for women."

Still, Fauzia fought to keep the language in. She understood why some women felt that this might be too much, too quickly. But she believed that radical change was the only option. She and Ilham both knew that thousands of years of tradition would not end overnight: they would not stop child marriage, prevent all violence against women, or block every man from taking a second wife if he no longer wanted the first one or wanted children with another. Both Fauzia and Ilham had been raised in families where women had no voice. They had no illusions about the magnitude of change the language represented. But having the words about women in there mattered, they believed.

"If we are not going to protect women's rights during the revolution, we certainly aren't going to protect them afterward," Fauzia said to others in her political party. It was a refrain the women had repeated for years, in political fight after fight, informed by what had happened all around the world: women helped lead political revolutions only to be rendered powerless afterward. "We have to do it now."

Fauzia didn't know how to think about the future. None of them did. They understood that in a given afternoon they could face Syrian government forces or a Turkish attack or a Russian offensive or an ISIS onslaught. Maybe all of those at once. They knew the Americans could abandon them the moment they judged that supporting the Kurds no longer served their interests. Whatever happened the next day would happen the next day. But for now they would stay organized, consolidate their gains, and build on them.

In thinking about the constitutional language, Fauzia looked to the example of Tunisia. In 2014, the same year that the Syrian Kurds issued their founding document for the Kurdish regions of northeastern Syria, Tunisia, the nation where the Arab Spring had taken root, passed a constitution that stated that women "have equal rights and duties and are equal before the law without any discrimination." Tunisia also required political parties to alternate the members of their candidate lists between men and women. If Tunisia could do this, Fauzia thought, so could their section of northern Syria.

In December 2016 the representatives of the Syrian Democratic Council gathered in the town of Remeilan to complete the draft constitution and vote on it. Council members also approved a change to the region's official name. No longer would "Rojava," the Kurdish word for "West," be included in it. The de facto government's title would reflect the push for inclusivity: the Democratic Federal System of Northern Syria.

The Kurds living outside the region objected swiftly to this rebranding, but two pressing factors accounted for it: first, the Syrian Democratic Council needed to win the backing of the Americans, who had been speaking frequently about increased Arab participation in the area's governance; and second, the council needed the support of Arab communities in Deir Ezzor and Raqqa. These largely Arab towns remained in ISIS hands, and the liberation of Raqqa, the de facto capital of the Islamic State, remained the most high-profile, symbolically potent military challenge up ahead for the United States and, by extension, its battlefield partner, the SDF. Getting ISIS out of Raqqa using an SDF ground force of Arabs and Kurds would be critical to the success of the campaign; the Kurds told the Americans that while they would put their troops' lives on the line for the fight for Raqqa, Arab forces must take the lead for the effort to have the legitimacy and acceptance it needed to succeed.

Once the naming discussion concluded, the group turned to the draft constitution. At that point, its ratification was largely a formality. Fauzia and Ilham had toiled to lay the groundwork: nights spent in consultation with local communities, as Murray Bookchin's grassroots democracy required; afternoons devoted to meeting with representatives on the constitutional council; strategy sessions among themselves to figure out whose votes they might be able to win.

On December 29, 2016, four and a half months after Manbij's liberation from ISIS, the constitutional committee announced the Social Contract of the Democratic Federal System of Northern Syria. More than 150 council members would share the document with the public and the awaiting local media. Capital punishment would be outlawed, the "international declaration of human rights and all related charters of human rights" would be adhered to, and all ethnic groups' languages would be recognized. Refugees would not be repatriated without their consent, natural-resource wealth would be shared, and freedom of the press would be protected, at least on paper. Communes, local councils, and unions would be part of the new "direct democracy" system.

And once again women's rights would form the spine of the document. The Social Contract mentioned women thirteen times. Women would co-lead towns that fell under the federal system's jurisdiction, in all areas it governed.

Article 13 reflected the Tunisian example: "Women's freedom and rights and gender equality shall be guaranteed in society," it stated.

And the next article of the document addressed families like

Znarin's, where girls had no voice in shaping their own fates: "Women shall enjoy free will in the democratic family, which is based on mutual and equal life."

"Violence, manipulation, and discrimination against women shall be considered a crime punished by law," Article 25 stated.

And in the next line was this defense of equality: "Women shall have the right to equal participation in all fields of life (political, social, cultural, economic, administrative, and others) and take decisions relevant to their affairs."

The judicial system would focus on the unique rights, roles, and needs of women: "Women's organizations and equal representation of women are the basis in the field of justice and its institutional activities. Women-related decisions are dealt with by feminine justice systems," the document stated. A "women's justice council" would "deal with all issues and affairs related to women and family."

For Fauzia, the document represented a victory born of years of work, and she decided to savor just a moment of triumph. That night, after the passage of the constitution, Fauzia sat sipping a cup of tea, brought to her by one of the young women who worked in her second-floor office, which had moved from the Congress Star outpost in Derek to the new government's headquarters in Qamishli, a town the Syrian regime had fully controlled five years before. She thought about how much had happened in the intervening half decade. She and her political teammates had succeeded in creating a constitution that stated clearly that women would be seen as equal under the law.

Still, she understood how fragile it all remained. No entity outside northern Syria acknowledged the document, and the Syrian regime would trample it in an instant given the chance. At any moment, Assad could decide to send tanks backed by Russia's airpower into their territories. Turkey constantly threatened to carry out an offensive against either Manbij or the city of Afrin or both. ISIS still controlled cities only a few hours' drive from where she now sat. The Americans offered the Syrian Kurds military support, but no one could say with certainty how long that would last. Given America's history of abandoning the Kurds, she found it hard to imagine that they would be enduring allies, even if she hoped she was wrong. If circumstances forced America to choose between a few million Syrian Kurds and Turkey, a populous and powerful NATO ally, the Kurds would lose every time. All these gains they had fought for since 2011 could vanish instantly if regional powers decided to attack.

The irony of the unintended consequences of ISIS's decision to attack Kobani was striking. By setting out to achieve its utopian vision of ideological dominance in such a splashy and barbaric way in 2013 and 2014, ISIS had inadvertently led the United States to counter with the only ground force that met its needs: the People's Protection Units. With America's support, the Syrian Kurds had turned Kobani into an opening that allowed their own utopian vision to come to life.

Now came the showdown for which many had waited: the battle to retake Raqqa, the capital of the Islamic State. ISIS members from all around the world had lived in Raqqa; some of these men had bought and sold women and girls out of cages at a market on the city's streets. Fauzia thought it only appropriate that women would lead the way in liberating the city.

CHAPTER NINE

Kobani had been the academy that trained a corps of leaders in urban warfare. Rojda, Azeema, Znarin, and Nowruz—all had emerged from that battle with the audacity required to win a street fight and were intimately familiar with the way the men of the Islamic State waged war.

Like Azeema, Rojda had proved herself in that fight, enough to earn plaudits from Nowruz and her commanders in the YPG and YPJ and the opportunity to lead battles after Kobani ended. In 2015, while Azeema went to Hassakeh, Rojda served as one of the commanders charged with defeating ISIS in the town of Ain Issa.

Ain Issa mattered because of its proximity to a far bigger prize: it was thirty miles north of Raqqa, the capital of the caliphate. The town sat along the main route between Raqqa and the other villages that remained in the hands of the Islamic State. The YPJ played a leading role in taking Ain Issa from ISIS after Kobani, and the fight for Raqqa got under way from there.

Rojda had not crossed the Euphrates River with Znarin and her fellow members of the all-women's unit in Manbij in the summer of 2016; at the time, she was part of a stabilization force focused on keeping secure other towns in the north that had been freed from ISIS. But she had gone to Manbij once the offensive had begun and had led forces as the SDF got closer to the city center.

A few months after the end of the battle for Manbij came the official start of the fight for Raqqa. While Ilham and Fauzia focused on the new constitution that summer and fall, Rojda and her team remained on the battlefield.

Rojda would lead around four thousand fighters, Arab and Kurdish, men and women, as the commander of the western front line in Raqqa. The scale of Rojda's leadership responsibilities spoke to the expansion of the larger group. The YPJ was no longer a band of several hundred fighters, defying their male counterparts to start their own unit back in Derek in 2013. By 2016, the all-women's force had reached a few thousand, with hundreds killed in battle; photos of smiling young people who had died in the ISIS fight hung from streetlamps and signposts across northeastern Syria, honoring them. The YPJ had won international media attention, which senior leadership welcomed, even if Rojda and other commanders found it grating and a distraction. There was no denying that all the attention in the press had bolstered the recruitment effort: young women had been motivated by watching women join and lead the battle.

Rojda long ago had stopped feeling fear in the same way she had when she first entered combat in Sere Kaniye—Ras al-Ain in Arabic—against Nusra in 2012. She had become accustomed to war; she understood its pace. She knew the sounds of Russian weapons versus American ones, the gathering roar of an approaching U.S. airstrike, and the smell of an AK-47 just fired. She understood what it felt like to lose a battlefield comrade she loved. After each loss, she asked herself whether her teammate would still be alive if she had made different decisions. She shared with Azeema and Znarin the desire for revenge against the men who killed her friends, took her lands, and enslaved her fellow women.

She thought frequently of the women tortured and beaten by ISIS whom she met in town after town. Rojda and others in the YPJ had rescued mothers and daughters from the Islamic State in every campaign; they found women—sometimes one or two, sometimes many more—who had been held as captives, some still wearing chains around their ankles. The memory of one young woman in particular remained fixed in her memory.

An Arab man had "bought" her from ISIS in order to free her, then delivered her to the YPJ. The rescued woman, named Dalal, rested in one of the YPJ's bases until the group could arrange for her transport back to Sinjar to reunite with her family.

When Rojda met her, Dalal wore a yellow dress and looked to be about thirty. Her full veil, mandatory under ISIS, hung from a hook outside the room where they sat. Rojda sat down next to her on the carpet and asked her what life had been like with the men who had enslaved her.

"When ISIS attacked Sinjar," she told Rojda, "they took the women from my village. They took everyone they didn't kill. I ended up being sold ten times."

She explained that she had been used as a sex slave by every one of the men who held her. When one of them was killed in the fight, she would be moved to the house of another ISIS member who had purchased her.

Rojda sat listening to her there on the carpet, her back pressed against the wall, her head resting on her right elbow and knee, her left leg tucked beneath her. She remained near-motionless while

Dalal shared her story, and her mind focused on the woman's words. As a human being, she couldn't imagine what this woman sitting before her had endured. But she knew that she could not stand for it.

"You are safe here," Rojda told her guest. She held Dalal's hands in her own, and they stayed up the entire night talking, Rojda mostly listening as Dalal shared stories about the men who had terrorized and brutalized her: the way they lived, whom they ate with, married, and fought alongside, and how they viewed their own futures. In the morning, when Rojda had to return to her command headquarters, she hugged Dalal close and told her that all would be better from here.

As she listened to Dalal's story, Rojda felt the desire to keep going until she made these men pay for the crimes they had felt free to commit against Dalal, her family, and all the other women whose lives and futures they'd destroyed.

Now, more than a year after that all-night conversation, the fight to retake Raqqa would at last begin.

WITH RUSSIAN ASSISTANCE from the air starting in October 2015, the same month the SDF was born, and with help from Iranian forces and the Iranian-backed fighters of Hezbollah on the ground, the Syrian government had survived its gravest existential tests. From the start, Iran and Russia had been all in on the regime's side, and now they saw their efforts rewarded. In December 2016, the Syrian Army and its allies at last won back the country's largest city, Aleppo, following a savage, months-long bombing campaign led by Russia. Fighter jets, barrel bombs, cannons, all of them were used to destroy Aleppo. The campaign sent hundreds of thousands of Syrians fleeing their homeland and ended up creating a crisis across the European Union as country after country tried to figure out how to respond to all the people seeking safety at their borders. Each time the United Nations Security Council took up a resolution to speak out against the regime's violence, Russia and China vetoed it. In February 2017, those two nations even thwarted language condemning Assad for using chemical weapons against his own citizens.

In 2011 the world had heard Barack Obama say that "the time has come for President Assad to step aside." But by 2017, few expected that step any time soon. As it turned out, Obama left office before Assad. On November 8, 2016, three days after the announcement of Operation Wrath of Euphrates, the name for the Raqqa campaign, a political earthquake shook Washington: Donald Trump was elected the forty-fifth president of the United States.

For the Americans, discussion about the Raqqa offensive had been consumed for months by two central questions: What force would lead the way in the battle to push ISIS out of its capital, and how could the policy groundwork be best laid for the new U.S. administration? Before November 8, the first question felt more urgent than the second, because conventional wisdom held that Hillary Clinton would be elected, and thus a continuation of the current president's policy was likely. Trump's election introduced another unknown.

Since the end of the battle for Manbij in August 2016, Turkey had insisted to the Obama administration that it could field a force to take Raqqa from the Islamic State. America's NATO ally argued that the Syrian Kurds could not be permitted to lead the way in this fight in the majority-Arab city. U.S. military leaders had listened to this discussion, and visited Turkey to tackle the conversation in person, as had senior diplomats involved in Syria policy, including Brett McGurk. The Americans who had watched the ISIS fight from a front-row seat for three years now felt strongly that the Syrian Kurds and, now, the SDF had to be the force with which they entered Raqqa. They argued that this force was the only one capable of teaming with Arab units to retake the city successfully. Discussions continued, but Turkey had delivered no viable alternative to the SDF.

One issue that had to be addressed if the Syrian Kurds were to lead the fight for Raqqa alongside the Arab components of the SDF: the U.S. would have to arm them directly. There was no way around it, given the scale of the fight they were about to undertake and the defenses ISIS would put in place to stop the SDF from taking the town. The Kurds wanted the tools the fight required: mortars, ammunition, heavy machine guns—such as the Soviet-era DShK, known as the Dushka—counter-IED equipment to stop vehicle-borne bombs, and up-armored Humvees to survive ISIS attacks. They also understood and sought the legitimacy that direct arming would confer.

As 2016 neared its end, the Obama administration, with McGurk advancing the discussion, decided it had to make a final call on the direct arming of the People's Protection Units. As McGurk and others saw it, their team had been wrestling with this question of "to arm or not to arm" for years, and it would be best to resolve this policy hot potato now rather than hand it off to a brand-new team. If the U.S. chose to arm the YPG, Turkey's reaction would be both public and vocal, and it would be best for the Obama White House to absorb the blowback. On the other hand, Obama noted, he would be saddling a new administration with a diplomatic maelstrom in its first few weeks, which he would not have appreciated back in 2008. In the end, the new administration weighed in. Trump's national security adviser, Michael Flynn, spoke with his counterpart in the Obama White House, Susan Rice. Flynn asked Rice not to proceed with the plan to arm the Kurds pending the Trump administration's review. The Obama administration understood. This decision was important, and the arriving White House should settle the issue for itself.

IN THE DARKNESS OF NIGHT on March 22, 2017, five hundred SDF fighters boarded American V-22 Ospreys and CH-47 Chinook helicopters bound for Tabqa, a town located less than thirty miles from Raqqa. The focus was Syria's largest dam. Rojda and her SDF teammates had wanted to launch this campaign in January, but winter weather had created delay after delay. American airstrikes had begun in the area earlier in the year, but would never be enough to dislodge ISIS. Now, at last, the campaign was under way. Along with the aircraft transporting SDF fighters into Tabqa, America offered protection in the form of Marine Corps artillery fire and Apache helicopters. Brady Fox, Mitch Harper's teammate who had first talked with him of the YPG's and YPJ's social media feeds back in 2014, had come to Tabqa as part of the Americans' advise-and-assist mission. Brady had trained a number of the best troops he could find from the SDF. He hadn't known if making the course coed was the right decision at first, until a twentysomething YPJ fighter blasted everyone on the fitness test. He noted her score to all the men and said she had set the standard for everyone else going forward.

The Tabqa Dam was a masterpiece of Soviet cement-and-steel engineering, built from French and German plans that had been created before the 1963 Syrian coup that eventually brought Hafez al-Assad, Bashar's father, to power. Construction launched in 1970, with thousands of Soviet experts dispatched to Syria to ensure the project's completion. The dam was a critical source of electricity, clean water, and irrigation for the area and pride for the Syrian regime. ISIS had controlled it for more than three years.

The SDF's first goal was to capture the dam. Two dozen miles from Raqqa, the dam would give ISIS a key path for troop reinforcements if the SDF didn't take it before moving on the capital. Rojda and Nowruz also feared that ISIS would release the water and flood the surrounding cities, a humanitarian tragedy that would be owned by the SDF and the Americans alike if it happened. Already, in January, the United Nations had warned of "massive scale flooding" in the area if more airstrikes occurred and the entrance to the dam was further damaged.

Rojda would help lead this campaign for the YPJ; her YPG counterpart, Karaman, had grown up in Tabqa. His father had served as an engineer at the dam when Karaman was a boy, and he knew the structure's complexity. The idea arose to use the blanket of darkness to fly in five hundred SDF fighters behind ISIS lines onto the south side of Lake Assad, the dam's thirty-mile-long reservoir and Syria's biggest water reserve and lake. Along with the SDF forces airdropped into ISIS territory came Bobcat loaders, small but powerful machines, some with their tops sawed off to fit in the helicopters, that could dig up earth and transport materials. The Bobcats would allow the SDF troops to quickly dig ditches to protect themselves from the massive ISIS car bombs they knew were sure to come. These forces would then begin the assault on the Tabqa Dam and be joined by reinforcements soon after.

The dam was built like a tank and was filled with ISIS snipers, including many foreign fighters, awaiting the SDF's arrival. ISIS set up remotely controlled machine guns in doorways so that it could shoot at the SDF fighters as they stacked up to enter a room. Brady had watched ISIS's tactics and noted to himself how much chaos could be created if you were tactically proficient and mentally prepared to die. By the third failed SDF attempt to take the dam's towers, which claimed the lives of seven fighters trained by Brady and the Americans, Karaman and Rojda and the U.S. advisers decided that they had to figure out another way in. Crossing the Euphrates was the only answer.

The crossing took place the night of April 3, following several days of training on nearby Lake Assad. The YPG men who led the boat crews, which were thwarted by powerful currents, took until dawn to reach the southern riverbank, which meant the crossing had to be aborted. Rojda watched with dismay; Brady and the Americans, impatient, stressed that they had to have a leader strong enough to manage all the contingencies of the crossing. Rojda told the Americans that she would take care of it. The next night, a young woman in a camouflage uniform and matching cap, carrying a walkie-talkie, stood on the northern side of the Euphrates, calling out the first wave of Zodiacs, and then the second and the third, to take around two hundred people across the river and reinforce the fighters who already had arrived there by helicopter. No glitches this time as the mission finished in the allotted window of darkness.

Rojda had felt confident in her field commander's ability to complete the job, though she was unhappy about the first night's missteps. But she allowed herself a little laugh when Brady joked that the SDF leaders should have given the assignment to the women in the first place, as they had in Manbij.

Meanwhile, after the airdrop into Tabqa, SDF forces surrounded the city and the ISIS fighters still inside it by moving in separate units, village by village. By April 6, after more than a day and a half of continuous fighting in a town four miles east of Tabqa, the SDF had completed another important piece of the mission: ISIS fighters in Tabqa were now cut off from any further reinforcements or resources. Now the work of retaking the city itself would begin. By April 15, the SDF had entered Tabqa; two days later, it captured the radio station that ISIS used as its broadcast center. The fight to retake the city continued from there as the Islamic State's men used snipers, human shields, and all manner of explosives to stop the SDF from advancing. Snipers claimed SDF lives, including that of a fellow YPJ commander and friend of Rojda's.

ISIS would not abandon the Tabqa Dam easily, just as the SDF had predicted. The jihadists dispatched a group of well-trained foreigners, including what the SDF thought to be Chechens and North and West Africans, to guard the tunnels below the dam on the southern end of Lake Assad. ISIS foreigners, despite being cut off from supplies and communications, also held the dam's control rooms and floodgates.

Still, by the start of May, the SDF controlled nearly all of the city as the campaign to free Tabqa from ISIS advanced even while the fight for the dam continued. Some ISIS fighters and their families were said to have withdrawn from the city and headed for Raqqa, but hundreds of others were estimated to have been killed. Even while surrounded and isolated, the ISIS fighters in the dam remained committed to their positions and forced the SDF to pursue them. At last, on May 10, Rojda and the SDF announced that they had taken full control of the Tabqa Dam after the ISIS fighters holed up inside it surrendered or were killed.

. . .

THE DAY BEFORE the SDF announced the successful conclusion of the Tabqa campaign, the Trump administration approved the direct arming of the Syrian Kurds. The White House had evaluated all the options and concluded that the decision offered America the best path to retaking Raqqa and defeating ISIS. Like the previous administration, the new White House had no intention of deploying U.S. ground troops in Syria. And, like its predecessor, it found that no other force could credibly serve as America's partner infantry for this fight. The new administration also faced the same challenges in explaining the decision to NATO ally Turkey.

"We are keenly aware of the security concerns of our coalition partner Turkey," the Pentagon said in a statement. "We want to reassure the people and government of Turkey that the U.S. is committed to preventing additional security risks and protecting our NATO ally."

The Americans could still sever ties with the Syrian Kurds the moment they didn't need them, but in the meantime the U.S. had signaled publicly to the world that it had chosen the Kurdish-led forces for the highest-profile fight yet. This step toward international legitimacy mattered a lot more to the Syrian Kurds than any of the American weapons.

Now Nowruz and Rojda and the fighters serving under them sought battlefield victories resounding enough to convince the U.S. that remaining aligned with them would serve America's counter-terrorism interests while buying time for their own political project to grow.

On June 5, one month after both the battle for Tabqa and the Washington decision to arm the YPG, Rojda and her team launched the campaign for Raqqa. Znarin, who had begun taking on a larger leadership role in Manbij, would be among the commanders serving alongside Rojda.

The battle began in the district of al-Mishlab, to the south and east of the city center, just as U.S. weapons shipments started to arrive. As the SDF forces entered the city, they saw gutted buildings standing in some places and crushed to the ground in others, evidence of the U.S. and counter-ISIS coalition airstrikes that had preceded them. They also encountered the expected ISIS response: car-borne explosives, suicide bombers, and mines left in just about every place imaginable.

Rojda's forces had been exhausted by the battle for Tabqa. Brady could see it and worried about their lack of rest as Raqqa approached. The fight had lasted weeks longer than many had expected. They had just a brief respite before starting the Raqqa campaign. She hoped it would be enough, because she felt certain that however grueling the fight in Tabqa had been, Raqqa would be far worse.

WHEN BRADY FINALLY headed back home to the U.S., nearly a year after he arrived and a half year later than he expected, his teammate Jason Akin took over. He would work with Rojda on the tactical level, advising on the movement of forces and the firepower and air support they would require, and Nowruz on the strategic side, planning the trajectory of the overall Raqqa campaign. Commanders from the YPJ now led both the eastern and western fronts in the greatly anticipated battle to retake the city. Rojda was one of them.

Initially, Jason and the small contingent of Americans focused on the Raqqa fight lived about twelve miles from the Syrian forces with whom they worked. The U.S. didn't want any of its people inside Raqqa, given how dangerous the fight would be. The guidance had not changed much since 2015: no Americans in the line of fire or in direct combat. Period. Mitch Harper had underlined that over and over to his forces back then, and the Syrians had internalized it. For the Syrian Kurds, the worst development would be if an American died in the battle.

For Jason, however, who had spent much of his adult life at war for the United States, this would not work. He told his commanders that he had to have a clearer and closer view of the front line to do his job and give battlefield leaders his best advice. This was not work he could do remotely. He stressed to his superiors that the half hour—minimum—of required driving at least once each day was precious time wasted. So they established a base on the western side of town that would house about one hundred Syrians and seventy to eighty Americans, including a surgical team charged with operating on any and all comers, so that the U.S. and SDF leaders could remain in constant contact.

At the outset Jason had wondered how he would establish battlefield rapport with women, including those who commanded the western and eastern front lines. He didn't know whether it would be different from working with men. What he understood quickly was that their mentality as leaders was the same as his. They had faced years of uninterrupted war without complaint and were willing to fight alongside anyone who shared their enemy. They were all grounded in the same warrior ethos.

ON THE OCTOBER MORNING when she listened on the radio for updates from a team of fighters she had assigned to take the central hospital, the most dominant piece of terrain in the city ISIS still held, Rojda had been leading the fight in Raqqa—what the SDF now called the Great Battle—for four months. She had been at war for more than four years and battling ISIS for three and a half of them. The Islamic State had reshaped her life.

The Raqqa fight had begun as predicted: a long, hard slog. ISIS had taken beatings but then regrouped: at the end of June it managed to retake neighborhoods it had lost to the SDF. By the first week of July, Rojda's teammates held one quarter of the city. If Kobani had taught these soldiers urban warfare, the far larger Raqqa offered a master class in its hellishness. Snipers and mortar fire slowed every advance the SDF attempted; in addition, some units outside the SDF that had come to join the fight decided it was too brutal and retreated, leaving SDF leaders to figure out how to replace them. How do you persuade people to keep advancing when either a sniper's bullet or an IED awaits them at just about every step? Rojda and her team wondered. Despite the airpower targeting its locations, ISIS dug in further and resorted to even more car bombs, suicide bombs, and mines programmed to detonate the moment the SDF fighters entered a building, stepped in a doorway, tripped over a teakettle, or opened a kitchen cabinet. Her forces lost twenty people in east Raqqa alone in only a little more than a day.

These are the same animals we fought in 2014, Rojda thought. *Their tactics haven't changed.*

International rights groups raised questions about the sheer intensity of coalition airstrikes targeting Raqqa and whether enough care was taken to protect the tens of thousands of civilians stuck inside the city. ISIS mined the roads, positioned snipers on roofs, and shot anybody trying to flee. Rojda wanted to finish the fight as quickly as they could: the longer the battle, the more willing ISIS was to use civilians as human shields to keep the Americans from striking its fighters. Surveying Raqqa with Rojda and others in the SDF leadership, Mitch Harper had been amazed by the level of destruction required to defeat ISIS. And he felt deeply concerned about what came next. They hadn't yet beaten the extremists, but already he worried about how the U.S. would keep them from returning. The Islamic State's forces remained committed to their ideology regardless of certain defeat and he saw few in the coalition to stop ISIS who were all-in when it came to winning the peace.

BY THE END OF AUGUST, the SDF held nearly two-thirds of Raqqa; the U.S.-backed forces had linked their southern and western fronts and at last had shaken ISIS from most of the Old City, but their progress had cost dearly: civilians held hostage by ISIS died while fleeing, coalition airstrikes—usually around two dozen a day—leveled buildings, and more than one hundred SDF fighters were killed. In mid-September, the Syrian Observatory for Human Rights reported that it had documented the deaths of 1,029 civilians since the fight's start. Refusing to give up, ISIS forces, particularly the foreigners, burrowed into buildings, waited for SDF troops to get close, and then blew themselves up when they did. A forty-six-minute audio message from ISIS leader Abu Bakr al-Baghdadi released September 28 showed that he remained alive despite reports to the contrary. He urged fighters to stay true to their faith and avoid surrender.

Just as she had in Kobani and in every battle since, Rojda's mother called at least every other day, just to hear Rojda's voice. Sometimes she hung up the moment Rojda said hello. Rojda's brother served as a medic in the Raqqa fight and often tracked his sister down at their mother's behest.

When word spread of a twenty-four-hour clash or a particularly awful vehicle-borne IED on the west side, Rojda's brother would listen continuously for his sister's voice on the radio. If he didn't hear it, he would find her and make sure she remained alive and uninjured. Then he would report back to their mother.

So far in Raqqa, Rojda had brushed up against death twice. The first time, a car bomb nearly rolled right into her. The second time, an ISIS drone with a grenade connected to it was about to explode in front of her when one of her teammates shot it down with an AK-47. Both times, she escaped untouched.

At the start of October, the fight to wrest the central hospital and stadium from ISIS control had reached an apparent stalemate. By that point, the SDF had taken almost all of the city, but ISIS held hostages and had fortified its position in both structures. The hospital served as the ISIS command and control center, and its size, as well as the hostages inside, made it difficult for the SDF to capture. The SDF had tried already to close in on it from two different directions in a maneuver known as a pincer movement. The goal was to pin ISIS down and stop reinforcements from arriving. That plan had failed. The SDF had instead been forced to move toward the northern edge of the city and push downward from there.

Each day since June, Rojda had faced the task of coordinating the operations of around four thousand fighters—Arabs and Kurds, men and women—moving several hundred at a time to take ground with the help of the airpower provided by the U.S. and its coalition partners. And each day as her troops advanced, they made some moves Rojda later would call mistakes. The SDF forces sometimes spent days taking only a few streets, and they lost fighters to snipers and explosives, a fact she would never get used to. But they could not afford to stop moving forward. It would only result in more deaths. ISIS had left all of Raqqa booby-trapped.

In the years the Islamic State held Raqqa, the group had created tunnels from which its members could pop out and blow themselves up. This meant that after the SDF forces had cleared a building or even taken it to use as a base, ISIS fighters could come tunneling into the structure and attack. This killed SDF soldiers, sowed confusion, and forced commanders to deal with the threat before they could return to trying to advance against ISIS. The Islamic State's troops benefited from the hospital's high ground, and each time Rojda's teammates got near enough to effectively respond to enemy fire, ISIS would use heavily laden car bombs to push them backward.

In early October, Rojda traveled out to the front line to see for herself what kept the SDF forces from advancing. That day they managed to move forward and take some ground. They had help from mortars fired by the Bethnahrin Women's Protection Forces, the all-female Assyrian militia, which Dean Walter and his U.S. special operations teammates had encountered on the side of the road in early 2016 as they headed into the battle for Shaddadi. Rojda planned to stop her troops' advancement for one to two days to do ground reconnaissance and give them a bit of rest. She herself would visit a few points on the front line before returning to the command base that her leadership team shared with Jason Akin and the other Americans.

Just as she began checking in with the frontline fighters focused on the central hospital, ISIS launched a new round of attacks. As Rojda observed the conditions on the ground and talked to the Americans over the radio, about one hundred ISIS fighters attacked her forces from two sides at once.

Nearly immediately Rojda began leading the clashes from there on the front line, where she, as a commander, knew she was not intended to be; taking out her own weapon, she joined the battle.

As she called out commands to move her forces forward, Rojda received an update over the radio: ISIS had killed six SDF fighters positioned farther forward and was burning their bodies. This meant that their families would not be able to bury them properly. ISIS combatants continued to come at their position, now in groups of four of five, with a seemingly unlimited supply of men. A team of SDF fighters had just gone to the roof of a shelled building to launch a rocket-propelled grenade at ISIS.

The way the Americans saw it, the SDF had not put enough people in place to secure this critical location. Jason argued this point to Rojda, among others, noting that every time they got close to the hospital, ISIS would bring in forty or fifty fighters to battle the SDF's eight or ten. But for Rojda and her team, which had fought lean since 2014 and had managed to survive until now by putting only the minimum number of fighters required at risk—far fewer than the Americans would put toward an offensive—not deploying en masse remained a key to success and survival.

The face-off lasted all that day and well into a second. At last Rojda's forces managed to push the ISIS fighters back, aided by U.S. airstrikes and several good shots that managed to stop the driver of a car bomb barreling toward their position. Rojda wanted to advance with her forces past a mosque behind which the SDF had established a secure point and get closer to the hospital, which was now gutted, its blue-and-brown painted walls facing a moonscape of disemboweled and abandoned cars. One of her fellow commanders stopped her as she tried to move forward with her troops.

"You have to stay here where it is safe," the commander said while Rojda spoke on the radio to her forces, discussing their next steps. Nowruz, too, had told Rojda that she needed to get back to their command base rather than remain on the front line, where she put herself—and, by extension, those she led—at risk.

Now that the immediate danger had passed, Rojda agreed. She had seen for herself why her fighters had not been able to press forward as fast or as far as she and her fellow commanders had sought. ISIS forces wanted to die here. They would use their mines, tunnels, and car bombs to make sure a lot of SDF troops did, too. She would spend that night and the next day with her leaders, and with Jason Akin and the Americans, figuring out the best way to take the hospital and the stadium and at last end this fight.

CHAPTER TEN

While the battle in Raqqa was brutal and filled with misery, the end of the Islamic State's hold on its onetime capital was inevitable. The question was not whether the U.S.-backed SDF forces would capture Raqqa, but how many would die, how long the fight would take, and how bloody ISIS would make it. The summer of 2017, I saw firsthand the crushing slog on silent streets the SDF undertook to win back the city. ISIS wanted to kill as many as it could even while the SDF backed it into a corner, and the more time passed, the more the SDF advanced, the more committed some in the Islamic State's ranks—particularly foreign fighters—became to holding out as long as possible. For many ISIS members, Raqqa signified the end of the road.

By mid-October, soon after Rojda returned to her base as Nowruz had wanted, the fight for the hospital and the stadium slowed to a stop. The ISIS fighters were surrounded. They had run low on water and food and had no way to get more supplies. The Islamic State had lost nearly all of Raqqa and now stood both dug in and encircled in two difficult-to-clear locations. They had reached the moment at which they must choose whether to fight until death or negotiate what came next.

Some on the U.S. side saw no need to give ISIS this option or any other. But tribal elders in Raqqa had made clear they wanted no more bloodshed and said they would take responsibility for the remaining ISIS fighters. The Raqqa Civil Council (RCC), chaired by men and women who would lead Raqqa going forward and work to restore services to the collapsed city, agreed. Similar councils now led Manbij and Tabqa. The Raqqa Civil Council posted a statement online appealing to the SDF for the ISIS men's safe exit.

"We are organizing transportation to remove these local fighters in order to save the lives of civilians used as human shields and save the rest of the city from destruction," the RCC statement said. "We tribal leaders will be the guarantors for those removed."

The Americans acknowledged the need for the deal, but they would not state that they were supporting it publicly nor that they would refrain from targeting ISIS fighters as they made their way out of the city. This was a local deal the Americans had to live with, regardless of whether they agreed with it. Some of Rojda's forces didn't love the deal any more than the Americans did, but they, too, accepted it.

On October 15, a convoy of more than a hundred vehicles carrying roughly three hundred ISIS fighters and more than three thousand civilians, including four hundred ISIS hostages, departed the Raqqa stadium for the town of Markada, which sat on the road linking Hassakeh with Deir Ezzor, which ISIS still held. The following day the line was clear: either ISIS fighters get on the buses out or they would face the next SDF offensive there in Raqqa. Among those who didn't board: a small group of foreign fighters who, though encircled and running low on ammunition, stayed committed to the idea of fighting to the end.

Two days later, Rojda's forces no longer faced ISIS bullets or car bombs during their operations to clear the rest of the city. The black flag of the Islamic State had vanished from the stadium. In its place was the SDF's yellow flag, carried by Rojda and other YPJ leaders. The battle for Raqqa had reached its exhausted end. The caliphate that sought to extend its rule as far as Rome could not even claim Raqqa as its capital. The idea of ISIS, however, would be far harder to conquer. Both the Americans and, much more deeply, the SDF knew that it was easier to kill a terrorist than to slay an ideology.

ON OCTOBER 17, 2017, Rojda rode to Raqqa's Naim Square— also known as Paradise Square—in one of the SDF's white HiLux trucks to do something she had not dared to do for years: share publicly and with her forces the satisfaction of victory. The SDF had at last pushed the Islamic State out of Raqqa. ISIS forces no longer attacked them from either the stadium or the hospital. The shooting, the mortars, the car bombs, the suicide attacks—those had all stopped. Now, in Paradise Square, a roundabout right in the city center, Rojda would mark the occasion of the Islamic State's defeat.

This place had witnessed so much. Before the civil war, Raqqa's families would enjoy gatherings in the roundabout's garden. Children ran across its lush grass. In the summertime, gleeful little boys splashed each other and jumped up and down and dunked their heads in the green-blue waters of the fountain to ward off the relentless city heat. ISIS ended all that. The rulers of the Islamic

State turned Paradise Square into their gruesome public stage. Instead of seeing the space as a heavenly respite from urban life, Raqqawis renamed it Hell Square. The terrorists would assemble there to blindfold, line up, and shoot in the head those who opposed the Islamic State. In the roundabout, ISIS cut off the hands and heads of anyone judged to be an enemy or found to be guilty of breaking the rules. Thick spikes lined the fence along the outer edge of Naim Square. ISIS placed the severed heads of those it executed atop the bent metal stakes that pointed toward the sky, looking like arrows aiming toward hell that somehow had gotten lost. ISIS forced Raqqa's residents, including the smallest citizens, to bear witness to the killings it carried out. ISIS security forces rounded up those who happened to be passing by on the street to come and watch, without looking away, how the group dealt with its enemies. The executions sent the message: this was the fate of ISIS's opponents.

Now SDF fighters who had battled and killed ISIS forces for months—and, in many cases, years—assembled in the roundabout. Women and men who had served under Rojda arrived in the square after surveying buildings where ISIS had ruled until only a day or two earlier, dodging all the booby-trapped explosives and unexploded shells the group had left behind. And Rojda—giving the troops a huge smile and carrying a yellow Syrian Democratic Forces flag on a wooden stick, her hair shaking loose from its braid, the flag waving in the wind—at last relaxed for the first moment since Manbij in 2016. Joy, relief, and disbelief pumped through her in competing pulses.

All around Rojda was the wreckage of the last five months, a rolling devastation from which the city's residents would not soon recover. Rubble coated streets lined with bombed-out buildings buckling under the weight of munitions dropped on them during months of airstrikes. But there, in the beaming October sunshine, whose bright rays contrasted with the sagging, ghost-ridden wreckage of the streets that led to Naim Square, SDF fighters marked the end of a battle that had claimed so many of their friends. Above Naim Square, a YPJ sniper stood guard, scanning the horizon for any signs of ISIS forces. A slew of smaller green-and-gold flags, in honor of the Women's and People's Protection Units, respectively, flew in the square.

ISIS had not disappeared even as its forces stopped firing; some of the group's members had blended in with civilians and fled, and many had headed to the next towns that would become battlefields: Deir Ezzor and Baghouz. A hive of mines ISIS had left to maim and murder Raqqa's residents had to be cleared before the city's families could return home. The work of rebuilding would be long and costly. Right now, a cleaned-up Raqqa restored to habitability seemed nearly unimaginable. The challenge of reviving the city would fall to the Raqqa Civil Council. From its start, the group faced questions about its legitimacy, a funding shortfall resulting from a lack of international support, and demands from desperate citizens whose homes and livelihoods had been destroyed. The council would soon confront the challenge of bringing services back to life in a city decapitated by war, with almost no money available for any of the work required.

But those worries would come another day. Today, the SDF, including the all-women's forces that fell under its umbrella, would stop for a moment to acknowledge all that they had sacrificed since 2014 to make this victory possible. In Naim Square, Rojda's fighters hoisted a picture of Arin Mirkan, the young YPJ fighter who had blown herself up in Kobani just feet away from ISIS forces during the grimmest hours of the town's siege in order to kill as many of them as possible when all looked nearly lost for the Kurds. Jason Akin, the American noncommissioned officer who had worked alongside Rojda just about every day for the past four months, gathered with SDF forces back at the base he had helped to establish that summer in Raqqa. The men and women he worked with sang and danced and used their phones to snap pictures and log video of them all together, as a team, before they each went on to whatever came next. Similar to Mitch Harper in Kobani in 2015 and Leo James in Manbij a year later, Jason had experienced an unexpected first on this tour: Commanders had assigned him and his team the task of supporting Rojda and the SDF in the seizing of Raqqa, which had not yet begun when the Americans arrived. Now, in October, the black flags of ISIS no longer flew over the city. Never before in his experience in the post-9/11 conflicts had the mission started and finished in the time allotted.

Sailing above Naim Square, however, was a sight that gave the Americans diplomatic heartburn.

There, high above all the women fighters who had come to commemorate the end of the battle, forming an unlikely sea of green patches, camouflage, braids, digital watches, patterned socks, and hiking boots, smiled the jovial image of the man whose ideas had made that day possible: Abdullah Ocalan. It was exactly what many within the State Department had said would happen if the U.S. partnered with the fighters of the People's Protection Units: eventually they would reveal themselves to be ideological zealots with a political agenda opposed to American interests. In reality, they had never pretended to follow any other ideology—indeed, it gave them the discipline that held their forces together.

The Americans had planned for a press conference in the Raqqa stadium where ISIS made its last stand. U.S. military leaders would appear alongside SDF commanders after the announcement of the end of the battle for Raqqa. Once the Ocalan posters went up, however, that plan collapsed. "We condemn the display of PKK leader and founder Abdullah Ocalan during the liberation of Raqqa," said Defense Department spokesman Maj. Adrian Rankine-Galloway. The Americans would do no public events alongside their battlefield partners, even while they put out statements congratulating the SDF and praising them for fighting "tenaciously and with courage against an unprincipled enemy."

For Rojda and Znarin and others in their all-women's units, Ocalan had to be a symbolic part of their celebrations. They would not have been in this fight, battled ISIS for years, or stood there before the cameras without him and his philosophy of women's liberation, which they had placed in the center of their military campaign. They had spread his ideas and, emphatically, his focus on the emancipation and the rights of women, as they fought, bled, and died, street by street, village by village, town by town, while at war with a force that taught and practiced women's enslavement.

Rojda, for her part, now had no idea what to do with herself, even while she marched across Naim Square. What do you do when the fight that has occupied all corners of your imagination and shaped each moment of every day is suddenly pushed into the fading past, replaced by a whole new set of challenges? She and her fellow leaders strode all around the square, flags waving and fists pumping. They ran and danced and didn't give even one thought to the mines all around them that ISIS had left behind. Joy ruled, not fear. In that moment, Rojda allowed herself to hope that this square, which had been a hell for Raqqa's citizens, would become a permanent haven for them once again before too long.

. . .

IN THE SUMMER OF 2018, eight women stood in a row under
the August sun and held hands. Then the eight became twelve.
The twelve became twenty, and the twenty became too many to
count.

With the pounding bass of the music bursting through the
courtyard's speakers and the unmistakable pitch of women's voices
calling out in joy, the dancing began. Men in the crowd joined in
the expression of happiness and began celebrating alongside them.

Side, side, forward, back. Men and women held hands and spun
their bodies, moving round and round to the beat in their shared
circle, smiling in the hundred-plus-degree heat of a Raqqa summer.
Some wore jeans and T-shirts; others wore pants and button-downs,
brightly colored ankle-length traditional dresses and matching head-
scarves, or military caps and the camouflage uniforms of the Wom-
en's Protection Units; one even wore a Zara jacket that declared, "I
really don't care, do u?"

Until ten months before, ISIS had bought and sold women on
the streets of Raqqa. Now women and men had come together to
celebrate the opening of the Raqqa Women's Council. Women had
worked barefoot and with sleeves rolled up cleaning the floors and
walls of the new council building in the neighborhood of Bedo—
the third such council in the city.

The council was one more part of the push for women's equality that had accompanied the military victories of the SDF. These
women's councils would organize women on economic, social, and
political issues and push the civil councils to address women's
needs. And there, on that second Saturday in August, a women's
council serving all of Raqqa, including some already established

neighborhood chapters, would open right in the center of town. Playing music, dancing, holding hands with someone of the opposite sex, being outside without a full black veil—any one of those activities could have ended in death or imprisonment and torture at the hands of ISIS. Now women had gathered to share a moment of joy, to celebrate the lives they were rebuilding for themselves, and to discuss all the work for women that lay ahead.

So much remained to be done in Raqqa. The city was still choked by rubble, as no significant international funding had yet materialized to assist with rebuilding, just as Mitch had worried about a year earlier, during the war for ISIS's former capital. None looked likely to arrive any time soon, either. So many homes still looked just as they had immediately following the airstrikes: entirely uninhabitable. Water and power came only in short supply for most of the city's residents. Security remained the greatest source of worry: ISIS waited eagerly to carry out sleeper-cell attacks and car bombings, and no matter how many were prevented by YAT, the U.S.-trained counter-terrorism force of the SDF made up of both men and women, not all of the threats could be stopped.

Still, Raqqa's resilience shone as the city's residents—teachers, shopkeepers, hairdressers, perfume sellers, women's council staff members, police officers—came back to their town to begin rebuilding their homes and their lives. The opening of the new women's council was the latest sign of Raqqa's citizens' refusal to be broken.

Alone in the center of the circle, surrounded by dancing adults in outfits of all kinds and colors as the music blared, stood a little girl in a short-sleeved red dress overlaid with lace, pearls hanging from its bottom ruffle at her shins. She looked to be around six or seven years old and wore her shoulder-length hair in a ponytail. A thin gold bracelet shone on her wrist. Her shadow moved back and forth in front of her as she swayed to the beat, a small, solo, red-clad representative of the future.

ROJDA SPENT much of the time following the fall of Raqqa training and leading new YPJ recruits in Tabqa. In 2018, she introduced my colleague Mustafa and me to the young women from Raqqa who had joined the all-women's force. At an SDF military base with a majestic view of the Euphrates River, which Rojda's teammates had crossed on Zodiacs during the campaign to push ISIS out of Tabqa, I sat with two dozen young Arab women in uniform who were now part of the YPJ. Recruits a decade younger wearing her same camouflage uniform rushed to shake Rojda's hand and deliver us hot tea, which we passed around the circle. After introducing Mustafa and me, Rojda sat silently while her fighters spoke. The only sound interrupting their stories was the clink of Rojda's sunflower seed shells falling into the glass bowl before her.

One young woman told us she had not left her house in more than three years of ISIS rule in Raqqa and spent the time reading the complete works of Egyptian writer Naguib Mahfouz. Another said that ISIS had imprisoned her for the crime of her arm showing from under her veil. Then I asked a young woman sitting silently to my left what had made her leave her family and join the all-women's force. She sat cross-legged, leaning forward, her hands lightly pressing each other, with a still kind of grace that struck me. Her long braid hung over her left shoulder and a thick wave of bangs swept across her forehead. She told me her name was Hala.

"When ISIS came to Raqqa, two of my cousins joined and they

pushed my brother to join as well," she said. "After a while he picked one of his 'brothers' and told me I had to marry him. I did not want to. I was eighteen. I said no, but I had no voice at all in my house.

"I had to marry a fighter from Homs," she continued. "He made the house a prison for me. He didn't want me to go out and he didn't let my family come visit."

She tried to escape to her mother's house, but her brother sent her back.

"I had heard that after the liberation of Tabqa, the SDF was planning to liberate Raqqa. I went to court and tried to get a divorce. But my husband found out and sent me to a home where ISIS held wives and widows. Eventually they took us to Idlib and put us in a jail. In this place, they raped a lot of women so many times. It was a rape camp.

"All the women there, we got together and said that we had to escape. We had nothing to be afraid of by then. ISIS told us that we had no place to go; we would be killed by a minefield."

Hala stopped and looked up. She had peered at the ground while telling most of her story.

"We said that if we are going to die, let us do that now; it will be better to die than to live like this," she said. The women escaped and eventually made it to SDF-held Manbij, which Znarin had worked to liberate two years earlier.

I asked her why, after all she had endured, she had decided to join this all-women's force.

"I wanted to join after all I saw," Hala answered. "Women being raped in front of my eyes. I wanted revenge. As a woman, why should we be raped? Why should we face this? Now at least I feel I am doing something for myself."

. . .

THIRTY-FIVE MILITARY band musicians stood in the corner of the courtyard of the base at the al-Omar oil field on the sunny morning of March 23, 2019, wearing heavy, tomato-red jackets with gold piping and gold buttons, gold leaves embroidered on the collar, and gold-fringed epaulets adorning their shoulders. In front of the musicians, filling rows of blue and orange plastic chairs, sat a few hundred fighters, politicians, local leaders, and reporters. Larger than both life and death, suspended dozens of feet in the air, hung yellow-and-green posters with photos of young people killed by the Islamic State.

Among the crowd, five or six rows from the front, were Azeema and Rojda. The two friends sat next to each other, just as they had as teenagers in Qamishli, sipping tea and awaiting the start of the proceedings. Azeema quietly snuck a cigarette despite the cameras from local media; if she scooted far forward in her seat and folded her chest onto her knees, her puffs would not be visible to Nowruz, who stood with the dignitaries right in the front. Not far from the two sat Znarin, who had come from Ain Issa for the event.

Just behind the musicians in their red-and-gold hats, holding their instruments high, the stars and stripes of the red, white, and blue American flag swayed gently in the mild March breeze as the brass band played the U.S. national anthem. White-gloved players crashed their cymbals together at the finale of "The Star-Spangled Banner."

Thus opened the ceremony that would mark the end of the territorial fight against the Islamic State. The Americans may have canceled their press conference in the stadium in Raqqa back in

2017, but seventeen months later, their flag stood proudly along-side their battlefield partner's, and so did their ambassador.

After the Raqqa battle, the SDF had taken down ISIS in the smaller towns of Deir Ezzor and Baghouz. Defiant until the end despite encirclement, airstrikes, and the pounding barrage of artil-lery, ISIS fighters pushed away offers of surrender for weeks. But the global "utopia" that ISIS had promised to transplant from its version of the seventh century right into the twenty-first had finally crumbled.

At last, on March 22, 2019, ISIS had had no choice but to accept its territorial loss. Tens of thousands of families had already streamed out of the last ISIS enclave, some people raising their index fingers while they left as a defiant demonstration of their steadfast alle-giance to the Islamic State. Many left simply desperate to get bread and something to drink for their children after having been trapped in Baghouz by ISIS fighters who used their own followers as human shields. The foreigners who exited Baghouz at the end came from Bangladesh, Seychelles, Egypt, France, Tunisia, Guyana, Australia, and Russia, to list only a few. Together these international followers formed a distorted United Nations of ISIS.

As of the twenty-second, the Islamic State had ceased to be a physical entity; it now governed nothing and held no land. Indeed, its high point sat close to a half decade in the rearview mirror: it had come in the fall of 2014, as the campaign to take Kobani, which would become the beginning of the Islamic State's territo-rial end, got under way.

It had maintained its hold on its believers' imaginations, how-ever. And Mazlum and Nowruz and Rojda and the others who had fought ISIS for five years knew better than anyone that that was the most dangerous weapon ISIS had.

Still, since 2014, two views had collided on the battlefield in northern Syria: those of Abu Bakr al-Baghdadi and Abdullah Ocalan. The Islamic State's leaders and followers alike had carried a vision of a caliphate that would stretch across borders to reshape the region and "endure" and "expand," words they used to describe the caliphate until the end. ISIS had met an equally ambitious project with quite different values that had stopped its expansion and rolled back its goals—for the moment, at least. It was that victory and all the sacrifices behind it that the SDF celebrated that afternoon in Baghouz.

All around the ceremony hung the images of the women who had come to define the People's Protection Units. Photos of women who died fighting ISIS were displayed parallel to photos of men who were killed in battle. The yellow-bordered green shield of the YPJ was painted on one white wall. Another wall featured a huge, square, orange-and-yellow airbrushed painting, in the style of American graffiti, featuring a woman holding an AK-47, its grip resting on her shoulder, her face turned toward the sunset.

As for the women who had led the battles—for Raqqa, for Manbij, for Tabqa, for Hassakeh, for Kobani—things had changed for them, even in their own families. Rojda's uncle, the same who had dressed up as a ghost to scare her and her cousin out of playing soccer in their grandmother's village, now called her for advice about family and real estate matters. Znarin's uncle, who had pulled her out of school and who had nearly succeeded in forcing her to marry one of his sons, now considered her a friend and adviser. The once-loathed cousins had become her friends, and they joked with her that they were ready to marry her any time she wanted.

When he took the stage to give his remarks, the American ambassador William Roebuck, the current deputy special envoy to the Global Coalition to Defeat ISIS, congratulated both Mazlum and Nowruz and shook their hands. Roebuck's North Carolinian lilt offered a genteel contrast to the war of which he spoke:

"We cannot forget that this accomplishment also came at significant costs. . . . We could not have achieved any of this without the unwavering commitment and unity of our coalition and the tremendous sacrifice of our Syrian partners on the ground, who have lost thousands of lives taking back their homeland and helping to protect the coalition homeland at the same time. We honor the sacrifices and the valor of the Syrian Democratic Forces in achieving this victory. . . . We will continue to support the coalition's operations in Syria to ensure this enduring defeat."

While the military defeat of the Islamic State's territorial hold was the focus of the day, the political future wasn't far from anyone's mind, especially that of Ilham, co-head of the Syrian Democratic Council.

"Liberating the land is not enough," she said to the assembled crowd. As she had during the founding of the SDC, she urged the world to stay engaged and to keep its focus on the next phase of the fight, against ISIS sleeper cells sure to upend any stability that the region enjoyed. "It is important that international support continue. We need a political solution for all of Syria—and we are hopeful that this liberation helps in that regard."

She ended by pushing for the acknowledgment of political legitimacy that Mazlum had discussed with Brett McGurk back in January 2016, when McGurk had wanted the SDF to press on to Shaddadi. The Syrian Kurds made clear they sought recognition and a seat at the negotiation table that would, one day in the future, decide Syria's political future.

"Any political solution without our participation will fail," Ilham said.

That unsettled future loomed over the ceremony. The previous December, after the U.S. president expressed on Twitter a desire to withdraw from northeastern Syria, the SDF and its political arm, the SDC, had faced an immediate existential crisis. Would their project's adversaries and challengers—Turkey, the Assad regime, Iran, Russia, ISIS—renew their efforts and undo the gains that the Kurds' fight against ISIS, supported by the Americans, had yielded? For a moment, before the Americans eventually reversed their decision, it had seemed that the U.S.-Kurdish partnership hung in the balance and would collapse.

McGurk had resigned as a result of that December withdrawal decision. He sent a message that a spokesman for the SDF read aloud at the ceremony.

"You have helped make the world a safer place, and we owe you a debt of gratitude," McGurk wrote. "You have suffered many losses in this four-year campaign, including many fighters I have known well. I have sent my deepest condolences to all those lost in the battle against Daesh; they are heroes."

Near the end of the event, U.S. military officials who had been part of the campaign to stop ISIS stepped onto the stage to receive a plaque from Mazlum and Nowruz.

As Nowruz handed the gift to him, a microphone picked up Mazlum's words:

"We hope our relationship will continue for a long time."

EPILOGUE

Barely six months after "The Star-Spangled Banner" played in Baghouz at a ceremony in which he had spoken of the valor of the SDF, America's deputy special envoy on Syria policy, U.S. ambassador William Roebuck, penned an extraordinary State Department memo. Its subject line: "Present at the Catastrophe: Standing By as Turks Cleanse Kurds in Northern Syria and De-Stabilize our D-ISIS Platform in the Northeast." A recent Turkish military operation, wrote Roebuck, "represents an intentioned-laced effort at ethnic cleansing."

Named Operation Peace Spring by the Turks, the offensive against Kurdish-led northeastern Syria began October 9, 2019, three days after a Sunday-night White House release stating that President Trump had spoken with Turkey's president, Recep Tayyip Erdogan, by telephone. The statement noted that "Turkey will soon be moving forward with its long-planned operation into Northern Syria."

Soon meant almost immediately. The Turkish Air Force launched strikes against towns that sat along the Syrian border and sent Syrian opposition groups to serve as its ground force. On October 12, a Turkish-backed group executed Syrian Kurdish politician Hevrin Khalaf, who had served as the secretary general of the Future Syria Party and had spent years working to build understanding among Christians, Arabs, and Kurds. More than two hundred thousand Syrians were displaced and at least two hundred died as a result of the Turkish offensive.

"We asked these people to take on this fight. It was our fight, and Europe's, and all of the international community's," Roebuck noted in his memo. "But we . . . put almost exclusively on their shoulders this burden of taking down what remained of the Caliphate."

"Our SDF partners did everything they told us they would do to fight ISIS, and did it with motivation," he wrote.

In many ways the SDF, with the Syrian Kurds at its center, had always been heading toward this moment of reckoning. The U.S. had never pledged to protect the People's Protection Units against Turkey, even as it encouraged them to take more terrain, and for years Turkish leaders had made clear they perceived the YPG's alliance with the United States and its territorial advances as an existential threat to which they would respond. As Roebuck noted, working with the Americans had placed a bull's-eye on the backs of the Syrian Kurds as they had grown in visibility, capability, and reach, and they had worked with the Americans knowing that each side pursued its own interests. But the same external factors that had thrust this little-known non-state actor into the international spotlight back in 2014 now came crashing down on it once the territorial fight against the Islamic State concluded. As American public disapproval of the Turkish offensive mounted swiftly and loudly, the U.S. pressed for a cease-fire and moved to sanction Turkey for its actions.

On the ground in Syria, however, the SDF faced the wrath of a NATO ally all on its own.

FOR CLOSE TO A HALF DECADE, since the start of U.S. cooperation with the People's Protection Units, Turkey had threatened to attack the Syrian Kurds. Now it had swerved from telegraphing its intent to carrying out its threat. In Kobani, Nowruz heard the news on October 7 from the Americans themselves at the military base they shared—the one Mitch Harper first found for the Americans in 2015—and listened in disbelief. The U.S. was pulling out of Kobani and would not stand in the way as its NATO ally Turkey moved into the area. Nowruz had been part of the contingent working closely with the U.S. on an agreement with Turkey that would address its fears about the YPG's encroachment on its border. Indeed, at America's direct request, the SDF had recently destroyed all its positions built to defend against a Turkish incursion.

Rojda first heard the news of the incursion from her teammates on WhatsApp and social media. She had just arrived in Rome along with several other members of the YPJ. They had come to speak at a conference organized by the Kurdish Democratic Council in France, an association for Kurds from across the country (such diaspora organizations are active throughout Europe). They had flown out of their area of Syria for the first time in their lives. The flight had frightened Rojda; its strong turbulence sent oxygen masks tumbling out of their cubbyholes in the airplane's ceiling. She felt more fear while flying than she ever had battling the Islamic State, because she had even less control of the outcome. She vowed never to get on another airplane once she got back to northeastern Syria. Then she heard the news about the Turkish offensive. Plans of sightseeing and touring around the city vanished. She could do nothing other than sit in her room, following every development on social media and waiting impatiently for her return flight.

Znarin was in Manbij. Azeema in Kobani. After their initial shock at the speed with which the Americans pulled back, they each went to work defending their respective towns. It would be back to war for all of them.

WHEN I FIRST BEGAN WORKING on this book in the fall of 2017, I understood that no one could know how it would end. Uncertainty appeared to be the only constant. Some journalists asked me why I would bother writing about people who would be overrun by the Turks or abandoned by the Americans or both before I even started my first interviews.

Yet every few months when I traveled to Syria, I saw nascent but real signs that people were rebuilding their lives and capitalizing on a fragile stability while it lasted. And what I saw looked different from any other U.S. presence in the post-9/11 conflicts. Indeed, the U.S. had become the invisible, Oz-like presence hanging over the area and enabling this stability to endure. Local officials governed and local forces kept the area safe.

Women were everywhere. That was the first thing I noticed in January 2018: women at checkpoints, women when you went to have your security papers signed, women when you walked into the defense ministry. In Raqqa, female shopkeepers I visited every few months throughout that year talked to me about how they saw their and their daughters' futures. Young Arab women were joining the new security forces to protect their cities and swatting away my questions about whether this was "appropriate" work for women in the views of their families. If their families didn't approve, they answered, they wouldn't be there in the first place.

That is what brought me to this story and what kept me working on it even after the ISIS territorial fight ended and international interest waned: the sense that something important was happening in a place the world wanted to forget.

IN DECEMBER 2019, I sat with Nowruz at the base the SDF used as its headquarters following the American withdrawal from Kobani. Her father had just died, and she had been home in Hassakeh with family. Her face wore the difficulty of the past several months, but her calm and her poise remained just the same as when we had visited the previous May. I ended our discussion by asking her whether she thought all the fighting was worth it, given ten thousand SDF lives lost to ISIS and another war under way.

"I say it is worth it because when I see a child, I wonder how will they live. I fight so people can live freely," she said. "Many of my relatives were martyred in the fight against ISIS. It is much more difficult to start a family and have children without a future, when you know you can't obtain education in your language, can't live in freedom on your own soil, and constantly live in fear of death.

"Like any other person, I love life—I am not tired of life," she continued, and sipped on the cup of tea a young member of the People's Protection Units had put before her. As rain poured down outside, a newly established camp filled with Arab and Kurdish families displaced by the Turkish offensive sat just a few minutes' drive away. "I love my people and children; I don't want them to live in the painful life that I lived in. I don't regret the sacrifices I have made."

She told me that the all-women's units had intended to host a women's conference that fall for organizations from around the region to talk about advancing women's rights. That idea had been put on hold during the Turkish attacks, but it remained part of their plan for the future.

AT THE TIME OF THIS WRITING, Turkey holds a corridor of northeastern Syria along its border. More attacks have been threatened in Kobani and beyond. The Americans remain in Syria with a far more limited presence, but that presence is helping the Syrian Kurds to maneuver and to maintain some degree of leverage with the Russians and the Syrian regime as they seek to plot out a future after the Syrian civil war, whenever that might be. The Russians have threatened to allow Turkey to attack Kobani if Mazlum and the SDF do not meet Russia and the regime's terms for returning to Assad's control.

I saw firsthand the diplomatic balancing act the SDF is managing in December 2019, my first visit to the area following Turkey's offensive. In the towns of northeastern Syria that Turkey and its allied militia did not capture, on the surface remarkably little has shifted. The SDF continues to control checkpoints in and between towns, and the civil and women's councils Ilham and her fellow political leaders helped put in place are very much intact—even in Raqqa, which the Russians and the Syrian regime nominally control. Women are still visible across the region.

Rojda is living in Ain Issa, the town where she freed enslaved Yazidi women and in 2016 launched the campaign to retake Raqqa.

We sat together late at night in Kobani after my team and I finished a long day's drive from Qamishli to Kobani. That drive had taken three hours before the Turkish campaign. It now took more than six, because the Turkish-backed groups controlled the highway between the towns; few used that route now out of concerns for their security.

It was the first time I had seen Rojda out of uniform. In her jeans and dark sweater, she looked somehow younger and out of place in my imagination. She said the same thing that Nowruz had told me for months: they had not wanted to fight Turkey—they understood the military mismatch better than anyone—and were seeking any way to avoid war. "In the end it wasn't in our control," Rojda said.

"It is really painful to have to fight Turkey in the same places we liberated from ISIS."

THE FUTURE OF NORTHEASTERN SYRIA remains a question written in invisible ink in a language no one can yet decipher.

What I know is that the young women I met across northeastern Syria, from all its communities—Arab, Kurd, Christian—want the same things from their lives as thousands of girls I have met every other place in the world, including the United States: a chance to go to school and an opportunity to forge their own future. The world has a way of telling girls and young women what they should want from their lives, and of telling them not to ask for too much. In northeastern Syria, these young women tell you exactly what they want for themselves. I have heard it over and over again. When the world stops speaking for them, you can actually hear what they have to say.

"We are trying to build a little lake in the middle of the desert," Fauzia Yusuf told me in her offices in Qamishli in 2018. "It doesn't happen quickly, and it is so very difficult to build something in the middle of destruction."

I asked Nowruz during our tea what she wanted a girl in the region born twenty years from now to understand about the war women waged in the fight against ISIS. She told me that she wanted girls from across communities to know their own worth and to be strong enough to forge their own way.

"I want her to know how to protect herself, how to be independent, and how to be powerful," she said. "I want her to grow up with this mentality, to have her own strength and not allow any obstacles in her way.

"We might not be alive then, but this must stay as part of history," she said.

ACKNOWLEDGMENTS

This book owes gratitude to many, as do I.

First, to Cassie, who called me and insisted I hear this story. Thank you.

The team at the *PBS NewsHour* is world-class, world-changing, and filled with people as smart as they are generous. Thank you to the unflappable Morgan Till, Dan Sagalyn, Emily Carpeaux, Sara Just, and Judy Woodruff, to name only a few. Jon Gerberg was a friend and trusted colleague there at the start, as was Gary, who told me with a smile as we drove into the silent city of Raqqa how much he loved his work with journalists.

No one could ask more than to work with Mustafa Alali, who toiled and translated and talked our way through five reporting trips with an indefatigable commitment to the story and a willingness to work eighteen-hour days. His guided tour of Kobani and Mishtanour also was invaluable. A young person who has seen so much, he will be a great part of his country's future, I feel certain. Kamiran Sadoun is a skilled journalist and astute problem solver who possesses an ability to make all work a joy and all stress vanish; he is a tremendous storyteller and friend, and our WhatsApps are always illuminating. Kamiran is a keen observer who cares deeply about Syria and I know he will make its future more just. Abdulselam Mohamad helped with research and insight and his friendship is appreciated.

I also owe thanks to all those who served America in uniform and as diplomats who shared hours upon hours of insight and perspective on their experiences working with this unconventional force.

Thank you to Zuzan, my Kurdish teacher, who worked to help me understand Kurmanci and translated all the videos and transcripts I sent with accuracy, precision, and such care. She is the best guide I could have asked for in language, and all failings in Kurmanci owed to the student, not the teacher.

My team in Erbil always made me feel so very welcome and gave me something to look forward to even as I left home. To Basel, thank you for all the music in our car rides and for letting me drive the roads of northern Iraq. And to the wonderful team at the Arjaan, you made every visit a real joy.

On the research front, Rebecca Perchik Hughes worked diligently to help us get this right, pouring in hours of meticulous research on Bookchin, Ocalan, the YPG, the PKK, and the rise of the Islamic State, to name only a few of our topics. Latreshia Hamilton offered swift and valued help with sourcing. Gina Hosler Lamb is a friend and thought partner who brings a love of copy editing and narrative that is contagious. I hope she will allow more authors to know the joy of working with her. Thank you to colleagues Henri Barkey, Steven Cook, and Bruce Hoffman at the Council on Foreign Relations for the scholarship and insight, to Patrick Costello for the constant outreach, and to Rachel Vogelstein, Meighan Stone, and Rebecca Turkington for talking through topics that touched our shared work.

With appreciation to colleagues and peers who read early versions of this manuscript.

Ellis W. tracked my moves in Syria and was the best friend I could have asked for in trying to navigate safely. He and his team of folks focused on security and service stand up for people who do work that matters, and I am thankful to be part of it. No one could ask for more generous and spirited colleagues than mine at Shield AI, who have always rooted for and supported me during travel to Syria and who are driven to make a difference for the better.

My team of Elyse Cheney and Kassie Evashevski are the folks you want in your corner. Through three books, Elyse's wit, humor, and sharply precise instincts have been a guiding star and an intellectual home base. She pushed me to do this book and fought for this story in all the right moments, as she always has. Knowing Kassie is excited about a book affirms that you have a story that is special, and I couldn't ask to work with anyone better than either of them. Claire Gillespie and Ali Lefkowitz offered help and a shot of energy along the path.

A huge thanks to the team that helped bring this book to the world. The indefatigable Gail Brussel worked each day to bring this story to readers, along with Danielle Plafsky, Liz Mahoney, Matt Haberman, and Celena Madlansacay, and the Narrative team worked to make sure this book reached its audience. Julie Fairchild, Monique Sondag, Catherine Binkley, Lucas Fairchild, and Michael Conrad were a joy to work with, and it was a delight to be on the 130A team. Thanks to Nadie Maenza for all the support and insight. Shelley Cheung Claudon and Eddie Claudon are beautiful video editors and collaborators. Paria Sadighi and Ashley Osei are friends and creative partners you want by your side at all times. Thank you to all for the work and heart and dedication.

Ann Godoff at Penguin Press is a publishing legend with whom I wanted to work. I am delighted to have had that opportunity. Ann wanted to see this story become a book and made me believe I could write it and you would read it, which sums up her ability to create magic from the love of an idea and the irresistible pull of a great story. Emily Cunningham sweat and strode beside me each step of the way with grace and determination to bring this book to you. Her ability to cut to what mattered and cut away much else made this book far stronger and allowed me to stay focused on introducing you to the people who sit at the very center of this history.

To Gloria Riviera and Jim Sciutto, who offered me a London refuge during *Dressmaker* reporting and remain dear friends; to Melissa Perold, who did the same; to the team at Lyceum who always share encouragement, my thanks. Arash Ghadishah, Laurye Blackford, Nada Bakos, Julia Cheiffetz, Juleanna Glover, Lee Gonzalez, August Cole, Syria travel colleague Hardin Lang, Alyse Nelson, Annik LaFarge, Jennifer Littlejohn, Diane Beasley, Melissa Magsaysay, Biola Odunewu, Robin Wood Sailer, Maxine Armstrong, Tara Luizzi, Sarah Smith, Max and Michelle Brooks, and Brenda Spaulding are among the dear friends and family who pushed me to press forward on this book and I am thankful for them. Sebastian Junger and David Ignatius generously and frequently shared with me their enthusiasm for the project, which meant a great deal. Defense One's Kevin Baron loved this book from the start. Hassan Hassan, Amberin Zaman, Aliza Marcus, and Wa'el Alzayat were among those experts who offered early thoughts, and I am thankful for their wisdom, insight, and time. Thanks to Aveen Alzayat as well. To the unstoppable and unflappable Lisa Shields and the communications team at CFR for always being ready to fight for this story, my thanks. To Willow Bay and

Mary Boies, thank you for sharing your excitement for the book when it was only an idea. Christy Morales Mann kept me on track, on time, and full of laughs. To Lesley Blum, my thanks for the shared exhales as we brought books into this world. Gaylan Lemmon always listened to my stories, shared laughs and perspective, and helped our entire family a great deal while I traveled. Rose Addis—thank you and know that you have achieved all you have sought for yourself and your family.

To all those who spoke with me for this book, from Washington to Palo Alto, in New York and all across the U.S., thank you. Your generosity, wisdom, and willingness to share primary documents remain with me and inform this history. To the Syrians who spoke with me, I do not have sufficient words to say thank you. It is not easy to trust someone to share your story. It is harder still in war, with translators, and when the work of fact-checking grows tedious by hour three of the interview. Know that I think of you daily and always will. Your willingness to talk and share with me, in Kurmanci and Arabic, in Kobani and Tabqa, from Manbij to Raqqa to Qamishli, has meant more than I can confine to words. These pages are my effort to live up to your trust.

Finally, to Justin, my gratitude. Your belief in this project supported me in the most trying moments and carried this book to readers. Your humor, strength, and grace in the face of my absence for weeks at a time and my confinement in the office during weekends, holidays, and nights made this book possible. Hudson, Beckett, and Alexandra, I hope you see in these pages that your future informs all that I write and work for. And to Elaine Cameron and Gloria Rojas, thank you for being the best guardian angels and godmothers I could ever want.

FURTHER READING

A Road Unforeseen: Women Fight the Islamic State by Meredith Tax

Assad or We Burn the Country by Sam Dagher

Black Flags by Joby Warrick

Blood and Belief by Aliza Marcus

Guest House for Young Widows by Azadeh Moaveni

ISIS: Inside the Army of Terror by Hassan Hassan and Michael Weiss

No Turning Back by Rania Abouzeid

Shatter the Nations by Mike Giglio

The Girl Who Beat ISIS by Farida Abbas

The Kurds of Northern Syria by Harriet Allsopp and Wladimir van Wilgenburg

The Last Girl by Nadia Murad

The Unraveling by Emma Sky

Under the Black Flag by Sami Moubayed

NOTES ON SOURCES

CHAPTER ONE

In this chapter, I consulted a number of works about Abdullah Ocalan and the Syrian Kurds, including the work of Aliza Marcus on the history of the Kurdistan Workers' Party, or PKK. I also consulted think tank papers on the history of the Kurds, including from the International Crisis Group, U.S. Institute for Peace, and the Carnegie Endowment; recent books by Meredith Tax and a cowritten volume by Michael Knapp, Anja Flach, Ercan Ayboga, David Graeber, Asya Abdullah, and Janet Biehl; and Central Intelligence Agency archives. A number of pieces from contemporary news outlets, including *The Atlantic*, Liz Sly and David Ignatius at *The Washington Post*, and Rukmini Callimachi at *The New York Times*, as well as the writings of Ocalan himself, also informed this chapter. Multiple extended interviews with Syrian Kurdish political actors as well as accounts from bloggers and close observers of the Syrian conflict also served as sources.

SOURCES INCLUDE:

"Balance Sheet of War of YPG-SDF 2013–2017." Transnational Middle-East Observer, June 2, 2013. https://vvanwilgenburg.blogspot.com/2019/06/bal ance-sheet-of-war-of-ypg-sdf-2013.html.

Barkey, Henri, and Direnç Kadioglu. "The Turkish Constitution and the Kurdish Question." Carnegie Endowment for International Peace, August 1, 2011. https://carnegieendowment.org/2011/08/01/turkish-constitution-and -kurdish-question-pub-45218.

Callimachi, Rukmini. "To Maintain Supply of Sex Slaves, ISIS Pushes Birth

Control." *The New York Times*, March 12, 2016. https://www.nytimes.com/2016/03/13/world/middleeast/to-maintain-supply-of-sex-slaves-isis-pushes-birth-control.html.

Cutler, David. "Timeline: Kurdish Militant Group PKK's Three-Decade War with Turkey." Reuters, March 21, 2013. https://www.reuters.com/article/us-turkey-kurds-dates-timeline/timeline-kurdish-militant-group-pkks-three-decade-war-with-turkey-idUSBRE92K0I320130321.

"Fear of Torture/Incommunicado Detention/Possible Prisoner of Conscience." Amnesty International, May 19, 2005. https://www.amnesty.org/download/Documents/88000/mde240272005en.pdf.

"Flight of Icarus? The PYD's Precarious Rise in Syria." International Crisis Group, May 8, 2014. https://www.crisisgroup.org/middle-east-north-africa/eastern-mediterranean/syria/flight-icarus-pyd-s-precarious-rise-syria.

Gambill, Gary C. "The Kurdish Reawakening in Syria." Middle East Intelligence Bulletin, April 2004. https://www.meforum.org/meib/articles/0404_s1.htm.

Gunter, Michael M. *Historical Dictionary of the Kurds*. 3rd ed. Lanham, MD: Rowman & Littlefield Publishers, 2018.

Ignatius, David. "Al-Qaeda Affiliate Playing Larger Role in Syria Rebellion." *Post Partisan* (blog). *The Washington Post*, November 30, 2012. https://www.washingtonpost.com/blogs/post-partisan/wp/2012/11/30/al-qaeda-affiliate-playing-larger-role-in-syria-rebellion/.

Katzman, Kenneth. "The Kurds in Post-Saddam Iraq." Congressional Research Service, October 1, 2010. https://fas.org/sgp/crs/mideast/RS22079.pdf.

Khalaf, Rana. "Governing Rojava: Layers of Legitimacy in Syria." Chatham House, December 2016. https://syria.chathamhouse.org/assets/documents/2016-12-08-governing-rojava-khalaf.pdf.

Knapp, Michael, Anja Flach, Ercan Ayboga, David Graeber, Asya Abdullah, and Janet Biehl. *Revolution in Rojava: Democratic Autonomy and Women's Liberation in Syrian Kurdistan*. London: Pluto Press, 2016.

Krajeski, Jenna. "The Iraq War Was a Good Idea, If You Ask the Kurds." *The Atlantic*, March 20, 2013. https://www.theatlantic.com/international/archive/2013/03/the-iraq-war-was-a-good-idea-if-you-ask-the-kurds/274196/.

"The Kurds in Turkey." Congressional Research Service, n.d. https://fas.org/asmp/profiles/turkey_background_kurds.htm.

Lowe, Robert. "The Syrian Kurds: A People Discovered." Chatham House, January 2006. https://www.chathamhouse.org/sites/default/files/public/Research/Middle%20East/bpsyriankurds.pdf.

Macleod, Hugh. "Football Fans' Fight Causes a Three-Day Riot in Syria." *The Independent*, March 15, 2004. https://www.independent.co.uk/news/world

/middle-east/football-fans-fight-causes-a-three-day-riot-in-syria-5354
766.html.

Makovsky, Alan. "Defusing the Turkish-Syrian Crisis: Whose Triumph?"
Washington Institute for Near East Policy, January/February 1999. https://
www.washingtoninstitute.org/policy-analysis/view/defusing-the-turkish
-syrian-crisis-whose-triumph.

Marcus, Aliza. *Blood and Belief: The PKK and the Kurdish Fight for Independence.*
New York and London: New York University Press, 2007.

Martins, Alice. "A Photographer's Journey into the Dying Center of the Islamic State." *The Washington Post*, July 3, 2017. https://www.washingtonpost
.com/graphics/2017/world/the-battle-against-isis-in-raqqa/.

Morris, Harvey. "Sykes-Picot: The Centenary of a Deal That Did Not Shape
the Middle East." *Time*, May 13, 2016. http://time.com/4327377/sykes-picot
-the-centenary-of-a-deal-that-did-not-shape-the-middle-east/.

Ocalan, Abdullah. "Liberating Life: Woman's Revolution." International Initiative, 2013. http://www.freeocalan.org/wp-content/uploads/2014/06/liberating
-Lifefinal.pdf.

Prados, Alfred B., and Jeremy M. Sharp. "Syria: Political Conditions and Relations with the United States after the Iraq War." Congressional Research
Service, February 28, 2005. https://fas.org/sgp/crs/mideast/RL32727.pdf.

Schøtt, Anne Sofie. "The Kurds of Syria: From the Forgotten People to World-
Stage Actors." Royal Danish Defence College, June 2017. https://pure.fak.dk
/ws/files/7248264/The_Kurds_of_Syria.pdf.

Sharp, Jeremy M., and Christopher M. Blanchard. "Armed Conflict in Syria:
U.S. and International Response." Congressional Research Service, July 12,
2012. https://www.everycrsreport.com/files/20120712_RL33487_7eeec59a
699d44be29548919207f56e7957534d7.pdf.

Sly, Liz. "In Syria, Defectors Form Dissident Army in Sign Uprising May Be
Entering New Phase." *The Washington Post*, September 25, 2011. https://
www.washingtonpost.com/world/middle-east/in-syria-defectors-form
-dissident-army-in-sign-uprising-may-be-entering-new-phase/2011/09/24
/gIQAKef8wK_story.html.

"Syria: Address Grievances Underlying Kurdish Unrest." Human Rights Watch,
March 18, 2004. https://www.hrw.org/news/2004/03/18/syria-address-griev
ances-underlying-kurdish-unrest.

"Syria's Kurds: A Struggle within a Struggle." International Crisis Group, January 22, 2013. https://www.crisisgroup.org/middle-east-north-africa/eastern
-mediterranean/syria/syria-s-kurds-struggle-within-struggle.

"Syria: The Silenced Kurds." Human Rights Watch, October 1996. https://
www.hrw.org/reports/1996/Syria.htm.

Tax, Meredith. *A Road Unforeseen: Women Fight the Islamic State*. New York: Bellevue Literary Press, 2016.

Weiner, Tim. "U.S. Helped Turkey Find and Capture Kurd Rebel." *The New York Times*, February 20, 1999. http://www.nytimes.com/1999/02/20/world/us -helped-turkey-find-and-capture-kurd-rebel.html.

Ziadeh, Radwan. "The Kurds in Syria: Fueling Separatist Movements in the Region?" United States Institute of Peace, April 2009. https://www.usip .org/sites/default/files/resources/kurdsinsyria.pdf.

CHAPTER TWO

For this chapter, I consulted sources documenting the timeline of the Syrian civil war as well as the creation of the Democratic Union Party. I also went back to primary sources from dates I remembered well, such as statements from the Obama administration urging Assad to step aside and reported pieces on the uprising against Assad in Homs. I also read reports and think tank papers on Turkey's treatment of the Kurds. In January 2019, I spent a morning with Murray Bookchin's daughter Debbie, and several phone and email exchanges afterward, interviewing her in New York City about her father and his work, and reviewed some of his correspondence with representatives of Ocalan. I conducted nearly a dozen interviews with Democratic Union Party leaders and YPJ fighters in Syria between 2017 and 2019 about their political project and the early battles with Nusra. The work of academics and think tank scholars such as Mona Yacoubian, Jordi Tejel, and Emile Hokayem proved invaluable in rounding out my understanding of both the Kurds and the tragedy of the broader Syrian civil war.

SOURCES INCLUDE:

Ahmed, Akbar Shahid. "America's Best Allies against ISIS Are Inspired by a Bronx-Born Libertarian Socialist." *The Huffington Post*, January 12, 2017. www.huffingtonpost.com/entry/syrian-kurds-murray-bookchin_us _5655e7e2e4b079b28189e3df.

Caves, John. "Backgrounder: Syrian Kurds and the Democratic Union Party (PYD)." Institute for the Study of War, December 6, 2012. http://www.under standingwar.org/backgrounder/syrian-kurds-and-democratic-union -party-pyd.

Enzinna, Wes. "A Dream of Secular Utopia in ISIS' Backyard." *The New York Times Magazine*, November 24, 2015. https://www.nytimes.com/2015/11/29 /magazine/a-dream-of-utopia-in-hell.html.

Ferdinando, Lisa. "Coalition Continues Strikes to Defeat ISIL, OIR Spokes-

man Says." U.S. Central Command, July 22, 2016. https://www.centcom
.mil/MEDIA/NEWS-ARTICLES/News-Article-View/Article/912082
/coalition-continues-strikes-to-defeat-isil-oir-spokesman-says/.

"Flight of Icarus? The PYD's Precarious Rise in Syria." International Crisis
Group, May 8, 2014. https://www.crisisgroup.org/middle-east-north-africa
/eastern-mediterranean/syria/flight-icarus-pyd-s-precarious-rise-syria.

Greenhouse, Steven. "After Convictions of Kurds, U.S. Presses Turkey on
Rights." *The New York Times*, December 14, 1994. www.nytimes.com/1994
/12/15/world/after-convictions-of-kurds-us-presses-turkey-on-rights.html.

Gunter, Michael M. "An Interview with the PKK's Ocalan." *Journal of Conflict
Studies* 18, no. 2 (1998). https://journals.lib.unb.ca/index.php/JCS/article/view
/11697.

Hokayem, Emile. *Syria's Uprising and the Fracturing of the Levant*. London:
Routledge, 2013.

Hubbard, Ben, and an Employee of *The New York Times*. "Kurdish Struggle
Blurs Syria's Battle Lines." *The New York Times*, August 1, 2013. https://www
.nytimes.com/2013/08/02/world/middleeast/syria.html.

"Italy Urged to Prosecute PKK Leader Ocalan." Human Rights Watch, November 20, 1998. https://www.hrw.org/news/1998/11/20/italy-urged-prosecute
-pkk-leader-ocalan.

"The Kurdish Democratic Union Party." Carnegie Middle East Center, March
1, 2012. https://carnegie-mec.org/publications/?fa=48526.

Makdesi, Marwan. "Assad's Forces Take Homs, 'Capital of Syrian Revolt.'"
Reuters, May 8, 2014. https://www.reuters.com/article/us-syria-crisis-homs
/assads-forces-take-homs-capital-of-syrian-revolt-idUSBREA470LX
20140508.

Marsh, Katherine. "Syrian Regime Launches Crackdown by Shooting 15 Activists Dead." *The Guardian*, March 23, 2011. https://www.theguardian.com
/world/2011/mar/24/syria-crackdown-shooting.

Martin, Douglas. "Murray Bookchin, 85, Writer, Activist and Ecology Theorist, Dies." *The New York Times*, August 7, 2006. www.nytimes.com/2006
/08/07/us/07bookchin.html.

Peuch, Jean-Christophe. "Turkey: Government under Growing Pressure to
Meet Kurdish Demands." *Radio Free Europe*, August 17, 2005. https://
www.rferl.org/a/1060741.html.

"Syria's Assad Grants Nationality to Hasaka Kurds." *BBC News*, April 7, 2011.
https://www.bbc.com/news/world-middle-east-12995174.

Tejel, Jordi. "Syria's Kurds: Troubled Past, Uncertain Future." Carnegie Europe, October 16, 2012. https://carnegieeurope.eu/2012/10/16/syria-s-kurds
-troubled-past-uncertain-future-pub-49703.

van Wilgenburg, Wladimir. "Syrian Kurds Win Support in Battle with Al-Qaeda Forces." *Al-Monitor*, October 25, 2013. https://www.al-monitor.com/pulse/originals/2013/10/al-qaeda-fight-prompts-kurds-support-pkk.html.

Wilson, Scott, and Joby Warrick. "Assad Must Go, Obama Says." *The Washington Post*, August 18, 2011. https://www.washingtonpost.com/politics/assad-must-go-obama says/2011/08/18/gIQAelheOJ_story.html.

Yacoubian, Mona. "Syria Timeline: Since the Uprising against Assad." United States Institute of Peace, June 4, 2020. https://www.usip.org/publications/2019/11/syria-timeline-uprising-against-assad.

CHAPTER THREE

This chapter drew on my experiences with the Yazidi community in northern Iraq and in Syria, along with histories of the Obama administration and interviews I conducted with former Obama administration officials. I also drew heavily on interviews from Syria between 2017 and 2019 and conversations with those who endured life under the Islamic State. I spent a lot of time talking in person and electronically with U.S. diplomatic, security, and military officials about the role of Sinjar in the U.S.'s decision to intervene in Kobani, and about the decision to return to Iraq in 2014 after the U.S. withdrawal a few years earlier. *The Washington Post*'s reporting from Sinjar, as well as survivor accounts and interviews with YPJ fighters conducted in Syria, were consulted for this chapter. In northern Iraq in 2018 I also met with local charities working with Yazidi survivors, and between 2018 and 2020 I interviewed U.S. officials who remembered vividly the day Sinjar was overrun by the Islamic State.

SOURCES INCLUDE:

Al-Salhy, Suadad, and Tim Arango. "Sunni Militants Drive Iraqi Army Out of Mosul." *The New York Times*, June 10, 2014. https://www.nytimes.com/2014/06/11/world/middleeast/militants-in-mosul.html.

Debenedetti, Gabriel. "Hillary Clinton Notes Distance from Obama on Syria Rebels." Reuters, June 17, 2014. https://www.reuters.com/article/us-hillary-syria/hillary-clinton-notes-distance-from-obama-on-syria-rebels-idUSKBN0ES31M20140618.

Jones, Jeffrey M. "Three in Four Americans Back Obama on Iraq Withdrawal." *Gallup*, November 2, 2011. https://news.gallup.com/poll/150497/three-four-americans-back-obama-iraq-withdrawal.aspx.

Landler, Mark. *Alter Egos: Hillary Clinton, Barack Obama, and the Twilight Struggle over American Power*. 1st ed. New York: Random House, 2016.

McCants, William. *The ISIS Apocalypse: The History, Strategy, and Doomsday Vision of the Islamic State*. New York: Picador, 2016.

Murad, Nadia. "Outraged by the Attacks on Yazidis? It Is Time to Help." *The New York Times*, February 10, 2018. https://www.nytimes.com/2018/02/10 /opinion/sunday/yazidis-islamic-state-rape-genocide.html.

Remnick, David. "Going the Distance: On and Off the Road with Barack Obama." *The New Yorker*, January 27, 2014. https://www.newyorker.com /magazine/2014/01/27/going-the-distance-david-remnick.

Roussinos, Aris. "'Everywhere Around Is the Islamic State': On the Road in Iraq with YPG Fighters." *Vice*, August 16, 2014. https://www.vice.com/en _us/article/3kee89/everywhere-around-is-the-islamic-state-on-the-road-in -iraq-with-ypg-fighters.

Shelton, Tracey. "'If It Wasn't for the Kurdish Fighters, We Would Have Died Up There.'" *PRI's The World*, August 29, 2014. https://www.pri.org/stories /2014-08-29/if-it-wasn-t-kurdish-fighters-we-would-have-died-there.

"Syrian Kurdish Fighters Rescuing Stranded Yazidis." *Fox News*, August 12, 2014. https://www.foxnews.com/world/syrian-kurdish-fighters-rescuing-stranded -yazidis.

Tharoor, Ishaan. "A U.S.-Designated Terrorist Group Is Saving Yazidis and Battling the Islamic State." *The Washington Post*, August 11, 2014. https://www .washingtonpost.com/news/worldviews/wp/2014/08/11/a-u-s-designated -terrorist-group-is-saving-yazidis-and-battling-the-islamic-state/.

van Zoonen, Dave, and Khogir Wirya. "The Yazidis: Perceptions of Reconcili-ation and Conflict." Middle East Research Institute, October 2017. https:// www.usip.org/sites/default/files/Yazidis-Perceptions-of-Reconciliation -and-Conflict-Report.pdf.

Warrick, Joby. *Black Flags: The Rise of ISIS*. 1st ed. New York: Anchor Books, 2016.

Weiss, Michael, and Hassan Hassan. *ISIS: Inside the Army of Terror*. 2nd ed. New York: Regan Arts, 2016.

Wille, Belkis. "Four Years On, Evidence of ISIS Crimes Lost to Time." Human Rights Watch, August 3, 2018. https://www.hrw.org/news/2018/08 /03/four-years-evidence-isis-crimes-lost-time.

CHAPTER FOUR

For this chapter, I drew on in-person interviews conducted between 2017 and 2019 with multiple YPJ and YPG members who fought ISIS in Kobani. In 2018, I also spoke with doctors who remained in Kobani during the city's siege and who spent hours recounting what the city felt like during those months. I in-terviewed multiple current and former U.S. military and diplomatic officials who watched Kobani unfold from northern Iraq and from the United States, and I took a walking and driving tour with people from Kobani who showed me their memories of what happened where in the war. I also listened to radio reports from the time in both English and Kurmanci, the latter of which were translated for me. Think tank papers from Brookings and the Bipartisan Policy Center—and reporting from the BBC, Al Jazeera, and NPR—that took a longer look at the history of the town and its role in the conflict also proved useful.

SOURCES INCLUDE:

"Battle for Kobane: Key Events." *BBC News*, June 25, 2015. https://www.bbc.com/news/world-middle-east-29688108.

Bowman, Tom. "How a Single Town in Syria Became a Symbol of the War against ISIS." NPR, January 27, 2015. https://www.npr.org/2015/01/27/381942714/how-a-single-town-in-syria-became-a-symbol-of-the-war-against-isis.

Cafarella, Jennifer, Jessica D. Lewis, and Theodore Bell. "Syria Update: September 24–October 02, 2014." Institute for the Study of War, n.d. http://www.understandingwar.org/sites/default/files/Syria SITREP 02 OCT.pdf.

Caris, Charlie, and Jennifer Cafarella. "Syria Update: September 12–19, 2014." Institute for the Study of War, n.d. http://www.understandingwar.org/sites/default/files/Syria SITREP 19 SEPT.pdf.

Dews, Fred, and Jane Miller. "On Fifth Anniversary of Global Coalition to Defeat ISIS, Former Leaders Reflect on Successes and Future Challenges." Brookings, September 16, 2019. https://www.brookings.edu/blog/brookings-now/2019/09/16/on-fifth-anniversary-of-global-coalition-to-defeat-isis-former-leaders-reflect-on-successes-and-future-challenges/.

Dosky, Reber. *Radio Kobani*. Journeyman Pictures, 2017.

Goudsouzian, Tanya. "Kobane Explained: What's So Special about It?" *Al Jazeera*, October 21, 2014. https://www.aljazeera.com/news/middleeast/2014/10/kobane-explained-what-so-special-about-it-201410216033364111.html.

Misztal, Blaise, and Jessica Michek. "The Importance of Kobani." Bipartisan Policy Center, October 29, 2014. https://bipartisanpolicy.org/blog/the-importance-of-kobani/.

Mohammed, Arshad, and Lesley Wroughton. "U.S.'s Kerry Hints Kobani Not Strategic Goal, Buffer Zone Merits Study." Reuters, October 8, 2014. https://www.reuters.com/article/us-mideast-crisis-usa-kerry-idUKKCN0HX1TG20141008.

Obama, Barack. "Statement by the President on ISIL." The White House. National Archives and Records Administration, September 10, 2014. https://obamawhitehouse.archives.gov/the-press-office/2014/09/10/statement-president-isil-1.

"US Warns Kobani May Be About to Fall as ISIS Advance Further into Town." *The Guardian*, October 10, 2014. https://www.theguardian.com/world/2014/oct/10/kobani-isis-advance-kurdish-resistance-surprise.

CHAPTER FIVE

The battle for Kobani became a duel of two narratives, playing out on the world stage and on TV in real time. The question was whose tale would carry the day and who would win the right to shape the histories that would be written afterward. For this chapter, I drew on sources focused on the airdrop of weapons and medical supplies into Kobani and spoke for more than two hours late at night with a doctor in Kobani who treated wounded YPG and YPJ members throughout the battle for the town. He talked with me about what it meant to him personally as he watched the pallets of supplies hit the ground. I also consulted pieces and papers on the Turkish–Syrian Kurdish relationship, U.S.-Turkish relations, the Islamic State, and the role of women inside ISIS, including work from scholars such as Mia Bloom and Steven Cook, and reporting by *The New York Times*. Finally, the perspectives shared in extended interviews with U.S. policy makers who were close to the decision on the airdrops proved invaluable in understanding the policy choice and consequences perceived at the time by the Obama administration.

SOURCES INCLUDE:

Almukhtar, Sarah, and Tim Wallace. "Why Turkey Is Fighting the Kurds Who Are Fighting ISIS." *The New York Times*, August 12, 2015. https://www.ny times.com/interactive/2015/08/12/world/middleeast/turkey-kurds-isis.html.

Al Rifai, Diana. "Kurdish Recapture of Syria's Kobane Reported." *Al Jazeera*, June 27, 2015. https://www.aljazeera.com/news/2015/06/kurdish-forces-recap ture-syria-kobane-isil-150627091855899.html.

Arango, Tim. "More Than a Battle, Kobani Is a Publicity War." *The New York Times*, November 19, 2014. https://www.nytimes.com/2014/11/20/world /middleeast/more-than-a-battle-kobani-is-a-publicity-war-.html.

Binetti, Ashley. "A New Frontier: Human Trafficking and ISIS's Recruitment of Women from the West." Georgetown Institute for Women, Peace and Security, 2015. https://giwps.georgetown.edu/wp-content/uploads/2017/10 /Human-Trafficking-and-ISISs-Recruitment-of-Women-from-the-West.pdf.

Bloom, Mia. *Bombshell: The Many Faces of Women Terrorists*. London: Hurst and Company, 2011.

Brannen, Kate. "U.S. Ramps Up Push to Save Key Syrian Town." *Foreign Policy*, October 20, 2014. https://foreignpolicy.com/2014/10/20/u-s-ramps-up-push-to -save-key-syrian-town/.

Callimachi, Rukmini. "Inside Syria: Kurds Roll Back ISIS, but Alliances Are Strained." *The New York Times*, August 10, 2015. https://www.nytimes.com /2015/08/10/world/middleeast/syria-turkey-islamic-state-kurdish-militia -ypg.html.

Cook, Steven A. "Neither Friend nor Foe: The Future of U.S.-Turkey Relations." Council on Foreign Relations, November 2018. https://cdn.cfr.org /sites/default/files/report_pdf/CSR82_Cook_Turkey.pdf.

Harf, Marie. "Daily Press Briefing: October 20, 2014." U.S. Department of State, October 20, 2014. https://2009-2017.state.gov/r/pa/prs/dpb/2014/10 /233166.htm.

Letsch, Constanze. "US Drops Weapons and Ammunition to Help Kurdish Fighters in Kobani." *The Guardian*, October 20, 2014. https://www.theguard ian.com/world/2014/oct/20/turkey-iraqi-kurds-kobani-isis-fighters-us -air-drops-arms.

McClam, Erin. "U.S. Drops Weapons to Kurds Defending Kobani." *NBC News*, October 20, 2014. https://www.nbcnews.com/storyline/isis-terror/u-s-drops -weapons-kurds-defending-kobani-n229446.

Mironova, Vera. "Is the Future of ISIS Female?" *The New York Times*, February 20, 2019. https://www.nytimes.com/2019/02/20/opinion/islamic-state-female -fighters.html.

Schmitt, Eric. "U.S. Airdrops Weapons and Supplies to Kurds Fighting in Kobani." *The New York Times*, October 20, 2014. https://www.nytimes.com/2014 /10/20/world/middleeast/us-airdrops-weapons-and-supplies-to-kurds -fighting-in-kobani.html.

CHAPTER SIX

This chapter drew on dozens of hours of interviews with YPG and YPJ fighters in Syria from 2017 to 2019, as well as extensive conversations with U.S. policy makers in 2018 and 2019 and social media histories on Twitter and Facebook. It also was informed by academic papers from think tanks such as the Hoover Institution, the Carnegie Middle East Center, and the Washington Institute for Near East Policy, and journalism pieces that dealt with the question of PKK and YPG relations and that chronicled the daily events of the Syrian civil war as it unfolded. I also interviewed Assyrian Christian fighters in 2018 who joined their community's women's units, and read histories of their local fights in 2015 and 2016. News sources from the immediate aftermath of the 2015 Paris attacks also were key to this chapter, along with in-person and electronic interviews with U.S. policy makers in 2019 and 2020 about the consequences of the Paris attacks.

SOURCES INCLUDE:
Al-Khalidi, Suleiman, and Tom Perry. "New Syrian Rebel Alliance Formed, Says Weapons on the Way." Reuters, October 12, 2015. https://www.reuters

.com/article/us-mideast-crisis-syria-kurds/new-syrian-rebel-alliance -formed-says-weapons-on-the-way-idUSKCN0S60BD20151012.

Arango, Tim, and Eric Schmitt. "A Path to ISIS, through a Porous Turkish Border." *The New York Times*, March 9, 2015. https://www.nytimes.com/2015 /03/10/world/europe/despite-crackdown-path-to-join-isis-often-winds -through-porous-turkish-border.html.

Balanche, Fabrice. "The United States in Northeastern Syria: Geopolitical Strategy Cannot Ignore Local Reality." Hoover Institution, 2018. https:// www.hoover.org/sites/default/files/research/docs/383981576-the-united -states-in-northeastern-syria-geopolitical-strategy-cannot-ignore-local -reality_1.pdf.

Barfi, Barak. "Ascent of the PYD and the SDF." Washington Institute for Near East Policy, April 2016. https://www.washingtoninstitute.org/uploads/Docu ments/pubs/ResearchNote32-Barfi.pdf.

Barnard, Anne, and Hwaida Saad. "ISIS Fighters Seize Control of Syrian City of Palmyra, and Ancient Ruins." *The New York Times*, May 20, 2015. https: //www.nytimes.com/2015/05/21/world/middleeast/syria-isis-fighters-enter -ancient-city-of-palmyra.html.

Bennett, Brian, and W. J. Hennigan. "Congress Likely to Cut Failed Pentagon Program to Train Syrian Rebels." *Los Angeles Times*, October 5, 2015. https:// www.latimes.com/world/middleeast/la-fg-syria-rebels-training-20151005 -story.html.

Callimachi, Rukmini, Alissa J. Rubin, and Laure Fourquet. "A View of ISIS's Evolution in New Details of Paris Attacks." *The New York Times*, March 19, 2016. https://www.nytimes.com/2016/03/20/world/europe/a-view-of-isiss -evolution-in-new-details-of-paris-attacks.html.

Muir, Jim. "Syria Crisis: Kurds Fight to Keep Out Encroaching Jihadists." *BBC News*, March 15, 2014. https://www.bbc.com/news/world-middle-east -26512863.

"Paris Attacks Planners 'Killed in Syria.'" *BBC News*, December 13, 2016. https://www.bbc.com/news/world-us-canada-38306615.

Phipps, Claire, Kevin Rawlinson, Nicky Woolf, Angelique Chrisafis, Nicholas Watt, Jessica Reed, Dan Roberts, and Raya Jalabi. "Paris Attacks Kill More Than 120 People—as It Happened." *The Guardian*, November 14, 2015. https://www.theguardian.com/world/live/2015/nov/13/shootings -reported-in-eastern-paris-live.

Sayigh, Yezid. "The War over Syria's Gas Fields." Carnegie Middle East Cen-ter, June 8, 2015. https://carnegie-mec.org/diwan/60316.

Schmidt, Michael S., and Richard Pérez-Peña. "F.B.I. Treating San Bernardino Attack as Terrorism Case." *The New York Times*, December 4, 2015. https:// www.nytimes.com/2015/12/05/us/tashfeen-malik-islamic-state.html.

Stern, Jessica, and J. M. Berger. "ISIS and the Foreign-Fighter Phenomenon." *The Atlantic*, March 8, 2015. https://www.theatlantic.com/international /archive/2015/03/isis-and-the-foreign-fighter-problem/387166/.

Yuhas, Alan, Julian Borger, Spencer Ackerman, and Shaun Walker. "Russian Airstrikes in Syria: Pentagon Says Strategy 'Doomed to Failure'—as It Happened." *The Guardian*, September 30, 2015. https://www.theguardian .com/world/live/2015/sep/30/russia-syria-air-strikes-us-isis-live-updates.

Zanotti, Jim. "Turkey-U.S. Cooperation against the 'Islamic State': A Unique Dynamic?" Congressional Research Service, October 21, 2014. https://fas .org/sgp/crs/mideast/IN10164.pdf.

CHAPTER SEVEN

This chapter was informed by more than two dozen interviews with U.S. officials and YPG members who planned the Manbij campaign, including Mazlum. I also drew on think tank and human rights reporting and social media histories, and I matched the memories of those who took part in the push to rout ISIS with published news accounts from the time. I visited Manbij four times between 2017 and 2019, including the location where the nighttime crossing began. I also interviewed, on two occasions in 2018, several young Arab women from Manbij who joined the Manbij Military Council. I turned further to news reports from the Paris attacks and pieces examining the Kurds' clashes with Al Qaeda–linked groups before ISIS.

SOURCES INCLUDE:

"Arab-Kurdish Alliance Savors a Victory over ISIS after Two Months of Ferocious Fighting." *PRI's The World*, August 10, 2016. https://www.pri.org/sto ries/2016-08-10/arab-kurdish-alliance-savors-victory-over-isis-after-two -months-ferocious.

Ferdinando, Lisa. "Coalition Continues Strikes to Defeat ISIL, OIR Spokesman Says." U.S. Central Command, July 22, 2016. https://www.centcom.mil /MEDIA/NEWS-ARTICLES/News-Article-View/Article/912082 /coalition-continues-strikes-to-defeat-isil-oir-spokesman-says/.

Gibbons-Neff, Thomas. "The Islamic State Just Took a Page from the 'Battle of Stalingrad.'" *The Washington Post*, June 29, 2016. https://www.washington post.com/news/checkpoint/wp/2016/06/29/the-islamic-state-just-took -a-page-from-the-battle-of-stalingrad/.

Graham-Harrison, Emma, and Spencer Ackerman. "US Airstrikes Allegedly Kill at Least 73 Civilians in Northern Syria." *The Guardian*, July 20, 2016. https://www.theguardian.com/world/2016/jul/20/us-airstrike-allegedly -kills-56-civilians-in-northern-syria.

McKernan, Bethan. "All-Female Yazidi Militia Launches Operation for Revenge on ISIS in Northern Iraq." *The Independent*, November 14, 2016. https://www .independent.co.uk/news/world/middle-east/isis-iraq-kurdish-trained-yazidi -women-launch-operation-revenge-free-women-a7416906.html.

Moore, Jack, and Rena Netjes. "Exclusive: Private ISIS Letter Outlines Group's Merciless Tactics ahead of Mosul Battle." *Newsweek*, October 15, 2016. https://www.newsweek.com/2016/10/28/exclusive-isis-letter-merciless -mosul-tactics-battle-iraq-508719.html.

"More Than 2,000 ISIS Hostages Freed from Syrian City of Manbij." *The Guardian*, August 13, 2016. https://www.theguardian.com/world/2016/aug /12/isis-kidnaps-human-shields-manbij-syria.

Schmitt, Eric. "U.S. Secures Vast New Trove of Intelligence on ISIS." *The New York Times*, July 27, 2016. https://www.nytimes.com/2016/07/28/world/middle east/us-intelligence-isis.html.

Stewart, Phil. "Exclusive: U.S.-Backed Syria Forces Launch Offensive for Manbij Pocket—U.S. Officials." Reuters, June 1, 2016. https://uk.reuters .com/article/us-mideast-crisis-syria-offensive-idUKKCN0YN377.

"Syria: Improvised Mines Kill, Injure Hundreds in Manbij." Human Rights Watch, October 26, 2016. https://www.hrw.org/news/2016/10/26/syria-impro vised-mines-kill-injure-hundreds-manbij.

"'They Came to Destroy': ISIS Crimes against the Yazidis." U.N. Human Rights Council, June 15, 2016. https://www.ohchr.org/Documents/HRBod ies/HRCouncil/CoISyria/A_HRC_32_CRP.2_en.pdf.

van Wilgenburg, Wladimir. "SDF Official: ISIS Militants Have Only Two Options in Manbij: Give Up or Die." *ARA News*, July 13, 2016. https://web .archive.org/web/20160714201822/http:/aranews.net/2016/07/sdf -official-isis-militants-two-options-manbij-give-die/.

CHAPTER EIGHT

This chapter drew on local news reports from the time about the political structures of northeastern Syria's founding, as well as extensive interviews from 2017 to 2019 with Syrian Kurdish political leaders who were part of form-ing those organizations, and with those who opposed them. I also spoke with U.S. officials who were then focused on Syria to understand their views on developments in the northeast during this time. I looked at sources, including from the U.S. Institute of Peace, discussing Arab leaders' involvement in these structures, as well as the role of women in advocating for change in the Middle East broadly and in Tunisia specifically. Papers examining the Democratic Union Party, the YPG, and their relations with the U.S., such as a report by the Congressional Research Service, were also consulted.

SOURCES INCLUDE:

Gunter, Michael M. *Historical Dictionary of the Kurds*. 3rd ed. Lanham, MD: Rowman & Littlefield Publishers, 2018.

"Kurdish-Arab Coalition Fighting Islamic State in Syria Creates Political Wing." *PRI's The World*, December 10, 2015. https://www.pri.org/stories/2015-12-10/kurdish-arab-coalition-fighting-islamic-state-syria-creates-political-wing.

"Kurdish-Arab Coalition in Syria Forms Political Wing." *Al Jazeera America*, December 11, 2015. http://america.aljazeera.com/articles/2015/12/11/kurdish-arab-coalition-in-syria-forms-political-wing.html.

"The Kurdish Democratic Union Party." Carnegie Middle East Center, March 1, 2012. https://carnegie-mec.org/publications/?fa=48526.

"Kurds in Iraq and Syria: U.S. Partners against the Islamic State." Congressional Research Service, December 28, 2016. https://fas.org/sgp/crs/mideast/R44513.pdf.

McGurk, Brett. "Hearing on the Evolving Threat of ISIS." *C-SPAN*, February 10, 2016. https://www.c-span.org/video/?404388-1/hearing-evolving-threat-isis.

Schwoebel, Mary Hope. "Women and the Arab Spring." United States Institute of Peace, May 5, 2011. https://www.usip.org/publications/2011/05/women-and-arab-spring.

"Social Contract of the Democratic Federation of Northern Syria." Co-operation in Mesopotamia. Constituent Assembly of the Democratic Federation of Northern Syria, December 29, 2016. https://mesopotamia.coop/social-contract-of-the-democratic-federation-of-northern-syria/.

"Syria Crisis: Russian Air Strikes against Assad Enemies." *BBC News*, September 30, 2015. https://www.bbc.com/news/world-middle-east-34399164.

"Syria: Russia's Shameful Failure to Acknowledge Civilian Killings." Amnesty International, December 23, 2015. https://www.amnesty.org/en/latest/news/2015/12/syria-russias-shameful-failure-to-acknowledge-civilian-killings/.

Tisdall, Simon. "Turkey's Rising Tension with Russia over Kurds Puts Erdoğan in a Corner." *The Guardian*, February 9, 2016. https://www.theguardian.com/world/2016/feb/09/ever-heightening-tension-putin-puts-turkey-in-a-corner.

"Tunisia's New Constitution: A Breakthrough for Women's Rights." U.N. Women, February 11, 2014. https://www.unwomen.org/en/news/stories/2014/2/tunisias-new-constitution.

"Under Kurdish Rule: Abuses in PYD-Run Enclaves of Syria." Human Rights Watch, June 19, 2014. https://www.hrw.org/report/2014/06/19/under-kurdish-rule/abuses-pyd-run-enclaves-syria.

CHAPTER NINE

This chapter drew on extensive reporting from Raqqa by *The New York Times* and the Associated Press during the battle for the city, as well as several dozen hours of in-person interviews with Syrians who fought in that campaign. I consulted primary documents from the U.S. policy realm at the time, and I interviewed U.S. officials close to the Raqqa campaign. Scholarship by Henri Barkey and Graham Fuller on the history of U.S.-Turkish-Kurdish relations, as well as pieces from the Migration Policy Institute on the evolution of the People's Protection Units and on civilian displacement, were also included.

SOURCES INCLUDE:

Barkey, Henri J., and Graham E. Fuller. *Turkey's Kurdish Question*. Lanham, MD: Rowman & Littlefield Publishers, 1998.

Barnard, Anne. "Battle over Aleppo Is Over, Russia Says, as Evacuation Deal Reached." *The New York Times*, December 13, 2016. https://www.nytimes.com/2016/12/13/world/middleeast/syria-aleppo-civilians.html.

Brown, Daniel. "Look Inside the Tunnels ISIS Uses to Launch Sneak Attacks in Raqqa." *Business Insider*, August 30, 2017. https://www.businessinsider.com/look-inside-the-tunnels-isis-uses-to-launch-sneak-attacks-in-raqqa-2017-8.

Dettmer, Jamie. "Battle to Retake Raqqa a Desperate House-to-House Fight." *Voice of America*, July 10, 2017. https://www.voanews.com/middle-east/battle-retake-raqqa-desperate-house-house-fight.

Filkins, Dexter. "Trump and Syria." *The New Yorker*, November 11, 2016. https://www.newyorker.com/news/news-desk/president-trumps-policy-on-syria.

Fratzke, Susan. "Displacement Reaches Record High as Wars Continue and New Conflicts Emerge." Migration Policy Institute, December 17, 2015. https://www.migrationpolicy.org/article/displacement-reaches-record-high-wars-continue-and-new-conflicts-emerge.

"Handful of Islamic State Jihadis Stall Push on Raqqa, Syria." *The Australian*, May 11, 2017. https://www.theaustralian.com.au/world/the-times/handful-of-islamic-state-jihadis-halt-push-on-raqqa-syria/news-story/515542cddab24fb33e6063e7e9ee3152.

Issa, Philip, and Robert Burns. "US Forces Ferry Syrian-Kurdish Fighters Behind IS Lines." Associated Press, March 22, 2017. https://www.ksl.com/article/43588481.

Jamieson, Alastair, and Ziad Jaber. "Operation 'Euphrates Anger' Begins to Liberate Raqqa from ISIS, Supported by U.S." *NBC News*, November 6, 2016. https://www.nbcnews.com/storyline/isis-terror/operation-euphrates-anger-begins-liberate-raqqa-from-isis-supported-u-n678591.

McKernan, Bethan. "'We Want Revenge': Meet the Yazidi Women Freeing Their Sisters from ISIS in the Battle for Raqqa." *The Independent*, October 8, 2017. https://www.independent.co.uk/news/world/middle-east/raqqa-latest-yazidi-women-fighters-ygs-isis-massacre-syria-iraq-a7988461.html.

"Pentagon Reassures Turkey on Equipping Kurdish Elements in Syria." *U.S. Department of Defense News*, May 9, 2017. https://www.defense.gov/Explore/News/Article/Article/1177677/pentagon-reassures-turkey-on-equipping-kurdish-elements-in-syria/.

Snow, Shawn. "ISIS Releases Baghdadi Audio as the Group Crumbles in Iraq and Syria." *Military Times*, September 28, 2017. https://www.militarytimes.com/flashpoints/2017/09/28/isis-releases-baghdadi-audio-as-the-group-crumbles-in-iraq-and-syria/.

Tax, Meredith. "When Women Fight ISIS." *The New York Times*, August 18, 2016. https://www.nytimes.com/2016/08/18/opinion/when-women-fight-isis.html.

CHAPTER TEN

This chapter drew on extensive interviews with the YPJ and YPG fighters who led the Raqqa campaign, as well as media releases from the counter-ISIL coalition. It also includes perspectives of U.S. diplomatic and military leaders gained during in-person interviews from 2017 to 2020. Analyses by RAND's Brian Michael Jenkins and by think tank scholars at the Atlantic Council and New America were also consulted. I spent two days in 2018 with young Arab women from Raqqa who joined the YPJ in some of the most unforgettable interviews I have ever conducted, conversations I think about nearly daily. Video feeds of the Baghouz ceremony provided direct quotes of translations, and on-the-ground interviews with women and men I met multiple times during six visits to Raqqa from 2017 to 2019, including shopkeepers, teachers, and entrepreneurs, rounded out the perspectives included in this chapter.

SOURCES INCLUDE:

al-Khuder, Khalifa. "The Conflict Has Torn Apart Syrian Tribes, but They Remain an Important Player." *SyriaSource* (blog). Atlantic Council, July 11, 2019. https://www.atlanticcouncil.org/blogs/syriasource/the-conflict-has-torn-apart-syrian-tribes-but-they-remain-an-important-player/.

Enders, David. "Naim Square, One of Raqqa's Main Roundabouts, Became Symbol of ISIL Brutality." *N World*, October 17, 2017. https://www.thenational.ae/world/mena/naim-square-one-of-raqqa-s-main-roundabouts-became-symbol-of-isil-brutality-1.668127.

Ferguson, Jane. "After the Fall of ISIS Caliphate, Its Capital Remains a City of the Dead." *PBS NewsHour*, April 4, 2019. https://www.pbs.org/newshour/show/after-the-fall-of-isis-caliphate-its-capital-remains-a-city-of-the-dead.

Hanoush, Feras. "Tokenism or Empowerment? Syrian Women and the SDF." *SyriaSource* (blog). Atlantic Council, March 12, 2019. https://www.atlanticcouncil.org/blogs/syriasource/tokenism-or-empowerment-syrian-women-and-the-sdf/.

Ismael, Yousif. "Interview with Ilham Ahmad Co-chair of Syria Democratic Council (MSD)." Washington Kurdish Institute, February 13, 2017. https://dckurd.org/2017/02/14/interview-with-ilham-ahmad-co-chair-of-syria-democratic-council-msd/.

Jenkins, Brian Michael. "Options for Dealing with Islamic State Foreign Fighters Currently Detained in Syria." *CTC Sentinel* 12, no. 5 (May/June 2019). https://ctc.usma.edu/options-dealing-islamic-state-foreign-fighters-currently-detained-syria.

Pirovolakis, Christine. "Pentagon Condemns Display of PKK Symbols in Raqqa." *TRT World*, October 20, 2017. https://www.trtworld.com/mea/pentagon-condemns-display-of-pkk-symbols-in-raqqa-11529.

"The Raqqa Diaries: Life under ISIS Rule." *The Guardian*, February 26, 2017. https://www.theguardian.com/books/2017/feb/26/the-raqqa-diaries-life-under-isis-rule-samer-mike-thomson-syria.

Rosenblatt, Nate, and David Kilcullen. "How Raqqa Became the Capital of ISIS." New America, July 26, 2019. https://www.newamerica.org/international-security/reports/how-raqqa-became-capital-isis/executive-summary/.

Schmitt, Eric. "U.S. Envoy in Syria Says Not Enough Was Done to Avert Turkish Attack." *The New York Times*, November 7, 2019. https://www.nytimes.com/2019/11/07/world/middleeast/us-envoy-william-roebuck-syria.html.

"SDF Preparing for Victory Ceremony in Baghouz." *ANF News*, March 23, 2019. https://anfenglish.com/rojava-northern-syria/sdf-preparing-for-victory-ceremony-in-baghouz-33796.

Specia, Megan. "From Playground to Killing Ground: An ISIS Legacy." *The New York Times*, October 18, 2017. https://www.nytimes.com/2017/10/18/world/middleeast/raqqa-syria-isis.html.

"Syrian Democratic Forces Liberate Raqqah." Combined Joint Task Force–Operation Inherent Resolve, press release, October 20, 2017. https://www.inherentresolve.mil/Releases/News-Releases/Article/1348988/syrian-democratic-forces-liberate-raqqah/.

van Wilgenburg, Wladimir. "Top US Commander Visits SDF Leadership in Syria amid Turkish Threats." *Kurdistan 24*, July 22, 2019. https://www.kurdistan24.net/en/news/ba1529aa-b4ab-40d4-99c8-698a15b1eb34.

INDEX

A PENGUIN READERS GUIDE TO

THE DAUGHTERS
OF KOBANI

Gayle Tzemach Lemmon

ABOUT THIS GUIDE

The questions, discussion topics, and other material that follow are intended to enhance your group's conversation of Gayle Tzemach Lemmon's *The Daughters of Kobani*.

A CONVERSATION WITH GAYLE TZEMACH LEMMON

Why do you think we hadn't heard the story of these Women's Protection Units told before?

I wanted to understand this too—I asked, how was it that this far-reaching experiment in women's equality took place on the ashes of the Islamic State? How did we not realize who had helped to hand ISIS their very first battlefield loss? Even in the towns these women visited, people would come up to them and say, "We didn't think you were real." And I just don't think we'd ever seen, collectively, the image of thirty young women wearing fatigues, smiley-face socks, braids in their hair, wielding AK-47s and going off to fight the Islamic State. I don't think we'd heard enough stories that showed women in all their complexity.

You talk in the book about being tired of trying to make Americans care about people in faraway places. What do you think is the importance of telling these Kurdish fighters' stories, especially to Americans who might not have heard of them?

When I first heard about the YPJ taking on the Islamic State, it struck me as such a David and Goliath story. Except David, in this case, is a woman. Here were these all-female militias, formed to protect their neighborhoods during the Syrian Civil War, fighting ISIS, which had experienced no battlefield losses at that point, back in 2014. And then comes this extraordinary battle in Kobani. I wanted readers in the U.S. to know this story and spend time with these women.

What stayed with you as you traveled to the region to write The Daughters of Kobani?

What struck me most, and what I want readers to keep in mind, was that these women weren't superhuman. They were just ordinary people who happened to meet extraordinary circumstances, and who rose to the challenge put in front of them. They thought they had done nothing extraordinary and would always joke with me, "Gayle, you're back again? We have to sit down and talk again?" I wanted to capture their sense of doing this for themselves and for women across the region, and to introduce them to readers in all their facets.

How has your personal experience shaped your approach to writing this book?
My father was born in Iraq and lost his country and his home as a boy because of his religion. I grew up in Prince George's County, Maryland, raised in a community of single moms, none of whom had graduated from college. My mom worked two jobs—she worked at the phone company by day and sold Tupperware at night—and my godmother worked at the government printing office. These were the kind of women who were completely underestimated by the outside world. But they taught us how to hustle and work hard, and they taught us about generosity. My mom used to tell me growing up, "On a scale of major world tragedies, yours is not a three." Hearing that makes me get up in the morning now and think, "Where can I make a difference?"

How can people outside the country show solidarity with the women of Syria across communities?
I think paying attention and engaging is the first step. There are Syrian women in civil society across communities who are really speaking up and making their voices heard, making sure they're not left out of their own future. It's not just for the sake of women that they're speaking up—it's for the sake of the durability of peace that everyone's voice is represented at the table. Organizations across communities are working hard to ensure that half their population is not seen as a special interest group when it comes to their country's future.

QUESTIONS AND TOPICS FOR DISCUSSION

1. Before reading this book, what did you know about the conflict in Syria, including the involvement of the United States?

2. A main motivating factor in the establishment of the Women's Protection Units is women's independence and equality. Did the oppressions that the women in this story faced recall other movements for gender equality, in the past and at present? How are these women ahead of their time in standing up to tradition and following their own path?

3. From 2011 onward, the U.S. stance toward the Assad regime and ISIS changed drastically. Did you agree with the Obama and Trump administrations' tactics and decisions in response to ISIS and the plight of the Kurds? Discuss the balance of maintaining international diplomacy while defending human rights and America's relationships with Turkey and Russia as the civil war unfolded.

4. Discuss how the Women's Protection Units were able to overcome the highly trained forces of ISIS prior to the arrival of American support. What motivated them to keep risking their lives against such an enormous threat? Once the American commanders arrived, how did they treat the Women's Protection Unit members? What surprised you about the relationship between the two groups?

5. What role did the internet and social media play in the international coverage of and response to this war, as well as the ways it was fought on the ground? Consider how the women kept in touch with their families and each other even in battle. What was the role of cameras and TV?

6. Compare and contrast the personalities and leadership styles of Azeema, Rojda, and Znarin. How did they maintain morale and resiliency after injury and defeat?

7. Return to some of the key battle scenes of the war, such as Kobani, Manbij, and Raqqa. How did you experience these retellings of combat through the eyes of the women? What is similar and what is different about the nature of this conflict compared to other wars throughout history?

8. Parallel to the combat on the ground was the fight to codify the freedoms the all-women's units were struggling for. How did the government handle the introduction of radical new ideas about women in 2012–2014? During and after the fall of ISIS, how did those ideals and decrees manifest?

9. The book ends in a moment when the future of Syria is still unclear, and threat looms from major international powers. At the time of your reading, how has this situation evolved, if at all?

10. The author describes her "sense that something important was happening in a place the world wanted to forget" (209). Why would the world want to forget Syria? How have Western nations erected and maintained boundaries to other parts of the world, despite globalization and increased access to technology? Does social media make you feel more or less engaged with world events?

Alien Dawn

And just as every baby is a fully grown adult in embryo, so he's also a complete human being in embryo. But this is the interesting thing. Because, you see, no human being on Earth has ever become a complete human being... We all stop growing before we reach that stage.

Colin Wilson (*Janus Murder Case*, 1984)

Alien Dawn

An Investigation into the
Contact Experience

Colin Wilson

FROMM INTERNATIONAL

NEW YORK

LIBRARY OF CONGRESS CATALOGING-IN-PUBLICATION DATA

Wilson, Colin, 1931–
Alien dawn : an investigation into the contact experience
/ Colin Wilson. — 1st Fromm International ed.
p.   cm.
Includes bibliographical references and index.
ISBN 0-88064-259-9
1. Human-alien encounters.   I. Title
BF2050.W54   1998
001.942—dc21   98-27660

Analytical Table of Contents

of radar. Leavengood and cell changes. Baron Zuckerman inter-
venes. Gerald Hawkins buys *Circular Evidence*. The geometry
of crop circles. The theorems that Euclid missed. The Martian
canals. The Face on Mars. Hawkins's fifth theorem. 'Euclid's
ghost.' The rune message. The conference on abduction at MTT.
Mind Steps to the Cosmos. Contact with extraterrestrial civilisations? The anthropic cosmological principle. Is man on the
point of a new mindstep?

5 Goblins From Hyperspace

The woman who saw a scorpion man. Ted Holiday's *The Goblin Universe*. 'Pan is not so funny when you encounter him.' Holiday investigates the Loch Ness monster. Sir Walter Scott's water horse. A ghost in Egypt. The phantom who walked through walls. 'Mind the cows.' Holiday sees a UFO. Are UFOs 'psychological projections'? The phantom menagerie. A UFO lands near Loch Ness. The man in black. UFOs in West Wales. The Mystery of Ripperston Farm. Humanoids in silver suits. The translocation of cattle. The horse in the hay loft. The Virgin in a caravan. John Keel and the poltergeist. Keel and the ghost of Frankenstein. In quest of jadoo. Sheik Abdul kills a snake. Are UFO witnesses 'selected'? The lama who floated in the air. Keel becomes famous. The saucer flap of 1966. Keel subscribes to a press-cutting agency. Two thousand sightings in a month. The UFOs that responded to thought. *Operation Trojan Horse*. The 1896 airship sightings. The first cattle mutilation. The Scandinavia sightings. Window areas. Good guys and bad guys? Connie Carpenter sees a bird-man and gets conjunctivitis. Can UFOs change their frequencies? Marconi stops car engines. 'Another world of intelligent energy.' Keel and telepathy. Keel's mystical experience in New York. Bucke's *Cosmic Consciousness*. 'The first faint beginnings of another race.'

force'. T.H. Huxley: 'I simply could not get up an interest in the subject.' The history of the atom. Planck invents the quantum. Is light waves or particles? Bohr's picture of the solar system atom. Dirac, Schrödinger and Heisenberg: three statements of the same idea. 'The uncertainty principle.' The Copenhagen Interpretation. Waves of probability. Einstein objects. Bell's Inequality Theorem. Are photons telepathic? The double-slit experiment. Hugh Everett and multiple universes. The new reality. John Wheeler's 'Participatory Anthropic Principle'. The way of the left brain. Deconditioning consensus reality. The abduction of John and Sue Day. Paul Roberts sees a UFO. Roberts and Sai Baba. 'All things are made by you.' David Bohm's 'living plasma'. Bohm and the hologram. What is zero-point energy? Donald Hotson's *Virtual Quantum Reality*. Was Einstein wrong about the ether? Special relativity. Does the old ether theory make more sense? 'The body alpha.' Did the Big Bang really happen? Hal Puthoff on zero-point energy. Does zero-point energy create gravity? The riddle of inertia. 'The SHARP drive.' Parallel realities and T.C. Lethbridge. The mind of the dowser. Psychometry. The 'vibratory rate'. Lethbridge sees a UFO. The universe as pure energy. *The Outsider* and the Romantic vision. Van Gogh understood the underlying reality of the universe. The philosophy of meaninglessness. The ETs as 'evolutionary midwives'. Ian Watson's theory of UFOs. *Miracle Visitors*. Ralph Noyes and the psychosphere. Patrick Harpur's 'daimonic reality'. 'Psychic reality runs parallel to physical reality.' A Martian visit to earth. Neanderthals and Cro-Magnons. History of civilisation. Julian Jaynes and the bicameral mind. The problem of left-brain awareness. Mankind in a spiritual cul de sac. Boredom. The robot and left-brain consciousness. Mankind's basic problem: leakage. Religion and 'high-pressure consciousness'. Synchronicity. William James and the energies of men. 'To be free is nothing; to *become* free is heaven.' Closing the leaks. Miraculous powers. 'It is part of the change.' H.G. Wells's *Star Begotten*. Are we all Martians? Rupert Sheldrake's morphic resonance. Odd synchronicities: a digital clock. The Information Universe. The seven levels of consciousness. *Seeing the Invisible*. Abductions and human evolution. Andrija Puharich and 'unusual children'.

Illustrations

Acknowledgments

Over the years I have made many friends who are interested in UFOs, and I had no idea what a piece of good luck this would prove. So when it came to the writing of this book, I was able to ask assistance from John Keel, John Michell, Bob Rickard, John Mack, Gerald Hawkins, Archie Roy, Jacques Vallee, and many others. Jacques sent me a copy of his journal, *Forbidden Science*, which proved invaluable in understanding the early history of UFO sightings. Archie Roy suggested that I should ring Ralph Noyes, who in turn put me in touch with Hilary Evans, John Haddington, John Spencer, Linda Moulton Howe, Colin Andrews and Timothy Good. And, in fact, they ended by providing me with such a wealth of material that I have been unable to use half of it. I particularly regret not having found space for a discussion of Mario Pazzaglini's study of the structure of alien languages, *Symbolic Messsages*, and for Paul Goddard's remarkable *Space and Time, The Conceptual Answer*, which, with deep reluctance, I dropped from an overlong final chapter. Gerald Hawkins's fascinating research into the crop-circle code, insofar as it concerns the initials of presidents of the Society for Psychical Research, was also a victim of lack of space.

I am also grateful to Richard Brozowski, who arrived for a visit with a copy of a magazine – which he had picked up at a Canadian airport – with Paul Roberts's article on his UFO encounters, Paul being one old friend I had not thought of approaching. Richard's wife Anne Stephenson also sent me a remarkable book on Canadian UFO sightings. So did my Toronto friend Ted Brown (not the same book). Linda Tucker went to some trouble to get me the striking material by the South African shaman Credo Mutwa. Michael Baldwin, my host in Marion, Massachusetts, sent me David Morehouse's *Psychic Warrior*, which arrived at exactly the right moment. My friend – and publisher – Frank DeMarco sent me Joseph McMoneagle's book on remote

viewing, and allowed me to quote from his own private journal describing his week at The Monroe Institute. Brenda Dunne and Robert Jahn
have provided extraordinary material. So have Ian Watson and Patrick
Harpur.

A large proportion of the books I bought for research were provided
by John Wright of Santa Monica and Stephen Shipp of Sidmouth. My
secretary Pam Smith-Rawnsley recorded for me Matt Punter's UFO
sighting. Paul Newman provided me with *Alien Discussions*, the transcript of the MIT conference on UFOs, while John Van der Does sent
me Bryan's *Close Encounters of the Fourth Kind*. Finally, I am grateful
to Lorna Russell, of Virgin Publishing, for asking me if I would like to
write a book on the possibility of extraterrestrial life. Neither she nor
I had any idea of what this would turn into.

Cornwall, Dec 1997

1 A Problem With Too Many Solutions?

IN MARCH 1995, I spent a few days in a small town called Marion, near Boston, at a conference on Consciousness Evolution; my fellow speakers were Rhea White, Peter Russell and Stanislav Grof. Marion is one of those old fashioned New England towns that looks as if it is still in the middle of the nineteenth century.

I had met Grof in California in the 1980s, and admired his work. As a young man in commmunist Czechoslovakia, Grof had read Freud, and been deeply impressed by the clarity of the style, and Freud's ability to 'decode the obscure language of the unconscious mind'. Grof decided to become a psychologist, and went to medical school. He later trained in psychoanalysis under the president of the Czech Psychoanalytic Association. But, when it actually came to applying Freud's ideas to real people, he became thoroughly frustrated. They either didn't seem to work, or, if they worked, took a very long time. Freud himself had often spent years over a case, with minimal success.

One day, a package arrived from the Sandoz Pharmaceutical Laboratories in Basle. It was a new drug called LSD, and the Sandoz Laboratories were sending it to psychologists all over the world and asking them to test it.

Grof himself tried it, and it changed his life. 'I was treated to a fantastic display of colourful visions, some abstract and geometrical, others filled with symbolic meaning. I felt an array of emotions of an intensity I had never dreamed possible.'

And when lights were flashed in his eyes, 'I was hit by a radiance that seemed comparable to the light at the epicentre of an atomic explosion . . . This thunderbolt of light catapulted me from my body . . . My consciousness seemed to explode into cosmic dimensions.'

'I found myself thrust into the middle of a cosmic drama that previously had been far beyond even my wildest imaginings. I experienced the Big Bang, raced through black holes and white holes in the universe, my consciousness becoming what could have been exploding super-novas, pulsars, quasars and other cosmic events.'

What impressed him so much was the sense of the *reality* of what he was seeing. Like Aldous Huxley, and so many others who have experimented with 'psychedelics', he felt that this was far more than a mere drug trip.

Shaken to the core by what he recognised as a 'mystical' experience, Grof realised that 'this drug could heal the gap between the theoretical brilliance of psychoanalysis and its lack of effectiveness as a therapeutic tool'. People suffering from mental illness are trapped in a kind of subjective hell; Grof saw that LSD might be used to restore contact with reality – not just ordinary 'objective reality', but a far wider reality.

He began a research programme, administering doses of LSD to patients. The effect of small doses, he found, was to bring back all kinds of childhood memories – just as in orthodox Freudianism. But larger doses brought on mystical experiences that sounded like those described in the classic texts of Eastern mysticism – even though few of the patients knew anything about Eastern philosophy. It looked as if the LSD had established communication with the Jungian collective unconscious.

In due course, Grof moved to America, continued his experiments with LSD and other forms of 'consciousness expansion' (such as hyperventilation), and became known as one of the minds at the 'cutting edge' of a new psychology.

Stan Grof is a huge man, with mild brown eyes, and a manner so serene and gentle that it is impossible to imagine him losing his temper. When I went across to say hello on that first morning, he introduced me to the man he was talking to – Professor John Mack of Harvard. In fact, I already knew John – I had met him at some conference such as this, and had told him then how much I admired his biography of Lawrence of Arabia, which seemed to me the best book on Lawrence ever written. I had just reread it, in preparation for a television pro-gramme on Lawrence that I was scripting. Now we exchanged a few polite words, and I left them to their interrupted conversation.

In fact, I saw very little of John Mack during the next few days; conferences of this sort demand a high level of social interaction with people who have paid for tickets. We occasionally nodded to each other in the distance or passed the salt at meals. It did not occur to me to ask him what he was doing nowadays.

There was plenty to absorb during the three-day conference. Rhea White talked about 'exceptional human experience', and described how she had become interested in the subject in her teens, when the car she was driving was sideswiped by a skidding coal truck in a snowstorm. She suddenly found herself floating above the car, so high that she thought she could see the eastern seaboard. Then the thought struck her: 'So this is what it's like to die.' She experienced a sense of total peace – and suddenly found herself lying on the bonnet of her car in the snow. She had been hurled through the windscreen and had thirteen fractures. Her companion, she found later, had been killed outright.

The experience led to her reading books on religion and philosophy, and finally becoming an assistant to J.B. Rhine at his Institute of Parapsychology at Duke University.

But what impressed me most at that conference was an anecdote that surfaced by chance. The four of us – Rhea, Peter Russell, Stan Grof and I – were engaged in a symposium, when Stan mentioned that he thought he had once had contact with an active force of evil. When I asked him to elaborate, he said the story was too long. Backed up by the others – and the audience – I asked him to tell it all the same.

When he had first been in America, he said, he had attended a psychiatric conference. One of the psychiatrists was presenting the case of a twenty-eight-year-old woman named Flora, a depressive with violent suicidal tendencies. At the age of sixteen, Flora had taken part in a robbery in which a night watchman had been killed, and she was sentenced to prison. Released on parole after four years, she became a drug addict and an alcoholic. She had to fight impulses to drive her car over a cliff or collide with another car. Then she got into further trouble after wounding her girlfriend with a gun she was cleaning while under heroin.

At the end of the conference, Grof was asked by her psychiatrist if he would give her LSD treatment. It was a difficult decision, because there was already considerable hysteria about psychedelic drugs, and, if Flora murdered somebody after the LSD treatment, it would be blamed on the drug. But, since Flora had no other prospects, Grof decided to take the risk. He began to treat Flora back at the Maryland Psychiatric Research Center, where he was working.

Her first two sessions with high doses of LSD were not unusual. She relived struggles in the birth canal, and came to recognise that many of her conflicts and suicidal tendencies were due to birth trauma. Yet, although she discharged large amounts of tension, her progress seemed minimal.

Two hours into the third session, the facial cramps from which she normally suffered became stronger and more painful. Sudddenly, her face froze into what Grof describes as 'a mask of evil'. She began to speak in a deep male voice, and she seemed to undergo a total change of personality.

The male voice introduced itself as the Devil. He ordered Grof to stay away from her, saying she belonged to him, and that he would punish anyone who tried to take her from him. Then he began to utter threats: what would happen to Grof, his colleagues in the room, and the research programme, if Grof persisted in treating her. Grof says they could all feel the 'tangible presence of something alien' in the room. The threats showed an amazing insight into Grof's own personal life and those of his assistants. Flora herself could not possibly have acquired such detailed knowledge – she was not even a patient in the hospital.

Grof's mixture of fear and aggression seemed somehow to feed the entity. He even thought of using a crucifix to try to drive it away. Instead, he placed himself in a meditative state, and tried to envisage a capsule of light around them both.

The next two hours were the longest he had ever spent. Gradually, her hand – which had become clawlike when the 'Devil' took over – relaxed in his own, and the 'mask of evil' vanished.

After the session, she remembered nothing of the 'possession' state – only what had led up to it, and what had followed later.

Quite suddenly, Flora improved dramatically. She gave up alcohol and drugs and began to attend religious meetings. The facial spasms ceased. She even experimented with heterosexuality and was married for three months, but found heterosexual intercourse painful. She returned to lesbianism – this time without the guilt that had tormented her – and took a job as a taxi driver.

We all listened, fascinated; there could be no doubt that the story was the highlight of the symposium.

Grof was disinclined to accept the 'possession' hypothesis, preferring to regard it as the manifestation of some 'Jungian archetype' – in other words, as some manifestation from the distant human past. But I, who had written a great deal about multiple personality, felt that there was no particular advantage in the Jungian explanation. After all, if Rhea White could leave her body, then there seemed to be no obvious reason why someone – or something – else should not take up temporary residence in Grof's patient.

The following day, my wife and I were driven to Boston, where we had to spend the day before catching our night plane. At that time, I was gathering material for a book on the world's religious sites, and I asked our driver whether there was a large bookshop in Boston. He recommended Waterstones. So the next morning we made our way there.

I not only found some useful books on religious sites, but also saw a copy of *Abduction: Human Encounters with Aliens*, by John Mack, which I was not aware he had written. And since it was a paperback, and easy to carry, I bought it to read on the plane.

I must admit that it was not a subject in which I felt any compelling interest. In the previous autumn I had attended the 'Fortfest' in Washington, run by Phyllis Benjamin, in which David Jacobs, the author of *Secret Life*, had given a talk entitled 'Abduction and the Paranormal'. It left me totally bewildered, because he assumed that the audience knew all about 'the abduction phenomenon', and my knowledge of it was almost nonexistent.

I *had* come across the case of a police patrolman, Herb Schirmer, who had seen a UFO at a crossroads in Ashland, Nebraska, then saw it take off. Back at the police station, he realised that it was later than he thought – he seemed to have lost a period of about twenty minutes. Regressed by a hynotist, he recalled being taken on board by aliens, who told him that they were conducting some breeding programme concerning humans. Then he was released – with his memory erased.

But that was in 1967, almost thirty years before. I was unaware that there had been a mighty wave of abduction reports since the 1970s.

Now, through John Mack's book, I found out. Its opening paragraph made me aware that my ignorance was nothing to be ashamed about. In 1989, Mack had been asked by a psychiatrist friend if he would like to meet Budd Hopkins. Mack asked, 'Who's he?' When told that Hopkins was a New York artist who tried to help people who believed they had been taken into spaceships, Mack replied that he must be crazy, and so must they.

But Mack is a reasonable, open-minded sort of person, and a few months later agreed to meet Hopkins. And he learnt, to his amazement, that all over America there are people who claim that they have been taken from their beds by little grey-skinned aliens with huge black eyes, transported aboard a UFO, and there subjected to medical examination, often painful and traumatic. Sometimes they suffer nosebleeds because a tiny ball has been inserted through the top of the sinus. Back in their own beds, they usually have no memory of what happened, or only some vague impression which they mistake for a bad dream. Under hypnosis, they could frequently recall the experience in great detail.

Mack's natural suspicion was that their 'memories' of the abduction were somehow implanted by the 'leading questions' of the hypnotist. He also suspected that such people were neurotics who needed some drama to brighten their lives, and that they had probably derived their ideas about little grey aliens from TV, or books like Whitley Strieber's *Communion*. But, when he met some of the abductees, he was struck by their normality; none of them seemed psychiatrically disturbed. Moreover, a large percentage of these people had no previous knowledge about abductees and little grey men (a claim I found easy to accept in view of my own ignorance about the whole phenomenon). There was an interesting sameness about their descriptions of the inside of the spacecraft, their captors, and what happened to them. Clearly, they were telling what *they* felt to be the truth.

When Hopkins suggested that he should refer cases from the Boston area to Mack, Mack agreed. Between spring 1990 and the publication of *Abduction* four years later, he had seen more than a hundred 'abductees', ranging in age from two to fifty-seven. They came from every group of society: students, housewives, secretaries, writers, business people, computer industry professionals, musicians, even psychologists.

A typical case concerned Catherine, a twenty-two-year-old music student and nightclub receptionist. One night in February 1991, she suddenly decided to go for a drive after working at the nightclub. When she arrived home, she was puzzled to discover that it was so late: about forty-five minutes seemed to be missing. She was also suffering from a nosebleed – the first in her life. The next day, she saw on television that a UFO had been seen in the Boston area. Someone recommended that she see John Mack.

After a number of hypnotic sessions, memories of abduction began spontaneously. She recalled that her first abduction had occurred when she was three, and another when she was seven. Finally, she recalled what had happened in the missing three-quarters of an hour. She had found herself driving into some woodland, where she experienced a kind of paralysis. She was taken out of her car by aliens, and guided into a UFO, where her abductors began to remove her clothes. When she asked them angrily why they didn't go and rent a porn movie, they looked blank, and it dawned on her that they didn't know what a porn movie was.

She was taken into an enormous room, with many tables, with human beings lying on them. She was made to lie on a table, and an instrument was inserted into her vagina. When it came out, there seemed to be a foetus on the end of it, about three months old. (Three months before, she had found herself driving along deserted roads in the middle of the night, and pulled in at a rest stop; although she had no further memory of what happened, she believes she may have been impregnated at this time.) Her experience would seem to support the statement by Herb Schirmer's captors that the aliens are engaged in some kind of breeding experiment.

Her attitude towards the aliens was at this time one of rage, but, during the course of the sessions with Mack, she came to take a more balanced view, suspecting that the aliens may be 'more advanced spiritually and emotionally than we are'. She finally became one of the most active members of Mack's support group, reassuring others who found the abduction experience terrifying.

The Catherine case occurs about a third of the way through Mack's book, and by that time I was beginning to suffer from information overload. There was also the obvious question of whether people like Catherine are suffering from 'false-memory syndrome' induced by the hypnosis.

Yet it was also clear that, even if this were so, the problem remains just as baffling. A poll conducted over three months by the Roper organisation in 1991 indicated that hundreds of thousands of Americans believed that they have undergone abduction experiences. If all these are false memories, then we have merely shifted the problem; it now becomes: why do such a vast number of people experience hallucinations about abduction?

The case that most fascinated me – and I finished the book between leaving Boston and arriving home in Cornwall twelve hours later – was that of a young man whom Mack calls Paul. Sessions with a female psychiatrist had been unsuccessful in resolving 'weird' problems, for she found herself unable to cope with the 'alien' material that was beginning to emerge. Once, during a session, he asked for some sign of the reality of his experiences, and a loud bang occurred, which frightened the psychiatrist. Later, at home, she experienced something like poltergeist phenomena: her bed had bounced up and down, as a result of which she had made some kind of attempt to exorcise the house of 'evil spirits'. Presumably she was not sorry when Paul terminated the treatment.

At his last session with the psychiatrist, Paul had recalled an abduction when he was about three. The alien had come into his room and taken him by the hand into a 'ship'. There he felt that something had been injected into his leg, causing numbness.

Paul also recalled how, at the age of six and a half, he had one night experienced 'a familiar voice in his head' telling him to go outside. On the porch, he saw the 'ship' overhead, huge and round, and brightly lit. Then he was joined by a group of aliens, all about the size of a six-year-old child (although one was taller), with whom he felt at home. He was placed naked on a bench in the UFO, and examined. Later, one of the beings showed him the controls, and explained that 'you're from here'. He was taken to a 'floating' bed, which he was told was his own. In fact, the quarters felt oddly familiar, as if he had been there many times.

At this point in the hypnotic session, Paul seemed to break through an 'information barrier', and to recognise that he had a dual identity, as an alien and a human being. He came from another planet, and 'there are a lot of us here'. Their purpose was to integrate with humans, but it was slow work. 'Everyone here is so wrapped up in power.' The aliens, Paul said, had access to a higher form of consciousness. Yet, with all their intelligence, they could not understand why human beings are so destructive, and so resistant to change.

At one point, Paul remarked plaintively, 'I want to go home.'

He went on to comment that the aliens had been to Earth thousands of years ago, and had made an earlier attempt to influence its life forms, in the days when the highest life forms were reptilian.

Like Catherine, Paul ended by becoming an active and valuable member of the abductee support group. Another member of this group told Mack that she believed she had met Paul on 'the ships', and Mack comments that such 'recognition' is common among abductees.

The case of Paul interested me more than any other I had read so far because it reminded me of Stan Grof's experience with Flora. Both were apparently dual identities, although Paul's 'secondary personality' was less menacing than Flora's. It seemed to me that the most important thing they shared was that they could both be regarded, from a purely psychiatric point of view, as fascinating examples of dual personality and self-delusion, yet that there was something about both of them that resisted such an interpretation.

Flora's childhood had been traumatic: she became a criminal and a drug addict, and suffered feelings of guilt about her lesbianism. So a violently antisocial alter ego might well have developed on an unconscious level, which expressed itself as her 'demonic' personality. As to Paul, he admitted that he had his first glimpse of an alien – on the stairs – after smoking marijuana. Paul had also had a difficult childhood and been physically abused by his stepfather. He had always felt a misfit. So the fantasy of being 'one of them', an alien in disguise, charged with some mission on earth, would obviously provide him with a satisfying sense of identity.

Yet, plausible as these explanations seem, both leave behind an element of doubt – particularly when viewed in the light of other similar cases. I had written extensively about multiple personality, and had at first accepted the standard notion that the 'other selves' are dissociated fragments of the total personality. But some cases described by psychiatrists like Adam Crabtree, Ralph Ellison and (more recently) David Cohen had refused to fit the pattern, and reluctantly led me to conclude that 'spirit possession' must be considered a possibility. And, where Paul is concerned, Mack himself notes how many abductees feel that they themselves are part alien, and belong elsewhere than on earth.

I had bought the book mainly to find out what John Mack had to say about UFOs; by the time I had finished, I was convinced that, whether abductions are a delusion or not, they demand to be taken very seriously.

Now I have to admit that, before encountering Mack's book, I had always found it difficult to work up any deep interest in Unidentified Flying Objects. The first widely publicised sighting had occurred two days before my sixteenth birthday. On 24 June 1947, a businessman named Kenneth Arnold had been piloting his private plane near Mount Rainier in Washington State, when a brilliant flash had drawn his attention to nine 'bright objects' flying at a tremendous speed – he estimated it at 1,700 miles an hour – and bobbing up and down as they flew, like boats on a rough sea. Arnold concluded that they were some secret weapon of the US Air Force. When he later told a journalist that the craft had bobbed up and down 'like a saucer being skipped over water', the term flying saucer was born.

The news unleashed a flood of sightings – no fewer than eighty-eight on Independence Day, 4 July 1947, alone – four hundred people spread across twenty-four states. And four days later, the commander at the Roswell army base announced that a flying saucer had been found and recovered from a ranch seventy-five miles away – only to take back the statement almost immediately. By that time, there were reports from England, Chile, Italy, Japan and Holland – the Chile sighting was made at the De Salto Observatory, where astronomers estimated that the saucer was travelling at 3,000 miles an hour.

All this failed to arouse my interest. In a few days' time I was due to leave school, and my family expected me to find a job and contribute to the household budget. Since I had failed to achieve a credit in mathematics, I would be unable to apply for a job with Imperial Chemicals, where I had hoped to begin a career as a scientist. That meant I had to take some kind of a labouring job in a factory.

But that was not all that dragged on my spirits at the age of sixteen. For the past three years I had been burdened by a feeling that life is meaningless and futile. It had started one day in the clay-modelling class, when we had started a discussion on where the universe ended. If you could travel in some spaceship to the end of the galaxies, how far would empty space extend? For ever and ever? I had read Einstein, and the assertion that space is spherical, and curves back on itself, but the notion that space – which is merely another name for emptiness – is curved struck me as absurd. Yet the idea of infinity seems equally absurd. We talk about infinity, but we never actually think about what it means – something that goes on *for ever*, totally contradicting our idea of a world where everything has an ending.

As we talked, I began to feel a horrible sense of insecurity. I had always lived in a good, solid world, a world of my parents and my grandparents and my home and school. There *were* unanswered questions, but science was busy looking for the answers . . . And suddenly, I was confronting a question that had no answer. It was as if the ground beneath my feet had collapsed. I left the class that day with a sense of dizziness, and a deep-seated fear, as if some terrible disaster had occurred. It was suddenly horribly clear to me that the apparently solid, normal world around us was a very thin façade, and that what lay behind it might be very disquieting indeed. We had no idea of who we were or where we came from or where we were going.

I had no way of knowing at the time, but this insight was just about the ideal preparation for looking into the problem of UFOs.

From that point, my universe went on crumbling; new cracks appeared all the time. I could see that the pleasant securities of childhood, all of those warm little human emotions, all of those trivial aims and purposes that we allow to rule our lives, were an illusion. We were like sheep munching grass, unaware that the butcher's lorry is already on its way. I got used to living with a deep, underlying feeling of uncertainty that no one around me seemed to share. It was rather like living on Death Row.

Even so, periods of intense depression were interrupted by flashes of the feeling I called – after a phrase of G.K. Chesterton – 'absurd good news'. It often happened early on a summer morning, when I set out on a long cycle ride, with a bag of sandwiches and a bottle of lemonade in a knapsack: the feeling that the world was infinitely rich, and that the problem lay in *the limitedness of consciousness itself*. In this state, the feeling that all our human values are illusions seemed unimportant, for our values are part of our ordinary state of consciousness. And these moments seem to offer the possibility of a far richer form of consciousness. Even in my states of deepest depression, I could recognise that depression is merely another name for low pressure, and that our inner pressure depends, to a large extent, on our assumptions. If we wake up feeling today is going to be futile, it probably will be.

These, it seemed to me, are the really interesting questions: how we could raise the intensity of consciousness, how we could cease to be what Nietzsche called 'human, all too human'. It seemed obvious that the feeling of happiness and expectation is a state of mind, which has nothing to do with the actual circumstances of our lives. You could feel it as easily in a rubbish tip as standing on top of Mount Everest. In that case the great riddle lay *inside* us, not in what happens around us.

All of which explains why I was totally uninterested in news items about flying saucers. If they were visitors from another planet, no doubt they would finally make themselves known. But I could not really believe that they were Martians or Venusians. And, to tell the truth, I didn't care much.

I felt rather the same when my grandmother had talked to me about spiritualism. As a child, I had taken an interest in ghosts and spirits; now they seemed absurdly unimportant in comparison with this question about the meaning of human existence.

A few years later, when I read George Adamski's claims that he had been taken to Venus in a flying saucer, I was confirmed in my belief that people who believe in flying saucers must be idiots.

In due course, events caused me to broaden my perspective. In the late 1960s, I was asked to write a book about the paranormal. As soon as I began to look into such matters as telepathy, precognition, second sight, out-of-the-body experiences, it became obvious to me that they cannot be shrugged off as delusions. I remained convinced that most people are interested in the paranormal for the wrong reasons – out of a kind of escapism – but felt nevertheless that the evidence for ghosts or poltergeists or precognition is as strong as the evidence for atoms and electrons.

Towards the end of *The Occult*, I felt obliged to include a section on flying saucers – merely for the sake of completeness. I discussed Kenneth Arnold's sighting and the crash of Captain Thomas Mantell's plane when chasing a UFO in January 1958. Then I went on to discuss a case that, in retrospect, I now see to have far more significance than I realised at the time.

A Californian friend, Richard Roberts, told me the story of a Dutch yogic practitioner named Jack Schwarz, who was able to lie on a bed of long sharp nails, with a heavy man sitting on top of him. The nails would sink deep into his body, yet the wounds would not bleed, and Schwarz obviously suffered no discomfort.

In 1958, Schwarz had been the welfare officer on a Dutch ship going through the Suez Canal. The troops were being entertained by a magician. Suddenly, a tall, thin Arab approached Schwarz, announced, 'You are my master', and kissed his feet. Then he walked away. Schwarz tried to follow him, but he had disappeared, and the watch at the gangway had not seen him.

A year later, as he was leaving a lecture in Los Angeles, a small man approached Schwartz and said he wanted to talk to him. In spite of his wife's misgivings, Schwarz got into his car. The man kissed his hand, then reminded Schwarz that he had once kissed his feet and called him his master. Schwarz was baffled; this little man bore no resemblance to the lanky Arab. But the man – apparently reading his mind – said, 'We can appear in any shape we desire' – and explained that 'we come from a tribe of people who crash-landed in a rocket ship on earth thousands of years ago'. He then told Schwarz that he was bringing him a message from *his* master in Nepal. The message was that 'You should now begin teaching the spiritual truth that is being given to you inspirationally. You are God's vehicle to bring the truth that is meant to be.' Promising to be in touch, the little man let him out of the car.

A few years later, Schwarz began receiving telepathic messages about his 'mission'. And a woman patient spoke in a metallic voice, telling Schwarz that he was from Pluto and that he – the voice – was from

Venus. The Venusian, who called himself Linus, went into technical detail about the 'gaseous' inhabitants of Venus, which was completely beyond the intellectual capacity of the woman patient (who was amazed when the tape was played back). Two months later, Linus again spoke to Schwarz through the mouth of another patient. And a psychic girl in Vancouver told him that she had travelled astrally to Venus the previous night, and that she had seen him there in company with Linus.

And that was the story, insofar as it had developed at the time I wrote *The Occult*.

At the time it seemed simply baffling. I now see that it fits a familiar pattern: men with some unusual ability begin to receive apparently supernatural communications assuring them that they are destined to become messiahs, and perhaps save the earth. Often, certain 'signs' are given – for example, prophecies of the future that prove accurate. But, if the recipient of the message is naive enough to commit himself to total belief, what follows is chaos and confusion – for example, some prophecy of a tremendous disaster, or even the end of the world, which simply fails to materialise, leaving the 'avatar' feeling rather foolish.

My next encounter with this bafflingly ambiguous world of UFOs occurred two or three years later, in the mid-1970s. *The Occult* had been well received, and I suddenly found myself invited to take part in projects involving the paranormal – such as presenting a series on BBC television, and serving on the editorial board of a series of books called *The Unexplained*. It was in this latter capacity that I came to meet Uri Geller, who had achieved overnight fame for bending spoons by gently rubbing them.

Prepared to believe that Geller was – as his critics alleged – merely a skilled conjuror, I was quickly convinced of his genuineness when he read my mind, reproducing a drawing I had made on the back of a menu card while he sat with his back to me – a sketch of a grotesque little creature that I invented to amuse my children. After I had turned over the menu card and covered it with my hand, Geller turned round, and asked me to stare into his eyes and transmit the drawing. Suddenly, he reproduced it on his own menu card, slightly less precise, but undoubtedly the same little cartoon character, with big floppy ears and huge eyes.

At that point, I asked him a question that had been troubling me ever since I had read *Uri: A Journal of the Mystery of Uri Geller*, by Andrija Puharich. Like most people, I had found the book extremely difficult to finish. The problem, quite simply, was that it was too unbelievable. It was not that I felt that Puharich was an out-and-out liar – simply that I found it impossible to take him seriously.

I wanted to know whether everything described in the book had really happened. Geller, I knew, had now broken with Puharich, not without some ill feeling, so would have no reason not to answer my question truthfully.

In fact, he told me with obvious sincerity, '*Everything* happened as Andrija describes it.'

'And do you believe that your powers come from some extraterrestrial source?'

'I don't know. I don't know where they come from.'

'But don't you feel that they could be a manifestation of your own unconscious mind – in other words, a kind of poltergeist effect?'

He shook his head. 'I find that hard to believe because whatever lies behind my powers seems to be intelligent. Sometimes it plays jokes. In my book[1] I say that maybe it is a Cosmic Clown.'

The reason for my question can be found in Chapter Three of Puharich's book. He describes how one day, under light hypnosis in a hotel room in Tel Aviv, Geller said that he was in a dark cave in Cyprus, where he used to sit and absorb learning. 'What are you learning?' asked Puharich, and Geller replied, 'It is about people who come from space. But I am not to talk about these things yet.'

Geller went on to describe how, in 1949, just after his third birthday, he was in a garden in Tel Aviv when he saw a huge, bowl-shaped light in the sky. Then a radiant figure appeared in front of him, its hands above its head, holding something that shone like the sun.

And it was at this point that I had begun to find Puharich's book frankly unbelievable. For he goes on to describe how, in the midst of the hypnotic session, Geller stopped speaking, and a strange, metallic voice began to issue from the air. It stated that 'it was us who found Uri in the garden when he was three'. 'They' had programmed him to serve their purpose, although his memories of contact have been erased. Their purpose was to avert a world war, which would begin as a war between Egypt and Israel. Geller would somehow be an instrument of their purpose.

'They', it would emerge later, were a group of superhuman beings called the 'Nine'. Puharich had first come across them when he was studying a Hindu psychic called Dr Vinod, who had suddenly begun to

---

[1] *My Story*, by Uri Geller, 1975

speak in a voice quite unlike his own, with a perfect English accent. The being was highly articulate, highly intelligent, and explained that it was a member of 'the Nine Principles and Forces', whose purpose is to aid human evolution.

Four years later, in 1956, Puharich had met an American couple, Dr Charles Laughead and his wife, who also passed on a lengthy message from 'the Nine Principles and Forces', which referred back to the earlier messages through Dr Vinod. Unless the new message was some kind of trick, it certainly looked as if the 'Nine' – or at least their spokesman – was some kind of disembodied intelligence. (But Laughead himself would later prove an example of the danger of getting mixed up with 'channelled' messages – he was to lose his post at Michigan State College after he announced that the world would end on a certain date, and the date passed without incident.)

All this explains why Puharich was inclined to accept the metallic voice in Tel Aviv as yet another manifestation of the Nine.

When Geller emerged from the hypnosis, he had no memory of what had occurred. When Puharich played back the tape recording describing what had happened in the garden, Geller muttered, 'I don't remember any of this.'

When the metallic voice began, Geller suddenly ejected the tape and ran from the room. Puharich swears he saw the tape vanish from Geller's hand as he seized it. When Geller was found, half an hour later – apparently still suffering from shock – the tape was nowhere to be found.

This is the beginning of a series of events so apparently preposterous that the reader begins to suffer from a kind of astonishment fatigue. Geller causes a ring in a closed wooden box to vanish, then to reappear. Puharich decides that this curious power to materialise or dematerialise objects might lead them to what they want to know. 'If we could be certain that the power of vanishing objects resided solely in Uri, it would simplify our problem. However, if this power was controlled by an extraterrestrial intelligence, we would be faced with one of the most momentous revelations in human history.'

So, by way of finding out, Puharich scratched code numbers on the three parts of a Parker pen. Then the pen was placed in the wooden box. Geller held his hand above it for nine minutes. When the box was opened, the pen was apparently intact. But, on closer examination, its brass cartridge had vanished.

Later in the day, while Geller was under hypnosis, the metallic voice spoke again, explaining that 'they' were in a spacecraft called *Spectra*, 'fifty-three thousand sixty-nine light ages away'. Puharich is told to take good care of Geller, who has an important mission to fulfil on earth. The voice adds that they have the missing pen part, and will return it in due course.

That evening, as they were driving in Tel Aviv, a 'round white luminous spacecraft with side fins' appeared in the sky at the end of the street.

Two days later, Puharich wanted to see a spot where Geller had had another UFO sighting. When he arrived to pick him up at the apartment of Uri's girlfriend Iris, Geller had not yet eaten. Iris took three eggs out of the refrigerator and filled a saucepan with water. When she went to pick up the eggs, she screamed with fright: they were hot, and proved to be hard-boiled.

Later, as they drove through a remote part of Tel Aviv with Geller at the wheel, they heard a chirping sound like a cricket. Then they saw a pulsating blue light in the air. Geller told Puharich and Iris to wait, while he walked in the direction of the chirping sound and the blue light. Sometime later he returned, looking as if he was in a trance. In his hand he carried the missing pen cartridge. Later, Geller told them that, as he approached the flashing blue light, his mind went blank. Then he found himself returning with the pen cartridge.

Understandably, all this left Puharich in no doubt that he was dealing with intelligent space beings, who were probably telling the truth when they said that they had been watching Earth for eight hundred years from a spacecraft as big as a city. All suspicion that Geller was playing tricks vanished as a series of strange events occurred in front of his eyes. The tape recorder would turn on of its own accord, then turn off, leaving messages from the metallic voice. The tapes actually dematerialised as he watched. A leather camera case which he had left behind in New York appeared in Tel Aviv. The time on his watch would change abruptly. On one occasion, as the watch lay on the table, Geller gave a startled cry as it materialised on his wrist. A piece of massage equipment that Geller thought of ordering from America, then decided was too expensive, suddenly appeared in Geller's room in its sealed box. One day, when the tape recorder began to record, the wall plug was snatched out of its socket; Puharich tried to replace it several times, but it was snatched out each time.

Now it is easy to put oneself in Puharich's place. Ever since he had met Geller, miracles had been taking place on a daily basis. A mysterious voice, speaking from the air, had assured him that he and Geller had an important task to perform, a task on which the future peace of the world could depend. Puharich began to feel that they were in the same position as the ancient Hebrew prophets, in direct contact with supernatural forces. He had always believed that, when the Bible says that the voice of God spoke to the patriarchs, this was merely a manner of speaking. Now he felt it was literally true.

Everyone will also agree that, under those circumstances, most of us would accept that the 'supernatural' (or extraterrestrial) forces were genuine, not some kind of hallucination or confidence trick. With the laws of nature being contradicted on a daily basis, as the 'voice' proved its power by making things happen before their eyes, the most hardened sceptic would believe.

Often it was for their eyes only. Driving in the desert, Geller, Puharich and another witness saw a giant spacecraft; yet the three military personnel in the front seat were unable to see it. The space intelligences obviously had strange powers of mind control.

But what was their purpose? If Geller had been selected for some tremendous task, what was it? The voice explained that 'they' would soon be involved in a mass landing on planet earth, which would finally convince the human race of the reality of supernatural forces. But when Puharich protested: 'We need some clarification about what our work is about', he was told: 'You must be patient, very patient. You are working twenty-four hours a day for us, but you don't even realise it.'

The reader finally begins to suspect that the space intelligences are not quite clear about their own objectives. Puharich was told: 'Do a movie on Uri.' But the movie fell through. (In due course, I was hired by Robert Stigwood, the theatre impressario, to work on a film about Uri, but that also fell through.) When Uri was ordered to go to Germany, the space intelligences seemed to believe that public demonstrations of his powers would somehow convince everyone of the reality of spiritual forces. But, in spite of stopping an escalator and a cable car, Uri's feats quickly ceased to interest the Germans.

The space intelligences also seem to have mishandled Geller's subsequent American trip. For some reason, they had ordered him to refuse any scientific testing. Geller went ahead anyway – with Hal Puthoff and Russell Targ at Stanford University – and the test results were impressive, with clear evidence of telepathy, and the ability to influence compass needles and bend and break small metal objects.

But American magicians, backed by *Time* magazine, had already decided he was a fake, and *Time* had a louder voice than a few Stanford scientists. Geller became increasingly angry and embittered, and he and Puharich began to have disagreements. Geller began to feel doubts about the 'voice', wondering if it might be just 'a goddam little clown that is playing with us'.

In spite of which, the space intelligences continued to demonstrate their powers. One day, Puharich's dog vanished in front of their eyes and reappeared in the garden. And when Puharich quarrelled with Geller, and expressed his disgust with the space intelligences, there was a gigantic thunderstorm, and a grandfather clock was hurled across the hall and smashed into pieces.

Yet still the space intelligences seemed to have no clear idea of what they wanted Puharich and Geller to actually *do*.

Finally, Puharich was instructed to break his vow of silence and write a book about it all. The result, of course, was *Uri: A Journal of the Mystery of Uri Geller* (1974). But it seemed that once again the occupants of *Spectra* had miscalculated. The result of the book was simply that Puharich's reputation as a serious investigator took a nose dive. His obvious sincerity and truthfulness ought to have carried the day, and demonstrated that *something* had been happening. But the events he is describing pass beyond the credulity barrier after about fifty pages, after which the book turns into a confusion of oddly monotonous miracles. It brought Geller and Puharich celebrity, but of a kind they would have been better off without.

My own acquaintance with Uri failed to bring any enlightenment on the subject of UFOs. I was to get to know him fairly well, and wrote a book called *The Geller Phenomenon*. During several days I spent with him in Barcelona, a number of minor 'miracles' occurred, but nothing that would convince a sceptic. Objects occasionally fell out of the air, but never actually in front of me, so that I could say with conviction that Uri had not thrown them. I do not, in fact, believe that he had, for, although I had misgivings about his enjoyment of publicity, I came to feel that he was totally honest.

My own conviction, at the time, was that Puharich had something to do with Geller's powers. Puharich himself describes how, in Tel Aviv, he went for a meal with Uri's mother and Uri's inseparable friend Shipi Strang, and how he suddenly discovered that he could pick up telepathic signals from Uri. 'We tried numbers . . . colours, and words in English, Hebrew and Greek. I was truly prodigious in my telepathic abilities.' Uri believed that Shipi's presence increased his own powers, which may be so. But my own feeling was that Puharich himself had strong paranormal powers – I suspect, as this book will make clear, that we all have – and that, when he came together with Uri, the combination of the two caused the sudden outbreak of strange events. And, since Puharich was already convinced of the reality of the Nine, it was almost inevitable that Geller's trance messages should come from them.

In the following year, 1976, I met Puharich, and spent an evening with him and his friend Joyce Petschek. He was a short, grey-haired man with a bushy moustache and a manner that was casual, good-natured and unpretentious. When I explained my theory about his 'psychic interaction' with Geller, he brooded on it for a moment, then said, 'You could be right, but I doubt it.'

During the course of that extremely interesting evening, it became clear that he had had so many strange experiences that he had come to take them almost for granted. Utterly weird events would drop briefly into the conversation, then vanish again as we discussed the mechanisms of telepathy or his extensive tests with the late psychic Peter Hurkos.

I told him my view that his book on Uri had failed to make an impact because it was too full of utterly unbelievable events. He assured me that he had, in fact, cut out some of the more preposterous anecdotes, because he was aware that he was overloading the reader's credulity.

He gave me an example. A couple were making love in a bedroom two hundred miles from Puharich's home in Ossining, New York. There was a knock on the door, and the man opened it to be confronted with Uri Geller, holding out a large chunk of stone. The man took it, and was bewildered when Uri left without a word.

In fact, the stone was some rare archaeological specimen from Puharich's collection. But Geller himself was actually in the house in Ossining at the moment when his doppelgänger knocked on the door two hundred miles away and handed over the stone.

Moreover, on one occasion in November 1973, Geller had actually been 'teleported' from a New York street to the house in Ossining.

I had to agree with Puharich that it was as well that he left out these stories from the book.

In my book *Mysteries* (1978), I comment: 'Puharich obviously found my theorising about subconscious poltergeist activity unnecessary. He had long ago reached the conclusion that the Nine are a reality, and that our earth has been observed by space men for thousands of years. He believes that the earth has reached a point in its history where the Nine feel that slightly more intervention is necessary.' And, after quoting the views of Puharich and Joyce Petschek, I go on: 'I found all this convincing up to a point. Nothing is more obvious than that Puharich and Mrs Petschek are totally sincere in everything that they say. Does that mean that I am convinced of the existence of the Nine? Obviously not.'

By the time I met him, Puharich had already been involved in another astonishing adventure with the 'space people'; it is described in detail in a book called *Prelude to the Landing on Planet Earth* (1977) by Stuart Holroyd.

After the break with Geller – which came shortly after the events described in *Uri* – Puharich began to receive more messages from the Nine via a medium named Phyllis Schlemmer. This time, no 'miracles' took place – at least, nothing more spectacular than the dematerialis- ation of Phyllis Schlemmer's earring, and its rematerialisation a few hours later. Puharich, together with an Englishman named Sir John Whitmore, were assured that, together with Phyllis Schlemmer, they were now the channels for the energies of the Nine, and that their task was to avert a world war that would start in the Middle East when Egypt, Lebanon and Syria launched an attack on Israel.

This time, the messenger of the Nine was a being who called himself Tom (short for Atum), who spoke via Phyllis Schlemmer, while she was in a trance. The three of them travelled around the world, meditating and praying in various hotel rooms to avert world catastrophes – for example, a meditation in Moscow apparently averted the assassination of Yasser Arafat at a press conference in Cuba.

But the main purpose of the Nine was to announce a mass landing of UFOs on Earth, which would last for nine days, and would finally convince the human race of the reality of the space beings.

According to Tom, the purpose of the Nine is to bring about an alteration in the consciousness of 'planet Earth', which has become a kind of bottleneck in the universe. 'This planet was originally created to teach [human beings] balance between the spiritual and the physical world, but in this physical world they got involved in the material world, and so [they] never evolve beyond the belt of this planet . . . It is important for the level of consciousness of this planet to be raised.'

But, by the time Puharich, Whitmore and Phyllis Schlemmer had averted another Middle East war by meditating in a hotel room over- looking the Golan Heights, 'Tom' had apparently forgotten about the mass landing on planet earth.

It is, of course, easy to dismiss Puharich as a gullible romantic, led astray by 'spirit messages' that probably originated in the medium's unconscious mind. Yet, when we take an overall view of his experiences, it becomes difficult to maintain this attitude. The first messages from the Nine came in 1952 via Dr Vinod. In 1956, they seemed to be confirmed by the encounter with Dr Charles Laughead, who passed on more messages from the Nine. This certainly seemed to suggest that the Nine were not a creation of Vinod's unconscious.

So, when the Nine again spoke in a Tel Aviv hotel room while Geller was in a trance, Puharich had every reason to believe in their genuineness. If he had any doubts, the 'miracles' that followed must have removed them. UFOs that hover at the end of the street, tape recorders that record without being touched, cassettes that dematerialise in front of the eyes – these are enough to convince anyone that he or she is dealing with real forces.

Here I have to admit that my own attitude has changed since I first read *Uri* in 1974, and wrote my own book *The Geller Effect* a year later. At that time, I took it totally for granted that so-called 'poltergeist' activity was a kind of unconscious 'psychokinesis' (mind over matter) caused by the minds of disturbed teenagers. I had no doubt that our minds are full of extraordinary unconscious forces over which we have no control. I found it difficult to explain the manifestations that took place when Geller and Puharich were together, since neither was a teenager, but that still seemed to me the only logical explanation.

Five years later, in the early 1980s, I was commissioned to write a book on poltergeists, and began to research the subject, beginning with a visit to a house in Pontefract where violent poltergeist activities had taken place over a long period. To my embarrassment, I soon found myself in no doubt whatever that poltergeists are disembodied spirits, who can make use of the energies of psychologically disturbed people.

I also began to believe that 'spirit possession' cannot be explained away as a kind of medieval superstition. This was why, when Grof told the story of Flora, I had no doubt that it was not a case of possession by some 'archetype of the collective unconscious'. I do not accept that the 'spirit' that possessed Flora was the Devil, or even *a* devil, but it was certainly some extremely unpleasant disembodied entity.

The result was that when I came to reread *Uri: A Journal of the Mystery of Uri Geller*, in the course of researching the present book, I found that my whole attitude towards it had changed. By then, I had read John Mack's *Abduction*, as well as Budd Hopkins's *Missing Time* and *Intruders*, and David Jacobs's *Secret Life*, and I could see that the subject was far more bizarre and complex than I had at first assumed. Now I saw why Geller and Puharich had disagreed with my theory that they themselves had been responsible for 'poltergeist effects'. They must have thought me appallingly obtuse, and been too polite to say so. They had *seen* tapes dematerialise, plugs pulled out of sockets, car engines immobilised. They knew they were dealing with some kind of paranormal force, not their own powers of psychokinesis. Both of them knew that when Uri snatched the first tape, and it vanished in his hand, he was being controlled – used as an instrument of these forces – just as John Mack's Catherine was being controlled when she experienced an odd desire to drive around Boston suburbs in the early hours of the morning. Which certainly suggests that the unseen entities possess some alarming powers . . .

But what are these entities? Are they, as Puharich believed, intelligent beings from space, who have been watching our planet for thousands of years, and who have intervened in human history more than once? Or are they, like most poltergeists, simply the juvenile delinquents and time wasters of the spirit world?

This is the question that I set out to answer soon after the trip to Marion. The first thing I wanted to know was: can they be considered intelligent? Most poltergeists show little more than a kind of rudimentary intelligence, often downright stupidity. If these 'space beings' demonstrated more than that, it would certainly be a strong argument in favour of some of their claims.

And it was at that point that I heard about the investigations of the astronomer Gerald Hawkins into crop circles.

2 Crop Circles and Frozen Music

ESTBURY, FIFTEEN MILES from Stonehenge, is a small weaving and glove-making town, whose most famous feature is the great White Horse cut into the turf of Bratton Down. It was first cut to celebrate King Alfred's victory over the Danes there in 878, but was recut in 1778 in a form that looks like an exceptionally tired and dispirited carthorse.

The farm of John Scull lies within sight of the White Horse, on the Wiltshire downs. In mid-August, 1980, Mr Scull was walking around the edge of his oat field when he was outraged by the sight of what looked like wanton vandalism. Someone had been trampling his oats on a vast scale. But, when he surveyed the damage at close quarters, he realised that it was more organised than it looked. There were three immense circles, each sixty feet in diameter, spread out over the field. The ripening oats had been neatly flattened in a clockwise direction, yet without breaking the stalks – the horizontal oats were continuing to ripen.

It looked as if some practical joker had worked out an elaborate hoax – elaborate because the circles must have been produced manually rather than mechanically; there was no sign of the disturbance that would have been made by some kind of machine. In fact the circles were surrounded by undamaged oats, which made it hard to see how anyone had approached. But then, all cornfields have 'tramlines' – double lines made by the farmer's tractor as he adds fertiliser or weed-killer – and a careful hoaxer could have trodden carefully along the tramlines without leaving any signs of disturbance.

But to what purpose? What kind of a madman would want to spend a whole night making three sixty-foot circles – presumably with long planks, or a piece of rope stretched from the centre?

The *Wiltshire Times* printed the story on 15 August 1980, together with a photograph. The report brought Dr Terence Meaden, editor of the *Journal of Meteorology*, to Mr Scull's farm. And, as he examined the three sharp-edged circles, Meaden realised that they had not all been made on the same night, but on three different dates between May and July. John Scull had simply not noticed them.

But made by what? Meaden was baffled. The only suggestion he could come up with was a summer whirlwind. But that seemed unlikely. Many country people have seen a summer whirlwind – a spiral of dust that dashes around a field and sucks up anything in its path. But summer whirlwinds are not usually sixty feet across – that would be a tornado. Neither do they stay in the same place. A summer whirlwind would have made a random path through the crop. Meaden's explanation was untenable even at the time, but it was the best he could do.

Later, he was to elaborate his theory, suggesting that when a gust of wind meets a hill, it forms a vortex, which meets the stationary air on the other side of the hill to create a spiralling column.

The next expert on the spot was another magazine editor: Ian Mrzyglod. He carefully measured the circles, and made the interesting discovery that they were not circles, but ellipses. Radiuses drawn from the edge of the circles to their centres varied by several feet, from twenty-six and a half to thirty-five. So the idea of a man with a long plank or a length of rope had to be abandoned.

If anyone had been interested, they might have learnt that John Scull's circles were not the first – that other farmers in the south of England had found their corn flattened in a clockwise circle since 1978. But, since there is something oddly boring about a mystery with no obvious solution, nobody had paid much attention. And now, for the same reason, everyone soon forgot the three circles in the Westbury oat field.

A year went past. Then, in August 1981, it happened again. This time it was in Hampshire, in a natural amphitheatre called Cheesefoot Head, where Eisenhower had addressed the troops before the 1944 D-Day landing. In dry weather, the foundations of some old building, possibly Roman, show through the turf. And when it is used for wheat – as it usually is – the great circle of golden yellow stands out sharply among the surrounding green hills.

In this 'punchbowl', on 19 August 1981, there appeared three circles in the wheat. Unlike the Westbury circles, which had been spread all over the field, these three were neatly in line: one large circle, about sixty feet across, and two smaller ones, about twenty-five feet, placed neatly and symmetrically on either side. They were again slightly elliptical. And they had been made on the same night.

If they were caused by a whirlwind – as Meaden still maintained – then it had to bounce three times. In fact, the Cheesefoot Head circles seem almost designed to refute Meaden's theory, as if they are saying: 'No, we, couldn't be due to whirlwinds, because we are in a straight line, and are of different sizes.'

The following year, 1982, was quiet, with only a few single circles over southern England. Then, in 1983, once more in the punchbowl field at Cheesefoot Head, no fewer than five circles appeared on the same night: a large central circle, and four circles spaced neatly and symmetrically around it. This was the *coup de grâce* to the whirlwind theory – although Meaden refused to acknowledge it. There was obviously no way that a whirlwind could bounce five times in a neat pattern. And, as if delighted to have made its point, the invisible prankster went on to make 'fivesomes' all over the south of England – one below the White Horse, another below the Ridgeway, near Wantage, in Oxfordshire, and another at Cley Hill, near Warminster, a town that had been noted for its sightings of UFOs.

Suddenly, the media discovered crop circles. The British press often refers to summer as the 'silly season', because for some odd reason, there is often a shortage of good news stories in the hot months, and the newspapers have to manufacture stories out of events that would be ignored in the winter. Crop circles were ideal for the purpose, and they were soon featuring regularly in most British newspapers, then all over the world. 'Artistic hippies' were widely suspected, although UFO enthusiasts insisted that the only plausible explanation was flying saucers.

When yet another 'quintuplet' found below the White Horse turned out to be a fraud, the sceptics seemed to be justified. Bob Rickard, the editor of the *Fortean Times*, a magazine dedicated to 'anomalies' and the memory of the late Charles Fort, was one of those who went to look at this new circle, and noted that its edges seemed less clear-cut than in most circles. He pointed this out to Ian Mrzyglod, who proceeded to investigate, and soon uncovered a hoax. The *Daily Mirror*, irritated that its rival the *Daily Express* had scooped so many crop-circle stories, had paid a family named Shepherd to duplicate the 'quintuplet' below the White Horse. They did this by entering the field on stilts, and then trampling the corn in a circle. Yet the fact that they *needed* to enter the field on stilts, and that their hoax was so quickly detected, seemed to argue that the other circles were either genuine or created by far more skilful hoaxers.

Now crop circles were reported not only from England, but from all over the world: Australia, Japan, France, Italy, Sweden, Norway, the United States, Canada. In fact, Canadian circles had been reported from as early as 1974. On 1 September 1974, Edwin Fuhr, a farmer, of Langenburg, Saskatchewan, was driving his tractor in a field of rapeseed when he noted a round, shiny disc, about eleven feet across, whirling above the crop and causing it to sway. Then he noticed four more, all doing the same thing. He sat frozen with fear, and watched them for fifteen minutes, until they took off, going straight up in a grey vapour. And his rapeseed had five crop circles, eleven feet in diameter. They drew crowds of journalists.

Circles that appeared in a field near Rossburn, Manitoba, in 1977 seemed to refute Meaden's whirlwind theory, in that they were in flat prairie land, with no hills to form vortices.

As the number of circles also increased, so did their variety. There were circles with 'rings' around them – flattened pathways that ran around the outer edge – double rings, triple rings, quadruplets, quintuplets, sextuplets, even swastikas. It was as if the circle makers were trying to outflank the sceptics. When someone pointed out that all the circles had been flattened anticlockwise, a clockwise circle promptly appeared. When someone suggested that the circles could be made with the aid of a helicopter, a circle appeared under a power line.

In August 1991, a British couple were present when a circle was formed. They were Gary and Vivienne Tomlinson, and they were taking an evening walk in a cornfield near Hambledon, Surrey, when the corn began to move, and a mist hovered around them. They reported a high-pitched sound. Then a whirlwind swirled around them, and Gary Tomlinson's hair began to stand up from a build-up of static. Suddenly, the whirlwind split in two and vanished across the field, and, in the silence that followed, they realised they were in the middle of a crop circle, with the corn neatly flattened.

This certainly seemed to support Meaden's whirlwind theory, and he had himself photographed with the two witnesses. Meaden's response to the question of why, if the circles are formed by whirlwinds, they started in the late 1970s, and were not (apparently) found before that, was that they *had* been. He cited a pamphlet of August 1678 called *Mowing Devil*, concerning a field in Hertfordshire in which a circle was found in the corn, and attributed to a demon. But this still failed to explain why no crop circles were found between 1678 and the modern outbreak.

In a book called *The Goddess of the Stones*, Meaden speculates that the spirals often found carved on old stones were inspired by crop circles. But again, the problem is: why, in that case, do we not find references to crop circles in ancient literature?

Bob Rickard's interviews with witnesses – people who claimed to have been present when circles were made – may or may not be taken as confirming Meaden's whirlwind theory: these are a patchwork of their comments:

> Suddenly the grass began to sway before our eyes and laid itself flat in a clockwise spiral . . . A perfect circle was completed in less than half a minute, all the time accompanied by a high-pitched humming sound . . . My attention was drawn to a 'wave' coming through the heads of the cereal crop in a straight line . . . The agency, although invisible, behaved like a solid object . . . When we reached the spot where the circles had been, we were suddenly caught up in a terrific whirlwind . . . [The dog] went wild . . . There was a rushing sound and a rumble . . . then suddenly everything was still . . . It was uncanny . . . The dawn chorus stopped, the sky darkened . . .

In Bolberry Down, Devon, on 16 June 1991, a ham radio operator named Lew Dilling heard a series of high-pitched blips and clicks that drowned Radio Moscow and the Voice of America. He had heard them before – at the time of crop-circle incidents. The next day, a seventy-foot circle, with a 'bull's eye' in the middle, was found in the centre of a nearby field. But this differed from earlier crop circles, in which no serious damage had been done. In this case, the owner of the field, Dudley Stidson, found his corn burnt, as if a giant hot plate had been pressed down on it.

The landlord of the local pub, Sean Hassall, could work out what time the circle had been made from the fact that his spaniel had gone berserk in the night and had begun tearing up the carpet, doing considerable damage.

A few days before this, a Japanese professor had announced that he had solved the crop-circle riddle. Professor Yoshihiko Ohtsuki, of Waseda University, had created an 'elastic plasma' fireball in the laboratory – a plasma is a very hot gas in which some electrons have been stripped away when atoms collide violently. Fireballs, or ball lightning, are still one of the unsolved mysteries of science. They are created during storms, and drift around like balloons before exploding – often causing damage – or simply vanishing like a bubble. So Ohtsuki's achievement in manufacturing one in the laboratory was considerable. His fireball created beautiful circular rings in aluminium powder on a plate. This certainly sounded as if it could be the solution to the crop circles that everyone was looking for. Then someone pointed out that many of the latest crop circles had had rectangles associated with them, and that one at Alton Barnes (of July 1990) had keylike protuberances sticking out of its side. (In fact, this one was so complex that it should have taken far more than a night to create.)

A critic had pointed out to Professor Ohtsuki that most fireballs are about the size of grapefruit, and that a seventy-foot fireball would attract attention for many miles around. Besides, no fireball of that size had ever been known.

Stories of crop circles began to appear in the Japanese media. On 17 September 1989, on Kyushu Island, a rice farmer named Shunzo Abe found two wide circles in his fields. He thought at first that they were caused by a wild boar, then noted that there were no footprints in the soft earth.

Back in England, another curious phenomenon had been noted: that the 'circle makers' responded to the suggestions, and even the thoughts, of the investigators. In August 1986, Busty Taylor was flying home near Cheesefoot Head, when he remarked to his passenger George Wingfield that he would like to see a pattern with a central circle surrounded by satellites and rings. In his mind, he said, were the words 'Celtic cross' – a form of cross with arms emerging from a central circle. The next day, flying over the same spot, he was astounded to find a Celtic cross in the field below him. Colin Andrews, another of the first 'cereologists' (as crop-circle students came to be called) lay in bed one night and visualised a Celtic cross, literally asking for it to appear in a nearby field. The next day, a local farmer rang him to report an elaborate Celtic cross in his field.

On 18 June 1989, six investigators, including George Wingfield, were in a crop circle at Cheesefoot Head when a trilling noise began. It seemed to circle around the group in the corn. A female member of the group said: 'If you understand us, stop', and the trilling stopped for a moment, then resumed. Then Wingfield called: 'Please will you make us a circle?' The following morning, a new circle had appeared 500 yards away, in the direction in which the trilling noise had finally moved away.

The six also noted that when the trilling stopped their watches showed them – to their astonishment – that it had gone on for an hour and a half, far longer than any of them remembered.

At exactly the same time the following year, 1990, a group including George Wingfield, John Haddington (the present Lord Haddington) and the publisher Michael Cox decided to set up a vigil at Wansdyke, near Silbury Hill. On the first night, Wingfield and Haddington saw lights along Wansdyke, while elsewhere Michael Cox again recorded the trilling sound. The following evening, the sound began again, and the lights moved from Wansdyke into the middle of the cornfield where they were standing: 'They would flash on and off very quickly,' wrote Haddington, 'and were an orange, red or greenish hue.'

Then, as they watched, hundreds of black rods began to jump up and down above the wheat. (In 1987, Busty Taylor had succeeded in capturing this phenomenon in a photograph.) Michael Cox tried to pursue the trilling sound with his tape recorder, but was suddenly overwhelmed with nausea, and his knees gave way. He had to stagger to the fence and sit down; but he had again captured the trilling noise on tape. Haddington remarks: 'To the human ear this most musical sound has the most beautiful bell-like quality, really indescribable as it is so high-pitched. This does not translate on to a tape in a true fashion, coming out covered by a harsh crackling, static-like noise which is presumably caused by the discharge of high energy.' He is obviously correct: there is no reason why a tape recorder should not accurately record any sound, unless the sound is a by-product of some energy vibration that spoils the recording.

When the American television investigator, Linda Moulton Howe, was in England in 1992, Colin Andrews told her the story about visualising a Celtic cross, and remarked that he thought investigators could influence the circles. On 22 July a group of them went out circle-spotting, including a 'psychic' named Maria Ward. She told them that, on the previous day, she had received a mental impression of a design of a triangle with a circle at each of its points – she drew it on request. She added that she felt it had to do with Oliver Cromwell. Two days later, this exact design was found in nearby Alton Barnes, in a wheat field below Oliver's Castle Hill, where Cromwell had fought Charles I in 1643.

The problem with such data is that, scientifically speaking, it is worthless. Even the two published accounts of the Busty Taylor episode differ slightly: he says he only *thought* of a Celtic cross, but did not mention it; George Wingfield, who was with him in the aeroplane, says he mentioned it. We can see how events are changed slightly in recollection. And a scientist would point out that no one could prove that Colin Andrews visualised a Celtic cross the night before one appeared, and that some hoaxer may have created the Alton Barnes triangle after hearing that a psychic had predicted it.

In fact, hoaxers quickly threw the whole phenomenon into doubt. In September 1991, two elderly landscape painters named Doug Bower and Dave Chorley, who lived in Southampton, claimed that they were the authors of most of the crop circles, and that their main piece of equipment was a short plank. Their claim was reported in the press around the world, and many people felt that this was the solution to the mystery – without reflecting that crop circles were now being reported from all over the world. Doug and Dave – whose names became a synonym for hoaxing – were commissioned by a documentary film maker to create a circle design at East Meon, and responded with an admirable pattern like a dumbbell, with additional designs at either end – it took an hour and a half. But they did it by trampling the wheat, and using short planks, often snapping stalks; on the whole, genuine crop formations show bent stalks – as if, Linda Howe says, rushing water had flowed over them.

The question is not whether they were telling the truth – they obviously were, in the sense that they had undoubtedly made dozens of hoax circles. But could they be taken seriously when they claimed that they – together with a few unconnected hoaxers – made *all* the circles since 1978? If so, why did they wait until September 1991 to claim credit? It seems clear that they finally approached the now defunct *Today* newspaper because they wanted to claim the prestige due for what they regarded as a kind of artistic endeavour. And obviously their story would be far less impressive if they claimed that they had been making circles only for the past two or three years. If they were going to make their bid for notoriety, they would *want* to claim credit for all the circles. But is it likely that two 'artists' would want to hide their light under a bushel for thirteen years?

That many of the crop circles are the work of hoaxers cannot be doubted; but the notion that they are *all* by hoaxers – including a circle in a Japanese rice field, whose soft earth would show footprints – is hard to believe.

It was an investigation by Terence Meaden in 1991 that made it clear that the hoaxer theory was inadequate. It was called 'Blue Hill', and was funded by Japanese universities, and associated with a BBC film project. Both Meaden and the BBC installed radar equipment whose aim was to detect both hoaxers and whirlwinds. Most of the six weeks of the project were uneventful, although new circles appeared further afield. But, towards the end, two circles were found close at hand in the radar-booby-trapped area, demonstrating fairly conclusively that they had not been made by either hoaxers or whirlwinds.

Between 1991 and 1993, an American biophysicist, W.C. Levengood, examined samples from known hoaxed circles, as well as some believed to be 'genuine'. He discovered that the 'genuine' samples showed changes in the cell-pits (in Britain called pips or seeds), enlargements that he was able to reproduce only in a microwave oven. He also noted cell changes in the hoax samples – a lengthening of the pits – but these were due to being trampled on and squeezed through the cell wall. Even though Levengood concluded, 'Whatever is doing these formations is affecting the fundamental biophysics and biochemistry of the plant', cereologists, who had hoped for an instant test to distinguish hoaxes, had to admit that it was not as clear-cut as they might have wished.

Linda Howe tells how, in September 1992, Levengood was contacted by a farmer from Clark, South Dakota, about a 600-foot circle that had appeared among his potatoes. The plants were all dead. Levengood studied the dead plants, and again found pit enlargement, often of more than a quarter, while the potatoes themselves had yellow streaks and cracks.

In Austinburg, Ohio, a gardener named Donald Wheeler discovered a large rectangle in his maize; the stalks had been flattened but not broken, and were all lying in the same direction. The wet ground showed no sign of footmarks. Dr Levengood examined maize from inside the rectangle, and undamaged maize from outside. The 'tassels' on the undamaged corn were closed, while those on the damaged corn were open, indicating that their growth had been somehow accelerated. Linda Howe published photographs of the wheat, potatoes and maize examined by Levengood in her *Glimpses of Other Realities*, where the difference can be clearly seen.

One startling development – although at the time no one recognised how startling – was a long review of three books on crop circles in the *New York Review* on 21 November 1991. What was so unusual was that it was by Baron Zuckerman, one of the most distinguished members of Britain's scientific establishment – perhaps *the* most. He had ended a brilliant academic career as chief scientific adviser to the British government. And, by 1991, he was eighty-seven years old. So why was such a man getting involved in a subject that most scientists dismissed as lunacy?

The answer may lie in the fact that Zuckerman had retired to a village near Sandringham in Norfolk, and that Sandringham happens to be one of the royal residences. There is, among cereologists, a persistent rumour that crop circles appeared on the Queen's estate at Sandringham, and that the response of Prince Philip was to send for their old friend Baron Zuckerman to ask his opinion. Zuckerman certainly went to the trouble of personally examining a number of crop circles.

One result was the *New York Review* article, written two years before his death, and two years after his alleged visit to Sandringham.

'Creations of the Dark' is a curious piece. There is no hint of that carping tone that has become the standard response of scientists to such bizarre matters. He begins by speaking of mysteries of the British landscape, like Stonehenge, Silbury Hill and the white horses cut in the chalk, then, moving on to crop circles, mentions that almost a thousand appeared in England between 1980 and 1990. He goes on to speak sympathetically and at length about Pat Delgado and Colin Andrews, authors of *Circular Evidence*, one of the books he is reviewing.

They believe that the circles are 'caused by some supernatural intelligence', he explains – yet still with no touch of the critical scepticism one would expect of a senior scientist. Even when he mentions that one of the cornfield inscriptions reads WEARENOTALONE, it is with no hint of scorn. This appears only at the end of his summary of the views of Terence Meaden, when he says: 'How a downwardly directed turbulent vortex ... could explain the more elaborate circle designs is not touched on ...', and goes on to quote Colin Andrews's criticism that even a bouncing vortex could not make geometrical patterns. And, a few sentences later, he quotes with satisfaction Wingfield's remark that rectangular boxes in the corn have 'driven the final nail into the coffin of the atmospheric vortex theory'.

Why, he wants to know, have scientists not taken a more active interest in the phenomenon? The owner of one farm where Zuckerman went to look at circles told him it was owned by New College, Oxford, but that none of the science fellows there had shown any interest. Neither had the science teachers at Marlborough School, only ten miles away.

One useful step, Zuckerman suggests, would be to train university students to make hoax circles. If it proved to be easy, that at least would be one established fact. And if it proved to be difficult . . . well, we would be back at square one, still faced with the mystery. What is perfectly clear, from Zuckerman's admission that he has studied many of these circles, is that he does not accept either that they are natural phenomena, due to whirlwinds, or that they have all been created by hoaxers. The final impression left by the article – and by the very fact that a man as distinguished as Zuckerman had taken the trouble to write it – is that he is far from dismissive of the suggestion that at least some of the circles are the work of nonhuman intelligences, and that he feels that scientists ought to be trying to find out.

It so happened that, on the other side of the Atlantic, another scientist had been corresponding with Zuckerman and was following his advice. Gerald S. Hawkins was a British radio astronomer who had been Professor of Astronomy at Boston University, and had achieved international celebrity through his book *Stonehenge Decoded* in 1965. In 1960, he had used a computer to investigate an idea that had been planted in his head when he attended a lecture on Stonehenge at London University in 1949: that Stonehenge may be a complex calendar or computer to calculate moonrise and sunrise over the 18.6-year moon cycle. The idea, which caused fierce controversy at the time, is now generally accepted, and has become the basis of the new science of archaeoastronomy. Subsequently he went on to apply the same techniques to the pyramids of Egypt.

Hawkins started Boston University research in 1989, the year that *Time* magazine published a long article on the crop-circle controversy. He was intrigued by the photographs, and by the comment of a few colleagues that perhaps the circles might provide him with another problem for computer analysis. After all, they were mostly in the same county as Stonehenge. Later that year, on a visit to England, he picked up a copy of *Circular Evidence* by Andrews and Delgado – which had become an unexpected bestseller, demonstrating that the phenomenon was now arousing worldwide interest.

Andrews and Delgado had carefully measured eighteen of the circles, and included the measurements in their book. A glance told Hawkins that this was not suitable material for computer analysis. The obvious alternative was a mathematical or geometrical approach – to compare the size of the circles.

As a typical scientist, Hawkins had already plodded through *Circular*

Evidence page by page. Being an astronomer he was treating the book like a star catalogue. Andrews and Delgado had measured twenty-five circle patterns with engineering precision, and gave them in order of appearance. The first forty pages were large circles with satellites, and the diameters revealed a musical fraction, accurate to one per cent. Anyone can check this from the book by just taking a pocket calculator and dividing the large by the small. One per cent, by the way, is high precision for the circle maker. It is only just detectable in a symphony orchestra, and totally unnoticeable in a rock group.

But after 1986 things changed. From this time on circles appeared with rings around them. Hawkins found the simple fraction was now given by the *area* of the ring divided by the *area* of the circle. From schooldays we recall that ancient area formula, pi-r-squared. Modern computer experts would say: 'Ha! Data compression. We get a larger ratio from the same sized pattern.'

The first step in his reasoning was that, if the first circles had been made by Meaden's vortices, then all patterns involving several symmetrical circles must be ruled out, since a whirlwind was not likely to make neat patterns. Which meant that the great majority of circles since the mid-1980s must be made by hoaxers. But would hoaxers take the trouble to give their patterns the precision of geometrical diagrams? In fact, would they even be capable of such precision, working in the dark, and on a large scale? They would be facing the same kind of problem as the makers of the Nazca lines in the desert of Peru – the great birds, spiders and animals drawn on the sand – but with the difference that the Nazca people worked by daylight and had an indefinite amount of time at their disposal, whereas the circle makers had to complete their work in the dark in a few hours.

Hawkins began by looking closely at a 'triplet' of circles which had appeared at Corhampton, near Cheesefoot Head on 8 June 1988. To visualise these, imagine two oranges on a table, about an inch apart. Now imagine taking a small, flat piece of wood – like the kind by which you hold an ice lolly – and laying it across the top of them. Then balance another orange in the centre of the lolly stick, and you have a formation like the Cheesefoot Head circles of 1988 (*see plate no. 1*).

Now even a nonmathematical reader can see that the lolly stick forms what our teachers taught us to call a tangent to *each* of the oranges. And, since all the oranges are spaced out equally, you could insert two more lolly sticks between them to make two more tangents. The three sticks would form a triangle in the space between the three oranges.

That is a nicely symmetrical pattern. But, of course, it does not prove that the circle makers were interested in geometry. Perhaps they just thought there was something pleasing about the arrangement. When he had been at school, Hawkins had been made to study Euclid, the Greek mathematician, born around 300 BC, who had written the first textbook of geometry. Euclid is an acquired taste; either you like him or you don't. Bertrand Russell had found him so enjoyable that he read right through the *Elements* as if it were *Alice in Wonderland*. As an astronomer, Hawkins had always appreciated the importance of Euclid, in spite of having been brow beaten with him at school. So now he began looking at his three circles, and wondering if they made a theorem. He tried sticking his compass point in the centre of one circle, and drawing a large circle whose circumference went through the centres of the other two circles. He realised, to his satisfaction, that the diameter of the large circle, compared with that of the smaller ones, was exactly 16 to 3.

So now he had a new theorem. If you take three crop circles, and stick them at the corners of a small equilateral triangle, then draw a large circle that passes through two centres, the small circles are just three sixteens the size of the larger one.

He looked up his *Elements* to see if Euclid had stumbled on that one. He hadn't.

Of course, it is not enough to work out a theorem with a ruler: it has to be proved. That took many weeks, thinking in the shower and while driving. Eventually, he obtained his proof – elegantly simple.

After this success, he was unstoppable. Another crop-circle pattern, in a wheatfield near Guildford, Surrey, showed an equilateral triangle inside a circle – so its vertices touched the circumference – then another circle *inside* the triangle. Hawkins soon worked out that the area of the bigger circle is four times as large as the smaller one.

Another circle used the same pattern, but with a square instead of a triangle. Here, Hawkins worked out, the bigger circle is now twice as large in area as the smaller one.

When another circle replaced the square with a hexagon, he worked out that the smaller circle is three-quarters the size of the larger one.

Now so far, you might say, he had proved nothing except that crop-circle patterns – which might have been selected by chance, like a child doodling with a pair of compasses and a ruler – could be made to yield up some new theorems. But, early in the investigation, he had stumbled upon an insight that added a whole new dimension.

It so happened that his wife Julia had always had an ambition to play the harp. So Hawkins bought her one. And, although he was not a musician, he decided to tune the harp himself. Which in turn led him to teach himself the elements of music.

The musical scale, as everyone knows, has eight notes – doh, re, mi, fa, so, la, ti, doh. The top doh completes it, but also begins a new octave. These are the white notes on a piano keyboard – we also call them C, D, E, F, G, A, B and top C – and we feel that they are somehow natural and complete. But of course the keyboard also has black notes, the semitones. Hawkins found that the harp sounded better if he tuned it according to the white notes – which are also known as the diatonic scale – and used mathematical fractions.

Now the reason that each sounds different is that they all differ in *pitch*, which is the number of times the piano string vibrates per second. The doh in the middle of a piano keyboard is 264 vibrations per second. And the top doh is exactly twice that – 528 vibrations per second. And since, to our Western ears, the remaining six notes sound 'perfectly spaced', you might expect each note to increase its vibrations by a jump of one seventh, so that re is one and a seventh, mi is one and two-sevenths, and so on. But our Western ears deceive us – the notes are not perfectly spaced. In fact, re is one and an eighth, mi is one and two-eighths, fa is one and a third, soh one and a half, la one and two-thirds, and ti one and seven-eighths.

However, the points is that these *are* simple fractions. The black notes are a different matter. While re is one and an eighth above doh, the black note next to it (called a minor third) is 32 divided by 27, which no one could call a simple fraction.

Now, as Hawkins went on measuring and comparing crop circles, he discovered that most of the ratios came out in simple fractions – and, moreover, the fractions of the diatonic scale, listed above. The 16:3 of the Cheesefoot Head formation was the note F. Three well-known circle formations yielded 5:4, the note E, 3:2, the note G, and 5:3, the note A. A few, where circles and diameters were compared, yielded two notes.

If Doug and Dave, or other hoaxers, had been responsible for the crop circles, then the odds were thousands to one against this happening (Hawkins calculated them as 25,000 to 1). In fact, Hawkins studied a number of circles that Doug and Dave admitted to, and found no diatonic ratios in any of them.

Now it is true that not every circle revealed this musical code. Out of the first eighteen Hawkins studied, only eleven were 'diatonic'. The answer may be that Doug and Dave had made the other seven. Or that some of the 'circle makers' were not musical. Yet almost two-thirds was an impressive number, far beyond statistical probability.

So Hawkins felt he had stumbled on a discovery that was as interesting as any he had ever made. If the 'circle makers' were human hoaxers, then they had devised a highly sophisticated code.

But why bother with a code? Why not simply spell out the message, like the WEARENOTALONE inscription, which is claimed by Doug and Dave? An obvious answer suggests itself. WEARENOTALONE sounds like Doug and Dave. But a code of diatonic ratios is almost certainly beyond Doug and Dave.

Following the advice of Lord Zuckerman, Gerald Hawkins sent off an account of his findings to *Nature*, the prestigious magazine for publishing new and yet-to-be-explained discoveries. In 1963, *Nature* had published his work on Stonehenge, but now in July 1991 the editor balked, saying: your findings do not 'provide a sufficient advance towards understanding the origin of crop circles to excite immediate interest of a wide scientific audience'.

It was like asking an astronomer to explain the origin of the stars, sun or moon. Hawkins, like any careful research scientist, does not rush in with a theory. He looks at the facts that are there. Edmund Hilary did not ask for the theory of origin of Mt Everest, he climbed it because it was there.

Even now as I prod and poke, I cannot get Hawkins to come out with an origin. For him the game's afoot. He continues to investigate the theory of hoaxers as Zuckerman suggested, but what he has found in the intellectual profile has made him even more cautious. Now he talks about 'circle makers', a tautology that neatly covers hoaxers and all possible origins.

But let us go back to the basic question. *If* there is a complex geometry hidden in the circles, does this not suggest that *nonhuman intelligences are trying to communicate with us*? If Hawkins's geometry leads us to conclude that the answer is yes, then we have decided a question that has been preoccupying scientists for well over two centuries: the question of whether we are alone in the universe, or whether there are other intelligent beings.

But then, others have believed they had solved that problem, and have been proved mistaken. In 1877, the Italian astronomer Giovanni Schiaparelli studied Mars on one of its closest approaches to Earth, and believed he saw lines that looked like rivers on its surface. He called them *canali* and included them on his map of Mars. *Canali* means 'channels', but it was translated into English as 'canals', and soon half the civilised world believed that Mars was the home of a superintelligent but dying race who had built canals to bring water from the polar icecaps to the tropics; the idea inspired H.G. Wells to write his novel *The War of the Worlds*. Then the American astronomer Percival Lowell looked at Mars through a more powerful telescope, and saw the canals even more clearly. His books arguing that there is life on Mars caused great excitement. But all these dreams of Martian civilisation came to an end when the Mariner 4 space probe sped past Mars in 1965, and its photographs showed a surface as bleak and dead as the moon – and without canals. Our eyes join up dots that are close together to form lines, and Lowell and Schiaparelli had been victims of this illusion.

In July 1976, when the Viking 1 orbiter began sending back photographs of the surface of Mars, a NASA researcher named Toby Owens observed what looked like an enormous face in the Plain of Cydonia. Mentioned at a NASA press conference as a kind of joke, the 'Face on Mars' was soon exciting widespread attention. Richard Hoagland, a former NASA adviser, argued that the face, and what look like other 'man-made' (or Martian-made) structures in the same area, prove that Mars was once the home of a technically accomplished civilisation. Sceptics replied that the face, and other such structures, are natural features, and that they are no more significant than the face of the man in the moon.

There is, however, a basic difference between the approaches of Lowell and Hoagland, and that of Hawkins. Lowell's evidence depended on what he saw – or thought he saw – through a telescope, Hoagland's upon blurry photographs taken from miles above Mars. Hawkins has argued that many of the crop circles show too much geometrical sophistication to be by hoaxers, and that, moreover, the underlying pattern of diatonic ratios is too precise to be an accident. 'For the crop circles, the odds against an accident are about 400,000 to 1, something like getting 7 sixes in ten throws of the dice.'

Moreover, Hawkins's work on the four theorems made him aware that they were all special cases of a *fifth* theorem. One of his advantages as a scientist was a naturally visual imagination, the ability to see shapes and patterns in his head. (It is sometimes called eidetic imagery.) He drew the second theorem in his head, then contracted the circles and changed the shapes until he had the third and fourth theorems – then realised they all sprang out of a more general theorem about triangles in concentric circles.

The existence of this fifth theorem was revealed in *Science News* for 1 February 1992, in an article entitled 'Euclid's Crop Circles', by Ivars Peterson. He begins by describing crop circles, and how farmers are plagued with 'some enigmatic nocturnal pest'.

Peterson takes, of course, the view that the circle makers are quite definitely human hoaxers. After all, if a respectable science magazine is to agree that crop-circle theorems are not a matter of chance, then it is also forced to conclude that someone put them there. And, since extraterrestrial intelligences are unthinkable, then it had to be hoaxers.

The article goes on to say that Hawkins wrote a letter to Doug Bower and Dave Chorley, asking them how they had managed to incorporate diatonic ratios into the 'artwork', and concludes, 'The media did not give you credit for the unusual cleverness behind the design of the patterns.'

Doug and Dave, apparently, decided not to reply.

Peterson goes on to describe how Hawkins had discovered the 4:3 ratio in the Cheesefoot Head design, and how he had then discovered three more theorems in designs involving triangles, squares and hexagons. But then he realised that these could all be derived from a fifth theorem.

The hoaxers apparently had the requisite knowledge not only to prove a Euclidean theorem but also to conceive of an original theorem in the first place – a far more challenging task. To show how difficult such a task can be, Hawkins often playfully refuses to divulge his fifth theorem, inviting anyone interested to come up with the theorem itself before trying to prove it.

What Hawkins now has [Peterson concludes] is an intellectual fingerprint of the hoaxers involved. 'One has to admire this sort of mind, let alone how it's done or why it's done,' he says.

Did Chorley and Bower have the mathematical sophistication to depict novel Euclidean theorems in the wheat?

Perhaps Euclid's ghost is stalking the English countryside by night, leaving his distinctive mark wherever he happens to alight.

Hawkins learnt later that the editor had cut out the reference to Euclid's ghost, which was originally in the first paragraph. Somehow, the writer got it reinstated at the end of the article. 'Euclid's ghost' clearly implies more than two hoaxers called Doug and Dave.

In September 1995, another magazine, the *Mathematics Teacher*, ran an article on Hawkins called 'Geometry in English Wheat Fields'. This also accepted that the four theorems were not simply being 'read into' the crop circles. And, like *Science News*, it took it for granted that the circle makers were hoaxers. It challenged its 70,000 readers to work out the fifth theorem from which the other four were derived (none succeeded), adding that, so far, the circle makers themselves had not shown any knowledge of it.

They were behind the times.

At one point, wondering what patterns would appear next, Hawkins had hoped that it would be four concentric circles, with a triangle whose sides formed chords to three of them – the basic diagram of his fifth theorem. In fact the circle makers went one better.

At Litchfield, Hampshire, on 6 July 1995, a 250-foot circle appeared with *eight* concentric circles, as well as a surround of half-circles made to look like intestines. Hawkins realised that the circle makers were ahead of him. They were pointing out that there was a whole geometry of concentric circles. He felt that it was as if they were sticking out their tongues and saying: 'Get a move on!'

Hawkins contacted the *Mathematics Teacher*, and told them that the circle makers *had* now demonstrated knowledge of his fifth theorem. But the editor said that the article was already in the press, and it was too late to change.

Hawkins's increasing conviction that the circle makers were intelligent was increased by the curious affair of the runic cipher.

In late July 1991, an American named John Beckjord cut out – with the farmer's permission – a message, TALK TO US, in a field near Alton Barnes, Wiltshire. He wrote it on a double row of straight tractor lines. A week later, a circle spotter in an aeroplane saw a curious set of markings at Milk Hill, not far from Beckjord's message, which was also on a double row of straight tractor lines. But the 'letters' made no sense; Beckjord thought the message was in Korean, while someone else suggested Atlantean.

Clearly, the obvious assumption was that this was the work of a hoaxer.

Someone sent Gerald Hawkins a copy. The first thing that struck him was that the whole thing showed a care and precision that argued that someone *meant* something by it. This was also the opinion of a number of trained cryptologists to whom he showed it. And three sets of parallel lines at the beginning, middle and end suggested that they were intended as word-dividers. In which case, the message seemed to consist of two words – the first of six letters, the second of five.

Meanwhile, one of the cryptologists had recognised that the symbols were runes – letters of the ancient Germanic alphabet. But that brought the solution no closer, for in runes the message spelt 'DPPDSD XIVDI', where the 'X' is a non-runic letter looking like a capital 'I'.

Sherlock Holmes had been confronted with a similar problem in a story called 'The Dancing Men', in which the newly married wife of a Norfolk squire is driven to despair by a series of strange notes containing matchstick men in various positions. They are sent by a former lover who is determined to get her back.

Holmes recognises that the dancing men stand for letters of the alphabet, and, since the most frequently used letter is 'e', is quickly able to identify the 'e'. He also reasons that, when the figures hold a small flag, this symbolises the end of a word. A chain of similar reasoning gradually breaks the code – although not before the husband has been murdered and the lady attempted suicide.

In the Milk Hill message, the first word contains the same letter – a kind of square-looking 'U' – at the beginning, middle and end. And the opening letter is followed by two identical letters looking like square 'C's.

We use double consonants – BB, CC, DD, FF – far more than double vowels. So the chances are that the first letter is a vowel, followed by a double consonant, followed by the same vowel, followed by an unknown consonant, followed by the same vowel again. It could, for example, be 'effete'. And the same vowel occurs as the penultimate letter of the second word.

Julia Hawkins, an anthropologist, had Sylvester Mawson's *Dictionary of Foreign Terms*, a book containing 18,000 common phrases in forty-two languages, from French and Latin to Hindustani and Russian in her library. Hawkins plodded steadily through it until he finally found a word of six letters that fitted. It was the Latin 'OPPONO', meaning 'I oppose'.

If that was correct, the penultimate letter of the last word was 'o'. And since that was followed by an unknown letter, the word ending was probably 'os'. That also gave the second letter, so the message now read 'OPPONO __S__OS'. What would the writer be opposing? Another long search suggested 'astos', meaning 'acts of craft and cunning' – or frauds. So the script could be translated as 'I am against frauds' or 'I am against hoaxes' – a sentiment that might well be felt by a genuine circle maker.

But, if the circle makers were using a runic alphabet, why did they change its letters? The answer may be that they didn't. For example, the runic 'P' *is* a square C, as in 'OPPONO'. And, in a slightly different version of the runic alphabet used by the Knights Templars, 'O' is identical with the 'O' used here, except that it is upside down. Runes were not standardised, like our modern alphabet; the circle makers may have been using another version of the runic alphabet.

Hawkins's solution was published in the magazine *The Cereologist* (no. 3). The magazine also offered a prize of £100 for a more plausible rendering; many tried, but no one succeeded.

Even those who feel that Hawkins was wasting his time will acknowledge that his approach was impeccably scientific. Given his initial assumption that the script was not a meaningless jumble of symbols, the rest follows – although it is just possible that some other solution might be found in Korean or Armenian or Icelandic.

What may bother other readers is the assumption that the script *was* meaningful. If it was a hoaxer, perhaps responding to Beckjord's TALK TO US, then he would be much more likely to write random nonsense. But if it was not a hoaxer, then we are asked to believe that some extraterrestrial intelligence was writing in Latin to express its annoyance with hoaxers like Doug and Dave. Surely that is too far-fetched to make sense?

But then, the same argument applies to crop circles in general. Is it not more likely that they were simply patterns made for fun?

Against this objection, two facts stand out clearly. One is that, for whatever reason, Lord Zuckerman decided to make a close study of the circles, and ended by being more than half convinced that they were not the work of hoaxers or whirlwinds. The second is that Gerald Hawkins concluded that the circles showed signs of more care and intelligence than would be expected of hoaxers. If two scientists, both pre-eminent in their own field, decide that the circles are worth serious attention, then are most of us justified in dismissing them as unimportant?

For me, an equally interesting question is: *why* did Zuckerman and Hawkins take the risk of having their names associated with the 'lunatic fringe' by displaying an interest in crop circles? There can be only one answer: that both were carried away by a powerful first impression that this was no hoax – that *something or someone* was trying to communicate.

And, although Hawkins decided to hold back on publishing his investigation in 1993, after Linda Howe had published the first four theorems in her *Glimpses of Other Realities*, his communications with me up to the end of 1997 make it clear that he remains as actively interested as ever.

In due course, his fifth theorem became available on request from the National Council of Teachers of Mathematics. But the *Mathematics Teacher* decided against publishing it for the time being, perhaps feeling that mathematics in a cornfield was getting beyond the bounds of scientific propriety.

If so, they were not far wrong. Looking back over the history of crop circles since 1980, it looked as if the circle makers were engaged in a kind of argument with those who did not believe they were real. First the circles were blamed on midsummer whirlwinds, but, as the circle makers began making several at the same time, this explanation became more and more unsatisfactory. As multiple whirlwinds – and other such absurdities – were postulated, they began adding lines, which could hardly be formed by whirlwinds. When Hawkins recognised their geometry, and their diatonic ratios, they began making them increasingly complex, with triangles, squares and hexagons, and finally targets.

But a change in direction had been apparent since a design that had appeared at Alton Barnes in July 1990, with more than half a dozen circles joined by lines, and with objects like keys or runes sticking out of the side (*see plate no.2*). The same night, its twin appeared near the Allington White Horse. (Crop figures had always shown a tendency to appear near ancient sites.) From then on, an increasing number of circles seemed to have a symbolic rather than geometrical significance – some, for example, resembled signs of the zodiac.

If hoaxers were responsible, then we might have assumed that their passion for practical jokes would diminish after Doug and Dave confessed. In fact, their number has remained undiminished – in 1996, according to Bob Rickard, it actually increased. Perhaps hoaxers have turned it into a sport, like bunjy jumping. On the other hand, perhaps the circle makers have decided to go on trying to communicate until they are understood.

I came upon Hawkins and his theory by a fortunate accident. After my lecture at the Fortfest in Washington in 1995, I strolled to the back of the hall, and met the conference organiser, Phyllis Benjamin. The man standing with her looked vaguely familiar. She asked me, 'Do you know Gerald Hawkins?'

In fact, we had met at some academic conference years before. We exchanged greetings, and I mentioned that I had recently reread his *Beyond Stonehenge* in the course of writing a book on the Sphinx and ancient civilisations; then the next lecture started, and we had to curtail the conversation.

After John Mack's *Abduction* had aroused my interest in the abduction phenomenon, I began adding to my out-of-date collection of books on UFOs, which I had picked up *en masse* in a second-hand shop in Plymouth in the mid-1960s – such works as *The Case for the UFO* by M.K. Jessup and the books of George Adamski. Seeking out the latest books on the phenomenon, I came upon *Close Encounters of the Fourth Kind* by C.D.B. (Courty) Bryan. It was an account of a five-day conference on UFO abductions held at the Massachusetts Institute of Technology in June 1992. MIT is, of course, one of the most prestigious institutions of scientific learning in the USA, and I was surprised that it should be willing to play host to a subject which, only a few years before, had been regarded by scientists with contempt and derision.

Bryan, an American journalist, went to the conference in a mood of total scepticism. His large book makes it clear that he ended by recognising that open-mindedness is a better attitude.

One of the people he met at the conference was Linda Moulton Howe, author of *An Alien Harvest*, one of the first to conduct extensive investigations of cattle mutilations, and their possible connection with UFOs. It was Linda Howe who told him about crop circles – how there had been around 2,000 in the 1980s, from all over the world. She mentioned the conclusions of Dr Levengood, who stated that the affected corn would have had to be subjected to the kind of heat found in a microwave oven. She then went on to discuss the ideas of Gerald Hawkins at some length.

Here, I felt, was something that looked a little more solid than 'contact' stories like those described in *Uri* and *Prelude to the Landing on Planet Earth*. I lost no time in ringing Phyllis Benjamin to get Gerald Hawkins's address and phone number. Soon after that I was speaking to him on the phone.

He is an easy man to talk to, generous with his time and ideas. He began by advising me to purchase the *Harvard Dictionary of Music* to pick up the necessary technical background. (Although I have always been an avid listener – and collector of gramophone records – I have never learnt to read music.) And, not long after this, a fat envelope arrived, containing articles about his investigations, accounts of the five theorems, and even a copy of Zuckerman's 'Creations of the Dark' review.

By this time, I had also laid my hands on the most important of his later books, *Mind Steps to the Cosmos* (1983). The premise of that book is that mankind periodically goes through what Hawkins calls a 'cosmic mindstep', a new, revolutionary change in man's perspective on the universe.

Hawkins is talking about 'mindsteps' in astronomy, but they could apply just as well to the whole field of human evolution.

To begin with, says Hawkins, man was little more than an animal, stuck firmly on earth. Then he began to take notice of the heavens, and to invent myths in which the heavenly bodies are gods – he demonstrates that the Babylonian *Epic of Gilgamesh* is about gods who are also the sun, moon and planets. This was Mindstep 1. Then came the Greeks, who studied the heavens, and tried to explain the movements of the heavenly bodies – Mindstep 2. But, since Ptolemy placed the earth firmly at the centre of the universe, his scheme was impossibly complicated. It was not until Copernicus placed the sun at the centre of the solar system that the next great mindstep took place. The invention of printing also brought about a 'knowledge explosion'.

The next step was the age of space, when man began looking to other galaxies, and finally began to grasp the size of the universe. This was Mindstep 4.

And the next mindstep? Could it be some totally new technology, enabling us to explore the universe? Or perhaps contact with extra-terrestrial civilisations?

And now, suddenly, I began to see why, unlike most of his fellow scientists, Hawkins was willing to admit the possibility that the crop circles might be some form of intelligent communication. *Mindsteps to the Cosmos* is a book about a vision – a clear recognition of how far man has come in a few thousand years. But, as man looks outward to a universe of black holes and cosmic gushers, the question of meaning becomes more insistent. Is man alone in the universe? Or is he a part of some vast and intelligible pattern of life? Should our knowledge of the size of the universe make us feel more lonely and frightened? Or should it make us feel that, in some strange sense, we 'belong', that we are a part of the universe, as our individual cells are a part of our bodies?

A few decades ago, a scientist who looked for 'meaning' in the universe would have been regarded by his colleagues as downright dishonest. The universe is self-evidently made of matter, and it operates according to material laws. Man is merely a product of these material laws, and has no more 'meaning' than the wind and the rain. Man's notion that he is a priveleged species is a delusion. He is a product of mere chance.

But there were a few scientists who questioned these views – on purely scientific grounds. Around the turn of the century, a Harvard biochemist, Lawrence J. Henderson, noted that life could not exist without certain unique and quirky properties of water, such as surface tension and the tendency to expand when frozen. Similarly, the astronomer Fred Hoyle has argued that the universe seems oddly suited to the existence of life: alter just one or two of the conditions very slightly – like the way carbon is converted into oxygen by collision with a helium atom – and life would be impossible. It is, he says, as if some 'superintendent' has 'monkeyed with the physics' to make life possible.

In the early 1970s, the astronomer Brandon Carter, of the Paris Observatory, also noted these 'coincidences' that made life possible. For example, if the relative strength of the nuclear force and the electromagnetic force were different, carbon could not exist, and carbon is the basis of life. Noting the high number of such 'extraordinary coincidences', Brandon Carter suggested that the universe *had* to create observers (i.e. us) at some stage. This became known as the 'strong anthropic principle' – the notion that intelligent life had to come into existence.

In their book *The Anthropic Cosmological Principle* (1986), John D. Barrow and Frank J. Tipler – an astronomer and a physicist – point out that, so far, life seems to have had very little effect on this vast material universe, and that, if it died out at this stage, it would be with a whimper rather than a bang. So why did the universe bring it into existence in the first place?

This may sound like the familiar complaint of poets and philosophers: why does God permit tragedy etc.? But that is to miss its point. For the question is not based on the assumption of a benevolent god, but upon such matters as 'extraordinary coincidences' in physics, and the 'Large Numbers Hypothesis' of the cosmologist Paul Dirac.

Barrow and Tipler ask: if life *had* to come into existence, does not this at least suggest that it must eventually go on to colonise the whole universe? The question sounds as if it contains some element of religious optimism, so again it must be emphasised that it is strictly logical and scientific. If the laws of nature brought life into existence – laws that sometimes look as if some superintendent has been monkeying with the physics – is it not conceivable that the same laws dictate that life will never die out?

Of course, it is also possible that the laws contain some principle that dictates that life *must* die out – for example, when the universe reaches the limits of its expansion, and begins to contract. Yet it is hard to see that this makes sense. Think of an ordinary explosion – a bomb, for example, or a volcano. It creates only chaos. But, when the universe came into existence fifteen billion years ago – as most cosmologists think it did – with a big bang, it produced huge stars, whose immense inner pressure produced the heavy elements, which in turn produced life. Now life may be an accidental by-product, like fungus on a wall, but it is also intelligent and adaptive and enduring. So what Barrow and Tipler call 'the Final Anthropic Principle' could be correct after all.

But perhaps this discussion is taking us too far away from the simple facts with which we began – such as crop circles, abductions and entities that claim to have come from the stars. Let us take a deep breath and return to the facts.

3 How to Get People Confused

N THE THIRD week of November 1996, I was in Los Angeles, filming part of a television documentary at the famous tar pit of La Brea – which can be found, still bubbling ominously below a watery surface, in the grounds of the George C. Page Museum. Thousands of animals died as they wandered incautiously into the oily swamp to drink the water, including giant sloths, mammoths, mastodons and sabre-toothed tigers. But, as far as the television programme was concerned, I was less interested in these animals who had died over tens of thousands of years than in the evidence of a sudden mass extinction around 11,000 BC. The evidence seemed to show that more than a dozen species had been simply wiped out over a period of a mere twenty-five years. That suggested some sudden catastrophe, such as the impact of a giant meteor, or some convulsion of the Earth's crust that caused earthquakes and volcanic eruptions.

Now my own suspicion was that a professor of anthropology named Charles H. Hapgood had correctly diagnosed the cause of the extinction. He had first suggested the theory in a book called *Earth's Shifting Crust*, in 1959. What Hapgood suggested was that the crust of the Earth was a thin skin, which rested on a liquid mantle rather like the skin that forms on boiled milk or gravy. The build-up of ice can induce a sudden wobble that causes the crust to slip on the mantle; the result is that whole continents move. Lands that were subtropical, like Siberia, move into colder regions, while India and Africa, once buried under ice sheets, slide towards the equator. Einstein was so impressed by the theory that he wrote an introduction to Hapgood's book.

Now it has been known for a long time that movements of the crust cause continents to rearrange themselves – England was on the equator during the Devonian period, about 400 million years ago. But it has always been supposed that such movements take millions of years.

Hapgood thought it could happen quite suddenly – his own view was there had been an enormous slippage of the earth's crust some time since 15,000 BC, before which Antarctica had been 2,500 miles further north, and had a temperate climate.

While Hapgood was writing *Earth's Shifting Crust*, he learnt of a discovery that seemed to throw an interesting new light on it. In 1956, the US Hydrographic Office became aware that it possessed a strange map that had been presented by a Turkish naval officer. This was a medieval map which had belonged to a Turkish admiral (and pirate) called Piri Re'is, who had been beheaded in 1554, and it appeared to show the east coast of South America, and the coast of Antarctica – which was not officially discovered until 1818. Moreover, it appeared to show certain bays on the coast of Queen Maud Land that were now no longer visible, since they were completely covered with ice. Yet a 1949 survey team, which had taken soundings through the ice, had established that they were precisely where the map showed them to be. What made it so baffling was that, as far as anyone knew, Antarctica had been covered with ice for thousands of years – possibly since about 5000 BC.

Of course, it was not Piri Re'is who had made the original map – he had merely had it copied. His map was of a kind widely in use among medieval sailors, and known as a portolan (meaning 'from port to port'). Hapgood began to study other portolans – the Library of Congress proved to have hundreds – and was astonished to find that they were far more accurate than the maps being made by well-known mapmakers working in the same period. One map in particular intrigued him; it was made by one Oronteus Finaeus, and showed the whole South Pole, as if photographed from the air, and again, the coastal region was shown free of ice.

Obviously, they were based on far more ancient maps. But that in itself was baffling. Historians generally agree that writing was invented by the Sumerians about 3500 BC. We can assume that maps did not exist before that time, since a map is of very little use without writing on it. So how could there have been maps that showed Antarctica as it was at least a thousand years earlier than the Sumerians, and possibly several thousand?

After years of study of portolans (aided by his students), Hapgood finally concluded that there existed a worldwide maritime civilisation around 7000 BC. He stated this extraordinary conclusion in a book entitled *Maps of the Ancient Sea Kings*, which was published in 1966.

It was Hapgood's misfortune that, six years before the publication of *Maps of the Ancient Sea Kings*, a book called *The Morning of the Magicians* had appeared in Paris, and quickly became a world bestseller. Its authors, Louis Pauwels and Jacques Bergier, discuss the Piri Re'is map and other portolans, and ask, 'Had they been traced from observations made on board a flying machine or some space vessel of some kind?' And in 1968, two years after Hapgood's book, the Swiss writer Erich von Däniken went even further in *Chariots of the Gods?*, stating that Hapgood had claimed that the portolans had been based on photographs taken from the air by 'visitors from space'.

Von Däniken's idea that the earth had been visited in the remote past by 'ancient astronauts' was by no means implausible; in fact, it had been suggested in 1962 by the Russian astronomer Josef Shklovskii in a book called *Universe, Life, Mind*, published in America in 1966 under the title *Intelligent Life in the Universe*, in collaboration with Carl Sagan. The problem was that von Däniken's book was full of wild and absurd inaccuracies, such as multiplying the weight of the Great Pyramid by five, and suggesting that the Nazca lines, scratched on the surface of the Peruvian desert, might have been intended as an airport for spacecraft. It was inevitable that Hapgood should be condemned through 'guilt by association'.

Yet Hapgood's book has never been truly discredited – merely ignored. Not only had the 1949 Antarctic soundings revealed that the ice-covered bays shown by Piri Re'is actually existed, but a 1958 survey had shown that the Philip Buache map of 1737, which represented Antarctica divided into two islands, was also correct. The Dulcert Portolano of 1339 showed accurate knowledge of the geography between Galway and the Don basin in Russia. Another portolan showed the Aegean with numerous islands that do not now exist. And, since the islands were probably drowned as melting ice caused the sea level to rise, it sounds as if the map was made before the end of the last ice age. Altogether, there is strong evidence that civilisation appeared on earth thousands of years before it arose in the Middle East, and that Hapgood was probably not far out when he talked of a worldwide seagoing civilisation around 7000 BC. To study *Maps of the Ancient Sea Kings* is to be impressed by the sheer weight of corroborative evidence.

So, although most of von Däniken's evidence about visitors from space cannot be taken seriously, the portolans certainly raise the possibility that Earth might have been visited by ancient astronauts in the remote past. Shklovskii and Sagan suggest:

> Some 25 million years ago, a Galactic survey ship on a routine visit to [Earth] may have noted an interesting and promising evolutionary development: Proconsul. The information would have filtered at the speed of light slowly through the galaxy, and a notation would have been made in some central information repository . . . If the emergence of intelligent life on a planet is of general scientific interest to the Galactic civilisations, it is reasonable that with the emergence of Proconsul, the rate of sampling of our planet should have increased, perhaps to about once every ten thousand years . . . But if the interval between sampling is only several thousand years, there is a possibility that contact with an extraterrestrial civilisation has occurred within historical times.

They go on to point out that, when primitive people record some important historical event in the form of a myth, the oral tradition often preserves the essence of the event with remarkable fidelity, even when it is embellished with certain mythological details. Shklovskii cites the first encounter between the Tlingit Indians of North America and the French expedition of La Perouse, in which the sailing ships are remembered as great black birds with white wings.

Such 'proofs' can, of course, be deceptive. The archaeologist Henry Lhote suggested that a fresco found in cliffs overlooking the Sahara at Tassili might be a man in a spacesuit, and labelled it 'the Martian god'. But a little research revealed that the Martian god was simply a human being dressed in a ritual mask. (Von Däniken would nevertheless use it as evidence for his ancient astronauts.)

But there is a myth that seems to the authors altogether more likely to represent a contact between earth and aliens from space. ' . . . the legend,' they say, 'suggests that contact occurred between human beings and a non-human civilisation of immense powers on the shores of the Persian Gulf, perhaps near the ancient Sumerian city of Eridu, in the fourth millennium BC or earlier.'

This legend can be traced to Berosus, a priest of the god Bel-Marduk in the city of Babylon at the time of Alexander the Great. Berosus would have had access to cuneiform and pictographic records (on cylinders and temple walls) dating back thousands of years before his time.

In one of his fragments, Alexander Polyhistor describes how there appeared from the Persian Gulf 'an animal who was endowed with reason, who was called Oannes'. This creature had a fish's tail, but also had feet like a man, and spoke with a human voice. It taught men letters and science, and every kind of art, as well as how to build houses and temples. 'In short he instructed them in everything which could tend to soften manners and humanise mankind.' Oannes used to spend his nights in the sea, for he was amphibious. And after him came more creatures like him.

Another chronicler, Abydenus – a disciple of Aristotle – speaks of Sumerian kings, and mentions 'another semi-demon, very like to Oannes, who came up a second time from the sea'. He also mentions 'four double-shaped personages' – by which he presumably means half-man and half-fish – who 'came out of the sea to land'.

Finally, Apollodorus of Athens mentions that in the time of King Ammenon the Chaldean there 'appeared the Musarus Oannes, the Annedotus, from the Persian Gulf', and later 'a fourth Annedotus, having . . . the shape of a fish blended with that of a man'. And in the reign of King Euedoreschus there appeared yet another fish-man named Odacon.

Apollodorus speaks about Oannes the Annedotus as if it is a title rather than a proper name. I spent half an hour looking in encyclopedias, trying to find the meaning of 'annedotus' and also 'musarus', and finally succeeded in finding 'musarus' in Liddell and Scott's Greek lexicon – it means 'abominable'. But I could not find 'annedotus'. Then, recalling that Robert Temple had mentioned the fish gods in *The Sirius Mystery*, I looked in that work, and found that I could have saved myself so much effort – Temple had done the work for me. 'Annedotus' means 'the repulsive one'. It was amazing: the Musarus Oannes the Annedotus means 'the abomination Oannes the repulsive'.

Temple feels – and I am inclined to agree with him – that this is an indication that we are dealing with truth rather than invention. You would expect a mythical account to glorify the godlike teachers of civilisation, not describe them as frankly disgusting. But we have only to conjure up an image of a fishlike being with slippery scales, huge white eyes and a large mouth to understand why frankness compelled men to admit that they found them repulsive. They may not even have felt the description to be pejorative – merely factually accurate, as in the case of Ivan the Terrible or Akbar the Damned.

Now Temple's *Sirius Mystery* happens to be by far the most scholarly and convincing book on the possibility of 'ancient astronauts'. Temple's interest was aroused when he stumbled on an article about an African tribe called the Dogon, who live in northern Mali, and learnt that the Dogon believe that fish gods called the Nommo came from Sirius, and brought civilisation to earth some three thousand years ago.

The dog star Sirius (so called because it is in the constellation Canis) is 8.7 light years away. And the Dogon tradition declares that it has an invisible companion, which they call *po tolo* (meaning 'star grain' – and since the grain they refer to is their staple diet, digitaria, it can be translated 'digitaria star'), and which is made of a matter far heavier than any on Earth. They declare that this invisible star moves in an elliptical orbit, and takes fifty years to do so.

In fact, Sirius *does* have an invisible companion, called by astronomers Sirius B; it is a 'white dwarf' – that is, it is made of atoms that have collapsed in on themselves, so that a piece the size of a pea could weigh half a ton. It moves in an elliptical orbit, and takes fifty years to do so. The Dogon also showed a remarkable knowledge of astronomy. They said that the moon was 'dry and dead', and they drew Saturn with a ring around it – which is not visible to the naked eye. They knew about the moons of Jupiter, and that the planets revolve around the sun. *Encyclopaedia Britannica* says that the metaphysical system of the Dogon is 'far more abstract than that of other African tribes'.

It was inevitable that, when western scholars heard about the astronomical knowledge of the Dogon, they should try to prove that it was probably picked up from European travellers.

Western astronomers had known about Sirius B since 1862, so it *was* possible that the Dogon had learnt about it from a tourist or missionary. But it was not until 1928 that Sir Arthur Eddington postulated the theory of white dwarfs. And the two anthropologists who studied the Dogon – Marcel Griaule and Germaine Dieterlen – arrived in Mali in 1931. It seemed unlikely that another traveller had visited the Dogon in the intervening three years and brought them up to date on the latest cosmological theories.

There is an even better reason for dismissing the tourist theory (which, typically, was later espoused by Carl Sagan). Griaule had been studying Dogon mythology and religion for sixteen years before the priests decided that his dedication deserved to be rewarded by initiation into their deepest secrets. One of their wisest men was appointed to be his tutor, and to teach him the four degrees of religious knowledge. It went on for years, and, when the teacher died, another was appointed. Griaule realised, to his astonishment, that the Dogon religion is as rich and complex as, say, the Christian theology enshrined in Aquinas's *Summa Theologica*. There can be no question of the fish gods being introduced during the past century as a result of an encounter with an astronomically inclined missionary: they form the foundation stone of a religious mythology that has taken thousands of years to formulate.

If we add that the Sumerian language has nothing in common with any other Semitic or Indo-European language, and that Sumerian specialists are puzzled that the civilisation seems to have appeared out of nowhere, we can see that there is at least a strong prima facie case for Shklovskii's notion that the fish-god myth might have been a record of the contact with an extraterrestrial civilisation. And if we also take into account the Dogon and their Nommo myth – of which Shklovskii and Sagan were unaware at the time – the argument begins to look very plausible indeed.

This was to strike me even more strongly in March 1997, when the TV documentary took me to the ruined city of Tiahuanaco, near Lake Titicaca, in the Andes, and I wandered around that vast courtyard called the Kalasasiya, the sacred place of the remote ancestors of the Incas. Some time in the 1890s, Professor Arthur Posnansky, of La Paz, who spent his life studying Tiahuanaco, calculated from the astronomical alignment of the temple (most ancient temples are aligned on the heavens) that it was built about 15,000 BC, a time when our ancestors were supposed to be living in caves. His colleagues were outraged – their own estimate was about 500 AD – but in the 1920s a German astronomical team confirmed Posnansky's estimate, which was based on the fact that there are two observation points on the Kalasasiya that mark the winter and summer solstices, when the sun is directly over the Tropic of Cancer or Capricorn. Because the earth rolls slightly as it travels around the sun, the position of the tropics changes by as much as two and a half degrees over 41,000 years. The Germans confirmed Posnansky's calculation – that the position of the tropics built into the temple indicated 15,000 BC.

Of course, it is easy to make some slight mismeasurement when dealing with half a degree or so, and the Germans finally suggested that the date indicated could be more like 9,000 BC. That still caused outrage, and, by taking other variants into account, the German team suggested that the date might be further reduced to 4,500 BC. Posnansky decided to accept that estimate – probably muttering under his breath, like Galileo, 'But it moves all the same.'

Four thousand five hundred BC is close to the date of the rise of

Sumerian civilisation, and I was reminded of that fact when, on my second trip to Tiahuanaco, I summoned the energy to walk to a remote corner of the courtyard. (Tiahuanaco is two and a half miles above sea level, and the thin air produces a sensation like carrying two heavy suitcases.) I had seen there another statue, not unlike the 'Great Idol' that stands in the centre of the courtyard, looking down on a sunken temple. Even my producer, Roel Oostra, had not felt it worth his while to walk that far. But we both agreed that the effort was worth it. The statue is known as 'the Friar' (El Fraile) – heaven knows why, because it looks nothing like a friar. It is actually a fish god, with huge eyes and scaly lower body, and is at least as impressive as the Great Idol which stands a hundred yards away, and which also seems to have a fish-scale design on its lower half. And, looking at this strange and powerful piece of sculpture, I found myself thinking of the fish god Oannes, who is represented on Babylonian and Assyrian cylinder seals. Could it really be pure chance that the fish god is found on opposite sides of the world?

I felt the same when I looked at the giant Olmec heads in the park of La Venta, in Villahermosa, southern Mexico (*see plate no. 13*). There can be no possible doubt that these are African negroes – and that they represented kings who ruled about 1500 BC in Central America. There could hardly be a stronger proof for Hapgood's worldwide maritime civilisation.

Now we know that, at some point in prehistory, the whole plateau containing Tiahuanaco and Lake Titicaca was at sea level; we know this because Titicaca is a saltwater lake, and has many sea creatures in it. At some remote epoch, a great convulsion of the Earth thrust it more than two miles in the air. But we also know that Tiahuanaco was once a port on Lake Titicaca – which is now a dozen miles away. It may be that Lake Titicaca has simply shrunk over the years. But Tiahuanaco itself suggests another reason. What used to be its port area, the Puma Punku (Puma Gate), is covered with massive blocks of stone, once part of a dock, then tossed around like ninepins by some convulsion of the Earth. The so-called 'Great Gate of Tiahuanaco' or Gateway of the Sun, a kind of miniature Arc de Triomphe which stands in the opposite corner of the courtyard from the fish god, was never finished, and has a crack running from one of its corners to the gateway in the middle (*see plate no.14*). It looks as if this might also have been damaged in some cataclysm.

Could it have been the same cataclysm as caused such havoc in the area of La Brea around 11,000 BC?

Let me admit that I feel slightly inhibited about posing such questions. It is one of von Däniken's most irritating habits: 'Why are the oldest libraries in the world secret libraries? What are people afraid of?' etc. I am fully aware that modern archaeology dates Tiahuanaco from around 500 BC to AD 700, and that these are the dates you will find on the chart in the Tiahuanaco museum. But the truth is that nearly all such dates are educated guesswork. And since modern archaeologists are determined to sound factual and scientific – in reaction against their nineteenth-century forebears, who were unashamedly romantic – they prefer to err on the side of conservatism, and make their dates as recent as possible. In the 1960s, Stonehenge was believed to date from 2500 BC; now the date has been pushed back to 3100. Civilisation in the Middle East was supposed to have started around 5000 BC; now we know there were cities 3,000 years earlier. Conventional archaeology dates the Sphinx around 2500 BC, at the time of the Great Pyramid, in spite of powerful evidence (which I discussed in *From Atlantis to the Sphinx*) that it must be thousands of years older. And we have seen that, in the 1920s, Tiahuanaco was believed to date from about AD 500; now it is accepted by the most conservative archaeologists to be a thousand years earlier. So I do not feel too concerned about suspecting that Posnansky may have been roughly correct about the age of Tiahuanaco and modern archaeologists wrong.

This feeling was strengthened when I spent a morning in the Library of Congress, looking at some of the portolans that had inspired Hapgood. My companion was Rand Flemath, who, together with his wife Rose, wrote a book called *When the Sky Fell* (1996). The Flemaths had studied myths of many tribes of American Indians, and found again and again tales of a sudden violent catastrophe that had darkened the sun, and caused massive earthquakes and floods. And it was Rand who, as we looked at a map of the American continent and talked about the cataclysm of La Brea, remarked casually that Hapgood believed that the great crust movement that had caused the catastrophe had run from north to south through the American continent, and spared most of the rest of the world. Such a movement would be an obvious candidate for the cataclysm that cracked the Gate of the Sun, and tilted Lake Titicaca so that it retreated a dozen miles from Tiahuanaco.

And so, as I talked to John Harris, the director of the George C. Page Museum, about the catastrophe of 11,000 BC, my thoughts were never far from Hapgood. Admittedly, 11,000 BC was 4,000 years earlier than the worldwide maritime civilisation suggested by Hapgood on the basis of the portolans. Yet the fish god of the Kalasasiya suggested a connection with Oannes, and with Shklovskii and Sagan's theory of extraterrestrial contact, and with Robert Temple's impressive evidence about the Dogon and their fish gods from Sirius. I had a feeling that it was all beginning to come together.

In fact, only that morning, I had found a number of books that would provide new pieces of the jigsaw puzzle.

When I woke up in my Los Angeles motel, I knew that I had a few hours to spare before I was due at the La Brea museum. I might have stayed in bed and tried to get over my jet lag, but that would have seemed a waste of time. I asked Roel, my producer, what he intended to do, and he said that he had to drive over to Santa Monica to interview someone about a future programme.

That seemed a good idea. I had known Santa Monica – on the northern outskirts of Los Angeles – since the 1960s, when I was lecturing in Long Beach, and came there to see Christopher Isherwood and Henry Miller. More recently, in the late 1980s, I had spent some time there with my friend John Wright, who runs a bookshop on Santa Monica Boulevard – I had given a number of lectures there.

It was seven or eight years since I had last seen John, and I no longer remembered clearly where the bookshop was situated. But I got Roel to drop me off at the end of Santa Monica Boulevard, and strolled south, suffering from the heat of a dazzling November morning. After a few blocks, it dawned on me that I had been rash to assume I could still find the shop – or even that it was still there.

Finally, I found a bookshop – though clearly not the right one. But there were copies of books on Gurdjieff in the window, and on religious mysticism, so I pushed on the door handle. The door was locked; I looked at my watch; it was a few minutes after ten o'clock. I was about to turn away when there was a shout of 'My God, Colin!', and John Wright appeared at the door.

A few minutes later I was seated at the counter, drinking coffee. It seemed that John had relocated further along the boulevard. It was lucky for me that he had happened to look out of the window at that moment.

I picked up a new book by Budd Hopkins called *Witnessed*, and told John that I would like to take it with me. I had his earlier books *Missing Time* and *Intruders*.

'Are you interested in UFOs?'

I explained that I had been commissioned to write a book on extraterrestrial life, and that I suspected it was going to turn into a book about UFOs.

'We've got a big section on UFOs. You may remember, it's a subject we specialise in.'

I didn't, because I hadn't been particularly interested in UFOs last time I had seen John. But now, as I began to look through a whole corner of the room devoted to them, my heart sank at the sheer number of books I had never heard of.

Some of them looked so weird they made you doubt the sanity of the authors – huge self-published volumes, some of them several inches thick, devoted to such propositions as that the aliens came from inside the earth, or that they had gigantic underground bases in locations like South Dakota, and that these had been built with the connivance of the US government. There were dozens of volumes and even magazines about 'conspiracy theories'. But there were also dozens of volumes with titles like *UFO Report, 1991*; *Close Encounters of the Fourth Kind*; *UFOs: African Encounters*; and *UFO Chronicles of the Soviet Union*, the last by my friend Jacques Vallee. It was obvious that the subject had so many remote byways that I could spend a lifetime exploring them.

As if to increase my depression, John's assistant Ramon told me that a local New Age bookstore, with even more books on UFOs, was closing, and that all books were being sold at 60 per cent discount. With a sense of plunging even further out of my depth, I agreed to let him take me there. The owner, whose lease was running out, cheered me by telling me that most of the UFO books had already gone, but that the few remaining could be found on the shelf between yoga and vegetarian cooking. In fact, there must have been a hundred or so titles. And Ramon, who was highly knowledgable in the field, kept holding out volumes to me and saying, 'That's very important', or 'That's a real classic'. So, having established that the books could be airmailed back to England, and that I could pay by credit card, I ended by buying a couple of dozen.

Back in John Wright's bookshop, Ramon was equally helpful about books I ought to read, and I ended with a pile of fifty or so on the counter. My credit-card bill for that morning was approaching a thousand dollars. But, as I took a taxi back to my motel, I felt that at least I had made a start on the research for my book.

On the plane back to Heathrow, I read a remarkable book called *The Holographic Universe* by Michael Talbot. Its early chapters are about the brain and the theory of holograms, but towards the end Talbot devotes a few pages to the UFO phenomenon, and they left me more confused than ever.

Summarising the views of a number of writers, like Jacques Vallee, Michael Grosso and Kenneth Ring, he seems to conclude that UFOs are largely a subjective and psychological phenomenon. He points out that in that classic early abduction case of Barney and Betty Hill, the commander of the UFO was dressed in a Nazi uniform, which sounds as if the event was closer to a dream or hallucination. He goes on:

> Other UFO encounters are even more surreal or dreamlike in character, and in the literature, one can find cases in which the UFO entities sing absurd songs or throw strange objects (such as potatoes) at witnesses; cases that start out as straightforward abductions aboard spacecraft but end up as hallucinogenic journeys through a series of Dantesque realities; and cases in which humanoid aliens shapeshift into birds, giant insects, and other phantasmagoric creatures.

But at least Talbot's book provided me with a possible explanation of one thing that had bothered me since I read Hopkins's *Missing Time*: why the aliens seem so inefficient at blotting out human memory. As noted earlier, abductees are often unaware that anything has taken place, but cannot understand why several hours out of their lives have gone missing. Then a few vague memories begin to return, and they often undergo hypnosis – or the memories return spontaneously – and recall that they have been kidnapped, subjected to medical examination, then returned to their cars or bedrooms.

Talbot begins *The Holographic Universe* by describing Karl Lashley's attempt to locate the source of memory in the brain by training rats to perform certain tasks, and then surgically removing various parts of their brains, in an attempt to eradicate the memory. But, no matter how much of the brain he cut away, he was unable to destroy the memory.

To explain this baffling result, his student Karl Pribram came up with a fascinating and plausible explanation: that the memories are stored in the brain like a hologram.

Everyone knows that a hologram is a three-dimensional figure that looks quite solid, but which turns out to be a mere projection of light, like an image on a cinema screen. This is done by passing two beams of laser light (light in which all the waves march in step, like a platoon of soldiers) through a photographic plate creating a kind of ripple pattern.

The ripple pattern is made when two beams of laser light interfere with each other. It is rather like throwing a stone into a still pond, and watching the ripples spread outward, then throwing in another stone, and watching the two lots of ripples interfere.

Imagine now that the two beams interfere with each other on a photographic plate, and one of them has just bounced off some object, like a human face or an apple. The pattern on the plate does not look in the least like a face or an apple – merely like rings of ripples – until a direct laser beam is passed through the plate or bounced off it, making the face or the apple suddenly appear, hanging in space, and indistinguishable from the real thing.

That pattern on the plate is actually the hologram. But it has a strange quality. If you break the plate in half, and shine a beam through it, the result is not half a face, but the whole face, only slightly less distinct. You can even break off a small corner of the plate, and the result will still be the complete face. The only difference is that it will now look far blurrier than the original made from the whole plate. In other words, every part of the plate contains the whole hologram. And if, when we learn something, the result of that learning is somehow photographed in the whole brain, then it would explain why Lashley could not eradicate the rats' memory – to do so he would have had to destroy the whole brain. So long as there was even a small part of the brain left, the rats remembered.

Which would seem to explain why aliens cannot totally eradicate the memory of the abductee – they only seem to be able to block it, rather in the way that a hypnotist can block a memory by suggestion. But, when a hypnotist does this, another hypnotist can unblock it, and hypnotists can apparently do the same with the abductee.

The books arrived a few days after I returned to Cornwall, and were soon cluttering up my bedroom floor. I always get up between 5 and 6 o'clock in the morning, so that I can get a couple of hours' reading before it is time to make breakfast for my wife. I plunged in head first, taking books virtually at random: Hynek's *The UFO Experience*, Linda Howe's *Alien Harvest*, Charles Bowen's *The Humanoids*, Jacques Vallee's *Messengers of Deception*, Hans Holzer's *The Ufonauts*, Michael Craft's *Alien Impact*, Timothy Good's *Beyond Top Secret*,

Arthur Shuttlewood's *The Warminster Mystery*, Whitley Strieber's *Communion*, Kevin Randle's *The UFO Casebook*, Ralph Noyes's *The Crop Circle Phenomenon*, and more than a dozen others.

As I read, I began to find all this research unexpectedly exciting and satisfying. This is because I had started out with memories of the scepticism inspired in me by Andrija Puharich's *Uri*, and Stuart Holroyd's *Prelude to the Landing on Planet Earth*, and I more than half expected to find all this reading an exercise in 'believing six impossible things before breakfast'. But I very soon began to feel exactly as I had when researching the paranormal in 1969: an intuitive conviction that this all made sense, and that it rang true. I found my feelings expressed in a book called *Tapping the Zero-Point Energy* by Moray B. King, a systems engineer who remarks: 'It was in the summer of 1974 that I had the misfortune of reading *Beyond Earth*, a book about UFOs. I picked it up just for fun, to read like science fiction. But what impressed me were the witnesses. Many were credible, such as airline pilots and police, who had everything to lose by reporting what they saw.'

And it was the sheer credibility of witnesses, and their testimony to the ability of UFOs to make hairpin turns at incredible speeds, that led King to wonder about the possibility of antigravity.

Now I found myself reacting in exactly the same way. Whatever else they were, these people were not liars. Their total honesty and normality came over again and again.

And, as with the paranormal, this not only rang true, but it all seemed to fit together. This could not be explained away as hysteria, or some kind of misunderstanding. There might be huge pieces of the jigsaw missing, but you got a feeling that the puzzle made sense; you could see a half of it, and you knew there must be missing pieces that would make up the rest.

Not long after the Los Angeles visit, I discovered a bookseller in Sidmouth who specialised in second-hand flying-saucer books, and picked up such classics as Edward J. Ruppelt's *Report on Unidentified Flying Objects* and Harold Wilkins's *Flying Saucers on the Attack*. I bought these solely for the sake of reference, suspecting that they would now be too out of date to provide any interesting ideas – then quickly realised that this was a naive error. For reading some of these early works not only brought a sharp sense of perspective, but made me clearly aware of basic facts that should be the starting point of any investigation of UFOs.

For example, Ruppelt – official head of Project Blue Book – describes an encounter of May 1952, when a Pan American Airlines DC-4 was flying towards Puerto Rico. Over the Atlantic, about 600 miles off Jacksonville, Florida, the copilot noticed a light ahead, which he took to be the tail-light of another aeroplane. That was odd, since they had just been advised by radio that there were no other planes in the area. He glanced down at the controls, and, when he looked up again, was horrified to see that the light was now directly ahead, and was much larger. As he and the pilot watched, the huge light closed in on a collision course. Then it streaked by the left wing, followed by two smaller balls of fire.

The pilot said later that it was like travelling along a highway at seventy miles an hour when a car from the opposite direction swerves across into your lane, then swerves back so you miss it by inches. 'You know the sort of sick, empty feeling you get inside when it's over? That's just the way we felt.'

Which raises the obvious question: why should the UFO have set out to give them a scare? For it certainly looks as if it changed course for precisely that purpose. What *point* was there in behaving like a juvenile delinquent in a stolen car? There seems to be only one obvious explanation: to get themselves noticed, and to add one more to the hundreds of reports of such encounters that were pouring in to the Air Force.

The same suspicion seems to fit another case described by Ruppelt. Soon after the DC-4 episode mentioned above, Ruppelt was called to Washington, DC, where a crowd of top military brass had witnessed a UFO incident. One of the most senior officials in the CIA was throwing the party at his hilltop home in Virginia, with a panoramic view of the surrounding countryside. While he was engaged in conversation, he noticed a light approaching in the dusk. At first he assumed it was an aeroplane until, as it came close, he realised it was soundless. It began to climb almost vertically, and he drew the attention of other guests to it. It climbed further, levelled out, then went into a vertical dive, before it levelled out again and streaked off to the west.

They began to argue; one thought it was a lighted balloon, another an aeroplane, another a meteor. They made some telephone calls – and, Ruppelt adds, their rank was such that they got swift results. Radar said there had been no aeroplane in the past hour, and the weather station said there were no weather balloons in the air. The station also checked on high-altitude winds, and discovered that none were blowing in the right direction. The light had been in sight too long to be a meteor – and, in any case, meteors do not climb and dive.

After Ruppelt had checked the story, he agreed that they had seen an 'unidentified flying object' and left it at that.

So we have a light that flies until it is almost directly above the garden full of distinguished guests, and then performs some absurd manoeuvres to draw attention to itself, then flies away, having demonstrated to a large number of Pentagon officials that UFOs were more than a hysterical rumour.

Ruppelt tells how they – the Air Force – decided to subscribe to a press-cutting service, just to see how many UFOs were reported in the newspapers. For the first month or so the cuttings came in ordinary-size envelopes, then in large manila envelopes, and finally in shoe boxes. All this was between March and June 1952, and by June they were aware that there was a major 'flap' (which Ruppelt defines as 'a condition . . . characterised by an advanced degree of confusion that has not quite yet reached panic proportions'). Project Blue Book – the official investigation – had only just got started, and it was immediately overwhelmed by hundreds of sightings. There was even a wave of sightings over Washington itself. Many flying-saucer enthusiasts predicted an imminent invasion from space; but nothing happened. It seemed that the flying saucers were merely occupied in an exercise to get themselves noticed.

Half a century later, this still seems to be the case. I did not have to look further than my own doorstep to find an example. My part-time secretary, Pam Smith-Rawnesley, told me that one of the first-year students at the local drama college where she works had seen a UFO a few days before, and I asked her to tape-record him describing what had happened. This is what Matt Punter said in June 1997:

I was travelling from my friend's house in Liskeard, at a quarter past eleven at night, to where I live in Pensilver. After about three miles, I was passing a place called Rosecraddock, and as I drove up the hill, and – basically – four different-coloured bright lights came over the top of my car, so low that I instinctively ducked my head. My first thought was that it might be an aeroplane about to crash on top of me, or just in front of me. So I slammed on my brakes. Then – I had no stereo on, and I realised there was no sound to the thing – that's when I thought: Mmm, it's a bit weird. Then, after stopping, the four lights stopped about ten metres in front of me, and stayed there for a second, and for that second, it really did seem that whatever it was was looking at me, and I was looking at it. Then they shot off in the air – so quickly that I couldn't see them once I looked up. But there were four different-coloured lights, blue, red, yellow and white – there were possibly two white lights – in a shape of a – er – parallelogram.

Pam asks whether he could see metal above the lights – obviously wondering if they were on the underside of a flying saucer. He says: 'No, I could actually see the road through them. All I saw were the four suspended lights in midair.'

After more questions, Matt goes on:

'I got home, and I woke my mum up – I wouldn't usually do that because she works early in the morning – but I woke her up and told her about it, and she calmed me down. She could see I was telling the truth, because I actually had tears in my eyes, my heart was going like nothing on Earth.'

It seems an oddly pointless event: four lights in the shape of a parallelogram swooping down over the car, and halting for a moment in front of him, so that he can see the road (he was driving uphill) through them. He feels as if they are watching him. Then they take off, so fast that when he looks up, they have already gone.

Matt Punter remarks that 'the weird thing was, there was absolutely no traffic on the road'. This seems to be a curious recurring feature in UFO cases – empty roads, empty streets, and so on; it has been labelled 'the Oz Factor', after Dorothy's journey down a yellow brick road apparently used by no one else. In Matt's case, this meant that there was fairly certainly no other witness, no car going in the opposite direction, who might have seen lights rise into the sky.

But the Oz Factor does not always apply. On 4 September 1997, while I was writing this book, my wife went out into the garden at about 11 o'clock at night, to give the dogs a final airing, when she saw an orange globe, about the size of the moon, which moved in the direction of an orange streetlight on the estate below, then turned and went back the way it came. She had time to go indoors and call my son Rowan to come and see it before it vanished behind trees. Yet she was so little struck by it that she did not even bother to tell me for several days, when I happened to mention that a large number of UFOs are orange globes, and she realised that she had probably seen a UFO.

One of the first questions raised by sceptics is that of the credibility of witnesses. As the philosopher David Hume said: is it more likely that a miracle occurred, or that someone is telling lies? But the UFOs seem to have taken care to neutralise this objection by overwhelming us with sheer quantity. And, even without David Hume, I find it impossible to believe that Matt Punter and my wife were not telling the truth. And Ruppelt obviously felt the same about the pilots of the DC-4, and the CIA officials at the garden party – in spite of the fact that every one of them had undoubtedly been drinking.

But it is important to be fair to the sceptics. Those who accept the reality of UFOs tend to be harsh on them – particularly those with some official position. At best, they think that sceptics are stupid or intellectually dishonest, at worst that there is a sinister conspiracy.

This, I feel, is missing a vital point: that the sceptic is often a totally honest person who, for perfectly good, sound reasons, simply cannot see a case for belief. In fact many – like Courty Bryan – admit that they would *like* to be convinced, but find it impossible.

A case in point is an official investigator called Roy Craig, author of *UFOs, An Insider's View of the Official Quest for Evidence*. Typically, it is published by the University of North Texas Press, for it is the kind of book that would not be taken on by a commercial publisher – they know that the public is not willing to pay money for books written by nonbelievers.

Craig was a member of the Condon Committee, hated and derided by all good ufologists. This was set up in 1966, after the termination of Project Blue Book, with the aim of studying all the available evidence for UFOs, and deciding whether the United States government ought to take them seriously. Two years later, their highly sceptical report was denounced as a whitewash, a cover-up, an attempt to let the defence establishment 'off the hook'. *The UFO Encyclopedia*, edited by John Spencer – one of the most balanced and objective writers on the subect – comments, 'There is some doubt as to Dr Condon's impartiality in respect of this (sceptical) conclusion, and in any case it appears clear that the conclusions of this report do not necessarily mirror the actual findings of the investigation.'

Craig's book makes it clear that both these statements are disputable. It also makes it clear that the truth is far more fascinating, and far more subtle, than most believers in UFOs are willing to concede.

Craig tells how, in October 1966, newspapers announced that Dr Franklin Roach would be one of the chief investigators for the Condon Committee, and how, that same day, he happened to meet Roach at a party, and remarked that he envied him. Roach said that, if he was interested, he ought to speak to Bob Low, the coordinator of the project – another name that makes ufologists wrinkle their noses. As a result, Craig was appointed an investigator for the committee.

His first 'case' was in May 1967. Many people in Hoquiam, near Seattle, had heard strange beeping noises originating from above the ground, and there was no obvious explanation. Cattle seemed worried by the noise, dogs cowered, and frogs stopped croaking. Ornithologists said it was not a bird. The story reached the newspapers, and Craig went to investigate, together with camera, tape recorder and ultrasonic translator-detector.

He and five fellow investigators spent an uncomfortable night lying in damp vegetation. They had hoped the beeping would start early and they could go home to bed. But, although it started briefly, there was not time to turn on the tape recorder. They left, cold and hungry, at dawn.

The next night it was raining, and they sat in a car with the window open and tape recorder at the ready. Again, nothing happened. They were so exhausted that they left at midnight.

The next day they phoned the local sheriff's office, and were told that a man who lived close to the site of the beeping had shot a tiny owl, the size of a sparrow, called a saw-whet owl. He had got sick of people trampling over his yard looking for the noise, and killed it with with a shotgun.

After that, the unearthly beeping stopped. The lesson was obvious. Look around for a local countryman who knows what a saw-whet owl sounds like. The people who had reported the beeping were not countrymen, neither did they know it was the saw-whet owl's mating season.

Craig's next case was more significant, for it involved one of the most famous encounters in ufology.

On Saturday, 20 May 1967, a fifty-one-year-old Polish-Canadian named Stephen Michalak returned to his home in Winnipeg with first-degree burns on his chest, and complaining of nausea. His story was that he had been out prospecting – looking for quartz – in Manitoba's Falcon Lake Park, when the local wild geese began to cackle loudly. When he looked up he saw two cigar-shaped objects descending from the sky, glowing with a scarlet colour. One of them remained in the sky, while the other landed on a flat-topped rock. The second UFO began to fly away, its colour changing from red to orange, then grey.

About to disappear behind clouds, it changed to orange again. It was moving very fast, and without sound.

Michalak now saw that the craft on the ground was changing colour, from red to grey-red, then light grey, then to the colour of 'hot stainless steel, with a golden glow around it'.

There was an opening in the top of the craft, and a brilliant purple light, which hurt his eyes, poured out. Then he felt wafts of warm air, smelt burning sulphur, and heard a whirring noise like a small electric motor running very fast. There was also a hissing sound, like air being sucked into the craft. A door stood open in the side.

By now his fear and astonishment had subsided, and he concluded that it was an American space project, and that someone would appear at the door at any moment. He went close to it, and heard muffled voices above the rush of air. He called to ask if they were having trouble but received no reply. He tried calling out in Russian, German, Italian, French and Ukrainian. Still receiving no reply, he approached closer, placing green lenses over the goggles he was wearing (to avoid chips of flying quartz), because the light hurt his eyes.

He stuck his head inside the opening, and saw a maze of lights – beams of light like a laser light show (although he did not use this image), flashing randomly. When he withdrew his head, the door closed, and another 'door' dropped down from above. He touched the craft, and found it was hot enough to burn his glove.

Then, very quickly, the craft tilted, and he felt a scorching pain in his chest. As it took off, his shirt and undershirt burst into flames. He tore them off and threw them on the ground. Meanwhile, the craft changed colour, then disappeared. Michalak vomited and passed out several times as he struggled back to the main road.

This was Michalak's story, and Craig went to investigate it two weeks later. A friendly taxi driver told him that Michalak had been in hospital, although Craig understood he was at home. Apparently he had been out in a helicopter to try to locate the site of the UFO landing, without success.

Craig met Michalak, and felt he was genuine and sincere. He saw the burnt undershirt, and photographed remains of burns on Michalak's body, and also studied Michalak's sketch of the craft – a typical flying saucer, with a dome on top and curved underside. And Michalak finally agreed to try to locate the site of the landing.

The next day they drove eighty-five miles out of Winnipeg, then off the highway to an abandoned gravel pit. Michalak proceeded to lead them, and often pointed out spots where he had chipped off rock with his hammer. Craig said that he got the impression Michalak was pretending to search rather than really searching. Finally, Michalak said he could not find the site that day, and would try another day. Craig suggested he should at least try a little longer. Michalak agreed, but was unsuccessful. Craig felt that, although Michalak talked as if he was leading them deep into the bush, they were really exploring the same area about two miles from the gravel pit. Finally, they gave up. Craig interviewed witnesses who had seen Michalak when he reached the highway, and men who manned a fire-watch tower; no one had noticed any UFOs that Saturday. And, after two or three more unsatisfactory days investigating this and other UFO reports, Craig went home.

Michalak had promised to telephone if he located the landing site, but he never phoned. Craig heard at second hand that he had finally located it. In a booklet he later published, Michalak said that when he had finally located the site, he also found the remains of the burnt shirt and a six-foot rule he left behind. A large circle of burnt grass, visible on a photograph of the site, left no doubt that *something* had landed there. Cracks in the rock on which the UFO landed showed traces of radioactivity. But Canadian officials told Craig that the radioactive material was similar to uranium ore from a nearby valley. Craig decided that it had probably been planted, and that the case was not worth pursuing.

Who can say whether he was right or wrong? Anyone who reads Craig's account can sympathise with his feeling that he was wasting his time. He was quite obviously doing his best. If Michalak had located the site, he might have been more convinced.

On the other hand, why should Michalak have concocted the story? Even if he received his burns in some other way – by some accident – it is still hard to see why he claimed he had received them from a UFO.

Craig obviously felt that Michalak was reluctant to take him out to try to find the site of the encounter. But is that so strange? Surely anyone would prefer to go alone to try to locate the site – and then take witnesses there after it had been located. It is always embarrassing to do things under the gaze of other people – particularly an official 'investigator'. The sheer desire to produce results may be counterproductive.

As to Craig's impression that Michalak was crisscrossing the same site, about two miles from the road, it was probably correct. If Michalak felt that it was somewhere in the area, then he would obviously keep on looking there.

What *is* clear is that, as a member of an official committee, it was not Craig's business to believe or disbelieve – simply to look for evidence. And, while he was in Winnipeg, this evidence was not forthcoming. He had every right to be unconvinced.

As to why Michalak should have concocted a false story, Craig would undoubtedly reply by relating the curious and instructive story of Major Y.

One day, two photographic slides were delivered to the Condon project office in Boulder, both of the same UFO. One was small and the image rather blurred, but the other was the best picture of a flying saucer they had seen – flat-bottomed, with a dome on top. It was brick-red in colour.

It had, apparently, been taken eighteen months earlier by an Air Force officer engaged on his last official flight before he retired. If this was genuine, it proved the existence of flying saucers beyond all doubt.

Major Y, who took the photograph, was apparently of the highest reliability. He had taken off in July 1966, intending to take some photographs of the mountains in western Utah, so had his camera with him. His copilot was studying a navigation problem when the UFO appeared off their wing, looking as if it was flying in a great arc to survey the plane. Major Y snapped a picture, then took another a few seconds later as it came closer, in the centre of his windscreen. It all took only a few seconds, and the copilot did not even look up.

But why, Craig wondered, had Major Y not reported it at the time, as he was obliged to under Air Force regulations?

Another puzzling point was the numbers on the slide mountings (which the developer had added). The 'first' picture, the blurred one, bore the number 14, yet the second one was labelled 11. Was Major Y mistaken about the order in which they were taken? And had he taken another two in between?

Craig and a colleague went to call on Major Y, now in a responsible civilian job, at his home in Denver. It was a beautiful house, and Major Y's wife quite obviously believed that the photographs were genuine, and seemed slightly offended that the investigators wanted to ask questions that implied doubt.

The major himself seemed a decent man, honest and reliable; it seemed unlikely that he had any reason for faking the photographs.

Craig asked if the major had told the copilot what he had seen. The major said that he told the copilot that he had just photographed something, and the copilot had replied, 'That's nice.' The major then said he asked the copilot if he had seen the object he had just photographed, and the copilot said he hadn't.

So the copilot ought to be able to verify that Major Y had photographed something.

But why had Major Y not reported what he had seen? There were two reasons: first, he did not want to be ridiculed; and second, he had been piloting the plane without authorisation – he had been removed from flight status.

Craig asked about the misnumbering of the slide mountings, and the major said that most of the slides from that roll had been misnumbered when they were developed.

Other slides were produced from the same roll of film. It had been developed in December, nearly six months after the UFO photograph had been taken. The major and his wife explained that they had taken the remaining photographs on the roll during a drive across the Rockies, after his retirement. They had also taken some photographs of a big snowstorm in October 1966.

Craig was not entirely happy. Would not a man who had just photographed a UFO shout at his copilot, 'I've just photographed a UFO'? And would he wait six months before getting the film developed?

Back at the project office, Craig examined the photographs more closely. Each frame of such a roll is numbered before it leaves the factory. And the numbering on these frames left no doubt that the UFO pictures were taken later than the October snowstorm pictures – that is, months after the major's retirement.

Craig tried to arrange a second interview with the major, to press him further, but the major was elusive – very busy with the garden. Finally, Craig asked him over the telephone about the misnumbering on the films. The major admitted that he did not even know that the slides themselves were numbered. Asked about how this discrepancy could have occurred – how the UFO pictures were numbered later than the snowstorm – he said that he might well have got mixed up about the rolls.

The fact that the major was unaware that the films themselves were numbered explains why he had thought he could get away with two fake UFO photographs. But it did not explain why such an apparently reliable and mature man had decided to perpetrate the hoax. Craig never found out, for after he returned the photographs – with a request for further explanations – he never heard from the major again.

Craig goes on to describe his experience with Jim and Coral Lorenzen, the founders of the Aerial Phenomena Research Organization (APRO). They told him that they actually possessed a fragment of a flying saucer, a piece of magnesium far more pure than any then being created in any Earth laboratory. It came from a town called Ubatuba, near São Paulo, in Brazil. A man and his friend had been fishing on the beach when, it was claimed, a UFO swooped down at an incredible speed towards the sea. But, just before it hit the water, it managed to turn, and flew upwards. Suddenly, it exploded, showering fragments that looked like sparks from fireworks. The man and his friend picked up many fragments that had fallen on the beach, and they were as light as paper. The fisherman wrote an account of his experience to a newspaper columnist in Rio de Janeiro, although his signature was illegible.

Jim and Coral Lorenzen came into possession of one of these fragments, and sent it for analysis which, they said, revealed that it was incredibly pure magnesium.

The Lorenzens agreed to lend their sample to the Condon Committee. Craig had it analysed in a laboratory; but alas, it was not as pure as magnesium produced by the Dow chemical company.

Later, Craig came upon a report on the same sample from another laboratory – apparently made for the Lorenzens. It said that the magnesium was not at all pure – in fact, less so than commercially manufactured magnesium. And he was saddened to read, in a book by Coral Lorenzen, the comment that 'it was not possible to determine whether the detected impurities were in the electrodes (used for analysis) or in the sample'. That, he felt, was just wishful thinking. Understandably, his opinion of the Lorenzens and their UFO research organisations took on a negative tinge.

The Lorenzens also told him that there *was* a strong piece of evidence in favour of a 'close encounter', in the form of a bent arrow, fired by a man called Donald Schrum at an alien 'robot'.

The encounter, Craig learnt, had taken place in a remote wooded area called Cisco Grove, California, on 4 September 1964. Schrum had been out hunting with two friends, and had been separated from them. As dusk came on, he lit a fire, hoping they would see it. A light appeared in the sky, and Schrum thought it might be a helicopter, out looking for him. He climbed a tree, then saw a domelike disc with a flashing light on it. Some dark object fell to the ground. In the moonlight he saw some kind of craft land nearby. Then two small figures, dressed in silver suits, came out of the woods, and stood looking up at him. Later, a stocky creature, which seemed to be a robot, joined them; it had large red eyes and a slitlike opening for a mouth.

They seemed – to his relief – unable to climb. He tried lighting his cap, which was greasy with hair oil, and threw it down at them; that seemed to worry them. So Schrum went on lighting items of his clothing and dropping them down.

It seemed the robot's mouth was not for eating. It would drop open like a trap and emit a puff of smoke, which would spread like mist; when it reached Schrum, he lost consciousness. Fortunately, he was wearing a long belt, with which he attached himself to the tree. The siege went on all night, and the creatures were joined by a second robot. After one of these periods of unconsciousness, Schrum woke up to find that his attackers had left. When he finally rejoined his companions, one of them said that he had also seen the flying object.

Understandably, Roy Craig felt this was too silly for words. It sounded like an episode from a child's comic. But it seemed that the bent arrow was one of three that Donald Schrum had fired at the creatures, and so provided evidence of some sort.

First, Craig looked in an ephemeris to see what the moon had been doing that night; in fact, there was no moon. As to the arrow, with its tip bent at a right angle, he concluded this had been bent by a blow from the side, rather than by impact with a robot's chest. Disgusted with the whole bizarre story, he made no attempt to contact Schrum's hunting partners, but decided to forget the whole thing.

Now Jacques Vallee, who recounts the story in *Passport to Magonia*, agrees that it sounds unbelievable. But that, of course, is one of the basic problems about UFO encounters – at times, they sound as if they had been deliberately concocted to *create* incredulity. But if we dismiss the story as some kind of fantasy, we are left with the usual baffling problem: why did the witness invent anything so preposterous? Schrum did not seek publicity; the Lorenzens heard the story from Jacques Vallee and Allen Hynek, who had failed to persuade another investigation team, Project Blue Book, to take it seriously. If Schrum was lying for the fun of it, why did he not make his lie more believable?

This problem of what might be called 'deliberate unbelievableness' occurs again and again in UFO literature. Craig was lucky he was not asked to investigate the Sutton farm siege of 1955, one of the most outrageous examples of sheer absurdity in UFO history – it would surely have made him resign from the committee in disgust. The siege took place in Kentucky during the night of 21 August 1955, during which a family named Sutton, and married visitors named Taylor, stayed awake trying to hold off little shining men, who somersaulted backwards whenever struck by a bullet, with a noise like a shot being fired into a pail. One creature climbed on the kitchen roof; struck by two bullets, it fell – then floated forty feet and landed on a fence, and walked away. During a break in the siege, the whole family – eight adults and three children – fled in two cars to Hopkinsville, Kentucky, seven miles away, to summon the police. But the police could find nothing, and left – whereupon the siege resumed, with the shining men, three feet tall, peering in at the windows. They finally left at dawn.

It certainly sounds like a hoax – only one member of the group claims to have seen the UFO that brought the aliens, although a neighbour later said he saw its lights. Yet the whole family undoubtedly piled into two cars in the middle of the night to get the police, and undoubtedly did a lot of shooting. Those who have studied the case are unanimous in agreeing that something really happened that night; eleven people had no reason to lie.

The little shiny men did not even look like the 'greys' who feature in so many abduction cases. A sketch based on witnesses' reports shows them as having huge, floppy ears, long sticklike legs and arms that came almost to their feet. Only one witness said she had not seen the goblins, and that was because she was too scared to look up.

Any reader of Craig's book can see why he ended as a total unbeliever. As case after case failed to provide the solid evidence he hoped for, he must have become increasingly convinced that the whole thing was a tissue of illusions and deceit. I must admit that, even when I had reached only the halfway mark, I felt much the same.

The problem with this state of mind is that it induces a kind of irritable impatience that is the reverse of open-mindedness. And I have only to turn to Coral Lorenzen's book *Flying Saucers* (1965) to see what has gone wrong with even as honest an investigator as Roy Craig. She begins by describing how, when she was nine years old (in 1934), a friend pointed out a white object in the sky, which she thought was a parachute. Coral Lorenzen says she thought it was more like an open umbrella without ribs, and that it was travelling in a leisurely manner with an 'undulating' motion.

On 10 June 1947 – now a young married woman – she was sitting on her back porch looking for meteors when she saw a tiny ball that rose quickly and vanished among the stars. In fact, June 1947 was a month in which dozens of reported sightings occurred, the most famous of which was Kenneth Arnold's on 24 June. And there were many more sightings after this, which she lists and describes. The most impressive is described in a letter from a Mrs King, who was leaving Mombasa at the end of June when she saw a huge, cigar-shaped vessel as long as the ship, which travelled alongside them for a few moments, then sped away, shooting flames from its rear.

Now clearly, Coral Lorenzen is in a totally different frame of mind from Roy Craig. She did not say to Mrs King: 'Come on, prove you saw it.' She has seen one – perhaps two – herself, and then gone on to collect hundreds of sightings and interview dozens of witnesses. She doesn't need to be convinced that UFOs exist. She wants to know what they are, and what they want. She is half inclined to believe that they intend a mass landing, and that their intentions may not be entirely friendly. But her attitude throughout the book is one of intelligent questioning. There is no suggestion of a cultist, for whom flying saucers have become a kind of substitute for religion.

And, quite obviously, she and Roy Craig are never going to agree, simply because their minds are on completely different tracks.

Craig was never to find the answer he was looking for, and – to do him justice – hoping to find. But this is partly because, by the time he was six months into his investigation, he had become so wearily cynical that he was convinced there was very little to investigate.

The disadvantages of this attitude can be seen clearly in another of Craig's cases, that of Patrolman Herb Schirmer.

On the night of 3 December 1967, at about 2.30 a.m., the twenty-two-year-old ex-marine was on the edge of Ashland, Nebraska, when he thought he saw a stalled truck at an intersection of Highway 63. When he turned his spotlight on it, he was staggered to see that it was a UFO – a football-shaped object on three tripod-like legs, with red lights on it. Seconds later, it took off. He returned to the station, and wrote in his logbook: 'Saw a flying saucer at the junction of Highway 6 and 63. Believe it or not!'

One thing puzzled him. It was now 3 a.m., and it took only ten minutes to get from the spot where he had seen the UFO to the station. What had happened to the other twenty minutes? He felt sick, and had a tingling sensation all over his body. There was also the odd fact that he had a red welt on his neck.

Schirmer began to suffer nightmares. He woke up trying to strangle his wife, or to handcuff her. He also had a ringing noise in his ears.

His sighting came to the attention of the Condon Committee, who asked him to come to their headquarters in Boulder, Colorado. There he told his story of the football-shaped UFO. The committee was particularly interested in the missing twenty minutes, as well as in the welt on his neck and the tingling sensation he had experienced. 'They really hammered me on those missing minutes.'

The committee decided to try the effect of hypnosis, and a professional psychologist swung a pendulum back and forth in front of his eyes. After a while, the psychologist asked him if there was more to tell, and Schirmer said yes.

Craig's account is not as clear as it might be. He is obviously bored with the whole thing, and suspects that Schirmer was only pretending to be hypnotised. Instead of quoting a transcript of the session, he merely mentions that Schirmer said he had been taken on board, shown the propulsion system of the craft, and that it was from another galaxy, whose inhabitants were friendly. This, says Craig dismissively, is 'typical UFO lore'. And the psychology professor who did the hypnosis admitted that he personally believed that extraterrestrials are conducting a survey of the earth. The implication is that the psychologist asked leading questions that prompted Schirmer's replies.

Craig has no more to say about the case, except that he would like to see physical evidence of a landing, rather than witness a hypnotic session, where the interviewer may merely be stimulating the subject's imagination or responsiveness to suggestion.

What he does not go on to tell us is what happened next: that Schirmer went back home, and was soon promoted to head of the department, becoming Ashland's youngest police chief. But as the headaches continued, until he was 'gobbling down aspirin like it was popcorn', he quit the job.

It seems that the psychologist at Boulder had not told him what he had revealed under hypnosis, and he badly wanted to know. Therefore he contacted Eric Norman, a writer on flying saucers, who advised him to go to a professional hypnotist. On 8 June 1968, with Norman and the author Brad Steiger present, Schirmer was hypnotised by Loring G. Williams, and regressed to the day of the encounter.

Now he told how, when he switched on his spotlight, the object had flown over to him, and how its occupants had approached his car. One of the beings produced a device that enveloped the car in green gas.

When he tried to draw his revolver, the alien pointed a rodlike device at him, which paralysed him. And, soon after that, something was pressed against the side of his neck, which left the red welt.

The being asked, 'Are you the watchman of this place?' Then it pointed at a power plant and asked, 'Is that the only source of power you have?' He was also asked about a nearby reservoir. He gathered that the visitors wanted to charge up the power units of their spacecraft.

Next he was invited to come on board. A circular doorway opened in the bottom of the craft, and a ladder appeared. Schirmer noted that the ladder and the interior of the craft were unusually cold – an observation that tends to recur in abduction cases.

In a large control room, Schirmer observed video consoles which showed areas outside the ship. He was told that the ship was a small observation craft, made from pure magnesium, and that it generated a force field around itself when landing. He was also told that they had bases on Venus and other planets, as well as underground bases on Earth at one of the poles, and on the coast off Florida. All this was communicated in a kind of broken English, and the voice seemed to come from the creature's chest area.

The crewmen were between four and five feet tall, and wore silvery uniforms, with an emblem of a winged serpent on the right breast. They wore helmets with antennae sticking out of the left side. They looked at Schirmer with unblinking eyes, and he did not notice if they were breathing.

The 'leader' also made the interesting admission that the UFO inhabitants want to puzzle people, and to confuse the public's mind. Schirmer said, 'They put out reports slowly to prepare us . . .'

The leader was pushing buttons as he spoke to Schirmer, and he felt signs of headache. He was told that they were putting things in his mind, and that they always did that with everyone they contacted.

Contactees, he was told, were chosen at random, because they happened to be in a lonely place, or sometimes because they were the son or daughter of someone who was already a contactee. (This was 1967, long before Budd Hopkins and others began to suspect that abductions sometimes occurred repeatedly in families.) The 'aliens' had been observing earth for a long period of time, and felt that if contactees slowly released information about what had happened to them, it would somehow help the aliens.

They had a programme called breeding analysis, in which some humans had been involved.

He saw a kind of logbook on a table, but said that the writing was more like 'the stuff we see in movies about Egypt' (i.e. hieroglyphics). Schirmer was told, 'Watchman, one day you will see the universe.' He was also told that he would be contacted twice more in his life. The being then told him, 'I wish that you would not tell that you have been aboard this ship . . . You will not speak wisely about this night.'

And, the next thing Schirmer knew, he was watching the spacecraft take off, with no memory whatsoever of what had happened since he first saw it.

We can see why Craig felt dubious about the case – particularly in the light of his negative experiences so far. But we can also see that the whole story is a great deal more plausible than Craig lets on. He dismisses it all as possible suggestion by the hypnotist, ignoring the fact that Schirmer went back to the police station twenty minutes later and logged the sighting. The tingling sensation, the headaches and nightmares that followed suggest that something had happened during that twenty minutes, and that Schirmer was affected by radiation.

When Schirmer went home after the first hypnotic session, he became police chief, and yet resigned from a good job because of the headaches. This again suggests that he is not inventing the story for the sake of attention. Finally, his need to know what happened led him to a second hypnosis, when so much interesting information emerged – much of it anticipating things suggested by Budd Hopkins twenty years later – that it provides clues to many other abductions, and possibly to the motivation of the aliens in general. For all these reasons, the Schirmer case seems obviously genuine, and Craig's refusal to take it seriously demonstrates the danger of developing a negative attitude.

Was Craig *never* convinced by any of his witnesses? Only in one case – an Air Force colonel, Lewis B. Chase, who encountered a UFO when he was commanding a B-57 on 18 September 1957. They took off from Forbes, Texas, at night, and flew down the coast over the Gulf of Mexico, then towards the Fort Worth–Dallas area. Over Jackson, Mississippi, Chase saw a 'real bright light' coming towards them at about their own altitude. He told the crew to prepare for evasive action. The light came on at what Lewis called an 'impossible closure rate', so fast that the colonel had no time to react as it crossed the nose of the aeroplane. He asked the copilot if he saw it, and the copilot replied cautiously, 'I did if you did.' Then they joked about having seen a flying saucer. The radar operator soon said that he had picked it up again, staying abreast of them about ten miles away – at about 425 miles per hour. The colonel tried slowing right down, then accelerating to top speed; still it stayed alongside – although now visible only on radar. The colonel called Fort Worth–Dallas, and they told him they could see both of them on the 'scope'.

The invisible UFO now shot ahead of them. Then its light came on again – 'it was huge – not a small ball of fire'. Chase increased speed again, and had almost caught up when the light went out. The plane made a turn – at that speed taking about thirty miles to do so – and they saw the UFO again. Again they tried to close in, and again the UFO vanished – this time, even off the scope.

They decided it was time to return to base. Now the UFO again appeared on scope, and followed them for miles. They finally lost it over Oke City.

Chase and his copilot were deeply impressed by its ability to vanish, then appear elsewhere, as if it had instant 'relocation ability'. The copilot and radar operator verified Chase's story, and the radar operator commented, 'Two different people were tracking on radar sets, two people were watching it visually, and I was watching it electronically . . . Whenever we'd lose it, we'd all lose it. There were no buts about it. It went off!'

Craig's team tracked down the original report in the Blue Book archives, and Craig toyed with a few explanations, such as an optical mirage. But he has to admit that they all failed to fit the facts, and that this UFO seemed genuine.

In February 1968, the Condon Committee began to run into trouble when two of its members, David Saunders and Norman Levine, decided that Dr Condon was engaged in a kind of cover-up. They had found an office memorandum from Robert Low, one of the project's organisers, which seemed to demonstrate that the whole exercise was designed to pull the wool over the eyes of the public. Low had written:

> Our study would be conducted almost exclusively by nonbelievers who, although they couldn't possibly prove a negative result, could and probably would add an impressive body of evidence that there is no reality to the observations. The trick would be, I think, to describe the project so that, to the public, it would appear a totally objective study but, to the scientific community, would present the image of a group of nonbelievers trying their best to be objective but having an almost zero expectation of finding a saucer.

Craig had actually found this memorandum, and shown it to Levine. And Saunders and Levine had shown the memorandum to a critic of the Condon Committee's methods, Dr James McDonald, himself a 'believer'; as a result, Saunders and Levine were fired. They then decided to publish their own 'rival' report, and asked Craig to join the mutiny. Craig declined. He pointed out that Low's memorandum did not represent the views of Dr Condon, and that, in any case, Low had never had any power to set an agenda for the committee. Condon had agreed that *all* views would be fairly represented in the final report.

In fact, the publication of the report in January 1969 was a disaster. John Fuller, the author of a book about a UFO 'flap' at Exeter, New Hampshire, in the mid 1960s, wrote a devastating article for *Look* magazine, called 'The Flying Saucer Fiasco', with a subtitle: 'The Half-million Dollar Cover-up on Whether UFOs Really Exist'. Craig still feels that all this was unfair and unjustified. Condon was an honest man who did his best. The unfortunate Bob Low, who had only been expressing his own sceptical view (which he had no power to impose on anyone else) became a public scapegoat, and saw his world collapse around him; he was virtually sacked. The book itself, which according to *Newsweek* would be 'an automatic bestseller' was a flop. Condon became the subject of endless cartoons – one showing him being kidnapped by little green men, while a friend shouts, 'Tell them you don't believe in them.' And the name 'Condon Report' became a synonym for an official cover-up, a whitewash.

Craig's book makes it very clear that this was unfair, and that everyone did his best to be honest and unbiased. But he does admit that changes made in the introduction to his chapter on the physical evidence for UFOs, by the editor Dan Gillmor, enraged him by incorporating 'a cynical attitude which was not mine'.

What becomes quite clear is that a project like the Condon Committee investigation was simply the wrong way to reach an unbiased conclusion on UFOs. Most of the investigators claimed to be open-minded and unprejudiced. But they were men like Craig – decent, hard-headed and simply disinclined to believe that UFOs were real. And, after they had all encountered fiascos like Craig's owl incident, they were no longer unbiased, but strongly inclined to be dismissive.

Yet Craig himself encountered at least two cases that he found convincing. One was the B-57 incident with Colonel Chase, the other a sighting at Beverley, Massachusetts, in which three women saw a strange object, which came down right over their heads – a flat-bottomed metal disc about the size of an automobile, with glowing lights around its top. Two policemen also saw the object, and verified this to Condon and Norman Levine.

The 'alternative report', by David Saunders, came out under the title *UFOs – Yes! – Where the Condon Committee Went Wrong*. Craig points out that this also contained a certain amount of nonsense – for example, mentioning the Ubatuba magnesium sample as a convincing proof of the reality of UFOs, without mentioning the laboratory analysis which showed that it was not as pure as the Lorenzens said it was. But, from the publishing point of view, the alternative report was not a great deal more successful than the original. It seemed the public did not want Condon in any form. Condon died in 1974, five years after his report was published, saddened by the hostility of scientific colleagues, and baffled that his attempt to arrive at an honest conclusion about UFOs had ended in such disaster.

4 The Labyrinthine Pilgrimage of Jacques Vallee

A
S I READ Roy Craig's book, it slowly became clear to me why there is such a deep reluctance to take UFOs seriously. I think most of us are perfectly willing to concede that they may exist. But we also feel that, whether they do or not, they are never likely to impinge on our personal lives.

Now this could well be a major error. Ever since that early wave of sightings in 1947, their number has gone on increasing. To begin with, UFOs were merely distant objects seen in the sky, which might or might not have been weather balloons, helicopters, or some other terrestrial object. Cranks and imposters increased the sense of scepticism by describing how they had met the occupants of flying saucers and been taken on trips to the planets. It all sounded like harmless lunacy.

Then the abduction reports began, and became increasingly difficult to dismiss. And now that abduction reports run into thousands, and come from all over the world, it becomes clear that this is something we would be stupid to ignore. This is no longer a story that cannot possibly affect the rest of us, like the Loch Ness monster or the Abominable Snowman. This could conceivably affect the whole human race.

Of course, it *may* simply go away. But, if past decades are anything to go by, the phenomenon will keep on demanding our attention until it finally gets it.

Craig's section on J. Allen Hynek underlines the point. Craig refers to him as one of the 'casualties' of the Condon Report. And, in Craig's sense, this was undoubtedly true. For Hynek, once the official mouthpiece of the sceptics, slowly became convinced that UFOs really exist, and that to try to ignore them or dismiss them would be dangerously short-sighted.

Hynek was a curious figure. An astronomer and an expert on artificial satellites, he became involved in investigating UFOs in 1948, as astronomical consultant to the US Air Force. His job was to examine reports of flying saucers, and to apply his specialist knowledge to determine how many could be dismissed as sightings of the planet Venus, lenticular clouds, reflections due to 'temperature inversions', and so on. He admitted later, 'I had joined my scientific colleagues in many a hearty guffaw at the "psychological postwar craze" for flying saucers . . .' And when he was asked to act as consultant for the Air Force, he saw it as a 'golden opportunity to demonstrate to the public how the scientific method works, how the application of the impersonal and unbiased logic of the scientific method (I conveniently forgot my own bias for the moment) could be used to show that flying saucers were figments of the imagination'.

Hynek also tells a story about how, at a reception for astronomers in 1968, word spread among the guests that lights performing strange manoeuvres in the sky had been spotted. The astronomers joked and bantered about it, but not one went outside to look.

Such indifference is, of course, by no means unusual; it is part of the human condition – as demonstrated, for example, on 21 August 1955, when Billy Ray Taylor went into the farmyard of his friend Elmer Sutton to get a drink from the well, then rushed back and told everyone that he had just seen a UFO landing in a nearby gulch. Far from being excited, the assembled company was not even curious enough to go outside and look. Half an hour or so later, the 'siege of the Sutton place' at Hopkinsville – described in the last chapter – began.

Hynek demonstrated 'how the scientific method works' in March 1966, when eighty-seven female students of Hillside College, Michigan, observed a light the size of a football hovering over a swampy area; it approached the women's dormitory, and apparently reacted to passing cars. The next day, five people, including two policemen, saw a large glowing object over a swampy area. Allen Hynek, now the astronomical adviser to the official study of UFOs, Project Blue Book, went along to investigate, and suggested at a conference in the Detroit Press Club that the 'UFOs' might be swamp gas. (Swamp gas was *very* unlikely in March.) A howl of derision went up around the nation, and Hynek acquired a reputation as one of the ignoble instruments of an official cover-up. One UFO writer, John Keel, even declared that Hynek had been ordered to dismiss the sightings as swamp gas, on pain of being fired by the Air Force. This is almost certainly untrue. But Hynek suddenly became the man UFO enthusiasts loved to hate – although, oddly enough, the swamp-gas incident turned him into the best-known ufologist in the United States.

Two cases helped convince Hynek that UFOs had to be genuine. One was the extraordinary 'Socorro incident'. On 24 April 1964, patrolman Lonnie Zamora, of Socorro, New Mexico, saw a flame in the sky, then saw that it was coming down in the desert. Alarmed in case it landed on a hut containing dynamite, he drove to a hilltop in time to see a silvery object settle in the gully. It was shaped like an egg balancing on one end, and was standing on four legs. Two small figures – about the size of children, and wearing white overalls – were standing near it. Zamora radioed back to his sergeant at Socorro, and drove round the hill to get a closer view; when he looked again, the craft was taking off with a thunderous noise, and vanished at a great speed. The brush near it burnt for an hour. Two colleagues arrived, and found four V-shaped depressions in the ground where the module had stood.

There is a kind of sequel to this story. A year later, on 1 July 1965, a French farmer named Maurice Masse, who lived in the provincial village of Valensole, heard a whistling noise in the sky, and saw an egg-shaped craft standing on six legs, with two beings he mistook for boys standing near it. Since vandals had recently been pulling up his lavender, he sneaked up on them – then became aware that they were not boys, whereupon he walked openly towards them. One of them pointed a pencil-shaped object at him, and Masse found that he was paralysed. The machine then took off.

Masse described his visitors as being less than four feet tall, with pumpkin-like heads, high, fleshy cheeks, large eyes that slanted round the side of their heads, slitty mouths without lips, and pointed chins. They were wearing close-fitting grey-green clothes.

A French investigator, Aimé Michel, went to interview Masse, and took with him a photograph of a model spacecraft that had been based on Zamora's description. When Masse was shown this he was thunderstruck, and went pale. At first he thought this was his machine. Told that this one had been seen in America, he said, 'You see, I was not dreaming.'

As investigator for the Air Force, Hynek went to see Zamora, and set out to undermine his testimony by trying to get him to contradict himself. He did not succeed, and ended totally convinced of Zamora's honesty. He then went to look at the site, and saw the charred plants and the marks left by the craft. He also learnt of another witness, who had seen a 'strange flying craft' looking as if it was about to land, and then saw Zamora's squad car on its way across the sandy terrain towards it.

But the case that most impressed Hynek was that of the Rev. William Booth Gill, an Anglican priest who headed a mission in Boainai, Papua New Guinea. At 6.45 p.m. on 26 June 1959, he was leaving his house when he saw a huge light in the sky. He sent a servant to fetch other people, then found a pencil and paper, and recorded his observations. The light was close enough to see something – or someone – moving on top of it, then he thought he could see three men, 'doing something on deck'. A 'thin electric blue spotlight' was switched on. At 7.20 the UFO vanished through the cloud cover, but an hour later, when the cloud thinned, Gill saw it again. Then a second UFO appeared. Finally, a third was seen over a nearby village. Gill and numerous witnesses saw what they took to be a mother ship hovering, 'large and stationary'. Gill watched, on and off, until after 10 o'clock.

The next evening the UFOs were back again. Gill was walking with a nurse and a schoolteacher near the hospital, and the UFO came so close that the teacher was able to wave at a figure on its deck; the figure waved back. Gill and several other people waved, and received waves in return.

Hynek learnt of the case from the British Air Ministry, who handed Hynek the report (apparently glad to get rid of it), and Gill's notes, as well as some lengthy tapes he made. Hynek remarks, 'As a few excerpts from his tape show, Reverend Gill is utterly sincere. He talks in a leisurely, scholarly way, delineating details slowly and carefully. The manner and contents of the tapes are conducive to conviction.'

Typically, the Australian Department of Air decided to classify the UFOs as an 'aerial phenomenon . . . most probably . . . reflections on a cloud'.

Hynek had earlier dismissed hundreds of sightings of UFOs as misinterpretations of astronomical objects; these sightings led him to begin stating publicly that he now saw the UFO phenomenon as 'the greatest mystery of our age, perhaps the greatest mystery of all time'. The Air Force was understandably upset by this unexpected turnabout of one of its most reliable debunkers; but Hynek was by now too well known to be silenced by threats.

For the rest of his life – Hynek died in 1986 – he attempted to persuade governments and scientific bodies to take the study of UFOs seriously; to this end, he founded the Center for UFO Studies (CUFOS), whose purpose was to study the evidence scientifically. But it was uphill work. Most official bodies felt then – as they do now – that UFOs should be classified with ghosts and sea serpents, as something that could safely be ignored because it made no real difference whether they existed or not.

Yet Hynek failed to come to any ultimate conclusion about UFOs – apart from a conviction that a percentage of them are real. He compared his task to that of Marie Curie, trying to refine tons of pitchblende to obtain a fraction of a gram of radium.

His caution exasperated his friend Jacques Vallee, another astronomer who had been preoccupied with UFOs since 1954, when he was fifteen.

In that year there had been a deluge of sightings in Europe, and Vallee had heard a railway worker describe on the radio how he had been relieving his bladder in the night air when he saw a UFO and two small robots near the railway. Police found signs that a large machine had landed at the spot. In the following year, Vallee saw one for himself. His mother screamed from the garden, and Jacques rushed down three flights of stairs in time to see a grey metallic disc with a bubble on top, hovering above the church of Saint-Maclou, in Pontoise.

In 1958, Vallee came upon a book called *Mysterious Things in the Sky* (*Mystérieux Objets Célestes*) by an acoustical engineer named Aimé Michel. That same day, Vallee recorded in his diary the wish that he could one day become a UFO researcher, and wrote a letter to Aimé Michel. Two weeks later, Michel replied; but he also made the baffling comment that many UFOs simply vanished, as if they had dematerialised. In other cases, they had changed shape instantaneously; 'can you imagine a pyramid turning into a cube?' It was obviously not a simple matter of visitants from another planet.

By August 1961, when he was twenty-two, Vallee had found himself a job at the artificial-satellite station of the Paris Observatory, at Meudon. Yet he and his colleagues sometimes observed satellites that had no official existence. One night, they tracked an exceptionally bright satellite of which there was simply no record. Moreover, it was travelling the wrong way – in retrograde motion. It took a far more powerful rocket launcher to boost a satellite into retrograde orbit, and no nation possessed one at the time. Yet when he drew this to the attention of Paul Muller, head of the artificial-satellite service, Muller confiscated the tape and destroyed it. When Vallee asked why they didn't send the information to the Americans (meaning the Harvard College Observatory in Cambridge, under the Geophysical Year agreement), Muller replied, 'The Americans would laugh at us.'

In spite of which, the satellite *was* tracked by a number of observatories all over the world. Then it vanished.

A week later, Vallee went to call on Aimé Michel, 'an amazing gnome of a man, short and deformed, who barely reaches to my stomach. Yet he radiates a kind of beauty that is unforgettable, a beauty that comes from the mind, and the nobility of his piercing eyes.' Michel had suggested a notion that he called orthoteny – that UFOs tended to appear on straight lines. But Michel had collected so many observations – hundreds of reported sightings – that he was unable to handle them all. Vallee offered what help he could, extending a line that went through Bayonne and Vichy right around the world, so Michel could find out whether other sightings appeared on it. The result was an excited letter from Michel. The line went through three major concentrations of UFO sightings, in Brazil, New Guineau and New Zealand. (A New Zealander named Bruce Cathie, an airline pilot who had experienced four UFO sightings between 1952 and 1965, arrived at a similar theory independently.) Vallee now began using the IBM computer at weekends (it occupied a whole room) to perform more calculations. He was aided by his wife Janine.

Vallee found that this interest in UFOs was attracting unfavourable comment, and became afraid that he would lose his job. An astrophysicist called Pierre Guerin had joined the group, and scientists next door were wondering why an expert on planets was talking to satellite-trackers. 'It seems amazing to me', Vallee commented in his journal, 'that people should find it suspicious and undesirable for scientists of adjacent disciplines to talk to one another. Isn't that what science is all about?'

He and Janine made the interesting discovery that there was an apparent relationship between the frequency of sightings and the distance of the planet Mars, which comes closest to earth every twenty-six months. This might have led him to wonder whether flying saucers are from Mars; instead, he reflected that it is odd that, if the visitors are from space, they are not seen long before they reach Earth – after all, fairly small objects can be seen in space, even with the naked eye, when they are hundreds of miles away. Vallee was already beginning to suspect that the flying saucers were not necessarily from other planets, or anywhere else 'out there'.

On a bookstall by the Seine, Vallee discovered a book by Major Donald Keyhoe, one of the pioneers in the field of ufology, and noted that the attitude of American scientists and military men towards UFOs was disturbing: 'They behave like a well-organised insect colony whose life is suddenly impacted by an unforeseen event.' He observed that their idea of researching UFOs was to chase one and shoot it down. Keyhoe's book led Vallee to formulate the notion that UFOs are 'the first great collective intelligence test to which mankind has been subjected'.

Early in 1962, Vallee resigned from the Meudon observatory, sick of the small-minded attitude of French astronomers. His boss Muller actually reproached him with the words, 'You think too much.' He took a job with an electronics firm, which gave him more time and freedom.

Janine asked a friend to look at the computations, and he asked her if they had anything to do with Mars. It turned out that he had a friend named Michel Gauquelin, a statistician who had decided to discredit astrology by using the statistical method. In the 1930s, a Swiss mathematician named Krafft had studied the birth data of 2,800 musicians, and concluded that the result proved a relation between a person's sun sign (the sign of the zodiac he is born under) and temperament. Gauquelin had fed this data into a computer, and discovered that Krafft was deceiving himself. Carried away by his success, Gauquelin decided to explode another superstition: that a person's choice of profession is governed by his rising sign – the planet that is just rising at the moment of his birth. (Doctors are supposed to be born under Mars, actors under Jupiter, scientists under Saturn, etc.) To Gauquelin's embarrassment, his first sample – people born under Mars – showed that the Mars effect was real. The tests were repeated in four different countries, and showed the same result. Without intending to, Gauquelin had made it fairly certain that astrology is not pure superstition.

Jacques and Janine met the Gauquelins, and were amused to realise that they had both been working on a kind of 'Mars effect', and that both couples had been obliged to keep their work secret for fear of the scientific establishment. Vallee began thinking about moving to America, and, when Aimé Michel told him about Hynek, wrote him a letter, and sent him his Mars correlations.

A few days before leaving for America, in September 1962, Vallee paid a visit to a musician named Paul Misraki, who had just published a book called *The Extraterrestrials*, in which he suggested that some religious miracles, like that at Fátima, might have the same cause as modern saucer sightings. The Fátima sighting had occurred on 13 May 1917, when three Portugese children saw a white-robed woman who asked them to return every month for six months. On the second occasion, fifty people were there, and heard an explosion, followed by the sight of a cloud rising from a tree; the third time, there were 4,500 people, who heard a buzzing noise, saw a cloud ascending from the same tree, and again heard an explosion. The children were shown a vision of hell, and told that a second world war would occur if people did not mend their ways. (It would begin, said the vision, during the reign of Pope Pius XI, who died in 1939.)

By September, there were 30,000 people, and they saw a globe of light moving down the valley towards the children, and the air seemed to be full of glistening bubbles as the globe rose and disappeared into the sun. On the last occasion, in October, there were 70,000 people. The pouring rain suddenly stopped, and the clouds parted to reveal a revolving disc of a silvery colour, which radiated, in succession, all the colours of the spectrum. Then it plunged towards the Earth. Most of the crowd thought it was the end of the world and fell on their knees; but the disc suddenly reversed, and flew upward into the sun. When it had gone, the crowd discovered that their clothes and the ground were miraculously dry.

This suggestion of a connection between Fátima and UFOs was to be extraordinarily fruitful for Vallee.

A year after arriving in America, Vallee finally met Hynek in a Chicago hotel, and they talked continuously for twenty-four hours. Hynek mentioned a vacancy in the computer programming department at Northwestern University, where he worked, and Vallee applied and was accepted. Soon he was working as one of Hynek's research assistants on Project Blue Book. Hynek's wife Mimi thought the whole UFO business was nonsense, and that it would never be taken seriously. But Vallee, having read and disliked a number of books on UFOs – for their popular tone – decided to write one of his own. By this time, his computer calculations had convinced him that Michel's orthoteny was almost certainly a matter of chance.

By December 1963, Vallee was suggesting to Hynek that 'an extraterrestrial intervention might have been a factor in man's early history, specifically in the early development of civilisation and of biblical events . . . The return of such phenomena today could be explained by the need to boost our religious vacillations.' He thought that some benign group of cosmic beings, trying to guide us towards galactic status, would behave exactly as the saucer operators do.

*   *   *

We should pause here to glance briefly at this notion of UFOs and man's early history. It seems, at first sight, absurd, an arbitrary linking of two completely different phenomena – biblical miracles, which most of us take with a pinch of salt anyway, and flying saucers.

What is difficult to grasp is that, for more than five years, Vallee had been studying hundreds – in fact thousands – of UFO sightings, and hearing them described in the witnesses' own words. It was totally impossible for him to doubt that flying saucers were real, even though many of them sounded absurd (like the two little robots seen by the Frenchman).

But when did they begin?

Certainly not with Kenneth Arnold; there had been hundreds, even thousands, of sightings long before that day in 1947.

In his dictated book *The Song of the Stars*, the South African shaman Credo Mutwa writes:

There are things that fly through the night, that you call UFOs, which we in Africa call Abahambi Abavutayo, 'the fiery visitors' . . . Long before they were heard of in other parts of the world, we, the people of Africa, had contact with these things and the creatures inside them. I can only speak within certain constraints because we are not allowed to talk in any detail about these sacred things. Our people fear that should we do that, then the star ships would stop visiting us.

He goes on to speak about the Mutende-ya-ngenge, 'the grey or white . . . creature with a largish head whose face is chalk-white, with large green eyes that go around the creature's head so that it can look at you over its shoulder . . .' He adds that the Mutende sometimes captures human beings, cuts them open, then closes them up again, and makes them forget what has happened. 'It is only when a witch doctor puts this person into what we call the *godsleep* . . . that this fact comes out.'

Mutwa goes on to describe his own abduction encounter with 'fellows like little dolls' in the bush, who were able to paralyse him, then examined him painfully, sticking instruments up his nostrils. He then describes how a female creature made love to him: 'but there was nothing human or warm about it . . . only a feeling of coldness and violation'. Afterwards, he was shown a creature like a baby frog, suspended in a purplish liquid – a humanoid foetus?

He found himself back in the bush, and, when he approached a village, all the dogs tried to attack him, and he had to be rescued. He then learnt he had been missing for three days.

Mutwa adds, 'There are creatures who are watching over us curiously, and who, I think, are regulating human progress for some reason.'

In 1925, the Russian mystical artist Nicholas Roerich, who designed the set for Stravinsky's *Rite of Spring*, set out across the Himalayas, and described in his journal how his party had been staring up at an eagle when 'we all saw, in a direction from north to south, something big and shiny reflecting the sun, like a huge oval moving at great speed. Crossing our camp this thing changed in its direction from south to southwest. And we saw how it disappeared in the intense blue sky. We even had time to take our field glasses and saw quite distinctly an oval form with shiny surface, one side of which was brilliant from the sun.'

But as early as 2 January 1878, a farmer named John Martin, of Denison, Texas, had been out hunting when he saw a moving object in the northern sky, dark in colour, and of considerable size. It must also have been moving fast, for, after he had looked down to rest his eyes, he discovered that the object was already overhead, at a great height, and 'looking like a large saucer'.

Even this is by no means the first. The *Chronicle* of William of Newburgh, a thirteenth-century monk, tells how, in 1290, in Byland Abbey in Yorkshire, the abbot and monks were at a meal when a 'flat, round, shining silvery object' flew over the abbey and 'caused the utmost terror'. And *Flying Saucers on the Attack* (1954) by Harold Wilkins (which, in spite of the sensational title, is a serious and comprehensive study of UFOs) lists no fewer than 150 reports of strange lights and objects in the sky, from 200 BC to 1912. A typical description by the Roman Julius Obsequens in 90 BC speaks of 'a globe of fire, golden in colour', in the area of Spoleto, which 'fell to earth, was seen to gyrate . . . became greater in size, and was seen to rise from the earth, was borne east, and obscured the disc of the sun with its magnitude'.

Even Alexander the Great saw a UFO. In 322 BC, he was besieging the city of Tyre when 'a large silver shield', with four smaller shields behind it, circled over Tyre; it shot a beam of light at the city wall and blasted a hole through it. The other 'shields' then fired at the defence towers. Alexander lost no time in taking advantage of this supernatural intervention and invading the city.

The very first report that sounds like a UFO sighting dates from ancient Egypt around 1500 BC. A papyrus now in the Vatican describes how, in the reign of Thutmose III and his queen Hatshepsut, a 'circle of fire' came from the sky, and its breath had a foul odour. A few days later, in the evening, the sky was filled with the circles of light, which then ascended and vanished towards the south. Then, of course, there is the Bible. Vallee's musician friend Misraki had suggested in his book *The Extraterrestrials* that the vision of the biblical prophet Ezekiel, around 600 BC, of 'a great whirlwind', with 'a fire infolding itself', might well be a vision of some kind of UFO.

So it seemed to Vallee highly probable that flying saucers have been visiting our planet for a long time. And, in view of the Fátima sightings, it is hardly surprising that he should feel that these visitants might be associated with religion. Vallee's feelings were not unlike those of Andrija Puharich after hearing voices talking from the air, and seeing tape recorders working of their own accord; he felt that there was definitely some 'unearthly' component. And, since Vallee was beginning to suspect that UFOs might not be visitors from outer space, he was left with the supposition that they might be some form of paranormal phenomena associated with the Earth.

A few years later, such speculation was commonplace. In 1967, a newspaper serialisation of von Däniken's *Chariots of the Gods?* was entitled 'Did God Drive a Flying Saucer?' And a space engineer named Josef Blumrich, after rejecting the idea as nonsensical, then took another look at the prophet Ezekiel, and decided that his visions, when studied in detail, *did* sound like a spaceship; he carefully reconstructed it, with diagrams, in *The Spaceships of Ezekiel* (1973).

But, when Vallee suggested the idea to Hynek in 1963, it was virtually new. And, as far as the Air Force and their Project Blue Book were concerned, it would have sounded like insanity. Their two chief 'investigators', Captain Hector Quintanilla and Sergeant Moody, had no scientific training, and no interest in the nature of UFOs. Quintanilla told Vallee, 'The mission of the Air Force is to identify, intercept and destroy any unauthorised object that violates US air space.' As to Moody, he regarded people who claimed to have seen UFOs as nuts. When Vallee asked Quintanilla how he accounted for worldwide sightings, Quintanilla replied that that was not their business.

Vallee wrote satirically of Sergeant Moody: 'Moody deserves a Nobel Prize for fudging his bold UFO "explanations." Thus he is the discoverer of a new species of *birds with four blinking lights*.' It was also Moody who once decided that a certain observation was without merit because "the reported object did not match any known aerial maneuvering pattern".'

Yet as he studied reports, Vallee began to feel a sneaking sympathy with Quintanilla and Moody. Some UFOs, he noted, changed shape, others disappeared on the spot; and UFOs that were seen on the ground did not look adapted to interstellar flight. They sounded more like a joke than a serious phenomenon.

Hynek's position caused Vallee mild exasperation. He noted that Hynek preferred to sit on the fence, arguing that there was not enough evidence to present to the National Academy of Science. It was not the money he received from the Air Force that kept Hynek in line, but the fear of losing access to the Air Force's files on the sightings.

Vallee had by now finished a book about UFOs, *Challenge to Science*, but publishers were not interested; one turned it down on the grounds that it would simply not appeal to an American audience. In April 1964, he went to see the Chicago publisher Henry Regnery, who asked, 'Do you fly to Mars and Venus, like George Adamski?' Vallee said he didn't. 'Do you explain them away as clouds and atmospherics?' Vallee said he didn't do that either. 'Then that's final,' said Regnery. 'You don't have a book about flying saucers.'

But he agreed to pass on the typescript to his daughter, who could read French.

It was at the end of April that Hynek was called away to New Mexico, when Lonnie Zamora saw his flying egg, with its two occupants. Hynek was impressed, and Vallee delighted – he noted that the Socorro landing sounded exactly like something out of the French files for 1954. Vallee now decided to begin a new book, to be called *Anatomy of a Phenomenon*. When this was accepted by Regnery, Hynek wrote an introduction – then changed his mind, because it might compromise his position with the Air Force.

In December 1964, Vallee received a letter that filled him with excitement. It was from a captain in the Italian Air Force, who was working at the Ministry of Aeronautics in Rome – Vallee calls him Luciano. He had been studying UFOs since 1947, and had more than 6,000 index cards of sightings, 800 of them from Italy. Vallee was interested to learn that Italy had also experienced a 'UFO flap' in 1954, a year when countries as far apart as France, Brazil and Australia had experienced 'UFO invasions'.

Some reported sightings amused him: an Englishwoman living in

South Africa decribed seeing an object like a moon which came towards her window, then changed into a kind of golden football.

'If it was a saucer, if it had a crew and if they saw me at the window, I must say they probably went away with a strange impression of an earth creature: I am blonde, almost six feet tall; on the night in question I was naked because of the heat and the humidity, and my hair was in metal curlers! It is not surprising that they left and did not return.'

She noted that as the object came close, she smelt an odour 'like an overheated radio'. Early valve radios smelt of burning Bakelite when they overheated, and it seems just conceivable that this might have been the 'foul odour' complained of by the Egyptian scribe.

A friend of Vallee's publisher told him an interesting story about the 'Washington flap' of July 1952, when two lots of UFOs were picked up on radar over the capital, and seen by airline pilots. Two men were sent outside with a camera to try to photograph the objects appearing on the radar screen (no fewer than eight on the first occasion). Their photographs were developed on the spot, and two of them showed clear luminous objects. They were immediately confiscated, and everyone in the room was sworn to silence. Donald Menzel, the professor who had been Hynek's mentor, explained the sightings away as 'temperature inversions'.

On 23 March 1966, Vallee heard the radio item that convinced him that 'nothing would ever be the same again' – about the UFOs seen near Ann Arbor, Michigan, and one that was seen landing in a swamp near Dexter. Girls at a Hillsdale college had also seen them, making more than sixty witnesses in all.

Hynek rang Quintanilla to tell him, but Quintanilla said he was not interested. When Hynek protested that that was not very scientific, Quintanilla replied, 'I don't give a damn.' But, half an hour later, Quintanilla rang up and passed on an order to go to Michigan.

Hynek seems to have enjoyed suddenly being in the limelight, with dozens of pressmen and television reporters waiting to hear what he had to say. But, at his press conference three days later, Hynek caused universal hilarity by suggesting that the UFOs had been swamp gas. Vallee was astonished and furious when he heard about it. Hynek rang him to explain that he had been harassed by too many reporters, and that, although there were so many witnesses, their stories were too confused and conflicting to make sense.

Yet the fiasco served a useful purpose. As Hynek became a figure of ridicule, the public began to take a serious interest in UFOs, which crystalised into a consensus that they must be real. And the Republican congressman for Michigan, Gerald Ford (who would succeed Richard Nixon after his downfall), protested that the American public deserved a better explanation than swamp gas. As a result, the Condon Committee came into existence.

By this time, Vallee's second book, *Anatomy of a Phenomenon*, had been published, and had aroused a far wider interest than the publisher had expected. This was partly due to the Mariner 4 landing on Mars, partly to a sudden wave of sightings all over the world. With its long opening chapter on the history of sightings of unidentified aerial objects since the days of the Bible, and its chapter on the search for intelligent life in the universe, it was by far the most substantial and scientific assessment of the problem so far.

Challenge to Science had also been published, but only in French. The attitude of these books was new in the world of ufology. To begin with, by presenting such an impressive cross-section of cases from all over the world, Vallee was making it clear that they could not all be dismissed as lies, mistakes or hallucinations. Second, in approaching this as a scientist and mathematician, Vallee was trying to desensationalise the subject, and to persuade science to study it seriously.

Other writers – like Morris Jessup, Donald Keyhoe and Coral Lorenzen – had been tainted with the 'invaders from Mars' mentality, which in turn had led scientists to feel that flying saucers were the product of hysteria. Vallee was arguing that UFOs had been reported so often that there was no possible doubt that they were real; what was important now was to try to decide precisely what they were. He was pleading, in effect, for a new science. After all, psychology and criminology were not regarded as sciences until the late nineteenth century, and there are still many scientists who decline to accept parapsychology as a science. Sooner or later, Vallee was arguing, governments will have to be prepared to finance the scientific study of UFOs.

One academic took him seriously. He was James McDonald, professor of atmospheric physics at the University of Arizona. McDonald asked permission to spend two days at the Wright-Patterson Air Force base in Dayton, Ohio – now virtually the hub of official UFO investigation in the US – studying their reports on 'ball lightning'. What he saw quickly convinced him that most of their reports of ball lightning were actually UFOs. He insisted on seeing the general, and had a forty-five-minute interview – longer than Hynek had ever had – and ended by talking with him about the humanoid occupants of UFOs. He told Hynek and Vallee that the Air Force explanations 'were pure bullshit', and lost no time in contacting the various civilian organisations that collected sightings, such as APRO and NICAP. Hynek and Vallee had lunch with him, and Vallee was exhilarated. 'It is clear that an entire era has come to a crashing end,' Vallee wrote. 'This man has many contacts, many ideas, and he is afraid of nothing.'

Unfortunately, McDonald proved to be a mixed blessing. He was assertive, abrasive and rude, and made no secret of his belief that Hynek had sold out, and become a tool for the Air Force cover-up. He even tried to recruit Vallee to join the anti-Hynek, anti-bullshit camp. 'If it wasn't for your influence, and all the research you brought over from France, Hynek would still be arguing that ninety-three per cent of those reports are due to Venus or marsh gas.' But Vallee quickly sensed that he would never be able to work with McDonald as he worked with Hynek – he felt that behind McDonald's determination to drag UFOs into the light of public debate was a will to power, a need for ego-assertion. In 1971, after five years of beating his head against a brick wall, and being jeered at by the scientific community, McDonald committed suicide.

Hynek himself was increasingly prepared to stick his neck out. When *Challenge to Science* was published in America in 1966, Hynek wrote a foreword. In this he used the analogy of isolating radium from pitch-blende, and admitted that he now felt there *was* radium to be found in the vast pile of UFO sightings, and that 'Perhaps I should have spoken earlier; eighteen years is a long time.'

Meanwhile, Vallee was studying the Air Force files, and was excited to discover that a wave of UFO sightings had occurred in 1951, 'landings and cigar-shaped objects, just as in Aimé Michel's classic work'. He admitted, 'I am beginning to think like McDonald: how could Hynek have missed it?'

The Air Force was anxious to get rid of the responsibility for UFOs, and wanted to pass it on to some respectable university. Hynek and Vallee hoped that the job of computerising their reports would go to their department at Northwestern. They were angry and frustrated when the Dean got cold feet and turned down the proposal; he was afraid that Northwestern might be associated with 'crank theories'. Hynek was so furious that he considered resigning.

Vallee was glad to escape back to Europe at the end of the summer semester. He was beginning to feel disillusioned with America, and was learning that democracy had two faces. On the one hand, he was able to publish books about UFOs while not endangering his position at Northwestern; on the other, ambitious career scientists like Carl Sagan could sneer about UFOs, and declare that no government funds should be channelled into research, and effectively prevent the subject being taken seriously. Vallee noted: 'If the saucers turn out to be significant, Sagan will take the credit for having theorized about cosmic visitors. If they are discredited, he will claim he always saw clearly through their mythical character.'

It was a relief to be back in Paris. He loved strolling along the Seine and looking at the bookstalls. His interest in UFOs had always run parallel with an interest in mysticism, hermeticism and alchemy. (Hynek himelf was deeply interested in these subjects, and was a Rudolf Steiner enthusiast.) And his study of the history of UFOs since Biblical times had made him aware that some knowledge of the past was essential to understanding the phenomenon. At the end of August 1966, he picked up a copy of Paracelsus, the magician and scientist who lived in the early sixteenth century. Most scientists would have dismissed Paracelsus as a would-be scientist who was gullible enough to be taken in by the magical superstitions of his time. But Vallee's years of studying UFO sightings had made him less dismissive. He was struck by Paracelsus's comment on gnomes:

'They can appear at will small or tall, handsome or ugly . . . *Think twice before becoming allied with them. As soon as you are linked to them, you have to do their bidding. When they are angry they inflict heavy penalties. Sometimes they kill. There are proofs of it.'* Vallee underlined these last (italicised) sentences.

In fact, Vallee was encountering many cases that would have been described in the Middle Ages as encounters with supernatural beings. The experience of Eugenio Douglas is typical. In October 1963, he was driving a truck through heavy rain near Islaverda, Argentina, when a blinding light forced him to slow down. When he stopped the truck, the light vanished. But further down the road he encountered a disc-shaped craft, thirty-five metres high, from which three giant figures wearing luminous clothes and strange helmets emerged – Douglas estimated them at twelve feet tall. A red beam came from either the craft or the entities, and burnt him. Douglas fired back with a rifle, then fled. The red beam followed him to the village of Montemaiz, where the street lighting was affected. Douglas took shelter in a house, whose own lights were flickering; both he and the occupants noted a strong smell.

The next day, Douglas was suffering from radiation burns. And, back at the site where he had seen the 'giants', he found footprints twenty inches long.

Paracelsus had remarked that there were four main orders of supernatural being – nymphs, dwarfs, sylphs and salamanders – but added that giants should also be included. The Douglas encounter seemed a case in point.

In November, back in Chicago, Vallee and Hynek went to Boulder, Colorado, to meet the Condon team. The next day, Hynek addressed them, telling them the whole story of Project Blue Book, and occasionally requesting that the tape recorder should be switched off while he told them things that he would prefer off the record. Vallee then gave a talk suggesting how the computer might be used in UFO investigations. All went well, and, when Hynek gave a press conference, there was a general air of congratulation, as if he had finally been vindicated after years of trying to get UFOs taken seriously. But, when a Denver newspaper reported it next day, it merely stated that Hynek had announced that there had been no 'hardware', no tangible evidence of saucer visits.

Vallee's journal makes it clear that he was becoming increasingly disillusioned with Hynek. Hynek turned up an hour late for a meeting with Vallee's publisher, returned some phone calls, made a few distracted remarks, then rushed off, saying he'd be back later. Vallee commented, 'How I miss the days when he was not such a celebrity . . . Media men hire Allen as they would hire a guitar player. He rushes wherever he sees a spotlight, and if the spotlight moves, he moves with it.'

He was also becoming deeply disillusioned with the Condon Committee. Hearing about Roy Craig's encounter with the saw-whet owl, he commented, 'In [Fred Beckman's] opinion the owl explanation is a joke. A friend of his, who has done his own enquiry with the local civil defense authorities, has found out that high-quality recordings were made which show artificial signal patterns.' He was even less happy with Hynek's dismissal of the Stephen Michalak encounter in Winnipeg on the grounds that it was a one-witness sighting, pointing out reasonably that Michalak's burns proved he had encountered *something*.

In June 1967, Vallee noted with disgust that, while a wave of UFO sightings was taking place in America, the Condon Committee merely argued, dreamt and theorised, while its chief administrator, Robert Low, proposed to use a research grant to go to an astronomical conference in Prague, where he would be joined by Hynek.

One day when Hynek was away on holiday, Vallee went to his house to sort through the Air Force files, and found a chaos of unfiled material; he took this away, and proceeded to sort it out. In among this, Vallee found a letter that left no doubt that the Air Force had been in favour of a cover-up since the initiation of Project Blue Book in 1952.

What had happened was that when the whole country was talking about flying saucers, which had even flown over Washington, the public urgently wanted to know what was going on. So the CIA decided to convene a panel, under the chairmanship of a physicist, Dr H.P. Robertson. Hynek was a very junior adviser. The Robertson Panel sat for five days, looked at film of UFOs, and discussed the evidence at length. The panel eventually concluded that most UFO sightings were meteorological phenomena or misidentification of aeroplanes, planets, etc., and that they posed no threat to national security. Therefore, the panel recommended (in January 1953), future UFO reports should be debunked. It also recommended that civilian UFO groups, like the Lorenzens' APRO and Keyhoe's NICAP, should be 'monitored' (i.e. spied upon) because of their influence on public opinion. Hynek was unhappy about this, but was then too uninfluential to make his views felt.

Now Vallee went on to uncover a letter in the files that left no possible doubt that the Air Force was engaged in a 'disinformation' operation. This letter, headed 'Secret', and dated three days before the panel was due to meet, noted that certain areas in America had an abnormally high number of UFO sightings, and recommended that such areas should have observation posts with radar, cameras, etc. So far, its advice was unexceptionable. But it then went on to recommend that 'many different types of aerial activity should be secretly and purposefully scheduled' within such areas. The careful monitoring of every possible unknown flying object would enable the Air Force to learn precisely which objects *were* flying saucers. But it would also enable the Air Force to debunk the thousands of public sightings that would inevitably occur, explaining that the Air Force was operating in that area. Moreover, said the letter, 'reports for the last five years could be re-evaluated' – in other words, past UFO sightings could also be debunked. In this way, the great American public could be reassured – and, of course, deceived.

When Vallee later met two members of the Condon Committee, he asked what had happened about the Stephen Michalak case, and was told that the investigator had 'brought back some data'. He was not told that Roy Craig had decided not to wait around for Michalak's identification of the UFO landing site because he had decided that Michalak was a fraud.

One of the committee members, Mary-Lou Armstrong, told Vallee frankly that they were not interested in field investigations. They were at present pursuing a theory propounded by one of their members, a psychologist name Wertheimer, that motorists only *thought* their headlights failed when they saw a UFO, because they were blinded by the ball lightning, and failed to realise that their headlights were on . . .

In fact, Mary-Lou Armstrong would resign from the committee in disgust. The other committee member who was present that day with Vallee was Norman Levine, who was sacked for showing McDonald the famous cover-up letter from Low.

Fred Beckman, one of Vallee's closest associates, summarised the problem of the Condon Committee when he said, 'The public is expecting serious answers from a committee of experts. Yet the truth is, these people won't even take the trouble to become superficially familiar with the problem . . .'

What he meant, quite simply, was that the basic weakness in the approach of the Condon Committee lay in the assumption that all that was needed was a group of intelligent and honest men. This is rather like setting up a panel to investigate whether the Big Bang theory deserves to be taken seriously, and choosing professors of English rather than physicists. The assessment of UFO phenomena requires, at the very least, an extensive knowledge of UFO reports. The members of the Condon Committee simply did not possess this knowledge – or try to acquire it. Vallee and Hynek had studied thousands of cases; the Condon Committee studied a case only when it was drawn to their attention.

In the autumn of 1967, disillusioned with America, and the direction UFO research was taking, Vallee returned again to France, and took a job in Paris. He disliked De Gaulle's France almost as much as Lyndon Johnson's America, yet found that Paris moved him in a way Chicago never could. He was in Paris for the students' uprising of May 1968. And on the day the strikes ended, 15 June 1968, he returned home with a pile of second-hand books, and recorded in his journal the idea for a book drawing a parallel between UFO phenomena and the medieval tradition about fairies, elves and elementals. The writing of

Passport to Magonia went fast – even though he was writing in English – and, by 12 September 1968, it was completed – together with a list of reports of over 900 saucer landings. Vallee felt that this was a book that he could never have written in America; the subject had somehow needed the deeper intellectual roots of Europe. Yet as soon as he had finished it, he returned to America – this time, for good. Comparing America to France in his journal, he wrote:

> On the one side is the great creative wind of freedom, the immense potential of America. When I look for something to put in the balance on the French side, what comes to mind is not science or art . . . but the humble street scenes – that old woman I passed in the rue de la Verrerie, for instance, whose hand was shaking so much she could hardly hold her grocery bag . . .

So America won. He went back taking Papus's *Practise of Magic*, Flammarion's *Invisible World* and Margaret Murray's *God of the Witches*.

So *Passport to Magonia* is, on one level, a kind of nostalgic homage to Europe. The title is taken from a passage in the writings of the nineteenth-century Archbishop Agobard of Lyons, who speaks harshly of people who believe that there is a country in the sky called Magonia 'from which ships sail in the clouds'. Agobard tells how three men and a woman were dragged before him by a crowd who claimed the strangers had descended from one of these airships, and demanded that they be stoned to death. Agobard states briefly, 'But truth prevailed' – meaning, evidently, that he told them not to be stupid, that people did not descend out of airships. Presumably the four men and women were the first recorded 'abductees'.

Vallee then quotes St Anthony's circumstantial account of his encounter with a friendly 'elemental', and philosophers like Paracelsus who believed that there is a whole class of beings between the gods and humanity. Vallee goes on to speak of the scholar Jerome Cardan, whose father recorded how, on 13 August 1491, seven men 'appeared to him', dressed in garments like silken togas, who claimed to be 'men composed of air', and told him their age was three hundred years. Cardan's father recorded that they stayed with him for three hours, and engaged in lengthy theological discussion. One of them explained that God created the world from moment to moment, and that, if he desisted even for a second, the universe would disappear.

The account sounds preposterous – but not more preposterous than hundreds of modern tales of encounters with 'extraterrestrials', many of whom sound very much like traditional angels.

And what should we make of a story of the poet Goethe, who describes in his autobiography how, on the road from Leipzig to Frankfurt, he passed a sort of amphitheatre by the road in which there were hundreds of lights, some of which moved around, while others were stationary? Goethe was unable to stop and investigate – he was walking uphill behind the coach – but wondered whether they were will-o'-the-wisps or 'a company of luminous creatures'. But 'will-o'-the-wisp' (or 'jack-o'-lantern') is another name for methane – Hynek's swamp gas – which can ignite spontaneously, and it is obviously impossible that a whole amphitheatre could have been full of exploding methane.

Vallee goes on to cite modern cases that sound equally bizarre: the two little men seen by Lonnie Zamora at Socorro, the 'goblins' who besieged the Hopkinsville farm all night, the two midgets in space suits who paralysed the French farmer Maurice Masse – who, in spite of his fright, still felt that his visitors were 'good'.

It is important to understand that what Vallee is implying is not simply that modern 'aliens' seem to have a great deal in common with various 'supernatural' creatures of folklore (which is obvious anyway), but that we are wrong to dismiss the fairies, elves, sylphs and angels of folklore as delusions of people who did not know any better. In 1897, for example, the poet W.B. Yeats accompanied his friend Lady Gregory around local cottages in Galway, collecting fairy stories, and, to his surprise, learnt that the peasants not only believed in fairies, but told circumstantial stories of their encounters with them. Yeats came to accept the factual reality of fairies, and persuaded a young American academic, Walter Evans-Wentz, to spend some time in Ireland collecting accounts. These appeared in a classic work called *The Fairy Faith in the Celtic Countries*, in which the author concludes that the factual and scientific evidence for the existence of fairies is overwhelming. In his later years, Evans-Wentz returned to his native America, and studied the beliefs of the local Indians near San Diego, again concluding that there is evidence for the real existence of supernatural beings.

Yeats's friend George Russell (the poet AE) contributed a section to the book in which he describes his own fairy sightings with the precision of an anthropologist describing primitive tribes: shining beings, opalescent beings, water beings, wood beings, lower elementals. Russell was a mystic with 'psychic' abilities, and in this connection it is worth bearing in mind a comment made by the UFO investigator John Keel: 'I discovered that the majority of all [UFO] witnesses had latent or active psychic abilities, and . . . other independent investigators around the world confirmed this in their own research.'[1]

By the end of *Passport to Magonia*, the reader is certainly inclined to agree that the most carefully documented UFO sightings sound far more absurd than accounts of fairies, elementals and other beings of folklore.

Not surprisingly, *Passport to Magonia* created dismay among the UFO fraternity. 'Vallee has gone off the deep end,' said one critic. People who believed that flying saucers came from Mars, or some distant constellation, felt that Vallee's parallels with folklore were irrelevant and far-fetched. UFOs were shining silver discs that took off at a tremendous speed and could do right-angle turns in the air. But Vallee had noted that not all sightings were of shining discs. As Mrs Lotti-Dainelli, of Arezzo, Italy, passed a torpedo-shaped machine by the roadside, two odd little men in one-piece suits and red hats grabbed the pot of flowers she was carrying to the cemetery, and took it into the spacecraft. By the time she had returned with a policeman, the machine had taken off, leaving a blue and red trail. It sounds like a joke, or something out of a children's cartoon. It certainly sounds too absurd to interest a scientist – why should two munchkins snatch a pot of flowers?

But Vallee points out that many creatures of folklore – such as fairies – like to steal human products. And, in doing so, he is putting his finger squarely on one of the major paradoxes of the UFO phenomenon: that it seems to have been devised by someone with a surrealistic sense of humour – like the case presided over by H.B. Morton's Mr Justice Cocklecarrot, in which an eccentric lady used to knock on the plaintiff's door and push seven red dwarfs into his hallway. Any number of close encounters sound just as hilariously pointless. Why did little tin men besiege the Sutton farmhouse? Why did two gas-puffing robots keep Donald Schrum up a tree all night? What was the motive of the UFO that trailed Colonel Chase's B-57 bomber over Texas and Mississippi – in one of the few cases that impressed Roy Craig of the Condon Committee? In fact, why were hundreds of planes in World War Two trailed by UFOs (which were then known as foo fighters)?

[1] 'The People Problem', in *Phenomenon*, edited by John Spencer and Hilary Evans.

Common sense suggests that they were behaving like mischievous schoolboys who knock on a door and run away; but that implies that they had no serious purpose. *If* they had a serious purpose, could it simply be to make themselves known, to make us aware that they are there? Then why not simply land in the middle of a major city? Would this, perhaps, be too great a culture shock for the human race? Vallee speculates in the last chapter: 'Perhaps it enjoys our puzzlement, or perhaps it is trying to teach us some new concept. Perhaps it is acting in a purely gratuitous effort, and its creations are as impossible for us to understand as is the Picasso sculpture in Chicago to the birds who perch on it . . .'

But what fascinated him most about UFOs was what he called 'the psychic component' – the tendency of UFOs (observed by Puharich and Geller) to behave more like ghosts than solid spacecraft. His next book, *The Invisible College* (1976),[1] is devoted largely to this psychic component. ('The invisible college' refers to the small group of a hundred or so UFO investigators all over the world who keep one another informed of their data.)

Vallee was interested in the *effect* of UFOs on people who believed they had seen them, or even that they had been in them. In 1973, he had met an engineering executive who described how he had been on an archaeological field trip when he had seen a disc-shaped object, and had been taken on board. He was transported to a place where he was connected up to a 'teaching machine', a kind of computer, and had spent three hours having information fed directly into his brain. After what seemed a few hours, he returned to the spot where he had been abducted – to find that he had been absent for eighteen days, and that his influential father had had the military and the police out searching for him. He was still wearing the same flower in his buttonhole, his clothes were impeccable, and he did not need a shave.

When the engineer spoke of the encounter, he was soon surrounded by curiosity-seekers, and ended by 'confessing' that it had all been a joke, merely to get rid of pests. But he told Vallee that, for six months after the experience, he had needed an enormous amount of sleep – more than twelve hours a night – and after that his need for sleep then diminished until he needed only an hour or two every night. His powers of memory and concentration were enormously enhanced. Now he had

---

[1] Also published as *UFOs, The Psychic Connection*.

become convinced that some immense change was about to take place on Earth. And since the UFO experience, he had never been ill.

Vallee compares the engineer's experience to that of the three-year-old Uri Geller in the garden in Tel Aviv; he also adds that he does not believe that mankind is being contacted by benign intelligences from outer space, or that Geller is the new Messiah.

Yet how, asks Vallee, can you say that a man is a sincere witness, and nevertheless reject his beliefs? This is the question he sets out to answer in *The Invisible College* – and which has preoccupied him ever since.

Yet the case he goes on to cite – of a French doctor who wished to remain anonymous, preferring to be called 'Dr X' – seems to contradict his scepticism about benign intelligences. Dr X was awakened in the middle of the night by his child, who was pointing at a flashing light in the sky. He opened the window and observed two disc-shaped UFOs. Then the two came together and blended into one. This disc then turned into the vertical position, so its blinding light illuminated the front of the house. Suddenly there was a loud bang, and it vanished.

The doctor now found that a leg injury had suddenly healed, and so had an old war wound. Subsequently, he lost weight, and a red triangle formed around his navel. The same triangle formed on the child. Vallee notes that, as a consequence of the experience, both the doctor and his wife have developed an almost mystical attitude of acceptance towards life and death. Strange coincidences occurred, the doctor and his wife became telepathic, and on one occasion he experienced levitation.

Vallee then speaks of a case that occurred at Aveyron, in France, where a farmer and his son saw glowing spheres that floated in the air. Later, the son saw a disc with a green light inside it, and thought he could see two occupants, before it flew off at an incredible speed.

This witness also began to sleep far more than usual, and also had an occasional sensation of floating out of his body, during which time his body would become paralysed – a phenomenon that often accompanies 'out-of-the-body experiences'. He also began trying to persuade young people to study science and astronomy. When he declared that he had to write a book, and someone pointed out that he was almost illiterate, he replied, '*They* told me not to worry about that.'

Vallee had first-hand experience of official cover-up when he and Janine heard of a case in Normandy, and went to investigate soon after the event. A fisherman and his son had come to the beach at daybreak, and saw a bright object hovering over the place where their nets were spread. It was yellow and emitted a conelike beam towards the ground. Three months earlier the son had seen three yellow spheres above the beach. A radar installation had picked up the second UFO, and watched it move away over the sea. And a nearby French trawler went off course, its magnetic navigation system having apparently gone awry.

A few days later, French Intelligence announced that some diving gear found on a nearby beach indicated that divers had been using some equipment that explained the radar sighting and the malfunction of the trawler's navigation system. So the authorities created an atmosphere that suggested that the UFO sighting had now been explained away as something quite natural.

The UFO problem, Vallee feels, is analogous to a conjuror who baffles his audience by some incredible display of magic, then explains it all – the hollow tabletop, the collapsing cane, the rabbit in the coat tail. Back at home you congratulate yourself on knowing how it was done – then realise that the explanation simply does not add up. He was not telling the truth. 'The phenomenon negates itself.'

Later in the book he has an even better suggestion. He tells an anecdote about the psychiatrist Milton Erickson, who was standing on a corner when a man came round it in a hurry and bumped into him. Erickson glanced elaborately at his watch and said, 'It's exactly ten minutes to two', then walked on, leaving the man staring after him in astonishment.

This encounter gave Erickson the idea for what he called the confusion technique of hypnosis. When a subject was difficult to hypnotise, Erickson would give a number of contradictory suggestions – such as 'Your left hand is rising, while your right remains immobile' and 'Your right hand is rising while your left remains immobile.' The psychiatrist's apparent confusion would arouse sympathy in the patient and lead to a cooperative attitude which favoured hypnosis. Still further confusion would lead the patient to give up his resistance and retreat from the confusion by accepting all the hypnotist's suggestions.

This, Vallee suggests, could explain the confusion technique used by UFOs, with all their surrealistic absurdities. Such a notion obviously implies that the UFO entities are trying to make individual contactees drop their rationalistic attitudes in favour of unconscious acceptance. It also suggests, of course, that they might be trying to hypnotise us.

Certainly, these puzzling creatures seem to enjoy creating confusion.

Vallee describes how a midwestern woman named Mrs Keech woke up with an odd tingling feeling in her hand and arm, and proceeded to take up a pen and do automatic writing. The communicating 'entity' seemed kindly and protective, and signed himself 'Elder Brother'. Mrs Keech soon became convinced that she was channelling information from a higher level of reality. A small sect formed around her. Then Elder Brother informed them that there would soon be a tremendous disaster, involving earthquake and flood.

A small group of academics from a nearby university infiltrated the group to study the psychology of religious conviction. When the flood failed to occur, the group were not in the least disillusioned; they believed that they had averted it.

The parallels with Puharich and the 'landing on planet Earth' are obvious, and, in fact, Vallee goes on to tell the story of Geller, Puharich and the invisible beings from Spectra. And his purpose becomes clearer when he goes on to tell a story about a Mrs Swan, who had also been writing down messages from space entities. A man named Talman contacted Colonel Friend, head of Project Blue Book, to tell him about this. And, when Mrs Swan was interviewed by an investigator named Commander Curtis, she suggested that *he* should try to contact the entities.

Oddly enough, Curtis tried, and got results. The 'entities' told him that they were called AFFA, and were from Venus. And as a group of investigators sat in a Washington office, with Curtis writing down answers to questions, someone asked if they could see a flying saucer. They were told, 'Yes, look out of the window.' There was nothing outside. But at 2 o'clock that afternoon – 6 July 1959 – they *did* see a cigar-shaped object that flew over Washington. They called the radar centre, and were told that, for some reason, the radar beam was blocked in that direction. The official memo stated that 'there is no question that the object was seen over Washington that day'.

Again, this sounds like firm evidence for the extraterrestrial-intelligence hypothesis. Why does Vallee not accept it? Because he knew enough about automatic writing and psychic phenomena to know that they seem to be based on systematic ambiguity and misdirection. The entities seem to tell lies just as often as they tell the truth. Vallee's own experiments, with a man of well-tested psychic ability, produced answers that seemed sensible and consistent. Asked what UFOs were trying to do, the answer was, 'To harmonise this world with the rest of the universe.' (Phyllis Schlemmer's 'Tom' had said much the same thing.)

But Vallee's conclusion is that the answers were 'an instance of communication with a level of consciousness, possibly (but not necessarily) nonhuman. But (while) its nature may be understandable only in terms of a space–time structure more complex than what current physics places at our disposal . . . it is useful to keep in mind that aspects of it may be systematically misleading.'

The story of a Brazilian named Paul Gaetano is a case in point. On 17 November 1971, he was driving with a friend named Elvio when he told Elvio that a flying saucer was following them. All Elvio could see was a bus. The car engine seemed to lose power, and, as Gaetano pulled into the side of the road, Elvio fell asleep. The saucer then landed, and little men took Gaetano aboard and made him lie on a table while they X-rayed him, then took a blood sample by cutting his elbow. After showing him a town plan and a picture of an atomic explosion, they induced him to fall asleep. He woke up as Elvio helped him back into the car. Elvio saw nothing of the flying saucer. But the wound on Gaetano's arm seemed to support his story.

It seems that the little men not only had the power to make Elvio fall asleep, but also to make him mistake a UFO for a bus.

In a chapter on miracles, devoted to Fátima, Lourdes and the Guadaloupe Madonna, Vallee points out the same element of confusion. Witnesses at Fátima saw the oldest girl, Lucia (aged ten), addressing the empty air, although one thought he could hear a faint voice responding – or it might have been the buzzing of a bee. Lucia reported that, the day after the vision, she had 'no strength to do anything' – like the UFO contactees mentioned earlier. Witnesses at Lourdes saw Bernadette dig a hole in the sand with her hands – which immediately filled with water – then try to wash in the water, and, to everyone's amusement, smeared her face with mud. After this, she began to eat grass. Later, Bernadette explained that the lady had told her to wash and drink in a spring, but that, since there was no spring, she began to dig in the sand, where a spring promptly appeared. The lady had also told her to go and eat grass.

The next day, a clear stream was flowing from the new spring, and, when a blind man washed his eyes in it, he was suddenly able to see. A dying baby was restored to health. When Bernadette was praying in a state of ecstasy, a doctor held a lighted candle under her hand for fifteen minutes, but her flesh was not even blistered. Yet when the candle was held under her hand when she had finished praying, she snatched her hand away saying, 'You are burning me.'

One witness of the final 'miracle' at Fátima describes how the sun seemed to change into a spinning snowball, then come down to earth in a zigzag motion, causing panic. This was at the scene of the miracle, but, even in a town nine miles away, one cynic who had spent the morning mocking the people who had gone to Fátima 'to see an ordinary girl' fell on his knees, crying out to God. A schoolboy who saw it – and who subsequently became a priest as a result – described how everything suddenly shone with rainbow colours (*see plate nos. 3, 4 and 5*).

At the end of the chapter on miracles, Vallee prints a four-page table comparing religious miracles to UFO events, pointing out dozens of parallels.

The final chapter of *The Invisible College* begins with infectious optimism: 'I think we are close, very close, to understanding what UFOs are.' He then propounds the theory that UFO phenomena are basically a 'control system' for human consciousness – that is to say that an important part of their purpose is to be found in the *effect* they have on human beings. Their purpose seems to be to *change consciousness*.

A 'control system' is, of course, a system of thought control. Hitler's or Stalin's propaganda machines are crude examples; so are George Orwell's Thought Police in *Nineteen Eighty-Four*. But Vallee does not seem to have anything so simplistic in mind. He uses the example of a thermostat, which switches on when a house falls below a certain temperature. A naive observer might think that, for human beings, 'warm' is good and 'cold' is bad, and would be bewildered when, in summer, the thermostat keeps the house cool. What we need, says Vallee, is not to make moral judgments, but to understand the principle of the thermostat.

He goes on to quote the behavioural psychologist B.F. Skinner, who points out that the best way to reinforce a learning pattern is to combine periodicity with unpredictability – not regular and monotonous, but irregular and unexpected – what might be called a regular pattern of irregularity. Vallee's graph of bursts of UFO activity from 1947 to 1962 follows precisely this pattern.

His vision is hopeful. 'With every new wave of UFOs, the social impact becomes greater. More young people become fascinated with space, with psychic phenomena, with new frontiers in consciousness. More books and articles appear, changing our culture in the direction of a higher image of man.' He feels that our society is too oriented towards technological progress, and the next step may be a 'massive change of human attitudes towards paranormal abilities and extra-terrestrial life'.

This is fascinating, but it leaves two major questions unanswered: who is it who wishes to change our culture in the direction of a higher image of man and where do flying saucers come from? Vallee does not try to answer either of these questions – although he seems to feel that the answer might not be far away. But his general conclusion is clear enough. He rejects the simplistic view that UFOs are manifestations of beings from another planet who have recently – or not so recently – come to earth. He feels that they behave confusingly because they want to confuse us, but that their ultimate purpose is to nudge us in the direction of open-mindedness.

The Invisible College is probably Vallee's best book. It might well have been entitled *Clues*, for it reads like a detective story, communicating an enormous sense of excitement. Vallee is fascinated by how many pieces of his complex jigsaw puzzle seem to fit together, and by the way that the distinction between ufology and paranormal research is beginning to blur – supporting the intuition that had led him to write *Passport to Magonia*.

But his next book, *Messengers of Deception* (1979), has an altogether darker tone. The optimism about a breakthrough seems to have evaporated. It is clear that he has begun to feel that the answer to the UFO problem is not as close as he thought, and that, as the title implies, the UFOs and the 'aliens' may be engaged in a complicated piece of deception. He is even inclined to wonder whether some human group might not be responsible for many of the phenomena. His earlier conclusion that UFOs are 'psychotronic devices' whose purpose is to influence human consciousness has now given way to the suspicion that they might be merely 'terrestrial-based manipulating devices'.

This idea arose, to some extent, from the activities of a mysterious organisation that called itself UMMO, which Vallee had already discussed in *The Invisible College*. On 1 June 1967, a lens-shaped UFO had been seen over a suburb of Madrid, its bottom inscribed with a symbol like a capital H, with curved uprights and a vertical line the middle of the crossbar. Five rather poor photographs of the UFO were published the next day in a Madrid evening newspaper. Numerous other sightings followed, and local shopkeepers received a circular letter stating that a UFO had landed, and had apparently left behind a number of metallic cylinders. It offered rewards of $300 each for these cylinders.

One cylinder was apparently found. It proved to made of a pure form of nickel, and contained a piece of green plastic with the H symbol on it. This cylinder had been picked up by a twelve-year-old boy, and found itself in the hands of an invesigator by way of a man called Antonio Pardo, who, it seemed, was also responsible for the photographs published by the newspaper. The plastic was unusual, but not extraterrestrial – it proved to be the type used in American space rockets.

After this, a writer and government employee named Manzano, who had founded an organisation called the Friends of Space, began to receive an enormous amount of material that claimed to come from aliens who originated on the planet Ummo (spelt in capitals), about three and a half light years from earth; its symbol was the crossed H. These aliens claimed to be responsible for the UFO activity. Some of the Ummo material was scientific, some philosophical.

Manzano also received phone calls from a man with a strong foreign accent, who claimed to be a representative of the Ummans. Apparently they were not responsible for the flying saucers seen by Kenneth Arnold – they had landed on Earth only in 1950. It seemed they did not intend to interfere in the social organisation of the Earth – this was forbidden by a 'cosmic morality'.

Understandably, Ummo and the Ummans became a subject of excited discussion in UFO circles all over the world. But although the material was often philosophically interesting, it was curiously naive. One letter began by commiserating with human beings on the death of 'your brother, thinker and mathematician Bertrand Russell', who, it was suggested, was really an Umman – as, apparently, were Gandhi, Che Guevara, Karl Marx, Martin Luther King, Albert Schweitzer, Tolstoy and others. It sounds as if the list has been concocted by some typical liberal intellectual of the 1960s.

Vallee was not inclined to take the claims of Ummo very seriously, even though he admits that some of the Umman correspondence was 'profound and even illuminating'. After *The Invisible College*, he had turned his attention to other groups who claimed UFO connections, and seemed to be confirmed in his view that the UFO entities were far from trustworthy.

For example, he met an attractive girl called Helen by appointment in a Los Angeles coffee shop; she wanted to tell him about her own 'close encounter of the fifth kind'. She had, it seemed, been part of a pop group, who were travelling back from a gig in the summer of 1968, when all four of them saw a bright light in the sky, which finally hovered silently over their car. Then four funnel-shaped lights came down from the UFO – which was as wide as a freeway – and drew them up into it. They apparently left their bodies in the moving car. Then she suddenly found herself back in her body and in the car.

Suspecting that there was something she could not remember, she submitted to hypnosis, then was able to recall going on board the UFO, being shown its propulsion system by a man dressed in white, who looked like a normal human being, and also being shown a perpetual-motion motor. She was, she told Vallee, trying to build this machine. Vallee felt that it could never run in the way she explained it, and knew, in any case, that perpetual motion was impossible, since it would defy the law of the conservation of energy.

All the same, he went to the trouble of trying to contact other members of the group (who had split up), and succeeded with two of them – he was unable to track down the third. But the two he spoke to confirmed everything Helen said – one of them said the event had been a turning point in his life.

Vallee's conclusion was that the experience was probably hallucinatory, 'projected to alter the individual belief systems'. He even suggests that the UFO might have been some 'form of natural energy' (ball lightning?) that might have triggered the vision, and adds, 'Let us not forget that the society in question is badly in need of "space brothers" . . .' Yet this seems to avoid the question of why they experienced a collective hallucination. Her apparent 'contact' may have been 'a symbolic manifestation or a trap. Her "spacemen" may have been messengers of deception.'

The book is a fascinating and highly amusing study of various Californian cults investigated by Vallee, including a group called Human Individual Metamorphosis, led by a man called Applewhite, which self-destructed dramatically two decades later in a mass suicide – the purpose being to join a spaceship hidden behind the comet Hale-Bopp. (The event had been anticipated in *Messages of Deception* in a section eerily entitled 'It Only Costs Your Life'.)

Then there was Grace Hooper Pettipher, head of the San Francisco Order of Melchizedek, who was always bumping into people who had reincarnated from Atlantis, and had also been in direct contact with the inhabitants of a UFO.

Dr Pettipher had dissociated herself from another branch of the sect, known as Urantia, who studied a 'channelled' book of that title. In pursuit of Urantia, Vallee studied the book, and was impressed. He was even more impressed when he came across a book called *The Physiology of Faith and Fear* by Dr William Sadler, a sceptical examination of many religious sects claiming direct revelation, in which Sadler admitted that, in spite of his general disillusionment, he had been deeply impressed by *The Book of Urantia* – although he admitted that, after eighteen years of study, he was back where he started. Vallee remarks:

> We might ask ourselves the same question about UFOs and their alleged agents among us: a phenomenon that leaves physical traces must be taken seriously, but what can we say of the people who claim to be in contact with superior intelligences emanating from these objects? What should we do about their claim that the phenomenon of UFOs is directing the evolution of mankind?

Vallee's feeling is clearly that they do not deserve serious consideration.

Messengers of Deception introduces the subject of cattle mutilation, which he studied in more detail later – he has still not published his results. But he is inclined to agree with the comments of Frederick W. Smith: 'Someone has been delivering a message to the American people, to the government, to the intelligence community.' But by this he seems to mean that the cattle mutilations may be engineered to induce terror.

Yet he stresses that he believes that the UFO phenomenon 'transcends time as it transcends space'. However, he says, 'we still need to discover the source of this manifestation'. And this aim, which has been the central purpose of all his books, is still unfulfilled at the end of *Messengers of Deception*.

Vallee was to write three more books – a trilogy – to try to summarise his conclusions about the UFO phenomenon. But while *Dimensions* (1988), *Confrontations* (1990) and *Revelations* (1991) sparkle with ideas and insights, and are as obsessively readable as ever, they fail to bring us any closer to a total understanding of the phenomenon.

Dimensions is Vallee's longest book, and his most substantial. It is an attempt at a summary of all his previous books, and to catch up with the latest developments, such as abductions. In his introduction, Whitley Strieber, author of the bestselling *Communion*, remarks: 'If we come to a correct understanding of the UFO phenomenon, we may well in the process destroy the whole basis of our present beliefs about reality.' And Vallee comments that he does not believe that UFOs are extraterrestrial objects in the normal sense, but that 'they present an exciting challenge to our concept of reality itself'. This view is again expressed at the end of the book, when he suggests that the reality that surrounds us is a 'multiverse' rather than a universe, and cites Hugh Everett's suggestion that quantum theory can be made fully consistent only by assuming that there is not one reality, but a series of parallel realities or universes.

The only logical follow-up to this view would be a book that goes into further detail about quantum physics, and how it could help to explain some of the paradoxes of the UFO phenomenon – a topic we shall consider in the last chapter. In fact, Vallee's next book, *Confrontations*, is about some research that he and Janine Vallee conducted in South America, which made it clear that UFOs can kill, and that they sometimes appear to do so deliberately – as in the case of a Brazilian named Salvador de Santos, who was hit by a beam of light one day in 1946, and died with his flesh falling off his bones as if he had been boiled in water. (Vallee speculates that the beam may have consisted of microwaves.) The book is an important – and disturbing – piece of research, but brings us no closer to a solution.

Revelations, the last of the trilogy, returns to the problem of human deception already explored in *Messengers of Deception* – such as the strange affair of the 'Majestic 12' documents, apparently a revelation of the government's duplicity, but which are now generally regarded as forgeries (the signature of President Truman having been lifted from another document). He concludes that 'someone is going to an awful lot of trouble to convince the world that we are threatened by beings from outer space', and that 'the time has come to mount an effort to restore some sanity to this field of research'. Yet his penetrating criticisms of some of the wilder conspiracy theories bring us no closer to solving the problem he presented so clearly a quarter of a century earlier in *Anatomy of a Phenomenon*.

What is this 'new concept of reality' that Vallee is speaking about? It seems to me that one of the most interesting passages in his books occurs towards the end of *Messengers of Deception*.

This describes how, in 1976, Vallee was investigating the Melchizedek groups. He wanted to know more about the Biblical prophet Melchizedek but was unable to find more than brief entries in reference books. On 21 February 1976, he took a taxi to a Los Angeles radio station, and asked the woman driver for a receipt. It was signed 'M. Melchizedek'. He said that it was as if he had put a notice on some universal notice board: 'Wanted: Melchizedeks', and some incompetent guardian angel had presented him with a taxi driver.

Wondering if the surname Melchizedek was common in Los Angeles, he looked in the vast Los Angeles telephone directory. There was only one Melchizedek – his taxi driver.

This is an example of what Jung calls synchronicity, or meaningful coincidence. It was a subject that had interested me for many years, because I had noticed how often they seemed to occur in my own life – particularly when I was feeling highly motivated and optimistic. In 1971 I was writing a book called *The Occult*, and needed a reference on alchemy. I was not quite sure where to find it, and took the wrong book off my shelf. The next book fell off the shelf on to the floor – open at the right page.

In 1986, I was writing an article about synchronicity for an encyclopedia of unsolved mysteries, and I told various stories of synchronicities that had happened to me, and went on to cite the Jacques Vallee anecdote. Having written it, I broke off my work to take the dogs for a walk. About to leave my study, I noticed lying on the camp bed a volume I did not recognise; it was called *You Are Sentenced to Life* by W.D. Chesney, and was about life after death. I had bought it a long time ago, but had never even glanced at it. Now I took it upstairs to read when I got back from my walk. When I did so, an hour and a half later, the first thing I saw was a heading across the top of the last page: ORDER OF MELCHIZEDEK, followed by a letter from Grace Hooper Pettipher to the author of the book. It was as if the god of chance had whispered in my ear, 'You think Jacques's taxi driver is a preposterous coincidence – I'll go one better.'

Admittedly, Chesney is a Los Angeles doctor, so this reduced the odds. What still puzzles me is how the book got on to the bed, so I noticed it; it would normally have been tucked away on a shelf.

In the conclusion of *Messengers of Deception*, Vallee admits that he had not enjoyed writing it. The facts he has unearthed 'shocked earlier theories of mine'. He had started out, in *Anatomy of a Phenomenon* and *Challenge to Science*, with a scientific attempt to record and analyse the data. *Passsport to Magonia* had added an interesting new dimension: the recognition that the UFO phenomenon may be a manifestation of something that has been on earth for thousands of years. *The Invisible College* bubbles with excitement as he recognises the 'psychic dimension' – that there is undoubtedly a close parallel between UFOs and the kind of thing the Society for Psychical Research was investigating in the nineteenth century. But *Messengers of Deception*, while as stimulating as ever, seemed to be a step backward into conspiracy theories. Only the end, with its Melchizedek story, seems to break new ground, suggesting that perhaps reality is not as straightforward and rational as a library, where books are arranged from A to Z, but is more like a computer, where information is stored associatively, rather than sequentially. ('You request the intersection of "microwave" and "headache", and you find twenty articles you never suspected existed.')

It would seem to me that the Melchizedek story illustrates more clearly than anything elsewhere in his books what Vallee means by a new concept of reality. The Melchizedek incident could, of course, have been mere coincidence. But my own odd postscript to it makes me feel that this was a genuine example of what Jung calls synchronicity – which seems to imply either (a) that the unconscious mind is able to manipulate reality, or (b) that some unknown force manipulates reality.

Whichever is true, it suggests that our normal, down-to-earth way of viewing reality – which is also the way of science – is somehow mistaken.

5 Goblins from Hyperspace

A FTER GIVING A lecture at the Architects' Association in London, Jacques Vallee received a letter from a woman who had been in his audience, and who had been greatly struck by a slide he had shown of two 'scorpion men' on a Phoenician amulet, standing below a 'winged disc'. Vallee had been suggesting that the 'winged disc' might be a UFO.

In her letter, the woman described how, in the summer of 1968, she and a companion were driving towards Stratford-on-Avon to visit friends when, in broad daylight, they saw a shining disc in the sky. It was about the size of the full moon, and darted around, 'almost as if to show off its abilities'. When it vanished behind some trees, they drove on.

During the remainder of the drive, she had

some novel insights into what I can only describe as the Nature of Reality. These were connected in some way to this shining disc, and have had a profound effect on me, causing what is commonly known as a personality change. I won't try to explain what those insights were, since almost all the religions of the world have tried to do this and have failed. (In that afternoon I changed from an agnostic into a gnostic, if that means anything at all.) However, these insights hit me like bolts from the blue, as though from outside, one after the other. I've never had a similar experience since.

This semi-mystical experience was followed later by one that was altogether more disturbing. That evening, after dinner, they were sitting in a room that had French windows open on to the lawn. She crossed to the window to breathe fresh air, and on the lawn, in the light from the room, she saw a strange figure that reminded her of the Phoenician scorpion men, or the god Pan.

It had dog or goat-like legs. It was covered in silky, downy fur, dark and glinting in the light. It was unmistakably humanoid, and to my mind malevolent. It crouched, and stared unblinkingly at me with light, grape-green eyes that slanted upwards and had no pupils. The eyes shone, and they were by far the most frightening thing about it. It was, I think retrospectively, trying to communicate with me, but my panic interfered with any message I might have received. If it had stood to full height, it would have been about four to five feet tall. It had pointed ears and a long muzzle. It gave the impression of emaciation; its hands and fingers were as thin as sticks.

Thinking she might be hallucinating, she went and sat down until the fear had subsided, then went back again. It was still there, although it had moved further into the shadows. She kept away from the window for the rest of the evening.

The first thing that strikes us is the oddness of her reaction. We would expect her to call to her host, 'Come and look at this' or 'Can you see what I can see?' – or just to scream. In fact, we encounter her reaction again and again in people who have seen UFOs, aliens or other strange creatures. It is as if the entity is able to somehow block the thought of calling another person or reaching for a camera.

There are several possible interpretations of what happened to her. Jacques Vallee quotes her letter because it seems to confirm his view that UFOs and mythological creatures often go together. But we might also speculate that the UFO sighting aroused a sense of mystery, a feeling that the universe is a bigger and stranger place than we normally realise, and that this is why she changed from an agnostic to a 'gnostic' in an hour's drive. However, it is worth paying attention to her words that these insights hit her like bolts from the blue 'as though from outside'. They might suggest that such glimpses of the nature of reality were being *given* to her.

Then how do we interpret the appearance of the satyr or scorpion man? Had the insights somehow caused the veil that separates us from the paranormal dimension to become semitransparent, so that she saw some kind of Pan-like nature deity or elemental? Or was the creature an alien connected with the UFO? The slanting eyes without pupils certainly seem to support that interpretation. Then there is her interesting comment: 'It was, I think retrospectively, trying to communicate with me.' Was it simply trying to communicate telepathically, like so many aliens in contact reports? Or was it trying to communicate some further insight to supplement the 'bolts from the blue' of the afternoon?

Here, a personal comment. Immediately after writing the above lines, I picked up a book called *The Goblin Universe* by F.W. Holiday, to look up his views on the subject of what he calls 'the phantom menagerie' – of lake monsters, black dogs, Bigfoots and other semi-mythological creatures. I opened it casually while moving a book to make room for it. When my eyes fell on the page, I found it had opened at 'Pan, the goatfooted god, is not so funny when you encounter him.' He goes on to tell a story of a climber who had experienced sudden panic on Ben MacDhui, in the Scottish Cairngorms, after hearing crunching footsteps and sensing an invisible presence, and who fled all the way down the mountain. This climber was one of many who have experienced a sudden irrational panic on Ben MacDhui.

Although I had written the introduction to *The Goblin Universe* – more than ten years earlier – I had forgotten that he even mentions Pan. This seems to be typical of the kind of synchronicity that happens when you enter this field where one reality touches another – a point that Holiday notes repeatedly in his books.

At all events, because of the curious role synchronicity seems to play in the world of UFOs and the paranormal, I feel that this intervention of the god Pan may be an indication that this is the point where I should speak about Holiday and his work.

Frederick William Holiday – known to his friends as Ted – was a journalist who wrote about fishing and other topics relating to the open air. In 1962, when he was forty-one, he drove up to Loch Ness to try to catch a glimpse of the monster *(see plate no. 6)*, which had been reported so many times since 1933, when a road was built along the north shore. That first evening, preparing to settle down in his tent, he experienced an odd nervousness that he felt was more than imagination. 'After dark, I felt that Loch Ness was better left alone.'

It was a still night, yet at midnight, when he woke up in the totally silent glen, he was puzzled to hear waves crashing on the beach, even though there was no boat out on the loch.

Two days later, at dawn, he saw the monster. Peering through his binoculars, he observed something black and glistening appear above the surface – a huge hump. When it dived, it produced an upsurge of water, like a diving hippopotamus. He could still make out the shape below the surface, thick in the middle and tapering towards its extremities, blackish-grey in colour, and about forty-five feet long. Then a workman began hammering on a nearby pier, and it vanished.

He saw it again in 1965, from three different positions, as he raced along the shore of the lake in his car. After that, he felt that what he had seen was a kind of giant slug, which could probably change colour. In his 1968 book *The Great Orm of Loch Ness* ('orm' is old English for worm – or dragon), he suggests that the monster is a huge version of a slug called *Tullimonstrum gregarium*. Yet at the end of that book, he notes casually that, in folklore, dragons are associated with evil. He had spoken to two fishermen who had seen the monster at close range; they described it as having a head like a bulldog, very wide and ugly, and a fringe of coarse black hair round its neck. He wrote to a fellow monster-hunter, Tim Dinsdale: 'When people are confronted with this fantastic animal at close quarters they seem to be stunned. There is something strange about Nessie that has nothing to do with size or appearance. Odd, isn't it?'

He was also intrigued that lake – and sea – monsters seem so hard to photograph; he once had his finger on the button when the Loch Ness monster submerged. Could it be telepathic?

In 1968, his investigations took a new turn when he heard of a monster in Lough Fadda, Connemara, in Ireland; witnesses included two priests and a middle-aged librarian. Yet, when he went to Lough Fadda, he was puzzled: it was obviously too small to house a monster – anything as large as that would soon eat up all the fish. Many had noted this problem before – a man called Thomas Croker had published a book about Irish lake monsters, and, when he sent it to Sir Walter Scott, Scott observed that many people near his own home, Abbotsford, swore to seeing a 'water horse' emerge from a nearby loch which was certainly too small for anything of that size.

Ted Holiday also spent some time at Lough Nahooin, where a water monster had again been reported by many witnesses. Again it was too small for a monster; yet, when he set nets across the lake, something disturbed them in the night.

Ted had encountered the paranormal during the war, when he was in the RAF, and stationed in Egypt, near Heliopolis. A friend sitting in the guard tent heard approaching footsteps, which entered the tent; but no one was visible. He fled, and encountered Ted with a police patrol guard dog. But the guard dog was obviously afraid and refused to enter the tent. And close to the same spot, two nights later, two guard dogs behaved as if they were terrified, staring at something that Ted and his fellow guard could not see.

Back in England, he investigated a haunted house, with a poltergeist that switched the light on and off, and footsteps followed him around the house.

In 1969, while he was investigating Irish lake monsters, Ted went to stay at a haunted house on the Isle of Mull. He was awakened in the early morning by footsteps that he recognised – from previous experience – as 'peculiar', as if, he says, they had a kind of double echo. They were heavy boots coming upstairs. He sat up in bed, expecting a phantom visitant through the door. Instead, it took a short cut through the wall, and stood by the headboard of his bed. A Belfast voice demanded, 'Who the hell are ye?', and a heavy blow landed on the headboard of the bed. Then, slowly, the tension drained out of the atmosphere, the entity obviously having used up all its energy. Ted lay awake until dawn. It was clear to him that not only had he encountered a ghost, but the ghost had encountered him, and been indignant at finding its bed occupied.

He also had an odd experience when driving his motorcycle in open country, and, just before roaring round a steep bend, heard a voice say clearly, 'Mind the cows.' He slowed down, and found the road around the bend full of cows that had broken out of a field. Without the warning, there would certainly have been an unpleasant accident.

While he was investigating water monsters, personal experience also led him to take an interest in UFOs. In January 1966, fishing on a harbour wall near his home in Wales, he saw a luminous object skimming a hundred feet above the waves – a spherical mass of white light that pulsated once every two seconds.

In October of that year he saw another UFO – this time a small luminous cloud orbiting against the night sky in a circle. Then a dark object came out of the cloud, and beamed down a ray of intense ruby light on Ted and some other fishermen. Then both objects moved apart in opposite directions, and were quickly out of sight.

A week later, driving along a mountain road, he saw a moving light in the sky, and stopped to look at it through binoculars. It was a flattened oval, about twenty or twenty-five feet long, golden in colour, and apparently of some 'glowing, translucent substance'. It passed out of sight over the hills.

Ted was interested in Jung's notion that UFOs could be 'projections' of the unconscious mind, and later was fascinated by the work of John Keel and Jacques Vallee. If UFOs were 'paranormal', what about lake monsters that were described by respectable witnesses, yet were obviously too large for the small lakes they were supposed to inhabit? Lake monsters and flying saucers, dragons and discs – could they be connected? The English researcher John Michell (of whom I shall speak in the next chapter) was reaching the same conclusion independently. And it now struck Ted that Anglo-Saxon barrows (burial mounds) were disc-shaped, while others were cigar-shaped – like UFOs and their 'mother ships'. And in his book *The Dragon and the Disc* (1973) he speculated whether Bronze Age culture in Britain might, in fact, be a 'disc culture'. Could it be that the problem of lake monsters and the problem of UFOs were connected in the sense that neither was ultimately soluble?

In June 1973, UFOs and monsters came together in Ted's life. He was sufficiently convinced that the Loch Ness monster might be a member of 'the phantom menagerie' that he agreed to accompany an eccentric clergyman called the Rev. Donald Omand in an exorcism ceremony on the loch. Both felt oddly drained and exhausted afterwards. Ted wondered if they were stirring up dangerous forces.

Ted had heard of a UFO sighting near the loch. A Swedish journalist called Jan-Ove Sundberg had been wandering in the woods behind Loch Ness when he saw a strange craft in a clearing, and three odd-looking grey men, wearing what he took to be divers' helmets. Then, with a shock, he realised they were not human. They stepped in through a hatch, and the craft took off at great speed, but not before Sundberg collected his wits enough to snap one photograph. After his return to Sweden, Sundberg had been plagued by 'men in black', who left strange footprints in his garden; he finally had a nervous breakdown. Ted heard about the episode from John Keel.

Soon after the exorcism, Ted went to stay the night with a wing commander named Basil Cary, who lived above Loch Ness. Both the Carys had seen golden, globelike objects over the loch.

Ted was telling Cary and his wife Winifred about Sundberg, and saying that he intended to go and visit the landing site the next day. Mrs Cary warned him against it – she had heard about people being abducted. As she spoke, there was a rushing sound like a tornado from outside, and a series of violent thuds; through the French window Ted saw a pyramid of blackish smoke swirling. Then a beam of white light came through the window and focused on Ted's forehead. Mrs Cary screamed. The odd thing was that Wing Commander Cary, who was pouring a drink with his back to the window, saw and heard nothing. Ted himself failed to see the beam of light. They went to investigate the garden, but everything was normal. Winifred Cary obligingly wrote and signed an account of the incident.

The next morning, as Ted went out, he saw a man clad in black leather and goggles, who seemed to be waiting for him. Deciding he might as well confirm whether this was a real man or not, Ted walked up to him. In doing so, he removed his eyes from the man for a few seconds, and heard a whistling sound; when he looked back, the man had vanished. He looked up and down the road; there was nowhere the man could have gone to.

One year later, Ted was standing near the same spot when he had a heart attack. As he was being carried away on a stretcher, he recognised that they were passing over the spot where he had seen the man in black. He comments in *The Goblin Universe*: 'Synchronicity and the forces that control it never give up.'

Five years later, in February 1979, Ted died of a heart attack.

I had seen the typescript of *The Goblin Universe* soon after Ted completed it, in mid-1975, and found it his most satisfying and stimulating book so far. So I was greatly puzzled when he told me that he had decided not to publish it. After his death, I persuaded an American publisher to bring it out, and to give the royalties to Ted's mother.

And it was when Florence Holiday sent me the typescript of his last untitled book that I finally discovered why he had changed his mind about *The Goblin Universe*. In June 1975, just after he had completed *The Goblin Universe*, the American investigator Robert Rines took some photographs in Loch Ness with an underwater camera. One showed a large creature with a neck as long as a giraffe's, while two others showed what looked like an immense triangular flipper. And suddenly, Ted became convinced that the Loch Ness monster was a creature of flesh and blood after all, and that, moreover, the Loch Ness Investigation Bureau might soon come up with even more solid evidence – perhaps even a carcass. If so, then all his work since *The Great Orm of Loch Ness* was a waste of time, an excursion down a blind alley. It must have been a considerable blow. But he picked himself up, and instead wrote a more straightforward book about lake monsters – something that was closer in tone to *The Great Orm of Loch Ness*.

Then, as if to renew his belief in the goblin-universe theory, there was a sudden outbreak of UFO sightings and encounters not far from Ted's home in Haverfordwest. The first occurred on 14 February 1977, when a shining metal disc with a dome on top landed in the field beside the Broad Haven Primary School. Fourteen boys and one girl all saw it. Unfortunately, the headmaster could not be bothered to go and look when several boys came to tell him what they had seen. Meanwhile, the disc moved behind some bushes and was lost to sight. But a local UFO spotter named Randall Jones Pugh heard about it later in the day, and went to look at the landing site. He found nothing, but a local reporter wrote an article about the sighting, and the affair was publicised in the national press and on television. Thirteen days later, a UFO landed again in the same boggy field, and was seen by a schoolteacher and two canteen ladies.

Ted Holiday and Randall Pugh began to investigate, and soon found many other people who had seen UFOs in what was then Dyfed. A party of four in a car saw a bright lighted object with a dome on top; a crowd on the sea front saw a large orange light in the sky out at sea, which diminished in size and finally disappeared; and a woman looking out of her kitchen window saw a silver object in a field, which vanished into thin air.

Then humanoid sightings began. A woman who ran a hotel heard a humming noise in the middle of the night, and saw a disc in a field, pulsating with blue light, then saw two very tall men in 'boiler suits', who seemed to be faceless; when she tried to call her husband, she found she had no voice. A youth named Steve Taylor saw a glowing orange disc in the sky, and a black dog ran past him frantically. He stopped at the gateway into a field and saw a large, domed object. Then a very tall man with high cheekbones and a one-piece suit walked up to him, and Steve felt an inexplicable fear and tried to hit him. His fist hit nothing, and he turned and ran as fast as he could. Back at home, the family dog barked and growled at him 'as if I was someone else'.

Another dog, belonging to a family in Milford Haven, also in Dyfed, refused to sleep downstairs after several members of the family saw lights in the sky, and the seventeen-year-old daughter saw a three-foot-high humanoid standing on the windowsill and looking into her bedroom. Another family were startled when a red light filled the sky and their television went off. An hour later, the grandson arrived in a state of terror; he had also seen the red light in the sky, and a tall man in a silver suit had jumped out of the bushes and chased him.

Then came the strangest case of all: the events on Ripperston Farm.

The herdsman on Ripperston Farm was Billy Coombs, who lived with his wife Pauline and five children in a cottage overlooking St Bride's Bay near Haverfordwest. On 12 April 1977, Pauline Coombs was driving back to the farm after dark, with three of her children in the rear seat, when her ten-year-old son Keiron pointed at a luminous yellow object about the size of a football that was coming towards them, with a torchlike beam shining from its lower side. It passed overhead, then did a U-turn and followed them. Pauline Coombs accelerated to eighty miles an hour and flew between the high hedges, but her speed made no difference. As the football caught up with them, the headlights faded, and the engine cut out. She opened the door, grabbed her children, and ran the rest of the way home. When she shouted that something was following them, her husband and teenage son ran out, to see the shining football vanishing over the sea. When Billy climbed into the car, it started immediately.

A few days later, making a cup of tea at 10.30 in the evening, Pauline Coombes saw another UFO from the kitchen window. This one was about twenty feet across, silvery in colour, and was standing on three legs. Then it took off towards the sea; when they looked at the spot, there was a circular burn mark.

On 22 April, television interference was very bad as the Coombses watched a late-night film. Pauline Coombs noted a glow outside the kitchen window, but paid little attention – there was another cottage next door. But, about an hour later, Billy Coombs looked at the window, and was electrified to see a face looking in. It belonged to a very tall man wearing a silver suit, with a kind of visor concealing most of his face.

Billy phoned the farm manager, then Randall Jones Pugh, then the police. But by the time they arrived there was no sign of the man in silver. But the eight-year-old twin girls saw the same figure three weeks later, as they were playing in the grass of a field, and the figure walked past, then apparently disappeared through a barbed-wire fence.

Now the aliens began playing tricks. The dairy herd – of a hundred cattle – began escaping from the yard at night and wandering. But it should have been impossible for the cows to escape: there was a massive gate, and Billy Coombs not only locked it, but wrapped wire round the catch. Yet the herd kept escaping – six times in all – going past the house so silently that no one was awakened, and turning up at Broadmoor Farm, run by the farm manager. On one occasion, the herd disappeared so soon after they had been locked in, and reappeared so soon at Broadmoor Farm, that Billy Coombs swore there was no time for them to escape and make their way there . . . But, whether or not they were 'teleported', the cattle were certainly traumatised, and their milk yield dropped.

This relocation of animals is by no means unknown. In 1967, in Chitterne, near Warminster (another UFO 'hot spot'), a herd of cows vanished, and a night-long search failed to locate it; the next day they were back in their field.

And, in his account of Ripperston Farm in *The Unexplained*, Hilary Evans mentions an 1897 book called *Haunted Houses* by John Ingrams, which speaks of a farm at Birchen Bower, near Oldham in Lancashire, where a bizarre custom was observed. A former owner, terrified of being buried alive, left instructions in her will that her body should be embalmed, and brought to the house every twenty-one years. Whenever this was done, the horses and cows would be found wandering. One cow was found up in the hay loft, although the entrance was too small for it, and blocks had to be borrowed to get it down. The *Daily Mail* of 18 May 1906 reported that a horse was found in the hay loft and a wall had to be knocked down to get it out.

Evans also reports a poltergeist case from Italy in April 1936, where fires kept breaking out in a farm in Prignano, near Salerno, and a pair of oxen were carried from one stall to another.

All this certainly suggests that the disturbances on Ripperston Farm were of the poltergeist type. And the earlier history of Pauline Coombs lends support to this. The Coombses had earlier lived in a caravan, and Pauline Coombs repeatedly saw the image of the Virgin, wearing a white dress, in the glass of the window. (Pauline had been brought up a Catholic.) It was life-size, appeared at 10.30 at night, and remained for half an hour. Sometimes it was transformed into an image of Jesus standing with outstretched arms. The local Roman Catholic priest came to see it, accompanied by the whole Sunday school, and declared that it was beautiful. A group of teddy boys came to jeer, and were reduced to amazed silence.

Billy Coombs told Ted Holiday and Randall Pugh that when the vision appeared, the latch of the wardrobe door would lift and the door would swing open.

When Pauline was in hospital having a baby, the farmer moved the family to a new caravan, and burnt the old one. As a nonconformist he may have felt that a caravan in which the Virgin had appeared had no place on his farm. Or perhaps he was simply afraid that the place might become a kind of Lourdes.

So it seemed Pauline Coombs was the focus of poltergeist effects and religious visions before UFO phenomena erupted around her.

In *The Dyfed Enigma* (1979 – co-authored with Randall Jones Pugh) Ted Holiday concluded that 'a force existed at Ripperston which was distinct from humans, but could use the potential of humans for ends which seemed purposeless and obscure'. And at the end of the book, he returns to the question of the 'goblin universe', and writes:

> . . . the phenomena, whatever they are, exist externally in space. We assume, but we cannot by any means be sure, that they also exist in time as we know it. Nor do we know whether they objectively occupy space in any meaningful sense of the term. When the humanoid beings are perceived as occupying space, they appear to react in conformity to the laws governing perspective and optics. They give the appearance of being three-dimensional objects, although they are manifestly neither physically solid nor organic in any known sense of the word . . .

In other words, he has returned to the conclusions of *The Goblin Universe*, which means that the misgivings that made him suppress *The Goblin Universe* were not, after all, as important as he thought when he saw the underwater photographs of the Loch Ness monster, and suspected that it might prove to be as unmysterious as a hippopotamus.

Now all this, admittedly, sounds slightly insane. We seem to have left the baffling but straightforward world of UFOs for a world that seems to make no sense at all. What have lake monsters, black dogs and the great god Pan to do with flying saucers?

What Ted Holiday is suggesting is that the UFO problem cannot be solved in isolation. Those early attempts to explain it in terms of invaders from Mars or visitors from Sirius all collapsed as it became clear that the phenomenon is too rich and complex to be explained in such practical terms. As Vallee pointed out, it seems to enjoy defying every category we devise for it.

The investigator who has come closest to creating a plausible general theory is the New Yorker John Keel, the man who told Ted Holiday about the UFO sighting of Jan-Ove Sundberg above Loch Ness. The phenomenon has led Keel the same kind of dance it led Vallee. But he did not approach it from the same angle as Vallee. Keel was not a scientist, but a writer with an irresistible attraction to the unknown.

John Keel's father was a bandleader and crooner who lived in Hornell, New York; when his band went out of business in the great depression, John – born in 1930 – went to live with his grandparents. His childhood hero was Houdini, and from the beginning he was fascinated by magic. He delighted his schoolfellows with simple conjuring tricks. When he was ten, he went to rejoin his mother, now divorced and remarried, on a remote farm, where entertainment was minimal. There he lay in the hayloft, reading books on magic, hypnotism, ventriloquism and the Black Arts, and daydreamed of travel to Egypt and the Himalayas.

When he was eleven or twelve, he experienced his own personal poltergeist. He used to sleep in a room at the top of the house, and, when he heard knocking sounds on the wooden wall close to his head, he at first assumed they were due to squirrels. But he found that, if he rapped back, the knockings imitated his rapping. Then he discovered that he could ask simple questions – by speakng them aloud - and receive the correct answer in knocks. Intrigued, he went to the local library and explored the section on ghosts and the paranormal. But his invisible companion seemed to resent this research – or perhaps the phenomena had run their course anyway – for the knocks stopped about six months after they had started.

He was fourteen when he first saw his name in print over a humourous column in the local newspaper, for which he was paid two dollars a week. At fifteen he sold his first article for five dollars. With an enormous appetite for knowledge, he spent all his days in the local library, and taught himself electronics, radio, chemistry, physics, aviation and a dozen other subjects, almost as if he was unconsciously training himself to work on the UFO problem.

At seventeen, he hitch-hiked the 400 miles to New York, and found lodgings in Greenwich Village. There he made a scanty living writing articles with titles like 'Are You a Repressed Sex Fiend?' He was – and is – a natural writer, apparently incapable of writing a dull sentence.

Then the Korean War broke out, and he was drafted – fortunately, not to Korea, but to Frankfurt, where he worked for American Forces radio. And there suddenly he achieved his first major success, with a Hallowe'en broadcast from Castle Frankenstein, where a monster *was* actually killed by Baron Frankenstein in the thirteenth century. The programme had much the same effect as Orson Welles's famous Martian invasion broadcast of October 1938. Three announcers were told that the monster returned every hundred years on Hallowe'en in search of his slayer, and were sent off in the dark to intercept it; some of their genuine terror (particularly when a fake monster came striding out of the night) conveyed itself to the listeners, and people all down the Rhine double-bolted their doors, while a convoy of military police with drawn guns converged on Castle Frankenstein.

The result was that Keel was offered a civilian job after his national service was finished, and was allowed to do what he had always dreamt of doing: roam around freely, making programmes – Paris, Berlin, Rome, and eventually Egypt, where he made a Hallowe'en broadcast from the King's Chamber of the Great Pyramid.

Again, it was successful, and Keel's taste of the Middle East awoke his old hunger to travel the world in search of mystery. In 1954, when he was twenty-four years old, he resigned from his radio job, drew his savings out of the bank, and went back to Cairo. He had decided to support himself by writing articles about the magic of the East.

The story of the next four years is told in *Jadoo* (a Hindu word meaning magic), one of the funniest and most fascinating travel books ever written. As a conjuror, Keel wanted to know the secret of some of the most famous magic tricks of the East, such as driving hatpins through the tongue and cheeks, or chopping off a pigeon's head and then restoring it. He was later to discover that he could drive hatpins through his own cheeks without much inconvenience – the needle hurts momentarily as it goes in, but otherwise there is no pain. The pigeon trick was done by sleight of hand – the pigeon's head is tucked under its wing, making it look decapitated, while the magician flourishes the head of another pigeon. Walking on water, Keel discovered, is accomplished by stretching a rope just under the muddy surface. As to the Indian rope trick, he was informed that it has to be performed at dusk, when poor light prevents the audience from seeing the fine wire, on to whch the rope is hooked, stretched overhead.

Yet Keel did encounter real magic. A sheik called Abdul Mohammed sat in front of him, and told him the precise amount of money he had in his pockets, including his reserve in his watch pocket. The same old man pointed out that there was a desert viper under Keel's chair, and, when the snake lashed out with its fangs, held out a hand over its head, and killed it merely by staring at it. Keel examined the snake and verified that it was dead.

It was on a trip to Aswan and Upper Egypt that Keel encountered the greatest mystery of the twentieth century. Above the dam, in broad daylight, he saw a metallic disc, with a rotating outer rim, hovering for several minutes. As it happened, Keel had already produced a radio programme about flying saucers, and his research had convinced him that they had been around on earth throughout human history.

In a later article on UFOs, Keel was to write: 'Although many UFO believers choose to assume that most UFO sightings are random chance encounters, there is evidence to show that *witnesses are selected* by some unknown process, and that strictly accidental sightings are rare, if not non-existent.' Certainly, the sighting of the UFO over the Aswan dam was to have important consequences for his own future.

In Bombay, Keel learnt snake charming, and almost died when bitten by a cobra. In Benares he allowed himself to be buried alive for half an hour, surviving by rationing his breath.

Crossing the Himalayas, Keel heard a great deal about the Yeti, or Abominable Snowman, and caught a glimpse of two of them, enormous brown hairy creatures who fled up a mountain at his approach. In Tibet, he sat in a roomful of lamas, and heard one of them describe a fire in a northern village, which he had just seen by 'travelling clairvoyance' – the ability to project the mind to other places. Later, Keel was able to check, and discover that the lama had been telling the truth.

Finally, at Singhik, he met Nyang-Pas, a lama he had been seeking, who was reputed to be able to levitate. And, within a few minutes of sitting in Keel's bungalow, he revealed that it was more than a rumour. Placing one hand on top of his stick, he pushed himself up off the floor until he was sitting cross-legged in the air. Then he conducted the remainder of the conversation sitting in midair. He then offered to read Keel's mind. 'Think of an object.' Keel thought of a tree. 'That is too easy,' said the lama. 'You're thinking of a tree.' Keel switched his mental picture to a pair of boots, and the lama said immediately, 'Now you are thinking of a pair of boots.'

The trick of mindreading, the lama explained, was to choose a good subject, who can clearly visualise the object he is thinking about. Then the mindreader must concentrate and focus his mind on the subject, and, after a moment, the object being thought about will pop into his head. Keel found that these instructions worked, and that he was slowly able to perform mindreading. (Uri Geller clearly used the same technique when he read my mind and duplicated my drawing.)

Nyang-Pas claimed that travelling clairvoyance, or *kinga sharrira*, depends on relaxing deeply, and imaginatively conjuring up a familiar road, following it mentally and visualising every detail. Then the aspirant must continue to visualise some part of the road with which he is unfamiliar. One who is skilled in this discipline – which is virtually what Jung calls 'active imagination' – can finally see places that he does not know and events that are taking place at the moment. Many years after Keel's visit to Tibet, the New York clairvoyant Ingo Swann demonstrated travelling clairvoyance under scientific conditions at Stanford University, while Professor Robert Jahn (of whom we shall have more to say in Chapter 9) undertook a series of investigations that left no doubt that the ability can be found in many ordinary people.

Keel also heard about the ability of some lamas to create mental objects – known as *tulpas* – by concentration, although he was unable to witness any demonstration of this ability. (But the British traveller, Alexandra David-Neel, learnt how to do it, and describes in *Magic and Mystery in Tibet* how she once conjured up a phantom monk who looked so solid that a herdsman mistook him for a real lama.) Again, the concept proved to be of basic importance to Keel.

When Nyang-Pas took leave of Keel, he said, 'I hope you will never stop asking questions.' The rest of Keel's life has shown that he took this comment to heart.

His departure from Tibet was not the end of his travels. In late 1955 he stopped in Italy, then went to Barcelona and found himself another radio job with the wire services. There he lived in a hotel on a hilltop with his girlfriend Lite (pronounced Lita), and wrote *Jadoo*, which is dedicated to her. He had met her in Frankfurt, and she had accompanied him on some of his travels (when he was solvent). However, the American publisher who accepted *Jadoo* thought the book was better without romance, so Lite was deleted.

The publisher also insisted that Keel should return to America for publication, for interviews and television appearances. And the book had the effect of making him a celebrity – for a while it was impossible to open a newspaper without seeing photographs of him performing the Indian rope trick or handling snakes. Now there was a healthy market for his journalism and short stories, and, for most of the next decade, he worked in a variety of jobs, including television and publishing. And, as usual, he continued to investigate mysteries wherever he found them – he and Jacques Vallee were in Costa Rica at the same time, studying the giant stone balls whose purpose is still unknown.

Inevitably, if rather reluctantly, Keel became interested in UFOs. He was inclined to feel that the subject had been marking time for a decade or so, and there was nothing new to investigate. But at least the public had become more interested. Before Keel's departure for Germany in 1950, UFOs had been of only moderate interest to most Americans. But the death of Captain Thomas Mantell, chasing a balloon-like object, in January 1948, gave impetus to Project Sign, the Air Force study of UFOs, with Allen Hynek as adviser; this in turn became Project Grudge, which – as we have seen – was more intent on soothing and misinforming the American public than in uncovering new information. Eventually, this blatant cover-up irritated Keel into action.

In March 1966, there was a 'saucer flap' in America: sightings were reported from all over the country. And the Secretary of Defense, Robert McNamara, blandly assured the American public that UFOs were illusions. Then, on 25 March, Allen Hynek told the assembled reporters in the Detroit Press Club that the hundred or more witnesses who had seen UFOs in Michigan had been misled by marsh gas. All over America, a roar of outrage and derision went up.

Since Keel had himself seen a UFO, he regarded all this discussion of whether they existed as a waste of time. Finally, he was irritated into a full-scale investigation. After the television jobs, his bank account showed a healthy credit, and he now asked press-cutting agencies to send him every cutting they could find on UFO sightings.

The sheer quantity staggered him. On 30 March, the day that McNamara announced that he did not believe in UFOs, hundreds of newspapers from coast to coast carried reports of close-up sightings of spinning discs whose radiation seemed capable of stopping car engines. Keel rang the newspapers, and was assured that, far from exaggerating the stories to manufacture news, they had selected only the more interesting ones. He checked with witnesses, ringing them long distance, and learnt that, in fact, the newspapers had deliberately suppressed what they felt to be incredible. People described being chased in their cars by UFOs, which had sometimes landed on the road, and later reappeared over their homes. They often reported that their eyes were red and swollen for days after a sighting, and a few males confessed to pains in the genitals. Others had felt nauseating waves of heat. Being a natural sceptic, Keel was at first inclined to dismiss much of this as hysteria. But soon he was converted by the sheer quantity of the reports.

With the same obsessive thoroughness and curiosity he had displayed in his search for oriental magic, he took to the road and spoke to thousands of people all over the country. A few were obvious publicity seekers and hoaxers, but he found these easy to spot. Most people were obviously ordinary and honest, and many were reluctant to discuss their experiences until he had won their confidence.

Keel collected ten thousand clippings in 1966, and a further two thousand in the month of March 1967 alone. He set out to analyse this vast mass of data, and soon discovered one peculiar fact: that more than a fifth of the sightings took place on Wednesdays between 8 and 11 p.m. Moreover, the 'flaps' were often in specific states: for example, he found hundreds of sightings in Arkasas on 16 August 1966, in two belts running north to south, but none at all in surrounding states. He concluded that Martians – or meteors – would not group themselves so neatly. The data suggested that the UFO denizens know about human calendars and geographical boundaries. In other words, Keel was approaching the same conclusion that Jacques Vallee arrived at in *The Invisible College* – that the purpose of UFO activity is, to some extent, the effect it has on human beings. They have every intention of being seen. And when UFOs began to follow him around – like the one that accompanied him along the Long Island Expressway on 4 October 1967 – he realised that they could somehow focus in on his own mind.

He had another reason for believing that UFOs possessed intelligence. At the Washington Fortfest of 1995, Keel described how he had noticed that most of the press cuttings were not about flying saucers, but about lights – often green and purple blobs. (According to Keel, similar light balls were beings seen at about this time – 1964–68 – all over the world.) He learnt that they descended on cargo boats navigating the Ohio River at night, and that the boatmen soon realised that the balls of light did not like their searchlights, and would quickly move out of the way when the lights were directed at them. Keel himself sat on a hilltop near the Gallipolis Ferry in West Virginia, in early 1967, fascinated by the lights, which he describes as small clouds of glowing gas, purple in colour. There were twenty or more, and at first he thought they were some kind of natural phenomenon. But, when he directed his powerful torch at them, they skittered out of the way of the beam. That argued that they could be alive. So he tried flashing at them in Morse code, telling them to go left or right, or up or down; they followed his instructions precisely. Then he decided to invent his own code – a circle for left, a triangle for right, and so on. And, once again, the lights followed his instructions. That could mean only one thing: the code was superfluous – they were reading his mind.

After three years of investigation of UFOs, Keel set down his conclusions in *Operation Trojan Horse* (1970). By this time, he had gone back to all the source material, including the Bible and the ancient historians. He unearthed many interesting stories from the past, including one from Alençon, France, dating back to June 1790, described in a report by a Paris police inspector named Liabeuf. The witnesses, who included two mayors and a doctor, all told of an enormous globe that had crashed into a hilltop and started grass fires; then a door in its side opened, and a man came out, dressed in 'clothes adhering competely to his body' (i.e. a skin-tight suit), who, seeing the reception committee, ran away into the woods. A few moments later, the globe exploded like a bubble, leaving only fine powder.

Keel was also intrigued by the strange series of 'airship' sightings of 1896–97, when there were fairly certainly no airships in the United States. These began when a witness in Sacramento, California, heard a cry of 'Throw her up higher – she'll hit the steeple', and saw a huge, cigar-shaped object, with a lighted glass cabin underneath, sailing slightly above the level of the rooftops. Five nights later, on 22 November, it came back again, this time floating so high above Sacramento that it simply looked like a bright light, with something looming above it. One man who looked at it through a telescope reported that it seemed to rise and fall as it moved, like a ship on the high seas – or, as Kenneth Arnold might have put it, like a saucer skipped over water.

More reports came from San Francisco – of some high-flying object with a bright light. The mayor of San Francisco concluded that 'some shrewd inventor has solved the problem of aerial navigation . . .' By February 1897, reports came from Nebraska, then Illinois, Wisconsin, Missouri and Arkansas, before the phenomenon moved south to Texas. By April dozens of stories started to come in from all over Texas, and were reported in the newspapers. Colonel W.A. Robertson of Mississippi saw it from a train approaching Dallas, and reported that it was travelling faster than the train.

Many reports came from people who claimed to have seen the airship on the ground. In April, Judge Lawrence A. Byrne told a Texarkana newspaper that he had walked through a thicket, and found 'the airship I have read so much about'. It was manned by three men of vaguely oriental appearance (the judge thought they might be Japanese) talking in a foreign language. They obligingly showed the judge all over the ship.

A farmer named Alexander Hamilton, in Kansas, described in April how the airship stole one of his calves. It was about 300 feet long and had a brightly lit glass cabin underneath. There were six occupants, who talked in a foreign language. Then it rose off the ground, and seems to have lassoed a calf, which then became caught in a fence. Farmer Hamilton found it was held by a cable. He cut the wire of the fence to free the calf, and watched the animal sail away. Later, its hide, legs and head – complete with Farmer Hamilton's brand mark – were found on a farm four miles away.

The last people to report the airship were a couple called Captain and Mrs Scobie, of Fort Worth. On 12 May 1897, after dark, Mrs Scobie called her husband to come and see something strange. They both watched the large, dark object moving through the sky over Fort Worth, with a brilliant light underneath. (Various witnesses had claimed the airship had an 'electric searchlight'.) Then the airship vanished from history. There had been 109 recorded sightings in Texas alone.

There were further 'airship flaps' in America in 1909 and South Africa in 1914. And in Scandinavia, from 1932 to 1937, there was a wave of sightings of enormous aeroplanes, bigger than any commercial planes then in use – one was reported as having eight engines, twice the number on the largest plane of the time. What was so odd was that these craft appeared – over Norway, Sweden and Finland – in appalling weather conditions that kept all normal aircraft on the ground. Moreover, they would do something that would be regarded by most pilots as suicidal: cut their engines, then circle at increasingly low altitudes, often 'gliding' in this manner three or four times. They frequently flew low, and a powerful searchlight raked the countryside.

The air forces of the countries concerned were baffled by the planes. The only explanation seemed to be that a mad millionaire, like some villain out of a James Bond novel, had a secret base somewhere, with elaborate maintainence equipment and an army of skilled mechanics. But why, in that case, was he also deploying red, green and white lights, which were often seen far above the phantom aeroplane?

On the mad-millionaire hypothesis – or perhaps of some unknown foreign power – the military and air forces of Norway and Sweden mounted an extensive search, losing two planes in the course of searching wild and distant places. On 11 February 1937, there was a close-up sighting: a fishing boat called the *Fram* left the port of Kvalsik,

Norway, for some night fishing, and, as it rounded a cape sticking out into the sea, the sailors saw the lights of a large seaplane on the water. Assuming it might be in trouble, the *Fram* approached it. As it did so, its lights went out, and it was enveloped by a cloud of mist. Then it vanished.

This was, of course, the period between the wars, when nations like Germany were arming, so the phantom aircraft were assumed to be some form of spy plane – particularly since they were often sighted around military installations. But there were no aircraft at that time capable of such manoeuvres, and, when World War Two came, it was soon clear that Germany simply did not have such planes.

Yet, just as in the great airship wave of 1897, there was a convenient explanation to satisfy the popular mind. Only experts knew that large aircraft do not choose to fly in snowstorms or to cut out their engines and 'glide' in circles close to the ground. It was as if the phenomenon wanted to remain ambiguous.

In 1946, objects like rockets were sighted over Sweden, Norway, Denmark, Finland and Greece – Sweden alone had more than 2,000 sightings. Rockets were seen to plunge into Lake Mjosa in Norway and Lake Kolmjarv in Sweden, where something exploded. Yet a military investigation revealed nothing whatsoever. The Swedish military issued a statement declaring that 80 per cent of the sightings were 'celestial phenomena' (i.e. meteors), although it did not explain how meteors can be mistaken for rockets. In Greece, an investigation headed by Professor Paul Santorini concluded that the objects were not missiles. To begin with, they occasionally changed direction in mid-flight.

But Keel also has his doubts about meteors. He spends most of a chapter in *Operation Trojan Horse* talking about sightings that were explained as meteors, and pointing out that they could not possibly be meteors – for example, one of November 1779 'which appeared like a ball of fire' and 'was visible for near an hour'. No meteors remain visible for an hour – the slowest speed ever recorded for a meteor is 27,000 miles an hour, which would take it right round the earth's equator in less than an hour.

Keel details such anomalies for several chapters before returning to modern times, and demonstrating that all these sightings fit the same pattern of what he calls 'flexible phantoms of the skies'.

After studying thousands of reports of sightings, Keel concluded that they tended to occur repeatedly in certain areas; he labelled these 'window areas'. He calculated that every state in the US has from two to ten window areas, where UFOs appear repeatedly for year after year. A huge number lie along the arc of a circle drawn from northwest Canada, down through the central states of America, and back to northwest Canada. Another is centred in the Gulf of Mexico and covers much of Mexico, Texas and the southwest. And a majority of these are over areas of magnetic deviation – that is, areas in which the earth's normal magnetism is distorted. The famous disappearance of five planes on 5 December 1945 – one of the great mysteries of the Bermuda Triangle – took place off the coast of Florida in one of Keel's window areas. (The flight leader reported over the radio that 'his instruments were going crazy'.)

Keel also noticed a 'January cycle' of UFO sightings which led him to predict correctly that there would be a 'flap' in January 1969.

As to the significance of such absurd sightings as those of 1896–97, or the Scandinavian wave of giant aircraft of the 1930s, he reaches the conclusion to which the book owes its title. He is not inclined to accept the explanation that these were some kind of bizarre practical joke; the alternative seems to be that their purpose is associated with some kind of information gathering, and that they wish to deceive us into assuming that they are simply a piece of advanced human technology. Flying saucers, he suggests, may be a part of something else – of Operation Trojan Horse. In religious ages, the phenomenon has set out to convince us that it was of religious origin. When man came of age technologically in the nineteenth century, they began disguising it as balloons and aircraft. During World War Two, they could masquerade as 'foo fighters', which were assumed by both sides to be enemy secret weapons.

Yet this interesting theory hardly seems to make sense if, as Keel and Vallee believe, the 'ufonauts' have been visiting earth for thousands of years – they should surely have finished their surveying activities by now?

In a chapter called 'The Cosmic Jokers' Keel comes closer to a theory that has been suggested by many other writers on the subject, notably Brinsley Le Poer Trench – that there are two types of UFO entity, the 'good guys' and the 'bad guys', and that the bad guys can be dangerous. He tells the story of a man who had been investigating a UFO flap near Ithaca, NY, and left his home to drive to a meeting, then, for some inexplicable reason, returned to the house and rearranged some books. Back in the car, he switched on the ignition – then lost his memory. But subsequent events show that he drove to a railway crossing just in time to meet an oncoming train, which demolished his car – although he escaped with only minor injuries.

Then, of course, there are the Men in Black – men who pose as military intelligence or Air Force officers, who call on witnesses of UFO activity, question them for hours, and warn them to keep silent. Since it seems to be one of the aims of UFOs to be seen – presumably to make as many people as possible aware of their presence – then we have to assume that the Men in Black belong to the 'other side', and are trying to prevent publicity about UFOs. As a theory, this hardly seems to make much sense – but, then, neither does anything else about UFOs.

What Keel does not explain is why either good guys or bad guys should want to devise absurd encounters – for example, of a woman who found herself paralysed in the middle of the night, and watched a football-sized object float through the window and lower a ramp, down which tiny figures descended. After apparently carrying out repairs to their craft, they climbed on board again and vanished through the window – after which her paralysis disappeared. Are such encounters intended – as Vallee suggests – to re-create folklore and myth about 'little people' in modern terms?

Yet, although Keel comes no closer than dozens of other ufologists to solving the problem of the purpose of the UFOs, his remarks on their technology have a ring of common sense.

In late November 1966, Keel had interviewed an eighteen-year-old girl named Connie Carpenter. Connie was the niece of Mary Hyre, the stringer (local correspondent) for Associated Press in Point Pleasant, Virginia. On the morning of Sunday 27 November 1966, Connie had been driving home from church when she had suddenly seen a giant. The figure was grey, and shaped like a man, but far bigger, and it was staring at her with glowing red eyes. As she slowed down, a pair of ten-foot wings unfolded from its back, and it rose into the air, swooped towards her car, and zoomed past overhead. She drove home in a state close to hysteria.

It sounds as if she was suffering from hallucinations. But, in fact, her sighting was the first of more than a hundred. And many of the witnesses suffered the same effect as Connie Carpenter: severe conjunctivitis – her eyes reddened, watered and swelled until she could hardly see. Soon, half the nation's press and television were in West Virginia working on stories about the creature who became known as Mothman.

At first, Keel did not connect the appearances of Mothman with

UFOs, but a wave of UFO sightings over West Virginia – often accompanied by severe conjunctivitis – made it clear that there had to be some connection. A young couple who were making love naked in the back of a car were interrupted by a large ball of bluish fire that hovered close to them, and, the next morning, both were heavily sunburnt, and had red, swollen eyes.

Keel was soon convinced that UFOs are not high-tech craft from another planet, but 'paraphysical' entities, who are related to the 'manifestations involved in religious miracles and spiritual seances'. Like Jacques Vallee, he specifically cites Fátima as an example. But Keel believes that the secret of the UFOs lies in the electromagnetic spectrum.

He points out that visible light is only a tiny part of the spectrum of energy. Below the red end of the spectrum there is infrared (heat) and microwaves and radio waves. Above the violet end there is ultraviolet light and X-rays and gamma rays and cosmic rays. Our human senses are sensitive only to a tiny proportion of this enormous range of energies.

Keel also points out that there have been thousands of radar sightings of UFOs that cannot be seen with the naked eye. That can only mean that UFOs must be a form of energy beyond the light spectrum.

He mentions that one of the most puzzling aspects of UFOs – particularly those that are seen as balls of light – is that they often change colour, usually from orange to red to violet, which leads him to suggest:

Let us assume that UFOs exist at frequencies beyond visible light but that they can adjust their frequency and descend the electromagnetic spectrum – just as you can turn the dial of your radio and move a variable condenser up and down the scale of radio frequencies. When a UFO's frequency nears that of visible light, it would appear first as a purplish blob of violet. As it moves further down the scale, it would seem to change to blue, and then to cyan (bluish green) . . .

I have therefore classified that section of the color spectrum as the UFO entry field. When the objects begin to move into our spatial and time coordinates, they gear down from higher frequencies, passing progressively from ultraviolet to violet to bluish green. When they stabilize within our dimensions, they radiate energy on all frequencies and become a glaring white.

In the white condition the object can traverse distances visibly, but radical maneuvers of ascent or descent require it to alter its frequencies again, and this produces new color changes. In the majority of all landing reports, the objects were said to have turned orange (red and yellow) or red before descending. When they settle on the ground they 'solidify,' and glow red again. Sometimes reportedly they turn a brilliant red and vanish. Other times they shift through all the colors of the spectrum, turn white, and fly off into the night sky until they look like just another star.

Since the color red is so closely associated with the landing and takeoff processes, I term this end of the color spectrum the UFO departure field.

This would explain why Barney and Betty Hill – those early abductees – at first thought they saw a star, which then changed into a flying saucer, and why another famous abductee, the Brazilian Antonio Villas Boas, whose report of being seduced by a 'space woman' is generally accepted as reliable, first saw a 'red star' which turned into a saucer on a tripod, and later saw it turn red as it took off after his seduction.

The microwave end of the spectrum could explain the intolerable waves of heat often experienced – for example, by the unfortunate Brazilian Salvador de Santos, investigated by Jacques and Janine Vallee, who died with the flesh falling off his bones, as if cooked. Keel also cites the case of Eddie Webb, a trucker who was pursued by a white light on 3 October 1973 in southeastern Missouri, and who stuck his head out to look back; there was a bright flash, and he shouted, 'Oh my God, I'm burned.' A lens had fallen out of his glasses and the frames had melted. The result was temporary blindness.

The sunburn and conjunctivitis of other witnesses, like Connie Carpenter, points to the ultraviolet end of the spectrum (although microwaves also affect the eyes and testes).

And what about this curious effect of stopping car engines and causing lights to fade? In a chapter of a later book, *The Eighth Tower*, Keel points out that, during the 1930s, Marconi – the radio pioneer – began experimenting with waves of very low frequency (VLF radio waves) to short waves (which are beyond the upper end of the radio spectrum – i.e microwaves). And he was horrified to discover that his microwaves would kill animals in nearby fields. He switched to experimenting with VLF waves, and found that they would stop car engines by interfering with their electrical circuits. (Diesel engines, which depend on pressure-ignition, were unaffected.)

So if, as Keel believes, UFOs can change their energy vibrations and descend down the spectrum from cosmic rays to VLF, their various effects, from the stopping of car engines to inflammation of the eyes and testes, would all be explained.

In emphasising the narrow range of our physical senses, Keel is making an important point: that they are pathetically inadequate to grasp the reality that surrounds us. Physical experience gives us an illusory sense of 'knowing' the outside world. For example, when you bite into a peach, you feel that you know it about as thoroughly as it can be known: you can see it, taste it, smell it. But the range of your sense of taste and smell is as small as the range of your vision; a Martian might be able to see a wider range of colours, taste a wider range of flavours, smell a wider range of smells. Who has never felt that odd sense of frustration with the senses? They may seem adequate enough when you are hungry and eating a meal; but when we experience the beauty of a mountain or a lake, or even a sexually attractive person, we often feel like a colour-blind man in a picture gallery, or a deaf man at a symphony concert – what Dr Johnson meant in *Rasselas* when he said, 'There must be some sixth sense, or some faculty apart from sense, that must be satisfied before we can be happy.'

If Keel is correct, then the UFO occupants must see us as virtually blind and deaf. He speculates:

Somewhere in this tangled mass of electromagnetic frequencies there lies an omnipotent intelligence . . . This intelligence is able to manipulate energy. It can, quite literally, manipulate any kind of object into existence on our planet. For centuries the occultists and religionists have called this process transmutation or transmogrification. Thousands of books have been published on this process, many of them serving as secret texts for alchemists and sorcerers. The early occultists understood, at least partially, that energy was the key to the whole.

This is why the occultists attach so much importance to the human aura. Keel writes: 'You are a chemical machine made up of electromagnetic energy. Your brain is actually an electrical computer connected to all parts of your body by a wiring system of nerves . . . Although you can't see it, your body is surrounded by self-generated fields of radiation. The occultists have always called this radiation the aura.'

And what has this, he asks, to do with flying saucers? 'Perhaps a great deal. Many contactees have been told that they were selected because of their aura. Occultists have long claimed that each person is surrounded by an aura which reveals his spiritual state. An evil person has a black aura. A saintly type has a golden radiation.' And he cites an Australian contactee who was told by two aliens in spacesuits that they had been able to contact him because of his aura. He goes on to suggest that perhaps only certain types of people can see UFOs.

In *The Eighth Tower*, Keel writes: 'Another world of intelligent energy is intermingled with ours and is very aware of us, while we are only vaguely aware of it. Not only has it a clear view of future events in our dimension; it can manipulate past and present events to prepare the way for the more important future events.'

All of which raises a self-evident question. If there *is* such a superintelligence, why is it bothering with us? We can be no more important to it than – to use one of Keel's images – the microbes swarming in a drop of water to the boy who is looking at them through a microscope.

But what if it is not true that we are microbes in a drop of water? Keel says that this superior intelligence can foresee the future. In fact, so can many human beings. 'Precognition' *ought* to be impossible, but it is not. On 13 December 1949, for example, Mrs Eva Hellstrom fell asleep on a tourist bus as it left Heidelberg, and dreamt of a beautiful painting of a four-leafed clover in the shape of a cross, surrounded by spirals. Waking a few moments later, she made a sketch of the picture, and wondered if she might encounter it in Egypt, which was her destination. On her last day in Cairo, Mrs Hellstrom was taken to the Coptic Museum, full of ancient relics of the early Christian churches in Egypt and Abyssinia, and there she saw her picture, corresponding in detail to her sketch. It was a stone slab, and the four-leafed clover was known as a 'Coptic rose'. She had dreamt of the slab as it had been a thousand years earlier, when it was in full colour.[1] Hundreds of such examples could be cited, all leaving no doubt that human beings possess the power of foreseeing the future – but seldom use it. The same is true of many other powers – for example, the 'travelling clairvoyance' and levitation witnessed by John Keel in Tibet, or the simple ability to read someone's mind. In fact, Keel himself possesses this ability. He writes in *The Eighth Tower*:

> In my early teens I found that I could sometimes sense what other people were thinking, and I assumed that everyone had this

[1] See *Riddle of the Future* by Andrew Mackenzie, London 1974.

ability . . . Now and then I encounter someone whose mind is actually vulnerable to my own. I can not only sense what they are thinking. I can project my own thoughts into their mind and they accept these thoughts as their own. In short, I can control that person's mind on a modest scale. There are people who have this power to a very developed degree. They can control others, even from a great distance. It is probable that some world leaders, especially the evil ones like Hitler, possessed and exercised this ability. One famous psychic claimed he could hand a railroad conductor a blank sheet of paper and the man would punch it thinking it was a ticket.

So it seems fairly certain that we all possess a range of powers that extend far beyond our usual limited spectrum. Then why do we not make use of them? Because we take it for granted that the narrow spectrum is 'all there is'. We accept that our tunnel vision shows us 'the reality', when actually it shows us as little of reality as a mole sees, snuffling through its tunnel underground.

Then why do certain human beings seem slightly less blind than the rest? Some seem to be born with a wider vision – the so-called psychics, while some experience a kind of suffocation that drives them to struggle instinctively for a wider vision: poets, artists, philosophers. And some people experience a momentary glimpse of a wider reality which transforms their vision of the world.

Keel himself had such an experience when he first went to New York. He described it to me in a letter of 18 April 1984.

For many years now, I have been quietly interviewing warlocks and trying to develop a book based on the actual experiences of natural witches and warlocks – people who are born with the ability to perceive and control the elementals. They seem to be several steps beyond mediums. Mediums are used by the phenomenon. Warlocks, on the other hand, are able to use these forces. Unfortunately, most of them seem to come to a tragic end – suicides, murders, bizarre deaths. But it is apparent that thousands of people in each generation suffer from this uneasy talent. I think that I had it when I was an adolescent but I diverted my attention by studying physics, chemistry, etc., and lost it by the time I was 18. At 18, I woke one night in a furnished room near Times Square and had what can only be described as an illuminating experience.

For a few brief moments I suddenly understood *everything* and I was really one with the cosmos. The next morning I could remember very little of it but I'm sure it was all entered into my subconscious.

Before writing this section I telephoned Keel in New York – a difficult feat since, apart from the time-zone difference between New York and Cornwall, John is an insomniac who stays awake all night and sleeps all day, so that it is hard to find a good time to ring him. I succeeded by getting up at a quarter to five in the morning and catching him when he came home from dinner at midnight. Among other questions, I asked him about his mystical experience. He described how he had awakened in the middle of the night, and found his room suffused with a pink or orange glow, which led him to assume the house was on fire. He was about to leap out of bed, but, for some reason, changed his mind. Then followed the experience of thinking with amazing clarity, and seeming to know everything – the origin of the universe, the creation and purpose of human beings ... He felt he ought to get up and write it all down, but instead went back to sleep. The next morning he could remember the experience, but not what he had 'seen'.

He feels nevertheless that part of that 'gnosis' lodged deep in his mind, for he finds himself reading books and cosmology – for example, Hawking's *A Brief History of Time* – and feeling he knows it all.

In 1969, the novelist Robert Graves told me of a similar experience, which he had described in a story called 'The Abominable Mr Gunn'. He had been sitting on a roller behind the cricket pavilion when he received a 'celestial illumination', and suddenly 'knew everything'. Graves describes it as 'a simple method of looking sideways at disorderly facts so as to make perfect sense of them'. He could actually remember it after a night's sleep, but it vanished as he tried to write it down, and kept crossing things out.

Keel assumed that the experience was unique to himself until, in the 1960s, he came upon R.M. Bucke's classic *Cosmic Consciousness*, in which Bucke describes how, driving home in a hansom cab, he suddenly found himself 'wrapped in a flame-coloured cloud' which made him assume that a nearby building was on fire. This was followed by 'an intellectual illumination impossible to describe' including the recognition that the whole universe is composed of living matter. The experience led Bucke to study the mystics, and to include in the book

1. The triplet of crop circles which appeared near Cheesefoot Head, Hampshire on 8 June 1988 *(page 34)*

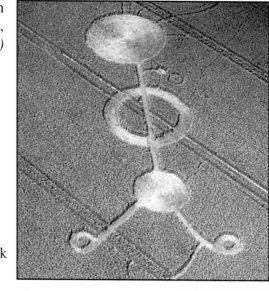

2. The 'letters' which appeared at Milk Hill, August 1991 *(page 40)*

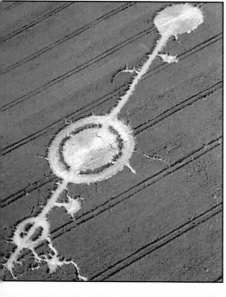

3. This formation appeared near Alton Barnes, Wiltshire in July 1990 *(page 43)*

4. Child witnesses Francisco, Lucia and Jacinta with local people, standing ben
a wooden archway erected at the site of the apparitions of the Virgin Mary a
Fatima, Portugal, in 1917 *(page 90)*

At the scene of the final miracle at Fatima on 13 October 1917, the crowd saw the sun dance in the sky. Here the people watch the solar phenomena

6. Jacinta is carried from group to group after the events of 13 October

7. The Loch Ness monster, photographed by Hugh Gray, 12 November 193[
(page 121)

8. A frame from the cine film of a Bigfoot (Sasquatch) *(page 223)* taken by Ro[
Patterson in 1967, at Bluff Creek, California

9. Enhancement of a frame from Patterson's film, to show how the creature might look

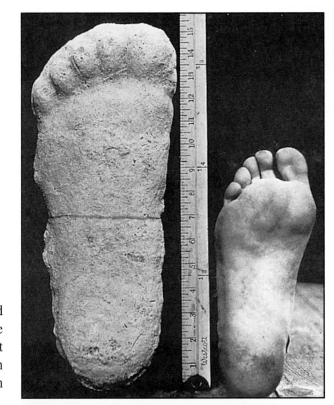

A man's foot compared with a cast of one of the gfoot footprints found at uff Creek after Patterson made his film

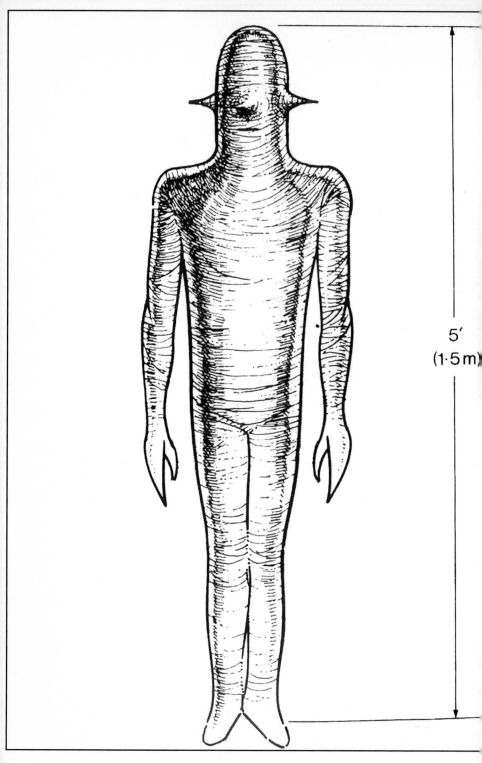

5′
(1·5 m)

11. An artist's impression of the UFO entity at the centre of the Parker and Hickson abduction case, Pascagoula, Mississippi, October 1973 *(page 213)*

12. An artist's impression of a 'grey', based on witness descriptions

13. Aliens drawn by an abductee from John Mack's support group

14. One of the giant Olmec heads in the park of La Venta, in Villahermosa Southern Mexico *(page 56)*

15. The Gateway of the Sun at Tiahuanaco *(page 56)*

fifty studies of mystics through the ages, all of whom had had a similar experience.

All of which would seem to indicate that what human beings need at this point in history – perhaps at any point – is something to rescue them from the tunnel vision that prevents them from grasping the extent of their 'hidden powers' and capabilities. It is interesting to note that the UFO experience sometimes seems to do precisely that. As, for example, in the case of Jacques Vallee's correspondent – with whom we opened this chapter – who experienced 'novel insights into . . . the Nature of Reality' connected to her sighting of the shining disc.

Bucke summarised his own conclusions:

> The simple truth is, that there has lived on the earth, 'appearing at intervals', for thousands of years among ordinary men, the first faint beginnings of another race; walking the earth and breathing the air with us, but at the same time walking another earth and breathing another air of which we know little or nothing, but which is, all the same, our spiritual life, as its absence would be our spiritual death. This new race is in the act of being born from us, and in the near future it will occupy and possess the earth.

In other words, these new people exist in this same physical dimension as the rest of us, yet at the same time walk another earth and breathe another air – as if living simultaneously in a kind of Fourth Dimension.

6 The Fourth Dimension

VALLEE AND KEEL were not the first to recognise the connection between UFO 'aliens' and creatures of folklore. In the mid-1960s, an Englishman named John Michell, who had studied Russian literature at Cambridge, became fascinated by UFOs, and also by Jung's book *Flying Saucers – A Myth of Things Seen in the Skies* (1958).

Jung had spoken of the major changes that might be expected with the coming of the Age of Aquarius (due around the year 2000). In fact, he felt that the human race was on the point of a leap to a new phase of psychic evolution.

He had noted that sceptical statements about UFOs were relatively unpopular compared with statements of belief, and reasoned from this that modern man experiences a sense of profound disquiet because of his lack of religious belief. (Jung believed that the religious impulse is as essential to man as the sexual impulse – 'the soul has a religious function.') He attached deep importance to the mandala symbol, a circle signifying completeness (and hence an image of God), and saw the widepread belief in flying saucers as an indication of man's longing for belief and certainty.

In *Flying Saucers*, Jung appears to be saying that he believes UFOs to be a 'projection' of the collective unconscious of mankind – a projection being essentially a kind of hallucination, like a drunk's visions of pink elephants. They are a projection of mankind's longing for a saviour – or for what Jung calls individuation, a state in which all the inner conflicts of the psyche are resolved.

John Michell's interest in flying saucers was due partly to his interest in the environment, and the fear shared by so many in the 1950s that man might destroy himself with atomic radiation. He points out that the 'UFO visitors' were warning of the increasing pollution of the environment long before Rachel Carson's *Silent Spring* suddenly focused awareness in 1962.

Michell's starting point is not dissimilar to that of Erich von Däniken or Robert Temple. 'The earliest myths describe the arrival on earth of an extra-terrestrial race who, by their example, altered the whole course of human history . . . Once we can accept the, at first sight, fantastic idea that our present culture is an inheritance from a former visit of people from space, a great deal of what is now obscure becomes clear.'

Evidence of these visitors from space can be found in myths, legends and folklore from all over the world. 'The evidence of mythology provides a general account of the days when the gods were known on earth.'

Michell notes that, according to legend, the arrival of the gods on earth was preceded by portents in the sky, such as fiery circles. The Egyptian 'eye of Ra' is symbolised by a winged disc. His first book *The Flying Saucer Vision* (1967) cites dozens of parallels between UFO lore and mythology, arguing, for example, that the dragon of folklore represents fiery discs in the sky.

He is also inclined to believe that, like the fish gods of the Dogon, or the white gods who landed in South America, these ancient visitors brought wisdom to mankind; this belief has the corollary that mankind evolved very quickly, not – as Darwin believed – through slow stages. In fact, man's brain *did* evolve with incredible speed – doubling in size so fast that scientists call it 'the brain explosion'.

The first thing that strikes the reader about *The Flying Saucer Vision* is the sheer range of its erudition. Michell seems not only to have read everyone from the ancient Greek geographers to modern anthropologists, but to have found much of his information in obscure byways of literature. This, he claims, was not due to a directed course of study so much as to synchronicities – Koestler's 'library angel' directing his attention to books by chance.

One of these serendipitous discoveries was the work of Alfred Watkins, the Hereford businessman who, as he was riding across country in June 1931, noticed that old churches, standing stones, barrows and hilltops were often connected by 'old straight tracks'. Watkins called them 'ley lines'.

He thought these ley lines were old trade routes. But in the late 1930s, a dowser named Guy Underwood concluded that they are lines of some kind of earth force, which is more powerful in the area of standing stones and other sacred sites – he speculated that the site was sacred *because* of this earth force. Michell noted that certain areas with a high level of UFO sightings – like Warminster in Wiltshire and Glastonbury in Somerset – were often crisscrossed with ley lines, and suggested some connection. He also noted that the Chinese version of ley lines are known as dragon paths (*lung mei*). In effect, he was observing the tendency of UFO sightings to occur on straight lines – Aimé Michel's 'orthoteny'.

Michell's interest in UFOs caused him to turn his back on the characteristic culture of the 1950s, in which most of the fashionable intellectuals were leftists who believed that socialism would bring about the millennium. (My own first book *The Outsider* was regularly attacked by leftist intellectuals as a 'fascist' work, simply because it was not concerned with left-wing politics.) Instead, he pursued the subject of ley lines and sacred geometry, and his book *The View Over Atlantis* (1969) brought them to the attention of a wide audience, with the incidental side effect of making Glastonbury a centre of pilgrimage for 'New Agers'.

The wide appeal of the book was due to its romanticism. John Nicholson wrote in an essay on Michell:

Hippies turned themselves into the new guardians of ancient skills and wisdom by rejecting industrial society and communing at old sites, or going for mystical rambles along ley lines, keeping an eye open for UFOs. Like Red Indians they touched the earth and felt the stones giving off psychic energies or 'vibes.' Some pop groups privately gave invocatory performances at the chosen time and place. It was all mixed up somehow as cosmic consciousness, and it gave many people many happy hours . . .[1]

The appeal of Michell was due, in fact, to what Jung called 'the flying saucer vision' – the power to see the world with new eyes. And here it is important to understand exactly what Jung meant. He wrote in an abstract, scientific style whose purpose was to guard against accusations of mysticism or irrationalism, and the result is that he often left a great deal unsaid. But what he left unsaid is made quite explicit by the illustrations. A painting called *The Fire Sower*, by E. Jacoby, shows a vast human figure towering above a city; the body and the head are made of fire, and the head, which is separated from the body, is a

[1] *An English Figure: Two Essays on the Work of John Michell*, p. 41.

flaming ball that seems to be spinning on its axis. Jung comments: 'Like an immaterial essence the fiery figure strides through the houses of the city – *two worlds which interpenetrate yet do not touch*.' Another painting, called *The Fourth Dimension*, by P. Birkhauser, shows a huge face hovering above a city. This, and other faces, look as if they are painted on a veil that hangs down in front of the city, and Jung comments: 'This painting, like the previous one, depicts the collision of two incommensurable worlds.'

But the clearest indication of his meaning can be found in a woodcut called *The Spiritual Pilgrim Discovering Another World*, which Jung believed to be a Rosicrucian work dating from the seventeenth century. In fact, later research suggested that it dates from the nineteenth century – but, in a sense, the nineteenth century, the century of romanticism, is even more appropriate. The picture shows a rainbow (or celestial sphere) arching over a pleasant land of woods and meadows, with the sun, moon and stars in the sky. But the pilgrim, crawling on hands and knees, has pushed his head through the rainbow, into a totally different world – a strange, symbolic landscape, with four great discs in the sky, two of which have spokes, and may be a reference to Ezekiel's chariots. The pilgrim has left 'this world' behind, and has broken through into another reality. This is what Jung meant by 'the flying saucer vision'.

What Jung has done is to make absolutely clear why flying saucers have exercised such a powerful influence on the human imagination in the second half of the twentieth century. It is the romantic – and religious – craving for 'another reality'. We are all so accustomed to struggling with the world of practical necessity – what Heidegger calls 'the triviality of everydayness' – that most of us have come to accept that 'that is all there is'. But, in the past few centuries, man has also developed the power of imagination. Unlike our down-to-earth ancestors, we have all become 'mental travellers', and those who have never been abroad can travel in an armchair watching a television set. We have all learnt to experience escape from the triviality of everydayness through the imagination.

However, that only sharpens the contrast between this everyday world and the world into which we 'escape'. Our deepest secret wish is to see the *real* world transformed. Rimbaud claims to have taught himself how to see 'a mosque in place of a factory, angels practising on drums, coaches on the roads of the sky, a drawing room at the bottom of a lake: monsters, mysteries'. But the increasing possibility that our planet is being visited by creatures from another world or another dimension seems to turn Rimbaud's dream into reality. Dozens of poets and artists of the nineteenth century committed suicide because they could not believe in their own dreams. And now, in the second half of the twentieth century, it seems that the creatures of that 'other reality' have decided to pay us a visit. And this is also what Jung meant by 'the flying saucer vision'.

Now it might seem that Jung is entangling himself in hopeless contradictions. He regards UFOs as hallucinations, projections of the collective unconscious, then admits that they are visible on radar screens and in photographs. During an interview with the aviator Lindbergh in 1959, Jung made it clear that he thought flying saucers were factual, and was rather cool when Lindbergh expressed his own disbelief. Lindbergh quoted his friend General Spaatz (of the US Air Force): 'Don't you suppose if there was anything true about this flying saucer business, you and I would have heard about it by this time?' Jung countered with, 'There are a great many things going on around this earth that you and General Spaatz don't know about.'

To disentangle all this, we need to know, to begin with, that Jung believed that the unconscious mind *can* produce physical effects – he called them 'exteriorisation phenomena'. In his autobiographical *Memories, Dreams, Reflections*, he tells how, as he and Freud were arguing about the reality of the paranormal, there was a loud explosion from the bookcase, which made both of them jump. Jung's diaphragm had begun to glow with heat as he and Freud argued, and Jung was convinced that he had caused the effect. 'There is an example of an exteriorisation phenomenon,' he told Freud. 'Bosh!' said Freud. 'It is not,' said Jung, 'and to prove my point, I predict that in a moment there will be another.' As he spoke there was another explosion from the bookcase.

Jung had been studying psychical research since his teens, and had no doubt of the reality of the paranormal. One day as he sat studying his textbooks, there was a loud report from the next room. He rushed in to find that a walnut table had split from the rim to the centre. There was no obvious reason: it was a cool day, and the wood had had seventy years to dry out. Soon after, there was a loud report from the sideboard, and Jung found that the breadknife had snapped into several pieces. Jung took it to a cutler to see if he could suggest an explanation; the cutler said it looked as if someone had inserted the knife into a crack and deliberately broken it.

Then his fifteen-year-old cousin, Helen Preiswerk, began to develop mediumistic powers. One day when the family was playing at 'table turning', she went into a trance, and began to speak in a voice totally unlike her own, and in literary German. When she woke up, she had a severe headache. Other 'spirits' later spoke through her, including a girl who chattered in a mixture of French and Italian – neither of which Helen could speak. Later, Helen was taken over by a woman who called herself Ivenes, and who claimed to be 'the real Helen Preiswerk'. She was obviously far more mature and intelligent than Helen. Eventually, Helen became a dressmaker, and died at the age of thirty.

In the fifth chapter of *Flying Saucers: A Myth of Things Seen in the Skies*, Jung points out that radar sightings do not prove conclusively that UFOs are spaceships, because there are cases where they are seen yet not picked up on radar, and cases where they are picked up on radar but cannot be seen. All this, of course, was written in 1958, when the erratic behaviour of UFOs was not fully recognised – although Jung admits that some cases are so weird that he prefers not to mention them. It was after that time that investigators like Jacques Vallee and John Keel became aware of their 'psychic' aspects. It seems fairly clear that Jung was actually the first to grasp intuitively the strangely dual nature of UFOs.

This again is underlined by his choice of illustrations – particularly *The Fourth Dimension*. In the early twentieth century, the notion of the fourth dimension – a dimension at right angles to length, breadth and height – was immensely popular, largely due to the works of the mathematician Charles Hinton. Many scientists believed that it was merely the limitations of the human mind that prevented us from seeing it, and a mathematician named Johan von Manen actually claimed to have had a kind of vision of a four-dimensional cube and sphere. Then Einstein suggested that the fourth dimension was simply another name for time. After all, if you agree to meet someone at a particular spot in a city, you not only have to specify where to meet them – in the second-floor lounge of a hotel on the corner of Third Avenue and Twenty-first Street – but *what time*, otherwise the other three-dimensional coordinates are useless.

Now it is quite plain that, by 'the fourth dimension', Birkhauser means something quite different from either Hinton's extra dimension of space, or Einstein's concept of time. The veil through which the strange faces seem to be staring is obviously not a part of the physical universe, but a kind of parallel universe. And that thought may well have come to Birkhauser from his own experience as a painter. A painter cannot stand before a canvas and turn on his inspiration like a tap, and the same applies to poets and musicians. If an artist feels dull and tired – entangled in the mere physical world – he cannot summon inspiration. The inner freedom responsible for inspiration requires a kind of mental 'push-up' from the world of space and time.

The apprehension of beauty cannot be explained in mere physical terms, for, if we feel dull, we fail to see it. It is doubtful whether a cow appreciates the view from its mountain pasture, no matter how magnificent, for it is too involved in the physical world. So to see beauty requires the same kind of inspiration that the artist requires to paint it. Living itself – insofar as it involves consciousness – means living in a kind of parallel universe, from which we view actuality, as a person looking out of the window of a skyscraper sees the street below as a separate reality.

Why do we not recognise this? Because the consciousness that forms a kind of fourth dimension is as transparent as the air that separates the person in the skyscraper from the street below. The world is made of solid matter and our bodies are made of solid matter, so we feel that we are merely a part of the world – although slightly less substantial and real than houses and buses.

In fact, consciousness is made of a different kind of substance from the world, and we exist as living beings insofar as we push ourselves away from it. It is not quite true, as Bucke implies, that mystics breathe a different air and walk a different earth from the rest of us. We *all* exist in two worlds at the same time.

The implications of this insight are revolutionary. If someone asks me what I thought of a television programme, I do not feel that I am being asked to do something that contradicts the physical laws of the universe. Yet if my parrot had been standing on the back of my chair, watching the same programme (as he occasionally does), he would have been unable to form any judgment. Because, in spite of being a bird, he would not have been able to take the same 'bird's-eye view' of the programme as enables me to form a judgment. Forming judgment, grasping meaning, appreciating beauty, all demand the same faculty as the artist calls inspiration, which consists, in effect, of pushing ourselves away from the world, taking a bird's-eye view of it.

The consequences are startling. When my senses are dull, reality seems curiously meaningless, as if I am watching a play by Samuel Beckett. But I remain convinced that I am awake and alive and 'grasping reality'. This is clearly a mistake. When I am cheerful and excited – for example, setting out on holiday – everything looks more meaningful: *in fact, I am seeing the world with what the artist calls inspiration.* And, if I can escape my prejudiced assumption that this is nothing to get excited about, any more than the glow that comes with a glass of wine, I can suddenly grasp that my senses are not passive receptors of reality. Looking at the world around me is much more like writing a symphony or painting a picture than taking a photograph.

And if I could, so to speak, push myself further and further from the world, into Birkhauser's 'fourth dimension', it would become steadily more meaningful until I was staggered by the revelation of its significance and complexity. The further I can push myself into the fourth dimension, which gives me detachment from everyday reality, the more I grasp the sheer strangeness of the world.

All this Jung knew intuitively, even if he never formulated it in precisely these terms. That is why he chose Jakoby's *Fire Sower* and Birkhauser's *Fourth Dimension* and the Rosicrucian woodcut of the pilgrim to illustrate the meaning of his book on flying saucers. He knew enough of the world of the paranormal to realise that mankind is being offered a revelation that could amount to a new kind of consciousness.

This is underlined by the book's curious epilogue. After he had completed the manuscript, Jung received a copy of a book called *The Secret of the Saucers* by a 'contactee' named Orfeo Angelucci, a person who describes himself as a nervous individual suffering from constitutional inadequacy, who suddenly became an evangelist of the 'flying saucer vision'.

Angelucci describes how, as he was driving home from the night shift on 23 May 1952, he experienced a sense of the dulling of consciousness, a dreamlike sensation, after which he saw a red, oval-shaped object on the horizon. Suddenly, it shot upward, releasing two balls of green fire, from which he heard a voice telling him not to be afraid. He stopped the car, and the voice told him that he was in communication with friends from another world. Suddenly, he felt very thirsty, and the voice told him to drink from a crystal cup he would find on the car wing. It tasted delicious. Then the space between the discs began to glow until it formed a kind of television screen, on which he saw a man and woman of supernatural beauty. They seemed strangely familiar to him.

Suddenly the screen vanished, and he once again heard the voice (which seems to have been telepathic), explaining that man had been under observation for centuries, and that every human being was precious to them, because 'you are not aware of the true mystery of your being'.

The UFOs, it explained, came from a mother ship; but the space beings did not need flying saucers, since they were 'etheric' entities; the UFOs were used only to manifest themselves to man. 'Cosmic law' prevented them from landing and interfering in human destiny. But Earth was in great danger.

Angelucci was exalted by these revelations, and felt that Earth and its inhabitants had become shadowy. Two months later, on 23 July 1952, it happened again – the same dreamlike sensation, followed by the appearance of a kind of huge hemispherical soap bubble, with a door in it. Inside, he sat in a comfortable chair. There was a humming sensation, and music came from the walls. He saw a coinlike object on the floor, and, when he picked it up, it seemed grow smaller. (It is trivial, apparently meaningless details like these that lend the story verisimilitude.) Then he was looking at Earth from outer space. The voice told him that Earth, in spite of its beauty, was a purgatorial world, full of cruelty and selfishness. He was told that human beings are simply mortal shadows of divinely created beings, and that they are trying to work out their salvation on Earth. Because Orfeo was not in the best of health, he had spiritual gifts which enabled the heavenly people to enter into communication.

As they were returning to Earth, there were more revelations, then Angelucci seemed to see all his previous incarnations, and understood the mysteries of life. He thought he was about to die.

When he was back on Earth, the UFO vanished. Going to bed that night, he noticed a burning sensation on the left side of his chest, and found a circular red mark with a dot in the middle, which he interpreted as a hydrogen atom.

Angelucci became an evangelist, preaching the gospel of the UFOs, and receiving a great deal of mockery for his pains. On one occasion, after seeing a UFO, he again met his ethereal companion, who told him his name was Neptune, and treated him to further insights about Earth's problems and future redemption.

In September 1953, he fell into a trance which lasted a week; during this time, he was transported to another planet, with noble, etheric beings who fed on nectar and ambrosia. He was told that his real name was Neptune; his male teacher was actually Orion, while his female teacher was called Lyra. When Lyra treated him with tenderness, he responded with human erotic feelings, which shocked his celestial friends. It was only when he had learnt to purge himself of these feelings that he was able to celebrate a kind of mystic union with Lyra.

It is clear that Jung accepts that Angelucci is telling the truth; but he feels that his story amounts to 'spontaneous fantasy images, dreams, and the products of active imagination' – Jung's term for fantasy that takes on a dreamlike reality. And Jung goes on to consider two fantasy novels – Fred Hoyle's *The Black Cloud* and John Wyndham's *The Midwich Cuckoos* – as symbolic accounts of the coming of UFOs to answer modern man's spiritual needs. In *The Black Cloud*, the cloud from space destroys most life on earth, but proves to be alive and intelligent. Its purpose is to regenerate itself by recharging its energies near the sun. Jung sees the black cloud as a symbol of the collective unconscious, man's dark side. In *The Midwich Cuckoos*, a whole village falls into hypnotic sleep, and when the villagers awake, they discover that all the young women are pregnant. The children prove to be of greater than human intelligence – the implication being that they were fathered by angels – and, when one of them learns something, all the others know it telepathically. (The same thing has happened in Siberia, Africa and an Eskimo settlement.) But human beings realise that these brilliant children will grow up to become masters of the Earth, and they destroy them. Wyndham's conclusion seems to be as pessimistic as that of H.G. Wells in *The Food of the Gods*, where human beings try to destroy a race of giants – 'we must needs hate the highest when we see it.'

Jung's reflections on 'the flying saucer vision' have clearly led him to some exciting conclusions – the major one being that UFOs presage a profound change in human consciousness, and an important step in man's evolution. He says of the strange events at Midwich, 'It is divine intervention that gives evolution a definite push forward.' And we can suddenly see why, although he regards UFOs as a kind of hallucination, he also regards them as far more than that. They are, he seems to feel, an expression of man's 'religious function', a kind of revolt of the soul, demanding a life with more meaning; therefore they should be welcomed as a precursor of the millennium.

Yet it is difficult to accept this conclusion without certain reservations. The story of Geller and Puharich, cited in Chapter 1, is a case in point; they received assurances from 'the Nine' that they were destined to change the world – but the sequel was anticlimactic. Similarly, Jack Schwarz was promised, 'You are God's vehicle to bring the truth that is meant to be' – but the promise was not fulfilled.

In the section on Puharich, we also encountered Dr Charles Laughead, who passed on to Puharich various messages from the Nine. Laughead had been receiving these messages via a trance medium, and the 'entities' made a number of predictions, which all came true. Then the entities announced that the world was going to end on 21 December 1954 – North America would split in two, the east coast would sink into the sea, and half of Europe would be destroyed. Only the chosen few – including Dr Laughead – would be rescued by spaceships.

Laughead announced the news to the press, and, since he was a respectable academic at Michigan State University at Lansing, he was given wide coverage. With a band of believers, Laughead awaited the catastrophe – which, of course, failed to arrive. Laughead lost his job.

The case of 'Dino Kraspedon' is even stranger. I first heard the name when I came upon his book *My Contact With Flying Saucers* around 1960, and bought it to read on the train. It was translated from the Portugese, and is told in a simple, unpretentious style which impressed me with its air of truth.

He tells how, in 1952, he and a friend were driving in mountains near São Paulo, Brazil, when they saw five flying saucers. They went back later and spent three days hoping to see more UFOs. But on the third day, 'after a series of episodes which we will not go into here for fear of digression', a saucer landed, and they were allowed to go on board.

The phrase about avoiding digression struck me as having the ring of truth; a liar would insist on going into minute 'factual' detail.

They went on board, were shown the craft and told how it worked, after which the captain promised to pay Kraspedon a visit some time.

A few months later, Kraspedon's wife told him that a parson wanted to see him. Kraspedon was puzzled; being an atheist, he did not know any parsons. When he went downstairs, he recognised the captain of the spaceship, looking very well dressed and wearing a dog collar. He told Kraspedon that the deception was due to his desire not to cause Kraspedon's wife anxiety. The parson stayed to lunch, and proved to be a man of considerable learning; he was able to quote the Bible in Hebrew and Latin, and also spoke English and Greek.

He explained that he was from a satellite of Jupiter, then proceeded to lecture Kraspedon on the nature of God and the universe.

At this point, expecting fantastic adventures – like George Adamski's trip to Venus – I was surprised when the book turned into a rather intellectually taxing dialogue. Electrons were defined as 'deformed magnetic space, propagated in wave form', and God as 'an oscillating charge superimposed on an infinite point, constantly causing a deformation in space'. Matter, he explains, is always being created from nothing, which is why the universe is expanding.

Kraspedon explains, in a chapter devoted to physics, that flying saucers make use of a limitless energy available in the earth's atmosphere. 'The atmospheric ionisation on one side gives rise to a fantastic pressure on the other. It is the detonator that unleashes a cyclone behind a saucer.'

And so it goes on. If Kraspedon is a crank, then he is certainly not a confidence man. The book is so dense with scientific discussion that few readers can have summoned the endurance to read right through it. Yet the chapter dealing with social ideas displays a reassuring common sense. He points out that even scientific progress has its dangers, and that if automation is developed (this was 1953) there would be a great loss of employment – a remarkable prediction of what has happened with the development of computers.

The space captain also suggests that most education could be conducted with the aid of sleep learning, and that criminality could be eliminated by the use of hypnosis. He predicts that man will learn to live far longer when he recognises that it is the force of the spirit that sustains the body. He shows considerable insight into the problem of atmospheric pollution, and how the atmosphere will cease to filter the rays of the sun. He predicts the gradual rise in earth's temperature, and the melting of the poles. The apocalyptic scenario that follows is hair-raising.

Finally, Kraspedon describes how he took leave of the spaceman at the Roosevelt station in São Paulo, and how the captain promised to return in 1956, or – if anything should prevent this – in 1959.

And that was all I learnt about Dino Kraspedon for many years – in fact, until I read John Keel's *Operation Trojan Horse* in the 1980s. It was from Keel's book that I learnt that Kraspedon's real name was Aladino Felix, and that, in 1965, six years after publication of his book, Kraspedon began to make prophecies of disaster – for example, of floods that would take place later in the year. He proved correct, and floods and landslides around Rio de Janeiro killed 600 people. In 1967 he appeared on television and foretold the assassination of Martin Luther King and Robert Kennedy, which duly occurred.

When Aladino began to predict an outbreak of terrorist attacks and murders in Brazil in 1968, no one was surprised when he proved to be correct. Public buildings were dynamited and there was a wave of bank robberies. Finally, the police arrested eighteen members of the gang responsible, and learnt that they had planned to assassinate government officials and take over the entire country. And the name of their leader was . . . Aladino Felix, alias Dino Kraspedon. Arrested on 22 August 1968, he explained, 'I was sent here as an ambassador to the Earth from Venus. My friends from space will come here and free me, and avenge my arrest. You can look to tragic consequences for humanity when the flying saucers invade this planet.'

But of course, Felix's space friends did not arrive to save him from prison, although no doubt they had assured him that they would.

John Keel himself almost became a victim of these strange hoaxers. In 1966, after he had begun his full-scale investigations of the UFO phenomenon, as described in the last chapter, the phenomenon 'zeroed in' on him.

Luminous aerial objects seemed to follow me around like faithful dogs. The objects seemed to know where I was going and where I had been. I would check into a motel chosen at random only to find that someone had made a reservation in my name and had even left a string of nonsensical telephone messages for me. I was plagued by impossible coincidences, and some of my closest friends in New York . . . began to report strange experiences of their own – poltergeists erupted in their apartments, ugly smells of hydrogen sulphide haunted them. One girl of my acquaintance suffered an inexplicable two-hour mental blackout while sitting under a hair dryer alone in her own apartment. More than once I woke up in the middle of the night to find myself unable to move, with a huge dark apparition standing over me.

Travelling all over America to check UFO stories, he came upon dozens of people he called 'silent contactees', who regularly experienced UFO contact, and kept it to themselves. And the contactees acted as intermediaries. When a contactee was being visited by one of these entities, he or she would ring John Keel, and he would sometimes converse with it for hours.

His later conclusion was that the phenomenon was slowly leading him from scepticism to belief – then to disbelief. 'When my thinking went awry and my concepts were wrong, the phenomenon actually led me back onto the right path. It was all an educational process, and my teachers were very, very patient.' In other words, it was, as Jacques Vallee has said, a 'control phenomenon' whose purpose was to alter his thinking habits. He notes: 'Other people who have become involved in this situation have not been so lucky. They settled upon and accepted a single frame of reference, and were quickly engulfed in disaster.' He has in mind people like Charles Laughead and Dino Kraspedon.

Keel had reason to be suspicious. The entities played absurd practical jokes.They would ring up Keel's friends, using Keel's voice, and impart disinformation. He once sent an article to an editor, who told him next time he saw him that he could not use it; Keel read it and was appalled: his article had been switched for a 'real piece of garbage', sent in one of Keel's envelopes. His phone bills became enormous, and he found out the reason one day when a friend accidentally misdialled his phone number, using the wrong last digit, and still got through to Keel. Keel discovered he was paying for two telephones. And the other was usually answered by someone who offered to take messages for John Keel. When Keel rang the number, and asked if there were any message, there was a gasp, and the receiver was slammed down.

In May 1967, the entities promised many of the silent contactees that a big power failure would occur. On 4 June 1967, there was a massive power failure in four states on the east coast. The contactees were then told – and in turn told Keel – that there would soon be an even bigger power failure across the whole country, and that the New York seaboard would slide into the sea on 2 July.

The day came and passed without incident. But now the entities repeated the strategy. Two plane crashes were predicted, both of which occurred. The rumour was spreading in hippie circles, and trance mediums and automatic writers repeated them. It was predicted that the Pope would be assassinated in Turkey, and that a three-day nationwide blackout would occur after that.

When Keel learnt that the Pope *was* scheduled to visit Turkey in July, he began to feel nervous. In the various 'flap areas' – where contactees had spread the word – hardware shops had sold out of candles and torches.

Finally, Keel decided to move to one of these flap areas to await the blackout. Leaving Manhattan for Long Island, he bought three quarts of distilled water, reasoning that a three-day power failure would be accompanied by a water shortage. On Long Island he called on a contactee, and was told that he had just received a visit from a UFO entity, and that the entity had left him a message: 'Tell John Keel we'll meet him and help him drink all that water.' No one but Keel knew he had the water.

The Pope was not assassinated, and the power failure did not occur. That weekend, Keel saw several UFOs.

The accurate predictions continued to occur. One 'UFO entity' called Mr Apol, who talked to him on the phone predicted a major disaster on the Ohio River, and that, when President Johnson pulled the switch on the White House lawn to turn on the Christmas lights, there would be a major blackout. On 11 December 1967, a mysterious phone caller informed Keel that there would be an aeroplane disaster in Tucson, Arizona. The following day an Air Force jet crashed on a shopping centre in Tucson.

The Ohio River was of particular interest to Keel, because – as already noted – he had spent a great deal of time during the past year at a place called Point Pleasant, in West Virginia, following up a UFO investigation which involved a strange winged figure who became known as Mothman, and every day he crossed the bridge from his motel on the Ohio side of the bridge into Point Pleasant. For a whole year, Point Pleasant had been virtually the UFO capital of America.

On 15 December Keel was sitting in his apartment with a friend, watching the television, which was showing the ceremony on the White House lawn. He was surrounded by candles and torches. Another visitor, a TV producer who was making a programme on UFOs, had decided to return to his own home to watch the programme and await the blackout. President Johnson threw the switch, and the tree lit up. And the lights stayed on.

A moment later, the programme was interrupted by a news flash. A bridge connecting Gallipolis in Ohio and West Virginia had just collapsed. Keel knew that there was only one bridge on that section of the river – the one he crossed regularly to Point Pleasant.

It was as if the UFO entities had wanted him to be watching television at that precise moment, and had told him the absurd story about the national blackout. If they had predicted the collapse of the Silver Bridge, he might have done something about it, for everyone knew that the traffic it was now carrying was far too great for its size (it had been built in 1928, when traffic was lighter), and a campaign in a Point Pleasant newspaper might have averted the tragedy.

A few hours later, the Australian Prime Minister, Harold Holt, went for a swim from a beach near Melbourne, and disappeared. The UFO entities had also predicted his disappearance.

Keel comments, 'I was lucky. I didn't cry their warning from the housetops. I didn't surround myself with a wild-eyed cult impressed with the accuracy of the previous predictions.' If he had – using his syndicated newspaper column – he would probably have found himself in the same unfortunate position as Charles Laughead.

Was that their aim – to discredit him, perhaps to silence him? It certainly begins to look as if the UFO 'entities' are, as Jacques Vallee phrased it, 'messengers of deception'. But why should they want to cause chaos and confusion?

The first step towards an answer probably lies in recognising that the term 'UFO entities' gives a spurious impression of unity, which quickly vanishes when we begin looking at the bewildering variety of cases. If, indeed, a UFO crashed near Roswell in July 1947 (as seems highly likely), then it must have been a 'nuts-and-bolts' spacecraft, even if its technology was centuries ahead of anything on earth. But the alien bodies reported by so many, and seen in an autopsy film (which may or may not be spurious), do not look in the least like the 'greys' of so many abduction accounts. And the greys reported so fully in the books of Budd Hopkins, David Jacobs and John Mack do not seem to bear any resemblance to John Keel's manic practical jokers, who often sound as if they stepped straight out of *Batman*.

As Keel points out, Mr Apol and his cohorts behaved far more like poltergeists. He remarks, 'Bedroom visitants and poltergeist activity are a common factor in the contactee syndrome.' This in itself suggests that many people who believe they are in contact with UFO visitants may really be dealing with the 'paranormal' entities that the Society for Psychical Research investigated so extensively in the last part of the nineteenth century.

Poltergeists, and other 'spirits' that manifest through ouija boards, automatic writing and so on, seem to be unreliable more often than not. Many paranormal researchers prefer to regard them as manifestations of the unconscious mind, as I was once inclined to myself; I had to abandon this pleasantly simplistic theory because it fails to fit most of the recorded cases – as, for example, the following.

On 15 September 1899, a boy working on the farm of George Dagg, near Quebec, was taken off to see the magistrate after two missing dollars were found in his bed; Mrs Dagg assumed that the boy was also responsible for streaks of ordure on the floor. But, while they were on the way to the magistrate, more streaks of ordure appeared, exonerating the boy.

After that, typical poltergeist phenomena began – overturned milk pails, smashed windows, small fires, water poured on the floor. The poltergeist particularly seemed to enjoy tormenting an eleven-year-old orphan called Dinah Maclean; one day it half severed a braid of her hair, so it had to be cut off. Unlike the others, she was also able to hear its voice.

An artist called Woodcock came to the farm, and Dinah told him that she had seen the spirit in the woodshed. They went there, and when she asked, 'Are you there, mister?', a gruff voice, which seemed to come from the air, replied with a stream of profanities. Woodcock asked, 'Who are you?', and the voice replied, 'I am the Devil. I'll have you in my clutches. Get out or I'll break your neck.'

Unintimidated, Woodcock fetched George Dagg, and a long conversation ensued. When Dagg asked, 'Why are you bothering my family?', it replied, 'Just for fun.' Asked why it had thrown a stone at Mary, the voice replied that the stone was intended for Dinah, but had missed. At Dagg's request, the entity also wrote a message with a pencil on a piece of paper, but lost its temper again when Dagg said, 'I asked you to write something decent.'

Requested to go away and leave them alone, the voice finally agreed that it would take its leave the following day, a Sunday. A large crowd gathered, and the voice held audience in the farmhouse. It seemed to have a remarkable knowledge of the personal business of the people who came in. When someone remarked that its language had improved, the voice replied that it was not the same spirit, but an angel – this was obviously untrue, since it was the same voice. But when, under questioning, it began to contradict itself, the old foul language reappeared.

This entertainment went on for hours. During this time, Woodcock drew up a statement of the poltergeist's activities which seventeen witnesses signed – broken windows, fires, a mouth organ being played by invisible lips, stones thrown, a large dining table overturned, and various other phenomena. It seemed that the children could see the entity, which gave its name, and mentioned that it had died twenty years earlier. (It asked for its name to be suppressed in the report.) The three children could see it as a tall man with a cow's head, horns and a cloven hoof, as a big black dog, and as an angel in white robes with a starry crown. (Note the black dog – a shape that has always been associated with spirits in folklore.)

Woodcock left in the evening, but the crowd found the spirit so interesting that they begged it to remain. By now it had ceased to speak in a rough voice and was singing hymns in high, flutelike tones. Finally it left, but said it would show itself to the children before it departed the next day.

The next day, the children rushed in in great excitement to say that a beautiful man in white robes had picked up Mary and Johnny in his arms. He had remarked that 'that fellow Woodcock' refused to believe he was an angel, but he would show that he was. Whereupon he floated up into the sky in a kind of fire that seemed to blaze up from his feet; little Mary said 'he was all red'.

The children all told the same story, and repeated it without variations many times.

If the same spirit had appeared a century later, it would undoubtedly have claimed to be the inhabitant of a UFO, and the children would probably have seen it climb aboard one as it departed into the blue. As it is, its departure recalls Elijah and his chariot of fire.

Dinah was clearly the 'focus' of the poltergeist activity. Poltergeists manifest themselves by taking energy from people, often children on the verge of puberty (as Dinah was) – probably because the sexual changes that take place during adolescence provide the necessary energy.

Poltergeists, like ghosts, seem to be what mediums call 'earth-bound spirits' – often people who do not know they are dead.

Now compare John Keel's comments about one of the UFO entities with whom he held long phone conversations in 1967:

> Mr Apol had assumed a definite personality . . . I studied his psychology, his quick temper, his mischievous sense of humour. I argued with him on the phone, sometimes for two or three hours at a stretch. And I felt sorry for him. It became apparent that he did not really know who or what he was. He was a prisoner of our time frame. He often confused the past with the future. I gathered that he and all his fellow entities found themselves transported backward and forward in time involuntarily, playing out their little games because they were programmed to do so, living – or existing – only so long as they could feed off the energy and minds of mediums or contactees. I could ask him any kind of obscure question, and receive an instant and accurate answer, perhaps because my own mind as being tapped, just like my telephone. Where was my mother's father born? Cameron Mills, New

York, of course. Where had I misplaced my stopwatch? Look in the shoebox in the upper right-hand corner of the bedroom . . .

Apol certainly behaves more like the Dagg poltergeist than the little green or silver-suited men reported by so many contactees.

UFOs seem to share another odd ability with poltergeists: to be visible to one person, but not to another. Andrija Puharich records a number of occasions when he and Uri Geller were able to see UFOs that were invisible to others who were with them. Dinah Maclean and the other two Dagg children were able to see (and hear) the poltergeist when no one else could. Moreover, the poltergeist was able to appear to them in different forms: as a thin man with a cow's head, as an angel, as a black dog.

By comparison, ordinary ghosts seem relatively conservative. But they also seem to have the same odd ability to be seen by one person and not another. One typical case will suffice.

In 1920, Cleve Court, near Minster, in Kent, was bought by the lawyer and founder of Northern Ireland loyalism, Sir Edward (later Lord) Carson. It had a pleasant atmosphere, but Carson and his wife soon realised it was haunted. There would be a knock on the door, and nobody there, and footsteps sounded along empty corridors in the old Elizabethan part of the house. Their six-year-old son told them he did not like the lady who walked along the passage outside his bedroom. A four-year-old girl named Patricia told them about the lady who often came into her bedroom, then pointed at the corner of the room. 'There she is.' She became quite annoyed because Lady Carson could not see her. One child who was invited to the house a second time asked if the 'poor lady' would be there; when asked what she meant, she said, 'The lady who walks in and out, and no one speaks to her.'

In December 1949, Lady Carson finally saw the ghost for herself. She had got up in the middle of the night because her spaniel wanted to go outside. In the hall, the dog began to whimper and ran away, and Lady Carson saw a woman in a grey dress coming downstairs. She looked so solid that Lady Carson was about to ask her what she was doing, then she noticed that the figure was making no sound, and realised it was a ghost. The woman walked through an open door to an older part of the house.

The researcher Andrew Mackenzie, who recounts the story in *The Unexplained* (1966), concluded that the ghost was the unhappily married daughter of a previous owner of the house – probably around

1700 – who had never had the children she hoped for, which may explain why she appeared so often to children.

At first sight, the dissimilarities between the Cleve Court ghost and John Keel's practical jokers may seem to outweigh the similarities. But that may be simply that we have all heard so many ghost stories that they have a deceptive ring of familiarity, arousing memories of Scrooge and Hamlet's murdered father. But if we try to forget these preconceptions, we can see that the Cleve Court case raises some fundamental questions. If we start with the assumption that the story is true – and Andrew Mackenzie is regarded as one of the most reliable of modern investigators – then we are faced with the notion that a woman who was alive in 1700 may still be wandering around Cleve Court, and almost certainly unaware that she is dead. So we reach our first conclusion: that, when we die, we undoubtedly do not simply cease to exist.

But why could the child Patricia see the grey lady when she was invisible to Lady Carson? The obvious assumption is that Patricia was somehow 'tuned in' to her. And this raises more questions. When a living person walks into a room, I do not need to be 'tuned in' to see them. So we tend to make the assumption that there is an objective world 'out there', like some gigantic television screen that we can all see. It differs from dreams in that they take place inside our heads. But, when one person can see something that is invisible to another, it raises the strong possibility that the outside world is not a massive television screen that we all share. Perhaps we all have our individual television screens, and some can tune in to things that others fail to pick up. It begins to look as if one of our most basic assumptions – that I am 'in here', inside my head, while the world is 'out there', common to all of us – may be false, or at least simplistic. Our minds may play a far greater part than we think in creating 'reality'. The grey lady's mind is obviously creating her own reality, in defiance of the present owners of Cleve Court.

This seems to be demonstrated by another episode in this strange story. Carson's family physician was called Dr E.G. Moon, and he confided to Lady Carson a baffling experience of his own. One day in 1930, he had called on Lord Carson, and was on his way out when he paused at the front door. What he saw was a totally different scene from the one he expected. His car had vanished; so had the thick hedge and the drive. Instead, there was a muddy cart track. Facing him, about to enter the house, was a man wearing a coat with multiple capes, a top hat, and gaiters. He stared at Dr Moon, who found himself wondering what on Earth was happening. He retreated back into the house – probably wondering if he had come the wrong way – then looked back again at the open door. The man had disappeared, and his car was parked where he had left it, among the familiar modern-day scenery. Dr Moon had experienced what is known as a 'time slip'. They are far less rare than might be supposed – in fact, Andrew Mackenzie devoted a whole book to them called *Adventures in Time* (1997). It contains, for example, a detailed account of the experience of the two English ladies at Versailles, who in 1901 were apparently transported back to the Versailles of Marie Antoinette, and ten years later described it in their book *An Adventure*. Then there is the account of the three Royal Naval cadets who walked into a Suffolk village one Sunday morning in 1957, and found themselves back in a deserted medieval village, probably at the time of the Black Death. Mackenzie also tells the story of the Scottish spinster who was returning to her home in the early hours of the morning when she saw flickering torches in the surrounding fields, and men in strange clothes examining corpses. A lengthy historical investigation revealed that what she had seen was probably a re-enactment of the aftermath of the battle of Nechtansmere, fought in AD 685.

One of the characteristics of virtually all these stories is that the participants experienced an odd sense of oppression, of dreamlike unreality – which, in the Versailles case, Charlotte Moberly and Eleanor Jourdain assumed to be a slight fever – and which, as Jacques Vallee points out, is often experienced in UFO sightings. (The contactee Angelucci reported the same thing.)

One of the oddest tales in the book, recorded by the Society for Psychical Research, concerned a Mr J.S. Spence, who spent several days in Devon in 1938. He experienced the same dreamlike oppression, and an odd feeling of being watched. At the top of a steep cliff he found a newly built dry-stone wall that stretched to the edge of the cliff. The next day, visiting the same spot, he was puzzled to find a very old, ivy-covered wall in bad repair.

Thinking that he must have taken the wrong path, he decided to go back the next day and try to solve the mystery. On the third day, he again found the new wall at the top of the cliff. But he had an odd feeling of dizziness. And as he moved forward, over apparently solid ground, he suddenly slipped and fell vertically. He found himself on a narrow ledge near the top of the cliff, with a twisted ankle. Far below, the sea was pounding on the rocks. Mr Spence succeeded in climbing back to the top – and found the old and broken wall, much of which had obviously collapsed into the sea when the edge of the cliff gave way. He had been trying to walk on 'solid ground' that had vanished in a previous century.

There are dozens of such recorded 'time slips' – probably hundreds. I myself collected one from a woman named Jane O'Neill, who visited Fotheringhay church with a friend in 1974, and was much impressed by a picture of the crucifixion behind the altar, with a dove over the cross. But a friend who accompanied her saw no such picture, as they discovered later when they compared notes. When they revisited the church, the friend proved to be right – there was no picture. But Jane O'Neill also failed to recognise the inside of the church. For she had seen it as it was when it was a collegiate church, which was pulled down in 1553.

There have been other recorded time slips at Fotheringhay. In August 1976, a schoolmaster named Priest and his wife were approaching the church when they heard sounds of 'a primitive kind of music' with trumpets and drums. They assumed some kind of rehearsal was taking place inside, but, when they opened the door, the church was deserted, and the music had stopped. Back at the church gate, they again heard the music, this time more faintly. They later discovered that they had visited the church exactly five hundred years after the funeral ceremony of Richard, Duke of York, but this may or may not be the answer.

In 1941, a policeman visiting the church with a female cousin heard the sounds of monks chanting, but the sounds stopped as abruptly as a radio being turned off when they opened the door and found an empty church. The 'ghost hunter' Peter Underwood has accounts of several other time slips at Fotheringhay, always on hot August days.

Other time slips have also occurred at Versailles – Mackenzie details no fewer than seven. In July 1908, an English family named Crooke, who lived in the village of Versailles, twice saw the same 'sketching lady' in old-fashioned dress described by Misses Moberly and Jourdain. They realised she was a 'ghost' because 'she appeared and disappeared several times, seeming to grow out of and retire into the scenery with a little quiver of adjustment'. And, in 1910, Major Robert Gregory – son of Lady Gregory – and his wife saw an 'old-fashioned' Versailles, including a thick wood. When they read *An Adventure* a year later, they returned to Versailles to find that the wood had gone, and that they were unable to recognise a single thing.

Fotheringhay and Versailles have been the scenes of many important historical events, and have witnessed a great deal of tragedy. Did Miss Moberly and Miss Jourdain see a 'ghost' of Versailles as it was about 1750? That seems unlikely – surely there is no such thing as the ghosts of a *place*? Then could their experience have been a kind of 'tape recording', the events of the past having somehow impressed themselves on the scenery? That is just possible – in 1960, in the cellar of the Treasurer's House in York, a heating engineer saw a Roman legion with round shields marching through the walls and across the floor, and felt that they did not perceive him. (Historians were later able to identify the legion, and verify that they carried round shields.) On the other hand, Miss Moberly and Miss Jourdain talked to some of the people in old-fashioned dress. And Dr Moon seems to have felt that the gentleman in the cloak and top hat actually looked at him.

So what is going on? Is time past still present in another dimension? Or is it present only in the minds of ghosts? Or can the individual television sets inside our heads tune in to other times and places, so they appear to be real? This would also imply that the world around us is perhaps not as real as it looks.

Then there is the baffling problem of precognition – the ability to foresee some event in the future in precise detail. It may be the immediate or distant future. A pianist friend of mine was returning along the Bayswater Road in a taxi after a concert when he knew, with total certainty, that, at the Queensway traffic lights, a taxi would try to jump the lights and hit them sideways on; it happened exactly as he had known it would.

Goethe, in his autobiography, tells how, having just said goodbye to his sweetheart, he was riding along a road in Alsace when he saw, coming to meet him, his own double (or doppelgänger), dressed in a grey and gold suit. Eight years later, on his way to visit the same girl, he realised that he was now dressed in the grey and gold suit. He had 'seen' his future self.

It would seem, then, that the commonsense view of time is somehow mistaken: the past and the future are in some sense present. There is also much evidence from psychical research that 'spirits' often confuse the past and future. During World War Two, an English woman with psychic gifts, Mrs A.M. Kaulback, conducted a series of telepathy experiments with her two sons, who were in the forces, and concluded that many of her impressions came from 'discarnate communicators', including her deceased husband. On one occasion, her husband told her that her son Bill had just been given command of a battalion, and described the scene in some detail. He was right – except that the events he described occurred a month later. When she asked her 'guide' to explain this, he told her, 'It is not easy grasping time between two planes.'

John Keel also found that his UFO entities were often confused about the sequence of events they predicted. The explanation might be that they were not actually UFO entities, but some of the more dubious denizens of the 'spirit world'. But, as Jacques Vallee points out, it cannot be assumed that the UFO entities encountered by 'contactees' like Herb Schirmer are telling the truth.

It seems clear, then, that there is a type of entity that enjoys deceiving and misleading. Why this should be so is a mystery, since it is hard to see how they can benefit from it. Perhaps they simply enjoy their contact with human beings, trying to impress, like some casual pub acquaintance who launches into self-glorifying autobiography. But, in the case of many of these entities, the result may be a kind of long-term confidence trick.

The novelist Jan de Hartog has described how this can come about. In a lecture to the American Society of Dowsers – and on another occasion, to me – he described how he had become interested in dowsing when he made the acquaintance of an animal healer at a health farm. The healer used a pendulum to make diagnoses. (It usually swings back and forward to indicate yes, and in a circle to indicate no – or whatever code the dowser chooses.) Together, they went to visit a 'druid' on the Cheddar Downs, and, practised dowsing and searching for 'energy spots'. Then the druid told his friend that he ought to speak to a disembodied woman called Imogen, who was standing ten paces away. His friend took ten paces forward, then stopped, apparently absorbed. Hartog learnt later that he had not only become aware of a female presence, but that Imogen was able to communicate with him. His friend remarked, 'I don't know who that was, but it was definitely a woman.'

Jan de Hartog describes the immense excitement that he and his friend felt, the sense of embarking on an amazing adventure. He went back to his farm in Pennsylvania, and his friend came and stayed, and taught him how to use the pendulum to receive messages. He would ask, 'Are you there?', and his pendulum would spin like an aeroplane propeller – there could be no doubt that he was not doing it himself. Then the message would be spelt out letter by letter.

Jan quickly learnt that the entity who was communicating with him was called Eleanor, that she had been a White Russian doctor, and that he and she had been lovers in a previous existence. And while his friend was receiving messages from Imogen – assuring him that he should give up animal healing and concentrate on humans, and that he was destined eventually to heal the whole human race – Jan was having long sessions with Eleanor, who was explaining how to lose weight by eating certain foods and avoiding others. Eleanor had a strong personality, and their relationship was stormy – on one occasion, when she ordered Jan to restrict his dinner to one hard-boiled egg, he threw his pendulum at her.

He also found himself in contact with an Indian called Old Oak, who instructed him about nature, and, on the whole, made more sense than Eleanor.

Soon Jan found he could abandon the old slow method of spelling out messages letter by letter; he became more and more intuitive about what Eleanor and Old Oak were trying to tell him, and would write as fast as his hand could cross the paper.

When winter came, both Eleanor and Old Oak advised him that there was going to be a cold spell, and it was time to invest in an electricity generator. He baulked at the cost, and eventually proved to be right – the cold front stopped a hundred miles away.

The family decided to go to a dude ranch in Montana, where his daughter could ride. There Jan lived in a little cabin, and his wife and daughter in another. And now Jan learnt that he had a new companion – Imogen had also joined him. His friend had told him that Imogen was the 'controlling spirit of all healing in the natural plane'. And Imogen lost no time in assuring Jan that he was a far more powerful healer than his friend. He was going to be one of the greatest healers of all time.

All this, Jan confesses, filled him with misgivings – he felt that it was somehow 'too big'. Yet it was all so fascinating – to be in communication with a disembodied intelligence – that he had no thought of giving up. He obviously felt as Geller and Puharich felt as they received messages from the Nine.

Imogen declared that it was time he embarked on his healing career. The next day, she explained, when a group of them rode under a waterfall, a horse would stumble, and a woman would be badly hurt. Jan was then instructed – in precise detail – how to heal her, exactly how far away to hold his hands, etc. All this would leave him in no doubt of his powers.

The next day, the riders approached the waterfall, and Jan prepared for the accident. But nothing happened. That night, in his cabin, Jan asked Imogen why. She explained that the spirit who had been detailed to trip up the horse had not turned up. Jan was horrified. 'You mean to tell me that some perfectly innocent woman was going to be thrown from her horse, merely so that I could heal her?' And, when it seemed that this, indeed, was what Imogen had intended, he suddenly knew beyond all doubt that he did not want to know her any more. He told her so, and suddenly all his powers vanished; the pendulum ceased to spin out messages, and he was once again alone.

Another friend of mine, Joe Fisher, had an equally disillusioning experience with 'spirits', which he describes in a remarkable book called *Hungry Ghosts*. He is a journalist in Toronto, and was one day contacted by a woman who, under hypnosis, had become the mouthpiece for 'discarnate entities'. He went along to see for himself, and a spirit with a reassuring Yorkshire accent spoke through her mouth and told him that he had a female guide called Filipa, a Greek girl who had been his lover in a previous existence, three centuries earlier, in a village called Theros, on the Greek–Turkish border. Joe was inclined to believe him, since he had always had a powerful affinity for Greece. Soon, like Jan de Hartog, he was in direct contact with Filipa. He would relax, and a buzzing noise in his head would precede a feeling of bliss and communication. Filipa was a sensual little thing who liked to be cuddled, and soon Joe's present love affair broke up, his girlfriend feeling she was no match for a ghost.

But, although he trusted Filipa, he began to experience doubts about some of the other spirits who came through at the seances. One claimed to be an ex-RAF pilot called Ernest Scott, who gave details of his wartime experiences. On a trip back to England, Joe decided to verify these stories, having no doubt whatever that they would prove genuine. The airfield certainly existed; so did the squadron with which Ernest Scott said he had flown. But Scott himself was not in the squadron records; he had never existed.

Joe tried to track down the farm where the Yorkshire spirit claimed he had lived in the nineteenth century. The geography was accurate; so were many other details. But the basic facts were simply wrong.

Joe also tried to verify the background a a lovable World War One veteran named Harry Maddox. Harry's accounts of World War One battles were accurate; but Harry himself had never existed.

In spite of these disillusionments, Joe had no doubt that Filipa was genuine. He felt that she 'possessed more love, compassion and perspicacity than I had ever known'. On a trip to Greece, he tried to locate the village of Theros, where he and Filipa had lived and loved. It did not exist. But he was able to locate a town called Alexandropouli, which Filipa told him had been nearby. When he got there, however, he learnt that Alexandropouli was a mere two centuries old; it did not exist when he and Filipa were supposed to have been lovers. Filipa, like the others, was simply a liar.

Now I agree that all this is extremely confusing: time slips into the past, glimpses of the future, poltergeists who play practical jokes, ghosts who do not know they are dead, entities who claim to be the spirits of living people, and who tell lies for the fun of it . . . What is it all about? How can we make sense of such a farrago of absurdity?

Only one thing seems to stand out with some certainty. This normal, solid world around us is just a façade, and, while we believe that it is *the* world, the *only* world, we are deceived. This assumption that we are in a perfectly ordinary, logical world, and that we know most of the rules, traps us in a kind of permanent tunnel vision. Gurdjieff even used the alarming simile of hypnotised sheep, who are kept in a state of trance by a magician who wants to save money on fencing, and so assures the sheep that they have nothing to be afraid of, and that nothing bad is going to happen to them. I am inclined to think his pessimism unjustified. But there can be no doubt whatever that this 'illusion of normality' causes us to waste our lives and fail to grasp our potentialities. If, instead of this vast façade of triviality that surrounds us, we could become aware of the complex realm that lies on the other side of it, we might stop wasting our lives.

Now it is this far wider, more inclusive view of reality that Jung and John Michell call 'the flying saucer vision' – clearly not a particularly appropriate name, since it applies to far more than flying saucers. John Keel seems to come closer to its essence when he says (in *The Eighth Tower*):

The extradimensional world is not a place where trees grow and politicians steal. It is a state of energy. All kinds of information about our trivial reality are stored in the energy field through a system of particles or units of energy in a negative or positive state, just as our brains store information by opening and closing billions of nerve switches called synapses. The field is like a massive radio wave and certain human brains have the ability to tune into it.

Some of these brains are adjusted to the frequency of the bank of future data. So they receive glimpses of the future in sudden thoughts, visions (images in the conscious mind), dreams (images in the unconscious mind), or a combination of all three. Since the superspectrum is outside our time frame, its system for measuring time is different from ours, and few humans with precognition are able to unscramble the time cycle of future events.

Keel admits:

I'm embarrassed now when I recall how I stood in darkened fields with contactees who suddenly began talking in a deep baritone, declaring themselves to be from outer space. No matter how devious and complicated the questions I asked, they always seemed to have a quick and reasonable answer. They seemed to know everything about everything, just as demons in religious cases of possession know the most minute details about the lives of their exorcists –

– as Stanislav Grof discovered when he tried to exorcise the girl with the criminal record.

Keel summarises: 'Demonic possession is just a game perfected by countless believers across the centuries. Spiritualism is another. And, of course, the outer-space game is the latest development, and currently the most important.'

Now we can begin to see why Jung thought that UFOs are 'psychic projections' which can nevertheless affect photographic plates and radar screens. He did not make some hard-and-fast distinction between the physical and mental worlds, but recognised that they are somehow intermingled. In 1928, Jung came upon alchemy in a Chinese work called *The Secret of the Golden Flower*, and came to the conclusion that alchemy is basically about the transmutation *of the mind*, and the discovery of the self. He asked a Munich bookseller to find him as many ancient alchemical works as he could, and, as he struggled with these infuriatingly obscure texts, came to feel that alchemy is a strange mixture of the physical and the mental. By sheer willed concentration, the alchemist can create states that Jung calls 'active imagination', whereby he can enter his own unconscious mind in a kind of wide-awake dreaming. So stories of alchemists – like Nicholas Flamel, who actually turned mercury into gold – may well be true; alchemy operates by the same strange laws as 'quantum reality', where the observer plays an all-important part.

So what might be called 'UFO reality' would seem to be a realm like alchemy and quantum reality, where two apparently incompatible realities come together. In fact, they are far from incompatible; they only appear to be so because we are trapped in our tunnel vision, which assures us that this world is physical, and that we are inescapably tied to it. Yet we are always catching glimpses of a larger reality that tells us this is untrue. Even as simple and commonplace an experience as setting out on holiday makes us aware of it: that curious feeling of happiness and excitement is far more than mere anticipation of leisure. It is a glimpse of something far richer and bigger and more complex, a feeling that we are on the verge of discovering some secret. And the secret somehow belongs to the same type as a young person's discovery of music or art – or, for that matter, sex. *It is a promise of freedom*, of far more freedom than we believe we possess, and also of control over our own lives.

7 'Oh no, not again!'

WE HAVE ALREADY encountered Harold Wilkins, as the author of one of the best of the early books on flying saucers. But in *Mysteries Solved and Unsolved* (1959) he recounts a tale that he certainly felt had no connection with flying saucers.

One day in the summer of 1906, three children went into a field known as Forty Acres, a mile outside Gloucester, and disappeared. They were a boy, age ten, and two girls, age five and three, the children of 'a rather uncouth railway guard, or brakeman, named Vaughan'. Harold Wilkins joined in the search. 'We paid particular attention to the north-east corner of the field, where the pasture was bordered by tall, old elms, a thick hedge of thorn and bramble, and a deep ditch, separating it from a corn-field. Every inch was probed with sticks, and not a stone left unturned in the ditch. Had a dead dog been dumped there, he would certainly have been found.'

The case was reported in the national press, and the Vaughan family received many postal orders from sympathetic readers. But, when the vicar called to express commiseration, he was turned away with the comment that Vaughan 'didn't want no bloody parsons rapping at his door'.

Four days later, at six in the morning, a ploughman going to work in the cornfield looked over the hedge, and saw the three children asleep in the ditch. The children simply had no idea of where they had been for three days and nights.

The ploughman was denied any share of the reward on the grounds that he had probably kidnapped the children to claim it – which was absurd, since the reward was not offered until after they had vanished. Besides, he lived in a small cottage in a tiny hamlet, where everyone knew everyone else's business, so it was impossible.

The missing boy was still alive after World War Two, and verified that he did not have the slightest idea of what happened from the time they went into the field to when they woke up four days later. This, Wilkins comments, is 'characteristic of the amnesia which marks these phenomena'.

Vallee would undoubtedly point out that the case bears an obvious resemblance to cases of abduction by fairies, as well as to the engineering student described in the Introduction to *The Invisible College*, who was taken on board a UFO and spent some hours connected to a 'teaching machine' – then returned to find he had been absent for eighteen days.

We also note its resemblance to the herd of cows that vanished and reappeared near Warminster in 1967. And John Mack would certainly point out its similarity to modern abduction cases. For example, one evening in 1943, as a normal American family was having dinner, the father – a violin teacher – stood up and said, 'I'm going to get a pack of cigarettes.' His family stared in astonishment – he was a nonsmoker. But he had been odd for some time, suffering strange lapses of memory. He drove away, and his car was later found parked outside the local grocery store. But he was never seen again. Nine years later, he was declared legally dead.

But why assume that he was 'abducted'? Because of the events that followed. More than half a century later, in June 1992, John Mack and other academics organised a conference on abduction at the Massachusetts Institute of Technology, and two of the many abductees who came to tell their story were women who lived and worked together on a horse farm: Anna Jamerson and Beth Collings – the latter the granddaughter of the man who vanished in 1943. And Beth Collings had reason to believe that she was at least the third generation that had been abducted, and that it might be happening to her son and granddaughter.

Years later, her father told her of an incident that had happened in 1930, when he was twelve. One morning, he and his brother were playing on a beach in Virginia, and he bent down to pick up a shell. When he looked up, his brother had vanished. Suddenly, dense sea mist rolled in. He walked up and down the seashore, calling to his brother. A shiny object caught his eye in the sand, and he bent to look at it. When he looked up, his brother was back. But his brother had also been searching up and down the beach . . . When they got home, their grandmother was frantic, and had called the police. The time was 3.45

p.m. – although only a short time before it had been 10 a.m. They had lost several hours.

After that, her father admitted, there had been frequent episodes of 'missing time'. In fact, he had shared one with Beth. In 1954, when Beth was five, she accompanied her father on a business trip to Doylestown, Pennsylvania. It was a hot day, and they were on a dirt road between fields when the car stopped. Her father got out to look under the bonnet, and Beth felt inexplicably nervous, and longed for him to come back. Then, suddenly, the car was full of freezing air, and she began shouting in alarm. Her father put his arm round her shoulder, and, as he was soothing her, the car started of its own accord. Yet he seemed unsurprised. When they finally reached Doylestown, there was a note on the office door saying, 'Sorry I missed you.' They were many hours late – yet the place where the car had stalled was only a short drive away.

Her father would later admit to many strange episodes of missing time – but said that he had thought he was dreaming or hallucinating. He also told her that his own father had been a concert violinist. But he had begun to behave erratically, occasionally failing to show up for concerts. He began teaching the violin to students in his own home, but still missed appointments. Then, that evening in 1943, he walked out and disappeared.

Beth had started to become aware of episodes of missing time in 1989. But they had obviously been going on since her childhood. When she was fourteen, she began to experience all the symptoms of pregnancy – cramps, morning sickness, tender breasts. Yet she was a virgin. Her father took her to a doctor, who performed pregnancy tests, which proved to be positive. She insisted that she could not be pregnant – she had never experienced sex. She had a boyfriend, but the affair was platonic.

One night, she went out to meet the boyfriend in a bus park. He was not there. She climbed on a bus, and woke up the next morning to find herelf in Little Rock, Arkansas. A woman pointed out a restaurant that would soon be open for breakfast. But as she sat outside, on a bench, her father's car pulled up. She climbed in, and she was driven home, without a word being spoken. Years later, when she was asking him about the 'missing time', she asked him how he had found her so far from home. He admitted that he did not have the slightest idea. He had simply 'known' where she was.

The same thing happened several times more during her teens, and each time her father somehow knew how to find her.

The implication would seem to be either that her father was 'psychic', or that he was somehow being *told* where to find her.

A few months after the Little Rock episode, she was taken for her prenatal examination, and the doctor announced that she was no longer pregnant – nor even showed signs of a miscarriage. Oddly enough, that was the end of it. No one else ever mentioned it again.

In 1987, after she had been married, divorced, and brought up a son alone, Beth saw an advertisement for a stable manager at a horse farm in Virginia. It was run by a woman of about her own age called Anna Jamerson. The two liked each other immediately, and Beth moved in. Oddly enough, Anna felt she had met Beth before; years later, they realised that they *had* met as children – in England – encountering each other by chance and having a long conversation. Such 'coincidences' occur with curious frequency in abduction cases.

Two years after Beth moved in, they saw three lights, in triangular formation, over the horse farm. It could have been an airliner, but there was no sound. Then the lights halted above them and one broke away, and disappeared.

On 15 December 1991, Beth was driving back after spending the day with her parents when she saw three bright lights over the top of the trees. She halted her car, feeling oddly alarmed. The lights were dazzling, and she got out to look more closely. One of the lights moved away from the others. And, quite suddenly, she found herself driving at a dangerous speed, five miles away, with no knowledge of how she got there. When she arrived back at the farm, she realised that it was far later than she thought – she was missing about two hours.

It happened again a few days later. Driving along, she saw the lights and groaned aloud, 'Oh no, not again!' She blinked, then found she was eight miles further on, having passed the farm. Strangest of all, a Christmas package she was carrying had been opened, and resealed with masking tape in a crude and clumsy manner. Apparently someone had opened it to find out what it contained, but had not touched the cookies in it.

Beth's parents received a visit from two Air Force officers. They explained that it was a routine check, due to the fact that Beth's son Paul had just been promoted in the intelligence branch. But, instead of asking about him, they asked questions about Beth; her father finally told them to go away and ask her themselves.

In April 1992, Beth woke up feeling sick, and discovered that she was bleeding from her navel. Over the next days she began to show all the signs of pregnancy – morning sickness, sore breasts, and obsessive house cleaning. But pregnancy was impossible – she had had a hysterectomy when she was twenty-three. Finally, she went to see a doctor, and tests showed she was three months pregnant. Her vagina was so inflamed that he asked her if she had been raped. The following day, her navel was bleeding again, but all signs of pregnancy had vanished.

The day Beth's symptoms disappeared, Anna went through the same experience – morning sickness and enlarged breasts. A home pregnancy test showed she was not pregnant – but she learnt later that, when an embryo is implanted direct into the womb (as is done in surrogate pregnancies), it does not show up on pregnancy tests. Then one morning she woke up to find herself normal again.

One day, Beth was sitting with her four-year-old granddaughter when she noted that the child was drawing a 'flying machine' with a red light, and faces looking out of the windows. Down in the corner was a small man; the child explained that this was 'Nu', and that he had taken her through a long tunnel. Nu, she said, was grey all over and had big eyes. As they were going to bed, the child turned to the open door and said, 'Goodnight, Nu.' Then she added, 'Nu is saying goodnight to you too, Grandma.'

Anna woke up in the night to find a huge man in her room. She felt no fear, but simply switched on the light. There was no one there. Then both of them woke up to see small grey figures in the room. It was at this point that Anna decided to contact a UFO help organisation. And this, in turn, led to their appearance at the UFO conference at MIT. There they met the newspaperman Courty Bryan, who would write about them in *Close Encounters of the Fourth Kind*, and also Budd Hopkins, who would invite them to New York and hypnotise them both.

During the conference, Beth had an odd experience. As she sat in the hall, everything suddenly became totally silent – as if she had become deaf. Then she found herself on a landing with a blue-tiled floor – she felt it was elsewhere on the campus. Someone seemed to be urging her to go back, and she resisted, then gave way. She found herself back in the conference hall, looking at herself and Anna (from above and slightly to one side, as has been reported by many people who have had out-of-the-body experiences), then she felt herself sink back into her body as if it was a feather mattress.

As they returned to the motel, the row of motorway lights blinked out in unison as they drove past. Beth was surprised, but Anna commented that it happened to her all the time – she records as much in the book *Connections* which she later co-authored with Beth. This book also contains an enormous mass of material for which there is no space here; unexplained electrical failures in their bedrooms but not in the rest of the house, lights and televisions turning themselves on, even when unplugged, pillows rearranged during the night. When Courty Bryan was tape-recording the two women, the tape recorder switched itself on when there was no one near it, and later the tape jammed in the mechine and refused to come out; it looked as if it would have to be taken out by force – until the women left the room, when it immediately ejected normally. There are as many of these small and relatively trivial events as in Puharich's *Uri*, and they would make equally exhausting reading if summarised here.

One of Beth's most crucial experiences happened in September, when she took a four-day holiday in the West Virginia National Park. On her first day there, a huge golden bee appeared, which she dubbed Goldie, and which followed her around like a pet bird.

That evening she saw a fog bank up above her cabin, and felt uneasy. Then she woke up and found herself in her bed; fully dressed. It was the next day, and she felt sick. When she removed her jeans, she was puzzled to find she was wearing no panties, which she had certainly been wearing the previous day.

Her car keys were missing, and the car proved to be in the middle of the roadway. As she was about to climb into it, she suddenly remembered what had happened the day before.

The fog bank had 'walked' down the slope; then three grey figures had emerged from it, and the fog had vanished. The small grey creatures seemed oddly familiar.

She grabbed her car keys and rushed for the car. The three 'greys' stopped in front of it, and one pointed his finger at the bonnet. The gear stick felt loose. Then a thought came into her head: 'Come with us.'

She agreed, but said, 'I want to remember this one.'

They climbed to the ridge where she had seen the fog bank, then she was engulfed in a blue-white light.

She found herself in a room, and a taller 'grey' approached her – over five feet; it had a huge head perched on a thin neck, and black almond-shaped eyes. He took her to another room, where there were three more like him; then she recalled that she had known him before, and that he was the 'doc'.

Liquid was injected into her hand below the thumb. When she cried out, she was told, 'There is no pain', and the pain went. Then she was undressed, and a needle driven into her navel. When she asked why this was being done, she was told, 'It is part of the change.' Later she was shown horses on a tiny screen, and told that they had also been 'changed'. So had cows. Then the 'doc' told her, 'You must eat only cow things.'

The creatures dressed her, forgetting her panties, and finally let her finish dressing herself. Once dressed, she took a step towards the 'greys', and was immediately paralysed; she realised they were afraid of her.

Then she woke up in bed, fully dressed . . . The 'greys' had allowed her to remember.

Her car refused to start, and a mechanic told her that the wires were all burnt out, and would be very expensive to repair. Anna arrived the next day, and the rest of their stay passed without incident.

The story sounds, of course, as bizarre and incredible as any of John Mack's cases, and even has touches of John Keel. (The women began to receive mysterious phone calls, one of them in a language that sounded like gibberish, although each word was carefully pronounced; the speaker became increasingly angry at his inability to make himself understood.) And, when Budd Hopkins – who entered the case as a result of meeting them at MIT – hynotised both women, he uncovered memories of abductions dating back to childhood. What was even more incredible, some memories indicated that Beth and Anna had been abducted *together* since childhood, which seemed to suggest that their whole lives had been manipulated by aliens. Hopkins was confirmed in the view he had formed as a result of years of study of such cases: that the 'greys' were engaged in some kind of biological experiment with human beings which involved implanting foetuses in the womb, and removing them when they were a few months – or weeks – old.

Anna had always been convinced that she had been raped by her father when she was twelve, when they were on a fishing trip. She could not recall how her pants had been removed, but thought that something had been inserted into her, and that, when she cried out, the assault stopped. Under hypnosis, she recalled this as her first abduction experience, during which her father was paralysed, and that it had resulted in the loss of her virginity.

If Beth Collings is to be believed, her family had been subjected to abductions for decades – at least since the late 1920s.

One of the most intelligent and perceptive of English ufologists, John Spencer, is inclined to doubt whether hypnosis is of any value whatever in abduction cases, on the grounds that it is too easy for the hypnotist to create false memories. But, while this is obviously true, it is hard to see how this should influence our view of the case of Beth and Anna. It would be easy to accuse them of a kind of *folie à deux*, and of simply being too imaginative. Certainly, if a book like *Connections* is taken in isolation, it would be easy for a sceptic to dismiss it as fantasy – lights going on and off on motorways, voices on the phone speaking gibberish, grey figures in the bedroom. Yet as soon as we turn from this to John Mack's *Abduction*, or Budd Hopkins's *Missing Time* and *Intruders*, or David Jacobs's *Secret Life*, or the vast transcript of the MIT conference, *Alien Discussions*, it is obvious that *Connections* fits neatly into a far larger pattern, and that, if we are going to dismiss the experiences of Beth and Anna, then we must dismiss everything else.

It is often stated that the 1961 abduction of Barney and Betty Hill is the first abduction case on record, and that little else happened until Budd Hopkins began to uncover cases of 'missing time' in the 1970s. In fact, one of the earliest recorded cases dates back as far as 1953. Two women who preferred to shelter under the pseudonyms of Sara Shaw and Jan Whitley were awakened at 2 a.m. by a bright light at their cabin in Tujunga Canyon, near Los Angeles; Sara knelt on the bed to look – and suddenly realised it was 4.20 in the morning, and she felt giddy and confused. Years later, under hypnosis, she described how she and Jan were floated up to a UFO and medically examined by aliens, then floated back.

The well-known psychic investigator Scott Rogo decided that the story was pure fantasy based on Sara's dissatisfaction with the lesbian relationship, but there is no evidence that this is true.

In 1957 there occurred the famous case of Antonio Villas-Boas, the Brazilian farmer who claimed to have been taken on board an egg-shaped craft, and seduced by a naked blonde. Although it sounds preposterous, his story has been subjected to detailed investigation, and is widely accepted as true. Villas-Boas later added that, in a second act of intercourse, the alien woman took a sperm sample, a fact that he had originally suppressed because it implied that he was merely being used. (Barney Hill probably had similar motives when he asked John

Fuller not to mention in his book that a sperm sample had been taken from him during the abduction.)

One of the most admirably detailed investigations of a sexual encounter with an alien was recorded by Hans Holzer in a book called *The Ufonauts* in 1976. As a result of an advertisement in a UFO magazine, Holzer established contact with a pretty blonde woman named Shane Kurz.

She told Holzer how, one evening in April 1968, she and her mother – who lived in Westmoreland, New York – saw a cigar-shaped object overhead. Later both women woke at 2 a.m. to find the bedroom flooded with white light, which came from behind the house of a neighbour across the road. Finally, the light moved up into the sky. The neighbour verified that he had also seen it.

On 2 May, Shane's mother realised that her daughter was not in her bed – they slept in the same room. She assumed Shane had gone to the bathroom. Later, she woke up to find that her daughter was lying on her bed wearing her robe, and mud-covered slippers. Muddy footprints led down the stairs to the open front door. More footprints led across the street to the field where they had seen the flashing light.

She shook Shane awake; the girl felt as dazed as if she had been given a sleeping tablet. When she showered, she noticed a red triangle on the lower part of her abdomen, and a red line running down from her navel.

For the next few days she felt deeply depressed, and found it hard to sleep. Her eyes were red and swollen, and, when she went to an oculist, she found that her vision had suddenly deteriorated. She suffered from headaches, and her periods stopped. Her hearing became abnormally acute – an effect noted by other abductees, including Beth Collings.

Shane's periods eventually started up again. But she then began to dream that she was in the field in her night robe, and that she was frightened of the UFO that hovered above her. In the dream a spotlight beam comes from the bottom of the ship, and she is floated up through a hole underneath.

Not long before she went to see Holzer, she woke up late, and noticed that her neck and face seemed to be heavily sunburnt. Again, she felt as though she had been drugged.

Holzer placed her under hypnosis, and Shane was able to recall the night in 1968 when she woke up with a feeling that someone was calling her name. 'I see this light and I want to get up.'

She sees the saucer, with a revolving rim, hanging above her, and she is 'floated' aboard. Then she is in a white room, and a small man wearing a kind of motorcycle jacket comes in. He asks her to lie on the table, and she refuses. He tells her to undress, then explains that he wants her to have a baby. She feels impelled to lie down. Then a long needle punctures her stomach.

After that, some kind of jelly is rubbed on her body, and she feels sexually stimulated. Finally, the naked man lies on top of her and makes love to her. 'I feel terrible . . . I am enjoying it.' Shane had been a virgin until then. Afterwards, she accuses the man of raping her, and he tells her she will forget it. She is dressed and floated down to the ground again.

What happened to the pregnancy? Holzer never found out. Shane had nightmares that made her refuse to submit to further hypnosis, so the case remained incomplete. But, since her periods came back, the assumption – based on other cases – is that she was abducted again and the foetus removed.

Ten years after Holzer's hypnosis of Shane Kurz, Budd Hopkins encountered a case that was in many ways similar.

After the publication of *Missing Time* in 1981, Hopkins was contacted by a woman named Kathie Davis (real name Debbie Tomey), who lived in Copley Woods, near Indianapolis. She sent him colour photographs, in which he immediately recognised typical signs of UFO landing – notably, a burnt circle of grass about eight feet in diameter. In July 1983, Kathie's mother had seen a bright light that had moved over the lawn. The dog hid under the car. That night, the grass was burnt, and nothing would grow there.

Kathie Davis also spoke of her sister Laura, who had felt a curious compulsion to drive into a car park, where she had seen 'something silver' hovering over a telegraph pole. Then, hours later, she found herself driving home in the dark.

Ten years later, Laura went to a hypnotist to lose weight, and that night found she was deaf and dumb. Hopkins reasoned that the hypnosis had probably awakened the abduction experience that had taken place in the car park.

Kathie herself had experienced missing time as a teenager, when both she and two girlfriends had seen a UFO hovering over their car one night; the next thing she remembered was arriving home at dawn.

Yet some of Kathie's experiences make us aware that, in abduction experiences, it is often hard to separate reality and unreality. One night, she drove to an all-night food store to get a drink. When she returned, she realised that she had still not bought anything to drink. She turned and drove back, and saw some large, brightly lit object in the sky, which she took to be an advertising balloon. After this, she went into the store, but the man she saw there was not the assistant who usually served her, and she recognised that the store was not a store, but some kind of spacecraft. Later that night, Kathie believes she had an abduction experience, and that so did her mother. It seems clear that the 'aliens' have the power to blur the sense of reality and make it dreamlike.

When Hopkins visited Kathie's house in Copley Woods, she told him how, on the night the lawn had been scorched, she and two friends had been swimming in her pool when – in spite of the heat – they all became freezing cold. (This, again, begins to look like a recurrent symptom in abduction cases.) Kathie's eyes started to hurt, and they all began to feel sick. Neighbours verified that some kind of bright light had landed on Kathie's lawn, and had made the lights flicker and interfered with the television.

When Kathie had been eighteen, she had found she was pregnant, and assumed that her boyfriend was responsible. A few months later, the pregnancy vanished – yet there were no signs of miscarriage.

Placed under hypnosis, Kathie remembered how, when she was nineteen, she had awakened to find two small grey figures by her bed. She remembered being floated into a place where she was medically examined, while a probe was inserted up her nose, and broke through the skin of the sinuses.

Her son Tommy also suffered a nosebleed, and the doctor who examined him found that his sinuses had been punctured. Hopkins had encountered many similar cases involving nosebleeds suffered by people who had had abduction experiences. He speculated that some sort of implant was some being inserted as a form of 'tagging'.

During a later hypnotic session, Kathie described how, during an abduction, she was allowed to see the child that had been removed from her womb; it was now a little blonde girl of about four, and she differed from a normal child only in that her head was slightly bigger than usual. ' . . . I felt like I just wanted to hold her. And I started crying.'

For Hopkins, these events were coming together into a pattern, and that pattern indicated that aliens were abducting women and implanting foetuses in their wombs, which were later removed. In 1961, Betty Hill had described having a kind of long needle inserted into her stomach.

At this time, there was no such needle in use in hospitals. But, ten years later, there was a device called a lamaroscope, a flexible tube containing fibre optics, which could be inserted into the patient's navel for looking inside her, and for removing ova for fertilisation – so-called 'test-tube babies'.

Hopkins mentions other cases that support this notion. A girl called Andrea described how, when she was thirteen, she dreamt of having sex with a bald man with 'funny eyes', and woke up to find the bed was wet. In subsequent months her stomach began to swell, and the doctor told her she was pregnant. Yet she was a virgin, and her hymen was still unbroken. The problem was solved with an abortion.

A girl called Susan described how, when she was sixteen, she had stopped her car to watch a light in the sky. She then experienced some telepathic communication with the UFO, and felt herself drawn up until she was lying on a table inside it. She was relaxed and unafraid, although she was naked from the waist down, and felt a probe inserted into her vagina. This experience, it seems, was simply an internal examination.

She told Hopkins that, a year later, she had spoken to her boyfriend about the experience. Hopkins rang him to check, and the boyfriend could not recall it. But he *could* recall a UFO they had seen together at this time – and which she had totally forgotten. All of which suggests again that that the 'aliens' are able to exercise some kind of hypnotic manipulation over humans.

At this point, it is important to state that most modern books on hypnosis propagate a fallacy: that people cannot be hypnotised against their will. It is true that medical hypnosis depends on the cooperation of the patient with the doctor. But there are dozens of cases of people being hypnotised against their will – or at least without their cooperation.

In a famous criminal case in Heidelberg in the mid-1930s, a swindler called Franz Walter travelled on a train with a young woman, and claimed to be a doctor who could treat her stomach pains. He asked her to come for a cup of coffee, but she was nervous and unwilling. But, as they stepped on the platform, he took her hand, and (she said) 'It seemed to me I no longer had a will of my own.' He took her to his room, told her she was unable to move, then raped her. He then ordered her to forget what had happened. Later, he ordered her to become a prostitute. Walter taught the men to whom he sold her a 'magic word', which would make her do whatever they asked. He took all the money she earned. After she married, he ordered her to kill her husband. When she failed, he ordered her to kill herself. Fortunately, three suicide attempts were thwarted by chance. Finally, the husband became suspicious and went to the police. And, after a long struggle, the police hypnotist succeeded in 'unlocking' the various inhibitions that Walter had implanted in her to prevent her remembering what had happened. Walter was sentenced to ten years in jail.

What seems clear is that Walter had immediately recognised her as the kind of woman over whom he could exercise control; he merely had to touch her hand to deprive her of will.

A case recorded in Robert Temple's classic history of hypnosis, *Open to Suggestion*, makes the same point. In January 1985, a Portuguese woman in Notting Hill Gate was accosted by a Portugese man who asked her the way. She was unable to help, and the man asked another passer-by, also Portuguese. This man introduced himself to her and took her hand. She immediately felt a dreamlike sense of unreality. She was then ordered to go home and bring her savings book, then to draw out all her savings – over £1,000 – and give it to the two men, who went off with her money. The two swindlers were caught by chance, and proved to have swindled several other people by the same method. Both were sentenced to prison and deported.

Temple demolishes the notion that people cannot be hypnotised against their will, and that people under hypnosis will not commit criminal acts that they would not commit in their normal state. He cites another woman who was assaulted by the hypnotist, and who said, 'He started to caress my lower body . . . I just let that happen, did not feel like, nor had the power to say no. He asked me if I liked it. Although I did not like it, I said yes.' And she adds the important statement: 'Only I did not have any fear which normally would have been there.'

In 1991, a hypnotist named Nelson Lintott assaulted 113 girls under hypnosis, often videoing the sex. He claimed to be curing them of nail-biting or smoking. When shown these videos later, the girls were horrified – they had no memory of being undressed and raped.

All of which makes clear that most skilled hypnotists have the powers attributed to aliens: can cause certain people to become 'will-less', to paralyse them, and to cause them to experience amnesia. In all probability, this does not apply to everybody; John Keel and Hans Holzer both suspect that 'contactees' may be chosen for certain reasons, including 'psychic' tendencies.

The American doctor Howard Miller, who practised hypnosis, was convinced that it involves some form of telepathy, in which the will of the hypnotist influences the will of the patient. And Ferenc Volgyesi's book *Hypnosis of Men and Animals* has many accounts of 'battles of will' between reptiles and animals – one photograph shows a battle of wills between a bird and a rattlesnake which ended in victory for the bird, while another shows a battle of wills between a toad and a cobra which ended in victory for the toad. So the notion that hypnosis is purely a matter of 'suggestion' is clearly in urgent need of revision.

The psychologist Pierre Janet was able to summon one of his patients, 'Leonie', with whom he had established hypnotic rapport, from the other side of Le Havre. It is quite clear that 'aliens' have a similar power over people with whom they have established a rapport, so that they can be 'summoned' in the middle of the night, often hearing their name called 'inside their heads'.

It also seems possible that the sight of a UFO – with its revolving rim and flashing lights – may induce hypnosis. We have seen a number of cases where people have entered a trance after seeing a UFO.

What most of us find so hard to understand is how 'contactees' can slip into a state that strikes us as totally irrational – like Kathie Davis when she was not sure whether she was in an all-night store or a UFO. This is as difficult to grasp as the idea of being hypnotised against our will. The philosopher James Mill believed it ought to be possible to argue madmen out of their madness, and so revealed that he suffered from a version of what Whitehead called 'the fallacy of misplaced concreteness'. Mill obviously believed that sanity is a norm which is common to all of us, like our perception that one and one make two, and that it ought to be easy to persuade anyone who deviates from the norm to recognise that he or she is being unreasonable. This is like assuming that, because sight is normal, we ought to be able to reason a blind man into acknowledging that he is only shamming.

In her book *The Human Brain*, Susan Greenfield points out that patients with damage to the parietal cortex often feel that parts of their body do not belong to them, and may even insist that their arm belongs to someone else. Oliver Sachs's title *The Man Who Mistook His Wife for a Hatstand* again makes us aware that brain damage can make quite bizarre perceptions seem normal. The truth is that there is no 'normal reality' that we all share; there is simply a *consensus* reality, which is like the consensus morality or consensus religion or consensus politics that is taken for granted by some remote tribe – or by most civilised societies.

The kind of scepticism we feel about contactees and abductees is a part of the consensus reality. But consensus reality changes. In 1950, only a tiny proportion of the population of Europe or the United States believed in the reality of UFOs; now the figure is more than 50 per cent. The UFO phenomenon has changed this aspect of our consensus reality – which seems to be part of its aim.

Of course, it would all be much easier if people who believe in the existence of UFOs could decide exactly what it is they believe in: solid metal spaceships from Sirius, semisolid craft from another dimension, or psychic vehicles from Ted Holiday's goblin universe that should be classified with ghosts and poltergeists.

To add to the confusion, the phenomenon itself seems determined to remain ambiguous, frustrating every attempt to reach definite conclusions. Every time someone arrives at a theory that sounds balanced and sensible, some contradictory new piece of evidence turns it on its head. Jacques Vallee, John Keel and John Michell spent years studying the phenomenon, and ended by feeling that it defies explanation. John Mack's original reaction to Budd Hopkins's claims about abductees was, 'They must be mad, and so must he.' A more careful examination of the subject convinced him that nobody was mad: they were telling the truth insofar as they knew it. Yet, years after becoming involved in the study of abductees, John Mack admits that he is no more enlightened than he was after six months.

Budd Hopkins is a good example of the nature of the problem. In *Missing Time* he concluded that abduction undoubtedly takes place, and that 'they' are able to induce amnesia. In *Intruders* he concluded that 'they' are involved in some biological experiment, probably breeding semihuman hybrids. But his next book, *Witnessed* (1996), not only fails to take the subject any further: it succeeds in making it sound too absurd to be taken seriously.

Hopkins had already described the case of the woman he calls Linda Cortile at the MIT conference. There he began by saying, 'This is the most important UFO abduction case that I've ever worked on. It concerns the abduction of a woman who recalled floating out of a twelfth-storey window in a downtown Manhattan building on November 30, 1989.'

Linda Cortile had written to Hopkins seven months earlier, to say that his book *Intruders* had awakened fears that she was an abductee.

In 1967, when she was twenty-three, she lay in bed and had the experience of feeling paralysis creep from her toes to her head. It happened several times. In 1969 she married, and went to see a doctor about a bump on her nose, which she feared might be a tumour. The doctor reassured her, but said she had a surgery scar inside her nose. She said she had never had surgerey on her nose; he assured her she had. This is what led her to write to Hopkins.

On the morning of 30 November 1989, she telephoned Hopkins to say that a small, grey-skinned alien had approached her bed in the early hours of the morning, and she had thrown a pillow at him. Then she had become paralysed. Two days later, under hypnosis, she described being taken to the window by three 'greys' and floated out to a UFO. There she was made to lie on a table, and she recalled speaking to them in their own language. One of them examined her nose, then ran his fingers through her hair with obvious tenderness, touched her cheek, and asked after her family. Soon after that she found herself back in her own bed.

Fourteen months later, Hopkins received a letter signed 'Police Officers Dan and Richard', which informed him that at 3.30 a.m. on 30 November 1989, they had seen a woman in a nightgown 'floated' out of a Manhattan apartment by 'three ugly but humanlike creatures', and into a large oval craft hovering overhead. The craft turned reddish orange, then flew away and plunged into the river near Brooklyn Bridge.

Hopkins was delighted – this looked like undeniable evidence for Linda's abduction, the positive proof that Earth was being invaded by aliens. Two weeks later, Richard and Dan called on Linda Cortile. She liked Richard, but Dan struck her as unfriendly and 'freaked out'. (Apparently the sight of the abduction had preyed on his mind.) Subsequently, Dan also wrote to Hopkins with his version of what had happened.

Now Hopkins learnt that Richard and Dan were not ordinary policemen, but the bodyguards of an important political figure. (The name that eventually emerged was Perez de Cuellar, former secretary of the United Nations.) He had also witnessed Linda's abduction from their car, which had broken down under Brooklyn Bridge.

The notion that an eminent politician had witnessed the abduction seemed wonderful – final proof not only of this abduction but of the abduction phenomenon in general. And soon Hopkins was even more delighted when a woman wrote to him saying she had also seen the abduction; at 3.30 in the morning, her car had been one of many that had stalled on Brooklyn Bridge; the streetlights had also gone out.

This was as much as Hopkins described at the conference at MIT. But, in his book *Witnessed*, it becomes clear that the story developed complications that make the reader wonder if he is having his leg pulled, or has gone mad.

First, Richard and Dan abducted Linda off the street to ask her if this was all some kind of trick, and insisted on looking at her feet to see if she was an alien. (Through binoculars they had noted that the aliens had no toes.) Then Dan took a holiday to get over the shock. Later, he wrote to Hopkins, disclosing more information about the night of 30 November 1989. Immediately after the abduction, he said, they had found themselves – inexplicably – on the seashore. And there on the sand was Linda, helping the 'greys' dig with shovels and putting their finds in rectangular boxes; she was talking to them in their own language. Then Linda and the aliens crossed over to the policemen and their distinguished charge, and held up a dead fish, saying, 'Look what you've done.' When Dan asked who she was, an alien replied, 'The lady of the sands.'

This obviously explained why the two policemen had abducted Linda and demanded to see her feet; they had every reason to believe she was acquainted with the aliens. Understandably, Richard and Dan were both in a state of psychological turmoil. Their transfer to the seashore meant that they were also abductees.

But what did the dead fish, and 'Look what you've done', mean? Hopkins decided that it was meant as a reproach to Perez de Cuellar about the Earth's ecology.

Incredibly, Linda confirmed this whole story at her next hypnotic session with Hopkins. She also confirmed the ecological interpretation of her words.

In October 1991, Dan abducted Linda once more and took her to a beach house on Long Island, where he asked her to put on a white nightgown he had bought her. He chased her across the beach, kissed her several times, and said he wanted her to go away with him and 'make a family'. Fortunately, Richard arrived and rescued her.

Richard later wrote to Hopkins confirming the abduction, as well as Dan's story about being transported to the seashore after Linda's original abduction. Richard added that Linda had spoken to them 'in their heads', and had warned Dan – who was thinking of using his gun – to keep his hands down. He also claimed that, the first time he and Dan

195

had abducted her, Linda had again spoken to them 'in their heads', and said, 'Be kind. Don't hurt me.' She also made Richard turn his head away by some kind of telepathic order.

Hopkins was forced to conclude that, in some weird sense, Linda was 'one of them' – without, apparently, consciously realising it. It seemed that, as a long-time abductee, she had become a kind of dual personality, unaware of her alien alter ego. Or was she merely under the total control of these aliens?

Mysteries multiplied. Linda went to see her niece, a foot doctor, and had her nose X-rayed. The X-ray showed some foreign body lodged in it. A few days later, Linda woke to find she had had a bad nosebleed in the night. And a further X-ray showed that the object had vanished.

Hopkins also received a letter from 'the Third Man' (de Cuellar?) verifying that he had been present when Linda was floated out of her apartment, and the seashore episode with the dead fish.

And now, as if the story were not complex and bewildering enough, it takes a twist worthy of Victorian melodrama. Richard accosted Linda one morning and she agreed to go with him – to a place of her choice – and talk. They wandered around New York – St Patrick's Cathedral, the Rockefeller Center, Central Park – and he made it clear that he had a romantic interest in her. On a bench in Central Park he suddenly kissed her, and she allowed it – in fact, participated with some enthusiasm. She felt guilty about her husband, but enjoyed it.

Subsequently, Richard wrote to Hopkins, mentioning that Dan had now been interned in a 'rest home'. He mentioned the outing with Linda – then went on to tell Hopkins that, since the age of ten, he had been dreaming of a girl, who was introduced to him in a white environment by two tall, emotionless beings. He called her Baby Ann; she called him Mickey. They took an instant liking to each other. Six months later he dreamt of Baby Ann again. It happened repeatedly over the years. When he was sixteen, and Baby Ann was thirteen, he gave her her first kiss. By the time he was twenty-five, he and Baby Ann wanted to marry, but since they knew each other only in dreams, this was obviously impossible.

When he saw – through binoculars – Linda being floated out of her apartment, he recognised Baby Ann.

Now he was inclined to believe that their love affair had not been a dream – it had happened in the 'UFO reality'. He even suspected that Linda's second son Johnny was really his own child. He and Linda had been abducted by aliens repeatedly from childhood, and had finally 'bonded' and become parents.

Hopkins's next step was obviously to find out whether any of this could be confirmed by Linda. He brought her to his apartment, and she told him that Richard had asked her if she had ever had imaginary playmates. Pressed by Hopkins, she recalled an imaginary playmate called Mickey, who called her Ann. And Hopkins was suddenly confronted with the incredible notion that Linda and Richard had been deliberately brought together by the aliens in a long-term psychological and breeding experiment. Linda was obviously deeply shaken when Hopkins read her Richard's 'Baby Ann' letter.

It was his first experience of this notion of the UFO occupants organising the lives of human beings like the mythical Fates. Later, he was to come across other cases. A couple called Jack and Sally kept having flashbacks to some earlier period together which, logically speaking, they knew they could not have shared. Under hypnosis they recalled being abducted together many times; like Richard and Linda, they remembered their nicknames for each other without any possibility of communicating.

Sally was in tears as she said, 'Jack and I love each other . . . but is this something the aliens are doing to us?'

Another couple met at a UFO conference, and gradually began to have flashbacks of meeting during abductions, and finally of becoming lovers. But each was happily married to someone else. She commented, 'It's not fair for the aliens to do this to anyone.'

Another couple lived as far apart as Scotland and the US, yet, when they met, instantly recognised each other. He recalled having had sexual intercourse with her during an abduction, which was unusual, since he was homosexual.

It is possible to see why Dan and Richard – and the 'third man' – were so shaken by their experience. They were top security men – Hopkins has a photograph of Dan standing with Reagan, Bush and Gorbachev – yet the aliens had made them feel like helpless children. Dan found it particularly hard to adjust. He felt that his answer to the problem was to marry Linda, who was the cause of all his insecurity, and planned to kidnap her.

In fact Dan escaped from the 'rest home', and made elaborate plans to kidnap Linda, drug her and fly with her to England. These were foiled by security men, including Richard, and Dan apparently ceased to be an 'official problem' – by which Hopkins understood Richard to mean either that Dan had been killed, or permanently incarcerated where there was no chance of escape.

There were still more strange twists. Richard admitted that they were not alone when their car broke down under Brooklyn Bridge: they were in an official motorcade of at least five cars, full of security men and important political figures. Their engines had simply stopped, and one security man later went on record as saying that he simply blanked out for an hour. During that hour, Richard, Dan and the 'third man' were abducted by being somehow sucked out of the car. They were taken to the seashore, and Richard put some sand in his pocket, which he later found. After the episode of the dead fish, when they became convinced Linda was an alien, they found themselves back on FDR Drive *outside* the car – in fact, with the 'third man' on the roof.

The story still has some further twists, but no purpose would be served in detailing them all. More witnesses to the abduction appeared. The 'third man' was apparently convinced that *he* had been abducted with Linda in the past, and might be the father of her child Johnny. He presented Johnny with a valuable sea-diver's helmet and wanted to hug him. Later, Hopkins succeeded in interviewing him at O'Hare Airport, but the third man (who was with his wife) professed to be bewildered by the strange story and to know nothing about it.

On a later occasion, Linda's whole family woke up simultaneously with nosebleeds in the right nostril, and the same was true of a neighbour's son who was staying the night. Hopkins later learnt that this boy had been having strange dreams of alien abduction since he was small.

What, then, are we to make of it all? The case has been attacked with a bitterness unusual even in ufological circles. Some critics have claimed that Hopkins is a liar, others that Linda Cortile is a fantasist who has duped Hopkins. It is pointed out that Hopkins has never met Richard or Dan – only corresponded with them and listened to tape recordings. John Spencer, while rejecting the notion that Hopkins is 'faking the case for money', thinks it possible that Hopkins 'oversold the case to himself, and then to the world'. Dennis Stacy, author of *UFOs, 1947–1997*, has said mildly that the case 'brings the abduction issue to a boil by raising the bar of believability'.

This may be regarded as one of the points in its favour. The same comment applies to *Witnessed* as to Puharich's *Uri*: that, if he had decided to tell lies, he would have made them believable.

In fact, there seems to be no good reason for assuming that Hopkins is lying, or even stretching the truth. *Missing Time* and *Intruders* are obviously sincere books, and Kathie Davis of *Intruders* has written her own book confirming it all. So it is impossible to believe that Hopkins or Linda Cortile is fictionalising.

Although it is true that *Witnessed* seems to demand a suspension of disbelief that is well beyond the average reader, this is largely due to the fact that 'its implications exploded almost exponentially', as Stacy puts it. What looks like a highly convincing case of a well-witnessed abduction begins to look more and more incredible when we learn that the witnesses were also abducted, and that one of them had known Linda – in some spacecraft – since she was four years old, and later impregnated her.

But then, we have already encountered something of the sort in the case of Beth Collings and Anna Jamerson, who met by chance as children, and came to believe that they had been abducted together in childhood. And, in this case, we are being asked to believe that the abductions took place over several generations, and are still going on.

The 'aliens' told Patrolman Herb Schirmer as long ago as 1967 that they were conducting biological experiments with human beings, and six years earlier they had taken a sperm sample from Barney Hill, and, four years before that, taken sperm from Antonio Villas-Boas. So it seems fairly clear that – assuming we accept the reality of aliens – the UFO beings are interested in human reproduction.

It also seems clear, from the number of abductees who have been shown scenarios of the end of the world, that the aliens are interested in warning us about the dangers of destroying ourselves. In a hypnosis session of October 1993, Anna Jamerson foretold a 'holocaust', and said that it had already started. It would get 'really bad' in 1997. I am writing this in August 1997, and have not noticed any holocaust that began in 1993 and has got worse recently. So it seems possible that, where these prophecies of doom are concerned, the aliens are, as Jacques Vallee suggests, 'messengers of deception'. On the other hand, pollution of the sea and atmosphere means that there *is* deep and immediate cause for concern, and adds plausibility to the notion that aliens may be warning us to take thought before it is too late.

Hopkins, oddly enough, rejects this notion:

Everything I have learned in twenty years of research into the UFO abduction phenomenon leads me to conclude the the aliens' central purpose is not to teach us about taking better care of the environment. Instead, all of the evidence points to their being here to carry out a complex breeding experiment in which they seem to be working to create a hybrid species, a mix of human and alien characteristics. A careful reading of the various witnesses' accounts suggests that here, as in many earlier cases, reproductive issues appear far more frequently than alien ecological concerns. Indeed, apart from the suspicious Lady of the Sands scenario, references to the environment are virtually nonexistent in the Linda Cortile case. But the possibility Richard raised – that the aliens may need a safer environment on earth in order to carry out their own central agenda – is not to be dismissed. Crudely put, one wants the hotel one stays in to be clean.

John Spencer, on the other hand, has written:

> The somewhat reductionist and simplistic view that alien astro-nauts are capturing literally thousands of people all over the world, over long periods of time, and performing genetic and sexual acts on them, as part of a programme of genetic engineering, seems to be the product of the science-fiction culture that gave us flying saucers in the first place. It is my view . . . that this scenario is created by the mostly accidental misuse of hypnosis . . .[1]

Yet such a view – which amounts to dismissing the whole abduction phenomenon as some kind of mass hysteria – is hardly consistent with the facts: such facts as women finding themselves pregnant, having their pregnancy confirmed by a doctor, then suddenly being no longer pregnant; or such facts as a whole family waking up at the same time with a nosebleed from the right nostril.

In any case, many abductees recall their experience without hypnosis. This wholesale attempt to make the abduction phenomenon go away has much in common with the attempt in the 1950s and 1960s to make the UFO phenomenon go away by talking about temperature inversions and weather balloons. We have already seen what happened to that attitude in the 1960s, with the Condon Committee, Hynek's 'conversion', and the seminal books of Jacques Vallee. The explanation, whatever it turns out to be, is certainly not that everybody was suffering from delusions.

[1] *Gifts of the Gods*, p. 140

In fact, John Spencer undermines his own case in the long section on 'The Abduction Phenomenon' in his important book *Perspectives*. After a long and critical account of Budd Hopkins's *Intruders*, he goes on to describe his own investigation of a case in Vallentuna, Sweden. On Saturday 23 March 1974, a man Spencer calls Anders left a political celebration and decided to walk home, about five kilometres (three miles) away. He had drunk a few glasses, but was still sober. It was a starry, moonlit night, and he decided to take a short cut that led over a hill. As he was climbing, a bright light came from behind, and, thinking it was a fast car, he moved off the road on to the grass and flung himself down – and realised that it was not a car: the light was right over him.

Then he found himself outside his home at a place called Lindholmen, and his wife opened the door to his frantic ringing. He was bleeding from a wound in the forehead, and his cheek was burnt.

The next day he called the National Defence, and was advised to contact a man called Hardy Brostrom, of the Home Guard, who was later to impress Spencer as a sober and thorough investigator. A UFO investigator called Stan Lindgren advised Anders to try hypnotic regression.

Under hypnosis, Anders remembered that he did not actually hit the ground. Some force lifted him into the air. He was then sucked into a vehicle by four 'semi-transparent entities' looking a little like Indians, but with no nose or ears. (He thought they could have been wearing hoods.) They were surrounded by a hazy glow. They approached him with some kind of 'instrument', which Anders would not describe, and he gathered that they intended to pierce him, and fought hard. In spite of that, the instrument was placed against his forehead, and caused a burning pain. After that, the aliens delivered him to his home.

There was no 'missing time': the walk would have taken him three-quarters of an hour, so the lift home meant that he arrived there about when he intended to.

Anders objected to the hypnotic sessions. But Brostrom found a way of overcoming his increasing unwillingness to help the investigation by introducing him to a man called Bertil Kuhlemann, who was on the staff of a scientific institution (and who later introduced Spencer to the case). And Bertil unearthed other witnesses.

A woman cyclist had seen the light at exactly the time Anders had been abducted. Two men independently saw a metal object in the field where Anders had his encounter. A woman and her fiancé, driving towards the spot, saw what they thought was a new water tower with lights shining out of its windows; later they saw that there was no water tower at the spot. There were numerous other sightings of a bright light the following night, including one of a bright yellow-white object that travelled over the forest and lit up the sky, moving off at a great speed. Televisions blacked out or showed interference, and telephones misfunctioned. And there were many more sightings over the next two years.

What is clear is that, in spite of the fact that Anders submitted to hypnotic regression, there was abundant evidence to show that the abduction was genuine.

Anders and investigator Arne Groth were inclined to believe that Anders was somehow under the influence of the 'aliens' from the moment he left the political celebration. This may or may not be so. What is significant is that Anders felt that the encounter had, according to Spencer, 'given him a feeling of one-ness, of unity, with the earth itself'.

The 'instrument' used by the aliens had left a scar on Anders's forehead. When he placed his left hand over the scar he felt a pricking, stinging sensation inside his head.

Groth had been studying the theories of Baron von Reichenbach, who discovered that certain people – particularly 'sick sensitives' – were responsive to magnets and crystals; one girl could tell when a magnet was uncapped even through a thick wall. (Reichenbach thought he had discovered a so-far unknown 'odic force'.) Groth found that Anders was sensitive to magnets at a distance of eight inches to a foot, and to rock crystal from six or seven feet. They gave Anders a stinging or sucking sensation in his head.

Anders clearly had some kind of paranormal talent, and felt that it had been heightened by his UFO experience.

A year later, Anders had a dream in which he heard the words, 'Search in yttrium'. He thought yttrium was a place, but Groth knew it was a rare metallic element. Groth obtained some and tried it on Anders; the effects were very powerful, and Anders felt something like an electric current.

Groth discovered 'lines' in Anders's body, similar to acupuncture lines, and that these were also sensitive to yttrium. Groth believed that his attention had been 'directed' to these lines of enquiry by the entities who had abducted Anders, and that their purpose was that Anders should enjoy a better association with the Earth. (Anders felt that the aliens were not extraterrestrials, but from Earth.)

Anders discovered that he could move a compass needle by passing his hand over it, and that he could cause 'patterns of force' to appear in iron filings placed on his stomach.

Anders told John Spencer that he could dowse – not only for water, but for 'earth force'. To demonstrate this, he got Spencer to hold a dowsing rod and placed him over an energy line. Nothing happened until Anders placed his hand nine inches above the rod, when Spencer felt a surge of energy, and the rod bent down, in spite of his efforts to resist.

Anders had dowsed the abduction site, and found that it was the convergence point of many lines of force (what are in Britain known as ley lines). There was also an ancient runic stone circle. Anders was able to see the aura of the Earth, which in places, he said, had diminished from a living blue or violet to a dull brown, a sign of pollution.

In one interesting experiment, Groth and Anders stood in their separate homes, twenty kilometres apart – that is about twelve and a half miles. One would touch gold, yttrium or a magnet with his rock crystal, and the other would know which had been touched. There were witnesses at both homes and the connection was established by telephone.

Spencer takes up the suggestion of Budd Hopkins that the purpose of 'implants' (like a ball in the nose) is to enable the aliens to contact the abductees subsequently – in other words, that it is a little like game wardens tagging an animal with a device that gives off a radio signal. Spencer adds that it ought to be possible to do it with the energy lines of each individual.

Significantly, a study of Anders's biorhythms revealed that he had been abducted at the exact moment when the three energies – physical, emotional and intellectual – peaked at a triple maximum, which happens only once every forty-six years. The implication is that Anders had been carefully selected for the abduction, and with some specific purpose involved with increasing certain paranormal abilities – a claim also made by Uri Geller.

Another implication is that the abductors meant no harm: on the contrary, they were trying to increase the powers and sensitivity of one human being.

This seems to be supported by another case Spencer looked into: of a Swedish woman called Kathryn Howard.

Like Anders, Kathryn felt that her experience had changed her, and that she had been 'born that day'.

In April 1969, she was out in the Swedish countryside with two men, Harvey and Martin. It happened around midday, and the three have no further memory until they found themselves sitting on a sofa in the home of one of them at 11 o'clock at night.

All three were highly 'politically conscious', and they were sitting in a meadow on a beautiful spring day discussing Vietnam and Biafra. Kathryn began to cry as she thought about the indifference of the civilised world to the sufferings of the masses. Then she and Martin looked up and saw an oval-shaped object with 'legs' against the sky. She asked, 'What's that?' A moment later, it vanished. Then she and Martin seem to have had a kind of vision. There was no longer blue sky, but 'a kind of colourless, almost fluidic, grey eternity', and against this background they saw the moon, as if at close quarters, with all its craters clearly visible. Martin could see it, but Harvey thought they were playing a joke on him. Kathryn said, 'We are sitting in the universe.' 'As I said that, the earth seemed to be expanding in front of my eyes. It was enormous and round.' She began to walk around, and said, 'I am walking upside down, sideways, every which way. The only thing that keeps me here is gravity.' And, as she spoke, she seemed to understand gravity. The earth continued to expand, and she seemed to be above it as well as standing on it. Then she heard a beating sound, like the heart through a stethoscope, except much slower. She knew this to be the rhythm of the universe.

Kathryn went on to say that it was the greatest joy she had ever known, and that she felt cosmic consciousness. Then she seemed to see the history of the human race flash past in a few seconds (an experience that has been confirmed by people who have been saved from drowning or survived some other life-threatening situation). She said, 'If everyone could see and feel as we do now, there wouldn't be any more wars, starvation, or anything negative.' Then she experienced a paradoxical insight: that all this didn't matter because 'that's just part of the evolution'.

After this they found themselves sitting on the sofa, having 'lost' about ten hours.

In 1986, Kathryn decided to try to regain the missing time by undergoing hypnosis. In a trance, she recalled that the 'legs' had withdrawn into the craft, and that she had been somehow sucked into it, and was looking down through a lens at the Earth. Then the Earth vanished, and she was terrified that she was being taken away permanently. After that she thought she was on another planet, and that the UFO entities were transparent (Anders had said 'semi-transparent'); she saw a cigar-shaped object taking off. She felt she was wearing a kind of crystal headdress or helmet, and states that clairvoyants have sometimes seen this around her head.

The experience caused an 'opening up'. Kathryn apparently had insights into past lives, 'and much more'. She also had a vision of Earth burning, and knew this was the end of civilisation. Subsequently, Kathryn felt that the experience had taught her that she had a message, to persuade people to open their eyes.

Certain things stand out clearly. First, she and Martin *saw* the UFO – presumably Harvey was not looking up. It seems, then, that the sight of the UFO may have triggered the experience. When Kathie Davis was driving back to a night food store, she saw a shining balloon in the sky; after that the experience became dreamlike, and she felt that the store was really a spacecraft. And, when Beth Collings's father was on the beach in Virginia, his attention became fixed on a shell, then he looked up and found his brother had vanished. Later, his attention was again fixed on a glittering object, and he found that his brother had returned. Hypnotists also work by 'fixing' the attention of the subject, often on some shining object. So it seems conceivable that, in Kathryn's case, the experience began with some hypnotic induction, possibly telepathic.

The case recalls John Keel's flash of cosmic consciousness in his New York bedroom (although, of course, this had nothing to do with UFOs), and Bucke's mystical experience in the carriage. Such 'flashes' – as in the case of Kathryn – have a permanent effect.

We also note that Kathryn, like Anders and so many others, became 'psychic' after the experience. It may be, of course, that she was already psychic, and that the experience simply released it or increased it.

John Spencer makes the point that, in these two cases, there was no suggestion of 'leading questions' in the hypnosis, which might lead to false memories. It is certainly a valid point; a TV programme on UFOs – part of the 1987 fiftieth anniversary of Kenneth Arnold's sighting – showed Hopkins asking a child 'leading' questions about whether he had ever woken up and seen strange figures in his bedroom. But the hypnotic transcripts quoted in his books – and in *Connections* by Anna Jamerson and Beth Collings – seem to show that this is not his normal practice. And we have seen that Beth Collings recalled her own abduction in the Virginia State Park without any help from hypnosis. In fact, an enormous number of 'abductees' recall their experience spontaneously.

But the main point is that the two Swedish cases show that Spencer accepts the notion of abduction as *some* kind of reality, and is not trying to argue that the whole abduction phenomenon is simply mass hysteria.

All the same, scepticism about the abduction statistics is easy to understand. In 1991, the Roper organisation polled nearly six thousand adults to find how many thought they might have been abducted. Budd Hopkins and David Jacobs devised eleven questions, such as whether a person could remember seeing unusual lights in the bedroom, missing time, flying through the air, mysterious bedroom figures who could deal out paralysis, and unaccountable scars on the body. The result showed that 119 people were possible abductees, or two per cent. Extrapolating to the population of the US, that meant about five million people. That clearly sounds preposterous – even though, under hypnosis, Anna Jamerson had stated that there are eight million 'changelings' on Earth.

Patrick Huyghe, co-editor of *The Anomalist*, wonders if something of the sort could be true. At the same time as Linda Cortile's abduction, another Manhattan woman claims to have been abducted from her apartment, and seeing fifteen or twenty other women moving through the streets towards a UFO on the bank of the East River; she saw two others in the sky.

We may also recall John Mack's case of Catherine, cited at the beginning of this book, who found herself in a spacecraft with between one and two hundred people lying on tables.

Anna Jamerson also recalled, under hypnosis, seeing in the spacecraft a wall full of hollow spaces with people lying in them.

I have mentioned that, when I met David Jacobs at the Fortfest in 1995, he told me that he hoped he might be on the verge of solving the UFO mystery. Patrick Huyghe tells of interviewing Jacobs in 1994, and how Jacobs mentioned a hypnosis session he had conducted the evening before, in which the abductee had seen fifteen other human beings on board the craft. Jacobs went on to suggest that a massive abduction programme may be taking place, 'twenty-four hours a day, seven days a week', to populate Earth with hybrids. This sounds as it might be Jacobs's notion of the solution of the UFO phenomenon.

But, leaving aside for a moment this question of statistics, what can be said about Budd Hopkins's theories in general? His belief that the aliens are conducting some kind of genetic experiment seems to be borne out by a certain amount of evidence. Aliens told Patrolman Herb Schirmer that they were conducting genetic experiments, long before anyone else suggested it. Shane Kurz and Beth Collings and Kathie Davidson did not simply invent their vanishing pregnancies. Villas-Boas had a sperm sample taken in 1957, Barney Hill in 1961 – while Betty Hill had a large needle inserted in her navel.

What is so baffling about the evidence is that the UFO aliens seem to possess powers that are far in excess of our human powers – so much so that it is hard to see why they should want to produce hybrids. Would human scientists want to produce hybrids of human beings and gorillas?

Another puzzle is that the aliens seem to possess powers that defy common sense. They seem to be able to transport human beings through walls and windows, and suck them out of their cars into UFOs. John Keel has explained how certain radio waves can stop car engines; but floating human beings through the windscreen of their cars sounds ridiculous.

Yet many cases also suggest that the entities also have some strange power over time. Linda Cortile told Budd Hopkins how she had first met 'Mickey'. She had been in the cubicle at a swimming bath on Coney Island; her family were in adjacent cubicles. The door opened, and, when she looked outside, she saw two men in skin-tight blue uniforms. They told her that she had to go with them and, in spite of her protests, took her to some strange environment where she was introduced to a little boy. As she left the swimming bath, people were standing as if in frozen animation. But they had not been paralysed, for, when she was returned three-quarters of an hour later, the splashed water in the swimming pool was suspended in the air, as if caught in a photograph. It seems that the aliens can somehow slow down time. But the only way to do that realistically would be to speed up Linda's psychological time, so a few seconds would seem to be a minute. An alternative would be that Linda was not taken physically, but subjected to an out-of-the-body experience, or an OBE. On the other hand, her physical body must have been present when she was impregnated by Richard in some alien environment.

When flying saucers first made headlines in 1947, writers like Harold Wilkins speculated that they came from Mars and were surveying Earth. That was interesting, but hardly of great concern to the rest of us, since there might well be some other explanation, such as weather balloons or experimental aircraft. Half a century later, the situation had suddenly become more menacing, with so many thousands of reports of alien abductions that it has become far more difficult to shrug them off.

Of course, it may be that this wave of UFO phenomena is, as Jung believed, some kind of 'projection' of our human need for religious belief. Or it may be simply a new manifestation of the nineteenth-century wave of occult or paranormal phenomena. Perhaps some semi-supernatural beings with whom we unknowingly share the Earth have been abducting humans – like the three children Harold Wilkins searched for – since the beginning of history.

But if – as that MIT conference on abduction seemed to imply – something new and strange is going on, then perhaps the human race ought to be looking for the answer with far more persistence and interest than we display at present.

8 High Strangeness

N THE 1850s, Paris was gripped by an amusing fashion called 'table turning'. People would sit around a light table – such as a card table – placed on a polished floor. All they then had to do was to link hands and concentrate, and soon the table was sliding around the floor, or rising into the air in spite of efforts to push it down. It would even answer questions by rapping in code with two legs. Table turning was incredibly easy to do (as it still is). If 'spirits' were responsible, then they must have been on duty all the time.

At that period, one of the capital's best-known intellectuals was an educator named Leon Rivail, who was to Paris what John Ruskin and Herbert Spencer were to London – a tireless lecturer on all topics from astronomy and electricity to art and botany.

Rivail had a friend called Becquet, and Becquet's daughter Christina was not only skilled at making tables dance around the room, but in automatic writing: both she and her sister could hold a pencil, and it would race across the page, filling it with many varieties of handwriting quite unlike their own. Moreover, the pencil seemed to be perfectly willing to answer questions.

Rivail had none of the modern prejuduce about such academically incorrect activities. He saw no reason why the realm of the 'spirits' should not be added to the many other subjects that fascinated his omnivorous mind. He asked the sisters if they would collaborate with him, and, when they agreed, proceeded to bombard the 'spirits' with questions.

If Rivail had been less of an ignoramus about the 'occult', he would never have done it. As we saw in the earlier brief digression on poltergeists, they seem incapable of telling the truth. But Rivail struck lucky. Armed only with enthusiasm and naivety, he proceeded to ask questions like 'What is God?' and 'What is matter?' and got sensible and coherent answers. In fact, some of the answers were well ahead of their time. When he asked if matter was naturally dense, he was told that this was true of matter as understood by man, but not of matter as a 'universal fluid'. 'The ethereal and subtle matter which forms this fluid is imponderable to you, and yet is nonetheless the principle of your ponderable matter.' This remark would not make sense for another half-century, with the discovery of electrons.

Recalling some recent poltergeist disturbances in the rue des Noyers, Rivail asked Christina's 'control' (or Master of Ceremonies) if he could speak to the spirit that had smashed all the windows. Soon a rough voice spoke from Christina's mouth: 'Why do you call me? Do you want to have some stones thrown at you?' But after a while, the spirit grew more polite, and admitted that he liked playing tricks – he had been a drunken rag-and-bone man during life, and now wanted to get his own back on the people who had treated him with contempt.

Did he have any help in creating the disturbances in the rue des Noyers? asked Rivail. Certainly, said the spirit, he used the energy of a maidservant in the house. And was she aware of what was happening? asked Rivail. Oh no, said the spirit, she was the most terrified of all. He explained, interestingly, that he 'joined his electric nature to hers', and made things fly through the air.

When Rivail asked about the subject of 'demoniacal possession', he was told that the influence of spirits is far greater than most people suppose; they often influence our thoughts *and* actions. 'A spirit does not enter into a body as you would enter a house. He assimilates himself to an incarnate spirit who has the same defects and qualities as himself . . .' These comments would certainly have struck a chord with Stanislav Grof, whose experience with the 'possessed' woman is described in Chapter One.

In due course, Rivail wrote down all he had learnt via the Becquet sisters in a work called *The Spirits' Book*, under the pseudonym Allan Kardec. In Brazil, where 'Spiritism' is one of the most widespread religions, it is still regarded as a kind of Bible.

And why discuss Rivail and poltergeists at this point? Because some of the material that follows raises 'the bar of credibility' so high that it is important to remind the reader that it is not quite as insane and unprecedented as it sounds. Rivail, a typical child of the materialistic nineteenth century, a believer in science and reason, suddenly found himself confronted with ghosts, poltergeists and demoniacal possession, which certainly struck him as no less extraordinary than the UFO abduction phenomenon strikes us. To Rivail's credit, he wrote is all down, studied it, and did his best to make sense of it.

A contemporary scientist called Brian O'Leary has shown the same kind of courage. O'Leary, born in 1940, started life as an astronomer and a trainee astronaut for NASA. Carl Sagan invited him to become an academic at Cornell University, and he later moved to Princeton. But, in his late thirties, he began to experience a vague dissatisfaction with being (as he puts it) a 'high priest of modern science', who mixed on a daily basis with some of the world's top physicists. And in the spring of 1979, he decided to use a five-day leave of absence attending a 'human-potential workshop' in Philadelphia.

Lying on the floor, beside a randomly selected partner, he decided to test his ability at 'remote viewing'. His partner, a woman from Allentown, Pennsylvania, gave him the name, address and age of a neighbour, and asked O'Leary to describe him. Although feeling pleasantly relaxed, he had no belief whatever in his own 'psychic' powers. Nevertheless, he felt he was looking at a man in his forties, who was walking alone on a beach in Maui, Hawaii, and who seemed rather forlorn. They had a kind of imaginary conversation – about the climate and weather – which seemed oddly real. When it was over, his partner told him that the man had just lost his wife, lived in Maui, Hawaii, and was a meteorologist.

Of course, it is conceivable that O'Leary picked up these facts by telepathy with his partner – but, if so, that is just as remarkable as 'remote viewing'. The experience made O'Leary aware that he had been living for thirty years in a false paradigm – the scientific paradigm that said that telepathy, remote viewing and psychic powers were delusions of feeble-minded New Agers. O'Leary now knew, beyond all possible doubt, that they were not.

When he began to tell Princeton friends about the experience, he received some odd looks. From their point of view, O'Leary had gone over to the enemy, the forces of irrationalism. But from O'Leary's point of view, he *knew* beyond all doubt that the paradigms of science were inadequate. They failed to explain how he could know about a man he had never met.

It would be another three years before another remarkable experience led Brian O'Leary to make the break with his past. In March 1982, when he was driving from New York to Boston, his car skidded on ice at sixty miles an hour, and overturned several times before it went through a crash barrier. The car looked like an accordion – yet O'Leary emerged unhurt and was able to walk away. As the car had been turning over, he had experienced a sense of floating above it. There was no panic – only of a kind of euphoria. He recognised what had happened later as a typical near-death experience (NDE for short). A month later he bought an old van and drove to California with all his possessions. One of the first results of his altered way of life was a book called *Exploring Inner and Outer Space*.

But he remained a scientist, attempting to explore the new paradigm with experimental methods. For example, he spent some time in the San Diego laboratory of Cleve Backster, the man who had discovered that plants can read our minds – Backster had attached a lie detector to a rubber plant, and found that it reacted when he thought of giving it water, or burning it with a cigarette. O'Leary was present at an even more extraordinary experiment. This time the machine recorded the electrical fluctuations in white blood cells donated by a young woman. As she and her boyfriend made love in a motel five miles away from the laboratory, the strip chart recorder registered wild fluctuations, then abruptly ceased. The next morning the recorder again registered fluctuations when the young couple woke and and began lovemaking again, and then once again stopped as the session ended. Although separated from her body, the blood cells in her saliva were still responding to her sexual excitement.

Like Leon Rivail, Brian O'Leary had recognised that we are living in a wider reality than that recognised by science, and that the paradigms of science can be an active hindrance to our personal development.

Inevitably, O'Leary became interested in UFOs. And a curious, if unsettling, experience left him in no doubt that there was some truth to the stories of abduction. In May 1987, O'Leary and a girlfriend went to stay with Whitley and Anne Strieber in their cottage in upstate New York; Strieber was just about to publish his bestselling *Communion*, describing his own abduction experiences. Before retiring for the night, O'Leary and his girlfriend did some meditations. Then he began to experience a strange lethargy and paralysis, accompanied by a sense of euphoria. 'We were being drugged without the help of an inducing substance.' Although he tried hard to stay awake, he fell deeply asleep, and woke up in the same position. His girlfriend had awakened four times in the night, still paralysed, and saw lights in the room. In the morning, all lights were off.

In the two years following this experience, O'Leary studied UFO reports and interviewed witnesses. He found himself agreeing with

Jacques Vallee, who wrote that UFO phenomena 'have had an impact on a part of the human mind we have not discovered. I believe that the UFO phenomenon is one of the ways through which an alien form of intelligence of incredible complexity is communicating with us *symbolically* . . . It has access to psychic processes we have not yet mastered, or even researched.' O'Leary's own conclusion was that 'through their experiences, an ever increasing number of people are telling us we are on a collision course with a destiny far beyond our conscious minds. My conclusion is that we cannot ignore the phenomenon any more than we can ignore the physical reality of an impending auto accident. Through the UFO phenomenon, the greater reality is being gradually but inexorably forced upon us.'

Carl Sagan had been one of the first to break with him after his 'travelling clairvoyance' experience, and O'Leary finally had some critical words to say about his old friend. In *Miracle in the Void* (1996), he comments:

> In his zeal to debunk the evidence, astronomer Carl Sagan seemed to go to extremes in distorting existing data on the 'face' on Mars and about the abduction phenomenon in popular articles for Parade Magazine. Sagan sees abductions as hallucinations, says there is no evidence of UFO phenomena, and seemed to contrive a second photograph of the Mars face which appeared to be doctored from the original version to look not like a face. Either Sagan is totally unaware of the available data, or has become a disinformation specialist for the existing world view.

In fact, Sagan had long been acting as a disinformation specialist. The year 1973 had seen one of those peaks of UFO activity – one sheriff's office in Mississippi was receiving two thousand calls a day. On 11 October, two shipyard workers, Charlie Hickson (42) and Calvin Parker (19) were fishing off the end of a pier in Pascagoula, Mississippi, when an oval-shaped UFO landed close to them, and three bizarre entities floated out *(see plate no. 10)*. They had pointed projections instead of ears and noses, and very long arms with clawlike hands. Hickson and Parker were 'floated' on board, and Parker fainted. (He later had two nervous breakdowns.) After being 'scanned' in some way, both were returned to the pier. They finally decided to call the sheriff's office. At one point the sheriff left them alone in a room with a secret tape recorder, and their conversation made it quite clear that they were not shamming. They also passed a lie-detector test. Expert after expert later concluded that they were honest – a conclusion John Spencer also came to when he met Hickson.

Sagan did not agree. Three months later, Hickson and Parker appeared on the Dick Cavett show on television with Allen Hynek, Carl Sagan and Larry Coyne, a helicopter pilot who, together with his crew, had almost experienced a midair collision with a cigar-shaped object that scanned them with a cone of green light. Says one writer who saw the interview:

> Sagan went last, giving one of his standard, suave, debunking performances. He took dramatic pauses to emphasise the scientific unlikelihood of interstellar visitation, chuckled dimissively in response to Hickson's story . . . and did everything but call Coyne a liar (responding to Hynek's observation that 'altimeters don't hallucinate,' he rejoined instantly with, 'I don't mean to attack Captain Coyne, but people who *read* altimeters hallucinate.')[1]

By this time, the UFO phenomenon was displaying a new and terrifying aspect: animal mutilation. On 9 September 1967, a three-year-old horse named Lady was found lying on her side on a ranch in the San Luis Valley of Colorado, her head and neck completely stripped of flesh. Her hoof tracks stopped a hundred yards from the place she was found. Strange lights had been seen in the sky in the past few days, and newspaper reports of the mystery mentioned UFOs.

By the 1970s, there was a wave of animal mutilations all over America. Inner organs had been neatly and bloodlessly removed; so, often, had the genitals. Newspapers spoke of 'Satanic rituals', but few Satanists were likely to be found out on the open ranges.

The cuts looked as if they had been done with some kind of laser, which seemed to explain the lack of blood. (Surgical lasers were not in use in 1967.) An investigator who went to look at the site of Lady's death months later noted that nothing would grow on the place where the carcass had lain.

At about the time of the Pascagoula abduction, a former Air Force security officer named Jim decided to retire to a ranch in Colorado, together with a business executive named John, his wife Barbara, and their teenage sons. In the investigation carried out by APRO (Jim

---

[1] From *Architects of the Underworld*, by Bruce Rux, p. 147.

and Coral Lorenzen's Aerial Phenomena Research Organisation) and by Dr Leo Sprinkle (a researcher of impeccable reputation, who had regressed Patrolman Herb Schirmer), the three asked for their anonymity to be preserved.

They soon found that the ranch they had selected in Colorado was virtually haunted by strange phenomena. There were electrical failures, sounds of someone walking outside the farmhouse, and sightings of 'Bigfoot'-type creatures in the woods.

On 16 October 1975, the cattle were braying with alarm, and the guard dog was trying to get into the house. John went out with a rifle, and saw a large lighted object hovering in the air. He decided to go back home. Jim had decided to go 'hunting' for cattle mutilators – for which a large reward had been offered – with a twelve-bore shotgun, but found himself unable to get up from the couch. 'It was like paralysis, like I was drugged.'

At the same moment, Barbara experienced a sudden increase in her heartbeat, a sense of panic, and a flood of memories. She screamed, and Jim managed to get up from the couch. But he was unable to speak. When Barbara tried to tell her husband about it, she could only stutter.

Sometime later, when it was snowing, they discovered a mutilated cow near the house. Huge eighteen-inch footprints were found in the snow, and even in the barn.

The cow's udders had been removed with surgical precision, and an eye and an ear were missing; there was no blood.

The incident was reported to a law officer in the nearest town; he promised to investigate, but never came. When a second mutilation occurred two weeks later – a bull – Jim asked the officer why he hadn't kept his promise. The answer was that there was no point. The mutilation was being done by extraterrestrials, and there had been about four hundred so far. Jim, understandably, thought this was an excuse for laziness, and told the policeman what he thought of him.

A few days later he was not so sure. Visiting friends went to investigate a noise coming from a cistern, and fled in terror as a huge, dark shape came through the barbed wire fence. Jim collected long strands of hair, and a Denver biogeneticist said they matched no known species.

Still Jim was inclined to believe that some real-estate man was trying to drive them out so he could sell the place to someone else; he began to sleep near the door with a shotgun. One day, awakened by a humming sound, he rushed out to see a disc-shaped object flying past. Another night he fired at a hairy creature and saw it flinch, but there was no blood.

One night, after more disturbances, Jim lost his temper, and swore, 'If we can't have this place, you won't either – I'll blow it up.' And, when he later went out of the house, a voice speaking from nowhere said clearly, 'Dr Jim, we accept.'

Jim asked the local lawman if he thought the boys ought to be moved away; the lawman said that, as far as he knew, no human beings had ever been harmed. But Jim was inclined to doubt this. He allowed two pilots to start putting an airstrip on the land, but, a week later, one was killed in a crash. He heard of other people who had died once they enquired too closely into the mutilations, including a magazine editor. After two Air National Guard interceptors crashed, the air above the farm was buzzing with aircraft. (The land overlooked an Air Force installation.)

One evening, no fewer than nine discs landed within sight of the house. Jim walked towards them. And, as Barbara watched out of the window, she was struck on the forehead, and knocked unconscious. While the others gathered round her, the discs vanished. Jim reflected later that it could have been a practical method of getting him back inside and stopping people looking out of the windows.

One night, with guests present, a mechanical-sounding voice spoke out of the radio and TV speakers. 'Attention. We have allowed you to remain. We have interfered with your lives very little. Do not cause us to take action you will regret. Your friends will be instructed to remain silent about us.' One of the guests, a computer expert, dismantled the stereo, but could find nothing unusual. (On the other hand, many radios – or even gramophones – pick up police broadcasts, so what happened is not beyond the reach of normal technology.)

Speaking again with the law officer, Jim learnt of an incredible incident. On patrol one night, the lawman had seen a box with a blinking light, in a group of trees. The officer returned to get a colleague – but by the time they returned, not only had the box disappeared *but the trees as well.*

One night in January 1977, Jim experienced an odd compulsion to go to the top of a nearby hill where grass refused to grow. There was a box on the ground with a light inside it, and it was making a noise like 'a bunch of angry bees'. Jim was with one of the teenagers, and told him to get back in the car. By the time he went back, the box had vanished.

Soon after, Jim saw another light, and walked towards it. He found two fair-haired men in tight-fitting clothes waiting for him, and one of them said, 'How nice of you to come.' (It sounds as if he had learnt his English from a phrasebook – 'How nice of you to come' is laughably inappropriate under the circumstances.) Down the hill was a disc. The light seemed to be coming from nowhere in particular. And there was also a Bigfoot present.

The men, sounding perfectly normal, apologised for the inconvenience they were causing, and talked about 'a more equitable arrangement'. They told Jim that he had been sensible not to approach the black box, and illustrated their point by ordering the Bigfoot to approach it; as it did so, the humming noise changed tone, and the Bigfoot collapsed. 'As you see, it is quite lethal.'

Oddly enough, Jim did not ask any of the dozens of questions he had in mind. Yet he still did not think he was talking to aliens – he thought that perhaps some government agency was responsible. After five minutes, he felt it was 'time to go', and went away, feeling 'pretty rocked', and wondered why they had wanted to talk to him.

When speaking to the investigators, whom they impressed as truthful, the three expressed bafflement about the whole bizarre story; Jim even wondered if he had been hallucinating. This is obviously possible – with the corollary that it looks as if something was deliberately causing them to hallucinate.

The whole story – recounted in Timothy Good's *Alien Contact* – sounds so fantastic (in the most precise sense) that the easiest way of dealing with it would be to assume that Jim and his friends are liars or madmen. But the APRO investigators, a psychologist, an anthropologist and a seismologist, had no doubt of their truthfulness, or of that of the witnesses, while the nearby Air Force base had also had so many sightings of 'Bigfoot' that they had instituted an official procedure for recording them.

As in Puharich's *Uri*, we note the strange phenomena of voices speaking out of the air or out of loudspeakers. We also note Jim's 'compulsion' to go to the hilltop, as if summoned – an indication that the 'aliens' can exercise the same form of mind control as (according to Rivail) disembodied 'spirits'.

As to the purpose of animal mutilations – Timothy Good quotes one investigator as saying, ' . . . the mutilations, involving the extraction of enzymes or hormonal secretions – were said to be essential to the aliens' survival.'

Linda Moulton Howe – whom we have already met in connection

with crop-circle analysis – was drawn into the problem of animal mutilation and alien abduction by chance. She had produced radio and TV programmes on medicine, and moved from Boston to Colorado in 1976. In 1979, she began researching a programme on animal mutilations. Oddly enough, the public was hardly aware that they were still going on – the initial publicity had died away almost entirely, and some people had never even heard of them.

She learnt that, only two years earlier, locals in Sterling, Colorado, had become accustomed to the sight of a huge white light in the sky, and smaller lights that were seen leaving and entering it so often that they became known as Big Mama and Baby UFOs. A local reporter named Bill Jackson had pulled into the side of the road when he saw what appeared to be an enormous aeroplane about to land on the prairie. What he saw fly over him, in complete silence, was a machine as big as a football field, with hundreds of lights – green, white, orange and red – that ran in lines along it. Sheriff Tex Graves tried tracking it down in a plane, but could get no closer than five miles.

Talking to locals about cattle mutilations and UFO sightings, Linda Howe soon began to suspect that they were connected, and subsequent investigation would strengthen this opinion.

When she heard of a Texas woman called Judy Doraty, who had experienced 'missing time' after seeing a UFO, she immediately contacted her. It seemed that, in May 1973, Judy had been driving back from a bingo game in Houston with four other people when they saw a bright light hovering overhead. She pulled up and found herself outside the car. Then they all experienced 'missing time', although no one recognised it then. Judy only knew that she got into the car feeling sick and very thirsty. Back at home, they were surprised by the lateness of the hour.

Five years later, she decided to undergo a hypnotic session to try to bring back what had happened. She then recalled seeing a calf being drawn up a beam of light into the UFO.

Later, under hypnosis by Dr Leo Sprinkle, with Linda Howe present, Judy Doraty described her experience in a way that suggests that it was neither wholly objective nor wholly subjective; it belongs, so to speak, to a third category between the two. She recalls feeling 'sick to her stomach' at the sight of the calf having parts surgically excised while it was still alive, yet she does not seem to be in the UFO at this point. She seems to be asking why they are doing this, and receiving the information mentally.

The aliens told her, she claims, that they are testing our soil for poison, and that for the same reason they are conducting tests on animal reproductive systems.

Later, she found herself watching her teenage daughter Cindy, who was also on a table on the UFO; Judy was terrified that they intended to harm her as they had harmed the calf. And, since she speaks of being 'pulled back to her body standing beside the car' after the experience, it would seem that the 'abduction' could have been basically an 'out-of-the-body experience', of the kind that 'Helen' described to Jacques Vallee.

The programme *A Strange Harvest* was broadcast on 25 May 1980, and the phones began ringing immediately. One caller told Linda how a group of ranchers, sick of the mutilations, had gone out heavily armed to a place where several mutilations had occurred. They saw a light overhead, although there was no sound, and a kind of searchlight beam came from it. The men were 'frozen in their tracks', and stood there with the hair standing up on the backs of their necks. No one thought of shooting. When the 'helicopter' had flown away, they went quietly home. The next day, two mutilated cattle were found within yards of each other in the pasture.

A teacher from Briggsdale rang, to tell of two calves found mutilated, the ground below them baked so hard that liquids would not soak in. It sounded as if the 'beam' might be, in part, composed of microwaves – which would also explain the nauseous feeling and running eyes.

Perhaps the oddest thing of all was that, when some of the mutilated tissue was examined under a miscroscope, the scissor-cut that had removed the portion showed cells destroyed by the scissors; but, in the actual mutilation, there were no broken or divided cells.

When Linda Howe drove back from a lecture, with some mutilated tissue in her car – which she was taking to a laboratory – there was a strange high-pitched sound in her car, which she was unable to trace, and which continued all the way home, ceasing only when she drove into her garage.

It seemed that no one had actually seen an alien near a mutilated cow – until she heard from a rancher in Texas. In April 1980, he was looking for a missing cow that was ready to calve when he saw two green-clad creatures, about four feet tall, carrying a calf between them. Their eyes were like 'large dark almonds', and they had egg-shaped heads with 'pointy' tops. Their clothes fitted as tight as leotards. The farmer decided not to wait to see more, but – he told Linda – ran all the way back to his truck. Later, he found the calf's hide and its skull on the ground, the hide turned inside out with the skull inside it.

Whether or not these aliens were basically well intentioned, their conduct was certainly terrifying. Dr Sprinkle worked on a case that had occurred near Cimarron, New Mexico, involving a twenty-eight-year-old mother, Myrna Hansen, and her five-year-old son. She had been driving when her car had suddenly filled with a blinding white light, after which she saw five UFOs in a field. One moved towards her and she felt herself paralysed. She was afraid for her son. Then she found herself able to drive, and her son was beside her. She carried on to her destination, and when she arrived, found it had taken her six hours to drive twenty-eight miles.

Under hypnosis, she revealed that she and her son had been taken to an underground facility, which she thought might be near Roswell. Struggling, she had been stripped, and a cold object inserted in her vagina. She also saw the aliens 'operating' on a cow that was still alive. 'They're pulling it apart.' She speaks of 'real hot light' and adds, 'Heat must come from the light.' One of the aliens was female, and seemed to be sorry for her as she was painfully examined. By now she was very cold. Then a taller being in white came in, and seemed to be angry with the others. She was allowed to get up, and was told that all this was necessary. Then she was taken to some kind of underground cavern with a river flowing through it. She saw a room with a humanoid figure floating in a vat of reddish liquid, which she thought had something to do with the tissues removed from animals, and that this somehow sustained the immersed creature.

As in many other accounts, this one suggests that some of the aliens are 'mindless robots', while others – the larger ones (or 'talls') – are some kind of doctors or scientists.

After the abduction, Myrna Hansen became seriously ill with a vaginal infection that the doctor was unable to identify; he said she survived only because he gave her massive doses of gamma globulin to boost her immune system. Her son seems to have been well treated – at one point she heard him laughing – and came to no harm.

In another Colorado abduction seven months later, a husband and wife were examined separately, and the husband felt that the aliens had somehow studied his memory bank, pulling it out of his head; meanwhile, there was a high-pitched sound. (It raises the possibility that Linda Howe's memory was being examined during her drive in the car with the high-pitched sound.) One of the aliens was a hairless tall man in a blue robe and high collar, and they both felt overwhelmingly drawn to him. But the woman felt violated and raped, and had a serious illness after the abduction, which resulted in a baby she was carrying being born two months prematurely.

Later, the couple recalled being told about a catastrophic event that would take place in their lifetimes, and which would destroy a large part of the world's population.

In her second book, *Facts and Eyewitnesses* (Part 1 of *Glimpses of Other Realities*, 1993), Linda Howe describes being present at the hypnosis of Judy Doraty's daughter Cindy. Judy had apparently not discussed the experience of seeing the UFO with Cindy, even after her own hypnosis five years later. Cindy was by then twenty-two years old and married, and had resisted the idea of hypnosis. But ten years later, in 1990, now divorced, she consented to hypnosis. It took place in Springfield, Missouri, and the hypnotist was Dr John Carpenter.

Cindy recalled the bright light, and crossing the field with someone she assumed to be her mother. Asked by the hypnotist to look more closely at her mother, she suddenly realised this was not her mother. 'She doesn't look right . . . They're screwin' with my mind.' That is, they were exercising some form of thought control or hypnosis to make her believe that it was her mother leading her across the field. 'It's my mom but it's not my mom.' There were two creatures, and they reminded her of some kind of 'bug' – skinny and sticklike, with large eyes. They moved 'mechanically . . . like a robot'. There was a kind of moisture in the air, which seemed to be associated with the light streaming down from the UFO. Then she saw the calf being raised in the yellow beam, and added, 'It acts like it's bawling, but you can't hear it.' This seems to suggest that the aliens have some method of cutting off sound – which may explain why UFOs are so often silent.

After that she was taken on board, and described a 'kind of sweet, smelly air'. They made her lie on a table, and seemed astonished at the braces she wore on her teeth. Then a probe was placed against her forehead, and she felt deeply relaxed, 'almost like a sedative . . .' They examined her stomach and navel, and looked down her throat with some sort of instrument. Finally, she was allowed to sit up – she had the impression that the aliens felt she was too young and undeveloped for their purposes. She saw her mother looking at her through a kind of window, obviously frantic.

So Cindy's analysis seemed to confirm in detail the account of her mother.

Linda Howe also spoke to a Missouri horse-farm owner named Karl Arnold, who in 1975 had been turning into his driveway when he and his son saw a small grey-suited entity with a plastic bubble over his head, standing near the gate. As they watched, it faded away. Later, he and his wife saw a silver disc in their horse pasture, and the soil under it was as hard as ceramic. In the same pasture, five of their horses were found mutilated.

The 'strangeness' increases suddenly in the next account. In July 1983, Ron and Paula Watson of Mount Verson, Missouri, saw bright silver flashes in a pasture across the road. Looking through binoculars, they saw a black cow lying on its side, and two silver-suited beings running their hands over it. As they watched, the cow floated up from the grass and into a cone-shaped craft that was almost invisible, because its mirror-like surface reflected the leaves, grass and sky.

Standing by the ramp that led into the craft was a creature like a cross between a man and a lizard, with green skin, and on the other side of the craft was a 'Bigfoot' covered in hair. After they had all entered the UFO, the craft disappeared. Paula found the whole thing, apart from its strangeness, deeply worrying, and begged Ron not to intervene.

When the farmer who owned the pasture told the couple that one of his cows had vanished, they tried to tell him what they had seen – but he did not want to hear. Understandably, he regarded this talk about lizard men and Bigfoots as some kind of lunacy.

Finally, after suffering from anxieties and insomnia, the Watsons asked John Carpenter to hypnotise them. The hypnosis seemed to reveal that she had been abducted ten days earlier by the same beings. This was why she had experienced such intense anxiety as they looked through the binoculars.

Another of Linda Howe's cases seems to shed some possible light on this complicated problem. Jeanne Robinson, of Springfield, Missouri, a single mother, wrote to Budd Hopkins because she was convinced that she had been abducted since she was four, by small, grey creatures with almond-shaped eyes. Hopkins referred her to John Carpenter. A battery of psychological tests revealed that she did not suffer from any kind of mental instability or proneness to fantasy.

Like Rivail's Becquet sisters, Jeanne Robinson would experience a sudden urge to seize a pencil and allow her hand to rush across a sheet of paper, trying to set down the thoughts that poured into her mind, then the urge vanished just as suddenly. She explained that she felt that 'something out there' was communicating telepathically.

According to Jeanne Robinson's 'messages', the 'greys' are 'manufactured replicates', or some kind of robot. But the other type of alien – sometimes described as the 'praying mantis' type – are the 'ancients', the 'Great Mother of many species'. Now unable to reproduce, they can only pass on their genetic ancestry by creating hybrids.

The 'reptilians', according to Jeanne Robinson's 'communicators', are servants, possessing great bodily strength – 'what your dinosaurs would be had they survived'.

There are also blond 'Nordics' who have been on earth for many thousands of years. 'They are your early ancestors.' While the 'praying mantis' type need human genes to reproduce, the Nordics are still able to do so normally. 'They are more concerned with your spiritual evolvement.' They are of an emotional, more gentle race, whose nature baffles the 'ancients' as much as human violence does.

The messages explained: 'We use substances from cows in an essential biochemical process for our survival. The material we use from cattle contains the correct amount of protein substances needed for biochemical absorption . . . While we respect all life, some sacrifices must be made . . .'

The animal mutilations, apparently, are performed by a 'concentrated beam of photon energy'.

In a vivid dream, Jeanne Robinson saw a bull on a raised platform. A computer-like screen had some kind of X-ray image on it.

A grey being took a penlike tube with a light on the end and stuck it in the bull's rectum. Somehow, the light continued to move inside the body after the 'pen' was removed. There was a smell of burning flesh and hair. On the screen a moving dot showed the 'light' cutting around rectal tissue, which was then pulled out.

Merely a 'dream', of course. But we still have to explain how the excisions can be bloodless, why they leave a peculiar hard, serrated edge, and how they manage to cut 'around' cells, leaving them intact, when we possess no technology that can do this.

In the second volume of *Glimpses of Other Realities – High Strangeness* – Linda Howe describes the experience of a man who prefers to be known as Steve Bismarck, a Seattle shipyard worker. On the Saturday before Easter, 1977, he was uprooting vine maples on his parents' farm near Everett when he saw a Bigfoot, or Sasquatch, *(see plate nos. 7, 8 and 9)* walking out of the woods. It was about eight feet tall, had a cone-shaped head, and long black hair. He lay down, hoping the creature would not notice him, and it vanished into the trees. He hurried home, and was asked by his father, 'Goddam it, kid, where have you been?' He protested that he had only been gone about fifteen minutes; his father pointed out that it was nearly dark, and that he had been gone several hours.

He told friends at work, but was laughed at. Then snatches of memory began to return – memory of small creatures and some kind of UFO. He contacted the sheriff's department, and an investigator there put him in touch with a hypnotist.

Under hypnosis he recalled that the experience had started when he saw a small man, about four feet tall, wearing a 'sparkly blue metallic suit'. This being stepped into a kind of transparent egg with a device like a helicopter blade on top. Another similar creature came out of the woods, and both of them flew above the trees in these one-man helicopters. A large UFO then descended at such speed that he thought it was going to crash; in fact, it hung suspended above the trees, causing a kind of whirlwind. He then became aware of 'specks' in the air like the 'snow' on an old black-and-white TV set; these suddenly came together into a shape like a wolf, which moved swiftly towards him; as it reached him he received an electric shock. He was aware that the wolf was some kind of illusion. The same thing happened several times. Then he saw a Sasquatch being lowered from the craft on a cable – presumably to intimidate him. (The evidence of hundreds of sightings make it clear that the UFO denizens are nervous of humans.)

After that, he remembered – dimly – being taken aboard the craft, and being paralysed by a kind of mild electric current. He could recall a radio, from which there came the sound of voices speaking many languages, including English and Russian. Then he recalled a man with a shaved head who removed Steve's eyeball to examine it. His next clear memory was of being back on the ground, and seeing the Sasquatch walk out of the trees – apparently all other memories had been blotted out.

The sheriff's office had told Steve Bismarck that they had appointed an investigator because so many people were reporting strange lights and unusual animal deaths. Linda Howe quotes a man named Dwain Wright, a UCLA graduate, who describes how, in 1980, he and a friend were in Sand Springs, Oregon, a place where, in the previous year, Wright had found a dead cow lodged in the upper limbs of a huge Ponderosa pine. They met a cowboy who asked, 'Do you believe in flying saucers?' When Wright said he did, the cowboy told him, 'Well, they come across the desert here at night. I want to show you something.' He then took them to a dead bull that had dented the ground as if it had fallen from a great height; it had been castrated, and various other organs were missing. The cowboy told them that coyotes would not touch these mutilated animals, and even flies failed to congregate around them. The cowboy had seen cattle floated up off the ground, into glowing discs.

High Strangeness is certainly one of the most extraordinary books ever written on the subject of UFOs. Some of its bewildering suggestions are presaged in the opening chapter, 'Military Voices', containing interviews with military personnel who claim to have had encounters with aliens, and had often been debriefed by military intelligence. One of them is a staff sergeant who was at the Bentwaters Air Force Base in Rendelsham Forest, in Sussex, UK, when a famous 'close encounter' took place during Christmas 1980. That a UFO was seen at close quarters was acknowledged publicly by the Deputy Base Commander, Lt Col. Charles Halt.

Staff Sergeant James Penniston claims not only to have seen the UFO at close quarters, but to have touched raised symbols on its surface, from which he received some kind of information. This seems to have been received telepathically. Penniston recalled under hypnosis that the UFO entities were engaged in research. Asked, 'To help them with what?' Penniston replied, 'Themselves. *They are time travellers. They are us . . .* From the future.' The entities, Penniston said, are here to take chromosomes, mainly from the head and stomach. Asked why, he replied, 'They are in trouble.'

This notion that the UFO entities are time travellers from the future occurs a number of times in *High Strangeness*. Penniston explains later that the entities can travel only backward in time, because it is impossible to travel into the future. But a moment later he makes it clear that he means the future of the entities, not *our* future. And this raises obvious contradictions. Why should they be able to travel backward and forward in *our* time, but not into their own future?

In fact, the whole notion of time travel will strike most people as self-evidently absurd. If I reverse a film showing a child falling down, I can make him stand up again. But life is not a film; it seems to be 'for real'. Besides, if I could travel back to yesterday, I could speak to the 'me' of yesterday, and perhaps even persuade him to come back with me into tomorrow – in fact, I could accumulate billions of 'me's, one for every instant of my life. (This notion, as we shall see in the last chapter, is known as the 'many-worlds' interpretation of quantum theory.)

But no sooner have we dismissed time travel than we recall cases of precognition, and of time slips into the past, which seem to leave no doubt that time *is* rather more strange and complex than our common-sense view suggests. If the two women at Versailles can go back into the past, then perhaps the UFO entities can do the same . . .

Linda Porter, a Californian woman who contacted Linda Howe in 1991, told her, 'They can manipulate time. They can take a person out of our time frame, and keep him, or her, as long as they please. Then reinsert them back into time so the person wouldn't even know he's been gone . . .'

The story of Linda Porter is one of the oddest in *High Strangeness*. Troubled by recurrent images of huge 'grasshoppers', and moving inside a light beam, she was referred to a hypnotist, but found the memories that began to return so frightening that she refused to continue. But memories then began to return spontaneously – for example, of being inside the grey corridor of some kind of craft, and seeing a mantis-type being about eight feet tall. She was then about fifteen. On another occasion, she recalled being taken to some kind of undersea base off the coast near Santa Barbara where, above bright-coloured doors, there was writing that looked like Arabic or hieroglyphics. (This recurs in case after case.) At the age of seventeen, she woke to find a hole in the middle of her bedroom floor, and grey, shadowy beings climbing out of it. She also recalled being lowered down a shaft of light at such a speed she was terrified that she would die as she hit the ground; but she slowed suddenly when about four feet above the ground.

But her strangest story is of how she 'changed bodies'. When she was twelve, she almost died of a badly infected throat, and had an out-of-the-body experience. Her parents did not believe in doctors, so she was left to recover without medical help.

Later, on board a craft, she saw a middle-aged man who was close to death, and watched as his soul lifted out of his body and moved to another identical body, which then came to life; she was told that the old body would be scrapped, since old bodies are no more than 'empty beer cans' – that the ETs are amused by the human obsession with funerals. Then Linda Porter went through the same process – her soul was lifted out and placed in another body, since the infection had damaged the old one beyond repair.

She was afterwards shown her former body, and an alien scientist held her heart in his hand. The instrument he used to cut out the heart was a small silver-coloured tube with a blue light on the end, which used vibrations to cut the flesh without causing damage to the cells.

Linda Porter received the impression that the ETs who performed this operation were 'trying to hide all this from some "higher" form of life – whatever the "authority" is that prohibits this soul tranfer also prohibits them from interfering on this planet'. This authority is much more highly evolved than the ETs are, 'and wields a great power over many, many other realms of existence'.

Like so many other abductees, Linda Porter was told that Earth is in immediate danger because of pollution and destruction of the environment: ' . . . there is a chemical poison spreading in our land . . . the result of some kind of secret testing done by our government in outer space. A dangerous by-product of that testing was created, and is now falling back into our atmosphere.' It would eventually lead to a deadly chain reaction culminating in 'ignition' or 'sky fire'. (Linda Howe points out that Judy Doraty had told her something very similar in 1980.)

The language of the ETs, according to Linda Porter, is much more precise and compact than ours, and consists of 'symbols that create emotions'. These appear as three-dimensional holographic sculptures. The universe itself is 'built on sound patterns, which is why so many different worlds/dimensions can exist in the same space. Each is on a different frequency. . . . There are countless different worlds/dimensions occupying the same space without being aware of one another, because of having their own individual octaves.' (These ideas seem to echo those of Gurdjieff, or those of the Cambridge archaeologist T.C. Lethbridge.)

Like so many abductees and contactees, Linda Porter did not wholly trust the aliens and the account they gave of their purpose. 'I still feel there's something fishy going on, something they don't want us to know.'

She also told Linda Howe that she had a 'gut feeling' that crop circles were a subliminal message.

One of the purposes of the abductions, she thought, was to bring the abductees to emotional maturity through fear. 'When the person becomes thoroughly saturated with this emotion, it causes them to move beyond it.' The people who had passed this test would be prepared for the time when 'the great changes begin'. But she also seemed to feel that abductees are themselves 'aliens'. 'We are like exchange students in that we were created to come here, and live an earthly life within the limited human experience.' This seems to fit in with the notions that John Mack suggests at the end of his own book *Abduction*.

Another abductee, Wanna Lawson, described how she and her family were travelling near Harrisburg, Pennsylvania, in two cars when they saw lights in the sky, and she seemed to hallucinate lights and figures, 'swinging what appeared to be lanterns'. Then, although the car was still travelling fast, her daughter Netta slumped over the steering wheel without causing the car to swerve. Both cars pulled into a rest area and they found themselves on the New Jersey Turnpike, a hundred miles or so from Harrisburg – yet both cars still had full petrol tanks.

The rest of the family wanted to forget the whole thing, but Wanna and her daughter had vague memories of being examined by humanoids. They submitted to hypnosis, and Wanna remembered a large room of humanoid bodies in glass containers. Linda Porter had described the same thing. Somehow, Wanna Lawson was transferred from her own body into that of a tall humanoid female – although she also recognised this new body, says Linda Howe, as 'her own'. In her new body she had sex with a male humanoid whom she recognised as a long-time companion. Linda Howe comments, 'The implication is that humanoid bodies were put on and taken off at will for a specific goal.'

This goal seems to involve 'seeding' the human race with a higher species, for which purpose certain beings like Wanna, who are actually aliens, return to earth again and again in a kind of reincarnation. The aim of what she calls 'the watchers of man, the creators of man' is to 'take a sub-creature and evolve it to (their) level'. One problem they have encountered is that 'some humans are so evil that it just about cripples us [aliens] to be around them'.

At a UFO conference, soon after she met Wanna Lawson, Linda Howe gave a lecture on the different types of entity she had encountered in her interviews with abductees – praying mantis, lizard, Bigfoot, Blond Hairs, Greys, and so on – and was startled by the number of people present who also claimed to have encountered one or other. And a man whose identity she conceals under the name Ken Rose spoke of being taken on board a craft and seeing three female human bodies in glass cases, with cavities where the stomachs should be; they were covered in a gold-coloured dust, to preserve them from bacteria, and seemed to be in the process of being constructed.

Linda Howe encountered the reincarnation theme raised by Wanna Lawson in interviews with an abductee named Jim Sparks, who has described his own experiences in a book called *Star People, Outsiders*

– *Us or Them?* (1996). Sparks, born in 1954, describes how he is usually 'taken' at about 3.30 in the morning; he experiences a 'whirling' sensation in the pit of his stomach, which expands to his head; he blacks out, and finds himself on board a craft. There he is subjected – whether he likes it or not – to a learning experience, being forced to learn the alien alphabet. Noncooperation brings a burst of physical agony. The alien symbols are not, like ours, designed to be drawn on a flat surface, but in three dimensions. It took seven years, from 1988 until 1995, for him to learn these symbols.

One day, in the alien environment, Sparks found himself reading a story, written in English, about a close friend, which depicted the friend's life in accurate detail. But, when the story reached the present, it continued, describing the future. He was so enthralled that when the story continued in the alien language, he carried on reading, and found he could understand it. Finally, he found he could understand one small symbol, the size of a fifty-cent piece, and see that it contained information that would normally occupy twenty pages.

Jim Sparks's account of the alien language was sent to a psychologist, Dr Mario Pazzaglini, who has become an expert in symbols reproduced by abductees since the 1980s. His lengthy analysis is presented in full in Linda Howe's book, and concludes: 'While we cannot definitely say that the Sparks script is alien (nothing is definite in this field), we can say that it does not follow the common characteristics of hoaxed or made-up script. It is the description of a complex system which possibly is capable of forming a communication between totally dissimilar minds.'

When Sparks asked the aliens, 'Why me?', they made him write his question in the writing they had taught him. When he had done this, he was shown a holographic scene that seemed to be of World War Two. He saw German and Italian officers conspiring in some kind of a coup, and recognised himself as one of the Italians. (Sparks is Italian.) This scene made him feel somehow ashamed for the human race.

Next he was shown a scene that seemed to be in the late nineteenth or early twentieth century: there was a horse-drawn buggy in front of a factory building, and he recognised himself in the buggy, wearing a black suit and top hat; he sensed he was the factory owner.

Then he saw a scene which he guessed to be about the fifteenth or sixteenth century: a man and a woman were in a field overlooking the sea, farming the crop; the man reminded him of himself. After this, there was a medieval inn, with men and women around a crude wooden table, drinking from pewter mugs. Again, one of the men reminded Sparks of himself.

In the next scene he saw the Roman senate, and he himself listening to the others speak in some important debate, 'as if he had all the power'.

When he asked how far they had followed his family line, he was shown a scene of the African savanna, with patches of trees and apelike creatures. From this, Sparks understood that the aliens were telling him that they were responsible for human creation – a theme Linda Howe had already raised at the beginning of the previous volume.

She also points out the parallel between Jim Sparks's learning experience and a similar scene described by Betty Andreasson, whose case has been presented in four volumes by researcher Raymond Fowler. Betty Andreasson described how she had seen her daughter Becky tracing raised alien symbols with her fingers on a console, and was told by a 'grey' that they were training her.

In another scene described in Jim Sparks's book, he found himself in a huge hangar, in which a man and a woman were inside two transparent containers. Sparks became angry as an alien touched the woman with a metal rod, and was disciplined by a being who seemed to be human, who pressed the back of his hand repeatedly with a rod that stung, and which left red marks afterwards. A friend of Sparks confirmed to Linda Howe that he had seen Sparks's hand coverd with red marks, and that Sparks had obviously been unwilling to discuss it. (Sparks explained to Linda Howe that he did not *want* it to be real.)

Sparks also explained that, in his view, there were three levels of American government. The first was the normal US government; the second was the level that covers up secrets like the recovery of the Roswell craft; the third, which Sparks called the Black Budget Boys (or BBB), is a Secret Club, whose existence is unknown to the other two levels.

Sparks believes that the aliens have been among us for thousands of years, and that they have been 'farming us'. (Charles Fort suggested once that 'We are property.') 'We are a self-perpetuating crop.' But now humans have taken a path that seems to lead to inevitable self-destruction, with nuclear waste and environmental pollution, the aliens have to face the possibility that all their 'farming' has been wasted. Jim Sparks feels that the decade from 1996 until 2006 may be crucial to the question of whether the human race can survive. The present interaction of aliens and human beings – the whole emergence of the UFO phenomenon – is, he believes, an attempt on the part of the aliens to avert this catastrophe.

Sparks's view is, relatively speaking, optimistic. Other abductees have stated that nothing can avert the catastrophe, and that part of the Earth will be destroyed. The human race will continue, but on a smaller scale. Sparks clearly feels that the situation is not yet as extreme as this – something *can* be done, but it is urgently necessary for us to be awakened out of our complacency.

There is another aspect of Linda Howe's work that I have deliberately refrained from raising until this point: her conviction that there *has* been contact between the aliens and the US government, and that the 'Black Budget Boys' are deliberately concealing this from the public.

At the beginning of *High Strangeness*, she quotes a long passage from Major Donald Keyhoe's 1960 book *Flying Saucers, Top Secret*, which makes it very clear that the military is fully aware of the reality of UFOs, and is engaged in a deliberate cover-up. In 1958, Keyhoe was asked by the director of television programmes at Lackland Air Force Base in Texas if they could quote from his book *The Flying Saucer Conspiracy.* He was sent a script of the programme which acknowledges the reality of UFOs, and cites such cases as the disappearance of an F-89 interceptor fighter pursuing a UFO over Lake Superior on 23 November 1953. On radar, the UFO 'blip' had merged with the oncoming fighter, and both had simply vanished.

The programme also acknowledged that there was an official order muzzling all military personnel, members of the Defense Department and other agencies, on the subject of UFOs, backed by threats of fines and imprisonment.

Not surprisingly, the programme – which was for internal consumption at Lackland only – was cancelled; it is hard to fathom how the director came to believe that it could ever have gone ahead. But, since the Air Force script is quoted at length by Keyhoe, it is undoubtedly genuine.

In 1983, three years after *A Strange Harvest* was broadcast, Linda Howe was asked to make a programme about UFOs and extraterrestrial involvement. Two UFO organisations had tried to sue the American government to obtain information about UFOs under the Freedom of Information Act, but the Supreme Court turned them down.

Based on later information, it seems that what happened next is that the Air Force decided to take action to anticipate future attempts to force its hand by launching a campaign of disinformation, which began with an apparent surrender. Peter Gersten, the attorney who had presented the case under the Freedom of Information Act, was invited to have dinner with Special Agent Richard C. Doty, of the Air Force Office of Special Investigations (AFOSI).

Over the meal, Doty acknowledged that there had been a UFO landing at Kirtland Air Force Base in 1983, and that, when a guard had approached the disc-shaped object with a shotgun, it took off vertically at great speed. Moreover, when a UFO had landed at Ellsworth Air Force Base six years earlier, in 1977, a guard who pointed a gun at an 'alien' had his gun disintegrated by a 'light beam', which also burnt his hand. Gersten and Doty discussed a highly classified study group, set up by the military to examine UFOs, called Majestic 12, which included some prestigious names, including (incredibly) the arch-sceptic Professor Donald Menzel.

Doty told Gersten that the US government had been in contact with aliens, and had made an agreement, according to which the aliens were given a base at Groom Lake, near Las Vegas (and known as Area 51), as well as permission to mutilate cattle and abduct human beings, in exchange for teaching US experts about alien technology.

This certainly sounds conclusive. Or was Doty deliberately trying to spread confusion by simply repeating back some of the wilder theories of the conspiracy theorists?

Linda Howe was herself granted a meeting with Doty, for which purpose she flew to Albuquerque, New Mexico. Doty was supposed to meet her, but failed to turn up at the airport. Finally, with the help of Jerry Miller, a scientific adviser at the base, she met Doty, who claimed he *had* been waiting at the airport.

As they drove back, he went on to confirm another story Linda had heard recently: that a UFO had actually landed at Holloman Air Force Base, New Mexico. But he said she had got the date wrong. It was not May 1971, but April 1964. The same craft had landed the day before at Socorro, and been seen (in a famous incident) by Patrolman Lonnie Zamora (see p. 85) – this was because there was some confusion about the place and time. The following day, it landed, as scheduled, at Holloman, for its official meeting with the US Air Force . . .

In his office, Doty told her that her programme *A Strange Harvest* 'came too close to something we don't want the public to know about'. He then showed her a paper entitled 'Briefing Paper for the President of the United States', which began by admitting a number of crashes of UFOs, beginning in 1946, and including Roswell (two of them), Aztec, New Mexico, and Kingman, Arizona. Alien bodies and discs had been recovered from the later crash near Roswell in 1949 (not the famous one in 1947), and taken to Los Alamos for analysis. Five dead aliens had been found, and one alive. This creature, known as Ebe (extraterrestrial biological entity), told investigators (telepathically and in words) that its civilisation originated on a planet five light years from Earth, and have been visiting Earth for 25,000 years. There is a colony of them underground on Earth. They have been manipulating DNA, and aiding human evolution. It was also stated that Jesus was an extraterrestrial, created by the aliens, placed on earth to teach men about love and nonviolence.

Linda Howe was not allowed to copy or make notes on any of this. But she was told that Doty's superiors intended to release to her film footage of crashed UFOs, aliens, and the alien called 'Ebe'.

Understandably, she was wildly excited at this scoop, and lost no time in telling the backers of her programme about it. They were just as excited. Then nothing happened. The promised film footage and information never arrived. Discouraged, the backers dropped the whole idea of a programme on UFOs.

This, it seems obvious in retrospect, was the intention. By offering so much information and raising such expectations, Doty was almost certainly setting out to wreck the project.

A year later, in 1984, another briefing paper for the US President (Eisenhower) was sent anonymously to a television producer named Jaime Shandera. It was on a roll of film, claimed to be by the CIA Director Admiral Hillenkoetter, and was about the 'Majestic 12' group. It claimed that four dead aliens had been found at the earlier crash at Roswell in 1947. Unfortunately, the signature of Harry Truman was almost (but not quite) identical to one on another document. The highly respected UFO investigator Timothy Good published the document in his book *Above Top Secret*, stating his belief in its genuineness, but later concluded that it was a hoax. He continues to feel that Majestic 12 *did* exist, and that the document contains a mixture of truth and falsehood.

Linda Howe is inclined to believe in the authenticity of the Majestic 12 document, as does another well-known investigator, Stanton Friedman. Jacques Vallee, who devotes a chapter to the affair in *Revelations*, is deeply sceptical, and talks about his disgust with the gullibility of UFO believers in general. He is equally sceptical about Area 51, the aliens' underground base.

In 1995, it looked as if new and conclusive evidence had come to light. A television producer named Ray Santilli announced that he had found film footage of a dead alien recovered from the Roswell crash. Santilli said he bought it from an old retired cameraman who wished to keep his identity a secret. This man had filmed the post-mortem on the alien at the request of the Air Force, and simply held on to it.

But is the film genuine, or is it a fake? The explanation about the cameraman who wishes to remain unidentified, and who therefore cannot be questioned more closely, throws doubt on the whole story. Japanese buyers were offered a filmed interview with the cameraman, 'Jack Barnett', who explained the poor quality of the film by saying that it was difficult to work around doctors. He referred to the aliens he had seen (and whose dying screams he had heard) as 'freaks', Santilli explained that he was a devout Christian whose beliefs would not allow him to entertain the existence of life on other worlds – which in itself sounds unbelievable for someone who has actually filmed them. Linda Howe includes the cameraman's statement in full in *High Strangeness*.

In 1997, a book appeared which seemed to confirm everything the conspiracy theorists had suspected about a government cover-up. *The Day After Roswell*, by retired Colonel Philip J. Corso, claims that not only were bodies and alien technology retrieved after Roswell, but that this technology – lasers, microchips, fibre optics, even the 'death ray' deployed in the Star Wars project – was stolen from the aliens.

Corso claims that in 1947, when he was at the Fort Riley base in Kansas, he sneaked into a storehouse on the night of 6 July 1947 (four days after the famous Roswell 'incident') and levered the top off an oblong box – one of several delivered that afternoon from New Mexico, where there had been a plane crash. Inside, in a kind of glass coffin, was a four-foot alien with a head shaped like a light bulb.

In 1961, Corso, now an assistant to General Trudeau in the Pentagon, found he had inherited a filing cabinet full of alien technology from the Roswell crash. Trudeau explained that the Air Force, the Navy and the CIA all wanted to lay their hands on it, which is why they had to keep it hidden.

Corso describes how he headed a research-and-development team to study the technology, and 'seed' it at various large American corporations, such as IBM and Bell Laboratories, where it gave the

Americans a leading edge over the Russians in the space race and the Cold War.

It is virtually impossible to assess such staggering information. Trudeau is dead, so cannot support or deny the story. Senator Strom Thurmond, Corso's boss after he retired from the Army in 1963, who wrote a foreword to Corso's book, is on record as protesting that he had no idea of the contents of the book, and should not be seen as endorsing it. Certainly, it seems strange that alien bodies should be sent to Washington by road and stored overnight, rather than refrigerated and sent by air. But Linda Howe, who interviewed Corso for several hours at Roswell, during the fiftieth anniversary celebration of the 'incident', received the impression that Corso is genuine and telling the precise truth.

If so, it raises a difficult problem. The solution Corso wants us to accept is that UFOs are metal spacecraft from some other planet whose civilisation is more techologically advanced than ours. Their intentions are basically hostile; they perform cattle mutilations and abduct human beings in the knowledge that we can do nothing about it. Star Wars technology with its high-energy beams put them on notice that we can now defend ourselves. According to Corso, the enormous build-up of atomic weapons during the Cold War was not to defend the West against the Russians, or vice versa, but to warn the aliens that, if they tried annexing a part of Earth, they could be totally destroyed.

A number of objections are immediately obvious. If we have put the aliens on notice that we can destroy them, why are the numbers of UFO sightings and abductions not decreasing? And, if the build-up of atomic weapons during the Cold War was to convince them that we could destroy them, would they have not have seen through our bluff – seen that we would also have destroyed ourselves, by filling the atmosphere with atomic fallout and poisonous radioactivity?

The whole story of the 'capture' of a living alien sounds dubious. A large number of the UFO reports cited in this book suggest that, if the aliens wanted to recover a lost comrade, they would have no difficulty whatsoever. The same reports suggest that their technology is so far ahead of our own that to speak of intimidating them with Star Wars technology sounds as ludicrous as fighting a modern war with cavalry and muskets.

But the real objection to Corso's scenario is that it puts us back more than half a century to the view that UFOs are nuts-and-bolts craft from outer space, whose technology is simply more sophisticated than our own. Jacques Vallee started from this assumption, as did John Keel. Both were soon forced to abandon it as they became aware of the complex nature of the phenomenon. Vallee's *Invisible College* begins with a chapter called 'The Psychic Component', then goes on to speak about the visions at Fátima and the Virgin of Guadaloupe. John Keel's experiences in West Virginia left him in no doubt that he was dealing with some kind of psychic phenomenon, with an element of mischief that has something in common with poltergeists. Most of Linda Howe's abductees – Jim Sparks, Wanna Lawson, Linda Porter, Judy Doraty – would also agree that the 'nuts-and-bolts craft' theory fails to even begin to cover their experiences.

In a book called *Open Skies, Closed Minds* (1996), Nick Pope, a British Ministry of Defence official who investigates UFOs for the government, comments that he is often asked, 'Is there an official cover-up?' and always replies, 'Not in Britain.' If that is true – in spite of the assertions of 'witnesses' who claim that sites like Rendlesham are underground UFO bases – then it seems a reasonable assumption that Vallee and Keel are correct, and that there is no significant cover-up in the United States either.

Somehow, Corso's explanation of the UFO phenomenon seems too crude and simplistic. And our basic intuition tells us that, whatever the final explanation of the phenomenon, it will not be as straightforward as that.

9 Alien Powers?

N *THE INVISIBLE COLLEGE*, Jacques Vallee discusses the curious experiences of Robert Monroe, a broadcasting executive who, in the late 1950s, began to have spontaneous out-of-the-body experiences. Monroe's description of these, in *Journeys Out of the Body* (1972), makes a powerful impact of sincerity and honesty. Professor Charles Tart, who studied Monroe, had no doubt of his genuineness. Monroe went on to form the Monroe Institute, a non-profit-making organisation whose aim is to teach people how to induce out-of-the-body experiences and 'altered states'. Monroe's subsequent books, *Far Journeys* (1985) and *Ultimate Journey* (1994), have – no matter how impossible they sound – the same air of painstaking honesty.

Yet their implications are as bewildering as anything described in this book. If Monroe is telling the truth, then we live in an even stranger universe than some of those astonishing abductee reports suggest, and there is something wrong with our basic assumption that we are simply material beings living in a material world.

And this, at least, sounds a promising starting point for trying to understand what lies behind the UFO phenomenon.

Monroe was a businessman, whose career was in radio and electronics. He was experimenting with sleep-learning devices, and this almost certainly influenced what happened to him.

One Sunday afternoon in the spring of 1958, when he was forty-two, he listened to a tape whose purpose was to induce aural concentration. Later, after a light lunch, he was seized with abdominal cramps, which he thought might be food poisoning. They continued until midnight, then went away. He wondered whether they might have something to do with the tape he had played.

Three weeks later, as he lay on the couch on a Sunday afternoon, 'a beam or ray seemed to come out of the sky to the north at about a 30 degree angle from the horizon'. He described it as 'like being struck by warm light. Only this was daylight and no beam was visible, if there truly was one.'

He began to 'vibrate', and became paralysed. With a great effort he forced himself to sit up. 'It was like pushing against invisible bonds.'

To his alarm, it kept on happening. He was afraid that he was seriously ill, but medical checks showed nothing wrong with him. Then one day, with his hand hanging over the edge of the bed, he felt he could push his fingertips through the rug and the floor, to the ceiling of the room below.

A few weeks later, he found himself floating against the bedroom ceiling, with his body below in bed. Terrified that he might be dead, he swooped down to his body, and re-entered it.

When the 'vibrations' came again, he imagined leaving his body, and found himself floating in midair. When he willed himself to stop, he stopped. Again, he was able to re-enter his body.

Next time, he tried leaving by simply willing, and again it worked. A powerful sexual urge made him feel ashamed, and he returned to his body.

Oddly enough, he had never heard of out-of-the-body experiences – OBEs – and learnt about them only when he was recommended to read some of the classic texts by Sylvan Muldoon and Oliver Fox. Muldoon had experienced his first OBE when he was twelve, waking up in the middle of the night and finding himself floating above his bed. His book *The Phenomena of Astral Projection* (1951) surveys dozens of examples taken from the enormous literature of OBEs. Oliver Fox learnt to 'astral project' through 'lucid dreaming' – becoming aware that he was dreaming as he lay in bed, and then controlling the dream. Later, he learned to induce OBEs by lying down and relaxing into a semi-trance state.

Robert Monroe was soon able to leave his body at will. On one occasion, he decided to call on a doctor friend who was ill in bed, and saw the doctor leaving the house with his wife and walking to the garage. He checked later and found that the doctor had felt better and decided to accompany his wife on a drive to the post office. Monroe was also correct about what they were wearing.

He paid an astral visit to Andrija Puharich – having warned him that he might 'visit' – and found him writing in his study. Puharich broke off his work and spoke to him; he later confirmed that Monroe's description of his study was accurate, but he had no recollection of the visit, or the conversation that Monroe remembered.

Monroe was inclined to wonder if he had somehow fantasised the conversation with Puharich. But later similar experiences showed that he often received information known only to the other person.

This is interesting. Does it mean that Monroe's astral being was communicating with Puharich's, without the latter's knowledge? Or is it possible that such events are somehow blotted out, as when we wake up from sleep? If so, could this, perhaps, explain why so many abductees suffer amnesia about their experiences?

Monroe did not enjoy astral projection in 'this world' (which he calls Locale I). It presents the same problems that a diver with a face mask would encounter diving to the bottom of the sea. But he felt at home in a realm he calls Locale II, a nonmaterial world which is the natural environment of the astral body, and to which we move after death. Here, he says, 'thought is the wellspring of existence . . . As you think, so you are.' He says that Locale II 'seems to interpenetrate our physical world', and that the best explanation for it is the concept of vibrations, 'an infinity of worlds all operating at different frequencies, one of which is this physical world'. Once again, this is a notion we have frequently encountered in this book.

It is also, he says, a timeless world, 'where past and present exist coterminously with "now".' Perhaps the best way to understand this is to think of a novel. It has 'time', yet when you have finished it, you can turn back fifty pages and travel back to earlier events.

Oddly enough, Locale II *does* have some solid objects; these, he thinks, are created by thought – a notion that, again, might have some bearing on UFOs.

The area of Locale II nearest our physical reality is peopled with 'emotionally driven' beings who have never learnt any kind of self-discipline in our world; Monroe sees the acquisition of self-discipline as one of the most important purposes of our life on earth. 'If it doesn't happen in physical life, it becomes the first order of business upon death.'

Immediately beyond our physical reality there is an area that Monroe calls 'the H Band Noise'. This is the hubub of all the thought that emanates from all living things on earth, a kind of 'disorganised, cacophonous mass of messy energy' and emotions.

There is also an area that Monroe calls 'the Belief System Territory'. Since, in Locale II, you are what you think, people who are deeply involved in some religious belief remain trapped in their beliefs, which are fortified by other believers. In *Ultimate Journey*, Monroe even describes an encounter with a Neanderthal woman who is trapped in a system that demands that she sacrifice herself to the sky god. These believers have to outgrow their 'system' before they can progress. (All this bears a remarkable similarity to Swedenborg's descriptions in *Heaven and Hell*.)

Monroe also had experiences with the dead. Sleeping in a strange house, he saw a woman, who clasped his hand in both of hers; the next day he learnt that she had died in the same bedroom, and that she had a habit of taking people's hands in both of hers. He visited a doctor friend who had died, but failed to recognise him because he was so much younger; it was only when he saw a photograph of his friend as a young man that he knew he had met him 'out of the body'.

Monroe notes that sex can take place in the astral plane, but that it is a kind of sexual 'shock' that occurs when two entities come close. And he makes the interesting observation that the human sexual act is only a feeble attempt to duplicate another intimate form of communion that occurs beyond the body.

In his second book, *Far Journeys*, Monroe goes on to tell something of what happened after he opened The Monroe Institute, at about the time of the publication of his first book. His group developed a technique he calls hemi-sync, or hemisphere synchronisation.

This depends on the fact that the left and right hemispheres of the brain are virtually two different people. The left hemisphere of our brain deals with logic, language and practical matters; it has the temperament of a scientist, and is known as the dominant hemisphere because it is more assertive than the other half. The right deals with intuitions and feelings, and recognition of patterns; it has the introverted temperament of an artist.

The odd thing is that it is the left half that we call 'me.' This becomes apparent in patients who have had the 'split brain operation' – severing the nerves between the two halves – to prevent epileptic attacks. They become literally two people. In one experiment, a patient was shown an apple with the right eye (connected to the left brain) and an orange with the left (connected to the right brain) in such a way that neither eye knew what the other was seeing. Asked what he had just seen, he replied 'Apple'. Asked to write with his left hand what he had just seen, he wrote: 'Orange'. Asked what he had just written, he replied 'Apple'.

One patient was shown a dirty picture with her left eye, and blushed.

Asked why she was blushing, she replied truthfully, 'I don't know.' The left half of her brain – where she lived – *didn't* know.

These two people inside our heads operate on different wavelengths. Monroe developed methods of using patterns of sound to create an identical wave form in both hemispheres, so the two halves ceased to be out of step. He found that it could produce a marvellous calming effect which was conducive to 'altered states' and OBEs.

Monroe's experiments with a team of 'explorers' led him to some important conclusions about extraterrestrial life. His out-of-the-body explorers were sent to the moon and other planets, and found no sign of life, not even vegetation. Even outside the solar system, they found nothing worthwhile. 'It seemed to us a sterile universe.'

Then there came a major change. It came about through a small alteration in the 'affirmation' that subjects were asked to memorise before they began, which was basically the assertion that 'I am more than my physical body.' When another paragraph was inserted about desiring the help and cooperation of other intelligent beings, the subjects began to experience frequent contact with nonhuman entities. One 'explorer', a physicist, had lengthy telepathic contact with two beings, whom he felt to be a man and a woman, but their attempt to answer his questions led to frustration. The physicist suspected that he saw them as male and female because he was imposing on them the shapes he found most familiar, and that they probably saw him in the shape *they* found most familiar. Another subject, an electronics engineer, talked to a being who said Earth was his 'territory', and got the impression that the being was some kind of helper.

Ultimate Journey is certainly the strangest and most controversial of Monroe's books. A reader who comes to it without reading the first two might well dismiss it as fantasy. A long chapter is devoted to Monroe's work in helping spirits who did not realise they were dead – for example, the woman who had died in the same bedroom proved to be still there, waiting for her husband to return. When these 'earthbound spirits' had been successfully convinced, they would suddenly vanish – presumably to a more productive level.

Monroe explored his own past incarnations, discovering that in the twelfth century he had been an architect who had been beheaded because he objected to the cost in human life when stones fell from crude scaffolds. When his son visited Louris Castle, near Munro Fields, in Scotland, and sent his father a picture, Monroe was amazed to see that the main octagonal tower of The Monroe Institute (which he had designed) was virtually identical to the castle tower. He enquired about the name of the architect of Louris, and discovered that it was Robert Munro.

When Monroe's wife died of breast cancer, he was able to visit her on what he calls 'Level 27', but found the explosion of emotion too overwhelming. A second attempt brought the same result. Monroe ends the book, published in 1994, wondering whether he can continue to live on two levels at once. In fact, he died in 1995, at the age of eighty.

Monroe was modest about his achievement: he says at one point that he expects his name to be forgotten in a decade or so. Yet, if his books are as factual as they seem to be, there can be little doubt that he will rank as one of the major pioneers of paranormal research in the twentieth century. There are many books about 'astral travel' whose authors – like Hereward Carrington and Robert Crookall – are highly regarded in the world of paranormal research; but parapsychologists and scientists who have tested Monroe in the laboratory seem to agree that his results are among the most striking so far. But is Monroe really being objective and accurate about these other dimensions of reality which he describes so circumstantially? Or is it partly subjective fantasy? In fact, are OBEs some form of elaborate dream, as some parapsychologists believe?

The American military certainly does not seem to think so. In a book called *Psychic Warrior* (1997), a professional soldier named David Morehouse describes how he was trained to use remote viewing for spying. In the spring of 1987, leading a combat platoon on manoeuvres in Jordan, he was knocked unconscious when a stray bullet penetrated his helmet. He found himself in a kind of mist, standing in a circle of white-robed figures, one of whom told him that his choice of a career in the military was wrong. 'Pursue peace.' Then he came back to consciousness among his own platoon. A few days later, in the sacred place above Petra, he saw the same being, who advised him to seek peace, then to teach it.

Back at home, he found himself undergoing odd experiences, glimpsing visions and images. Then, camping with his family in the woods, he had an odd sense of 'being closer to everyone, to everything. It was like I was tuned in to a different frequency.' That night, he had an out-of-the-body experience. He found himself rising towards the moon and seeing the Earth spread out below him, before he descended and re-entered his body.

He was now working for army intelligence, and, when he told a doctor about the experience, was surprised that it aroused such interest. He had expected to be treated as if he was mentally ill. The doctor handed him a folder, and when he opened it, back in his room, he found it was labelled 'Remote Viewing'. Someone was being instructed to identify a 'target' and describe it. He spoke of a meeting in which an angry man was talking about American hostages. The 'remote viewer' was being asked to find out what had happened to the Americans taken captive in the Teheran Embassy.

Morehouse now found himself assigned to a top-secret operation whose purpose was to use 'astral projection' and remote-viewing for collecting intelligence.

This is less bizarre than it sounds. As far back as 1972, the American psychic Ingo Swann had taken part in remote viewing experiments, and later, with the scientists Hal Puthoff and Russell Targ (who also studied Uri Geller), had scored some remarkable successes under test conditions at Stanford University. And these experiments, it seems, were closely observed by the military, who saw the potential of remote viewing for Cold War spying, and for such problems as keeping in touch with submarines under the polar icecap. They began a programme for remote viewing in 1974.

Morehouse became part of a group who were being taught 'astral projection' aimed at particular targets. He was introduced to a trainer named Mel, and to other remote viewers. And he was trained to find his way to a given 'target' through a set of coordinates.

Morehouse devotes only a footnote to the theory behind this, but that is perhaps one of the most extraordinary pages of the book. He explains that the coordinates are randomly assigned by a remote viewer to a target he has already 'visited', and that these coordinates can then serve to guide *any* remote viewer to the same target – the theory, he explains, is based on Jung's notion of the collective unconscious. In other words, once these numbers have been assigned, they become part of the 'psychic ether', much as the letters assigned to a website on the Internet will enable anybody to access the site. The parallel is interesting, for it suggests that the 'psychic universe' – Monroe's Locale II – should be thought of as a kind of abstract cyberspace rather than as having some 'real' location in space and time.

In his first remote-viewing exercise, Morehouse was sent to the Civil War Museum, although not told where he was going. He found he could rise above the building simply by imagining it, and then swoop down through the roof. He described the museum accurately – talking to his trainer Mel – then protested that the whole place tasted of death and blood. He saw a dirty, unwashed soldier staggering along, and realised that he was looking into the past, and that the man was dead. As he returned, he felt his 'phantom body' fall through a tunnel of light.

The second target was a Soviet landing craft in the Baltic. Morehouse started by plunging below the sea, and almost choked to death. But he was able to describe the landing craft accurately.

His next set of coordinates sent him to Dachau, the Nazi death camp, which he found full of a sense of hopelessness: 'I feel forgotten, and I've given up.' Although he had no idea of where he was, he felt 'filthy'. 'I want to come home and wash.'

But, interestingly, as he passed through the stone wall into the camp, he noted: 'It was at times like these that I learned that everything indeed has a spirit. The wall had its own history . . .'

After remote-viewing the Ark of the Covenant, he was told by Mel that it was part of a 'dimensional opening', the entrance to another dimension.

On a trip to a dead planet – which proved to be Mars – two identical linear depressions running parallel along the ground convinced him that they had once been made by living beings.

In another alien world, he saw crowds of people in a black amphitheatre, paying respect to some kind of lawgiver; Morehouse was certain that the lawgiver was aware of his presence.

Morehouse is discreet about his actual spying missions, although he mentions taking part in the war against drug traffickers in the Caribbean. He also describes targeting the Korean Airlines jet shot down by the Soviets in 1983, his mission being to find out whether the jet had drifted into Soviet airspace by mistake, or whether it was a spying mission, as the Russians believed; he concluded that the copilot had deliberately allowed the OO7 to drift off course, looking for holes in the radar coverage of the Russian coastline. And, during the Gulf War, he saw burning oil wells, and canisters that had contained Iraqi biological weapons, leading him to conclude that the Pentagon was aware that American troops had been poisoned, and intended to keep silent to avoid having to pay compensation.

Morehouse never ceased to feel that it was somehow wrong to use his powers for military and political purposes. Eventually, he decided to 'go public' – and immediately became the target of a dirty-tricks campaign, which even went so far as slashing the tyres of his car so they would burst when he was travelling at high speed. Eventually he resigned from the army, wrote his book, and became a panel member of the Gorbachev Foundation.

It is time to pause, and look carefully at some of the staggering implications of the ground covered so far.

For ten years or so after Arnold's sighting in 1947, the main question was whether flying saucers came from our solar system or another galaxy. By the 1960s it was clear that this was the wrong question, and that the entities behind the UFO phenomenon did not appear to share our limitations in space and time. Vallee pointed out that they seem to behave like creatures out of folklore, Keel that the phenomena resemble those investigated by the Society for Psychical Research in the nineteenth century. Abductions and crop circles did nothing to clarify the issue, except to make us aware that we seemed to be dealing with beings whose powers were far greater than our own. Their ability to manipulate human beings, to take over our lives, control our minds and monitor our thoughts, seemed designed to make it clear that our notion that we are the most intelligent life form on Earth needs some serious revision.

Yet the work of Robert Monroe makes it clear that we are seeing only part of the picture. If his experiences are to be taken seriously, *then there is something fundamentally wrong with the way we view ourselves.* If we truly understood ourselves, we might have far less reason for feeling inferior to these beings. Monroe's ability to leave his body strikes us as literally superhuman. The same is true of David Morehouse's powers of remote viewing. Yet it seems that Morehouse is only one of a team who can all do it.

In fact, shamans all over the world have always taken such powers for granted. In *From Atlantis to the Sphinx*, I quoted Sir Arthur Grimble's story of how, when he was Commissioner of the Gilbert Islands, he witnessed 'the calling of the porpoises'. The shaman fell asleep in his hut, then sent his 'dream body' to invite the porpoises to a feast; a few hours later, hundreds of porpoises proceeded to swim ashore, where they were slaughtered for meat. Clearly, the hypnotic power exercised by the shaman over the porpoises is not unlike that exercised by the alien abductors described by John Mack and Budd Hopkins.

Monroe gained his powers after experimenting with sounds in his ears, Morehouse after receiving a blow to the head. Jane O'Neill, whose 'time slip' at Fotheringhay I mentioned in an earlier chapter, was traumatised after helping rescue the victims of a traffic accident from a bus. She records how she was unable to sleep that night, seeing the terrible injuries of the passengers; on subsequent nights, she found that she could hardly sleep at all. Then she began seeing 'visions' that would suddenly obtrude on her normal consciousness; on one occasion, she told her friend Shirley, 'I have just seen you in the galleys,' and Shirley replied, 'That's not surprising. My ancestors were Huguenots, who were punished by being sent to the galleys.' All these experiences culminated in her 'time slip', when she saw Fotheringhay church as it had been in the time of Mary, Queen of Scots.

Now it is interesting to ask: why did Jane O'Neill's trauma not simply send her into depression or a nervous breakdown, instead of to flashes of 'second sight' and a time slip into a past century? The shock clearly caused some kind of 'short circuit' that enabled her, so to speak, *to tune in to stations we normally tune out*, because being tuned in to them would upset our normal balance. To know what Fotheringhay looked like in the time of Lady Jane Grey was certainly not essential to Jane O'Neill's survival. It might have been interesting if she was a historian writing about Fotheringhay; otherwise, it was simply a useless piece of information.

My own observation has convinced me that most animals are telepathic. I have often noted that when I am eating, and I decide to throw a scrap to one of the dogs, she suddenly looks up and pays attention, although, a moment before, she had been lying passively, pretending not to notice. Our parrot knows when my wife is thinking of putting him back in his cage, and takes cover. Ingo Swann noted the same thing about his own parrot. With rare exceptions, human beings have lost this kind of sensitivity to telepathic signals.

I have cited elsewhere the case of a Dutch house painter named Peter van der Hurk, who, during World War Two, fell off a ladder and fractured his skull. When he woke up in hospital, he realised that he could read the minds of his fellow patients. Moreover, he could see into the future; as he shook the hands of a patient who was about to be discharged, he not only 'knew' he was a British agent, but also that he would be killed by the Gestapo. As a result of his prediction, he came close to being executed by the Dutch underground, who thought he was working for the Germans; fortunately, he managed to convince them that he was psychic.

The disadvantage of his new powers was that he was unable to return to work; he was simply unable to concentrate. His mind was like a radio set picking up more than one station at a time. He might have starved if he had not had the idea of using his powers on the stage in a mind-reading act. In due course, he changed his name to Peter Hurkos, and achieved fame through using his new abilities to help the police solve crimes.

Man *needs* his powers of concentration, of focusing on the present and anticipating the future, in order to stay alive. This is why, at some point in his history, he instinctively got rid of his 'psychic powers'. For the same reason, carthorses used to be blinkered to prevent them being distracted by the traffic. David Morehouse's accident, like Jane O'Neill's and Peter van der Hurk's, removed the blinkers, and made life suddenly far more nerve-racking.

It is probable that man began to get rid of his psychic faculties the moment he began to live in cities, and had to pay more attention to bullock carts and jostling pedestrians than to predators. The moment we begin to focus intently upon any important problem, our senses automatically begin to cut out 'irrelevancies', and in cities psychic abilities were less important than commercial acumen.

The problem – as everyone must have noticed – is that, when we become narrow and obsessive, we end by cutting out far more than we intended, and end up with a rather bleak and depressing view of reality. This is what has happened to our own civilisation. Our narrowness no longer serves the function of allowing us to concentrate on survival – which, in any case, is hardly the prime concern of most well-protected city dwellers – but merely traps us in a kind of tunnel vision that deprives us of any wider sense of meaning. It is probably true to say that there has never been a point in human history when humankind had a more depressing view of itself.

We need to change – that is self-evident. But change to what?

Let me clarify the issue with another example.

In 1992, a Virginia publisher named Frank DeMarco received a typescript about the lives of Thomas and Martha Jefferson. He was struck by its vividness, and wondered how the author had learnt so much about the couple's relationship. Finally, she admitted that she *remembered* being Martha Jefferson, adding, 'You are free to regard me as a nut if you please.'

But DeMarco did not dismiss her as a nut. He believed in reincarnation, and at college had repeatedly hypnotised two friends and recorded their own impressions of past lives. And he suspected that he had also had glimpses of his own past lives, one of which involved a visit to Emerson at Concord.

DeMarco knew of Robert Monroe's work, and had visited The Monroe Institute in 1990. In 1992, he went there again, listened to tapes whose purpose was to sychronise the two halves of the brain, and recorded his experiences in his journal.

The instructor was a man called Joseph McMoneagle who, like David Morehouse, had worked for the military as a remote viewer.[1] Given geographical coordinates, he could send his mind to look at whatever they represented.

McMoneagle wrote coordinates representing latitude and longitude on a board, and the group was asked to relax and try to 'view' the place. DeMarco did not succeed in remote viewing, but he suddenly felt that the coordinates represented the St Louis Arch. He was certain he was wrong, for his own geography suggested that the place was in Kansas. But, when a photograph was projected on a screen, it was the St Louis Arch.

In a later session, he began to have glimpses that he connected with Concord. Having been there, he had no problem in visualising Emerson's house.

It was not, he says, like imagining Emerson's house, but like watching a movie. He saw the scene and dialogue in completely realistic playback. He went to the back door, and a maid went off to get Mr Emerson. He seemed to hear Emerson address him as Dr Atwood. In the dining room, he was introduced to Mrs Emerson, and formed clear impressions of her as a person. He also sensed that she was gratified that her husband's latest admirer regarded her as an individual, not merely as an adjunct of Emerson.

Thoreau arrived – he lived at the bottom of Emerson's garden – and Atwood felt he regarded him with a certain wariness, perhaps seeing him as a rival for the sage's attention. Atwood disliked Emerson's rather proprietorial attitude to his wife. Moreover, he felt he has seen her somewhere before. Emerson proposed that they walk down to Walden pond before dinner.

---

[1] See *Mind Trek, Exploring Consciousness, Time and Space Through Remote Viewing* by Joseph McMoneagle, Hampton Roads, 1993.

At which point, the voice of their instructor brought DeMarco back to the room in 1992.[2]

Now Jung had developed a therapeutic technique called 'active imagination', which involves visualising a scene so vividly that it takes on the 'movie-like' quality that DeMarco describes. DeMarco's experience may have been simply a kind of 'active imagination'. However, Monroe's laboratory results, and his tests with three thousand subjects over a ten-year period, seem to indicate that it was probably more than that. And some of DeMarco's own experiences at The Monroe Institute seem to support that view. He describes how, in a state of 'Focus 10' (body asleep – or deeply relaxed – and mind awake) he 'took a walk' down the corridor, down the stairs, and out of the door. Looking at the moon, he thought, 'I can go there', then decided instead to go to California, where Kelly, the author of the book on Jefferson, lived. Later, he received a letter from Kelly saying that she had seen him in her house.

There is strong evidence that the power of 'psychic projection' is more common than we generally suppose. One of the first works sponsored by the newly formed Society for Psychical Research in the 1880s was a vast study called *Phantasms of the Living* by Gurney, Myers and Podmore, containing hundreds of examples. One of the classic cases concerns a student named Beard who, with an effort of will, succeeded in 'projecting' himself to the house of his fiancée Miss Verity, so that he was seen there by Miss Verity and her sister. Beard himself was unaware that he had succeeded; he was sitting in a chair in his own room, in a kind of trance. Again, W.B. Yeats has described how, when he was thinking intently about delivering a message to a fellow student, the student suddenly saw him in his hotel hundreds of miles away, where Yeats delivered the message. Yeats notes that he had no knowledge of 'appearing' to his friend.

There is a clear distinction between out-of-the-body experiences, remote viewing and 'astral projection'. The remote viewer remains in his body, fully aware of it, while his consciousness is elsewhere. In OBEs, the body is left behind completely, connected only by some kind of psychic telephone line (Monroe was often drawn back by the need to urinate). In 'astral projection', a kind of 'double' appears in another place, apparently sent by the unconscious mind, while the conscious

[2] I am quoting from Frank DeMarco's unpublished account, with his permission.

mind usually remains unaware of what is happening. The basic condition for this type of projection seems to be an intently focused imagination, which suggests that it has some connection with Jung's active imagination.

Astral projection seems to depend upon some form of telepathy, or connection between minds. One of Brian O'Leary's Princeton colleagues, Robert Jahn, quotes Paracelsus: 'Man also possesses a power by which he may see his friends and the circumstances by which they are surrounded, although such persons may be a thousand miles away from him at the time.'

Jahn is a professor of applied sciences at the Princeton School of Engineering, and his researches are central to this argument. In 1977, a female student had asked him if he would oversee her project on psychokinesis – 'mind over matter'. She wanted to know whether a random-number generator could be influenced by human mental effort. Jahn at first refused, explaining that such experiments were not the kind of thing they did at Princeton. Finally, he gave way, telling her that they would have to keep quiet about it.

Her results proved so startling that Jahn himself began to repeat the experiments. These involved a machine called a Random Events Generator, in which binary pulses are generated by some random process, such as radioactive decay. It might be regarded as a kind of electronic coin-flipper. And if a coin is flipped often enough, the number of heads and tails will be equal.

Jahn, and his colleague Brenda Dunne, brought people in from the street and asked them to try to influence the coin-flipper to make it produce more heads than tails. And the rate of success was amazing. (The parapsychologist J.B. Rhine had conducted similar tests at Duke University, after a gambler came to his office, and told him he was able to influence the fall of the dice – a claim he went on to demonstrate as he and Rhine crouched on the floor of the office.)

Jahn and Dunne went on to study remote viewing. In one experiment described in their *Margins of Reality*, one subject, labelled 'Agent', went to downtown Chicago, while another, labelled 'Percipient', stayed behind in a TV studio.

When Agent arrived downtown, a random-number generator selected one of ten envelopes that had been prepared earlier, each one containing a different location within a thirty-minute drive. The target that was selected was the Rockefeller Chapel, on the campus of the University of Chicago.

Back in the studio, Percipient gave her impressions. She saw the arcade next to the *Tribune* building, and a fountain with a statue. She saw a building with turrets, and thin, long windows. She saw a heavy wooden door with a black bolt. It was, she felt, a church. She described the inside and outside the the Rockefeller Chapel in some detail, all of which proved to be accurate.

Now it may seem that this experiment is not about remote viewing so much as about telepathy between a sympathetic Agent and Percipient. But there is an interesting twist. Percipient gave her impressions of the chapel *an hour and a quarter before Agent arrived downtown and opened the envelope.* She was remote-viewing the future.

But then, we may recall, David Morehouse was able to remote-view the past – he had to travel back six years into the cockpit of the Korean airliner shot down by the Russians. However, we feel somehow that this should not be too difficult – the past has happened, and left its traces behind, as in the Civil War Museum. But to remote-view the future sounds absurd. Yet, as Jahn and Dunne point out, this is standard procedure in remote-viewing exercises carried out in many laboratories.

In other words, what Robert Jahn and Brenda Dunne are doing is demonstrating under test conditions that human beings – many of them selected at random from outside the lab – possess precisely the same kind of powers that contactees ascribe to aliens.

What is even more strange is that this is not only true of human beings. In another experiment, a random peanut dispenser was placed in a Californian forest, and the experiments found that skunks, racoons and foxes, in search of peanut snacks, were somehow able to influence it even more strongly than their human test subjects.

I have suggested in *From Atlantis to the Sphinx* that our remote ancestors took 'psychic powers' for granted, and that one of the turning points in human evolution was the discovery of hunting magic, as portrayed in the caves of Cro-Magnon man. This hunting magic, which almost certainly worked, gave man his first sense of control over nature and his own destiny. I have also suggested that the religion of early man was based on the 'collective unconscious', and that it gave a tribe a kind of psychic unity – the same unity as is displayed by a flock of swallows who wheel simultaneously in the air, without any obvious signal, or a shoal of fishes turning all at once in the water. Obviously, human beings in a modern city do not need that kind of unity. In the past four thousand years or so, the individual has had to learn to stand alone.

There would obviously be no point in trying to return to that earlier stage. But the kind of powers described by Robert Monroe and David Morehouse, and investigated by Robert Jahn in the laboratory, are a different matter. It is fairly certain that our Cro-Magnon ancestors could not have out-of-the-body experiences at will, or remote-view what a herd of bison was doing. Such powers were almost certainly possessed by their shamans, but were as rare then as they are today.

What is necessary at this stage in our evolution is not a 'return' to the psychic powers of our ancestors, but an expansion of our own potential powers, based upon *the certain knowledge that such powers exist.*

The truth is that there could be no simple return to the past. Things have changed inevitably and permanently. We are all members of a global culture, and, for better or worse, that culture is as practical and down-to-earth as ancient Rome.

And there is one respect in which it is definitely for worse. Our scientific culture is basically sceptical. So we have a suitably down-to-earth picture of ourselves as practical creatures whose chief business on Earth is to stay alive and provide for our children. When we hear about alien abduction, our first reaction is to dismiss it, and our second – if we get that far – is to wonder if we are about to be superseded by creatures to whom we must seem primitive and stupid.

This chapter introduces a third possibility: that the 'aliens' may not be so fundamentally different from us – that they have simply developed powers that are latent in all of us.

There is another reason why there can be no return to the past. Unlike every other creature on Earth, man has shown a voracious appetite for knowledge. In the time of Julius Caesar, most of that knowledge was stored in the great library of Alexandria. Now it is stored in hundreds of thousands of libraries and millions of computers. In other words, man's development has been primarily *left-brain*. He has not bothered overmuch with the development of psychic faculties, which seems to be a right-brain ability; he regards the practical, technical approach as far more rewarding. The result is that modern man is stuck firmly in a left-brain universe.

One UFO researcher, Donald Hotson, has thrown off an amusing and original theory that underlines this point. What, he asks, would have happened if, at some remote period in the past, the human race had split into two types, one of whom followed the left-brain path, while the other followed the right? The first thing that would certainly have happened is that the left-brainers would have developed a basic hostility to the right brainers, regarding them as 'weirdos'. And the right-brainers might, for their own protection, have withdrawn from the practical realm of the left-brainer, perhaps to one of these parallel worlds of which Monroe and Vallee speak. Perhaps, Hotson suggests, UFOs are visitors from our right-brain half-brothers?

It is worth trying to imagine what would have happened to a civilisation that decided to follow the right-brain path as obsessively as we have pursued the left. We have invented atomic power, computers and space travel. What would they have developed over the same period?

In the mid-nineteenth century, a group of philosophers and scientists, impressed by man's technological progress, decided to try to investigate scientifically the problem of life after death and psychic powers. For some reason, it didn't work. They accumulated a great deal of very impressive evidence about life after death, OBEs, second sight, precognition and telepathy. But they had not really annexed the paranormal in the way that nineteenth century science had annexed chemistry, geology and abnormal psychology.

We can see why. They were trying to annex the paranormal using the methods of science – measuring rods, flashlight photography, tripwires. And the paranormal was simply not willing to cooperate on those terms. As Brian O'Leary realised when he discovered that science had told him only half the truth, the investigator has to plunge in head first and look for first-hand experience. O'Leary had to learn that the paranormal exists as a separate realm, quite apart from our physical realm, which can be investigated with microscopes and telescopes and particle beams. It is literally a parallel universe.

Yet it *is* possible to approach it in a thoroughly scientific spirit. An interesting case in point is that of Peter Demianovich Ouspensky, born in Russia in 1878. Ouspensky struck his followers as hard, pragmatic, impatient of all talk of mysticism or religion. As a follower of the teacher and philosopher Gurdjieff, Ouspensky applied this same pragmatic, scientific approach, trying to organise Gurdjieff's 'system' into a practical methodology.

One of the things Gurdjieff taught Ouspensky was about 'self-remembering'. Self-remembering is looking at some object – say your watch – and being at the same time *aware of yourself looking at it*. This is extremely difficult to do. After a few seconds, you become aware only of yourself, and forget your watch, or of your watch, and forget yourself. Wandering around St Petersburg at night, Ouspensky would practise self-remembering, and he noted that, as he began to succeed, he would feel that the houses were somehow aware of him, and that he could sense the individual history of each house. 'They were living beings, full of thoughts, feelings, moods and memories.' We may recall that David Morehouse made a similar observation about Dachau. Passing through the stone wall into the camp, he noted: 'It was at times like these that I learned that everything indeed has a spirit. The wall had its own history . . .'

Ouspensky noted the same kind of thing looking at the Peter and Paul Fortress in St Petersburg, and a factory behind it. As a friend drew his attention to this, he says, 'I too sensed the *difference between* the chimneys and the prison walls with *unusual clearness* and like an electric shock. I realised the *difference between the very bricks themselves.*'

In a piece called 'Experimental Mysticism',[3] Ouspensky describes how he embarked on the study of altered states of consciousness by means of some method which he refuses to divulge, but which was almost certainly the inhalation of nitrous oxide, with which many psychologists were experimenting at the time. His first observation in this new state of awareness was that 'everything is linked together', and that it would be impossible to say anything about it without saying everything at once. Everything is connected.

Similarly, he describes looking at an ashtray in this heightened state, and becoming aware of 'a whirlwind of thoughts and images', including the history of tobacco, of copper, of mining, of smelting. He wrote down a few words in order to try to recall what he had glimpsed; the next day he read: 'One could go mad from one ashtray.'

In other words, Ouspensky is saying that the things around us – houses, bricks, ashtrays – contain endless depths of meaning, which is actually perceptible to us in certain states of consciousness. Aldous Huxley had noted the same thing in *Doors of Perception*: that, under mescalin, everything seemed to throb with meaning to an almost painful extent. Huxley suggests that our senses actually filter out most of this meaning, because it would overwhelm us and make practical, everyday life impossible. We are like blinkered horses. Our senses, Huxley suggests, are designed to keep things out as much as to let them in.

Could this, perhaps, explain some of the paradoxes of remote viewing – how, for example, David Morehouse could view a Korean airliner that had been shot down years earlier, and how Jahn's subject could

---

[3] In *A New Model of the Universe.*

foretell what her friend would be looking at in an hour's time? If, in fact, this world around us is suffused with infinite meaning, to which we have deliberately blinded ourselves, as if wearing a welder's dark goggles, then it is obviously possible that we might have access to all kinds of meanings that we assumed had ceased to exist. An antiques expert looking at an old carpet or piece of furniture can perceive things about its history that would be invisible to the rest of us.

There was, in fact, one eminent twentieth-century historian who believed that there *is* a sense in which we can gain access to the past. In the tenth volume of *A Study of History*, Arnold Toynbee describes ten occasions on which he felt himself transported back into the past, either as he stood on some historic site, or as he read some passage by a participant in the historic event.

At first, it sounds as if Toynbee is speaking simply about history 'coming alive' through the imagination. But it soon becomes clear that he means far more than that. He describes how, in March 1912, he rounded the shoulder of a mountain in Crete, and found himself looking at the ruins of a baroque villa, probably built for one of the last Venetian governors three centuries earlier. He describes how, looking at the house, he had 'an experience which was the counterpart . . . of an aeroplane's sudden deep drop when it falls into an air pocket'. It felt, he says, like falling into a time pocket, to a time, 250 years before, when the house was hastily evacuated. It seems clear that what Toynbee experienced was very similar to Ouspensky's feeling that the houses of St Petersburg were speaking to him, or Morehouse's experience as he passed through the walls of Dachau.

On another occasion, at the site of the battle of Pharsalus (197 BC), he seemed to see the Romans wiping out the army of Philip V of Macedon with such brutality that he averted his eyes. As he did so, he caught sight of a group of horsemen fleeing from the battle – he had no idea of their identity. A moment later, the whole scene vanished into thin air.

The full import of what Toynbee means by a 'time pocket' (if he had known the term, he might have called them time slips) becomes clear when he describes the experience that led him to write the *Study of History*. In May 1912 he had been sitting in the ruined citadel of Mistra, looking down on the vale of Sparta. Over 600 years it had changed hands again and again – Franks, Byzantines, Turks, Venetians. But then, in 1821, wild highlanders had poured through the city walls, massacring its fleeing inhabitants. And, from that day onward, Mistra had been a deserted ruin. His sense of this catastrophe was so real that he was suddenly overwhelmed by 'the cruel riddle of mankind's crimes and follies', and received the inspiration for his gigantic *Study of History*, in which he attempts to glimpse some meaning and purpose in human history.

What has happened is that the past has suddenly 'become alive'; it has become as real as the present. In the same way, Proust's novel *A la recherche du temps perdu* sprang from the single experience described by the narrator Marcel (who is Proust himself). Coming home one evening, cold and tired, Marcel tastes a little cake called a madeleine, which he has dipped in herb tea. It brings a strange sensation of pure delight: 'An exquisite pleasure had invaded my senses . . . I had now ceased to feel mediocre, accidental, mortal . . .' What has happened, he realises when he takes another taste, is that the cake dipped in tea has brought back his own childhood, when his Aunt Leonie used to offer him some of her madeleine dipped in herb tea when he came in from a long Sunday walk. The taste has revived the past, made it alive, as if the intervening years were a dream. His vast novel is an attempt to repeat this experience.

In a book called *The Occult* (1971), I coined a term for this curious ability to *grasp the reality of some other time and place.* I called it Faculty X.

But Faculty X should not be seen as some psychic ability. Toynbee's ability to 'relive' the past was based upon his exhaustive knowledge of it. He knew every detail of the manoeuvres at the Battle of Pharsalus. He knew all about how the Venetians had been driven out of Crete. He knew precisely how Mistra had been overwhelmed.

What happened, quite clearly, is that, as he looked down on the ruined citadel of Mistra, he experienced something akin to Proust's feeling as he tasted the madeleine; there was a kind of surge of vitality which, combined with imagination, suddenly made the past *totally real*.

Ouspensky had expressed this when he wrote: 'It seems to us that we see something and understand something. But in reality all that proceeds around us we sense only very confusedly, just as a snail senses confusedly the sunlight, the darkness and the rain.' In the flashes of Faculty X, the snail's-eye view vanishes; what had been merely an idea becomes *real*.

We can see that Toynbee was exercising a power that is peculiar to a modern man: it might, to some extent, be regarded as a paranormal faculty, but it is based on knowledge and the exercise of intellect. In this sense, it is quite unlike the powers traditionally exercised by shamans. These flashes of Faculty X could not have occurred if Toynbee had not spent years absorbing the history of Greece, and its language and literature and art. He had *prepared* the ground for Faculty X with *left-brain* discipline.

It may seem that, even if we could all learn to exercise Faculty X at will, our powers would still fall far short of those allegedly exercised by the kind of aliens described, for example, by Linda Howe. What I have tried to argue in this chapter is that this may be due only to our lack of insight into the powers that we *do* possess. The literature of paranormal research has always been full of extraordinary examples that few people have taken seriously.

Consider the following case from the French scientist Camille Flammarion:

> My friend Alphonse Bue was on horseback in Algeria, and following the edge of a very steep ravine. For some reason his horse made a mis-step and fell with him into the ravine, from which he was picked up unconscious. During this fall, which could hardly have lasted two or three seconds, his entire life from his childhood up to his career in the army, unrolled clearly and slowly in his mind, his games as a boy, his classes, his first communion, his vacations, his different studies, his examinations, his entry at Saint-Cyr in 1848, his life with the dragoons, in the war in Italy, with the lancers of the Imperial Guards, with the spahis, with the riflemen at the Château of Fontainebleau, the balls of the Empress at the Tuileries, etc. All this panorama was unrolled before his eyes in less than four seconds, for he recovered consciousness immediately.[4]

There are dozens of similar accounts of this kind of panoramic review of one's life – it really does, apparently, happen to drowning men – but this one is impressive because its sheer detail makes it clear that this was not just some vague impression of his life 'flashing before his eyes'. It was a kind of slowing down of time in which he saw his life in the kind of detail that would normally have taken hours. Clearly, the human

---

[4] Quoted by Hilary Evans in *Frontiers of Reality* (1989), p.111.

brain cannot only play back the past in detail (as Wilder Penfield discovered in the 1930s, when he touched a patient's temporal cortex with an electric probe, and the patient 'relived' detailed memories of childhood), but has the equivalent of a 'long-play' device on it, so that years can be compressed into seconds.

Hilary Evans cites the research of the American psychologist Milton Erickson, who found that hypnosis could also 'compress' time, so that a dress designer who would normally have taken several hours to design a dress produced a design in ten seconds. Yet it seemed to her that she had sat at a table, gazed out of the window, and spent several hours working on it.

Another subject was placed under hypnosis and asked to evaluate a painful moral dilemma in which a girl who wanted to marry had to choose between marriage and her invalid mother. The subject believed that she had spoken at length to the young couple, and as a result of this she produced a thoughtful and detailed analysis of the situation. The hypnotised woman believed she had devoted hours to the problem, and was amazed to find that it had taken her only ten seconds.

Clearly, the power to manipulate time is not restricted to the aliens.

Neither is the power to make people do things against their will.

The Polish psychic Wolf Messing, who fled to the USSR when Hitler marched into Warsaw, was tested by no less a person than Joseph Stalin. His first assignment was to walk into a Russian bank and attempt to 'will' the cashier into handing over 100,000 roubles. Messing, accompanied by two witnesses, handed the cashier a note, which the cashier glanced at, then opened the safe, and handed over several packets of banknotes. Messing put them in his briefcase and walked out. Then he went back into the bank and returned the money. When the bank clerk looked at the 'note', and realised it was a blank piece of paper, he was so stunned that he collapsed with a heart attack.

The second experiment was apparently impossible: to walk into Stalin's villa without a security pass. Messing strolled into the grounds and walked past the guards and the servants, nodding to them; they stood back respectfully. Then he walked into the study where Stalin was sitting at his desk. Asked how he had done it, Messing explained that he had simply willed the guards to think he was Lavrenti Beria, the greatly feared head of the secret police. In fact Messing did not look remotely like Beria.

All of which makes it clear that Hynek was exaggerating when he said that UFOs were the greatest mystery of our time. The greatest mystery of our time is the one that has puzzled mankind's greatest thinkers since Socrates said, 'Know thyself.' Two thousand five hundred years later, we are still as far as ever from understanding the mystery of human potential. The only thing that seems certain is that it is far, far greater than Socrates suspected.

10 The Way Outside

THERE IS A STORY by the science-fiction writer Brian Aldiss that has always seemed to me to have some bearing on human existence. It is called 'Outside'.

Six people live together in a house that seems to have no particular location: four men and two women. Every morning, they get up and look in a storeroom, in which their supplies of food appear mysteriously. They spend the day playing cards and amusing themselves, but never get bored. At the end of the day, they go to bed. They never seem to wonder what they are doing there, or how they got there.

One night a man named Harley feels uneasy, and forces himself to stay awake. He sees another man leave his bedroom, and go to the storeroom. When he peers into the storeroom, Harley sees that the far wall has swung open, and leads to a corridor.

Deeply worried, he rushes to shake one of his companions awake. 'Something's wrong. There's a way outside. We've got to find out what we are. Either we are victims of some ghastly experiment, or we're all monsters.' But as he speaks, his companion seems to dissolve, and turns into a kind of stick insect.

Harley succeeds in finding his way outside. He is gripped by a desire to find out who he is and what he is doing there, and feels that he has been cheated of the years he has spent in the house. He sees buildings and runs towards them, then pushes open the door to a lighted room.

A man sitting behind a desk comments, 'It has taken you four years to get out of there.' Then he explains. The Earth is in conflict with insect creatures called Nititians. They come to Earth, kill human beings, and take their place. They maintain their human body by a form of self-hypnosis. They are conditioned to behave exactly like human beings.

A group of five Nititians has been captured, and kept in a restricted environment. One human has been placed among them as an observer.

And, because the human sits around doing nothing, the Nititians also do nothing. They never ask where they are, or who delivers their food every day, or what lies outside the house. The men never even flirt with the women. They merely accept their situation.

The man Harley has seen leaving via the storeroom is the human observer, going off duty for the night.

Harley suddenly realises the implications of what he has just been told. He starts to shout, 'But I'm not a Nititian . . .', when he feels his body dissolving as he turns into an insect . . .

From that day at school, when we began to discuss where space ends, I have always felt rather like Harley. On the surface, this world looks straightforward enough. I was born in a certain town, I knew who my parents were, I went to school and learnt history, I became interested in science and learnt about the universe and about how human beings evolved. It all seemed very normal and secure, especially when I became devoted to H.G. Wells, and was told that science would eventually solve all the riddles of existence. But on the day I realised that I had no idea where space ends, I also realised that I had no idea who I am or what I am doing here. It all *seems* to have an answer; in reality, we are all in the position of Aldiss's Nititians, hypnotised into acceptance and passivity.

Most of my fellow human beings never seem to be bothered by these misgivings. They have their troubles, but they never seem to worry that the whole thing is an absurd charade or a confidence trick. As to me, I never cease to suspect that someone is pulling my leg. A forgotten poet called William Watson expressed it in a poem called 'World Strangeness':

> On from room to room I stray
> Yet my host can never spy
> And I know not to this day
> Whether guest or captive, I.

As a child I had become interested in spiritualism, and felt that the idea of life after death made more sense than Shakespeare's belief that our little life is rounded with a sleep. Yet I still feel that the basic question – 'What am I doing here?' – is not answered by saying that I shall survive my death. It merely replaces the question, 'What am I doing here?' with the question, 'What would I be doing *there*?'

One thing *is* clear to me: that the reason my fellow humans take so little interest in these amazing problems of the paranormal, or in whether aliens from other galaxies or dimensions are visiting our planet, is that, like those people in Aldiss's story, they seem to be in a strange, passive state that is akin to hypnosis. I share enough of their state of mind to understand their longing for security, and their objection to the intrusion of strangeness. Nevertheless, it seems to amount to burying your head in the sand.

I experience the same sense of absurdity when I listen to a cosmologist like Stephen Hawking telling us that the universe began with a big bang fifteen billion years ago, and that physics will shortly create a 'theory of everything' that will answer every possible question about our universe; this entails the corollary that God is an unnecessary hypothesis. Then I think of the day when I suddenly realised that I did not know where space ended, and it becomes obvious that Hawking is also burying his head in the sand. God may be an unnecessary hypothesis for all I know, and I do not have the least objection to Hawking dispensing with him; but, until we can understand why there is existence rather than nonexistence, then we simply have no right to make such statements. It is unscientific.

The same applies to the biologist Richard Dawkins, with his belief that strict Darwinism can explain everything, and that life is an accidental product of matter. I feel that he is trying to answer the ultimate question by pretending it does not exist.

And what is wrong with the 'scientific' view that ultimate questions do not exist? Only that we feel instinctively that it is an evasion. All living creatures need a sense of security, and that applies to human beings more than most, because we feel particularly vulnerable. Without a sense of security, we would be nervous wrecks. But it is possible to go to the opposite extreme, and to convince yourself that life is as comfortable and unproblematical as a Jane Austen novel. When that happens we vegetate – or, worse still, stagnate.

Let us try to take a bird's-eye view at how man found himself in this peculiar situation.

In the Middle Ages, the Church disapproved of people who thought for themselves, and the friar Roger Bacon spent most of his life in prison for pointing out that that is how we learn. But, during the Renaissance, the Church could no longer keep the lid on individuality, and the invention of printing soon made it impossible. So, when Copernicus suggested that the Earth was not the centre of the universe, and Kepler and Galileo went on to prove it beyond doubt, and then Newton outlined the first 'theory of everything', the old belief systems began to shake and crumble.

Yet the major figures of the Age of Reason – Voltaire, Diderot, Rousseau – were not great thinkers. In fact, they devoted most of their time to the less strenuous activity of attacking the Church. And the philosophers who followed were more interested in asking how we can be sure that our senses are telling us the truth than in understanding the universe. In fact, the whole idea of understanding the universe became thoroughly unfashionable.

In the nineteenth century, scientists were irritated by a sudden upsurge of interest in ghosts and poltergeists; they denounced it as a revival of the witchcraft superstition. One particularly violent outbreak of poltergeist activity, in the Fox household in New York state, led to the formation of the Spiritualist Church, which made the scientists angrier than ever. Yet intelligent men who studied the problem admitted that it could not be dismissed as superstitious ignorance. The mathematician Charles Dodgson – who wrote *Alice in Wonderland* – admitted: 'That trickery will *not* do as an explanation of all the phenomena I am more than convinced.'

In effect, the nineteenth century was faced with the same problem we face in UFOs. And its reaction was much the same: to pretend it did not exist.

In fact, Lewis Carroll suggested that it might be explained by some new force similar to electricity, but the investigations of the newly formed Society for Psychical Research showed that this would not explain thousands of ghost sightings. Yet most scientists went on refusing to pay attention to the paranormal. 'Darwin's bulldog', Thomas Henry Huxley, explained that he 'simply could not get up an interest in the subject'.

So the twentieth century still found science busily trying to create a 'theory of everything', while refusing to look at half the phenomena. By 1900, it began to look as if it might succeed.

And at that point, the edifice of science itself began to crumble. To explain why requires a brief – and I hope painless – digression on modern physics.

When J.J. Thomson discovered the electron in 1897, it became clear that atoms, after all, were not the smallest thing in the universe. He concluded that atoms are lumps of positively charged electricity, with negatively charged electrons embedded in them like raisins in a Christmas pudding.

And, just as it began to look as if science was getting close to the secret of the universe, a physicist named Max Planck introduced an awkward complication. He was trying to explain a problem that had been labelled the ultraviolet catastrophe. Expressed very simply: he wanted to know why, when you turn on an electric fire, you do not also fill the room with ultraviolet rays, X-rays, gamma rays, and all kinds of other dangerous radiation. After all, when you strike any note on the piano, it makes all the other strings vibrate, and the same ought to apply when you turn on a light or a bar fire, since heat and X-rays are – as Clerk Maxwell had shown – all part of the same keyboard of electromagnetic energy. But this clearly doesn't happen. Why?

In 1900, Planck made the suggestion that perhaps energy does not flow in continuous waves, but comes in small packets, called quanta. If you pour a cup of water on a table top, it will flow all over the place. But, if the water is frozen to make powdered ice, it will stay in a heap. This, in essence, was what Planck was suggesting about energy.

No one believed it – not even Planck himself. But, in 1905, a young patents clerk named Albert Einstein pointed out that Planck's idea could explain a puzzle called the photoelectric effect. When light falls on a sheet of metal, it causes particles to evaporate from its surface. Now if the strength of the light is increased – say, substituting a 150-watt bulb for a 60-watt – you would expect it to make the electrons fly *faster*. Instead, it simply increases their *number*. It looked as if the light consisted of shells being fired at the metal – in other words, quanta.

No one liked the idea. It took Planck several years to acknowledge that Einstein could be right. He then had to admit that light behaves like waves *and* particles. But how could a wave be a particle or vice versa? Quite suddenly, the 'theory of everything' began to look like a distant hope.

But at least the particle theory helped to build up a new picture of the atom. In 1908, Ernest Rutherford disproved the Christmas pudding picture when he fired alpha particles at a thin sheet of gold, and most of them went straight through. This proved that atoms must be made up mainly of empty space. He went on to suggest that the atom had a positively charged nucleus, like the centre of a roundabout, with the electrons somewhere round its edge. And in 1913 a young Danish physicist named Niels Bohr improved on this picture, suggesting that atoms are like miniature solar systems, with the electrons revolving around the nucleus like planets around the sun. But, unlike the planets, electrons can absorb or emit energy – in 'quanta', of course – and could jump from their orbit inward or outward.

Now there is a fairly simple way of finding out what is going on inside an atom. When light from some heated element (say hydrogen) is passed through a prism, it has a distinct spectrum. That spectrum is due to the vibration of electrons in their orbits, and can therefore tell us something about these orbits. The bright and the dark lines in a spectrum (called emission and absorption lines) are individual for each element, so it is even possible to tell what elements are present in a star. Bohr was able to use his knowledge of the hydrogen spectrum to explain what is going on in the hydrogen atom.

That still left many problems. When Newton had explained the solar system in his *Principia*, his mathematics described exactly why the planets moved as they did. But Bohr's mathematics failed to explain with the same exactitude what the electrons were doing inside the atom. Even when the German physicist Arnold Sommerfeld pointed out that the atom would work better if the orbits were elliptical, this still failed to solve the problem. For the next twelve years, quantum theory was in a state of confusion, taking one step forward and two steps backward, or, if it was lucky, just marking time. In 1922, Bohr met a brilliant young student named Werner Heisenberg, and admitted that he had reached an impasse. Atoms, he told Heisenberg, were not 'things'.

Then what could they be? In 1923, a student at the Sorbonne named Louis de Broglie had an apparently absurd idea. If light waves behave like particles, why should particles not behave like waves? The idea of 'matter waves' admittedly seemed a contradiction in terms. But, if the atom was not a 'thing', it followed that electrons were not things either. If an electron was not a little hard ball, perhaps it was a wave inside the atom, rather like a spring bent round into a circle, or a snake with its tail in its mouth. This would explain why electrons had orbits, since only certain wavelengths could fit into an exact circle. Or perhaps, de Broglie added as an afterthought, electrons consisted of a particle *associated* with a wave – an idea that was greeted with even less enthusiasm.

In spite of which, de Broglie's matter-waves were confirmed when beams of electrons were fired at a crystal. The crystal lattice is, in effect, a series of slits, and slits cause light rays to bend (diffract). The electron beam diffracted just as if it was a light beam. And so, in an experiment performed later, did a beam of neutrons. Particles *did* behave like waves.

By 1927, no fewer than three complete 'quantum theories' had solved

Bohr's impasse. They were proposed by Werner Heisenberg, Paul Dirac and Erwin Schrödinger

In 1925, on a holiday in Heligoland, Heisenberg decided to forget Bohr's 'solar system' atom, and concentrate on the mathematics. He pictured atoms as oscillators, or vibrators – rather like those mattresses that are supposed to induce relaxation. What he wanted to find was some connection between vibrations and the lines in light spectra. He finally succeeded in finding a mathematical formula that would describe all the states inside the atom. Heisenberg had broken the code of the spectrum. He was so excited that he left the house at 3 o'clock in the morning and spent the rest of the night sitting on top of a tall rock.

There was one point that troubled Heisenberg. In his quantum mathematics, p times q did not equal q times p, thereby apparently violating the laws of arithmetic (p and q stood for the position and momentum of a particle). This problem was solved when news of Heisenberg's breakthrough reached a Cambridge graduate student named Paul Dirac, a brilliant mathematician, who saw immediately that the paradox could be explained in terms of the work of a Dublin mathematician of the nineteenth century, William Rowan Hamilton. Hamilton had been working on this problem of whether light is made of waves or particles, and had produced a set of equations that would describe the motion of a wave *or* a particle, and in which A times B did *not* equal B times A.

Erwin Schrödinger, a physicist of the old school, was unhappy with this new tendency to turn quantum physics into complicated algebra; he continued to believe firmly that it ought to be possible to visualise an atom. During the Christmas of 1925, on holiday in the Tyrol with his latest mistress (he was a famous womaniser), Schrödinger had a sudden inspiration. Brooding on de Broglie's 'matter-wave', he produced a wave formula, which he called by the Greek letter psi, and which allowed him to think of an electron wave in the same terms as a wave on a pond. Or, rather, imagine a ball of dough which begins to dance to syncopated music, and shoots out waves as it does so; this is a crude approximation to Schrödinger's atom. Schrödinger's wave function was regarded as the greatest advance so far in quantum physics.

At first sight, these three great breakthroughs sounded contradictory; in fact, Schrödinger himself recognised that they were three statements of the same basic ideas.

It was Dirac whose 'quantum algebra' produced the next major breakthrough. One of his equations, dealing with an electron moving at almost the speed of light, had a plus as well as a minus in it, and seemed to predict the existence of a positive particle similar to the electron (which has a negative charge.) In due course, the positron was discovered in the laboratory, earning Dirac the Nobel Prize.

But by then another vital principle of quantum physics had been discovered by Heisenberg – the famous 'uncertainty principle'. Superficially, this sounds unremarkable. What Heisenberg stated – in 1927 – was simply that it is impossible to measure both the position and the speed (momentum) of a particle. It sounds unremarkable because it seems to be a merely practical limitation. To measure the speed and position of a billiard ball requires simply that you shine a light on it (otherwise you cannot see it), and then measure how long it takes to get from A to B. You cannot shine a light on an electron because it is too small; all you could do would be to make a single photon bounce off it, which would be like hitting the billiard ball with a golf club, and would obviously affect your measurement.

An analogy from everyday life might help. Imagine a behavioural psychologist writing a book about human behaviour (classical physics *is* a kind of behavioural science), and beginning a chapter on sex by explaining that it is an appetite exactly like eating and drinking. But, having embarked on this analogy, he realises that sex is in some respects quite different from the appetite for food. A starving man may die; no sex-starved man ever died from lack of sex. Starting from this recognition, he may end by grasping that sex, unlike food, is 90 per cent 'in the mind', and cannot be understood as a purely physical need. His position could then be compared to Bohr's recognition that an atom is not a 'thing'.

And in that same year, 1927, Niels Bohr dotted the i's and crossed the t's of Heisenberg's uncertainty principle. In discussions with Heisenberg, he produced what is known as the Copenhagen Interpretation, or the Principle of Complementarity. He said, in effect: forget whether an electron is a wave or a particle. If we ask an electron about its position (which is a particle property) we get an answer that suits a particle. If we ask it about its momentum (which is also a wave property) we get an answer that suits a wave. Stop asking which is correct, and recognise that the two answers complement each other.

In other words, not being able to measure both the speed and position of a particle is not just a practical limitation: it is inherent in the nature of reality itself.

Another quantum physicist, Max Born, had interpreted Schrödinger's wave function psi as a measure of the *probability* that the electron would be in one place or another. Schrödinger had protested, and made his point with his famous illustration of a cat locked in a box with a cyanide capsule. A quantum process – like radioactive decay – can trigger a hammer which may or may not smash the capsule and kill the cat. According to Born, said Schrödinger, the cat exists in a state that cannot be described as either alive or dead – until someone opens the box. And that, he said, is plainly absurd.

And yet that, in a sense, was exactly what the Copenhagen Interpretation was saying. Observing a subatomic process causes a collapse of the wave function, and makes it turn into a particle. But, before the wave function collapses, the electron is in a state of probability, which *cannot* be pinned down more accurately.

Einstein objected bitterly. He agreed with Schrödinger. Something is really happening inside the atom, even if experimental limitations prevent us from discovering what it is. 'God does not play dice,' he said indignantly.

He devised a 'thought experiment' to disprove Bohr – it is known as the Einstein–Podolsky–Rosen paradox, or EPR. Suppose, he said, two electrons collide at the speed of light, and bounce off in opposite directions. It *would* be possible to measure the speed of one and the position of the other; and since they are virtually identical – except for flying in opposite directions – this would amount to disproving the uncertainty principle.

Not so, said Bohr. The two electrons are part of the same system, so, if you cause one wave function to collapse, you cause both to collapse at the same time.

No, said Einstein, for since they are travelling at the speed of light, and it is impossible to exceed the speed of light, one particle cannot possibly know what is happening to the other.

But this argument was won by Bohr. In 1982, a group in Paris, led by Alain Aspect, carried out the two-particle experiment, and discovered that Bohr was correct. If you cause one photon to swerve upward at an angle of 45 degrees, the other will swerve downward by 45 degrees. So it would seem that, like identical twins, the photons somehow feel connected, even when flying apart at the speed of light. This also confirmed the work of the Belfast scientist John S. Bell, who had arrived at the same conclusion mathematically. (It is popularly known as 'Bell's Inequality Theorem'.)

There is one more step in this argument – a step that to the ordinary reader may seem to throw the whole question into hopeless confusion, yet brings us back, once more, to the problem of the nature of UFOs.

There is one particularly baffling experiment that underlines the Alice in Wonderland paradoxes of quantum physics. In its simplest form, it is known as the double-slit experiment. If I shine a beam of light through a narrow slit, with a screen on the other side, it will form a slit of light on the screen. If I now open up another slit at the side of the first, two overlapping slits of light will form on the screen. But there will be certain dark lines in the overlap portion, due to interference – the crest of one wave cancelling out the trough of another.

Now suppose that the beam is dimmed so that only one photon at a time can pass through either of the slits, and suppose that, instead of a screen, you have a photographic plate. Over a long period, you would expect two slits of light to appear on the plate – but no interference lines, since one photon cannot interfere with itself. Yet, when this experiment is performed, the result is still two slits of light with interference lines.

There is something stranger still. If a photon counter is placed over the two holes, to find which is used by each photon, the interference effect immediately vanishes, as if being watched made the photon behave itself.

How can this be? Does the photon split into two? Or does the wave somehow divide, and pass through both holes? If so, why does it hit the screen in a precise spot? And why does it behave like a wave when unobserved, and a particle when observed?

In the 1950s, Hugh Everett, a pupil of the physicist John Wheeler, suggested a bewildering interpretation. The fact that the photon becomes solid only when it is 'watched' suggests that, when it is not being watched, it still takes the form of Born's 'wave of probability', and can go through both pinholes at the same time. And the two 'waves of probability' interfere with each other. It is as if Schrödinger's cat existed in two universes at the same time, dead in one and alive in the other. Once the box is open, the two possibilities coalesce in our solid universe, and it is either one or the other.

But why just two universes? When a photon makes a choice between wave and particle, it is not, according to Everett, making a real choice: it is choosing *both* in parallel universes. And since an electron wave coalesces every time it collides with a photographic plate, or another electron, this implies a new parallel universe every time – thousands, in fact, billions, of parallel universes.

The idea sounds like a joke. Yet many scientists take it seriously. For example, a younger member of the quantum-physics establishment, David Deutsch, devotes a chapter in *The Fabric of Reality* (1997) to explaining the double-slit experiment, and speaks of 'tangible' photons and 'shadow' photons – the former existing in our universe, and the latter in parallel universes.

Aristotle had a concept called 'potentia', a strange realm that exists between possibility and actuality. It begins to look as if electrons – and cats – are perfectly comfortable in this realm.

The purpose of this detour into quantum physics is to make the point that, whether we like it or not, we have to learn to see reality in a completely different way. Like our sense of beauty, like our sense of humour, like our sexual preferences, reality lies mainly in the eye of the beholder. The physicist John Wheeler has even gone so far (in what he calls 'the Participatory Anthropic Principle') as to suggest that we *create* the universe in the act of perceiving it.

This is, of course, the notion to which Einstein objected so indignantly. Yet Einstein himself had played a central part in creating this new universe of physics in which the observer is all-important. And, by declaring that Planck was right about quanta of energy, he started a landslide that ended by carrying him away – cursing and shaking his fist.

Now it is true that this revolution has not yet affected you and me. We go about our business as if we lived in the old, solid universe of nineteenth-century physics. (In fact, a recent survey showed that one-third of all people in England and America do not even know whether the Earth goes round the sun or vice versa.) But it *has*, for example, troubled certain physicists, like Fritjof Capra and Fred Alan Wolf, and their books *The Tao of Physics* (1975) and *Parallel Universes* (1988) are devoted to a science that is becoming daily more like Eastern mysticism. We may also recall that, when Stanislav Grof's subjects were given large doses of LSD, they also had insights into the nature of reality that sounded like classic Eastern mysticism. Gary Zukav says the same thing in his book *The Dancing Wu Li Masters* (1979). We do not know it yet, but we are walking around in a different universe – a universe that seems to have very little connection with what we regard as common sense. We are in the position of one of those Walt Disney characters, who walks over the edge of a cliff, and carries on walking – until he looks down, and suddenly begins to fall.

The amusing irony is that all this has happened as a result of a problem we discussed earlier: that, at a certain point in its development, humankind chose the way of the left brain – practical advancement, leaving mysticism and psychic faculties to its tribal shamans. This choice is responsible for modern science and civilisation; it is also responsible for our tunnel vision and feeling of inadequacy. And now, absurdly enough, modern science is telling us that we suffer from tunnel vision, and that, if we want to understand the universe, we shall have to remove the blinkers.

Now it cannot have escaped the notice of readers that the UFO problem has brought us to exactly the same point. It began by looking quite solid and understandable. Kenneth Arnold's flying saucers raised the question: are we being observed by visitors from another world? Is it possible that the aliens are trying to prepare us for a mass landing on our planet?

Faced with that question, Jacques Vallee and John Keel quickly came to the conclusion that something altogether stranger was going on. Vallee concluded that it is a 'control phenomenon' – that is, that an important part of its purpose is *the effect it has on us*. And it was as if a problem in classical physics changed into a problem in quantum physics.

And what is the effect it has on us? John Mack speaks of 'the inconsistency between these [abductee] experiences and the consensus reality', and adds, 'There is no way, I believe, that we can even make sense, let alone provide a convincing explanation of this matter within the framework of our existing views of what is real or possible.'[1]

In other words, if an important part of the purpose of these phenomena is the effect on us, then that purpose would seem to be to *decondition* us from our unquestioning acceptance of consensus reality.

In many cases, that deconditioning can be both traumatic and strangely exciting – as epitomised in the case of John and Sue Day, who, on the evening of 27 October 1974, left the home of Sue's parents, and set out on the forty-minute drive home to Avely, in Essex, where they intended to watch a play on television. Their three children, age eleven, ten and seven, were in the back of the car. Their ten-year-old boy was the first to notice that an oval-shaped blue light was flying above them; they assumed it was an aeroplane. Then things became strangely silent, and, as they drove into a bank of green mist, the car

---

[1] *Other Realities, Noetic Sciences Review*, Autumn 1992.

radio began to crackle and smoke; John pulled out the wires. Then the engine went dead and there was a jerk. A moment later, they were driving again, and for a moment John had the odd impression that Sue was no longer present, and said, 'Is everybody here?' before he realised she was beside him.

When they reached home, they found the TV screen blank, and the clock showed that it was nearly 1 a.m. They had lost over two hours.

After this odd experience, the Days showed personality changes. John became more self-confident, more creative, and began writing 'poems about life'. Sue also became more self-confident. And the ten-year-old, who had been backward at reading, suddenly improved. They became vegetarians and almost gave up drinking. John, who had been a heavy smoker, gave up smoking.

Then poltergeist activity began to take place in the house. The back door flew open violently and crashed against the wall. Items would vanish, then reappear days later. There were unaccountable smells, such as lavender. Finally, under these bizarre trials, John had a nervous breakdown and lost his job.

When he heard a radio programme about UFOs, he contacted the researcher Andy Collins, who went to the house in Avely, and also witnessed poltergeist phenomena. Collins introduced John to a hypnotist caused Leonard Wilder, and, under hypnosis, John began to recall what had happened. To begin with, Susan was unwilling to be hypnotised, but began to recall spontaneously; later, she submitted to hypnosis.

John recalled a white light surrounding the car, and a sense of rising. He seemed to lose consciousness, then found himself on a balcony in a kind of hangar. He was looking down on a blue car which he recognised as his own, although his own was white. Two people were asleep in the front, and more in the back. Sue, who recalled standing beside him, saw John and her ten-year-old standing beside the car, although they were also beside her on the balcony. (John Spencer has suggested that this seems to indicate that the Days were actually undergoing an out-of-the-body experience.)

John was taken to an examination room, where he lost consciousness, then woke up on a table, being scanned by some apparatus. Three tall beings were watching, and two small, incredibly ugly creatures, rather like traditional goblins with huge ears, beaked noses and triangular eyes, were examining him with penlike instruments.

The tall beings wore silvery one-piece suits, and communicated by what John assumed was telepathy. When the examination was over, they showed John the rest of the craft, and the recreation area and the control room. In the latter he was shown images of the solar system (which flashed by very fast), and a holographic image of a planet that had been destroyed by pollution. Finally, left alone in another room, he was startled when an incredibly beautiful woman walked in, then vanished. At this point he found himself back in the car.

Sue recalled being taken to an examination room and strapped on a table, where she was painted a mauve colour and physically examined – she found she was wearing a gown, although she had no memory of being undressed. When the examination became too intimate, she screamed. One of the tall beings placed a hand on her forehead and, 'I went out like a light.'

Later, she was taken on a tour of the ship, and she was also shown images on a screen, including Earth from space, and the place where she lived.

At this point, she apparently told her captors that she did not want to go back, and they agreed she could stay. But when she saw John climbing into the car, and the car dematerialising, she changed her mind and said she wanted to go. Then she found herself sitting in the car. This may explain why John thought he was alone in the front of the car for a few moments before he realised Sue was there.

The Days struck everyone who spoke to them as exceptionally forth-coming and honest. It should also be borne in mind that the usual objection – that an abductee has been influenced by other stories of abductees – does not apply in this case, since this all took place in 1974 (although they were not hypnotised until 1977), when there *were* no other abductee reports in Britain (and even in America they were rare).

A number of important observations emerge from the case. The first is that the 'aliens' apparently intended no harm; apart from the uncomfortable physical examination, they seemed friendly, and treated the Days as intelligent fellow beings. The aftereffect was to make both of them more self-confident, and to cause them to become more aware of their own health and that of the planet. John's nervous break-down was apparently brought on by vivid dreams, and by the poltergeist activity. (Poltergeists have been responsible for more than one nervous collapse.) But he subsequently found another job involving more 'artistic' activity. Their ten-year-old improved at school. And the youngest, asked what he wanted to do when he grew up, declared that he intended to build a huge spacecraft to take thousands of people from Earth.

In general, then, the case seems to support John Mack's view that abduction experiences 'open the consciousness' of abductees. Mack also comments that his own experience of working with abductees provides a rich body of evidence to support the idea that 'the cosmos, far from being devoid of meaning and intelligence, is . . . informed by some kind of universal intelligence . . . one to which human intelligence is akin, and in which it can participate'.

But why the poltergeist activity? The likeliest explanation is that the poltergeists had nothing to do with the aliens, but that the experience had somehow 'opened up' the Days, weakening the divide that seems to separate human beings from other realms of reality – for example, Monroe's 'Locale II' – and making them vulnerable to attack. This again underlines the connection, noted so many times in this book, between UFO phenomena and the realm of the paranormal.

For me, the most interesting thing that has emerged during my research for this book is the connection between the UFO experience and the experience of wider – or deeper – states of consciousness: such as Jacques Vallee's case of the woman who experienced 'novel insights into the nature of reality', and who changed 'from an agnostic to a gnostic', after seeing a UFO on her way to Oxford. (This was followed, as in the case of John and Sue Day, by a 'supernatural' experience.) I have always been preoccupied with the oddly limited nature of human consciousness, and in my first book, *The Outsider*, I labelled it (rather arbitrarily) 'original sin'. In a later book on Gurdjieff I expressed it rather more precisely in the comment, 'Human beings are like grandfather clocks driven by watchsprings.' Human consciousness seems too feeble to take advantage of our occasional flashes of insight.

The nature of such insights is expressed by the writer – and student of Eastern mysticism – Paul Roberts, in an article he wrote on his own UFO experiences.[2] In 'Making Contact' he describes how he and two friends saw a flying saucer in 1969 in Cornwall. The enormous disc made a powerful electric whirring (unlike many UFOs, which are silent) and hovered motionless for over twenty minutes, during which it changed colour. Then seven or eight smaller discs came from somewhere, and merged with the larger one, although there was no visible opening. The saucer made off in a 'slow vague zig-zag' until over the

[2] *Why* magazine, autumn 1997.

Atlantic, then it banked and took off upward at a speed that one of them – a mathematician – thought be be over 20,000 miles per hour.

None of them reported the sighting, not wishing to be regarded as cranks, and they 'took it in their stride'.

Two months later, Roberts was again by the sea, this time with only one friend, on a moonlit evening. A policeman warned them to be careful because 'things have been happening around here'.

When the policeman had gone, they heard a voice behind them, succeeded by a powerful humming sound that made the beach vibrate. Nothing was visible in the sky. Then, suddenly, the night was lit up 'as if by a gigantic magnesium flare'. Before they could panic, a voice behind them said something like, 'There will be no harm for you.' Then two shining entities emerged from the shadows – Roberts's companion later described them as 'angels without wings'. Roberts was aware of others in the background. Then a vast egg of light descended, and they suddenly realised they were inside it. They seemed to be surrounded by a kind of liquid light that chilled them. They both had a dreamlike sensation, and a sense of telepathic communication.

Roberts writes:

I confess it grieves me to report – since this seems mandatory in every Close Encounter of the Third Kind – that a good deal of what we heard involved dire warnings about the planet's future unless we earthlings smartened up. The slight difference – and it's one that both of us have only come to appreciate some thirty years later – was that we were being told that the earth would be destroyed not so much by human actions as by the current human character. We were told that what we viewed as separate entities – people, flora, fauna, planet – are in reality but one entity. As was believed in the ancient world – and quite clearly, by such as Shakespeare – earthquakes and natural cataclysms are causally related to events in the human sphere, both as augurs or omens, and as reactions of cosmic outrage.

And there was also good news. It doesn't have to be this way. The planet's fate could be altered, as could our destinies – but only if we changed ourselves. And we'd be shown how this could be done in due time, as apparently everyone is eventually shown in some way or other.

After that, they saw the egg of light rise above them. The drone returned, and it streaked away into the night at 45 degrees.

Roberts says they sat in silence for hours, then his friend said, 'I suppose that changes everything.' They swore an oath not to speak of the experience – to protect themselves in academic circles – and Roberts records that, before writing the article, he had to get his friend's permission.

That is not quite the end of the story. In 1975, Roberts was with the Indian 'miracle man' Sai Baba in India – Baba is famous for being able to materialise objects from the air, and healing the sick. Roberts was talking with a nuclear physicist, S.K. Bhagavantam, and discussing space travel. Baba joined them and asked what they were talking about, and Roberts asked him about life on other planets and UFOs. In reply, Baba told him to shut his eyes. Roberts felt Baba's thumb pressed on his forehead.

Instantly, an inner vision of awesome beauty opened up before me. I saw world after jewelled world in a limitless cosmos of coiling self-illuminated spheres within spheres. I was in each world simultaneously, their myriad unique fragrances, textures, sounds, and landscapes, all apparent, their every inhabitant me and yet also not me. As with a dream, everything was projected from me, and yet existed independently of me, flowing in and out as fragile and as vital as breath. Yet it was truly infinite, no limit possible to the teeming life, which seemed made of undiluted joy. A universe that continued literally forever, worlds without end . . .

Baba told them, 'Outer space, inner space. Inner space the only real space.'

Roberts asked him if he was saying that UFOs came from within the mind. 'Not mind. Heart. Heart is God's mind, isn't it? Space men come from heart – heart of God.' He told them, 'Close your eyes, nose, mouth, ears . . . Is the world there? No smelling, tasting, touch, sight, hearing. Yes? World is gone. But you are not gone. See, my dears, all things are really made by you, but for now you are thinking that God is making the grandeur of this universe'.

When Baba was gone, Roberts and Bhagavantam experienced 'a monsoon of understanding'. 'The UFOs were real, all right. Yet their occupants are not flesh-and-blood beings like us. In spite of all the odds, we *are* unique. Nowhere in the universe is there a life form like us. The beings I'd seen with my friend were made of thought and light. They were ideas – but real ideas – and what they brought and still bring is a super-condensed form of truth.'

Now all this may sound as if it has very little to do with the UFO phenomenon as examined by Jacques Vallee or John Spencer. Yet there are interesting echoes. In Stuart Holroyd's *Prelude to the Landing on Planet Earth*, 'Tom' explained via Phyllis Schlemmer that Earth is of peculiar importance in the universal scheme of things, but that it is now acting as a kind of bottleneck, preventing the evolution of other planets.

Sai Baba's comment, 'all things are really made by you', sounds oddly like the view that seems to emerge from the Copenhagen Interpretation. The astronomer David Darling expresses it: 'It comes as a powerful corroboration . . . that the conscious mind is crucially involved in establishing what is real. That which reaches our senses is, at best, a confusion of phantasmal energies – not sights, or sounds, or any of the coherent qualities that we project outward onto the physical world. The universe, as we know it, is built and experienced entirely within our heads, and until that mental construction takes place, reality must wait in the wings.'[3]

As already mentioned, the physicist John Wheeler goes further. Starting from the position that a photon does not become 'solid' until it is observed, he points out that the double-slit experiment might be carried out with light from a distant star – light that started out billions of years ago. But, if light is a 'wave of probability' until observation causes the wave function to collapse, then we have to assume that the star (provided it is uninhabited) is also a wave of probability until its light is observed in the laboratory.

This is, of course, the position expounded by Bishop Berkeley in the early eighteenth century – that our senses 'create' the world, although its existence is sustained by God. And if, like Dr Johnson, you regard this position as mildly improbable (he kicked a stone to refute it), then you are unlikely to be convinced by Wheeler's expression of it.

Now another eminent physicist, David Bohm, was also unwilling to accept this new version of Berkeley. Being a Marxist at that time, he felt the Copenhagen Interpretation was a little too mystical, and was inclined to side with Einstein. Yet he was by no means a committed 'classical physicist'. In 1943, he was working on plasmas at the Lawrence Berkeley Radiation Laboratory – a plasma is a very hot gas most

[3] *Equations of Eternity*, p. 103.

of whose atoms have been stripped of outer electrons, which circulate freely. Bohm noticed that the plasma behaved in many ways like a living thing, that 'the plasma constantly regenerated itself and surrounded all impurities with a sheath, so as to isolate them completely',[4] just as our bodies do with viruses. He had the impression that the electrons were alive. He noticed the same thing at Princeton, working on the study of electrons in metals: that also led him to feel that he was dealing with a living ocean of particles, each aware of what the others were doing.

Talks with Einstein deepened his dissatisfaction with the Copenhagen Interpretation. Like Einstein, he wanted to feel there was something deeper than mere probability and uncertainty. He toyed with the idea of 'hidden variables', the notion of particles tinier than the electron that might account for its movements, then later suggested a kind of 'field' called quantum potential, rather like the nineteenth-century idea of the ether, in which all particles swam. These notions encouraged John Bell to formulate his Inequality Theorem, which led to the confirmation that two photons flying apart at the speed of light remain somehow in contact.

On a BBC television programme, Bohm saw a demonstration that provided a metaphor for these ideas. A drop of ink was suspended in a glass jar full of glycerine. A cylinder with a handle ran down the centre of the jar, and when the handle was turned clockwise, the ink became a streak, and gradually disappeared into the glycerine. But, when the movement of the handle was reversed, the 'streak' flowed the opposite way, and condensed back into a drop of ink. The 'order' in the ink drop was apparently scattered – but was there all the time, merely awaiting an anticlockwise turn of the handle.

Supposing, Bohm found himself thinking, there was a similar underlying order in the universe – like the order that seemed to govern the electrons in the plasma soup?

Then Bohm came upon the idea of the hologram (see p. 60), which gave him an even better metaphor. The holographic film has the appearance of a meaningless interference pattern, yet, when a beam of light is shone through it, a picture appears in space.

This led to the breathtaking idea that perhaps the universe itself might be a hologram that springs out of an underlying reality. As a child, Bohm had been struck by the way that water forms a vortex

---

[4] *Quantum Implications, Essays in Honour of David Bohm*, edited by B.J. Hiley and F. David Peat (1991) p. 3.

flowing down a plughole; it looks quite different from still water, yet it is merely water obeying hidden laws – laws of what Bohm later called 'implicate order', the order 'enfolded' in the hologram.

But, of course, what makes the hologram so fascinating is that every part of the photographic plate contains an image of the whole. The universe is not composed of disconnected parts: there is a fundamental 'interconnectedness'. An individual consciousness clearly plays a major part in converting the waves on the plate into a meaningful reality.

So Bohm has created his own answer to Einstein's objection to the Copenhagen Interpretation – that 'God does not play dice'. The notion of 'dice' is an illusion – there *is* an underlying order.

The book in which Bohm expressed this conclusion, *Wholeness and the Implicate Order*, appeared in 1980. For some odd reason that I have never discovered, his publishers decided to send me a proof copy (then entitled simply *Wholeness and Implicate Order*) to ask me for a quote for the dust jacket. It was obvious to me that Bohm was a tremendously exciting thinker, and that he was trying to bridge the gap between science and the philosophy of meaning. I said as much, and, in due course, found my quote – the only one, as it happened – on the dust jacket. Even so, it was some years before I grasped the seminal importance of the book I was recommending.

On page 191, I encountered a concept that left me puzzled and confused. 'It may be said ... that space is full rather than empty ... that what we perceive through the senses as empty space is actually the plenum, which is the ground for the existence of everything.' What space was full of, it seemed, was something called 'zero-point energy', so called because it still pervades space even at a temperature of absolute zero.

It was many years before I found out what he was talking about. A writer named Donald Hotson sent me the typescript of a book on the identity of Shakespeare's 'Mr W.H.' that was so erudite and amusing that I took the trouble of making his acquaintance when I next found myself in New York. There I was surprised to learn that he regarded Shakespeare scholarship only as a sideline – his uncle happened to be the Shakespeare scholar Leslie Hotson and the book sprang out of an argument with him. Donald Hotson's major interest was quantum theory and its bearing on cosmology. When I returned to England, he sent me the typescript of a book called *Virtual Quantum Reality*.

If the Shakespeare book had impressed me, this left me stunned. Short, clearly written, with a dry humour reminiscent of Mark Twain, it argued that Einstein was probably wrong – not just about the Copen-hagen Interpretation, but about virtually everything.

Now my friend Martin Gardner, in a book called *Fads and Fallacies in the Name of Science*, had argued that Einstein is the happy hunting ground of half-educated cranks, and that anyone who tries to disprove Einstein is a crank by definition. But Hotson was clearly no nut. His temperament was closer to that of Charles Fort, except that he knew far more about physics.

He began with Maxwell's discovery that light is a form of electromag-netic energy, and his assumption that the waves of this energy are carried by a medium called the 'ether', which permeates all space, although it cannot be detected. In 1897, two physicists named Mich-elson and Morley reasoned that if the Earth is passing through this ether like a ship through water, there ought to be an 'ether wind' whistling past us. To detect this, they shot one beam of light across the ether wind and back, and another up and down it for the same distance. Simple mathematics shows that a swimmer who goes up a river and back takes longer than he would take to swim the same distance across the river and back. The difference between the two times should have revealed how fast the ether wind was blowing. In fact, the experiment detected no ether wind whatever.

A Dutch physicist named Hendrik Lorentz was not discouraged by this. In 1904, he made the suggestion that perhaps our Earth itself is a huge 'standing wave' in the ether – a suggestion that nowadays makes far more sense than it did then, since we know our Earth is made of electrons, which *are* waves (until observation turns them into particles).

At this point, Einstein produced his Special Theory of Relativity. It sprang out of the thought that if he was sitting astride a beam of light, and travelling away from the clock in the Berne main square, the time would remain unchanged as he looked back. He went on to consider Maxwell's insistence that nothing could travel faster than light. But suppose you were sitting on the front of a train travelling at half the speed of light, and you shone a torch ahead of you, the torch beam surely *had* to be travelling at one and a half times the speed of light?

Not so, said Einstein. Something's got to give. And that something is time – or rather, space-time (for in the theory of relativity, space and time no longer have separate identities). For a train travelling at such a speed, space-time would distort in such a way that light would be found to travel at its usual speed.

In Einstein's theory, the ether also becomes unnecessary, for the negative results of the Michelson–Morley experiment are now explainable as a distortion of space-time. This, of course, still leaves the question of what light waves are 'waving' in. But, since Einstein thought light consisted of particles, that question did not arise. And, once quantum theory began to talk about 'wave mechanics', the question had been forgotten . . .

What Hotson is arguing is that the old ether theory made more sense. Lorentz thought the Michelson–Morley experiment failed because matter itself is made of waves, which contract in the direction of motion, and Michelson and Morley's apparatus would contract enough to nullify the result – a notion that is consistent with quantum theory. As it was, Einstein dispensed with the ether, and declared that all motion is relative. In the nineteenth century, physicists talked about some basically fixed reference point against which all motion could be measured – Ernst Mach, for example, suggested the stars. In 1869, Carl Neumann suggested calling the fixed reference system 'the body alpha'. Einstein threw all that into the bin, and said that all reference systems – trains, planets, stars – are equivalent.

Hotson argues that this was a fundamental error. He cites, for example, E.W. Silvertooth's 1989 'Michelson–Morley' experiment with a revolving laser apparatus, which showed that the wavelength of light varies with its direction, and which also registered the fact that the solar system is moving towards the constellation Leo. But, according to Einstein, it should make no difference if you measured the speed of light on a roller coaster moving at 10 million miles an hour – all reference systems should give exactly the same result.

Einstein went on to create the General Theory of Relativity, in which gravity is regarded as a warp in space. I have to admit that, as a teenager, I found it hard to understand this explanation, which was apparently proved in the eclipse of 1919 when light rays were shown to bend in the sun's gravitational field. But, if light consists of particles as well as waves, I felt, that is what you would expect. I was gratified to find that Hotson expresses the same doubts.

After that, he moves on to zero-point energy. When Dirac's mathematics appeared to reveal an antiparticle called the positron, and it was subsequently detected in the laboratory, he sugggested the existence of a great sea of energy pervading empty space – in effect, a sea of 'shadow electrons'. Now and then, something boosts the energy of a shadow electron so it becomes real, and leaves a kind of hole in empty space, called a positron.

This also answered the question of why electrons do not lose all their energy and collapse in on the nucelus of the atom. That basic level is already occupied by this vast sea of energy.

Hotson goes on to cite experiments that seem to show that Einstein was wrong about the speed of light. In 1921 the physicist Walter von Nernst predicted that light should lose tiny amounts of energy to the ether as it travelled through it. And, a few years later, Edwin Hubble noticed that light from the most distant stars is redder than that from closer stars. This 'red shift' seemed to show that the stars were moving away at a tremendous speed – the most distant at thirteen per cent of the speed of light. It looks as if the universe was exploding. But, if Nernst was correct, then light loses energy naturally as it travels long distances – particularly through 'empty space' that is seething with zero-point energy. As Hotson remarks, if your mother calls you out of the window, and her voice sounds faint, you do not assume she is travelling away from you: you assume her voice is attenuated by distance or the wind.

So, argues Hotson, the whole notion of the Big Bang becomes unnecessary. Some of the 'background hiss' of microwaves – particularly the higher frequencies – that astronomers believed to be a remnant of the Big Bang can also be explained as a consequence of zero-point energy, which makes a hiss in all microwave receivers; while, in a book called *The Big Bang Never Happened*, Eric Lerner points out that cosmic dust and microfilaments of plasma absorb and retransmit microwaves at a lower frequency.

On these basic assumptions, Hotson goes on to develop a bold theory of 'virtual quantum reality', which has something in common with Bohm's idea of the holographic universe. Unfortunately, discussing it in detail would take up more space than I have available.

Since Hotson quoted Hal Puthoff as his authority on zero-point energy, and I had corresponded with him back in the days when he was testing Uri Geller, I wrote to Hal to ask for his paper on ZPE. In reply, he sent me a dozen or so papers and popular articles that made me aware that I had been absurdly ignorant of an important development in modern physics.

Quantum theory led physicists to predict that particles would arise spontaneously in the vacuum, but would disappear before they could violate the uncertainty principle. This continuous appearance and disappearance of particles explains why the zero-point vacuum is often referred to as zero-point fluctuation.

The papers answered one obvious question: whether there is any proof that the zero-point energy exists? The answer is yes. If two metal plates are placed very close together, some force draws them into contact. This is because many waves in the zero-point vacuum are the wrong size to fit between the plates, so the radiation pressure outside is greater than inside, and pushes the plates together. It is known as 'the Casimir force'.

The physicist Willis Lamb noted another effect of the zero-point energy. When electrons jump from one orbit to another, it shows up in the frequency lines of the spectrum. Lamb noted a slight shift in frequency, due to the fact that electrons were 'jiggled' slightly in their orbit by zero-point energy (which produces a kind of jitter – or vibration).

In the early 1980s, the Soviet physicist Andrei Sakharov made the startling suggestion that the ZPE might be the true cause of gravity. As the two plates are drawn together by the Casimir force, it looks as if they are being pulled by gravity. Puthoff writes:

A particle sitting in the sea of electromagnetic zero-point fluctuations develops a 'jitter' motion ... When there are two or more particles, they are each not only influenced by the fluctuating background field, but also by the fields generated by the other particles, all similarly undergoing jitter motion. The coupling between particles due to these fields produces the attractive gravitational force.

Puthoff went on to develop the mathematics of the notion that not only gravity, but also the force we call inertia, is due to the jitter motion. Inertia is the tendency of things at rest to remain at rest, and of things in motion to remain in motion. You experience it if you try to move a heavy table, which takes a great push to get it started.

We take that so much for granted that Galileo was the first to notice it. But Newton realised that it was a real problem, like gravity. It is easy to suppose that it *is* the force of gravity that makes it hard to push a table, but that cannot be so, for if you take a bucket of water, and swing it in an arc above your head, the water will stay in the bucket even though gravity should pull it downward. This is inertia.

In 1993, Puthoff, together with his colleagues Bernhard Haisch and Alfonso Rueda, produced a paper called 'Inertia as a zero-point Lorentz force', arguing that inertia could also be due to zero-point energy, which resists the acceleration of energy through it. It came to the attention of

Arthur C. Clarke, who used it in his novel *3001* (1997), in which interstellar travel is accomplished by something called the SHARP drive, the letters standing for Sakharov, Haisch, Rueda and Puthoff. Clarke explains that Puthoff and his colleagues answered the question, 'What gives an object mass (or inertia) so that it requires an effort to start it moving?' by saying that both inertia and gravitation are electromagnetic phenomena resulting from interaction with the zero-point-energy field.

One zero-point-energy theorist, Timothy Boyer, has even developed a classical version of zero-point-energy physics, which he calls stochastic electrodynamics (meaning random), and has reproduced many results so far thought to require quantum mechanics, and is steadily adding new ones. So it looks as if quantum theory is still in a bewildering state of flux, and that anyone who dared to predict where it would go next would be insane.

If we look back to the science of the late nineteenth century, the present state of affairs seems unbelievable. Who could have foreseen that so much chaos could spring out of Planck's suggestion that energy might come in packets? From the perspective of the 1890s, it looked as if science had solved most of the major problems, and would soon clear up the few that remained. Geology had shown that earth was millions of years old, and the theory of evolution had explained how man came on the scene. The cathode-ray tube had led to the discovery of X-rays, then of the electron. Hertz had discovered radio waves and Bell invented the telephone.

All this explains why T.H. Huxley felt he could not 'get up an interest' in psychical research; it seemed totally irrelevant. Science would achieve the millennium without these remnants from a superstitious past.

A century later, scientists were still inclined to dismiss the paranormal as a superstition. At a meeting of the American Association for the Advancement of Science in 1979, John Wheeler called for the paranormal researchers, whom he called 'pseudos', to be 'driven out of the temple of science'. Yet it was this same John Wheeler who suggested that the universe does not exist until we observe it, and whose student Hugh Everett argued that there must be billions of parallel universes – ideas that Huxley would have regarded as even more outrageous than a belief in ghosts and spirits.

We have encountered this notion of parallel realities elsewhere in this book – such as Vallee's comment that 'the UFOs may not come from ordinary space, but from a multiverse which is all around us', or Air Marshall Dowding's suggestion that UFOs 'could be creations of an invisible world coincident with the space of our physical earth . . .' John Keel believes that UFOs 'move into our spatial and time coordinates' by 'gearing down from the higher frequencies', and into our colour spectrum. Again and again, there is the suggestion that some other reality exists on a level that is somehow parallel to ours, *but on a different vibration rate.*

Now this suggestion was first made, as far as I know, by a retired Cambridge don named T.C. Lethbridge, who had been keeper of the Anglo-Saxon Antiquities Museum. As an archaeologist, Tom Lethbridge had soon recognised the curious fact that a dowsing rod can not only detect underground water, but buried artefacts. This sounds absurd; for while we can believe that our bodies possess some natural device, inherited from our remote ancestors, for detecting water, it is far harder to understand why a forked twig should respond to solid objects. But Lethbridge found that it did, and used it constantly in his archaeological work for detecting potsherds, bronze artefacts and agricultural implements.

He also found that a pendulum – a piece of string with some sort of bob at the end – would do just as well. And, when he retired to Devon in 1957, the eccentric old lady who lived next door told him that the pendulum would respond to different substances according to the length of the string. Being incorrigibly scientific by temperament, he lost no time in conducting a long series of precise experiments.

What he did was to take some specific substance – like copper – and dangle over it a pendulum whose string was wound around a pencil, and could be lengthened or shortened. When the length of the string reached thirty and a half inches, the pendulum went into a circular swing. Silver was twenty-two inches, gold twenty-nine, tin twenty-eight. When he tried it in his back yard, it soon located a small copper tube. He discovered that truffles respond at seventeen inches, and used it to locate a truffle in his garden.

He wondered if these various substances give off some distinct vibration, which is picked up by the body, like a radio signal. But he finally came to agree with Sir William Barrett, the founder of the Society for Psychical Research, and Professor Charles Richet, another eminent psychical researcher, that it is the *mind* of the searcher to which the pendulum responds, and the mind that somehow 'picks up' the substance by somehow tuning in to it.

Now it is worth pausing to look at this a little more closely. I am not a particularly good dowser, yet even I know that a dowsing rod or pendulum responds as precisely as an ammeter does to a current. Any good dowser can detect, say, coins hidden under a carpet. What is more odd is that, if he places a mixture of copper and silver coins under the carpet, he can pick out which is which; if he 'tunes in' to copper, his rod will ignore the silver coins, and vice versa.

Even more odd is the ability of some people to hold an object in their hands and 'sense' its history. It was discovered (and exhaustively investigated) in the nineteenth century by Professor Joseph Rodes Buchanan, who labelled it 'psychometry', and it has since been the subject of hundreds of investigations by paranormal researchers. This is obviously simply a more sophisticated version of the ability that enables a dowser to respond to silver or copper coins.[5]

Lethbridge soon realised that the pendulum was simply responding to some unknown power of the mind. In which case, it ought to respond to thoughts as well as things. He tried it, thinking clearly of such notions as love, anger, jealousy, even evolution, and found that the pendulum again responded to each at a distinct rate. It responded to 'death' at forty inches, which seemed to be the pendulum's limit.

Sometimes, several substances – and ideas – shared the same vibrational rate, so that at ten inches the pendulum responded to graphite, milk, fire, the colour red and the direction east. But each item was characterised by the number of times the pendulum gyrated in a circle.

What would happen if he extended it beyond forty? He tried and found that it simply started all over again, merely adding forty to all the previous 'rates'. There was one difference. Held over a piece of copper – for example – it would not react directly above it, but slightly to one side. Why? Lethbridge speculated that, since forty was the 'rate' for death, the pendulum might be registering some realm beyond death where, for some reason, objects register as slightly displaced – like a pencil appearing bent in a glass of water. (People who have experienced OBEs often report that they find themselves above and slightly to one side of their bodies – as in the case of Beth Collings mentioned on p. 183.)

Beyond eighty inches, the same thing happened. All the rates were repeated plus eighty. Lethbridge concluded that there were probably

[5] See my book *The Psychic Detectives*.

any number of 'parallel realities' which could be detected if the pendulum could be made long enough.

These realities, Lethbridge came to believe, exist parallel with our own. They are around us all the time, but undetectable because they are on different vibrational rates. He cites an Indian tribe who believe that invisible people live among us.

It was not until *The Legend of the Sons of God*, the last of the ten books published in his lifetime (he died in 1971), that Lethbridge wrote about UFOs. He had seen a UFO as early as 1931 – a typical 'ball of light'; driving through a heavy rainstorm, he glanced down a lane, and saw a shining disc or globe, about three feet across, descending towards the road. Since it was raining heavily, he drove on without stopping. The reports of post-1947 UFO sightings led him to conclude that Earth has probably been visited by 'aliens' in the remote past, although he speculated that they may have been from 'another dimension', separated from us by its vibration rate. (We may recall Linda Porter's comments to Linda Howe: 'There are countless different worlds/dimensions occupying the same space without being aware of one another, because of having their own individual octaves.')

Lethbridge knew little about physics; if he had, he would have realised that his own speculations were converging with those of modern science. We now know that there is no such thing as matter – only energy. Zero-point-energy theory tells us that there is no such thing as empty space, only surging tides of energy. But quantum theory tells us that there is one more vital component in the universe, mind, and that mind seems to be able to somehow freeze waves into particles, or energy into matter. Mind does not seem to be part of the energy system, but somehow separate from it and above it, as indicated by the fact that Lethbridge found that the pendulum responded to different vibration rates, but that, where an abstraction was concerned, he had to clearly envisage it in his mind before the pendulum responded. His unconscious mind was reaching out and looking for something, and, when it had found it, caused his muscles to respond and the pendulum or downsing rod to move.

In the same way, when he was dowsing for archaeological artefacts with a dowsing rod, the rod would respond to what he was looking for, and not to other things. It was the mind that selected, then tuned in, to the vibration, just as a radio tunes in to a station.

This also implies that human beings are continually bathed in moving tides of energies, which they can select, and, to some extent, control.

We have all noticed how some people leave us feeling drained, while others seem to revitalise us; this seems to indicate that, without even being aware of it, human beings can exert some kind of unconscious control over vital energies, and possess some of the powers once attributed to vampires.

So even our science is beginning to point towards a strange new conception of the universe: as vast tides of energy, inhabited by minds that can tune in to it, and exert some control over it. This energy somehow carries information, which explains how a psychometrist can 'sense' the history of an object.

It is clear that modern man has almost no conception of his power to tune in to these energies. Thousands of years of left-brain dominance have left him completely out of touch with them. And the extraordinary growth of science and technology has encouraged a feeling that he is merely a pawn in a game that is too big for him to understand. In the meantime, our culture has developed an overwhelmingly pessimistic tinge which has been characteristic of the past two centuries.

Now it so happens that this was the starting point of my own work. *The Outsider* (1956) was about the number of men of genius in the nineteenth century who committed suicide or died of illnesses induced by 'discouragement'. The reason was obvious. They would experience moods in which the whole universe seemed glorious, and in which they felt that life could be a continuous ecstasy. Then they would wake up the next morning, and wonder what on earth it had all been about. And, since reality was very obviously cold, hard and problematic, they would conclude that the vision had been an illusion, and sink into depression.

What was happening was that in these 'moments of vision' they were experiencing the universe as pure energy, the energy that excites us in Shelley's 'Ode to the West Wind' or in the poetry of Goethe:

> *Es schäumt das Meer in breiten Flüssen*
> *Am tiefen Grund der Felsen auf,*
> *Und Fels und Meer wird fortgerissen*
> *In ewig schnellem Sphärenlauf.*

And all the towering cliffs among
In spreading streams upfoams the ocean,

> And cliffs and sea are whirled along,
> With circling orbs in ceaseless motion.[6]

It is the energy that excites us in the music of Wagner or in Van Gogh's painting *The Starry Night*. Van Gogh enables us to see the essence of the tragedy. In the later painting, we can see that he is experiencing this overwhelming sense of universal energy – the grass and trees and even buildings seem to surge upward like flames. Yet after these visions he came back to a world of endless financial anxiety, and the feeling that he was a burden on his brother and sister-in-law. This is why he killed himself, and left a note saying, 'Misery will never end.' The vision seemed a lie.

What is more, science told him it was a lie. Huxley and Haeckel and Tyndall and the rest assured the romantics that the world could be explained in completely material terms, and that mind is a product of matter, in the same way as fire is a product of combustion.

Contemporary scentists like Richard Dawkins and Stephen Hawking tell us the same thing. The absurd thing is that science itself tells us the opposite. It tells us that the universe is not made of matter but of vibrations of energy, and that mind seems to have some incomprehensible role in determining how this energy reveals itself.

It seems incredible that no one so far has noticed it. But modern science is telling us that the vision of the nineteenth-century romantics was true, and that their notion that matter is cold, hard and unyielding is untrue. Goethe, Wagner, Van Gogh and the rest were sensing the underlying reality of the universe.

Unfortunately, they did not know this. It seemed to them quite simply that their visions of affirmation were illusions, and this thought plunged them into depression. The result was a mood of self-pity, which became the main theme of much of the most typical poetry and art of the 1890s. In the twentieth century, self-pity developed into a stoical 'realism' that was based upon acceptance of human weakness and vulnerability, and which culminated in the work of writers like Graham Greene, William Golding and Samuel Beckett – the last of these epitomising the notion that human life is totally pointless and meaningless.

All this is understandable. To Goethe and Shelley and Wagner and Van Gogh and Nietzsche, it seemed that their vision of surging energy was contradicted by the brute force of matter. Now we know this is

[6] *Faust*, Prologue, translated by A.G. Latham.

untrue. That vision of universal energy, and of the mind's power to enter into creative interaction with it, is an accurate perception of the underlying reality.

It also enables us to understand why dowsing and psychometry seem to work. The energies of the universe have been 'stamped' with meanings by previous events, and some part of our mind has the power to decode these meanings. The sense of meaninglessness that seems such a typical part of everyday experience – particularly when we are tired or depressed – is an illusion, due to the superficial nature of everyday consciousness. To look for 'meaning' with everyday consciousness is like going to an art gallery and trying to appreciate the pictures through a pair of binoculars.

The philosophers who take this meaninglessness as their starting point – Schopenhauer, Heidegger, Sartre, Foucault, Derrida – are quite simply wrong. The most urgent necessity at the moment is to create a new philosophy based upon the recognition of underlying meaning.

Now let us look again at the problem of UFOs from the standpoint of this new understanding of the nature of reality.

It explains, to begin with, some of their paradoxical behaviour: their ability to appear out of nowhere, to defy the laws of inertia by changing direction at tremendous speeds, to disappear in one part of the sky and reappear simultaneously in another. Our chief mistake lies in thinking of UFOs as craft like our own space probes when all the evidence suggests that they are unknown energy forms.

And what about the entities who control them? We have seen again and again how those who have experienced 'close encounters' have felt that their powers far surpass our own. Human beings seem to be as helpless in their hands as babies. They can apparently make us do what they like, then wipe the memory clean. Yet although encounters with them can be downright unpleasant, there seems to be a general agreement that they are not malevolent or hostile. They simply seem to regard us as we would regard Neanderthals.

But one thing ought by now to be clear. It is not they who see us as Neanderthals: it is *we* who regard ourselves as Neanderthals compared with them. If this book has tried to make one thing clear, it is that human beings possess powers of which they are unaware.

So, from the point of view of the UFO entities, the human race is a species that is about to make the transition to a state that our visitors have already reached. I would argue that the evidence suggests that their purpose is to help us to make that transition.

We may note Brian O'Leary's comment that 'through their experiences, an ever increasing number of people are telling us we are on a collision course with a destiny far beyond our conscious minds', and Vallee's conclusion that UFO phenomena 'have had an impact on a part of the human mind we have not discovered'. He goes on to suggest that the phenomena are 'one of the ways through which an alien form of intelligence of incredible complexity is communicating with us *symbolically*'.

Again, we have also seen, in an earlier chapter, how Hawkins has predicted that man is on the point of a new 'mindstep to the cosmos.' Mindstep 1 towards understanding his universe was mythology. Mindstep 2 was early astronomy. Mindstep 3 was the Copernican revolution, aided by the printing press. Mindstep 4 was the modern space age, with its attempt at a 'theory of everything'. And the next mindstep, Hawkins speculates, could be a new technology for exploring the universe, or a contact with extraterrestrial civilisations.

But if these aliens are really extraterrestrials, or even interdimensionals from parallel worlds, why do they not tilt the balance by making their presence known so positively that no one could doubt it?

None of the ufologists I have quoted in this book has addressed this question – except for the occasional hint that downright interference in human affairs is somehow 'not allowed'. But why not? And not allowed by whom?

One of the few plausible attempts to answer these questions was made by the novelist Ian Watson, best known for his *tour de force, The Embedding* (1973), which has claims to be one of the best sciencefiction novels ever written. But *Miracle Visitors* displays a grasp of the UFO phenomenon that reveals someone who not merely studied it, but has tried to find an answer to the mystery.

The central character is a professor of psychology named Deacon, who has edited a book on the subject of consciousness. One of his students, Michael Peacocke, has seen a UFO on a Yorkshire moor, and experienced 'missing time'. Under hypnosis, Michael recalls being taken on board, and induced to have sex with a blonde alien who introduces herself as Loova. One of the aliens tells him that they are from a planet called Ulro. Deacon happens to know that Loova and Ulro can be found in William Blake's prophetic books, and assumes that Michael's abduction is simply an expression of his unconscious sexual urges.

Weird events ensue, most of them based on actual reports. The professor's dog is beheaded. Michael's girlfriend has a terrifying encounter with an alien, followed by a visit from men in black, and has a nervous breakdown. An Egyptian mystic has an encounter with Khidr, Master of the Saints, also known as the Green Man. Later, Michael has further UFO encounters which culminate in a visit to an alien base on the far side of the moon, accompanied by Deacon and an American investigator.

The climax of the novel occurs after the three have returned to Earth, and are separated in the Mojave Desert of California. There Deacon also encounters the Green Man, and has a mystical revelation about evolution:

> For all these inaccessibilities caused a fierce suction towards even higher patterns of organisation, towards higher comprehension. So molecules became long-chain molecules, and these became replicating cells that transmitted information . . . till mind evolved, a higher mind.
>
> The universe, he realised, was an immense *simulation*: of itself, by itself. It was a registering of itself, a progressive observation of itself from ever higher points of view. Each higher order was inaccessible to the lower order, yet each lower order was drawn towards the higher – teased by the suction of the higher.

Absorbed into this higher order, Deacon suddenly becomes aware that it was *he* who cut off his dog's head, failing to recognise that his touch could be fatal. He was the blonde woman who seduced Michael. He was the alien who caused Michael's girlfriend to have a nervous breakdown. As to why UFOs do not interfere more directly:

> There was a plus and minus factor at work too, he saw. When you inject a higher-order knowledge, something must change within the lower-order reality or be lost to it, to compensate. The trick was to make the loss the least negative one possible – to create merely mystery, not damage. UFO intrusions all too often scared the wits out of people, maimed them, slew animals, stole flesh and blood. 'You had to pay the Devil . . .' But really, the UFO wisdom was an awareness of the universe thinking itself, causing itself, evolving itself.

'To create merely mystery, not damage.' In other words, the mystery is essential, to open up the way to the perception of higher-order knowledge. More positive intervention would be self-defeating, since the aim is to persuade human beings to take the crucial step themselves. Every schoolteacher knows that education can achieve its real purpose only by making the pupil *want* to learn. The aim is to lure free will into expressing itself and recognising its own existence.

An equally striking view of 'UFO reality' has been expressed by Ralph Noyes, a Vice-President of the Society for Psychical Research and the editor of one of the first books on crop circles, in a novel called *A Secret Property* (1985). Noyes was a high-ranking civil servant, and the novel reflects his knowledge of the workings of government. Set in the Cold War era, it concerns attempts by the Russian and Western governments to make use of psychics for military purposes. It is based on the notion that Earth is surrounded not only by what Teilhard de Chardin called the biosphere – the living envelope of life – but by a 'psychosphere', an envelope of supersensible realities.

> Whipped up into local vortices, [the psychosphere] whirled saucer djinns into the innocent lives of a farmer in the Brazilian uplands, a housewife on the outskirts of Buenos Aires, a couple of vacationing Americans in Venezuela. It had not quite reached the force at which it would turn them into the blue-electric torches of spontaneous combustion. It merely singed their hair, arrested their vehicles, sucked them into saucer visions, gouged up the earth into traces which would remain, for ever, not quite evidential enough for a court of law.

Noyes is suggesting that UFO phenomena may not always be deliberately engineered: they may be meteorological eruptions from the psychosphere. He is also suggesting that spontaneous human combustion may also be one of its manifestations. The psychosphere, Noyes feels, is a realm whose laws we do not even begin to understand.

Another English writer, Patrick Harpur, believes that behind our material reality there is a 'daimonic reality', and, in a book of that title (1994), he argues that UFO phenomena can be understood only in the same terms as apparitions, fairies, religious visions and the 'other world' of the shamans. His thesis has much in common with Vallee's *Passport to Magonia*, but draws its evidence from a wider range of examples, and argues that the underlying reality of the universe is what Plato called *anima mundi*, the soul of the world.

In 1992, in an article for a Japanese magazine, I had made my own attempt to formulate an answer to the problem:

> More than twenty years of psychical research have led me to the conclusion that there is a 'psychic reality' which runs *parallel* to our physical reality. Ghosts, demons, poltergeists, fairies, even 'vampires', are incursions from this 'other reality' into our own. Like the human race, the denizens of this other realm probably change and evolve, so their methods of drawing attention to themselves also change and evolve.
>
> In ancient times, there were simply ghosts, believed to be spirits of the dead. In the Middle Ages came poltergeists. In the 17th century there were vampires. In the 19th century, there were all kinds of 'spirit communicators.' In the second half of the 20th century there are UFOs. In the 21st century, there will probably be some new wave of 'strange phenomena' which at present we cannot even imagine.
>
> Do these phenomena have a 'purpose?' That is impossible to say; but one thing is very clear: that their effect is to remind human beings that their material world is not the only reality. We are surrounded by mystery that cannot be understood in terms of scientific materialism. If psychic phenomena have a purpose, it is to wake us up from our 'dogmatic slumber', and galvanise us to evolve a higher form of consciousness.

The only sentence with which I would now take issue is the one about the twenty-first century, which implies that UFOs are simply another type of psychic phenomenon from this 'parallel reality'. Now I would say that their purpose is not simply to remind us that the material world is not the only reality, but to draw us by a kind of suction into consciousness of another kind of reality.

Imagine that you are a Martian, or a being from another star system, and that you are paying a visit to Earth to check on the green planet's evolution. Your predecessors had noted the progress of this upright, humanoid creature, so much more intelligent than his nearest relative, the ape. But the real distinction is that these humans are religious. All living creatures have a vague perception of a supernatural realm, but man's perception means that he sees the world around him peopled with spirits. Mountains fill him with a sense of awe; so do lakes and forests. There is no evidence that gorillas or horses feel that way.

When the cosmic expedition reaches Earth (about a hundred thousand years ago), its scientists are pleased to discover that the most intelligent creature on the planet is a type of man that we call Neanderthal (after the valley in Germany where his skull was later discovered). Neanderthal is small, and prefers to live in caves. He is known to eat his own kind – not for food, but because he thinks he takes on the vitality of his enemy. He has strong family feelings, and takes care of old and infirm members of the tribe. Above all, he worships the dead, whom he buries with elaborate ritual involving woven carpets of flowers. And, because the red clay called ochre is the colour of blood (due to iron oxide), he holds it in the same high regard as we feel for gold. In fact, he mines it from the ground – with appropriate rituals to propitiate the mountain gods – and later reseals it with more apologies to the gods. But, although one variety of Neanderthal hunts with the bow and arrow, he is not deeply intelligent. His lack of organisation is revealed in his cave dwellings, which are piled high with bones and other refuse. His brain is large – far larger than modern man's – probably because his social life is so rich and complex; but he cannot be said to use it much.

Sixty thousand years later, the Martians pay us another routine visit. This time, things look much more promising. The gentle, bumbling Neanderthal has been driven out by a newcomer who is more aggressive, and, in one vital respect, more intelligent. This is our ancestor, Cro-Magnon man, whose emergence has been so swift that the space visitors wonder if some previous expedition has been experimenting with a little genetic engineering.

What is so fascinating about this new man is that he has taken the one vital step that makes him truly human, and discovered science. Of course, we would not call it science, but 'magic', for his shamans play a vital role in his hunting activities: they make drawings of bison, deer and other animals on the walls of his caves, then perform a ritual which involves dressing up in a deer skin with antlers, and leading a ritual dance. Oddly enough, this actually works, removing a great deal of the element of chance from hunting. (Lethbridge would say that the shaman was simply locating the prey through some form of divination; but Cro-Magnon man undoubtedly believed he was drawing the prey into an ambush, and he may have been right.) This is why the Cro-Magnon population has increased in size, and why our ancestor has displaced the Neanderthals.

We can see that what was so important was that Cro-Magnon man had developed a new attitude to life. Animals feel helpless and vulnerable, accepting their lot and making no effort to escape it. They are not even capable of the thought of controlling the world around them. But this new type of man believed that his shamans had miraculous powers, and could intercede directly with the gods. The shamans – as we would expect – had become their tribal chieftains. So Cro-Magnon man no longer had the sheeplike acceptance of his destiny that characterised Neanderthal. He was beginning to develop the feeling that H.G. Wells caught in the phrase, 'If you don't like your life you can change it.'

This looks so promising that the visitors begin making more frequent checks, and even offer a little occasional instruction. (The humans, of course, regard them as gods.) But when they return about seventeen thousand years ago, and discover that civilisation is beginning to flourish, they become aware of a new problem. These simple people are not yet ready for civilisation. And this is due to a law that might be called the Law of Complication, which states that success brings expansion, and expansion brings complication. When that happens, life loses its spontaneity, and becomes an endless, exhausting struggle against complication. The same problem would later cause the downfall of the Persian and the Roman Empires.

What has almost certainly happened is that their shamans have achieved such power that small tribes have been absorbed by large ones, and 'civilisation' (which means literally 'citification') has become inevitable. But since it is still based on religion and magic, and its leaders are not ready for such full-scale expansion, the experiment is doomed to failure. There is evidence to suggest that, in fact, it ended with a geological catastrophe which scattered the survivors all over the world – particularly to Egypt and South America.[7]

The next attempt at civilisation, beginning about twelve thousand years ago, is altogether more successful. Man rediscovered agriculture, built cities, and developed writing. Ancient Egypt was the most successful civilisation so far, and this was largely due to its obsession with religion, as well as to its fortunate geographical position, with mountains on three sides to defend it from enemies. It was rather like an

[7] See my book, *From Atlantis to the Sphinx*, 1996

enormous village, whose ends are connected by the Nile, and its hier-archical structure, with the pharaoh regarded as a god, and the priests as its aristocracy, created the highest level of peace and prosperity humankind has ever known.

This could not last. Even in 2000 BC, the modern world was moving too fast for a theocracy.

At some point in history, man became a 'left brainer' – that is, the rational part of the brain became the dominant hemisphere, relegating the intuitive part to a supporting role. Julian Jaynes, in his book *The Origin of Consciousness in the Breakdown of the Bicameral Mind* (1976), has suggested a fairly precise date – around 1250 BC. Jaynes believes that, during the tremendous wars that convulsed the Middle East after 2000 BC, human beings were forced to acquire a new ruthless-ness and efficiency in order to survive. He believes that this 'change of mind' came about in Mesopotamia. Kings up to this point were regarded as gods, and carvings show them sitting on a throne beside the god. But a carving of 1250 BC shows the Assyrian king Tukulti-Ninurti kneeling in front of the *empty* throne of the god. Man is suddenly trapped in the left brain, and has lost touch with the divine. A cuneiform text of the period contains the lines:

> One who has no god, as he walks along the street
> Headache envelops him like a garment.

Jaynes may or may not be correct about when it happened. I am inclined to suspect that left-brain awareness developed slowly and inevitably with the coming of the cities. What matters is that it always produces the same effect. When the logical brain operates without the backup of its intuitive companion, life loses its richness, and we become subject to irritability and tension.

But that brings a certain compensation. Since the left brain's purpose is to 'cope' with everyday life and 'scan' it for problems, the narrower left-brain awareness permits long periods of concentration on small things. And concentration on small things is the foundation of science and technology. In due course, these became the foundation of modern civilisation.

But left-brain awareness has one enormous drawback. Being limited and obsessive, it narrows the range of consciousness. When we are happy and relaxed (that is, in a 'right-brain' state), we have a sense of 'meanings beyond' the present moment. When we are trapped in left-brain awareness, we lose all sense of 'meanings beyond'. We feel that this – the present moment – is all there is.

So our cosmic visitors would have noted that the human race has entered a kind of spiritual cul-de-sac, an evolutionary dead end. Left-brain dominance would lead to technological achievement and the 'conquest of nature'. But it would also lead to a vague sense of frustration and dissatisfaction, since we know instinctively that technological achievement is not the real purpose of life.

Unfortunately, our blinkered left-brain awareness can see no other purpose. Driven on by its own momentum, it has achieved immense technological development, and the problems that go with it – over-population, the endless proliferation of cities, and pollution of the environment.

But these are only the symptoms. Our visitors would be able to understand the deep, underlying problem: that, when the left brain feels there is nothing to 'scan', it tends to sink into a kind of hypnosis. We call it 'boredom', but it is more than that. It is a kind of judgment on the universe, a feeling that no effort is worth making.

The odd thing is that, when we are galvanised by a sense of emergency, it suddenly becomes obvious that it is perfectly easy to concentrate our energies. Hans Keller, the former head of BBC music, once described how, in prewar Germany, when he was in danger of being arrested and sent to a concentration camp, he prayed: 'Oh God, let me get out of Germany, and I swear I'll never be unhappy again.' It seemed obvious that, once this crisis was behind him, he could be happy all the time. And Graham Greene's 'whiskey priest', in *The Power and the Glory*, suddenly recognises, as he stands before a firing squad, 'how easy it would have been to be a saint'. Dr Johnson went to the heart of the matter when he said, 'When a man knows he is to be hanged in a fortnight, it concentrates his mind wonderfully.'

Why is it so hard to keep the mind concentrated, and to live up to our good resolutions? The problem is the basically *mechanical* nature of left-brain consciousness. We have a kind of robot servant who does things for us: we learn to type or drive a car, painfully and consciously, then our robot takes over, and does it far more quickly and efficiently. Because man is the most complex creature on Earth, he is forced to rely on his robot far more than other animals. The result is that, whenever he gets tired, the robot takes over. For the modern city dweller, most of his everyday living is done by the robot. This is why it takes an emergency to concentrate the mind 'wonderfully', and why we forget so quickly.

The problem of living with permanent low-pressure consciousness is that we forget what real consciousness is like. We all experience it in flashes, perhaps in what Abraham Maslow calls 'peak experiences', when we are flooded with sudden delight, or on spring mornings, when everything seems marvellously real and alive. But we then accept it as a kind of freak. Low-pressure consciousness seems, on the whole, more 'normal'. The trouble is that low pressure tends to prolong itself, because it can see no reason to do otherwise. When you are staring blankly in front of you, thoroughly bored and discouraged, you find it very difficult to see any reason to make an effort. It seems easier just to sit and stare. This is why the human race is marking time at its present stage of evolution.

Religion, on the other hand, has a tradition of high-pressure con-sciousness. That is why yogis sit cross-legged, focusing and concentrating the attention. That is why monks spend hours on their knees in prayer. That is why ascetics devote their lives to meditation. It gives them a glimpse of higher levels of *power* which make ordinary living seem futile by comparison.

Now it seems clear that our 'alien' visitors have long since risen beyond the stage of evolution in which humankind finds itself trapped. Many contactees have received the impression that they are in the presence of a more highly developed form of life. It also seems logical to assume that, at some stage, they went through the phase in which the human race now finds itself. If we could begin to formulate some notion of how they managed to find their way beyond it, we might begin to see our own way out of the cul-de-sac.

The answer is, I believe, more straightforward than we might assume. In fact, it is already inherent in what has been said already. The problem with left-brain consciousness is, quite simply, that it is inclined to *leak*. When we are driven by a deep sense of purpose, our energies become focused and concentrated. When we try to spread our attention over a dozen complications, it loses pressure, and half the energy dribbles away. Left-brain consciousness is like a leaky pump that seldom works at more than 50 per cent efficiency.

We have all noticed how, when things begin to go wrong, we experi-ence a sinking of the heart, which is actually a sinking of inner pressure. When this happens, things begin to get worse because a kind of feedback loop sets in.

On the other hand, we have all experienced those times when everything seems to be going right, and we have a curious certainty that they will continue to go right. *It is as if we knew that the mind somehow controls what happens to us.*

Goethe's friend Eckermann once pointed out to him that he had been born with a silver spoon in his mouth, and asked how he would have felt if he had been less lucky. Goethe replied contemptuously, 'Do you suppose I would have been such a fool as to be born unlucky?' He obviously felt that there is a sense in which our mental attitudes govern what happens to us.

Jung was implying the same thing when he coined the word 'synchronicity'. And Vallee's Melchizedek story (p. 115) underlines the point. It is almost impossible to dismiss the encounter with the only Melchizedek in the Los Angeles phone directory as mere coincidence. Vallee suggests that the universe may be constructed more like a computer with its random database (i.e. where information is conjured up by the correct word) than a library with its alphabetical order. But that still does not explain how he found a taxi driver whose surname was that of the cult he was researching. Here we are dealing with the same kind of puzzle as in the case of Lethbridge and dowsing. And the answer to that puzzle seemed to be that we are living in an 'information universe', where information is somehow encoded into energy, and is accessible to the mind. In which case, Vallee may have 'retrieved' his taxi driver as I can retrieve a computer file by typing in the right word, or as Lethbridge could retrieve information about underground artefacts with his pendulum, or as a psychometrist can 'retrieve' the history of an object by holding it. Or, for that matter, as a 'remote viewer' can find his way to some distant site by using an arbitrarily assigned code. But a solid female taxi driver is obviously quite a different thing from a computer file or a piece of information, and we need to formulate some very strange theories to explain how it could happen.

Whatever the explanation, the implications remain the same: that the mind – without knowing it consciously – has some sort of control over the material universe.

But how could human beings begin to achieve a conscious grasp of this control?

We must try to grasp what is wrong with us at present: that human consciousness habitually operates on half-pressure, and consequently loses half its energy in 'leakage'. When we operate on full pressure –

as, for example, when some emergency galvanises us to determined effort – we begin to glimpse the real possibilities of consciousness.

William James approached the problem in a little book called *The Energies of Men* (1899), in which he remarks:

> Everyone is familiar with the phenomenon of feeling more or less alive on different days. Everyone knows that on any given day there are energies slumbering in him which the incitements of that day do not call forth, but which he might display if these were greater. Most of us feel as if a sort of cloud weighed upon us ... Compared to what we ought to be, we are only half awake. Our fires are damped, our drafts are checked. We are making use of only a small part of our mental and physical resources ... There seems no doubt that *we are each and all of us to some extent victims of habit-neurosis* ... We live subject to degrees of fatigue that we have come only from habit to obey. Most of us may learn to push the barrier farther off, and to live in perfect comfort on much higher levels of power.

And he goes on to note that, when people have achieved this higher degree of will-drive, 'the transformation ... is a chronic one: the new level of energy becomes permanent'.

This is clearly getting altogether closer to the transformation we are talking about.

Another oddity about the human mind was noted by the philosopher Fichte: 'To be free is nothing; to *become* free is heaven.' Everyone must have noticed what it is to lie in bed on a frezing winter morning, when you have to get up in ten minutes, and the bed has never seemed so warm and comfortable. Yet when you can lie in bed as long as you like on a Saturday morning, you cannot recapture that delicious warmth and comfort. You have *too much* freedom.

What happens should be clear. When you have to get up in ten minutes, you *pay attention*, and close all your leaks. So you feel more alive and aware. When you can stay in bed as long as you like, you do *not* pay attention, and your 'robot' takes over.

This is connected with another main problem of human beings: our 'defeat proneness'. Difficulties not only cause the heart to sink: they often make us feel totally vulnerable. And, once life has got us on the run, difficulties seem to proliferate. This is a consequence of our tendency to 'leakage'.

On the other hand, once some powerful interest has made us close the leaks, we experience an increasing sense of inner pressure, and begin to feel curiously invulnerable. And suddenly it is as if we are standing at the beginning of the yellow brick road, with all kinds of fascinating prospects in front of us. This is quite clearly a glimpse of a different way of living, a way that no longer involves taking two steps forward and sliding two steps backward. For the past two centuries, from Goethe's *Werther* to Beckett's *Endgame*, the basic message of our culture has seemed to be 'You can't win'. But these states of non-leakage bring a breathtaking glimpse of the possibility that we *can* win.

I would suggest not only that many of the aliens we have encountered in this book are beings who have moved far beyond the stage in which humanity finds itself marking time, but that they originally moved beyond it by discovering the secret of closing the leaks and living on a level of higher inner pressure. But then, the same seems to apply to some of the unusual human beings – for example, the Tibetan lama Nyang-Pas, encountered by John Keel, who was able to hold a conversation while sitting in midair, and was able to read Keel's mind. He also explained to Keel how to practise 'travelling clairvoyance', which elsewhere in this book has been called remote viewing.

In fact, 'miraculous' powers are so commonplace among Hindu holy men that Ramakrishna warned his disciples against attaching any importance to them, since they are too easy to achieve, and can impede further progress.

I am, then, arguing that the UFO entities – or some of them – have passed beyond the 'leakage' stage of evolution, and have begun to learn what can be accomplished when consciousness is operated at full pressure – what should be 'normal' pressure. And certainly, there are enough examples of people who have encountered UFOs and experienced some kind of transformation. We may recall Vallee's engineer who spent three hours aboard a UFO, and found he has been away for eighteen days; he told Vallee that his powers of memory and concentration had been enormously enhanced, and that he was convinced that some immense change was about to take place on Earth. We may also recall 'Dr X', whose leg injury vanished after he had seen a UFO, and who told Vallee that he and his wife had become telepathic, that strange coincidences kept occurring, and that he had experienced levitation. There was also the Aveyron case, where the farmer's son began to have out-of-the-body experiences after seeing a UFO. Many other cases in this book – like John Spencer's Kathryn Howard, or the woman who saw a goat-footed man in an Oxford garden – leave no doubt that a UFO encounter can cause a basic change in awareness.

Moreover, it also seems likely that some of the incomprehensible operations performed on abductees are another method of inducing change. When Beth Collings asked a 'grey' why he was driving a needle into her navel, she was told, 'It is part of the change.' The same seems to apply to the instrument applied to the forehead of Anders, in the case described by John Spencer, and which left Anders with a deep sense of unity with Earth.

There is also considerable evidence for Budd Hopkins's suggestion that the entities are involved in some kind of breeding experiment. Hopkins has been accused of imposing this reading on his material. But there are too many other cases to take this objection seriously – for example, Hans Holzer's case of Shane Kurz, the virgin who in 1967 found herself pregnant after an abduction encounter, then ceased to be pregnant. This was a feature also described by Beth Collings and Anna Jamerson (see Chapter 7). Altering the human race by changing its breeding stock would seem to be another obvious method of bringing about evolutionary change.

Other cases – like that of Linda Cortile – point to a possibility even more startling: the notion that many human beings may be dual personalities, whose everyday selves are simply unaware that they have an alien alter ego. It would certainly be an interesting way to bring about change in the human species: to abduct thousands of individuals and 'engineer' their minds to turn them into part-aliens.

One of the most interesting of H.G. Wells's later novels, *Star Begotten* (1937), presented just such a notion. Its central character is a writer of popular history books who notices that more and more exceptional children are being born, and wonders if this might be caused by mutations due to cosmic rays. These children he calls 'Martians'. They seem to see the universe in a slightly different way from other people. They question accepted ideas.

The hero asks, 'Suppose there are beings, real material beings like ourselves, in another planet, but far wiser, more intelligent, much more highly developed . . . Suppose for the last few thousand years they have been experimenting in human genetics. Suppose they have been trying to alter mankind in some way, through the human genes.'

He has come to suspect that 'Martians' are deliberately bombarding Earth with cosmic rays. The idea disturbs him deeply. But when, at the end of the book, his wife asks whether he believes he is one of these 'fairy changelings', 'everything became coherent and plain to him. Everything fell into place.' Suddenly it is obvious to him that he *is* a Martian. And, as they look down at their sleeping baby, they know he will be a Martian too. (Significantly, their names are Joseph and Mary.)

But cosmic rays could hardly bring about the kind of change Wells has in mind. We now know that cosmic rays would not be a viable instrument for genetic engineering, being incapable of 'fine tuning'. A far more practical way of bringing about a 'change of mind' would be by altering the consciousness of individuals – as discussed above – and then relying on what Rupert Sheldrake has called 'morphogenetic fields' to spread the change. Studying the experiments of the psychologist William McDougal with white rats, Sheldrake noted that not only were the rats able to pass on their laboratory training to their offspring (thus challenging the dogma that 'acquired characteristics' cannot be inherited), but that other rats in the laboratory which had played no part in the experiment (the so-called 'control group') had also picked up the same learning – apparently by some form of telepathic induction. But it could not have been simply telepathy, because even crystals behaved in the same way. Some crystals are extremely difficult to crystal- lise in the laboratory; but once a single lot has been crystallised, others also crystallise more quickly, even in distant laboratories. Sheldrake suggested that this form of 'osmosis' was due to a kind of electrical induction, and called his theory 'the hypothesis of formative causation'.

There have been many experiments that have confirmed it. For example, English speakers memorised two rhymes in a foreign language, one of which was a well-known nursery rhyme, while the other had been newly composed. As expected, the subjects found it easier to memorise the well-known rhyme – presumably because millions of people already knew it.

So, if the UFO phenomenon is, indeed, a 'control phenomenon', then we would expect it to make an increasing impact on the human mind simply by this process of morphogenetic 'induction'.

During the writing of this book I have been experiencing an odd kind of synchronicity. Beside my bed there is a digital clock. And, when I look at it in the night, it often shows numbers in treble figures: 1.11, 2.22, 3.33, 4.44 and so on. Now the chance of that happening are obviously sixty to one. Yet it happens again and again – on one occasion, twice in one night. Once, I fell asleep after doing a particularly satisfying piece of thinking, and when I woke up, the clock showed 11.11. And this morning, when I knew that it must be sometime after four, I turned over, thinking (only half seriously) 'I bet it will be 4.44.' And, sure enough, it was.

This could be explained by various hypotheses. The first is coincidence, which I am disinclined to accept. The second is some sort of 'outside intervention', perhaps 'spirits', or even UFO entities, trying to tell me that I am on the right track – that bizarre phenomena and coincidences should not be dismissed as unimportant. This strikes me as just possible, but the principle of Ockham's razor – which warns against the multiplication of entities – makes me view it as unlikely. The third is the hypothesis I have already considered: that we are living in an 'information universe', and that my unconscious mind may be trying to tell me that I can make use of its facilities more easily than I think. This, on the whole, seems to me the most fruitful. Ian Watson told me that, while he was writing *Miracle Visitors*, UFOs seemed to 'home in' on him – not actual sightings, but endless snippets of information about them, including a number of reported sightings close by. And on one occasion, a man dressed in a black suit knocked on his door and asked if he could use the toilet – to Watson's puzzlement, since there was a public toilet nearby, as well as some convenient bushes across the road. The man may have been a normal passer-by, or he may have been one of John Keel's practical jokers.

The information-universe theory – implying that mind can directly influence matter – recalls Robert Monroe's observation about Locale II – 'As you think, so you are.' But then, there is no solid matter in Locale II, and our world consists of little else.

Yet it would seem that the UFO entities have no problems with solid matter. And it is likely that we would be the same if we had reached their level of evolution. Our problem, when we feel trapped in matter, is that we find it very hard to believe that it can be tamed by any mental discipline. Yet, on a lower level, everyday life supports this contention. Apparently insoluble problems yield to determined effort. I am inclined to believe that the matter of this world yields to effort just like the finer matter of Locale II. But it has immense inertia, and yields slowly and painfully, like some gigantic rusty door. Half the battle is realising that it *will* yield if you push hard.

When I began this book, my knowledge of UFOs was slightly wider than that of most newspaper readers, but not much. I had even written a small paperback on the subject. This did not prepare me for the effect of reading two hundred or so books about UFOs. These left me in no doubt that *something* was trying to communicate with us, but that direct communication would be counterproductive. It seemed to be an important part of the scheme to create a sense of mystery.

When I read *Miracle Visitors*, I felt that Ian Watson had come the closest so far to suggesting a plausible solution, and this was because he had been willing to consider that the answer might lie in the realm of the 'mystical'. But that notion obviously implied that the phenomenon could not be dismissed as practical joking or even the hybridisation of the human race. Something much stranger was happening.

Now I had always been interested in mysticism, and the Hindu saint Ramakrishna had occupied a central place in the first book *The Outsider*, while the second, *Religion and the Rebel*, was largely devoted to mystics.

In the early 1980s, I had formulated the notion that there are, for practical purposes, eight levels of consciousness. If we regard unconsciousness as Level O, then Level 1 is dreaming. Level 2 is mere passive consciousness, in which the mind is simply a reflecting mirror, taking no interest in its surroundings. In Level 3, the mind is now active, but feels a helpless pawn of 'fate', or its environment. Level 4 is so-called 'normal consciousness', the kind we experience every day. It still has a strong underlying feeling of helplessness and pessimism. But Level 5 is what I have labelled 'spring-morning consciousness', that wonderful sense of clarity and wide-awakeness, when the world seems to sparkle with meaning. This tends to last a few hours at most, so Level 6 was a more permanent version of Level 5 – such as might be experienced, for example, by a couple on honeymoon, for whom everything seems perfect. Level 7 is what I have called (in Chapter 9) 'Faculty X', the strange ability to grasp the reality of other places and times by some kind of imaginative effort. And Level 8 is mystical consciousness, about which it seems impossible to speak without contradicting oneself. (Ouspensky's chapter 'Experimental Mysticism' in *A New Model of the Universe* is probably as good an introduction to the subject as exists.)

It will be noted that, below Level 5, all the states are basically passive; after Level 5, they are all active. Above Level 5 we achieve 'nonleaking' consciousness, and the result is a glimpse of amazing possibilities. It is rather like scrambling to the top of a high cliff, and getting your head over the top, and seeing an extraordinary landscape that will take months or years to explore.

In a book called *Seeing the Invisible* (1990), a collection of religious and mystical experiences submitted by ordinary readers, I had been impressed by how often the 'glimpse' seems to come from 'outside'. For example, a wireless operator described how, in the Western Desert during World War Two, he was lying in a state of exhaustion after days of battle when a 'torrent of ideas' began to flow into his mind, insights about the universe, the meaning of reality, and infinity. He felt strongly that 'no effort of mine was involved in what was, for me, a highly superior piece of thinking'. He was flooded with delight, and, after perhaps ten minutes, seemed to hear a voice in his head saying, 'That's quite enough to be going on with.'

He states that he cannot believe that what happened originated inside him. 'Perhaps, unwittingly, I tapped some universal source of knowledge.'

And, as I came upon more and more people whose vision of reality had been transformed by contact with UFOs, it seemed to me that what he had experienced was a form of what Jung called 'UFO consciousness'.

Now I myself had had enough experiences of 'nonleaking' consciousness to know that it produces a tremendous feeling of delight. I once experienced it driving through very deep snow along a narrow country road, and concentrating for dear life to avoid landing in the ditch. When I finally arrived back on the main road, I realised that all this concentration had made my mind glow with a new kind of intensity, throwing light on places it had never reached before. Everything I looked at seemed immensely *interesting*, and I felt that, now I knew it could be achieved by effort, there was nothing to prevent me from exploring this fascinating realm at the top of the cliff. I have not achieved it on a regular basis, although I have succeeded on half a dozen occasions (once seated for hours in a passport control office in Damascus), but I can usually get somewhere near to it on long train journeys or car drives. It consists basically in 'closing the leaks' and then feeling consciousness begin to glow.

So I had no doubt that, if the UFO entities – specifically the 'talls' – had pushed their way beyond our present stage of evolution, then I had a good idea of what it felt like.

My long-term preoccupation with human evolution showed me the next part of the answer. Cro-Magnon man was probably the first human type to feel that he was no longer a mere animal at the mercy of nature, because his hunting magic gave him a sense of control, of being able to take a short cut to capture his prey instead of relying on luck. It seemed clear then that human evolution involves a slowly increasing sense of control *over the mind* (control over the material world follows), and that there is no obvious upward limit.

Accounts of abductions offered the final clue. Many of them seem to make no sense; nothing much seems to be achieved. But, when Beth Collings asked a 'grey' why he was driving a needle into her navel, he replied, 'It is part of the change.' And she later realised that she had been abducted since childhood, and that so had her father and grandfather, and probably her grandchildren. Why make an effort over several generations unless the purpose is to create a new kind of human being?

Not long before Andrija Puharich's death, I was asked to write an article about him, and rang him at his home in America. When I asked him what he was working on, he told me that he was studying supernormal children. 'You wouldn't believe how many of those kids there are out there. They seem to be on genius level. I know dozens, and there are probably thousands.'

And this, I suspect, is the beginning of the change that the UFOs are working on.

Selected Bibliography

Adamski, George, *Flying Saucers Have Landed* (with Desmond Leslie), The British Book Centre, New York, 1953.

Andrews, Colin and Delgado, Pat, *Circular Evidence*, London, Bloomsbury, 1989.

Ashpole, Edward, *The UFO Phenomena*, Headline, 1995.

Asimov, Isaac, *Extraterrestrial Civilisations*, Robson Books, 1980.

Bartholomew, Alick (ed.), *Crop Circles – Harbingers of World Change*, Gateway Books, 1991.

Bauval, Robert with Gilbert, Adrian, *The Orion Mystery*, Heinemann, 1994.

Bauval, Robert and Hancock, Graham, *Keeper of Genesis*, Heinemann, 1996.

Bracewell, Ronald N., *The Galactic Club, Intelligent Life in Outer Space*, Heinemann, 1974.

Bryan, C. D. B., *Close Encounters of The Fourth Kind*, Knopf, New York, 1995.

Cameron, Vicki, *UFO Experiences in Canada*, General Store Publishing House, Ontario, 1995.

Campagna, Palmiro, *The UFO Files: The Canadian Connection Exposed*, Stoddart, Canada, 1997.

Cathie, Bruce, *Harmonic 33*, A. H. and A. W. Reed Ltd, 1968.

Cathie, Bruce, *The Pulse of the Universe: Harmonic 288*, A. H. and A. W. Reed Ltd, 1977.

Chariton, Wallace O., *The Great Texas Airship Mystery*, Wordware Publishing, Texas, 1990.

Clarke, David and Roberts, Andy, *Phantoms of the Sky: UFOs – A Modern Myth?* Hale, London, 1990.

Collings, Beth and Jamerson, Anna, *Connections: Solving our Alien Abduction Mystery*, Wild Flower Press, 1996.

Colombo, John Robert, *UFOs Over Canada: Personal Accounts of Sightings and Close Encounters*, Hounslow Press, Ontario, Canada, 1991.

Constable, Trevor James, *Skycreatures: Living UFOs*, Pocket Books, New York, 1976.

Corso, Col. Philip J. with Birnes, William J., *The Day After Roswell*, Pocket Books, New York.

Craft, Michael, *Alien Impact*, St Martin's Press, New York, 1996.

Craig, Roy, *UFOs: An Insider's View of the Official Quest For Evidence*, University of North Texas Press, 1995.

David, Jay, *The Flying Saucer Reader*, Signet Books, New York, 1967.

Drake, Raymond, W. *Gods and Spacemen in the Ancient East*, Spearman, 1968.

Fiore, Edith, *Encounters, A Psychologist Reveals Case Studies of Abductions by Extraterrestrials*, Ballantine Books, New York, 1989.

Ford, Brian J., *The Earth Watchers*, Frewin, London, 1973.

Fowler, Raymond E., *The Andreasson Affair*, Wild Flower Press, Oregon, 1994.

Fowler, Raymond E., *The Watchers: The Secret Design Behind UFO Abductions*, Bantam, New York, 1990.

Fowler, Raymond E., *The Watchers II*, Wild Flower Press, Oregon, 1995.

Fowler, Raymond E., *The Allagash Abductions*, Wild Flower Press, 1993.

Fuller, John G., *The Interrupted Journey*, Dell, New York, 1966.

Fuller, John G., *Incident at Exeter*, Putnam, New York, 1966.

Good, Timothy, *Beyond Top Secret*, Sidgwick and Jackson, 1996.

Good, Timothy, *Alien Contact*, Morrow, New York, 1991.

Good, Timothy (ed.), *The UFO Report 1991*, Sidgwick and Jackson, 1990.

Good, Timothy (ed.), *Alien Update*, Avon Books, New York, 1993.

Grof, Stanislav, and Grof, Christina (eds), *Spiritual Emergency*.

Haines, Richard F., *Advanced Aerial Devices Reported During the Korean War*, LDA Press, Los Altos, Cal. 1990.

Hancock, Graham, *Fingerprints of the Gods*, Heinemann, 1995.

Harbinson, W. A., *Projekt UFO: The Case For Man-Made Flying Saucers*, Boxtree, 1995.

Hesemann, Michael, *The Cosmic Connection, Worldwide Crop Formations and ET Contacts*, Gateway Books, Bath, 1996.

Hesemann, Michael, and Mantle, Philip, *Beyond Roswell: The Alien Autopsy Film*, O'Mara, 1997.

Hill, Betty, *A Commonsense Approach to UFOs*, Betty Hill, PO Box 55, Greenland, NH, 1995.

Hind, Cynthia, *UFOs – African Encounters*, Gemini, Salisbury, Zimbabwe, 1982.

Hoagland, Richard, C., *The Monuments of Mars*, North Atlantic Books, Berkeley, 1987.

Holiday, F. W., and Pugh, Randall Jones, *The Dyfed Enigma: Unidentified Flying Objects in West Wales*, Faber and Faber, 1979.

Holroyd, Stuart, *Prelude to the Landing on Planet Earth*, W. H. Allen, London, 1977.

Holzer, Hans, *The Ufonauts*, Granada, 1976.

Hopkins, Budd, *Missing Time*, Ballantine, New York, 1981.

Hopkins, Budd, *Intruders*, Ballantine, New York, 1988.

Hopkins, Budd, *Witnessed*, Pocket Books, New York, 1996.

Horn, Arthur David, *Humanity's Extraterrestrial Origins*, PO Box 1632, Mount Shasta, California, 1994.

Howe, Linda Moulton, *An Alien Harvest*, Howe Productions, Pa., 1990.

Howe, Linda Moulton, *Glimpses of Other Realities: Volume One Facts and Eyewitnesses*, Howe Productions, 1993.

Howe, Linda Moulton, *Glimpses of Other Realities: Volume Two High Strangeness*, Howe Productions, 1998.

Hynek, Allen, J., *The UFO Experience: A Scientific Enquiry*, Regnery, Chicago, 1972.

Jacobs, David M., *Secret Life*, Simon and Schuster, New York, 1992.

Jessup, M. K., *The Case for the UFO*, Arco, 1955.

Keel, John A., *Jadoo*, Julian Messner, New York, 1957.

Keel, John A., *Operation Trojan Horse*, Souvenir Press, 1971.

Keel, John A., *Our Haunted Planet*, Spearman, 1971.

Keel, John A., *The Mothman Prophecies*, Dutton, New York, 1975.

Keel, John A., *The Eighth Tower*, Dutton, New York, 1976.

Keyhoe Major Donald, A., *Flying Saucers From Outer Space*, Hutchinson, London, 1954.

Keyhoe Major Donald A., *The Flying Saucer Conspiracy*, Hutchinson, London, 1957.

Keyhoe Major Donald A., *Flying Saucers, Top Secret*, Putnams, USA, 1960.

Lorenzen, Coral and Jim, *Flying Saucer Occupants*, Signet Books, 1967.

Lunan, Duncan, *Man and the Stars: Contact and Communication With Other Intelligence*, Souvenir Press, London, 1974.

Mack, John E., *Abduction: Human Encounters With Aliens*, Simon and Schuster, 1994.

Macnish, *Cropcircle Apocalypse*, Circlevision Publications, 1993.

McMoneagle, Joseph, *Mind Trek*, Hampton Roads Publishing Co., 1993.

Michel, Aimé, *The Truth About Flying Saucers*, Hale, London, 1957.

Michel, John, *The Flying Saucer Vision*, Abacus, 1974.

Morehouse, David, *Psychic Warrior*, St Martin's Press, New York, 1996.

Noyes, Ralph (ed.), *The Crop Circle Enigma*, Gateway Books, 1990.

Noyes, Ralph, *A Secret Property*, Quartet Books, 1985.

O'Leary, Brian, *Exploring Inner and Outer Space*, North Atlantic Books, Berkeley, 1989.

O'Leary, Brian, *The Second Coming of Science*, North Atlantic Books, Berkeley, 1992

O'Leary, Brian, *Miracle in the Void*, Kamapua'a Press, Hawaii, 1996.
Persinger, Michael A. and Lafreniere, Gyslaine F., *Space – Time Transients and Unusual Events*, Nelson-Hall, Chicago, 1971.
Pope, Nick, *Open Skies, Closed Minds*, Simon and Schuster, 1996.
Pope, Nick, *The Uninvited*, Simon and Schuster, 1997.
Randle, Kevin D., *The October Scenario*, Berkeley, 1989.
Randle, Kevin D., *A History of UFO Crashes*, Avon Books, 1995.
Randle, Kevin D., and Schmitt, Donald R., *The Truth About the UFO Crash at Roswell*, Avon Books 1994.
Randles, Jenny and Hough, Peter, *The Complete Book of UFOs*, Stirling Publishing Co., New York, 1994.
Ruppelt, Edward J., *The Report on Unidentified Flying Objects*, Doubleday, New York, 1956.
Rux, Bruce, *Architects of the Underworld*, Frog Ltd, Berkeley, Cal., 1996.
Sachs, Margaret, *The UFO Encyclopaedia*, Corgi, 1981.
Sagan, Carl (ed.), *Communication With Extraterrestrial Intelligence (CETI)*, MIT, 1973.
Sagan, Carl (ed.), *Other Worlds*, Bantam Books, 1975.
Schlemmer, Phyllis V., *The Only Planet of Choice*, Gateway Books, Bath, 1993.
Shklovskii, Isi. S., and Sagan, Carl, *Intelligent Life in the Universe*, Delta Books, 1966.
Shuttlewood, Arthur, *The Warminster Mystery*, Spearman, 1967.
Shuttlewood, Arthur, *The Flying Saucerers*, Sphere, 1976.
Shuttlewood, Arthur, *Warnings From Flying Friends*, Portway Press, 1968.
Spencer, John, and Evans, Hilary, *Phenomenon*, Futura, 1988.
Spencer, John, and Evans, Hilary, *Perspectives*, MacDonald, 1989.
Spencer, John, and Evans, Hilary, *Gifts of the Gods? Are UFOs Visitors or Psychic Phenomena*, Virgin, 1994.
Spencer, John, and Evans, Hilary, and Spencer, Ann, *Fifty Years of UFOs*, Boxtree, 1997.
Steiger, Brad and Whritenour, Joan, *Flying Saucers are Hostile*, Universal Tandem, 1967
Steiger, Brad and Whritenour, Joan, *The New UFO Breakthrough*, Universal Publishing, New York, 1973.
Strieber, Whitley, *Communion*, Century, 1987.
Strieber, Whitley, *Transformation: The Breakthrough*, Century Hutchinson, 1988.
Strieber, Whitley, *Breakthrough, the Next Step*, Harper Collins, 1995.
Talbot, Michael, *The Holographic Universe*, Harper Collins, 1991.
Trench, Brinsley, Le Poer, *The Sky People*, Spearman, 1960.
Trench, Brinsley, Le Poer, *Temple of the Stars*, Spearman, 1962.
Trench, Brinsley, Le Poer, *Operation Earth*, Spearman 1969.

Selected Bibliography

Trench, Brinsley, Le Poer, *The Eternal Subject*, Souvenir, 1973.

Thompson, Richard L., *Alien Identities: Ancient Insights Into Modern UFO Phenomena*, Govardhan Hill Publishing, Florida, 1993.

Vallee, Jacques, *Anatomy of a Phenomenon*, Regnery, Chicago, 1965.

Vallee, Jacques, and Janine, *Challenge to Science*, Regnery, 1966.

Vallee, Jacques, and Hynek, Allen J., *The Edge of Reality: A Progress Report on UFOs*, Regnery, 1975.

Vallee, Jacques, *Passport to Magonia*, Regnery, 1969.

Vallee, Jacques, *The Invisible College*, Dutton, 1975.

Vallee, Jacques, *Messengers of Deception*, Berkeley, 1979.

Vallee, Jacques, *UFO Chronicles of the Soviet Union*, Ballantine Books, New York, 1992.

Vallee, Jacques, *Dimensions*, Ballantine, 1988.

Vallee, Jacques, *Confrontations*, Ballantine, 1990.

Vallee, Jacques, *Revelations*, Ballantine, 1991.

allee, Jacques, *Forbidden Science, Journals 1957-1969*, Marlowe, New York, 1996.

Walton, Travis, *Fire in the Sky*, Marlowe, New York, 1990.

Warren, Larry, and Robbins, Peter, *Left at East Gate*, Marlowe, New York, 1997.

Wilkins, Harold T., *Flying Saucers on the Attack*, Citadel, 1954.

Index

Index

Index

Index